Great Source

Reading Advantage

TEACHER'S EDITION
LEVEL D

READING LEVEL GRADES 5–6

Laura Robb, James F. Baumann, Carol J. Fuhler, Joan Kindig

Avon Connell-Cowell, R. Craig Roney, Jo Worthy

GREAT SOURCE
A Division of Houghton Mifflin Harcourt Publishing Company

Reading Advantage Team

Laura Robb has more than forty years of experience in grades 4 through 8. Robb also coaches teachers of kindergarten through grade 12 in Virginia, New York, and Michigan. She speaks at conferences all over the country and conducts staff development workshops. Robb is a coauthor of these Great Source products: *Summer Success: Reading, Reader's Handbooks* grades 3, 4–5, 6–8, and *Daybooks* and *Sourcebooks* grades 2–5. In addition, she has written three books for Scholastic, *Teaching Reading in Middle School; Teaching Reading in Social Studies, Science, and Math;* and *Teaching Reading: A Complete Resource for Grades 4 and Up.*

James F. Baumann is a teacher and university professor. He has taught students in several school districts, and he has been a professor of reading education at three universities. His research and writing have examined how to provide students both rich, literate learning environments and effective instruction in reading skills and strategies. Baumann is also a coauthor of *Summer Success: Reading* (Great Source, 2001).

Carol J. Fuhler is currently an Associate Professor at Iowa State University. Dr. Fuhler is coauthor of *Teaching Reading: A Balanced Approach for Today's Classrooms* and contributed a chapter to *Young Adult Literature in the Classroom: Reading It, Teaching It, Loving It.*

Joan Kindig is an Associate Professor at James Madison University, where she teaches both Reading and Word Study courses. Dr. Kindig is also a frequent presenter at workshops and conferences.

Avon Connell-Cowell is a mentor for the New York City Department of Education. Dr. Connell-Cowell's area of interest is effective teaching practices in urban education.

R. Craig Roney is a Professor of Teacher Education at Wayne State University in Detroit, specializing in Children's Literature and Storytelling. He has also written numerous publications on these topics including *The Story Performance Handbook* (Lawrence Erlbaum Publishers, 2001), a research-based "how-to" text on reading aloud, mediated storytelling, and storytelling.

Jo Worthy, a former elementary- and middle-school teacher, teaches in the teacher preparation and graduate programs in literacy at the University of Texas at Austin. Her major research and teaching interests include reading fluency, struggling readers, and reading preferences of upper elementary- and middle-school students.

Editorial: Ruth Rothstein, Lea Martin, Sue Paro

Design/Production: Bill Smith Studio.

Printed in the United States of America

International Standard Book Number: 978-0-669-01390-0

1 2 3 4 5 6 7 8 9 10 - DBH - 13 12 11 10 09 08

Contents

Introduction to Reading Advantage

Unit 1 TRAVEL THE WORLD Magazine

Unit 2 REVOLUTIONS Magazine

Unit 3 MOUNTAINS Magazine

Unit 4 CHANGES Magazine

Appendix

Great Source Reading Advantage

Starts with Reading

The components in Reading Advantage were designed to help students

- develop essential reading comprehension skills, including decoding multiple-syllable words, comprehending complex syntax, and understanding context clues;
- strengthen reading fluency and gain experience reading a wide range of nonfiction genres including interviews, news articles, and photo-essays;
- build reading strategies, background knowledge, and vocabulary;
- transition from guided reading to independent reading;
- become proficient, confident readers who enjoy reading.

For the STUDENT

Reading, Reading, Reading

(6 copies of 4 different magazines)

Magazines At the heart of the program are high-interest magazines based on themes that offer original selections (primarily nonfiction) written below grade level.

Paperback Books (12 titles) for independent reading practice.

eZines CD-ROMs reinforce the skills and strategies taught in the program through additional theme-based magazine articles offering text highlighting, real voice audio, embedded strategy activities, and end-of-article comprehension quizzes and reports.

Activities

Student Journal copymaster that supports students as they read each selection and provides practice in comprehension and vocabulary (also available as consumable Student Journals).

For whole classroom instruction, purchase extra copies of Theme Magazines, Paperback Books, and Student Journals separately!

For the TEACHER

Instruction, Assessment, Support!

Teacher's Edition with point-of-use instruction wrapped around full-color theme magazine facsimiles; detailed lesson plans that follow the before, during, and after reading process; and comprehension, writing, vocabulary, and phonics/word study instruction.

Word Study Manual that serves as a teacher resource for expanded, in-depth word-building lessons, word sorts, and activities that target compound words, homophones, homographs, long and short vowels, multiple-syllable words, and word parts.

Assessment with instructions for determining students' reading level, mid- and end-of-magazine tests to track student progress, and checklists and observation notes for ongoing assessment.

Writing Advantage provides scaffolded instruction to support and extend students' writing.

Also Available!
Gates-MacGinitie Reading Tests® allow teachers to assess the reading level of individual students.

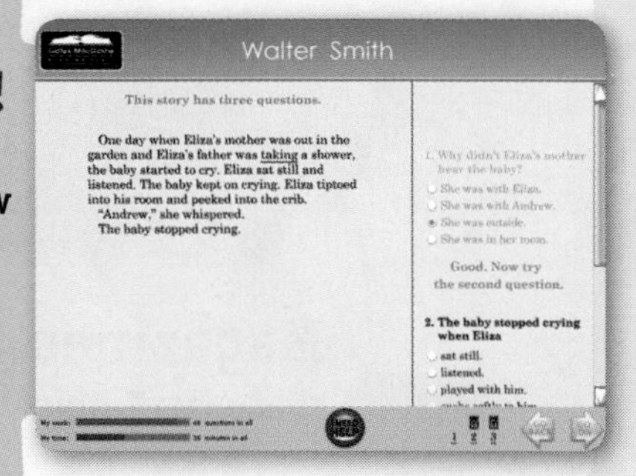

Seven levels to help your struggling readers!

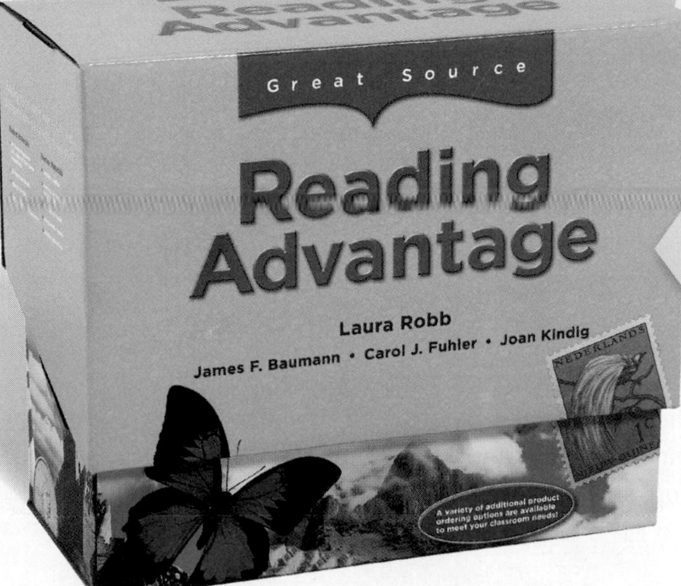

Each kit contains the items shown for student and teacher

Great Source Reading Advantage

Features the Reading Process

Reading Advantage is infused with the **Reading Process** to model for students that there are actions they can take **BEFORE** they read, **DURING** their reading, and **AFTER** they read to make themselves better readers.

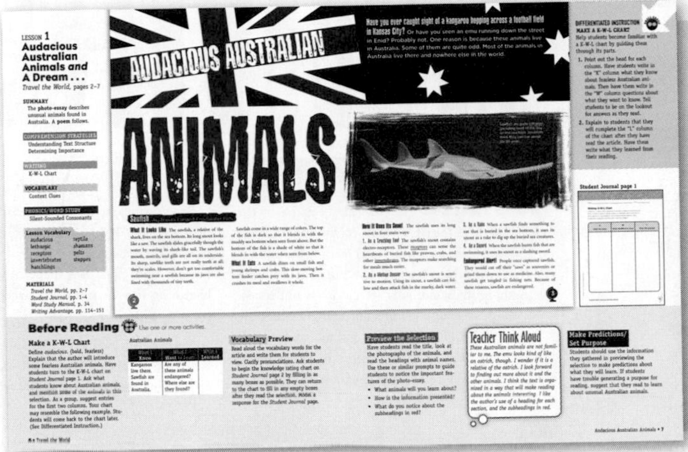

BEFORE

- Activate prior knowledge
- Preview the selection and vocabulary
- Set a purpose for reading
- Make predictions

DURING

- Check and adjust predictions
- Monitor understanding of a text
- Apply comprehension strategies

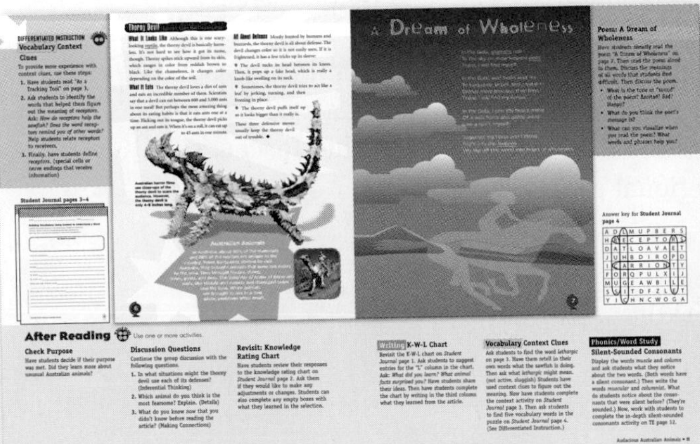

AFTER

- Respond to and discuss the selection
- Return to the purpose
- Write in response to reading
- Learn and apply skills and strategies

Annotated Lesson

Every lesson in *Reading Advantage* is set up to model the reading process:
BEFORE READING
DURING READING
AFTER READING
Each lesson is designed to last for three or four sessions when the reading period is about forty minutes long.

LESSON **1**
Audacious Australian Animals *and* A Dream . . .
Travel the World, pages 2–7

SUMMARY
The **photo-essay** describes unusual animals found in Australia. A **poem** follows.

COMPREHENSION STRATEGIES
Understanding Text Structure
Determining Importance

WRITING
K-W-L Chart

VOCABULARY
Context Cl

PHONICS/WORD STUDY
Silent-Sounded Consonants

Lesson Vocabulary

audacious	reptile
lethargic	shamans
receptors	pelts
invertebrates	steppes
hatchlings	

MATERIALS
Travel the World, pp. 2–7
Student Journal, pp. 1–4
Word Study Manual, p. 34
Writing Advantage, pp. 114–151

Sawfish Australia's Largest Freshwater Fish

What It Looks Like The sawfish, a relative of the shark, lives on the sea bottom. Its long snout looks like a saw. The sawfish slides gracefully though the water by waving its shark-like tail. The sawfish's mouth, nostrils, and gills are all on its underside. Its sharp, sawlike teeth are not really teeth at all; they're scales. However, don't get too comfortable swimming near a sawfish because its jaws are also lined with thousands of tiny teeth.

Sawfish come in a wide range of colors. The top of the fish is dark so that it blends in with the muddy sea bottom when seen from above. But the bottom of the fish is a shade of white so that it blends in with the water when seen from below.

What It Eats A sawfish dines on small fish and young shrimps and crabs. This slow-moving bottom feeder catches prey with its jaws. Then it crushes its meal and swallows it whole.

Magazine Pages
The magazine pages, shown as facsimiles throughout the Teacher's Edition, were designed to look sophisticated and, therefore, appeal to students. The text, however, was constructed to be clear, provide abundant context for vocabulary, and increase gradually in difficulty across the magazines within a level.

Before Reading
WHOLE CLASS Use one or more activities.

Make a K-W-L Chart
Define *audacious.* (bold, fearles Explain that the author will introd e some fearless Australian animals. Ha e students turn to the K-W-L chart on *Student Journal* page 1. Ask what students know about Australian anima , and mention some of the animals in th s selection. As a group, suggest entries for the first two columns. Your chart may resemble the following example. S u-dents will come back to the chart la r. (See Differentiated Instruction.)

Australian Animals

What I **Know**	What I **Want** to Learn	What I **Learned**
Kangaroos live there. Sawfish are found in Australia.	Are any of these animals endangered? Where else are they found?	

Vocabulary Preview
Read aloud the vocabulary words for the article and write them for students to view. Clarify pronunciations. Ask students to begin the knowledge rating chart on *Student Journal* page 2 by filling in as many boxes as possible. They can return to the chart to fill in any empty boxes after they read the selection. Model a response for the *Student Journal* page.

6 • Travel the World

BEFORE READING
The first part of each lesson prepares students to read through discussion, writing, and/or graphic organizers. The selection always suggests activities for building background, previewing the selection and vocabulary, and making predictions and setting a purpose. The more support a student needs for reading, the more substantive the introduction should be. Choose the part or parts that your students need to support their reading.

Build Background Use knowledge about students' abilities to select or adapt lesson plan suggestions or strategies as appropriate to accommodate students' needs and your instructional style.

Graphic Organizers
Graphic organizers are used throughout the program. Black-Line Masters of most organizers are in the Appendix of this Teacher's Edition.

Have you ever caught sight of a kangaroo hopping across a football field in Kansas City? Or have you seen an emu running down the street in Enid? Probably not. One reason is because these animals live in Australia. Some of them are quite odd. Most of the animals in Australia live there and nowhere else in the world.

Sawfish are quite lethargic, spending most of the day on the sea floor. Scientists think they can live about 25–30 years.

How It Uses Its Snout The sawfish uses its long snout in four main ways:

1. As a Tracking Tool The sawfish's snout contains electro-receptors. These receptors can sense the heartbeats of buried fish like prawns, crabs, and other invertebrates. The receptors make searching for meals much easier.

2. As a Motion Sensor The sawfish's snout is sensitive to motion. Using its snout, a sawfish can follow and then attack fish in the murky, dark water.

3. As a Rake When a sawfish finds something to eat that is buried in the sea bottom, it uses its snout as a rake to dig up the buried sea creatures.

4. As a Sword When the sawfish hunts fish that are swimming, it uses its snout as a slashing sword.

Endangered Alert! People once captured sawfish. They would cut off their "saws" as souvenirs or grind them down to use as medicine. Also, many sawfish get tangled in fishing nets. Because of these reasons, sawfish are endangered.

3

DIFFERENTIATED INSTRUCTION
MAKE A K-W-L CHART

SMALL GROUP

Help students become familiar with a K-W-L chart by guiding them through its parts.

1. Point out the head for each column. Have students write in the "K" column what they know about fearless Australian animals. Then have them write in the "W" column questions about what they want to know. Tell students to be on the lookout for answers as they read.
2. Explain to students that they will complete the "L" column of the chart after they have read the article. Have them write what they learned from their reading.

Student Journal page 1

Name ____________ Date ________

Writing: K-W-L Chart

K What We Know	W What We Want to Know	L What We Learned

Travel the World • Audacious Australian Animals

Differentiated Instruction

Students who need deeper instruction in and/or a different approach to a strategy or skill will benefit from instruction that provides more support, or scaffolding. Use the ideas in tutorials with individual students or with a small group of students who need the support for the same skill or strategy.

English Language Learners

Students who are acquiring English as a second language will benefit from a variety of techniques and tools embedded in *Reading Advantage*. In the magazines, text provides rich context to help define unfamiliar words, illustrations and photographs provide visual support, and plays offer a natural way to practice oral fluency. In the Teacher's Edition, background concepts, oral discussion, graphic organizers, and the Differentiated Instruction featre all work together to help students build confidence in using the English language.

Preview the Selection

Have students read the title, look at the photographs of the animals, and read the headings with animal names. Use these or similar prompts to guide students to notice the important features of the photo-essay.

- What animals will you learn about?
- How is the information presented?
- What do you notice about the subheadings in red?

Teacher Think Aloud

These Australian animals are not familiar to me. The emu looks kind of like an ostrich, though. I wonder if it is a relative of the ostrich. I look forward to finding out more about it and the other animals. I think the text is organized in a way that will make reading about the animals interesting. I like the author's use of a heading for each section, and the subheadings in red.

Make Predictions/ Set Purpose

Students should use the information they gathered in previewing the selection to make predictions about what they will learn. If students have trouble generating a purpose for reading, suggest that they read to learn about unusual Australian animals.

Teacher Think Aloud The Teacher Think Aloud makes the thinking of a good reader public knowledge for all students.

DIFFERENTIATED INSTRUCTION

Comprehension

UNDERSTANDING TEXT STRUCTURE

Use these steps to help students form a stronger understanding of text structure:

1. Explain to students that authors of informational articles organize their ideas in different ways. For example, the ideas in an article about events in history might be organized by dates. This article about Australian animals is organized by the kind of animal.
2. Have pairs of students read the headings and subheadings in each section and tell what they expect to learn in that section.

Student Journal page 2

Name______________________ Date__________

Building Vocabulary: Knowledge Rating Chart

Show your knowledge of each word by adding information to the other boxes in the row.

Word	Define or Use in a Sentence	Where Have I Seen or Heard It?	How Is It Used in the Selection?	Looks Like (Words or Sketch)
audacious				
lethargic				
nocturnal				
hatchlings				
raucous				

2 Travel the World • Audacious Australian Animals

Emu Australia's Largest Bird

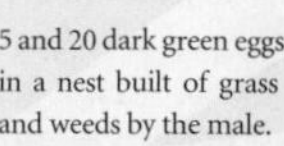

What It Looks Like The emu (EE myoo), the world's second largest bird, looks like its relative, the ostrich. (The ostrich is the world's largest bird.) Like the ostrich, the emu is flightless. Unlike the ostrich, it lives in Australia. Long, thick, drooping feathers cover its body. The feathers on its head are short, making its pointy beak, bright eyes, and blue throat stand out. Even though the emu can't fly, it runs very quickly. Using its long legs and three-toed feet, an emu can run up to 50 kilometers per hour (about 31 miles per hour).

What It Eats Living mainly on a diet of grass, flowers, and seeds, the emu sometimes likes a treat of a crunchy grasshopper. Emus drink water once or twice a day.

Hatching Baby Emu Emus pair up when they are about two years old. A female emu lays between 5 and 20 dark green eggs in a nest built of grass and weeds by the male. The male keeps the eggs warm for eight weeks. During this time, he hardly ever leaves the nest. To survive, he uses up a layer of fat that he built up by eating a lot before nesting. When the eggs hatch, the male cares for the young for about six to nine months. Emus are in the most danger as eggs because lizards love to eat them. They also are at risk as hatchlings, when they are in their very young stage, because foxes hunt baby emus for food.

Emus can grow to a height of 6 feet (185 cm) and weigh about 110 pounds (50 kg). The female is usually larger than the male.

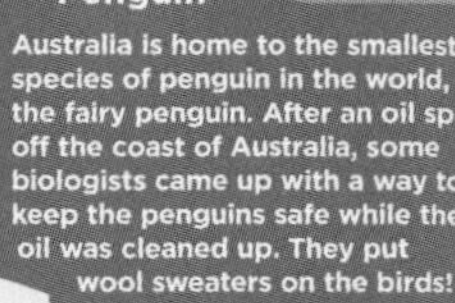

Australia's Smallest Penguin

Australia is home to the smallest species of penguin in the world, the fairy penguin. After an oil spill off the coast of Australia, some biologists came up with a way to keep the penguins safe while the oil was cleaned up. They put wool sweaters on the birds! The wool kept the penguins from cleaning their feathers.

4

During Reading

Comprehension

UNDERSTANDING TEXT STRUCTURE

Use these questions to model for students how to determine the classification text structure of the selection. Then ask students how this helps them understand the text.

- What do I notice about the way this article is structured?
- Why do I think the author chose this text structure?

(See Differentiated Instruction.)

Teacher Think Aloud

I notice that this article is divided into sections. Each section has a title. The titles are the names of different Australian animals. I think the author did this to help me understand the information by presenting it in small chunks. Also, the author used subheadings to break down the information more. The first two subheadings for each animal are the same.

Comprehension

DETERMINING IMPORTANCE

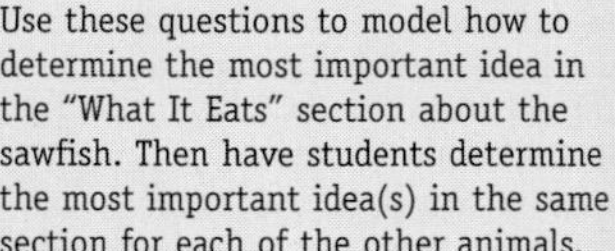

Use these questions to model how to determine the most important idea in the "What It Eats" section about the sawfish. Then have students determine the most important idea(s) in the same section for each of the other animals.

- What is the most important idea in this section?
- Why do I think this is the most important idea?

8 • Travel the World

DURING READING

Instruction is provided for strategies that students will learn to apply while they are reading. If students print the prompts on a bookmark or card, they will have a handy reminder for all their reading. While students are reading independently, meet with small groups or do "walk-by" conferences. In a walk-by conference, stop briefly beside a student and ask a couple of questions to assess how the student is doing. "Tell me about what you just read," "What does that word mean? How do you know?" and "Read aloud the paragraph you just finished reading" are prompts that allow you to do a quick check on a student's comprehension of text.

Each comprehension strategy features a **Teacher Think Aloud** that models the strategy.

Tasmanian Devil! Australia's Fiercest Marsupial

What It Looks Like You might have a hard time spotting Tasmanian devils in the daylight because they are nocturnal. But if you are lucky enough to catch sight of one, you will find that a real devil looks less cute than the familiar cartoon character! A typical devil is the size of a small terrier dog, is a bit plump, and has a foot-long tail. It is covered with black fur and is usually marked with a white patch of fur around its neck that looks like a collar. A Tasmanian devil's head is large and powerful. It has wide jaws with sharp, pointed teeth. Its pink ears turn red—like a devil's—when it is angry, upset or provoked.

What It Eats Tasmanian devils eat carrion, the flesh of dead animals. Gross as it might sound, a devil will eat anything that has been lying around, no matter how rotten, old, or smelly. Its powerful jaws allow it to crush bones. Devils have been known to eat entire animals—the meat, the fur, and the bones. They leave nothing behind.

Tasmanian devils are fairly calm except when it comes to mealtime. They are very protective of food and will even kill another devil that wants its food.

If you see a Tasmanian devil, you will probably notice many patches of missing fur, which are the battle scars from these food fights.

Baby in a Pouch Tasmanian babies are called joeys. Joeys are born blind, deaf, and about the size of a grain of rice. Up to fifty joeys can be born at a time. They race up the mother's belly, about three inches, to the opening of her pouch. Of the fifty joeys, only about four survive because of limited room in the pouch. When a joey reaches the pouch, it stays there for three months, drinking its mother's milk. At the end of that time, it will leave the pouch for a nest.

A Famous Scream If you miss seeing a Tasmanian devil, you might hear one. They are very raucous, especially when there is a group of them around a dead animal, battling for food. They snort, bark, and scream. These horrible noises, along with their mean looks, are two reasons why they've earned the name "devil."

A devil can eat 40% of its body weight in 30 minutes. That amount of food will keep a devil going for 2–3 days.

5

Teacher Think Aloud

The author presents several ideas in the "What It Eats" section about the sawfish. Which one is the big idea the author wants me to understand? I think it is the information in the first sentence because it tells me exactly what a sawfish eats. The other two sentences tell about how a sawfish catches its food and swallows it. These details are interesting, but they don't tell me about what a sawfish eats.

Fix-Up Strategies

Offer these strategies to help students read independently.

If you don't understand what you're reading:

- Reread the difficult section to look for clues to help you comprehend.
- Read ahead to find clues to help you comprehend.
- Retell, or say in your own words, what you've read.
- Visualize, or form mental pictures of, what you've read.

If you don't understand a word:

- Reread the sentence. Look for ideas and words that provide meaning clues.
- Find clues by reading a few sentences before and after the confusing word.
- Look for the base or root word and think about its meaning.
- Think about the topic or plot at this point to see if either offers meaning clues.

Fix-Up Strategies Each lesson includes fix-up strategy reminders to help students become independent problem solvers.

DIFFERENTIATED INSTRUCTION SMALL GROUP

Vocabulary Context Clues

To provide more experience with context clues, use these steps:

1. Have students read "As a Tracking Tool" on page 3.
2. Ask students to identify the words that helped them figure out the meaning of *receptors*. Ask: *How do receptors help the sawfish? Does the word receptors remind you of other words?* Help students relate receptors to receivers.
3. Finally, have students define *receptors*. (special cells or nerve endings that receive information)

Student Journal pages 3–4

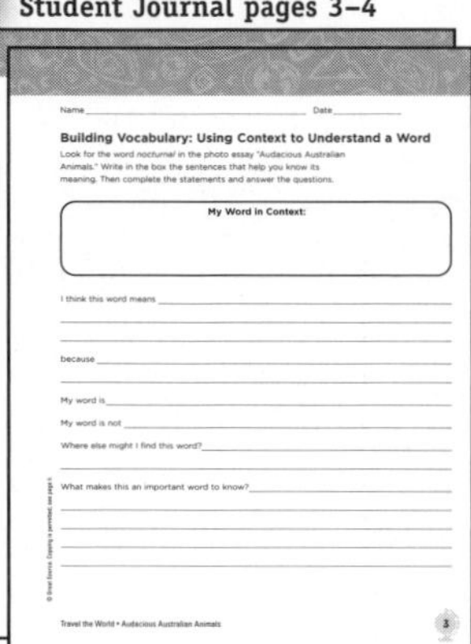

Thorny Devil Looks Can Be Deceiving

What It Looks Like Although this is one scary-looking reptile, the thorny devil is basically harmless. It's not hard to see how it got its name, though. Thorny spikes stick upward from its skin, which ranges in color from reddish brown to black. Like the chameleon, it changes color depending on the color of the soil.

What It Eats The thorny devil loves a diet of ants and eats an incredible number of them. Scientists say that a devil can eat between 600 and 3,000 ants in one meal! But perhaps the most amazing thing about its eating habits is that it eats ants one at a time. Flicking out its tongue, the thorny devil picks up an ant and eats it. When it's on a roll, it can eat up to 45 ants in one minute.

All About Defense Mostly hunted by humans and buzzards, the thorny devil is all about defense. The devil changes color so it is not easily seen. If it is frightened, it has a few tricks up its sleeve:

- The devil tucks its head between its knees. Then, it pops up a fake head, which is really a knob-like swelling on its neck.
- Sometimes, the thorny devil tries to act like a leaf by jerking, turning, and then freezing in place.
- The thorny devil puffs itself up so it looks bigger than it really is.

These three defensive moves usually keep the thorny devil out of trouble. ◆

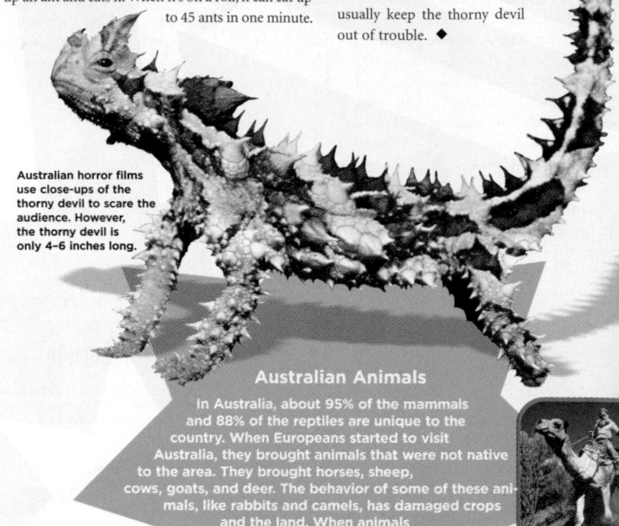

Australian horror films use close-ups of the thorny devil to scare the audience. However, the thorny devil is only 4–6 inches long.

Australian Animals

In Australia, about 95% of the mammals and 88% of the reptiles are unique to the country. When Europeans started to visit Australia, they brought animals that were not native to the area. They brought horses, sheep, cows, goats, and deer. The behavior of some of these animals, like rabbits and camels, has damaged crops and the land. When animals are brought to live in a new place, problems often result.

6

Student Journal Reduced facsimiles are placed near the point of use to help you quickly identify which pages are used in the lesson.

After Reading

WHOLE CLASS Use one or more activities.

Check Purpose

Have students decide if their purpose was met. Did they learn more about unusual Australian animals?

Discussion Questions

Continue the group discussion with the following questions.

1. In what situations might the thorny devil use each of its defenses? (Inferential Thinking)
2. Which animal do you think is the most fearsome? Explain. (Details)
3. What do you know now that you didn't know before reading the article? (Making Connections)

Revisit: Knowledge Rating Chart

Have students review their responses to the knowledge rating chart on *Student Journal* page 2. Ask them if they would like to make any adjustments or changes. Students can also complete any empty boxes with what they learned in the selection.

AFTER READING

The After Reading section provides a variety of response ideas that include discussion, instruction, vocabulary, writing, and phonics/word study. Select the activity or activities most appropriate for your students.

Discussion Questions Strategy- and skill-based questions allow students to review their reading and teachers to check comprehension. By discussing the questions together, students learn from each other. The technique called Think-Pair-Share is sometimes recommended for discussion. In it, students think through a question, talk about it with a partner, and then share with the whole group. This technique takes the pressure off students, especially English Language Learners, because it allows them time to think and the verbal support of a partner.

A Dream of Wholeness

In the Gobi, shamans ride
To the sky on snow leopard pelts.
There, I will find myself.

In the Gobi, wild herbs lead me
To turquoise, jasper, and crystal—
Stones more precious than time.
There, I will find my senses.

In the Gobi, I grip the heavy mane
Of a wild horse and gallop away
Like a spirit, myself.

Together, my horse and I blend
Right into the steppes.
We slip off this world into hours of wholeness.

Poem: A Dream of Wholeness

Have students silently read the poem "A Dream of Wholeness" on page 7. Then read the poem aloud to them. Discuss the meanings of all words that students find difficult. Then discuss the poem.

- What is the tone or "sound" of the poem? Excited? Sad? Happy?
- What do you think the poet's message is?
- What can you visualize when you read the poem? What words and phrases help you?

Answer key for **Student Journal page 4**

A	D	L	M	U	P	B	E	R	S
H	R	E	C	E	P	T	O	R	S
D	A	T	L	O	A	V	A	E	T
J	U	H	B	D	I	R	O	P	D
I	C	A	R	R	I	O	N	T	Y
F	O	R	Q	P	U	L	X	I	J
M	U	G	E	A	W	B	I	L	E
S	S	I	T	D	F	Z	L	E	T
Y	I	C	H	N	C	W	O	G	A

Writing K-W-L Chart

Revisit the K-W-L chart on *Student Journal* page 1. Ask students to suggest entries for the "L" column in the chart. Ask: *What did you learn? What animal facts surprised you?* Have students share their ideas. Then have students complete the chart by writing in the third column what they learned from the article.

Vocabulary Context Clues

Ask students to find the word *lethargic* on page 3. Have them retell in their own words what the sawfish is doing. Then ask what *lethargic* might mean. (not active, sluggish) Students have used context clues to figure out the meaning. Now have students complete the context activity on *Student Journal* page 3. Then ask students to find five vocabulary words in the puzzle on *Student Journal* page 4. (See Differentiated Instruction.)

Phonics/Word Study

Silent-Sounded Consonants

Display the words *muscle* and *column* and ask students what they notice about the two words. (Both words have a silent consonant.) Then write the words *muscular* and *columnist*. What do students notice about the consonants that were silent before? (They're sounded.) Now, work with students to complete the in-depth silent-sounded consonants activity on TE page 12.

Focus on... Two pages at the end of every lesson provide a choice of activities:

Phonics/Word Study lesson (with references to *Word Study Manual*)

Phonics/Word Study

Silent-Sounded Consonants

Place the following words on the board: *sign* and *bomb*. Ask students what is unusual about the spelling of these words. Students should notice that both words contain a silent consonant. The steps below will show students why these letters are present.

- Brainstorm all the words you can come up with that have the word *sign* in them. Students might come up with *signature, signal, signatory, signet, signify*, and others. (See *Word Study Manual* page 34 for a word list.)
- Ask students what they notice about the *g* in these associated words. (The *g* is sounded in all of these words.)
- Ask students if they can tell by looking at all of these connected words why the *g* is even in the word *sign*. Help them discover that although the *g* may be silent, it has a meaning connection, so it remains in the word *sign*.
- This change is an example of consonant alternations. The *g* consonant may alter (or change) in sound in related words, but the spelling remains the same. This is an example of the spelling-meaning connection that students will see over and over again in these lessons.
- Have students use their Word Study notebooks to write the following words in separate columns: *crumb, bomb, muscle, hasten, column, soften*, and *comb*. Have students underline the silent letter. Under each column, have them write as many words as they can that come from those words. Once they are done, create a list and discuss their selections.
- Remember, every discussion you have about words creates enthusiasm for words and helps build students' vocabularies.

crumb	bomb	muscle	hasten
crumble	bombard	muscular	haste
crumby	bomber		hasty
crumbly	bombardier		
column	**soften**	**comb**	
columnar	softer	combine	
columnist	softy		

For more information on word sorts and spelling stages, see pages 5–31 in the *Word Study Manual*.

Focus on . . .

Use one or more activities in this section to focus on a particular area of need in your students.

Comprehension STRATEGY SUPPORT

To help those students who need more practice using the strategies covered in this lesson, work one-on-one or in small groups to apply the strategy prompts below. Apply the prompts to a *Reading Advantage* paperback, a classroom library book, or a new or familiar selection in the magazine. Always model your own thinking first.

Understanding Text Structure

- What kind of text is this? (book, story, article, guidebook, play, manual)
- How does the author organize the text? (cause-effect, problem-solution, chronological order, description, question-answer, comparison-contrast)
- What details support my thoughts about the text structure?
- What is the cause (effect, problem, solution, order, question, answer)?
- If fiction, who are the characters? What is the setting, plot, conflict, and resolution?

Determining Importance

- What is the most important idea in the paragraph? How can I prove it?
- Which details are unimportant? Why?
- What does the author want me to understand?
- Why is this information important (or not important) to me?

Writing Animal Guide

Have students choose an ordinary or exotic animal to research. Have them create a short informational guide with headings such as *What It Eats, Where It Lives*, and other headings related to special features of the animal.

For instruction and practice writing informational paragraphs, see lessons in *Writing Advantage*, pages 114–151.

Comprehension, reteaching of strategies

Writing in response to the selection, with a reference to *Writing Advantage*

Fluency: Phrasing

Explain to students that it's important to read with correct phrasing. Phrasing describes how words are verbally grouped together in a meaningful way. After students have read the poem "A Dream of Wholeness" at least once, have partners read the poem aloud to each other.

As you listen to students read, use these prompts to guide them.

- Notice the line breaks and punctuation. They will help guide your reading.
- Think about the poem's message.

When students read aloud, do they—

✓ demonstrate quick recognition of words and phrases?
✓ exhibit an understanding of phrasal construction?
✓ incorporate appropriate timing, stress, and intonation?

English Language Learners

To support students as they learn about text structure, review the meanings of words they encountered in this lesson: *structure*, *title*, *heading*, *subheading*, and *photograph*. Then point out one or two words that have a distinct prefix, suffix, or root. Examples include *subheading* (*sub*, "under") and *photograph* (*photo*, "light" or *graph*, "written"). Have students brainstorm other words that contain the same word part. As a group, analyze the words to try to determine what the word part means.

Independent Activity Options

While you work with individuals or small groups, others can work independently on one or more of the following options.

- Level D paperback books, see TE pages 367–372
- Level D *eZines*
- Repeat word sorts from this lesson
- *Student Journal* pages for this lesson
- *Writing Advantage* independent lessons

Assessment

Strategy Assessment

To help you and your students assess their use of comprehension strategies, ask the following questions. Students can complete a written response or provide verbal answers in a one-on-one reading conference.

1. **Understanding Text Structure** In what ways did the text structure of the article help you understand the information the author presented? (Answers will vary, but students may say that the headings helped them know what they would be reading about, and that having the information presented in small sections helped them concentrate on one part at a time, rather than being overwhelmed with too much information.)
2. **Determining Importance** What are three important ideas about the thorny devil? (Answers will vary, but students should be able to defend their beliefs that the ideas they state are important.)

For ongoing informal assessment, use the checklists on pages 61–64 of *Level D Assessment*.

Word Study Assessment

Use these steps to help you and your students assess their understanding of silent-sounded consonants.

1. Write the words *crumb, crumble, crumby,* and *crumbly* on the board or on word cards.
2. Have students read the words aloud and identify which consonants are silent and which are sounded. (The *b* is silent in *crumb* and *crumby* and sounded in *crumble* and *crumbly*.)

crumb
crumble
crumby
crumbly

Assessment, ongoing assessment, helps you and your students assess what they have learned in the lesson with questions about the strategies and word study. A reference to the formal assessment appears in time for the Mid-Magazine and Magazine Tests.

Fluency suggestions focus on reading aloud with expression, pacing, and phrasing

ELL boxes target ways to accomodate English Language Learners

Independent Activity Options help teachers manage individuals and small groups

Great Source Reading Advantage

Is Supported by Research

No Child Left Behind has placed a national spotlight on the critical issue of reading proficiency. Educators across the nation face the challenge of helping their students read at or above grade level by the end of the third grade; however, many students continue to struggle with reading through high school. In fact, according to the National Center for Education Statistics (2003) **only 33% of eighth graders and 36% of twelfth graders are reading at or above the proficient level.**

Teachers want to help these students improve their reading and writing ability; however, the task is daunting because of a lack of appropriate instructional materials to address the specific issues with which these students struggle.

Reading Advantage, designed by **Laura Robb** with a team of nationally known university educators and master classroom teachers, including **James F. Baumann**, **Carol J. Fuhler**, and **Joan S. Kindig**, can help this adolescent population improve their reading and writing skills. The seven kits address the needs of at-risk adolescents who are reading between the middle of first grade and eighth grade reading level.

The program focuses on critical areas where students need the most support: comprehension, word study and phonics, vocabulary and fluency building, and assessment, and includes enough reading materials to support each student's progress.

Great Source Reading Advantage

Matches the Level to Your Classroom Needs!

Program Level	Grade Level	Lexile Measure	Guided Reading Level	DRA
Foundations Motion Fun and Games Survival Arts	**1-2**	350L-470L	J-L	18-24
Level A Mystery Space Odyssey Water Cities	**2-3**	500L-630L	M-P	28-38
Level B Flight Underground Heroism Music	**3-4**	630L-700L	M-Q	28-38
Level C Emotions Racers & Racing Boundaries Ecology	**4-5**	730L-780L	M-Q	28-40
Level D Travel Around the World Revolution Mountains Changes	**5-6**	820L-920L	N-R	30-40
Level E Communications Relationships Discoveries Money	**6-7**	940L-990L	T-W	44-50
Level F Adaptation Justice Sports Disaters	**7-8**	1030L-1100L	T-W	44-50

Lexile® is a registered trademark of MetaMetrics, Inc.
Guided Reading Levels are from *Guiding Readers and Writers, Grades 3-6* by Irene Fountas and Gay Su Pinnell (Portsmouth: Heinemann, 2001).
Developmental Reading Assessment® is a registered trademark of Pearson Education, Inc. DRA is a trademark of Pearson Education, Inc.

Great Source Reading Advantage

Offers Differentiated Instruction

Not all students in your class need the same instruction at the same time. Therefore, using the whole-class model is not always the most effective way to teach reading. Use a pattern of whole-class, small-group, and individual instruction to address the needs of all students.

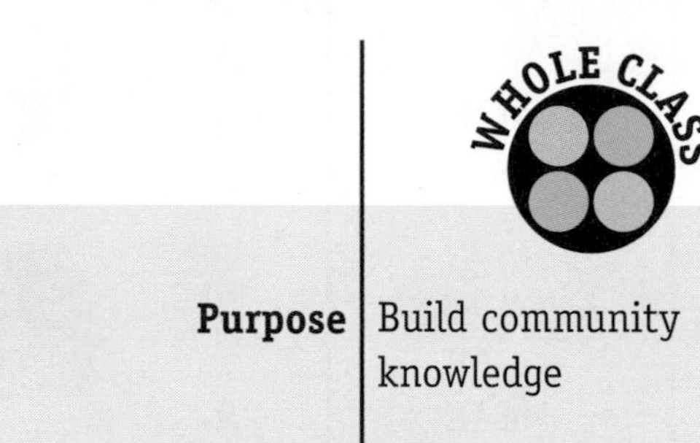

	Whole Class	Small Group	Independent
Purpose	Build community knowledge	Address students who have similar needs	Target individual needs and promote independent work
Instructional Activities	▶ Introduce theme ▶ Before-reading activities ▶ Lesson wrap-up	▶ During-reading strategy instruction and modeling ▶ Discussion questions ▶ After-reading skills & strategy instruction	▶ After-reading skills & strategy instruction ▶ Enrichment ▶ Self-evaluation ▶ *Reading Advantage* paperback collection

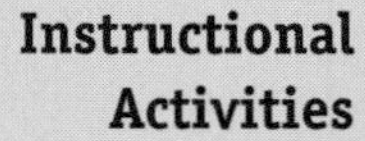

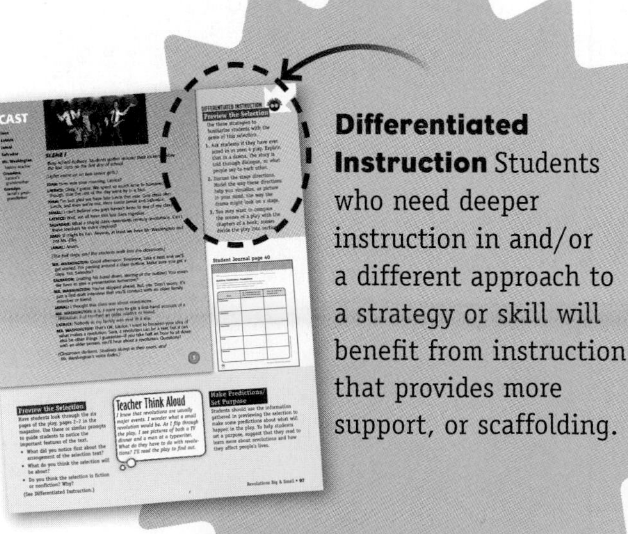

Differentiated Instruction Students who need deeper instruction in and/or a different approach to a strategy or skill will benefit from instruction that provides more support, or scaffolding.

More to Read!
Keep the *Reading Advantage* paperback books and the *eZines CD-ROM* available for students who have finished their assigned work. See the Teacher's Edition appendix for applying the reading strategies to the paperback books.

Great Source Reading Advantage

Is Easy to Manage

How can you address the needs of your students while still maintaining order in the classroom? Routines and schedules are key.

Establishing Routines

Students can work independently if they know

- what to expect each day;
- how to use the material;
- what they can do to solve most problems on their own;
- how to respect their classmates.

The following charts will help your students to work productively and independently will foster an atmosphere of respect.

Post guidelines, procedures, and schedules on a bulletin board or a wall. Have students in the independent groups take turns being the group leader to help keep the rest of the group on task.

Behavior Guidelines During Teacher-led Group Work

- Come prepared.
- Be a good listener.
- Respect ideas of others.
- Use details from the magazine article to support your position.
- Participate in the discussion.
- Talk quietly so others can work independently.

"I-Need-Help" Procedure Chart for Independent Work Times

If you need help, try the four steps below.
(If you need to speak, use a quiet voice.)

1. Think for a moment. Try to solve the problem yourself.
2. Ask a group member for support.
3. If that person can't help, ask another student from your group.
4. If none of the steps work, put your name on the "Needs Help" clipboard. Work on something you can do until the teacher helps you.

Is Easy to Manage continued

Class Gathering

Use this time to present an overview of the day's learning events. Explain which groups you will meet with and go over the directions for the independent work other groups will do. Writing the class schedule on the board as a reference and time-management guide for you and your students lets everyone know what the plan is.

Strategic Think Aloud or Minilesson

Present instruction that will benefit the whole class. Use this whole-class time to introduce a new theme, teach a new comprehension strategy, or to do the Before Reading activities. Support for all these teaching ideas is in the *Reading Advantage* Teacher's Edition.

Read Aloud

Why read aloud to older students? Research shows that reading aloud to students on a daily basis develops their listening capacity, builds their background knowledge, develops their vocabulary, and enlarges their knowledge of literary language and syntax by attuning their ears to the language of different genres.

What can you read aloud? The *Reading Advantage* Teacher's Edition provides a theme-related read-aloud selection for each magazine in the unit opener. Use articles from the *Reading Advantage* magazines or choose short selections such as poems, short stories and folk tales, or fascinating passages from nonfiction texts.

Small-Grouping Instruction

The following chart shows how two or three groups rotate through the major learning events related to *Reading Advantage*. Vary the rotation according to the number of groups you have (no more than 3 groups are recommended) and the length of time you have to spend on *Reading Advantage*.

TWO GROUPS

	Teacher-led Group	Student Journal Word Study Independent Reading
Time 1	Group 1	Group 2
Time 2	Group 2	Group 1

THREE GROUPS

	Teacher-led Group	Student Journal Independent Reading	Word Study Independent Reading
Time 1	Group 1	Group 2	Group 3
Time 2	Group 2	Group 3	Group 2
Time 3	Group 3	Group 1	Group 1

→ **WRAP-UP** Bring the class back together to give any instructions, such as homework or preparation necessary for the next class.

Establishing Schedules

Write the class schedule on the board as a reference and time-management guide. This technique enables your students to take responsibility for what they should be doing. A daily session could follow these schedules:

	Whole Class		Small Group / Independent		Whole Class	
30 minutes	Class Gathering	3 min	Small-Group Instruction Independent Work (1)	20 min	Wrap-up	2 min
	Strategic think-aloud or minilesson	5 min				
55 minutes	Teacher Read Aloud	5 min	Strategic think-aloud or minilesson	5 min	Wrap-up	2 min
	Class Gathering	3 min	Small-Group Instruction Independent Work (2-3)	40-45 min		
90 minutes	Teacher Read Aloud	5-10 min	Small-Group Instruction Independent Work (2-3)	65 min	Wrap-up and homework	5 min
	Class Gathering	5 min				
	Strategic think-aloud or minilesson	5-10 min				

Make Reading Advantage Your Own!

Use these schedules as a guide and tailor them to your schedule and teaching style.

If you use *Reading Advantage* as a supplement in your 90-minute block, for example, follow one of the shorter schedules and leave the remaining time for your other reading and language arts activities.

Great Source Reading Advantage

Comprehension

To become skillful readers, students must develop the reading strategies necessary to understand and learn from text. *Reading Advantage* provides for instruction in five high-utility reading strategies:

Monitor Understanding

The ability to determine whether comprehension is occurring and to take corrective (fix-up) action when comprehension becomes difficult

Making Connections

The ability to activate prior knowledge, predict, self-question, and make connections to personal experiences and other texts

Determining Importance

The ability to evaluate and determine the importance of ideas, and support one's beliefs with evidence

Understanding Text Structure

The ability to recognize and understand the organization an author uses to write a narrative or expository selection, which includes knowledge of text features and genre

Inferential Thinking

The ability to infer and synthesize ideas that are not directly stated in the text

These strategies are integrated into *Reading Advantage* lessons to provide students "point-of-use" strategy instruction and application using suitable texts. If you wish to extend these point-of-use instructional suggestions, there are references to the more robust Model Lessons that follow on pages xxiv–xxxiii.

Each Model Lesson provides a definition of the strategy, supporting research, and a three-part teaching sequence:

Explain:	Information to help you provide students with a verbal explanation of the strategy and how to employ it
Model:	Examples for how to demonstrate to students the application of the strategy
Practice:	Guidance for how to provide students practice in the strategy to promote its independent use

We encourage you to refer to and use the Model Lessons flexibly, drawing from them as needed when you determine that students would benefit from more extensive instruction in the strategies incorporated into *Reading Advantage*.

REFERENCES

Alvermann, D. E., & Hagood, M. C. (2000). Critical media literacy: Research, theory, and practice in "new times." *Journal of Educational Research, 93,* 193–206.

Anderson, R. C., & Pearson, P. D. (1984). A schema-theoretic view of basic processes in reading comprehension. In P. D. Pearson (Ed.), *Handbook of reading research* (pp. 225–292). New York: Longman.

Armbruster, B. B., Anderson, T. H., & Ostertag, J. (1987). Does text structure/summarization instruction facilitate learning from expository text? *Reading Research Quarterly, 22,* 331–346.

Baker, L. (2002). Metacognition in reading comprehension. In C. C. Block and M. Pressley (Eds.), *Comprehension instruction: Research-based best practices* (pp. 77–95). New York: Guilford.

Baker, L., & Brown, A. L. (1984). Metacognitive skills and reading. In P. D. Pearson (Ed.), *Handbook of reading research* (pp. 353–394). New York: Longman.

Barron, J. B., & Sternberg, R. J. (Eds.). (1987). *Teaching thinking skills: Theory and practice.* New York: Freeman.

Brown, A. L., & Day, J. D. (1983). Macro rules for summarizing texts: The development of expertise. *Journal of Verbal Learning and Verbal Behavior, 22,* 1–14.

Commeyras, M. (1993). Promoting critical thinking through dialogical-thinking reading lessons. *The Reading Teacher, 46,* 486–494.

Duke, N. K., & Pearson, P. D. (2002). Effective practices for developing reading comprehension. In A. E. Farstrup & S. J. Samuels (Eds.), *What research has to say about reading instruction* (3rd ed., pp. 205–242). Newark, DE: International Reading Association.

Ennis, R. H. (1987). A taxonomy of critical thinking dispositions and abilities. In J. B. Baron & R. J. Sternberg (Eds.), *Teaching for thinking* (pp. 9–26). New York: Freeman.

Hahn, A. L., & Garner, R. (1984). Synthesis of research on students' ability to summarize text. *Educational Leadership, 42*(5), 52–55.

Hare, V., & Borchardt, K. M. (1984). Direct instruction of summarization skills. *Reading Research Quarterly, 20,* 62–78.

Fitzgerald, J. (1989). Research on stories: Implications for teachers. In K. D. Muth (Ed.), *Children's comprehension of text: Research into practice* (pp. 2–36). Newark, DE: International Reading Association.

Fitzgerald, J., & Spiegel, D. L. (1983). Enhancing children's reading comprehension through instruction in narrative structure. *Journal of Reading Behavior, 15,* 1–17.

Gordon, C. J. (1989). Teaching narrative text structure: A process approach to reading and writing. In K. D. Muth (Ed.). *Children's comprehension of text: Research into practice* (pp. 79–102). Newark, DE: International Reading Association.

Griffin, C. C., & Tulbert, B. L. (1995). The Effect of Graphic Organizers on students' comprehension and recall of expository text: A review of the research and implications for practice. *Reading and Writing Quarterly, 11,* 73–89.

Hansen, J., & Pearson, P. D. (1983). An instructional study: Improving the inferential comprehension of good and poor fourth-grade readers. *Journal of Educational Psychology, 75,* 821–829.

Langer, J. A. (1995). *Envisioning literature: Literary understanding and literature instruction.* New York: Teacher's College Press.

Mandler, J. M., & Johnson, N. S. (1977). Remembrance of things parsed: Story structure and recall. *Cognitive Psychology, 9,* 111–151.

McGee, L. M., & Richgels, D. J. (1988). Teaching expository text structure to elementary students. *The Reading Teacher, 38,* 739–747.

Meyer, B. J. F. (1984). Organizational aspects of text: Effects on reading comprehension and applications for the classroom. In J. Flood (Ed.), *Promoting reading comprehension* (pp. 113–138). Newark, DE: International Reading Association.

National Reading Panel. (2000). *National Reading Panel: Teaching children to read: An evidence-based assessment of the scientific research literature on reading and its implications for reading instruction: Report of the subgroups* (NIH Publication No. 00-4754). Washington, DC: National Institute of Health and National Institute of Child Health and Human Development.

Nickerson, R. S. (1988). Improving thinking through instruction. In E. Z. Rothkoph (Ed.), *Review of research in education* (pp. 3–57). Washington, DC: American Educational Research Association.

Paris, S. G., Wasik, B. A., & Turner, J. C. (1991). The development of strategic readers. In R. Barr, M. L. Kamil, P. Mosenthal, & P. D. Pearson (Eds.), *Handbook of reading research, Volume II* (pp. 609–640). White Plains, NY: Longman.

Pearson, P. D., & Camperell, K. (1981). Comprehension of text structures. In J. T. Guthrie (Ed.), *Comprehension and teaching: Research reviews* (pp. 27–55). Newark, DE: International Reading Association.

RAND Reading Study Group. (2002). *Toward an R & D program in reading comprehension.* Santa Monica, CA: RAND Corporation.

Rosenshine, B., Meister, C., & Chapman, S. (1996). Teaching students to generate questions: A review of the intervention studies. *Review of Educational Research, 66*(2), 181–221.

Tierney, R. J., Sofer, A., O'Flahavan, J. F., & McGinley, W. (1989). The effects of reading and writing upon thinking critically. *Reading Research Quarterly, 24,* 134–173.

Monitor Understanding

DEFINITION: Monitoring understanding involves a reader's conscious effort to determine whether comprehension is occurring and to take corrective (fix-up) action when comprehension becomes difficult. Fix-up strategies include rereading, reading ahead, retelling, visualizing, asking questions, and using context.

RESEARCH SUPPORT

Thoughtful reading comprehension requires that readers critically analyze why and how authors write and use ideas (Alvermann & Hagood, 2000; Ennis, 1987; Tierney, Sofer, O'Flavahan, & McGinley, 1989). Research indicates that students can be taught to understand how to read critically and analytically (Barron & Sternberg, 1987; Commeyras, 1993; Nickerson, 1988).

MODEL LESSON

Explain: How the Strategy Helps and When to Use It

Explain to students that monitoring understanding will help them improve comprehension and learn new information. It's especially helpful with nonfiction but can be used with any challenging text. Self-monitoring is a multi-step process that happens during reading. Here's how it works:
In Step 1, the reader reads a section of text.
In Step 2, the reader asks: *Do I understand what I just read well enough to retell it?* The reader retells the section without looking at the text.
In Step 3, the reader looks back at the section of text and evaluates the retelling. If the retelling includes the most important details from the text, the reader reads on. If the retelling includes incorrect or few details, the reader chooses a fix-up strategy to try to resolve the confusion.

Five Fix-Up Strategies

- *Reread* a difficult section to see if that improves understanding. Rereading includes careful rereading of diagrams, captions, and photographic details. Rereading can also be done to connect newly read ideas with earlier text.
- *Read on* to see if the next section gives clues for comprehension.
- *Visualize* to form mental pictures of what's happening or of specific words and phrases.
- *Ask questions* to clarify confusing details. Then try another fix-up strategy to find the answer.
- *Use context clues* in the sentences before and after the difficult word and word-structure clues to help figure out meaning.

Model the Strategy

Materials *Travel the World,* "Ancient Artists of Lascaux," pages 8–14
Step 1 Name the strategy and explain to students what it is and how it helps them.
Think Aloud Here's a good way to break down the Monitor Understanding strategy: read/pause/retell/evaluate. This process will help you confirm your understanding of a text and pinpoint areas of confusion. After reading a paragraph, section, or page of text, pause and retell in your own words what you've read. Then check the text and evaluate yourself. Ask: *Did I recall enough details to show that I understand?* If you recalled several important details, then read on. If you had trouble retelling what you read, you probably didn't understand or remember enough. Try applying a fix-up strategy to make better sense of the passage.

Now, I'll model the whole strategy. Listen as I read/pause/retell/evaluate and apply a fix-up strategy.

Step 2 Read aloud the section called "Signs in Cave Art" on page 12.

Think Aloud Now I'll retell what I read, without looking at the paragraph.

Signs are a kind of cave painting and can be dots, lines, circles, and triangles. Scientists don't know the meanings of these signs.

When I look back at the paragraph, I see that I left out details. Even though I understood the text, I didn't remember much. I'll try rereading as a fix-up strategy. Here's my second retelling. Notice how I add more details.

Signs in a cave could be designs. But scientists don't know the purpose of the signs. Scientists use the signs to date pictures in different caves. When caves have the same signs, scientists believe the same people lived in them at different times.

Step 3 Discuss how to choose a fix-up strategy.

Think Aloud It can be hard to figure out which fix-up strategy to choose when you're confused about your reading. Ask yourself these questions to help you make the choice: *Do I need to slow down and reread? Do I need to connect ideas from this last section to text that came before? Am I having trouble visualizing images? What ideas are most unclear? Did a specific word confuse me?*

Guided Practice

1. Set aside time when you can observe students as they self-monitor, evaluate, and if necessary, apply a fix-up strategy.
2. Circulate and listen to students think aloud as they monitor their understanding. Support students who have difficulty by first modeling the entire process, then sharing the process, and finally having them complete the process on their own.

Independent Practice

1. Assign a section of text for students to monitor understanding on their own.
2. Give each student a piece of paper, have them write their retelling, evaluate it, and note the fix-up strategy they plan to apply.

Following Up

Continue to encourage students to self-monitor their reading, especially of new or challenging texts.

Making Connections

DEFINITION: When readers make connections to a text, they link their life experiences and prior knowledge to the information, characters, themes, and topics in the text. Connections can be to a reader's own experience, to other texts, or to the larger world.

RESEARCH SUPPORT

There are common patterns or structures for narrative (Fitzgerald, 1989; Mandler & Johnson, 1977) and expository texts (Duke & Pearson, 2002; Meyer, 1984; Pearson & Camperell, 1981). Research demonstrates that students can be taught to recognize and use narrative (Fitzgerald & Spiegel, 1983; Gordon, 1989) and expository (Armbruster, Anderson, & Ostertag, 1987; McGee & Richgels, 1988) text structures to enhance their comprehension, and there is evidence that the use of graphic representations of text structures can enhance students' understanding (Duke & Pearson, 2002; Griffin & Tulbert, 1995).

MODEL LESSON

Explain: How the Strategy Helps and When to Use It

Explain to students that when they make connections, they compare the information in a text to their own experiences, to other texts, and to issues in the larger world. The more connections they make to a text, the better they will understand and remember it. Making connections will also help students learn new information and better understand the experiences of the characters or people in a text. If a reader can't make a connection, the text will be harder to understand. In those cases, provide any necessary background and encourage students to read on and re-evaluate at the end of each section, page, or chapter. If students discover that their prior experience doesn't match what is in the text, discuss possible reasons for the mismatch.

Readers begin making connections before reading, as they preview the text to access prior knowledge. The process should then continue during and after reading. Encourage students to make connections with all texts.

Model the Strategy

Materials *Travel The World*, "End of Summer," page 37

Step 1 Name the strategy and explain to students what it is and how it helps them.

Think Aloud When you make connections with a text, it strengthens your comprehension in two important ways: It makes the text more interesting, which helps you stick with it, and it helps you remember what you read. The connections you make can be to your own experience; to other texts, movies, and TV shows you know; and to issues in your community and in the world.

Step 2 Explain that posing questions is a good way to make connections to a text. Display these questions so students can refer to them as they read:

- What do I connect to in the text?
- What makes me feel these connections?

Provide sticky notes to students and have them jot their connections on them. Students can place the sticky note next to the passage with which they connect.

Step 3 Have students read the poem called "End of Summer" on page 37. Show them how the questions help you connect to the title, the illustration, and the first stanza.

Think Aloud I make a strong connection to the title, "End of Summer" and to the ocean water and the beach. For years, I spent summers in a cottage near the ocean. I loved standing near the water's edge and listening to the waves lap gently over my feet. Sadness always enveloped me when it was time to return home and go back to school. I really connect to the part in the first stanza about packing the car. I remember the feeling of being crowded in the back seat with suitcases and bags. After we all piled in the car to go home, my parents always drove to the ocean one last time for all of us to see and smell the ocean air. These memories help me move beyond myself and better understand the boy and the girl in the poem.

Step 4 Point out that the more specific the connections, the deeper the understanding.

Step 5 Organize students into partners. Have partners discuss their connections to the rest of the poem, explaining why they feel them. Then have pairs share their thoughts with the class.

Step 6 After reading, post these questions to encourage students to self-reflect.

- Which connections made the reading more meaningful?
- How did these connections help me move beyond myself to thinking about other people, other texts, and larger issues that affect the community or the world?

Step 7 Have students share their insights with the class.

Guided Practice

1. Provide sticky notes for students so that they can respond to the questions in Step 2 as they read.
2. Point out that you want students to begin making connections before reading, as they preview the text and begin to access what they know.
3. Have students share their connections with a partner or small group. Circulate and listen so that you can identify students who need more guidance.
4. Support students who need your expertise to make connections and reflect on them.

Independent Practice

1. Continue to offer students opportunities to practice making connections.
2. Confer with students you supported during guided practice to make sure they can work productively on their own.

Following Up

Periodically review this strategy and point out that making connections is a part of inferential thinking, another important comprehension strategy.

Comprehension continued

Determining Importance

DEFINITION: Determining importance involves making decisions about what is important in a text. To determine the importance of ideas in a text, a reader must have a purpose for reading. Purposes can differ among readers and situations. By reflecting on important information in a text, a reader can infer big ideas and build new understandings.

RESEARCH SUPPORT

Students are presented with large amounts of information in texts, so it is essential for them to be able to identify and remember the important ideas in selections they read. Important ideas in expository texts are the main ideas, which are supported major details. A number of studies document that students can be taught to look for and identify main ideas and major details in expository text, enabling them to comprehend and recall important information (e.g., Armbruster, Anderson, & Ostertag, 1987; Sjostrom & Hare, 1984; Taylor & Beach, 1984). Important information in narrative texts consists of central story ideas, often represented in a story map. There is considerable research demonstrating that students can be taught to identify the key ideas in stories and that this enhances their understanding and memory for narrative texts (Fitzgerald & Spiegel, 1983; Idol & Croll, 1987; Singer & Donlan, 1982).

MODEL LESSON

Explain: How the Strategy Helps and When to Use It

Explain to students that finding important ideas in a text is an important skill for students. When students identify what's important, they will better comprehend and remember what they read. An awareness of important ideas will also help students create and infer new understandings. Determining importance is dependent on a purpose for reading. Students can set purposes before reading a passage, a chapter, an article, or an entire book.

Point out that students should begin setting purposes and determining importance during a selection preview. Then, they should use their purposes as support for selecting important ideas both during and after reading.

Model the Strategy

Materials *Travel the World*, "Sacagawea: Native American Navigator," pages 28–31

Lesson 1: Determining Important Details

Step 1 Name the strategy and explain to students what it is and how it helps them.

Think-Aloud Nonfiction often has a lot of information and fiction can be complex and detailed. It can be tough to sort out what is important in both kinds of texts. A helpful way to figure out the important details is to use the purposes for reading that you set before you started reading. I will show you how I set purposes. Be on the lookout that my purposes might change as I read and gather more information.

Step 2 Show students how you preview pages 28–31 and then set purposes for reading. Explain that to preview, you'll read the title, the introduction on page 28, and the headings; study the illustrations; and skim the sidebar on page 31.

Think-Aloud After previewing, I set these purposes for reading. I would like to discover

- why Sacagawea is called a navigator [from the title];
- why there's a statue of her and her baby and why she points west [from illustration on p. 30];
- how she helped Lewis and Clark on their journey [from heading on p. 30].

Step 3 Have students read page 30 and show them how you figure out important ideas. Be sure to point out any changes in importance that occurred.

Think-Aloud OK, now that I've read page 30, I see that the title refers to Sacagawea as navigator because she led the explorers on their journey west—that's why her hand on the statue points west. She helped Lewis and Clark by showing them edible plants and berries and where to hunt for animals. Her connections to the Lemhi Indians helped the expedition get food, horses, and more guides. At first, I thought these were the most important details, but, as I read, I changed my mind. Her sense of calm, which saved Lewis and Clark's journals and supplies when their boats overturned, was possibly more important because without the journals, we would have no record of the journey today.

Step 4 Have students comment on your think-aloud and add details that they believe relate to your purposes.

Lesson 2: Finding Big Ideas

Step 1 Explain that you will now show students how you reflect on your purposes for reading and important details to determine (or infer) a big idea.

Think-Aloud Now that I've read the article, let me think about my purposes for reading and all the important details I discovered. What big ideas grow out of everything I know? I think one big idea is that Sacagawea's presence on the expedition made a big difference. Sacagawea knew the land and the language and was a symbol of peace to the tribes they met. Her calm demeanor ended up saving the written record of the journey.

Step 2 Organize students into partners. Have pairs discuss and suggest other big ideas.

Guided Practice

1. Organize students into partners.
2. Have all pairs preview the same article and write their purposes for reading in a journal or notebook.
3. Have pairs discuss the selection, pinpoint important ideas, and jot them in their journals or notebooks.
4. Ask partners to share and discuss the important ideas they identified.
5. Have pairs use their purposes and important ideas to figure out a big idea. Pairs can share their big ideas with the class. Tell students that when they find big ideas, they are inferring.
6. Support pairs who need more practice with setting purposes and determining important ideas.

Independent Practice

1. Continue to give students practice with setting purposes and determining importance.
2. Confer with individuals to determine who needs more support with finding big ideas.

Following Up

Review this strategy throughout the year. Finding big ideas helps students comprehend, remember, and infer new meaning.

Understanding Text Structure

DEFINITION: Text structure involves the organization an author uses to write a selection. There are text structures for narrative and expository texts, and readers' knowledge and recognition of various text structures can enhance their text comprehension, recall, and learning.

RESEARCH

Students are presented with large amounts of information in texts, so it is important for them to be able to identify and remember the key ideas in selections they read. Research documents that, although creating summaries is a challenging task, preadolescents and adolescents can acquire this strategy through thoughtful instruction (e.g., Armbruster, Anderson, & Ostertag, 1987 Brown & Day, 1983; Duke & Pearson, 2002; Hahn & Garner, 1984; Hare & Borchardt, 1984; National Reading Panel, 2000).

MODEL LESSON

Explain: How the Strategy Helps and When to Use It

Explain to students that all selections are organized into one or more text structures. Before beginning to write, an author chooses how to organize the information. When students can identify and understand the text structures, their comprehension and recall improve. When reading fiction, students can use the **narrative structure** of **setting, characters, plot,** and **outcome** to better understand the story and remember the text. When reading nonfiction, students can identify the structures of **sequence, cause-effect, problem-solution, question-answer, compare-contrast**, and **description** to improve their understanding of the author's purpose and to identify details and big ideas. It's important to note that informational text often contains more than one structure.

Point out that skilled readers tune into text structure before reading, as they preview a text. Being aware of the text structure before reading will help students anticipate and predict what they will read. During reading, students can use text structure to comprehend, predict, and remember. After reading, students can discuss material in terms of text structure.

Model the Strategy

Materials *Changes,* "The Next Move," pages 29–34; *Changes,* "Changing the Definition of Pop Star: Stevie Wonder," pages 23–28

Lesson 1: Understanding Text Structure Before Reading

Step 1 Name the strategy and explain to students what it is and how it helps them.

Think-Aloud 1 Today, we'll preview a text to determine if it's narrative or informational. Look at pages 29–34; there are no section headings and there's dialogue between characters, two clues that this is narrative. To preview a narrative text, read the first two pages and look at the illustrations. We meet Sela, who might be the main character; we see the setting, Sela's old house and new house. The illustrations show an unhappy girl; it could be Sela. This is a narrative text.

Think-Aloud 2 Today, we'll preview to determine if this text is narrative or informational. If it's informational, we'll try to see what kind of structure the author uses. I know this is informational because it's about Stevie Wonder, a real pop singer. There are photographs, headings, and sidebars, all features of nonfiction. It looks like a short biography. Biographies are often written in a time-sequence structure so I'll look for clues that point to that. As I scan the article, I see dates that go from 1961 to 1999. That tells me that the main text structure is sequence.

Step 2 Organize students into pairs. Have pairs preview a text to decide whether the text is narrative or informational. Encourage students to give you the clues that led them to their conclusion.

Step 3 Have students read the texts. Then identify and discuss the structures(s).

Step 4 Remind students to use their knowledge of text structure as they read.

Lesson 2: Using Text Structure After Reading

Step 1 Organize students into pairs. Have them read "The Next Move."

Step 2 After reading the short story, have pairs complete a graphic organizer showing the structure of the story. (See TE page 387 for a plot organizer).

Step 3 Show students how you use the setting and plot to understand Sela's reactions and the illustrations. The opening shows a happy Sela who feels like she finally fits in at school. When Sela learns her family will be moving to California, she's angry and upset. She says, "You are going to ruin my life!" This line (along with the plot and setting) help you understand Sela's reactions and how she looks in the illustrations.

Step 4 Ask pairs to use setting and plot to explain another change in feelings and attitude that Sela experiences.

Step 5 After reading about Stevie Wonder, show how you use time sequence to figure out a big idea. The author details several hurdles that Wonder faced in the 1970s and 1980s. Explain that reading about these hurdles showed you that Stevie Wonder is very persistent and doesn't give up easily.

Step 6 Have pairs use time sequence to find another big idea.

Guided Practice

1. Provide guided practice before and after reading with other narrative and informational texts from the magazines.
2. Ask students to preview to figure out structure and then use structure to deepen meaning and recall.
3. Support students who need your expertise to help identify text structure to improve comprehension and recall.

Independent Practice

1. Provide students with opportunities to practice using text structure.
2. Confer with students you helped during guided practice to make sure that they are learning to identify and use text structure.

Following Up

Continue to review this strategy throughout the year.

Inferential Thinking

DEFINITION: Inferential thinking is the process of creating personal meaning from text. An inference is created when a reader combines prior knowledge with details from a text to create new, unstated meaning.

RESEARCH SUPPORT

Writers rely on readers' ability to use their prior knowledge and their ability to make inferences to fill-in information that is not explicit in text. This is a challenging task for many readers (Graesser, Singer, Trabasso, 1994; RAND, 2002). Fortunately, there exist a number of studies that demonstrate that students can be taught to make inferences about the texts they read by relying on prior knowledge and by making text-based and schema-based inferences (Dewitz, Carr, & Patberg, 1987; Hansen, 1981; Hansen & Pearson, 1983; McGee & Johnson, 2003).

MODEL LESSON

Explain: How the Strategy Helps and When to Use It

Explain to students that writers purposely do not include all the details in a text. Writers expect readers to combine their prior knowledge with the information in the text to create new, unstated meanings. When readers infer meaning, they deepen their comprehension by becoming more involved or connected with the text and create new understandings. Students can use this strategy with fiction, poetry, biography, and informational texts. Point out that inferential thinking starts before reading, when students make logical predictions, and continues during and after reading.

Model the Strategy

Materials *Revolutions,* "Sophie Germain; A Revolutionary Thinker," pages 30–32, *Revolutions,* "Middle Years: The Apache Sunrise Ceremony," page 16

Lesson 1: Biography

Step 1 Name the strategy and explain to students what it is and how it helps them. Display these questions to guide students' inferring:

- What does the text tell me?
- What do I already know about the topic?
- What new meaning can I infer?

Think-Aloud Today, I'll show you how to make inferences with "Sophie Germain; A Revolutionary Thinker," so you can better understand why Sophie Germain decided to study math. First, I'll notice what the text says and then I'll combine it with my prior knowledge to create an inference. I'll use the three questions to guide me.

Step 2 Read aloud page 30 and show students how you make an inference.

Think-Aloud First, here's what the text tells me: Sophie Germain was a child during the French Revolution. Because of the dangers that lurked outside her home, she had to remain inside. One day she happened to read the story of Archimedes, a Greek mathematician. Germain assumed that math must be pretty exciting if Archimedes didn't even notice a guard threatening him while he solved a math problem. She decided she would study it, too. Now, here's my prior knowledge: I know that women in the past were not always encouraged to study whatever they wanted. Finally, here's my inference or new meaning: Sophie Germain must have had a lot of confidence and drive to forge ahead with studying math despite the cultural norms at the time. The author does not state these ideas directly, but they make sense and help me understand Germain better.

Step 3 Organize students into partners.
Step 4 Have students read pages 32–34 and have them infer the character traits that Germain had that led to her win honorable mention in the contest.

Lesson 2: Informational Text
Step 1 Have students read page 16 in Revolutions.
Step 2 Show students how you use the three questions to infer. (See Step 1 in Lesson 1: Biography.)
Think-Aloud Here are the facts in "Day 1: Preparations": the godparents dance into camp; there's an opening speech; the girl's clothes are decorated; an eagle feather is put in her hair. Now, here's my prior knowledge about ceremonies: They mark important events that have great meaning. Finally, here's my inference or new meaning: This elaborate ceremony tells me that the Apache see a girl's first menstrual cycle as very important because it shows that the girl is now an adult, and is ready for more responsibilities like caring for others, working, marriage, and children.
Step 4 Have students find facts in one of the next sections and use the three questions to help them infer new, unstated meanings.

Guided Practice

1. Organize students into partners.
2. Use parts of fiction and nonfiction selections from the magazines. Have pairs read or reread the same selection.
3. Have pairs use what they know to explore implied meanings. Then have partners share their findings with classmates.
4. Circulate and listen to pairs working together. Identify students who can work on their own, and those who need your support.
5. Help pairs who need extra practice and guidance until they grasp making inferences.

Independent Practice

1. Continue to give all students practice with making inferences. Use fiction and nonfiction texts. Make sure students use the three questions to guide their inferring.
2. Confer with students in brief one-on-one meetings. Ask them to show you how they make inferences using part of an article from one of the magazines. Or have them write inferences they have made about a character, person, or information.

Following Up

1. Keep reviewing inferential thinking with students even though they're learning another strategy.
2. Support students who need your expertise by modeling how you infer from a magazine passage. Then listen to students infer.

Teacher Talk

Word Study

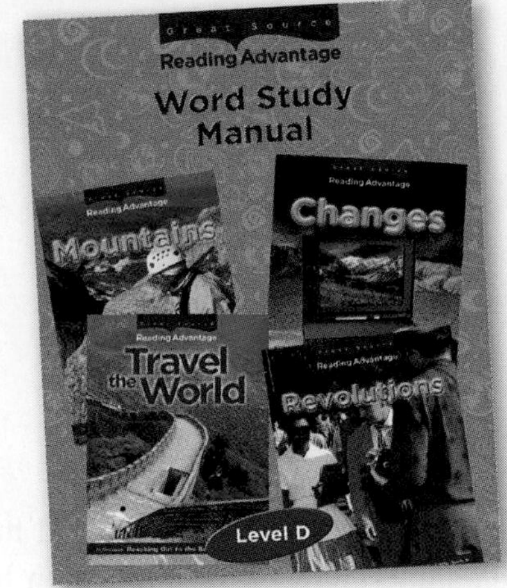

You remember the adage: *I hear and I forget; I see and I remember; I do and I understand.* This is why active learning is so important!

Why bother with Word Study?

Word Study promotes word knowledge and word fluency by having students take an active role in examining words and exploring patterns. Each word study activity has students engage in the following activities:

- **study** a group of words to find common features
- **sort** the words into categories
- **discuss** and explain the relationship between the words

How do I do Word Study?

The *Word Study Manual* has everything you need to know about Word Study. Use it as a resource to create your own free-standing word-study program or use it as a support for the Phonics/Word Study lessons right in the *Reading Advantage* Teacher's Edition. You can do Word Study with the whole class, but you might find it more manageable to do the activities with a single small group. This will also reduce the number of card sets that you will need for sorting.

Sorting words is an important—and the most engaging—part of word study. Try these steps to familiarize yourself with word sort.

- First of all, read through Chapter 5, "What Is Sorting?" in the *Word Study Manual* to build background for yourself.
- Try a practice sort with your students.
  - Prepare a set of about a dozen index cards for every two or three students by writing an animal name on each one (e.g., hippo, giraffe, deer, manatee, buffalo, whale).
  - Hand out the cards to pairs or triads of students. Read aloud each animal name to be sure that everyone knows the words.
  - Ask students to sort the cards into categories. Suggested categories for the animals above include these: number of syllables, double letters, land animals, water animals.
  - There are no right answers, but students must have a reason for each category! Ask them to share their categories and reasons with the class. Listening to students explain how they sorted the words gives you a window into their way of thinking about words.

Here's how to go about doing a Phonics/Word Study lesson in *Reading Advantage*.

Preparation

- Read through the activity.
- Open to the page in the *Word Study Manual* that has the words for the word sort. The page number will be in the Teacher's Edition lesson.
- There are three choices for sorting the words:
  - Students sort word cards.
  - Students write the words in categories on paper.
  - You and/or students work with a cut-apart transparency on an overhead projector.

If students will sort word cards, prepare a set of word cards for each pair or triad of students. Make a photocopy of the page from the *Word Study Manual* and cut apart the word cards.

If students will write the words on paper, make sure they have paper and pencil.

If you have an overhead projector, photocopy the page from the *Word Study Manual* onto a transparency and cut apart the word cards.

Word Study

Long e Vowel Sort from Level B

ee
agreed
speech
cheer
ie
chief
brief
shriek
eCe
these
theme
scene
Oddball
friend
rein
seize

Sorting the Words

- Explain the categories for the day. For example, the activity might focus on different spellings of the Long e sound (modeled on this page), or words with prefixes or suffixes.
- Read each word to be sorted aloud.
- Model how to sort the words by placing the first few words into the appropriate columns, explaining your thinking as you work: The word *chief* has *ie*, so I will place it in the *ie* category. The word *friend* also has *ie*, but the sound is different, so I will place it in the Oddball category.
- Have students continue to sort the words.
- Help students move misplaced words to the correct category.

Follow-up

- Discuss the sort and what students learned.
- Have students sort the words again, trying to increase their *personal* speed (this is not a competition!) and accuracy.
- If students keep a Word Study Notebook, they can record their sorts and add words that fit the patterns. (See *Word Study Manual*, page 13.)

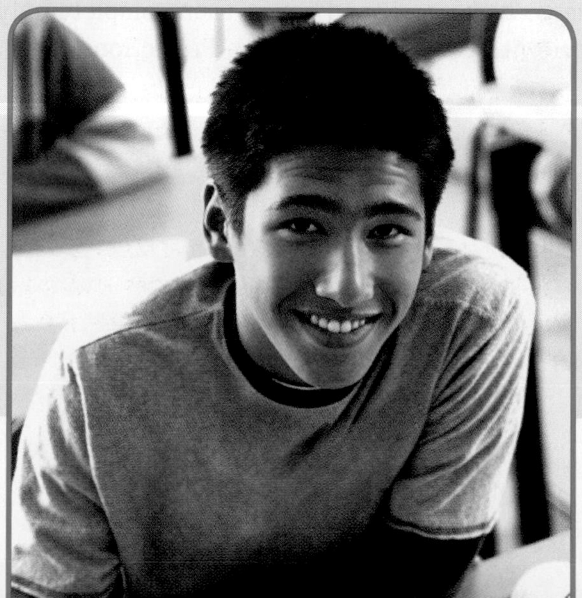

Teacher Talk

Planning a Reading Advantage Lesson

You open the *Reading Advantage* box. You lift out the Teacher's Edition and flip through the pages. Then you think, "Now what do I do?" What you want to do is to **skim through the lesson**, thinking about your students, and decide which activities will benefit them. **Then make a plan** to do those activities. (See the chart on page 30.)

Skim through the lesson

Look over the lesson to get a sense of the instructional opportunities available. Think about your students' needs as you skim the activity headings: Do your students need work in comprehension? Vocabulary? Make a note of the areas on which you will concentrate.

Choose how to introduce the magazine selection

Each lesson begins with a variety of activities to prepare students to read. (See Before Reading.) You know your students best and can decide whether they need a lot of support up front or just a little. Is this a topic or genre new to students? Then they might benefit from some extra pre-reading instruction. If students are comfortable with the topic and genre, then complete only Preview the Selection and Make Predictions/Set Purpose.

Decide how students will read the selection

Choose any one or more of these ways to have students read the selection.

- Read all or part of the selection aloud.
- Have students read with a partner or in small groups.
- Have students read independently.

While students are reading in a small group, with a partner, or on their own, use the questions in During Reading to monitor students' comprehension in brief one-on-one conferences.

Select after-reading activities for the whole group

The activities in After Reading, on the blue pages, are a follow-up to the reading selection. They work well in a whole-group setting.

Prepare the Phonics/ Word Study activity

Check the Phonics/Word Study activity for any preparation that needs to be done before class, such as creating word cards and using resources from the *Word Study Manual*.

Select follow-up instruction

Look over the activities listed under Additional Skills/Activities. Choose one or more activities that suit your students' needs.

Assign a time frame

How long are your class periods? That will determine how much you can do in a single day. You may want to break up a lesson into two or three parts if you have short periods. To fill in around the edges, make the paperback books (see Teacher's Edition appendix) and *eZines* available to your students to use independently.

Keep your students moving

Use the Self-Reflection questions at the end of each lesson to check whether students have understood the main concepts in each lesson. Use the more formal mid-magazine and end-of-magazine tests to monitor students' progress through a level. If students do well on the mid-magazine test, consider moving them up a level or accelerating the remainder of a level by using some of the magazine selections as independent reading (without the instruction).

Planning a Reading Advantage Lesson continued

Plan Your Lesson • 3-Day Plan

Here's one way to plan a *Reading Advantage* lesson! This plan is for Lesson 3 in Level C, but it serves as a model for all *Reading Advantage* lessons.

	Activity	Page Numbers	Time
Before Reading	KWL chart Preview the Selection Vocabulary Make Predictions Set Purpose	TE 20-21 SJ 8	Day 1 20 minutes
During Reading	Read aloud Independent reading Comprehension: Making Connections	TE 22	Day 1 20 minutes
After Reading	Discussion Questions Revisit the KWL chart Writing: Evaluate Masks	TE 24 SJ 9	40 minutes
Phonics/ Word Study	Plural endings –s, -es	TE 26 WSM 36	20 minutes
Additional Instruction	**2 groups:** ▶ Article: Say It with Emotions (read on their own) ▶ Comprehension: Understanding Text Structure (teacher-led group)	TE 26	20 minutes
When students finish their work	Paperback books EZines CD-ROM		

TE = Teacher's Edition SJ = Student Journal WSM = Word Study Manual

Great Source Reading Advantage
Assessment

Reading Advantage includes assessment options to help you place students in the program, check students' progress, and plan tailor instruction:

Place students in the right level

Use the Reading Advantage **Placement Test** to make sure that your students are reading text that is on their instructional level. When text is neither too hard nor too easy, students can attend to learning strategies and skills that will help them make progress in their reading ability. You have a choice of administering a Group Reading Inventory or an Individual Reading Inventory. Both have reading passages followed by multiple-choice questions and are available in each kit as well as online at http://www.greatsource.com.

Monitor students' progress informally

Each lesson ends with an opportunity for you to check your students' understanding of the featured comprehension strategy and word study skill for the lesson.

Assess students' progress formally

With each *Reading Advantage* kit, you will receive an Assessment book. Inside, you will find formal assessments for testing students' progress within a level. The **Mid-Magazine Tests** and **Magazine Tests** have reading passages followed by multiple-choice and extended-answer questions. The reading level and selection vocabulary in the passages match those in the magazine.

Observe students informally

At the back of the Assessment book you will find an **Interest Survey,** a **Reading Survey,** and four **Observational Checklists**. The purpose of the surveys is to help you learn about students' interests and feelings toward reading so that you can help them choose books they will enjoy. The main purpose of the Observational Checklists is to help you monitor students' progress during the year. The information you collect will enable you to make instructional decisions based on your observations and interactions with students.

Measure students' achievement

The *Gates-MacGinitie Reading Tests®* (*GMRT®*) are nationally recognized and respected for providing accurate assessment based on current research in reading. GMRT results have been directly correlated to Reading Advantage levels, so you can make the most of your *Reading Advantage* instruction by placing new students into the proper level, organizing instructional groups, targeting individual needs, and evaluating the effectiveness of *Reading Advantage*. GMRT is available online or in print.

Great Source Reading Advantage

Professional Development

Research is very clear that teacher expertise is one of the most important factors influencing student achievement. High quality professional development that is research-based, aligned with adult learning theory, and structured to promote the transfer of learning to classroom instruction is one of the most effective ways to enhance teacher expertise and student achievement.

Districts that partner with Great Source to create a sustained professional development plan for *Reading Advantage* benefit in many ways:

- **The professional development workshops** are based on a proven, research-based delivery model that will impact teacher instruction
- **Trainers are experts in the field of reading**, bringing years of experience to their work. They have used the *Reading Advantage* program and provide many suggestions for classroom use
- **Interactive and hands-on activities, trainer modeling, simulations, role playing, discussions, and practice teaching** prepare teachers for working with their students
- **The workshop** insures teachers will implement *Reading Advantage* appropriately
- **Well-trained teachers result in greater student achievement**

Great Source Reading Advantage

Scope and Sequence

The instructional lessons in Reading Advantage are set up in three parts: Before Reading, During Reading, and After Reading. Below is an outline of the skills and strategies that are taught throughout the program and where in the lesson they appear. All skills and strategies are addressed at each level.

Leveling, Strategies, and Skills	Foundations	A	B	C	D	E	F
Reading Level							
Grade 1 Reading Level	•						
Grade 2 Reading Level	•	•					
Grade 3 Reading Level		•	•				
Grade 4 Reading Level			•	•			
Grade 5 Reading Level				•	•		
Grade 6 Reading Level					•	•	
Grade 7 Reading Level						•	•
Grade 8 Reading Level							•
Before Reading							
Build Background Concepts	•	•	•	•	•	•	•
Vocabulary							
Context	•	•	•	•	•	•	•
Association	•	•	•	•	•	•	•
Categories	•	•	•	•	•	•	•
Word Meanings	•	•	•	•	•	•	•
Preview/Make Predictions							
Text Features (boldface, italics, headings, subheadings, captions, sidebars, graphics)	•	•	•	•	•	•	•
Text Structure (fiction, nonfiction)	•	•	•	•	•	•	•
Genre	•	•	•	•	•	•	•
Set purpose	•	•	•	•	•	•	•
During Reading							
Comprehension Strategies							
Monitor Understanding (read on, reread, retell, visualize, ask questions, context, word structure)	•	•	•	•	•	•	•
Making Connections (use prior knowledge, make predictions, compare to other texts)	•	•	•	•	•	•	•
After Reading							
Comprehension Strategies							
Monitor Understanding (read on, reread, retell, visualize, ask questions, context, word structure/breaking apart long words)	•	•	•	•	•	•	•
Making Connections (use prior knowledge, make predictions, make connections)	•	•	•	•	•	•	•
Determining Importance (ideas and details)		•	•	•	•	•	•
Understanding Text Structure (narrative [story elements], expository [description, sequence, cause/effect, compare/contrast information, problem/solution, question/answer]; text features; genre)		•	•	•	•	•	•
Inferential Thinking (make inferences, draw conclusions, identify themes)		•	•	•	•	•	•
Phonics/Word Study							
Vowels (long, ambiguous [e.g., *oo, ew, ou*])	•	•	•	•	•	•	•
Consonants (digraphs, blends, doubled)	•	•	•	•	•	•	•
Prefixes, Suffixes, Roots, Compound Words, Syllables	•	•	•	•	•	•	•
Vocabulary							
Synonyms/Antonyms, Homophones, Acronyms/Initialisms, Multiple-meaning Words, Idioms, Context, Denotation/Connotation, Classification, Association, Dictionary Skills	•	•	•	•	•	•	•
Writing	•	•	•	•	•	•	•
Ongoing Assessment	•	•	•	•	•	•	•

Integration with other Great Source Products

Great Source offers a variety of products that enable you to group students for instruction and reach every reader in your class.

What if my *Reading Advantage* students want more reading?

- The *Reading & Writing Sourcebooks* are an ideal supplement because they use a strategic approach and provide scaffolded reading and writing activities. Students in Level A of *Reading Advantage* can use Sourcebook grade 4, students in Level B can use Sourcebook grade 5, and students in Levels C and D will be comfortable using Sourcebook grade 6.
- Using the *Summer Success: Reading* program ensures a consistent instructional approach in summer school. Used alone, the magazines are perfect for additional independent reading.
- *Leveled Libraries* are ideal for independent reading and include nonfiction and fiction collections.

How can I meet the needs of English Language Learners?

- *Access*, a program for ELL students, provides materials and instructional guidelines to help students learn the content information their classmates are learning.
- *Leveled Libraries* in English and Spanish help students practice basic reading skills.

How can I extend reading and writing for my students?

- *Reader's Handbook* puts information about the reading process and reading strategies right into the students' hands.
- *Daybooks of Critical Reading and Writing* promote fine literature and improve students' critical reading and writing skills.
- *Lessons in Literacy* is a teacher resource that puts reading and writing skills and strategy lessons at your fingertips.
- *Science Daybooks* (Life, Earth, and Physical) help middle school students learn and review concepts in physical, life, and earth science.
- The *Write Source* program supports students' writing with student-friendly information on writing process, traits of effective writing, forms of writing, writing across the curriculum, and conventions.

TEACHER'S EDITION
LEVEL D

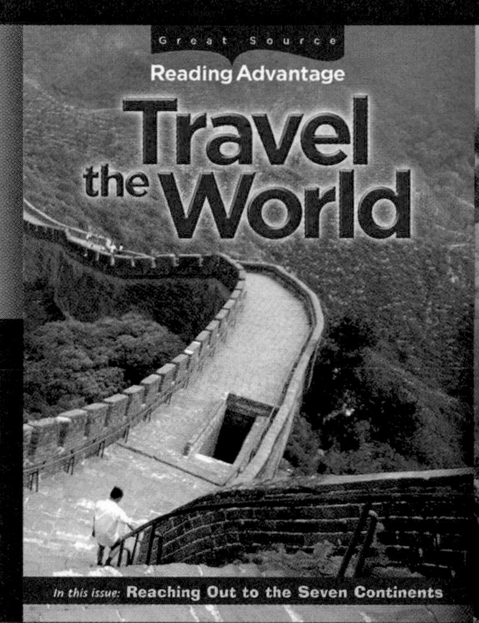

Level D, Magazine I

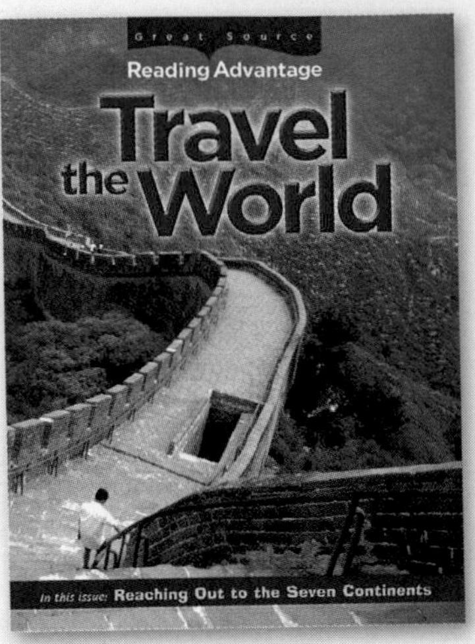

Travel the World

Magazine Summary

Travel the World magazine features a wide variety of literature, including a photo essay, poetry, a travelogue, a radio play, a diary, and a folktale. Each of these works focuses on a particular region of the world or travel experience.

Content-Area Connection: social studies
Lexile measure 820L

Travel the World Lesson Planner

LESSON	BEFORE READING	DURING READING	AFTER READING
LESSON 1 **Audacious Australian Animals** *and* **A Dream of Wholeness** (photo-essay and poem) page 6	K-W-L Chart Vocabulary Preview Preview the Selection Make Predictions/Set Purpose	Understanding Text Structure Determining Importance	Check Purpose Discussion Questions Writing: K-W-L chart Vocabulary: context clues Phonics/Word Study: silent-sounded consonants
LESSON 2 **Ancient Artists of Lascaux** *and* **Aspects of a Train** (memoir) page 14	Make a List Vocabulary Preview Preview the Selection Make Predictions/Set Purpose	Making Connections Monitor Understanding	Check Purpose Discussion Questions Writing: 5Ws chart/news story Vocabulary: root words Phonics/Word Study: consonant alternations
LESSON 3 **Stay Cool—Travel to Antarctica!** (question-answer article) page 24	Concept Web Vocabulary Preview Preview the Selection Make Predictions/Set Purpose	Making Connections Understanding Text Structure	Check Purpose Discussion Questions Writing: opinion chart Vocabulary: word root *therm-/thermo-* Phonics/Word Study: consonant alternations
LESSON 4 **Amazon River Adventure** (biography and poem) page 32	Association Web Vocabulary Preview Preview the Selection Make Predictions/Set Purpose	Making Connections Monitor Understanding	Check Purpose Discussion Questions Writing: notes for visualizing Vocabulary: prefix *pro-* Phonics/Word Study: vowel alternations: long to schwa

Overview

Preview the Magazine

Give students ample time to look through the magazine. Have them read selection titles and look at the photographs and illustrations. Tell students that the magazine contains literature about travel experiences in many different parts of the world. Then create a class chart with information about the continents.

Continent	What We Know
Africa	
Antarctica	
Asia	
Australia	
Europe	
North America	
South America	

PHONICS/ WORD STUDY	FOCUS ON	ASSESSMENT	HIGHER-ORDER THINKING QUESTIONS
Silent-Sounded Consonants	Writing: animal guide Fluency: phrasing English Language Learners Independent Activity Options	Understanding Text Structure Determining Importance Silent-Sounded Consonants	Choose two animals from the article to write about. In what ways are they similar? How do they differ? Use information and specific details from the article to support your answer. What special physical characteristics have these animals developed to defend themselves from predators or competitors? Use information and specific details from the article to support your answer.
Consonant Alternations	Writing: double-entry journal Fluency: punctuation English Language Learners Independent Activity Options	Making Connections Monitor Understanding Consonant Alternations	What factors led to the closing of the caves at Lascaux in 1963? Use information and specific details from the article to support your answer. Imagine your friends are traveling to France. What would you tell them about the caves in Lascaux to encourage them to visit there? Use information and specific details from the article to support your answer.
Consonant Alternations	Writing: journal entry Fluency: punctuation English Language Learners Independent Activity Options	Making Connections Understanding Text Structure Consonant Alternations	If you were planning a trip to Antarctica what kinds of planning would you do? Use information and specific details from the article to support your answer. Antarctica is not a friendly environment for people and animals. What must they do to survive there? Use information and specific details from the article to support your answer.
Vowel Alternations: long to schwa	Writing: journal entry Fluency: expression English Language Learners Independent Activity Options	Making Connections Monitor Understanding Vowel Alternations: long to schwa	How would you persuade a friend to sign your petition for saving the rainforest from over cutting and destruction? Use information and specific details from the article to support your answer. How does the way the article was written complement its subject matter? Use information and specific details from the article to support your answer.

Travel the World Lesson Planner

LESSON	BEFORE READING	DURING READING	AFTER READING
LESSON 5 **Sacagawea: Native American Navigator** (biographical sketch) page 40	Anticipation Guide Vocabulary Preview Preview the Selection Make Predictions/Set Purpose	Inferential Thinking	Check Purpose Discussion Questions Writing: biographical sketch Vocabulary: suffix *-ible/-able* Phonics/Word Study: vowel alternations: long to short
LESSON 6 **Brotherly Love** *and* **End of Summer** (short story and poem) page 46	Create a List Vocabulary Preview Preview the Selection Make Predictions/Set Purpose	Making Connections Understanding Text Structure	Check Purpose Discussion Questions Writing: journal entries Vocabulary: multiple meanings Phonics/Word Study: vowel alternations: short to schwa
LESSON 7 **The Grizzlies of Yellowstone** (radio play) page 54	Anticipation Guide Vocabulary Preview Preview the Selection Make Predictions/Set Purpose	Making Connections Monitor Understanding	Check Purpose Discussion Questions Writing: play scene Vocabulary: denotation and connotation Phonics/Word Study: vowel alternations review
LESSON 8 **When in Rome** (narrative) page 62	K-W-L Chart Vocabulary Preview Preview the Selection Make Predictions/Set Purpose	Understanding Text Structure Inferential Thinking	Check Purpose Discussion Questions Writing: compare-contrast Vocabulary: concept ladder Phonics/Word Study: Greek roots
LESSON 9 **On Safari** (diary entries) page 70	Make a List Vocabulary Preview Preview the Selection Make Predictions/Set Purpose	Monitor Understanding Understanding Text Structure	Check Purpose Discussion Questions Writing: timeline Vocabulary: multiple meanings Phonics/Word Study: Greek roots
LESSON 10 **The Beautiful Girl on Whose Lips Bloom Roses** (Bulgarian folktale) page 78	Folktale Features Chart Vocabulary Preview Preview the Selection Make Predictions/Set Purpose	Making Connections Understanding Text Structure	Check Purpose Discussion Questions Writing: story map/summary Vocabulary: synonyms Phonics/Word Study: Greek roots
LESSON 11 **The Great Wall of China** *and* **The World at Your Feet** (articles) page 86	Category Chart Vocabulary Preview Preview the Selection Make Predictions/Set Purpose	Determining Importance	Check Purpose Discussion Questions Writing: notes for visualizing Vocabulary: context Phonics/Word Study: Greek roots

PHONICS/ WORD STUDY	FOCUS ON	ASSESSMENT	HIGHER-ORDER THINKING QUESTIONS
Vowel Alternations: long to short	Writing: biographical sketch Fluency: pacing English Language Learners Independent Activity Options	Inferential Thinking Vowel Alternations: long to short	What evidence would you use in a debate about Sacagawea's importance to the Lewis and Clark expedition to support the idea that she was essential to the expedition's success? Use information and specific details from the article to support your answer. What of Sacagawea's character traits made her useful to the expedition? Use information and specific details from the article to support your answer.
Vowel Alternations: short to schwa	Writing: letter Fluency: expression English Language Learners Independent Activity Options	Making Connections Understanding Text Structure Vowel Alternations: short to schwa	Why is Luis envious of his brother? Use information and specific details from the article to support your answer. The title of the poem "End of Summer" suggests the end of a vacation. Which words suggest that the poet is thinking about other endings, too? Use information and specific details from the poem to support your answer.
Vowel Alternations Review	Writing: pamphlet Fluency: expression English Language Learners Independent Activity Options	Making Connections Monitor Understanding Vowel Alternations Review	If your friends wanted to travel to Yellowstone Park and observe bears, what advice would you give them to avoid danger? Use information and specific details from the article to support your answer. What causes bears in hibernation to be sluggish and hungry? Use information and specific details from the article to support your answer.
Greek Roots	Writing: description Fluency: pacing English Language Learners Independent Activity Options	Understanding Text Structure Inferential Thinking Greek Roots	If you were a middle class citizen of ancient Rome, what would you like about your life? Use information and specific details from the article to support your answer. Compare the comfort of a tunic and stockings to a toga. Use information and specific details from the article to support your answer.
Greek Roots	Writing: journal entry Fluency: expression English Language Learners Independent Activity Options	Monitor Understanding Understanding Text Structure Greek Roots	Compare and contrast two animals described in the journal. Use information and specific details from the article to support your answer. How did the author's planning for the trip contribute to her enjoyment of it? Use information and specific details from the article to support your answer.
Greek Roots	Writing: point of view Fluency: pacing English Language Learners Independent Activity Options	Making Connections Understanding Text Structure Greek Roots	In what ways are pearls and roses symbolic of tears and lips? Use information and specific details from the story to support your answer. Read and interpret the following quote from the selection: "Before the roses bloomed on her lips, he knew this girl was his true wife." Use information and specific details from the story to support your answer.
Greek Roots	Writing: friendly letter Fluency: pacing English Language Learners Independent Activity Options	Determining Importance Greek Roots	The author compares the Great Wall of China to a sleeping dragon. What facts about the Wall support such a characterization? Use information and specific details from the article to support your answer. Imagine that your friends are traveling to China. What would you tell them to persuade them to visit the Great Wall? Use information and specific details from the article to support your answer.

LESSON **1**

Audacious Australian Animals *and* A Dream . . .

Travel the World, pages 2–7

SUMMARY

The **photo-essay** describes unusual animals found in Australia. A **poem** follows.

COMPREHENSION STRATEGIES

Understanding Text Structure
Determining Importance

WRITING

K-W-L Chart

VOCABULARY

Context Clues

PHONICS/WORD STUDY

Silent-Sounded Consonants

Lesson Vocabulary

audacious	reptile
lethargic	shamans
receptors	pelts
invertebrates	steppes
hatchlings	

MATERIALS

Travel the World, pp. 2–7
Student Journal, pp. 1–4
Word Study Manual, p. 34
Writing Advantage, pp. 114–151

Sawfish Australia's Largest Freshwater Fish

What It Looks Like The sawfish, a relative of the shark, lives on the sea bottom. Its long snout looks like a saw. The sawfish slides gracefully though the water by waving its shark-like tail. The sawfish's mouth, nostrils, and gills are all on its underside. Its sharp, sawlike teeth are not really teeth at all; they're scales. However, don't get too comfortable swimming near a sawfish because its jaws are also lined with thousands of tiny teeth.

Sawfish come in a wide range of colors. The top of the fish is dark so that it blends in with the muddy sea bottom when seen from above. But the bottom of the fish is a shade of white so that it blends in with the water when seen from below.

What It Eats A sawfish dines on small fish and young shrimps and crabs. This slow-moving bottom feeder catches prey with its jaws. Then it crushes its meal and swallows it whole.

Before Reading

WHOLE CLASS Use one or more activities.

Make a K-W-L Chart

Define *audacious.* (bold, fearless) Explain that the author will introduce some fearless Australian animals. Have students turn to the K-W-L chart on *Student Journal* page 1. Ask what students know about Australian animals, and mention some of the animals in this selection. As a group, suggest entries for the first two columns. Your chart may resemble the following example. Students will come back to the chart later. (See Differentiated Instruction.)

What We **Know**	What We **Want** to Learn	What We **Learned**
Kangaroos live there. Sawfish are found in Australia.	Are any of these animals endangered? Where else are they found?	

Vocabulary Preview

Read aloud the vocabulary words for the article and write them for students to view. Clarify pronunciations. Ask students to begin the knowledge rating chart on *Student Journal* page 2 by filling in as many boxes as possible. They can return to the chart to fill in any empty boxes after they read the selection. Model a response for the *Student Journal* page.

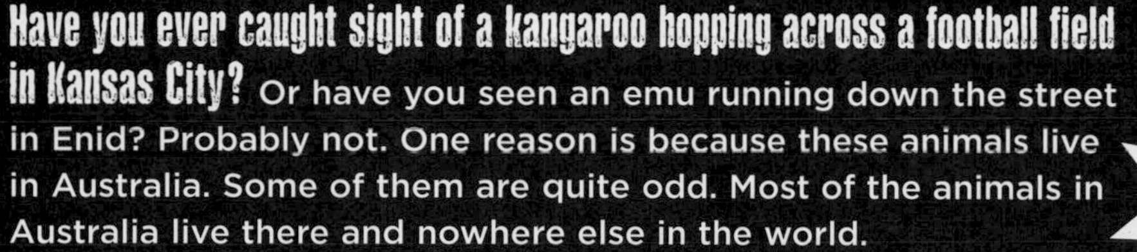

Have you ever caught sight of a kangaroo hopping across a football field in Kansas City? Or have you seen an emu running down the street in Enid? Probably not. One reason is because these animals live in Australia. Some of them are quite odd. Most of the animals in Australia live there and nowhere else in the world.

Sawfish are quite lethargic, spending most of the day on the sea floor. Scientists think they can live about 25–30 years.

How It Uses Its Snout The sawfish uses its long snout in four main ways:

1. As a Tracking Tool The sawfish's snout contains electro-receptors. These receptors can sense the heartbeats of buried fish like prawns, crabs, and other invertebrates. The receptors make searching for meals much easier.

2. As a Motion Sensor The sawfish's snout is sensitive to motion. Using its snout, a sawfish can follow and then attack fish in the murky, dark water.

3. As a Rake When a sawfish finds something to eat that is buried in the sea bottom, it uses its snout as a rake to dig up the buried sea creatures.

4. As a Sword When the sawfish hunts fish that are swimming, it uses its snout as a slashing sword.

Endangered Alert! People once captured sawfish. They would cut off their "saws" as souvenirs or grind them down to use as medicine. Also, many sawfish get tangled in fishing nets. Because of these reasons, sawfish are endangered.

3

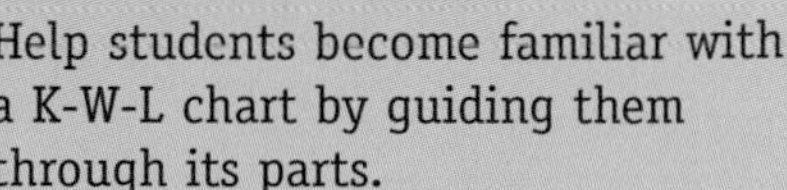

DIFFERENTIATED INSTRUCTION

MAKE A K-W-L CHART

Help students become familiar with a K-W-L chart by guiding them through its parts.

1. Point out the head for each column. Have students write in the "K" column what they know about fearless Australian animals. Then have them write in the "W" column questions about what they want to know. Tell students to be on the lookout for answers as they read.
2. Explain to students that they will complete the "L" column of the chart after they have read the article. Have them write what they learned from their reading.

Student Journal page 1

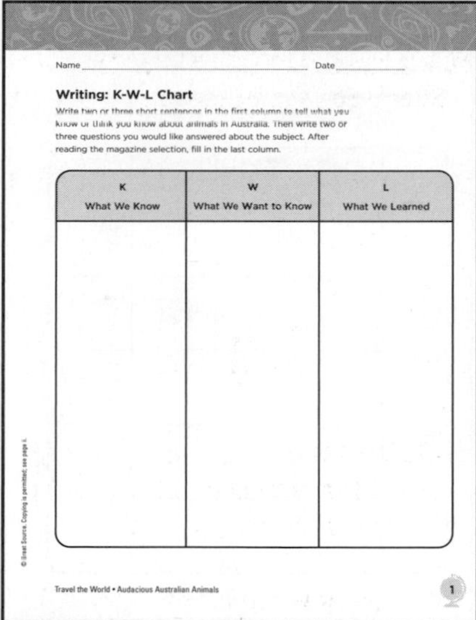

Name ____________ Date ________

Writing: K-W-L Chart

Write two or three short sentences in the first column to tell what you know or think you know about animals in Australia. Then write two or three questions you would like answered about the subject. After reading the magazine selection, fill in the last column.

K What We Know	W What We Want to Know	L What We Learned

Travel the World • Audacious Australian Animals 1

Preview the Selection

Have students read the title, look at the photographs of the animals, and read the headings with animal names. Use these or similar prompts to guide students to notice the important features of the photo-essay.

- What animals will you learn about?
- How is the information presented?
- What do you notice about the subheadings in red?

Teacher Think Aloud

These Australian animals are not familiar to me. The emu looks kind of like an ostrich, though. I wonder if it is a relative of the ostrich. I look forward to finding out more about it and the other animals. I think the text is organized in a way that will make reading about the animals interesting. I like the author's use of a heading for each section, and the subheadings in red.

Make Predictions/ Set Purpose

Students should use the information they gathered in previewing the selection to make predictions about what they will learn. If students have trouble generating a purpose for reading, suggest that they read to learn about unusual Australian animals.

DIFFERENTIATED INSTRUCTION

Comprehension

UNDERSTANDING TEXT STRUCTURE

Use these steps to help students form a stronger understanding of text structure:

1. Explain to students that authors of informational articles organize their ideas in different ways. For example, the ideas in an article about events in history might be organized by dates. This article about Australian animals is organized by the kind of animal.
2. Have pairs of students read the headings and subheadings in each section and tell what they expect to learn in that section.

Student Journal page 2

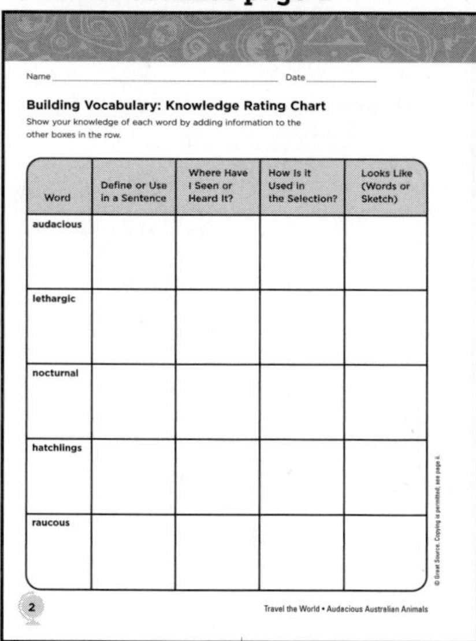

Name_______________ Date_______________

Building Vocabulary: Knowledge Rating Chart

Show your knowledge of each word by adding information to the other boxes in the row.

Word	Define or Use in a Sentence	Where Have I Seen or Heard It?	How Is It Used in the Selection?	Looks Like (Words or Sketch)
audacious				
lethargic				
nocturnal				
hatchlings				
raucous				

2 Travel the World • Audacious Australian Animals

Emu Australia's Largest Bird

What It Looks Like The emu (EE myoo), the world's second largest bird, looks like its relative, the ostrich. (The ostrich is the world's largest bird.) Like the ostrich, the emu is flightless. Unlike the ostrich, it lives in Australia. Long, thick, drooping feathers cover its body. The feathers on its head are short, making its pointy beak, bright eyes, and blue throat stand out. Even though the emu can't fly, it runs very quickly. Using its long legs and three-toed feet, an emu can run up to 50 kilometers per hour (about 31 miles per hour).

What It Eats Living mainly on a diet of grass, flowers, and seeds, the emu sometimes likes a treat of a crunchy grasshopper. Emus drink water once or twice a day.

Hatching Baby Emu Emus pair up when they are about two years old. A female emu lays between 5 and 20 dark green eggs in a nest built of grass and weeds by the male. The male keeps the eggs warm for eight weeks. During this time, he hardly ever leaves the nest. To survive, he uses up a layer of fat that he built up by eating a lot before nesting. When the eggs hatch, the male cares for the young for about six to nine months. Emus are in the most danger as eggs because lizards love to eat them. They also are at risk as hatchlings, when they are in their very young stage, because foxes hunt baby emus for food.

Emus can grow to a height of 6 feet (185 cm) and weigh about 110 pounds (50 kg). The female is usually larger than the male.

Australia's Smallest Penguin

Australia is home to the smallest species of penguin in the world, the fairy penguin. After an oil spill off the coast of Australia, some biologists came up with a way to keep the penguins safe while the oil was cleaned up. They put wool sweaters on the birds! The wool kept the penguins from cleaning their feathers.

4

During Reading

Comprehension

UNDERSTANDING TEXT STRUCTURE

Use these questions to model for students how to determine the classification text structure of the selection. Then ask students how this helps them understand the text.

- What do I notice about the way this article is structured?
- Why do I think the author chose this text structure?

(See Differentiated Instruction.)

Teacher Think Aloud

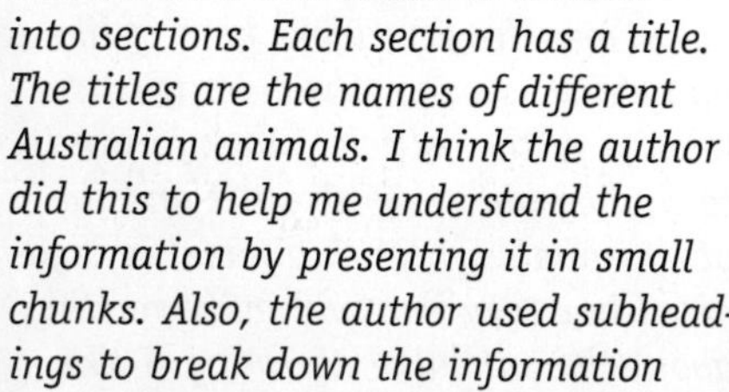

I notice that this article is divided into sections. Each section has a title. The titles are the names of different Australian animals. I think the author did this to help me understand the information by presenting it in small chunks. Also, the author used subheadings to break down the information more. The first two subheadings for each animal are the same.

Comprehension

DETERMINING IMPORTANCE

Use these questions to model how to determine the most important idea in the "What It Eats" section about the sawfish. Then have students determine the most important idea(s) in the same section for each of the other animals.

- What is the most important idea in this section?
- Why do I think this is the most important idea?

Tasmanian Devil Australia's Fiercest Marsupial

What It Looks Like You might have a hard time spotting Tasmanian devils in the daylight because they are nocturnal. But if you are lucky enough to catch sight of one, you will find that a real devil looks less cute than the familiar cartoon character! A typical devil is the size of a small terrier dog, is a bit plump, and has a foot-long tail. It is covered with black fur and is usually marked with a white patch of fur around its neck that looks like a collar. A Tasmanian devil's head is large and powerful. It has wide jaws with sharp, pointed teeth. Its pink ears turn red—like a devil's—when it is angry, upset or provoked.

What It Eats Tasmanian devils eat carrion, the flesh of dead animals. Gross as it might sound, a devil will eat anything that has been lying around, no matter how rotten, old, or smelly. Its powerful jaws allow it to crush bones. Devils have been known to eat entire animals—the meat, the fur, and the bones. They leave nothing behind.

Tasmanian devils are fairly calm except when it comes to mealtime. They are very protective of food and will even kill another devil that wants its food.

If you see a Tasmanian devil, you will probably notice many patches of missing fur, which are the battle scars from these food fights.

Baby in a Pouch Tasmanian babies are called joeys. Joeys are born blind, deaf, and about the size of a grain of rice. Up to fifty joeys can be born at a time. They race up the mother's belly, about three inches, to the opening of her pouch. Of the fifty joeys, only about four survive because of limited room in the pouch. When a joey reaches the pouch, it stays there for three months, drinking its mother's milk. At the end of that time, it will leave the pouch for a nest.

A Famous Scream If you miss seeing a Tasmanian devil, you might hear one. They are very raucous, especially when there is a group of them around a dead animal, battling for food. They snort, bark, and scream. These horrible noises, along with their mean looks, are two reasons why they've earned the name "devil."

A devil can eat 40% of its body weight in 30 minutes. That amount of food will keep a devil going for 2–3 days.

Teacher Think Aloud

The author presents several ideas in the "What It Eats" section about the sawfish. Which one is the big idea the author wants me to understand? I think it is the information in the first sentence because it tells me exactly what a sawfish eats. The other two sentences tell about how a sawfish catches its food and swallows it. These details are interesting, but they don't tell me about what a sawfish eats.

Fix-Up Strategies

Offer these strategies to help students read independently.

If you don't understand what you're reading:

- Reread the difficult section to look for clues to help you comprehend.
- Read ahead to find clues to help you comprehend.
- Retell, or say in your own words, what you've read.
- Visualize, or form mental pictures of, what you've read.

If you don't understand a word:

- Reread the sentence. Look for ideas and words that provide meaning clues.
- Find clues by reading a few sentences before and after the confusing word.
- Look for the base or root word and think about its meaning.
- Think about the topic or plot at this point to see if either offers meaning clues.

DIFFERENTIATED INSTRUCTION

Vocabulary Context Clues

To provide more experience with context clues, use these steps:

1. Have students read "As a Tracking Tool" on page 3.
2. Ask students to identify the words that helped them figure out the meaning of *receptors*. Ask: *How do receptors help the sawfish? Does the word* receptors *remind you of other words?* Help students relate receptors to receivers.
3. Finally, have students define *receptors*. (special cells or nerve endings that receive information)

Student Journal pages 3–4

Name ________________ Date ________

Building Vocabulary: Using Context to Understand a Word

Look for the word *nocturnal* in the photo essay "Audacious Australian Animals." Write in the box the sentences that help you know its meaning. Then complete the statements and answer the questions.

My Word in Context:

I think this word means ________________

because ________________

My word is ________________

My word is not ________________

Where else might I find this word? ________________

What makes this an important word to know? ________________

Travel the World • Audacious Australian Animals 3

Thorny Devil Looks Can Be Deceiving

What It Looks Like Although this is one scary-looking reptile, the thorny devil is basically harmless. It's not hard to see how it got its name, though. Thorny spikes stick upward from its skin, which ranges in color from reddish brown to black. Like the chameleon, it changes color depending on the color of the soil.

What It Eats The thorny devil loves a diet of ants and eats an incredible number of them. Scientists say that a devil can eat between 600 and 3,000 ants in one meal! But perhaps the most amazing thing about its eating habits is that it eats ants one at a time. Flicking out its tongue, the thorny devil picks up an ant and eats it. When it's on a roll, it can eat up to 45 ants in one minute.

All About Defense Mostly hunted by humans and buzzards, the thorny devil is all about defense. The devil changes color so it is not easily seen. If it is frightened, it has a few tricks up its sleeve:

- The devil tucks its head between its knees. Then, it pops up a fake head, which is really a knob-like swelling on its neck.
- Sometimes, the thorny devil tries to act like a leaf by jerking, turning, and then freezing in place.
- The thorny devil puffs itself up so it looks bigger than it really is.

These three defensive moves usually keep the thorny devil out of trouble. ◆

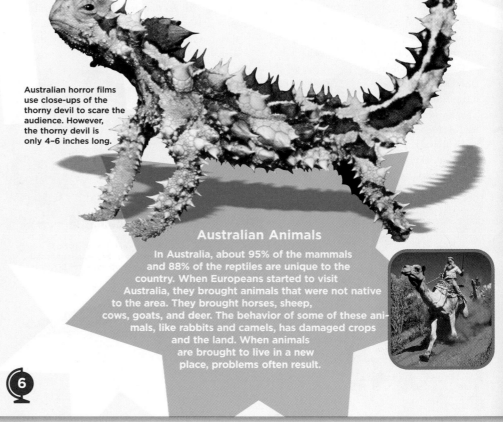

Australian horror films use close-ups of the thorny devil to scare the audience. However, the thorny devil is only 4–6 inches long.

Australian Animals

In Australia, about 95% of the mammals and 88% of the reptiles are unique to the country. When Europeans started to visit Australia, they brought animals that were not native to the area. They brought horses, sheep, cows, goats, and deer. The behavior of some of these animals, like rabbits and camels, has damaged crops and the land. When animals are brought to live in a new place, problems often result.

6

After Reading

Use one or more activities.

Check Purpose

Have students decide if their purpose was met. Did they learn more about unusual Australian animals?

Discussion Questions

Continue the group discussion with the following questions.

1. In what situations might the thorny devil use each of its defenses? (Inferential Thinking)
2. Which animal do you think is the most fearsome? Explain. (Details)
3. What do you know now that you didn't know before reading the article? (Making Connections)

Revisit: Knowledge Rating Chart

Have students review their responses to the knowledge rating chart on *Student Journal* page 2. Ask them if they would like to make any adjustments or changes. Students can also complete any empty boxes with what they learned in the selection.

A Dream of Wholeness

In the Gobi, shamans ride
To the sky on snow leopard pelts.
There, I will find myself.

In the Gobi, wild herbs lead me
To turquoise, jasper, and crystal—
Stones more precious than time.
There, I will find my senses.

In the Gobi, I grip the heavy mane
Of a wild horse and gallop away
Like a spirit, myself.

Together, my horse and I blend
Right into the steppes.
We slip off this world into hours of wholeness.

7

Poem: A Dream of Wholeness

Have students silently read the poem "A Dream of Wholeness" on page 7. Then read the poem aloud to them. Discuss the meanings of all words that students find difficult. Then discuss the poem.

- What is the tone or "sound" of the poem? Excited? Sad? Happy?
- What do you think the poet's message is?
- What can you visualize when you read the poem? What words and phrases help you?

Answer key for **Student Journal page 4**

A	D	L	M	U	P	B	E	R	S
H	R	E	C	E	P	T	O	R	S
D	A	T	L	O	A	V	A	E	T
J	U	H	B	D	I	R	O	P	D
I	C	A	R	R	I	O	N	T	Y
F	O	R	Q	P	U	L	X	I	J
M	U	G	E	A	W	B	I	L	E
S	S	I	T	D	F	Z	L	E	T
Y	I	C	H	N	C	W	O	G	A

Writing K-W-L Chart

Revisit the K-W-L chart on *Student Journal* page 1. Ask students to suggest entries for the "L" column in the chart. Ask: *What did you learn? What animal facts surprised you?* Have students share their ideas. Then have students complete the chart by writing in the third column what they learned from the article.

Vocabulary Context Clues

Ask students to find the word *lethargic* on page 3. Have them retell in their own words what the sawfish is doing. Then ask what *lethargic* might mean. (not active, sluggish) Students have used context clues to figure out the meaning. Now have students complete the context activity on *Student Journal* page 3. Then ask students to find five vocabulary words in the puzzle on *Student Journal* page 4. (See Differentiated Instruction.)

Phonics/Word Study

Silent-Sounded Consonants

Display the words *muscle* and *column* and ask students what they notice about the two words. (Both words have a silent consonant.) Then write the words *muscular* and *columnist*. What do students notice about the consonants that were silent before? (They're sounded.) Now, work with students to complete the in-depth silent-sounded consonants activity on TE page 12.

Phonics/Word Study

Silent-Sounded Consonants

Place the following words on the board: *sign* and *bomb*. Ask students what is unusual about the spelling of these words. Students should notice that both words contain a silent consonant. The steps below will show students why these letters are present.

- Brainstorm all the words you can come up with that have the word *sign* in them. Students might come up with *signature, signal, signatory, signet, signify,* and others. (See *Word Study Manual* page 34 for a word list.)
- Ask students what they notice about the *g* in these associated words. (The *g* is sounded in all of these words.)
- Ask students if they can tell by looking at all of these connected words why the *g* is even in the word *sign*. Help them discover that although the *g* may be silent, it has a meaning connection, so it remains in the word *sign*.
- This change is an example of consonant alternations. The *g* consonant may alter (or change) in sound in related words, but the spelling remains the same. This is an example of the spelling-meaning connection that students will see over and over again in these lessons.
- Have students use their Word Study notebooks to write the following words in separate columns: *crumb, bomb, muscle, hasten, column, soften,* and *comb*. Have students underline the silent letter. Under each column, have them write as many words as they can that come from those words. Once they are done, create a list and discuss their selections.
- Remember, every discussion you have about words creates enthusiasm for words and helps build students' vocabularies.

crumb	bomb	muscle	hasten
crumble	bombard	muscular	haste
crumby	bomber		hasty
crumbly	bombardier		

column	soften	comb	
columnar	softer	combine	
columnist	softy		

For more information on word sorts and spelling stages, see pages 5–31 in the *Word Study Manual.*

Focus on . . .

Use one or more activities in this section to focus on a particular area of need in your students.

Comprehension STRATEGY SUPPORT

To help those students who need more practice using the strategies covered in this lesson, work one-on-one or in small groups to apply the strategy prompts below. Apply the prompts to a *Reading Advantage* paperback, a classroom library book, or a new or familiar selection in the magazine. Always model your own thinking first.

Understanding Text Structure

- What kind of text is this? (book, story, article, guidebook, play, manual)
- How does the author organize the text? (cause-effect, problem-solution, chronological order, description, question-answer, comparison-contrast)
- What details support my thoughts about the text structure?
- What is the cause (effect, problem, solution, order, question, answer)?
- If fiction, who are the characters? What is the setting, plot, conflict, and resolution?

Determining Importance

- What is the most important idea in the paragraph? How can I prove it?
- Which details are unimportant? Why?
- What does the author want me to understand?
- Why is this information important (or not important) to me?

Writing Animal Guide

Have students choose an ordinary or exotic animal to research. Have them create a short informational guide with headings such as *What It Eats, Where It Lives,* and other headings related to special features of the animal.

For instruction and practice writing informational paragraphs, see lessons in *Writing Advantage*, pages 114–151.

Fluency: Phrasing

Explain to students that it's important to read with correct phrasing. Phrasing describes how words are verbally grouped together in a meaningful way. After students have read the poem "A Dream of Wholeness" at least once, have partners read the poem aloud to each other.

As you listen to students read, use these prompts to guide them.

- Notice the line breaks and punctuation. They will help guide your reading.
- Think about the poem's message.

When students read aloud, do they—

- ✓ demonstrate quick recognition of words and phrases?
- ✓ exhibit an understanding of phrasal construction?
- ✓ incorporate appropriate timing, stress, and intonation?

English Language Learners

To support students as they learn about text structure, review the meanings of words they encountered in this lesson: *structure*, *title*, *heading*, *subheading*, and *photograph*. Then point out one or two words that have a distinct prefix, suffix, or root. Examples include *subheading* (*sub*, "under") and *photograph* (*photo*, "light" or *graph*, "written"). Have students brainstorm other words that contain the same word part. As a group, analyze the words to try to determine what the word part means.

Independent Activity Options

While you work with individuals or small groups, others can work independently on one or more of the following options.

- Level D paperback books, see TE pages 367–372
- Level D *eZines*
- Repeat word sorts from this lesson
- *Student Journal* pages for this lesson
- *Writing Advantage* independent lessons

Assessment

Strategy Assessment

To help you and your students assess their use of comprehension strategies, ask the following questions. Students can complete a written response or provide verbal answers in a one-on-one reading conference.

1. **Understanding Text Structure** In what ways did the text structure of the article help you understand the information the author presented? (Answers will vary, but students may say that the headings helped them know what they would be reading about, and that having the information presented in small sections helped them concentrate on one part at a time, rather than being overwhelmed with too much information.)
2. **Determining Importance** What are three important ideas about the thorny devil? (Answers will vary, but students should be able to defend their beliefs that the ideas they state are important.)

For ongoing informal assessment, use the checklists on pages 61–64 of *Level D Assessment*.

Word Study Assessment

Use these steps to help you and your students assess their understanding of silent-sounded consonants.

1. Write the words *crumb, crumble, crumby,* and *crumbly* on the board or on word cards.
2. Have students read the words aloud and identify which consonants are silent and which are sounded. (The *b* is silent in *crumb* and *crumby* and sounded in *crumble* and *crumbly*.)

crumb
crumble
crumby
crumbly

LESSON **2**

Ancient Artists of Lascaux *and* Aspects of a Train

Travel the World, pages 8–15

SUMMARY

The **article** tells about the discovery and importance of the Lascaux cave paintings in rural France. A **poem** follows.

COMPREHENSION STRATEGIES

Making Connections
Monitor Understanding

WRITING

5Ws Chart/News Story

VOCABULARY

Word Roots

PHONICS/WORD STUDY

Consonant Alternations

Lesson Vocabulary

engravings	scaffolding
replica	deteriorated
decipher	speculations
inhabited	

MATERIALS

Travel the World, pp. 8–15
Student Journal, pp. 5–8
Word Study Manual, p. 35
Writing Advantage, pp. 30–56

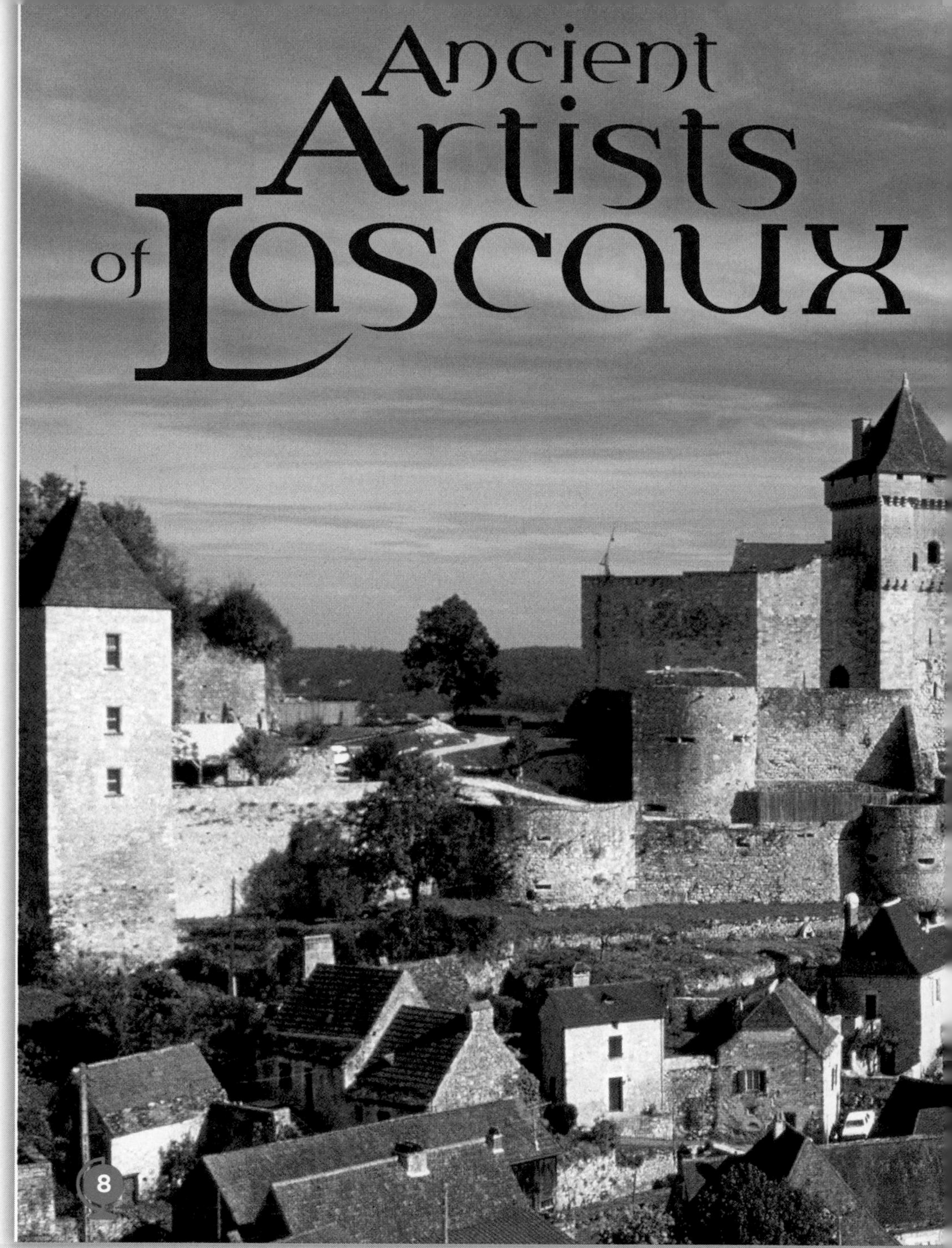

Ancient Artists of Lascaux

8

Before Reading

Use one or more activities.

Make a List

Brainstorm with students a list of reasons why people decorate the walls of their homes and personal spaces with pictures, murals, wallpaper, and so forth. Plan to revisit the list after reading the selection.

Why do people decorate?
1. To feel more at home
2. To add color
3.

Vocabulary Preview

Review the vocabulary list. Write the words on the board and read them aloud to clarify pronunciations.

Have students begin the predictions chart on *Student Journal* page 5. Ask for volunteers to share their thoughts.

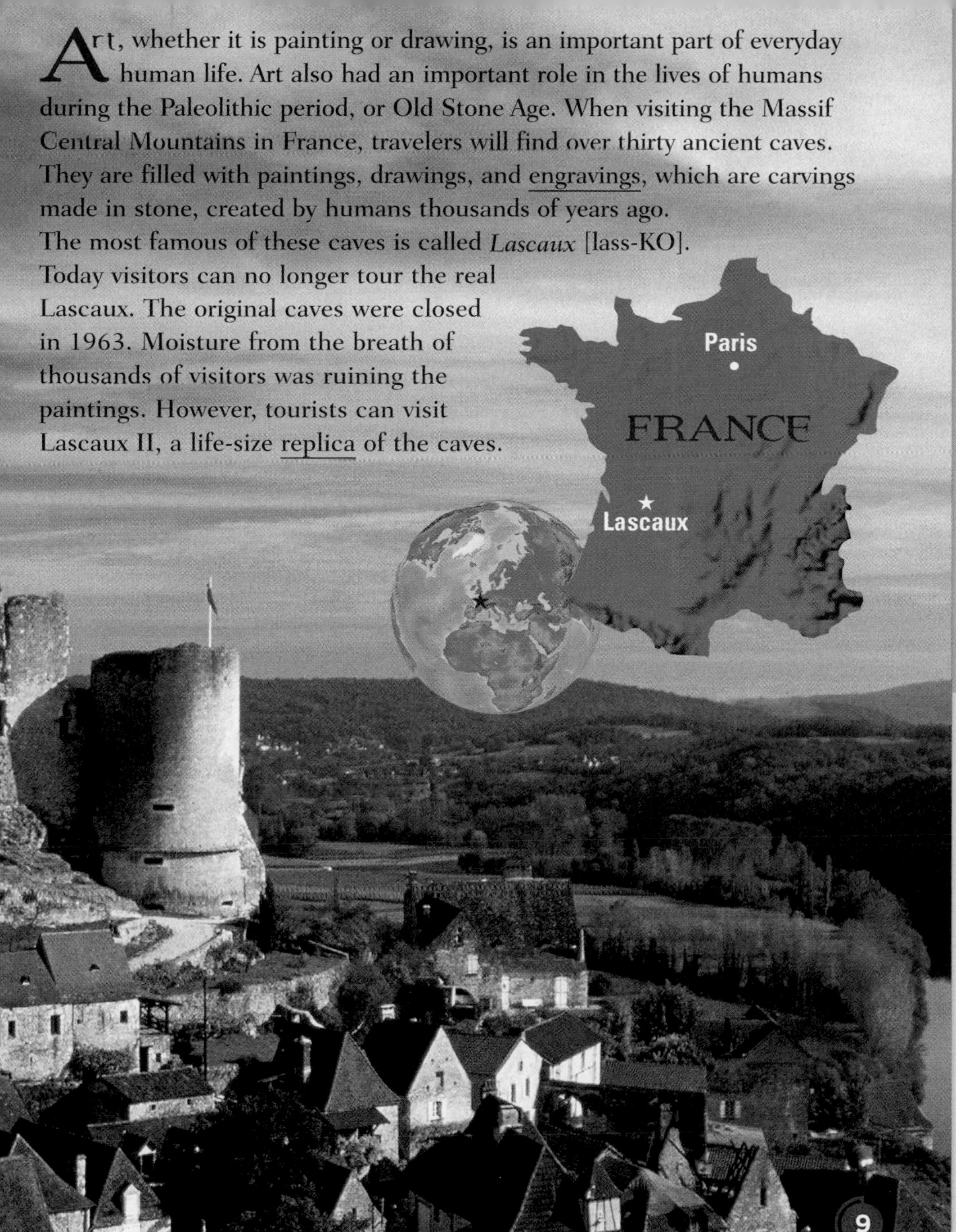

Art, whether it is painting or drawing, is an important part of everyday human life. Art also had an important role in the lives of humans during the Paleolithic period, or Old Stone Age. When visiting the Massif Central Mountains in France, travelers will find over thirty ancient caves. They are filled with paintings, drawings, and engravings, which are carvings made in stone, created by humans thousands of years ago.

The most famous of these caves is called *Lascaux* [lass-KO]. Today visitors can no longer tour the real Lascaux. The original caves were closed in 1963. Moisture from the breath of thousands of visitors was ruining the paintings. However, tourists can visit Lascaux II, a life-size replica of the caves.

9

DIFFERENTIATED INSTRUCTION SMALL GROUP

Make Predictions/ Set Purpose

Help students establish a purpose for reading.

1. Emphasize that having a purpose for reading gives the reader focus. The reader is always asking, "Are my questions being answered?"
2. Note that personal interests are often behind the reader's purpose for reading. Have students skim the article to look for headings, pictures, and special features that grab their attention. Explain that any of these can help set a reading purpose.

Student Journal page 5

Name ______________________ Date __________

Building Vocabulary: Predictions

Choose five words. How do you think the words will be used in "Ancient Artists of Lascaux"? Write your answers in the second column. Next, read the article. Then, clarify your answers in the third column.

engravings **decipher** **scaffolding** **speculations**
replica **inhabited** **deteriorated**

Word	My prediction for how the word will be used	How the word was actually used

Travel the World • Ancient Artists of Lascaux 5

Preview the Selection

Have students look through pages 8–14 in the magazine. Use these or similar prompts to quide students to notice important features of the text.

- Do you think this selection is fiction or nonfiction? Why?
- What do you notice about the headings?
- What do you think you will learn?

Teacher Think Aloud

The title of the selection tells me that it is about artists. At first, I think of people who create paintings, like the ones you see in museums. Then, I notice that the first heading is "Discovering the Caves," and the photographs are of paintings on cave walls. I am glad there are lots of photographs. I look forward to finding out more about these cave artists.

Make Predictions/ Set Purpose

Students should use the information they gathered in previewing the selection to make predictions about what they will learn. If students have trouble generating a purpose for reading, suggest that they read to find out why the caves at Lascaux draw thousands of visitors annually. (See Differentiated Instruction.)

DIFFERENTIATED INSTRUCTION

Comprehension

MAKING CONNECTIONS

Help students connect with the text by discussing their experiences with drawing and painting. Ask:

- Do you enjoy drawing and painting? Why or why not?
- Do you draw or paint things that are familiar to you, as the cave painters did? What kinds of things?
- Suppose that on your wall, you could paint something that tells a story. What story would you tell?

Discovering the Caves

On an early September morning in 1940, four French teenagers exploring the countryside around their homes came across a cave. The teenagers entered a room in the cave, now called *The Painted Gallery* because of the number of paintings on the walls. Those teenagers' eyes became the first modern eyes to look at the painted walls of Lascaux. The boys then discovered a large fallen tree, which had made a hole in the earth. This hole led to another opening in the cave. After widening the opening, the teenagers slipped through it. They fell into what is now known as *The Great Hall of the Bulls*. This cave contains one of the largest and most impressive walls of cave painting in the world. News of this amazing discovery spread quickly. Soon, villagers from near and far rushed to see the caves.

Amazing Sights in the Caves Some of the paintings on the walls of Lascaux are difficult to decipher, or understand. To our eyes, these paintings might look like scribbles for a few reasons:

1. Over time, the surfaces of the walls have been damaged. Many paintings are not whole.

2. Clay trickles down the cave walls. The clay leaves behind dirt and other build-up that slowly cover the paintings.

3. Some paintings were drawn on top of other paintings. This makes them hard to understand.

Anthropologists and other scientists who specialize in making sense of ancient civilizations spend their lives trying to "read" the paintings on the cave walls.

Three Kinds of Painting

The cave drawings fit into three main categories, or groups: humans, animals, and signs.

Humans in Cave Art Ancient artists rarely drew human figures. At Lascaux there is only one drawing of a human. This drawing is in the cave room known as *The Shaft of the Dead Man*. If you look closely at the drawing at the bottom of page 11, you will notice that the picture of the human isn't lifelike. Neither the body, the hands, the arms, nor the head seem correctly sized. Also, the drawing of the man contains no fine points, such as facial details or fingers.

On an early September morning in 1940, four French teenagers exploring the countryside around their homes came across a cave . . .

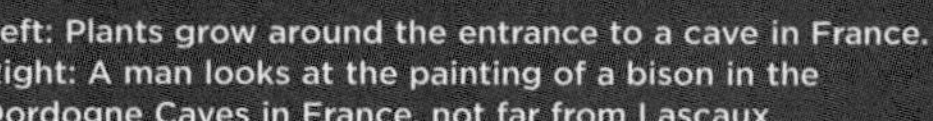

Left: Plants grow around the entrance to a cave in France.
Right: A man looks at the painting of a bison in the Dordogne Caves in France, not far from Lascaux.

10

During Reading

Comprehension

MAKING CONNECTIONS

Use these questions to model how to make connections with the text. Then have students make their own connections.

- What have I learned?
- What do I find the most interesting about this article?
- What would I like to learn more about?

(See Differentiated Instruction.)

Teacher Think Aloud

Teenagers finding one of the caves really got my interest. I usually think that only scientists such as archaeologists make important discoveries. I thought to myself, "I wish I had been with them." I wonder if the teenagers got some official credit for finding the cave.

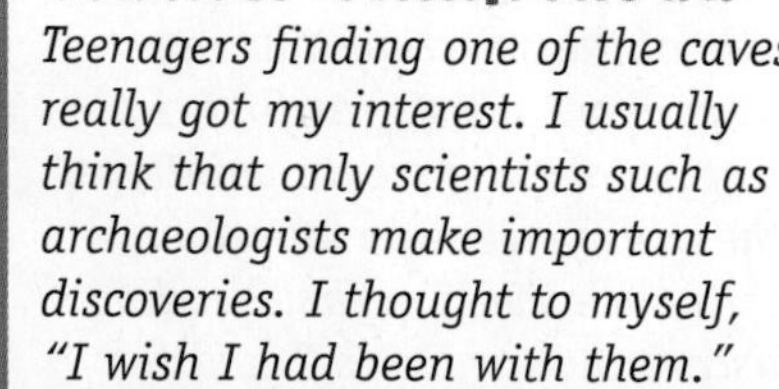

Comprehension

MONITOR UNDERSTANDING

Use these questions to model how to visualize. Then have students tell about a part they visualized.

- What do I picture in my mind as I read?
- Which details help me create this image in my mind?
- How does seeing this picture in my mind help me understand what I am reading?

Animals in Cave Art These ancient cave-artists didn't seem to care about drawing pictures of human life. Instead, most of the paintings on the cave walls are of animals, like horses and bison. At Lascaux there are over 600 animal paintings. Why? Perhaps all of these animal

Most of the paintings are of animals, like horses and bison . . .

paintings tell us how important animals were in the lives of ancient humans. Some people think that each drawing of an animal replaced an animal that was killed. Animals may have been important for these reasons:

- They provided food.
- They helped people with work.
- They fired the human imagination.

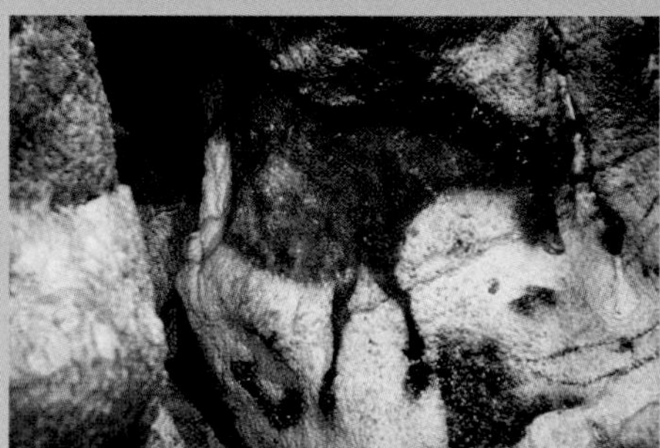

Scientists aren't sure what the cave paintings mean. They do know, however, that human figures *(bottom)* are rare. All three images are from the Lascaux Caves.

Teacher Think Aloud

The beginning of this article tells about the teenagers finding the cave and discovering cave paintings. The detail about clay trickling down the cave walls helps me see what it looked like in there and makes me feel as if I were there. It helps me understand why the paintings are hard to decipher.

Fix-Up Strategies

Offer these strategies to help students read independently.

If you don't understand what you're reading:

- Reread the difficult section to look for clues to help you comprehend.
- Read ahead to find clues to help you comprehend.
- Retell, or say in your own words, what you've read.
- Visualize, or form mental pictures of, what you've read.

If you don't understand a word:

- Reread the sentence. Look for ideas and words that provide meaning clues.
- Find clues by reading a few sentences before and after the confusing word.
- Look for the base or root word and think about its meaning.
- Think about the topic or plot at this point to see if either offers meaning clues.

DIFFERENTIATED INSTRUCTION

SMALL GROUP

DISCUSSION QUESTIONS

To help students become better critical readers, talk them through question 1.

1. First, ask students if they think the author feels good, bad, or indifferent about the discovery of the cave paintings. Have them look at the specific language the author uses. Encourage students to give examples that support their assessment of the author's viewpoint.
2. Now, recall that the cave paintings are off limits to the public. Ask: *Does the author in any way suggest an overly positive or overly negative reaction to the measure?* Have students look for evidence in the text.

In the Painted Gallery, the drawings cover almost the entire space of the cave. They climb up the walls to the ceiling.

Most paints were mixes of minerals, charcoal, and iron. Unfortunately, these natural materials disappear over time, which makes the paintings difficult to study.

Signs in Cave Art Signs are another group of cave paintings. These signs range from simple dots and lines to more complex circles and triangles. Scientists do not understand the meaning or purpose of these signs; perhaps they are just designs. However, scientists use these signs for dating the pictures. When they find signs that are alike in different caves, the scientists guess that people inhabited, or lived in, these different caves around the same time.

Paintings from Ceiling to Floor

The cave artists painted everywhere, not just in easy-to-reach places. Some paintings, like murals, span whole walls. Others reach high above the cave floor. Scientists who examine these paintings use ladders or build scaffolding to get a good, clear look at them. Scientists guess that the artists of these paintings also built ladders of their own to make their work easier.

Painting Styles and Tools The paintings and drawings on the walls of Lascaux are nearly 20,000 years old. Because the artists of these paintings drew on cave walls, they had to adapt their style to fit the surface of the walls. In some of the caves, the artists used stone tools to carve and scrape into the clay. Because the artists could not carve into very hard rock, they drew and painted instead. Most paints were mixes of

12

After Reading

WHOLE CLASS

Use one or more activities.

Check Purpose

Have students decide if their purpose was met. Did they find out why the caves at Lascaux draw thousands of visitors annually?

Discussion Questions

Continue the group discussion with the following questions. (See Differentiated Instruction.)

1. What do the cave paintings tell you about the lives of the cave painters? (Inferential Thinking)
2. What measures have been taken to preserve the original cave paintings? (Details)
3. Which picture in the article impressed you the most? Explain why. (Making Connections)

Revisit: List

Look back at the list started in Before Reading that shows students' ideas about the reasons why people decorate their homes and personal spaces. Do any of the students' ideas reflect the suggested motivations of the cave painters?

Revisit: Predictions Chart

Have students return to the predictions chart on *Student Journal* page 5. Have them complete the third column. How were the words actually used?

minerals, charcoal, and iron. Unfortunately, these natural materials disappear over time, which makes the paintings difficult to study.

Scientists have also found tools in and around the caves that they believe the artists used for painting. Tools like brushes that were made of wood, horsehair, and other organic materials deteriorated, or broke down, and disappeared. They can't be studied. However stone, shell, and bone blades for carving and engraving survived. More than 300 of these tools still exist.

Why Paint? Why did prehistoric people paint pictures? No one really knows why. However, it is known that people in different parts of the world made cave paintings. There are a number of guesses, or speculations, as to why ancient people created cave art. Indeed, there are more questions than answers about cave painting.

1. Did both men and women do the painting?
2. Why were human figures almost never shown?
3. Why were the land and plants outside the caves never shown?

Clearly, creativity is part of what makes us human. It separates us from plants and animals. The cave paintings show that the need to be creative isn't something new. Rather, it has developed over millions of years.

Damage to the Caves Scientists want to keep the caves in good condition so they can study them, but natural forces wear away the cave paintings in three ways:

1. When the weather changes from cold to warm, rocks wear away.
2. When there is more than one entrance to a cave, the extra water in the air causes the stone to decay.
3. Rainwater trickles down through cracks and ruins the paintings.

Creativity is part of what makes us human. It separates us from plants and animals. The cave paintings show that the need to be creative isn't something new . . .

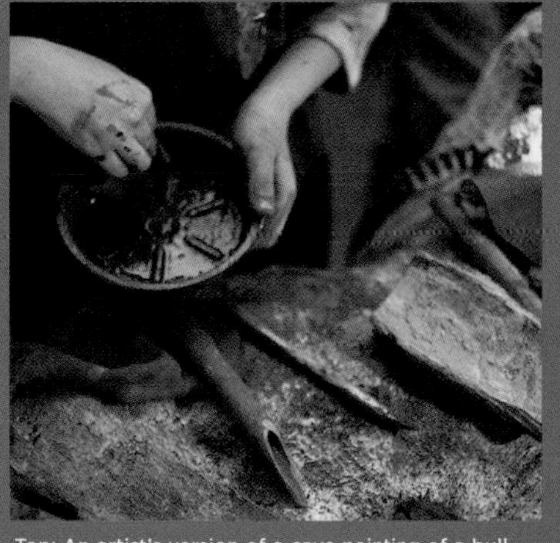

Top: An artist's version of a cave painting of a bull and a horse from Lascaux Caves
Bottom: An artist mixes paint using methods and materials of the cave dwellers.

13

Student Journal pages 6–7

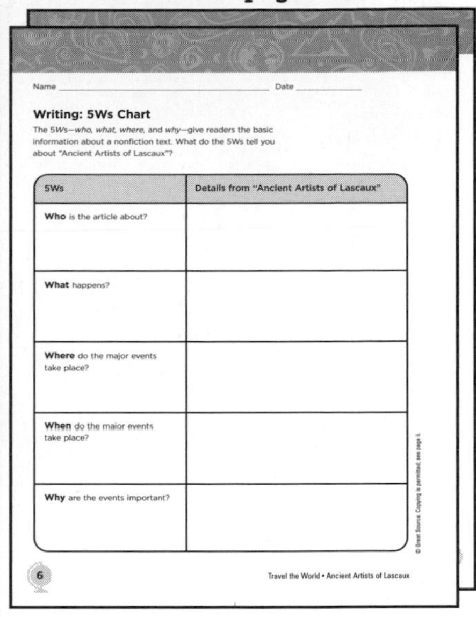

Name ______ Date ______

Writing: 5Ws Chart

The 5Ws—*who, what, where,* and *why*—give readers the basic information about a nonfiction text. What do the 5Ws tell you about "Ancient Artists of Lascaux"?

5Ws	Details from "Ancient Artists of Lascaux"
Who is the article about?	
What happens?	
Where do the major events take place?	
When do the major events take place?	
Why are the events important?	

© Great Source. Copying is permitted; see page ii.

6 Travel the World • Ancient Artists of Lascaux

Possible answers to **Student Journal page 8** include *spectacle, bespectacled, inspector*, and *speculate*.

Name ______ Date ______

Building Vocabulary: Word Roots

Write words you know that contain the Latin root spec-/spect-. Write a definition for each word. Use a dictionary to help you, if you wish.

spec-/spect- means "to see"

Words	Definitions
speculations	assumptions

© Great Source. Copying is permitted; see page ii.

8 Travel the World • Ancient Artists of Lascaux

Writing 5Ws Chart/ News Story

Ask students to think about what a newspaper reporter might have written when the Lascaux cave was first discovered. As a group, brainstorm some general ideas. Then have students complete the 5Ws chart on *Student Journal* page 6, in preparation for writing a short news story. Once the chart has been completed, students can use it to help them write their own news story on *Student Journal* page 7.

Vocabulary Word Roots

Display the word *speculations* and have students find it on page 13 of the article. Ask: *What context clues help you understand the meaning of the word?* Underline the root *spec-* in *speculations*. Identify it as a word part that comes from Latin and means "to see." Relate the root to *spectator* and *inspect*. (*spectator*: someone who sees something; *inspect*: to look into something) Then have students complete *Student Journal* page 8.

Phonics/Word Study

Consonant Alternations: Words that end with *-ian*

Display the words *magic* and *magician*. Ask students what they notice about the sound of the letter *c* in these two related words. (It has a hard /k/ sound in *magic* and a soft /sh/ sound in *magician*.) Repeat with *music* and *musician*. Now, work with students to complete the in-depth consonant alternations activity on TE page 22.

After World War II, the caves became popular visiting spots. Some days over 1,200 people walked through a cave. Soon scientists noticed that all of this traffic caused problems. They guessed that moisture in people's breath damaged the cave walls. Scientists tried to keep track of the damage, but in 1963, they closed the caves to the public. Today, the cave paintings are checked very closely. A high-tech computer system measures air pressure and temperature in the caves. ◆

Early Art

Some ancient humans created portable art. Portable art can be carried with you. It includes things like small sculptures of bison, reindeer, and (rarely) humans. It also includes tools and utensils that ancient humans used, like spoons. These objects were made of bone, ivory, antlers, and stone. The carved feline below is believed to be over 16,000 years old. It can be seen today in France, just outside Paris, at Le Musée des Antiquités Nationales.

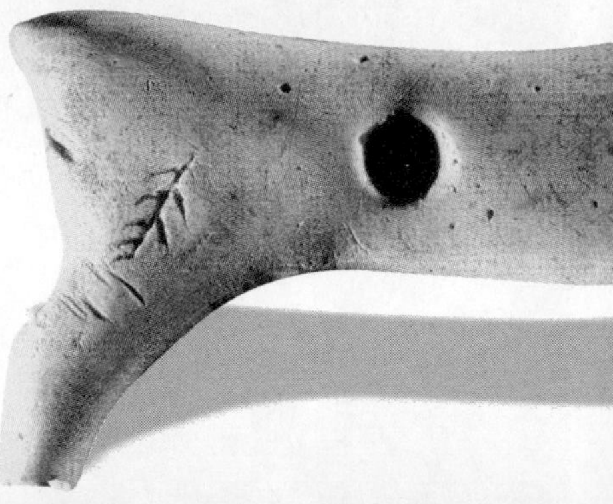

Cave Paintings

Cave paintings are not found only in France. People have discovered caves with paintings in Spain, Australia, Africa, and India. Each region's paintings have their own special characteristics.

Prehistoric rock painting of a bison, Spain

Stick-like figures painted on sandstone around 25,000 years ago, Australia

14

Aspects of a Train

I. The Namers

Conductors, always wearing blue,
as if they could lead the sky
into musty train cars of red-backed seats.
They yell out the names of cities:
Wilmington, Baltimore, Washington—
three-syllable cities,
balancing off their tongues,
landing in white-block letters
on station signs.

Conductors open doors
between the cars.
The earth rocks
side to side,
unsteady as water.
The ground moves
so quickly beneath their feet
they can't even call it
the ground.

II. Rite of Passage

A father turns his head to his son,
he is all profile. From this angle
he tells the boy:
every day, thousands of trains
thunder on the tracks: box cars,
flat cars, stock cars, streamlined
diesel locomotives.
The boy watches his father's nostrils
open and close. Air passes over
the black hairs, stiff as railroad ties.
His crooked nose, a bridge, rises
between his eyes.
His face is no longer a face.

Poem: Aspects of a Train

Have students silently read the poem on page 15, and then aloud with a partner. Use these or similar questions to talk about the poem.

- To which of the five senses does each of the two parts of the poem appeal? What words or phrases support your thoughts?
- Which of the two parts do you like better? Why?
- How does your phrasing change when you read aloud a poem versus an article?

Phonics/Word Study

More Consonant Alternations: Words That End with *-ian*

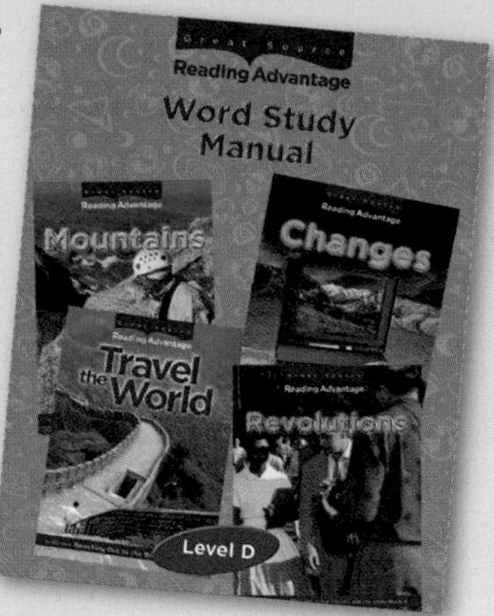

Place the following words on the board: *clinic* and *clinician*. Ask students what is unusual about the spelling of these two related words. Point out that the sound of the final *c* in *clinic* changes with the addition of the suffix *-ian*. Try the activity again with *politic* and *politician*. What exactly is the sound shift in these words? Students should be able to notice that the shift goes from a /k/ sound to a /sh/ sound.

- Put the following words on an overhead or on the board and ask students to change the words by adding the *-ian* ending: *cosmetic, technical, electric, pediatric*. (*cosmetician, technician, electrician, pediatrician*) Have students copy both forms of the words into their Word Study notebooks. (See *Word Study Manual* page 35 for a list.)
- Is there a spelling-meaning connection between these two forms? (Yes, the change is a sound change and a part of speech change.)
- Brainstorm any other words that change in the same way. Some others include *magic*, *statistic*, and *music*. Have students add any new words to their Word Study notebooks.
- Remember, every discussion you have about words creates enthusiasm for words and helps build students' vocabularies.

For more information on word sorts and spelling stages, see pages 5–31 in the *Word Study Manual*.

Focus on . . .

Use one or more activities in this section to focus on a particular area of need in your students.

Comprehension STRATEGY SUPPORT

To help those students who need more practice using the strategies covered in this lesson, work one-on-one or in small groups to apply the strategy prompts below. Apply the prompts to a *Reading Advantage* paperback, a classroom library book, or a new or familiar selection in the magazine. Always model your own thinking first.

Making Connections

- What does this story (article, passage) remind me of?
- What do I already know about this topic?
- Where have I heard about this topic before?
- What do I have in common with the characters, people, or situations in the text?
- What other books, stories, articles, movies, or TV shows does this text make me think about?

Monitor Understanding

- Do I understand what I'm reading? If not, what part is confusing to me?
- What fix-up strategies can I use to solve the problem? (See During Reading for fix-up strategies.)
- Why did a character say (do, think, ask) that?
- What images do I visualize from the text? What parts can't I visualize?
- Why did the author include (or not include) those details?

Writing Double-entry Journal

INDEPENDENT

Have students make double-entry journal notes about "Ancient Artists of Lascaux." Display the headings for a double-entry journal chart. (See TE page 380 for a double-entry journal BLM.) Have students look back through the article to find phrases, passages, and ideas that they felt were interesting or important to them. Explain that students should choose three quotations from the article and write them in the first column of the chart. Then they should write their thoughts and feelings in the second column.

To help students use sensory details and strong verbs in their writing, see lessons in *Writing Advantage*, pages 30–56.

Fluency: Punctuation

After students have read the poem, model how to read the poem at a smooth and even pace. Note that reading too quickly or too slowly makes it difficult for listeners to understand the content. Then have partners take turns reading aloud in the same way.

As you listen to students read, use these prompts to guide them.

- Let the line breaks and the punctuation guide your reading. They signal where to pause slightly.
- Keep your eyes on the text as you read so that you don't lose your place and either miss words or repeat them.
- Think about the message of the poem, and its tone. Use your voice to create interest and hold listeners' attention.

When students read aloud, do they—

✓ demonstrate appropriate meaning and usage of punctuation marks?

✓ incorporate appropriate timing, stress, and intonation?

✓ exhibit well-timed pauses between words and phrases?

English Language Learners

Help new language learners expand their vocabulary as they make connections to the article. Have them use phrases such as:

I enjoy . . .
I would like to learn/experience . . .
My favorite hobby is . . .

Have partners use this vocabulary as they make connections to the poem.

Independent Activity Options

While you work with individuals or small groups, others can work independently on one or more of the following options.

- Level D paperback books, see TE pages 367–372
- Level D *eZines*
- Repeat word sorts from this lesson
- *Student Journal* pages for this lesson
- *Writing Advantage* independent lessons

Assessment

Strategy Assessment

To help you and your students assess their use of comprehension strategies, ask the following questions. Students can complete a written response or provide verbal answers in a one-on-one reading conference.

1. **Making Connections** What in your own life or in the world today did you think of as you were reading the article? Explain. (Answers will vary, but students may mention their own painting or drawing, familiar animals, experiences with caves, or even experiences traveling.)
2. **Monitor Understanding** When you think about the article, what images pop into your mind? How did picturing those images help you better understand what you read? (Answers will vary, but students should be able to describe an image they have in their heads after reading the article. They should be able to indicate which details helped them create the image and explain how visualizing helped their understanding.)

For ongoing informal assessment, use the checklists on pages 61–64 of *Level D Assessment*.

Word Study Assessment

Use these steps to help you and your students assess their understanding of consonant alternations.

1. Write the words *tactic, electric, logic,* and *pediatric* on the board or on word cards.
2. Ask students to add *-ian* to each word and then pronounce both words. Does the sound of the letter *c* change when *-ian* is added? (Yes, in every case.)

tactic	tactician
electric	electrician
logic	logician
pediatric	pediatrician

LESSON 3
Stay Cool: Travel to Antarctica

Travel the World, pages 16–21

SUMMARY

This **question-answer article** describes scientific information about Antarctica.

COMPREHENSION STRATEGIES

Making Connections
Understanding Text Structure

WRITING

Opinion Chart

VOCABULARY

Word Root *therm-/thermo-*

PHONICS/WORD STUDY

Consonant Alternations

Lesson Vocabulary

stations	averted
remote	dehydration
hypothermia	frigid
discarded	contiguous

MATERIALS

Travel the World, pp. 16–21
Student Journal, pp. 9–11
Word Study Manual, p. 36
Writing Advantage, pp. 114–151

STAY COOL: TRAVEL TO ANTARCTICA

Warm sun, sand, and water—perfect for a relaxing vacation. But there are some adventurous folks out there who prefer a travel challenge. Antarctica might be just the place for them.

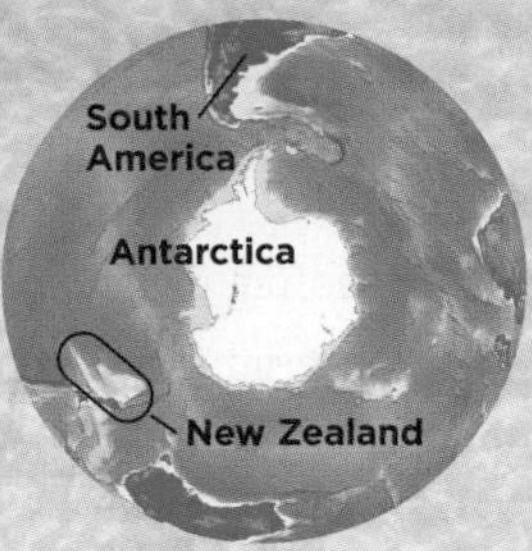

A dogsled team brings supplies to a remote area of the continent.

Scientific Information and Fabulous Facts About the World's Coolest Continent

Q How does a person travel to Antarctica?

A There is no direct flight from the United States. First, you fly to New Zealand. Once you reach New Zealand, you have to wait from one day to a week before another plane flies you to Antarctica. Flights do not leave for Antarctica every day. Plus, weather conditions in Antarctica can delay flights even further. The plane that flies to Antarctica is usually filled with a lot of supplies and food for the people staying at the stations there. (Nothing is grown or made in Antarctica, so everything has to be flown in.) So, it is not a roomy, comfortable ride.

Q How cold does the temperature get in Antarctica?

A The coldest temperature ever recorded in the world was recorded in Antarctica. The temperature fell to –128.6°F (–89°C). Luckily, scientists carry out most of their work in the Antarctic summer, when temperatures stay in the 20s. Not a heat wave, but a definite improvement.

16

Before Reading

Use one or more activities.

Make a Concept Web

Write *Antarctica* in the center oval of a concept web. Ask students:

- What do you know about Antarctica?
- What images come to mind when you think about the continent?
- What questions do you have about Antarctica?

Write students' ideas and questions around the web. When students finish reading the selection, have them revisit the web to add any new details or questions from the article. (See Differentiated Instruction.)

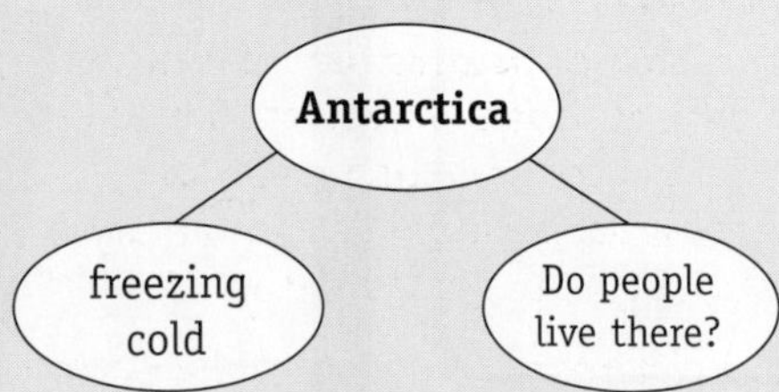

Vocabulary Preview

Review the vocabulary list with students and clarify pronunciations. Ask if students can make any associations with specific words. Ask: *Who has used this word? Does the word remind you of anything else? Does it look or sound like any other words you know?* Have students complete the word associations activity on *Student Journal* page 9.

Q What kind of clothing is worn in Antarctica?

A Most people wear clothes that are not that different from what you might wear at home: jeans, shirts, or sweatpants. However, when you have to fly out to a weather station or another remote (far-off) location, you need to wear your ECW, or Extreme Cold Weather clothes. This special clothing includes things such as fleece, leather gloves with special lining, wind parkas, wool socks, and snow goggles. It takes some time to get dressed to go outside.

Q What special training is needed for people who want to work in Antarctica?

A You would be trained in a number of ways. First, and maybe most importantly, there are special survival training programs that every person going to work in Antarctica must complete. During the class you learn about dangers specific to the extreme cold and harsh environment, dangers like frostbite and hypothermia. Teachers train you to carry out these basic skills needed for survival in Antarctica: how to set up emergency shelters, how to dispose of waste, and how to use a cook stove.

Antarctica
Antarctica is the fifth largest continent. It is about twice the size of Australia. Antarctica has land features like other places on earth—mountains, valleys, coastal areas. However, the land lies under a one-mile-thick layer of snow and ice. The ice could cover the United States with a two-mile-thick layer of ice. The ice contains more fresh water than exists in the rest of the world.

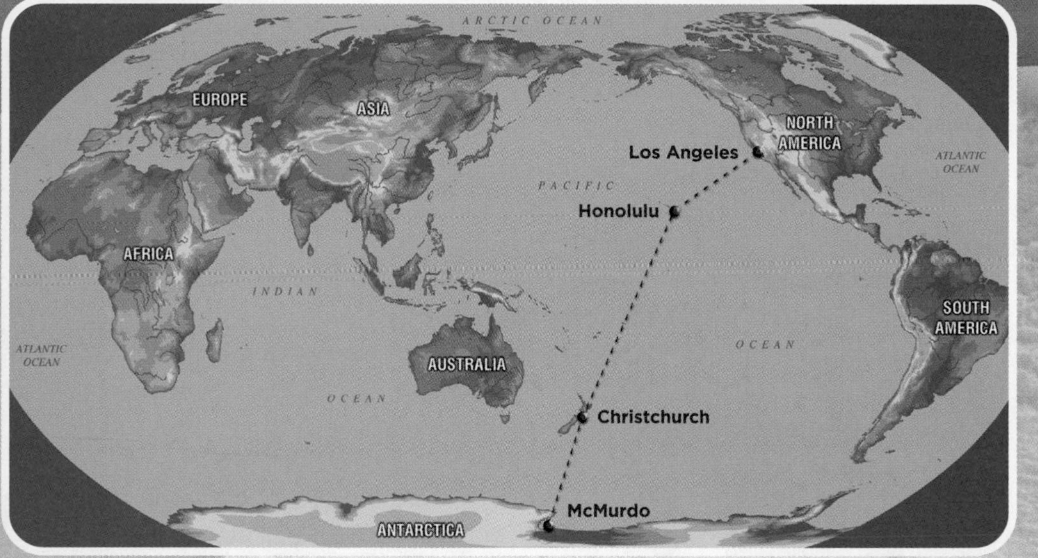

The flight route from the United States to Antarctica is from Los Angeles, California, to Honolulu, Hawaii; from Hawaii to Christchurch, New Zealand; and then from New Zealand to McMurdo, Antarctica.

DIFFERENTIATED INSTRUCTION

SMALL GROUP

MAKE A CONCEPT WEB

If necessary, use the following strategy to provide more background information:

- Show Antarctica on a globe or a map. Point out its location in relation to the equator. Engage students in a brief discussion about conditions in Antarctica. Ask: *Is Antarctica near the equator? What do you think the weather conditions might be like in Antarctica? Why?*

Student Journal page 9

Name ______ Date ______

Building Vocabulary: Making Associations

Pick two words from the vocabulary list below. Think about what you already know about each word. Then answer the questions for each word.

stations	hypothermia	averted	frigid
remote	discarded	dehydration	contiguous

Word ______

What do you think about when you read this word? ______

What does the word remind you of? ______

What do you already know about this word? ______

Word ______

What do you think about when you read this word? ______

What does the word remind you of? ______

What do you already know about this word? ______

Now watch for these words in the magazine selection. Were you on the right track?

Travel the World • Stay Cool: Travel to Antarctica 9

Preview the Selection

Have students look through the six pages of the selection, pages 16–21 in the magazine. Use these or similar prompts to guide students to notice the important features of the text.

- What information does the title give you?
- Do you think the article is fiction or nonfiction? Why?

Teacher Think Aloud

The title of this article tells me that it is about Antarctica. I think I will learn a lot about how cold it is in Antarctica, because I see lots of snow and ice in the photographs. I'm sure the article is nonfiction because the introduction mentions "scientific information" and "facts." Also, the question-answer format makes me think that the author is providing real information.

Make Predictions/ Set Purpose

Students should use the information they gathered in previewing the selection to make predictions about what they will learn. If students have trouble generating a purpose for reading, suggest that they read to learn why adventure seekers love Antarctica.

DIFFERENTIATED INSTRUCTION

Comprehension

MAKING CONNECTIONS

Help students make connections with the text by talking about visiting Antarctica. Ask:

- Who would like to visit Antarctica? Why?
- Who would *not* like to visit Antarctica? Why not?

Call on volunteers to explain why they would or would not like to visit Antarctica, on the basis of what they have read in the article and what they already know.

Q How do people go to the bathroom in Antarctica?

A If you are lucky to be at a permanent station, then you go in a room that looks like a regular bathroom. But privacy is not high on the list of important things. Since space is limited, chances are you have to share. At some stations there are heated outhouses about fifty yards from the camp. But, if you are at a remote camp, you go to the bathroom in a big plastic bag. Then, you seal the bag and bring it back to the main station to be discarded with the other trash.

Q Are there health risks to worry about when visiting Antarctica?

A One of the most serious health risks in Antarctica is one that can be easily averted: dehydration. The air in Antarctica is so dry that you lose a lot more water than you might think. You don't see yourself sweat. If you stop drinking, you most likely will pass out from lack of water. At the survival course, trainers teach you to carry a water bottle on your body so it won't freeze.

Q What kinds of animals live in Antarctica?

A There are many seals and penguins. However, no animals really live on the ice because they can't find food. But penguins, seals, and other birds spend a lot of time sunning and playing on the ice or the rocks near the sea. Seals and penguins get their food from the frigid ocean. Blubber, a thick layer of fat, protects the seals from the freezing waters. Penguins rely on both their fat and feathers to keep them warm.

Frozen Facts About Antarctica

- **About 5,100,000 square miles in area**
- **Highest point is Vinson Massif, 16,864 feet**
- **Average yearly temperature is 0°F**
- **Coldest temperature ever recorded on Earth, –127°F at Vostok Station in August 1960**

Penguins live in the wild only in the Southern Hemisphere. Here, Adélie penguins dive into the sea, where they spend most of their time. However, they lay their eggs and raise their young on the icy shore of Antarctica.

18

During Reading

Comprehension

MAKING CONNECTIONS

Use these questions to model making connections with the text. Then have students make their own connections.

- What does reading about Antarctica remind me of?
- Have I ever seen any of the things described in the article?

(See Differentiated Instruction.)

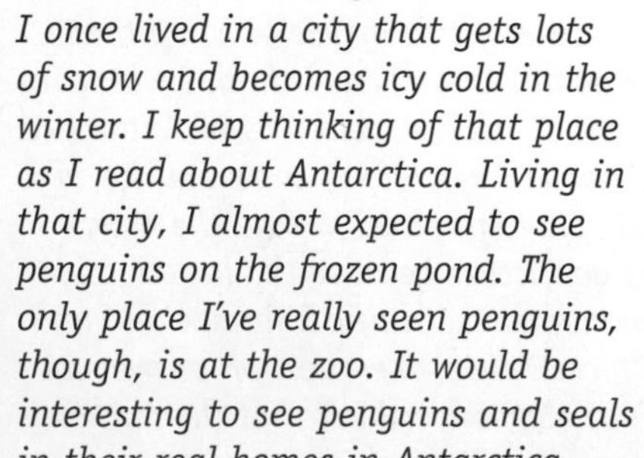

Teacher Think Aloud

I once lived in a city that gets lots of snow and becomes icy cold in the winter. I keep thinking of that place as I read about Antarctica. Living in that city, I almost expected to see penguins on the frozen pond. The only place I've really seen penguins, though, is at the zoo. It would be interesting to see penguins and seals in their real homes in Antarctica.

Comprehension

UNDERSTANDING TEXT STRUCTURE

Use these questions to model how to determine the question-answer text structure of the selection. Then have students tell how the text structure helps them understand the information.

- What do I notice about how the information is structured?
- Why do I think the author chose this text structure?

A gray seal pup wakes up from a nap.

Snow in Antarctica

Antarctica is a lot like a desert. It rains an average of about two inches per year. Believe it or not, that is the same amount of rainfall as in the Sahara Desert, which is in northern Africa. The dryness is the reason that less snow falls than you would expect in Antarctica. The air is too dry to make snow. The South Pole gets only about 4 to 6 inches of snow per year. The moister coast gets about 1 to 2 feet of snow per year. Compare that with northeastern Minnesota. There, the average yearly snowfall is almost 6 feet!

Q What would happen if the Antarctic ice melted?

A Antarctica is as large as the 48 contiguous United States plus half of Mexico. Antarctic ice is almost two miles deep. Imagine how much water that is! If all of that ice melted, the world's oceans would rise by nearly 200 feet. Water would cover large areas of dry land, and some islands would disappear. Don't worry too much, though. Even in the worst situation, the ice wouldn't melt for a few hundred years.

Icicles are formed when melting snow refreezes.

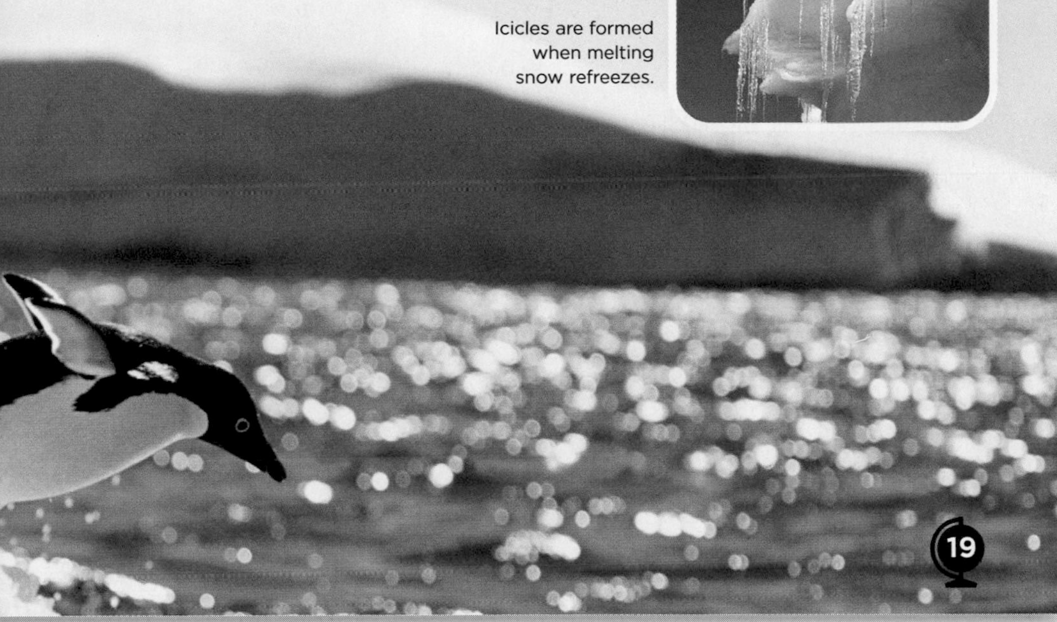

Teacher Think Aloud

The author wrote this article in a question-answer format. I find this format very helpful because I can absorb information in small pieces, without being presented by too much at once. Also, when I learn about something new, I always have questions of my own, so it seems natural for the author to have questions asked and answered.

Fix-Up Strategies

Offer these strategies to help students read independently.

If you don't understand what you're reading:

- Reread the difficult section to look for clues to help you comprehend.
- Read ahead to find clues to help you comprehend.
- Retell, or say in your own words, what you've read.
- Visualize, or form mental pictures of, what you've read.

If you don't understand a word:

- Reread the sentence. Look for ideas and words that provide meaning clues.
- Find clues by reading a few sentences before and after the confusing word.
- Look for the base or root word and think about its meaning.
- Think about the topic or plot at this point to see if either offers meaning clues.

Q Has anyone ever climbed Mount Erebus?

A Mount Erebus is 12,448 feet high, and it is really a volcano. The first person to climb Mt. Erebus was Ernest Shackleton, in 1908. It took him five days. Today there is an observatory, a place to view outer space, and a research center near the volcano's rim. Helicopters fly scientists in and out. They don't climb by foot anymore.

Q What kind of environmental problems does Antarctica face?

A Antarctica is the least polluted place on earth. The biggest concern for scientists is that it remains that way. Unfortunately, when the first camps of scientists were set up, people were not careful with trash. They placed it near the sea ice. When summer came and temperatures rose, the ice melted. Trash dropped right into the water. Today scientists collect all trash and waste, seal it up, and ship it back to the United States. Another problem that Antarctica will have to deal with in the near future is tourism. Today, more and more tourists visit Antarctica. They create a lot of trash.

Q Who runs Antarctica?

A Antarctica does not have a president, a king, or a queen. Instead, it is governed by a treaty, which is an agreement between countries. In 1959, twelve countries agreed to use Antarctica only for peaceful uses, such as scientific research. The Antarctic Treaty states that there can be no military bases, maneuvers, or weapons testing. Only military equipment used for scientific research or other peaceful goals is allowed. The Treaty now has 26 member nations. ◆

The national flags of the countries that signed the Antarctic Treaty encircle what is not the actual, but the ceremonial, South Pole.

20

Student Journal page 10

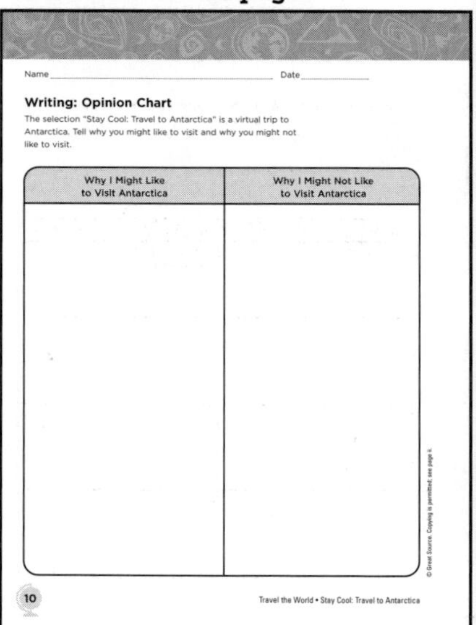

Name ____________ Date ________

Writing: Opinion Chart

The selection "Stay Cool: Travel to Antarctica" is a virtual trip to Antarctica. Tell why you might like to visit and why you might not like to visit.

Why I Might Like to Visit Antarctica	Why I Might Not Like to Visit Antarctica

© Great Source. Copying is permitted; see page ii.

10 Travel the World • Stay Cool: Travel to Antarctica

After Reading

Use one or more activities.

Check Purpose

Have students decide if their purpose was met. Did students learn why adventure seekers love Antarctica?

Discussion Questions

Continue the group discussion with the following questions.

1. In what ways do people manage the extreme cold in Antarctica? (Problem-Solution)
2. What do you know now that you didn't know before reading the article? (Making Connections)
3. Why might it be important to control the number of tourists who visit Antarctica? (Inferential Thinking)

Revisit: Concept Web

Return to the Antarctica concept web. What new information can students add?

Ernest Shackleton

Ernest Shackleton is a well-known Antarctic explorer. In 1908, he came within 97 miles of the true South Pole. In 1914, he captained a ship into the Weddell Sea, where it was crushed by ice. You can read more about the 1914 expedition in *Shipwreck at the Bottom of the World* by Jennifer Armstrong.

Mt. Erebus (12,448 feet) is the world's southernmost active volcano. It was discovered by explorer James Ross in 1841. In 1908, Shackleton and his crew were the first people to climb it.

21

DIFFERENTIATED INSTRUCTION

Vocabulary Word Root *therm-/thermo-*

Try these steps:

1. Display the words *thermostat, thermos,* and *thermal.*
2. Ask what students notice about the three words. (All have the word root *therm-*.)
3. Have students listen as you read the sentences. They should tell which word completes each sentence. (1) *The room is too hot; turn down the* ___. (2) *Put the coffee in a* ___ *to keep it warm.* (3) *I wear* ___ *underwear when it is very cold.*
4. Ask students what they think *therm-* means in each word. (relating to heat)

Student Journal page 11

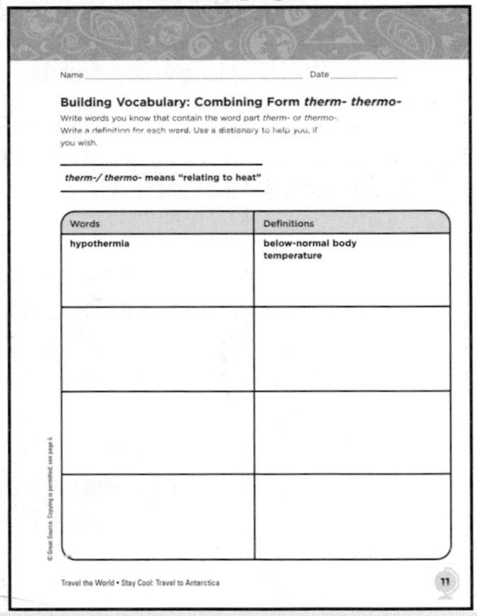

Name ______ Date ______

Building Vocabulary: Combining Form *therm- thermo-*

Write words you know that contain the word part *therm-* or *thermo-*. Write a definition for each word. Use a dictionary to help you, if you wish.

***therm-/ thermo-* means "relating to heat"**

Words	Definitions
hypothermia	below-normal body temperature

Travel the World • Stay Cool: Travel to Antarctica 11

Writing Opinion Chart

Discuss what students learned about Antarctica. Take a poll to see who would want to visit Antarctica. Then have students complete the activity on *Student Journal* page 10 that asks them to state why they might like to visit (or not visit) Antarctica.

Vocabulary Word Root *therm-/thermo-*

Display the word *hypothermia*. Point out that *therm-* is a word part that means "relating to heat." Explain that *hypo-* means "under, below, less than." If someone has hypothermia, he or she has a below-normal body temperature. Brainstorm a list of other words with *therm-/thermo-*. Have students work with partners to complete the chart on *Student Journal* page 11. (See Differentiated Instruction.)

Phonics/Word Study Consonant Alternations

Write the words *public* and *publicize* on the board. Ask students what they notice about the sound of the letter *c* in these two related words. (It has a /k/ sound in *public* and an /s/ sound in *publicize*.) Repeat with *politic* and *politicize*. Now, work with students to complete the in-depth consonant alternations activity on TE page 30.

Phonics/Word Study

More Consonant Alternations

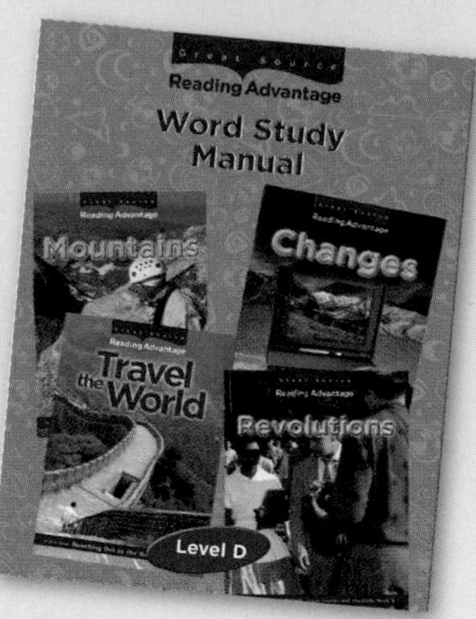

Place the following words on the board: *critic* and *criticize*. Ask students what is unusual about the spelling of these two related words. Point out that the sound of the final *c* in *critic* changes with the addition of the suffix *-ize*. Try the activity again with *public* and *publicize*. What exactly is the sound shift? Students should be able to notice that it goes from a /k/ sound to an /s/ sound in these words. This is different from the previous lesson. There, the shift went from /k/ to /sh/. Here, it goes from /k/ to /s/.

- Put the following words on an overhead or on the board and ask students to change the words by adding the *-ize* ending: *political*, *ethics*, and *italics*. Have students copy the words in both forms into their Word Study notebooks.
- Is there a spelling-meaning connection between these two forms? Yes, the change is a sound change and a part of speech change.
- Finally, using Consonant Alternations Sort One, have students take the words and find their appropriate match. (See *Word Study Manual* page 36.) Once students have found the match, they must define the word as well.

Consonant Alternations Sort One			
bomb bombard	diagnostic diagnostician	muscle muscular	public publicize
clinic clinician	ethicist ethics	music musician	sign signature
column columnist	haste hasten	pediatric pediatrician	technical technician
cosmetic cosmetician	italicize italics	physician physics	
crumble crumbly	magic magician	political politicize	

For more information on word sorts and spelling stages, see pages 5–31 in the *Word Study Manual.*

Focus on . . .

Use one or more activities in this section to focus on a particular area of need in your students.

Comprehension STRATEGY SUPPORT

To help those students who need more practice using the strategies covered in this lesson, work one-on-one or in small groups to apply the strategy prompts below. Apply the prompts to a *Reading Advantage* paperback, a classroom library book, or a new or familiar selection in the magazine. Always model your own thinking first.

Making Connections

- What does this story (article, passage) remind me of?
- What do I already know about this topic?
- Where have I heard about this topic before?
- What do I have in common with the characters, people, or situations in the text?
- What other books, stories, articles, movies, or TV shows does this text make me think about?

Understanding Text Structure

- What kind of text is this? (book, story, article, guidebook, play, manual)
- How does the author organize the text? (cause-effect, problem-solution, chronological order, description, question-answer, comparison-contrast)
- What details support my thoughts about the text structure?
- What is the cause (effect, problem, solution, order, question, answer)?
- If fiction, who are the characters? What is the setting, plot, conflict, and resolution?

Writing Journal Entry

What might a scientist who is stationed on Antarctica write in a journal entry? Have students create a journal entry that describes an entire day. Before students begin to write, have them look back at the article to jot down specific details about life on Antarctica.

For instruction and practice writing descriptive paragraphs, see lessons in *Writing Advantage*, pages 114–151.

Fluency: Punctuation

After students have read the selection at least once silently, have them pair up to read a portion of the article as an interview.

As you listen to students read, use these prompts to guide them.

- Preview what you will read. Notice the different punctuation marks and what these signal to you. Pause at commas and periods. Let your voice rise at the end of sentences marked with a question mark.
- Read with expression. Imagine yourself in the role you have chosen (interviewer or interviewee). How would an interviewer sound? How would an expert on Antarctic conditions sound?

When students read aloud, do they—

✓ demonstrate appropriate meaning and usage of punctuation marks?

✓ incorporate appropriate timing, stress, and intonation?

✓ exhibit well-timed pauses between words and phrases?

English Language Learners

To support students as they complete *Student Journal* page 10, review the concepts of fact and opinion.

1. Discuss clue words that often signal an opinion *(best, worst, should, shouldn't)*. Remind students that facts can be proven.
2. Provide students with five statements (two opinion/ three fact) of your own about the class. Have partners determine whether the teacher-generated statements are facts or opinions.
3. Have partners brainstorm factual statements and opinions about the text.

Independent Activity Options

While you work with individuals or small groups, others can work independently on one or more of the following options.

- Level D paperback books, see TE pages 367–372
- Level D *eZines*
- Repeat word sorts from this lesson
- *Student Journal* pages for this lesson
- *Writing Advantage* independent lessons

Assessment

Strategy Assessment

To help you and your students assess their use of comprehension strategies, ask the following questions. Students can complete a written response or provide verbal answers in a one-on-one reading conference.

1. **Making Connections** As you read the article, what connections did you make? (Answers will vary. Students may mention that the article reminded them of information they already knew, provided new information, or raised questions.)
2. **Understanding Text Structure** Besides the question-answer format, what else did you notice about how this article is organized? (Answers will vary, but students may point out that the classification of topics through subheadings helps them find specific information on snow or Ernest Shackleton, for example.)

For ongoing informal assessment, use the checklists on pages 61–64 of *Level D Assessment*.

Word Study Assessment

Use these steps to help you and your students assess their understanding of consonant alternations.

1. Write the following pairs of words on the board or on word cards: *electric, electrician; clinic, clinician; politic, politicize; music, musician; critic, criticize.*
2. Ask students in which pairs the *c* sound changes from /k/ to /sh/ (*electric, electrician; clinic, clinician; music, musician*) and in which pairs the *c* sound changes from /k/ to /s/ (*politic, politicize; critic, criticize*).
3. Have students explain why the sound changes are different. (The suffixes *-ian* and *-ize* affect the sound.)

electric	electrician
clinic	clinician
politic	politicize
music	musician
critic	criticize

LESSON **4**

Amazon River Adventure

Travel the World, pages 22–27

SUMMARY

This **article**, written in the form of journal entries, describes a four-day Amazon River adventure. It includes interesting facts about the Amazon River and the species that inhabit it.

COMPREHENSION STRATEGIES

Making Connections
Monitor Understanding

WRITING

Notes for Visualizing

VOCABULARY

Prefix *pro-*

PHONICS/WORD STUDY

Vowel Alternations:
Long to Schwa

Lesson Vocabulary

informative
propelling
accommodations

MATERIALS

Travel the World, pp. 22–27
Student Journal, pp. 12–14
Word Study Manual, p. 37
Writing Advantage, pp. 114–151

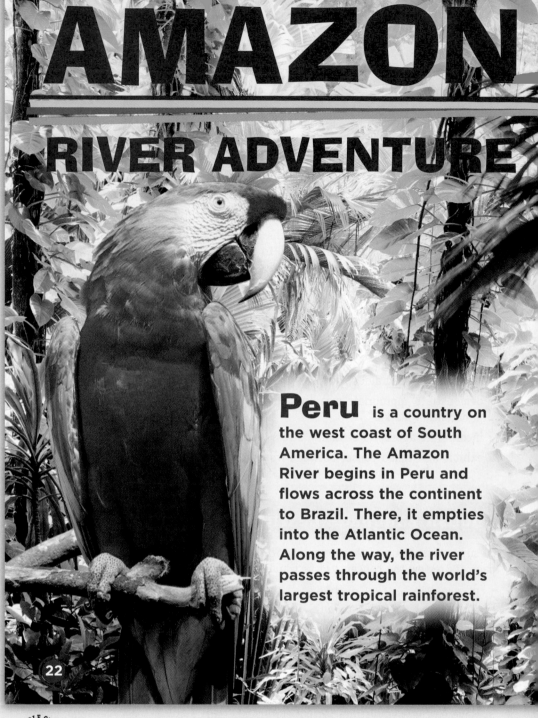

AMAZON RIVER ADVENTURE

Peru is a country on the west coast of South America. The Amazon River begins in Peru and flows across the continent to Brazil. There, it empties into the Atlantic Ocean. Along the way, the river passes through the world's largest tropical rainforest.

22

Before Reading

Use one or more activities.

Make an Association Web

Tell students they are going to read about the Amazon River and rainforest. Explain that a rainforest is a warm, rainy climate with tall trees, plant life, and unusual animals. Write *rainforest* on the board or on chart paper. Ask students to tell what they associate with a rainforest, and build an association web together.

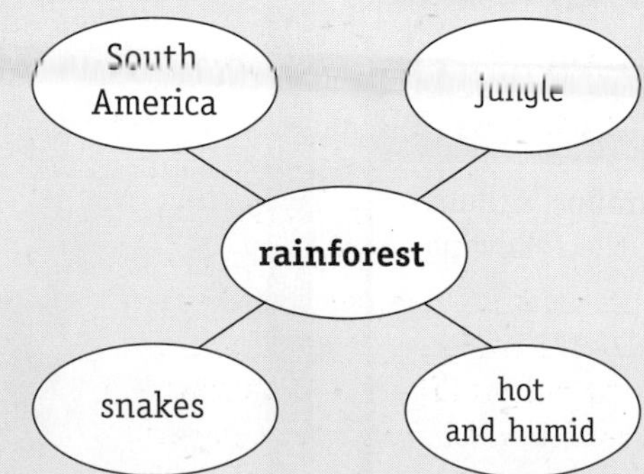

Vocabulary Preview

Display the vocabulary words. Ask volunteers to read the words aloud and briefly share what they know about them. Then have students fill in the second column on *Student Journal* page 12. Students can share their predictions with a partner

Model for students the process of predicting how a word will be used in the selection. Students will finsh the chart later.

Day 1— Landing in Lima, Peru

Tomorrow I'll be sailing down the Amazon River. But, today I began my adventure in Lima, Peru. I'm so excited about the next few days. I hardly slept at all on the plane ride from Miami because I tried to read as much about the Amazon as I could. I've learned a number of interesting facts:

- The Amazon River is about 4,000 miles (6,437 kilometers) long. By most accounts, it is the second longest river in the world behind the Nile in Egypt. It is about as long as the distance from San Francisco to New York City.
- Through most of its course, the river ranges from 1.5 to 6 miles (2.4 to 10 kilometers) wide.
- The world's largest snake, the anaconda, lives in the Amazon. (Wouldn't it be fantastic to see one?)
- Nearly half of the world's oxygen supply comes from all of the trees and plants around the Amazon River.

A gold spoon from a museum in Lima

The plane landed in Lima—Peru's capital city. Peru is south of the equator. That means that the seasons are opposite of what they are in the United States. So, even though I'm on my winter break, it's summertime in Peru.

After getting from the airport to the hotel, I decided to take a bus tour of Lima. The guide was very informative, I learned quite a lot about the city, and we visited some famous sites. My favorite was the Gold of Peru Museum. There must have been thousands of gold pieces on display: necklaces, drinking cups, nose rings, and weapons.

Finally, it was time for dinner. The guide suggested that we try some of Lima's traditional food, or "criollo." Many of the choices at the restaurant were fish and shellfish. I ordered ceviche (suh VEE chay)—raw fish marinated in lemon juice and seasoned with special spices. It was delicious. After dinner I was happy to get back to the hotel and go to sleep early. Tomorrow it's on to the river!

The Iglesia de San Francisco in Lima

A boat tours the Amazon River.

23

DIFFERENTIATED INSTRUCTION

SMALL GROUP

Preview the Selection

Guide students on a picture tour through the selection. Use the following steps:

1. Have students look at each individual photograph. Ask volunteers to talk about the details they see.
2. Have students use the photographs to predict what they might learn about in this selection. Write their predictions on the board.
3. Revisit their predictions after students finish reading the article. Did students learn what they thought they would?

Student Journal page 12

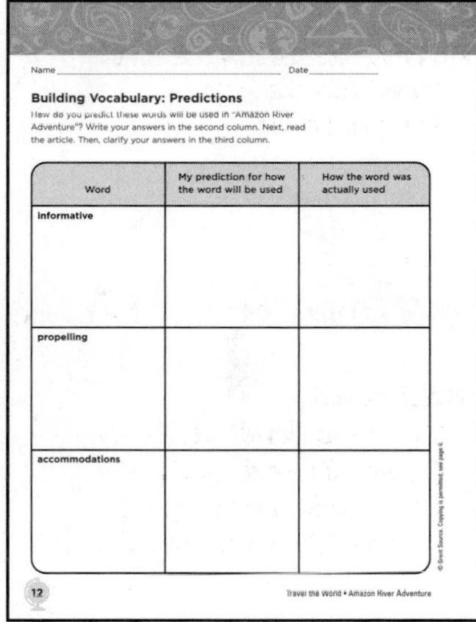

Name ______________________ Date __________

Building Vocabulary: Predictions

How do you predict these words will be used in "Amazon River Adventure"? Write your answers in the second column. Next, read the article. Then, clarify your answers in the third column.

Word	My prediction for how the word will be used	How the word was actually used
informative		
propelling		
accommodations		

12 Travel the World • Amazon River Adventure

Preview the Selection

Have students look through the six pages of the article. Use these or similar prompts to guide discussion.

- What do you think you will read about?
- How is the information organized?
- Why might an author write a selection in journal form?
- What can you learn from the photographs?

(See Differentiated Instruction.)

Teacher Think Aloud

The picture on the first page makes me think this will be an informational article about the rainforest. As I look at the other photographs and read the headings, though, I realize it is about a trip the author took down the Amazon River. I look forward to learning about what traveling on the river was like and what kinds of animals the author saw.

Make Predictions/ Set Purpose

Students should use the information gathered in previewing the selection to make some predictions about what they will learn from the article. To help students set a meaningful purpose for reading, have them read to discover what a trip down the Amazon River is like.

DIFFERENTIATED INSTRUCTION

Comprehension

MONITOR UNDERSTANDING

To help students monitor their understanding, use the following steps:

1. Explain that when you visualize what you read, you make pictures in your mind.
2. Read aloud the paragraph about macaws on page 24. Students should listen to visualize.
3. Then have students check their mental images against the photograph on page 24.

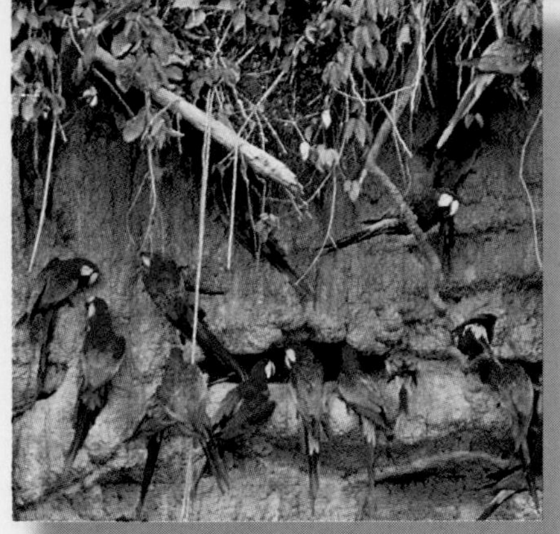

Macaws can live to be 70 years old.

River dolphins can be either pink or gray. Scientists consider them intelligent and friendly.

Day 2—On the River

After a quick coffee and roll for breakfast, I flew to Iquitos, where my cruise on the Amazon would begin and end. The river at Iquitos is so wide that ocean liners cruise into it! At the airport, people in my tour gathered by the baggage claim and waited for the boat crew to pick us up. Once everyone was together, we headed for the boat. I was surprised to see that the boat we were taking looked a lot like a riverboat on the Mississippi—except for the fact that it didn't have a big wheel propelling it along. The accommodations weren't bad either: the boat had eight bunk beds with curtains hung around each bed for privacy, a bathroom, and a shower! The water for the shower is pumped up from the river. I wonder how clean it will be.

The first amazing thing I saw was a flock of macaw parrots flying over the boat. Their feathers were so bright—reds, blues, and greens—and they were so loud! According to one of the guides, the macaws eat the river clay. Scientists aren't sure why these birds eat clay. They think the macaws need salts and minerals that they don't get from their regular diet of fruits and flowers.

"One thing I need to remember for my next visit to the Amazon is that it is so hot."

Note to myself: One thing I need to remember for my next visit to the Amazon is that it is so hot. By ten this morning, it was already 80°F in the shade. Our guide said it was 100°F in the sun.

After a lunch of rice and shrimp, I sat out on the boat deck. I had to look twice because I thought I saw a dolphin swimming close to the boat! I asked the man sitting beside me what it was. He said it was a river dolphin. A river dolphin can grow to be about nine feet long and weigh up to 190 pounds! I'd never heard of river dolphins before, so I asked him more about them. Apparently, during the rainy season, when the Amazon floods, the river water fills with berries and leaves. Fish come to eat the berries and leaves. The dolphins come to eat the fish.

24

During Reading

Comprehension

MAKING CONNECTIONS

Use these questions to model making connections with the text. Then have students make their own connections.

- Does anything I am reading sound familiar to me?
- What do I know about the animals mentioned in the text?
- Would I like to visit the Amazon River one day? Why or why not?

Teacher Think Aloud

I was really surprised to read on page 24 that there are such things as river dolphins. I thought dolphins lived only in the ocean. And I couldn't believe how big the river dolphins can grow to be. The article said that they could reach up to "nine feet long and weigh up to 190 pounds!" When I think about my own height and weight, I get a good sense of just how big that is.

Comprehension

MONITOR UNDERSTANDING

Use these questions to model visualizing. Then have students tell about a part they visualized.

- What do I visualize, or picture in my mind, as I read?
- What details help me create this image in my mind?
- How does visualizing help me understand the text?

(See Differentiated Instruction.)

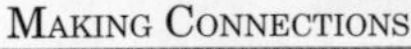

The anaconda can grow up to 20 feet long. The snake constricts, or squeezes, its prey.

Amazon River Facts

- The world's second longest river
- The main river in South America
- Starts in Peru and flows east across South America, through Brazil, and to the Atlantic Ocean
- Longer than the distance from San Francisco to New York City
- Ninety miles across at its widest point

For dinner, we had rice and beans, and for dessert we feasted on pineapple and papaya. Another thing I need to remember for my next visit is that mosquitoes swarm everywhere on this river. I am thankful for the netting around my bunk. Hopefully, it will protect me from some bites.

Papaya

Pineapple

Day 3—Caimans and Herons and Fish—Oh, My!

Our guide told us that people do not agree on how the Amazon River got its name. Some people say that it comes from a word that means "without source" because no one is sure where the Amazon River starts. Others say that the name comes from a type of canoe native people use on the river.

The guide spent a lot of his energy cutting away vines so our boat could pass through the rainforest. We stopped along the edge, and he pulled a baby caiman (KAY mun) out of the water. A caiman is a kind of crocodile. It was much darker than any of the crocodiles I had ever seen at the zoo or in books. Our guide said caimans eat snails and fish and should do well in the Amazon. But their numbers are dropping because people hunt them illegally. He dropped the caiman back into the river, and it slithered away. We all kept our eyes out on the banks for other unusual animals. I was hoping to see an anaconda, but I never did.

DIFFERENTIATED INSTRUCTION

Comprehension

MONITOR UNDERSTANDING

To help students with visualizing, follow these steps:

1. Remind students that when you visualize, you make pictures in your mind. Visualizing can help you better understand the text.
2. Have students close their eyes as you read aloud the paragraph about macaws, on page 24. Tell students to visualize the macaws as you read.
3. Have students check their mental images against the photograph on page 24. Discuss which details in the text helped students picture the macaws.

Teacher Think Aloud

I had trouble picturing the boat described on page 24. The text said that it was like a riverboat on the Mississippi, except that it didn't have a big wheel propelling it. I have never seen a Mississippi riverboat, so I didn't know what the author meant. I looked for a picture of the boat and found one on page 23. Once I saw that, I could picture the boat in my mind as I read about the journey.

Fix-Up Strategies

Offer these strategies to help students read independently.

If you don't understand what you're reading:

- Reread the difficult section to look for clues to help you comprehend.
- Read ahead to find clues to help you comprehend.
- Retell, or say in your own words, what you've read.
- Visualize, or form mental pictures of, what you've read.

If you don't understand a word:

- Reread the sentence. Look for ideas and words that provide meaning clues.
- Find clues by reading a few sentences before and after the confusing word.
- Look for the base or root word and think about its meaning.
- Think about the topic or plot at this point to see if either offers meaning clues.

DIFFERENTIATED INSTRUCTION

SMALL GROUP

CHECK PURPOSE

To help students determine whether their purpose was met, use the following steps:

1. Discuss with students what they learned from the article.
2. Ask students to write down some notes about what a trip down the Amazon River would be like.
3. Have students share some of their ideas with the group and compare their ideas with one another.

Student Journal page 13

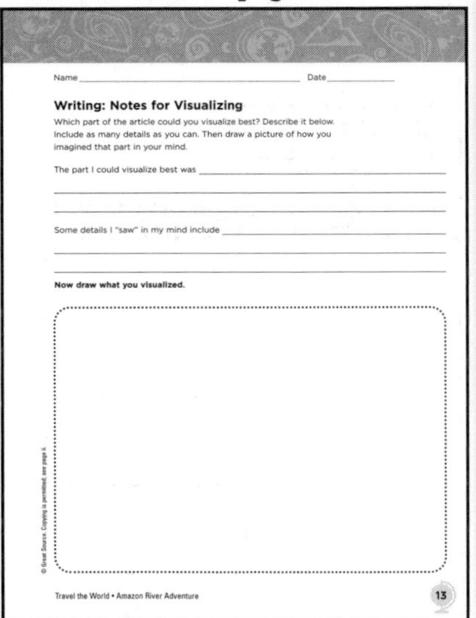

Name ______ Date ______

Writing: Notes for Visualizing

Which part of the article could you visualize best? Describe it below. Include as many details as you can. Then draw a picture of how you imagined that part in your mind.

The part I could visualize best was ______

Some details I "saw" in my mind include ______

Now draw what you visualized.

© Great Source. Copying is permitted; see page ii.

Travel the World • Amazon River Adventure 13

Close-up of a woolly monkey

The tour included a hike in the rainforest.

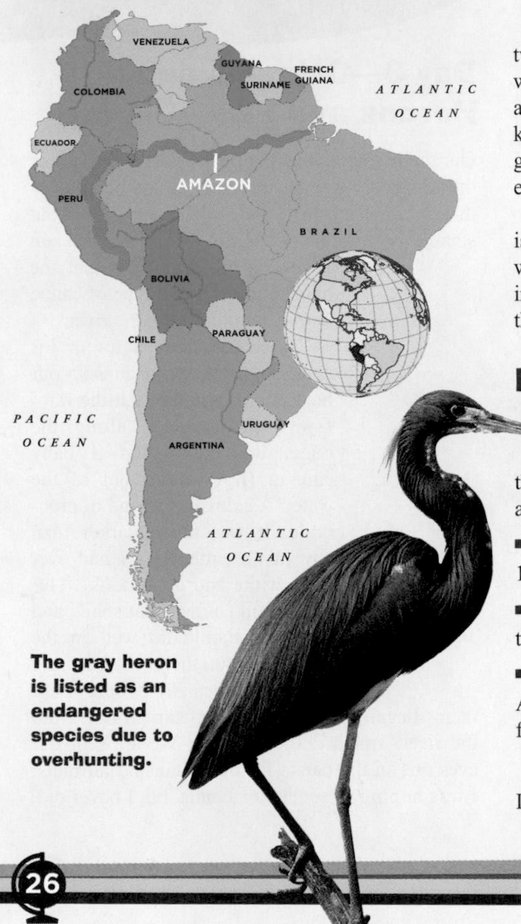

The gray heron is listed as an endangered species due to overhunting.

We stopped to lace up our hiking boots for a two-mile hike to a beautiful rainforest lake. Once we reached the lake, we canoed and paddled around it. From my canoe I saw amazing animals: kingfishers, herons, monkeys, and a family of giant otters. I went for a quick swim. Later, we all enjoyed the beautiful orange-gold sunset.

After dinner I treated myself to some flan, which is a delicious, pudding-like, caramel dessert. Then, we all sat on the deck and listened to the nocturnal insects and frogs. What a musical concert! Later that night the boat sailed us back to Iquitos.

Day 4—Heading Home

We all awoke before sunrise to catch our plane. Part of me was sad to leave the Amazon River and Peru. I learned some truly amazing information on this trip:

- Some places along the Amazon River get up to 19 feet of rain each year.
- The mouth of the Amazon, where it opens into the Atlantic Ocean, is 200 miles wide.
- Over 2,400 species of fish live in the Amazon. And some of them grow to huge sizes; river catfish can weigh 600 pounds!

I never did get to see that anaconda, but perhaps I will on my next trip to the Amazon River. ◆

26

After Reading

Use one or more activities.

Check Purpose

Have students decide if their purpose was met. What did they discover about what a trip down the Amazon River is like? (See Differentiated Instruction.)

Discussion Questions

Continue the group discussion with the following questions.

1. Which day of the trip did you find most interesting? What happened that day? (Sequence)
2. How would you describe the climate of the Amazon area? (Details)
3. Which animal that was discussed in the text interested you the most? Why? (Making Connections)

Revisit: Association Web

Revisit the rainforest association web. What new information can students add?

Revisit: Predictions Chart

Have students complete the predictions chart on *Student Journal* page 12. Encourage them to use context clues to confirm or correct their predictions.

An orange-gold sunset was the spectacular end to the journey.

Saving the Rainforest

Saving the rainforest might just be a life or death situation. Over half of all medicine that we use today comes from the rainforests. Seventy percent of the nearly 3,000 plants that scientists are studying as possible cancer cures come from the rainforests. Remember, too, that much of the oxygen we breathe comes from the Amazon rainforest. The facts below show the importance of saving the world's rainforests.

- Each year rainforest land, equal to the size of England and Wales combined, is destroyed.
- In the rainforest, an entire species dies out every 10 minutes.
- If the destruction rate continues, rainforests will disappear in fifty years.

27

Possible answers to **Student Journal page 14** include *proceed, to begin and carry forward an activity; progress, to move forward; promotion, advancement in rank or grade;* and *proposal, something put forward for acceptance.*

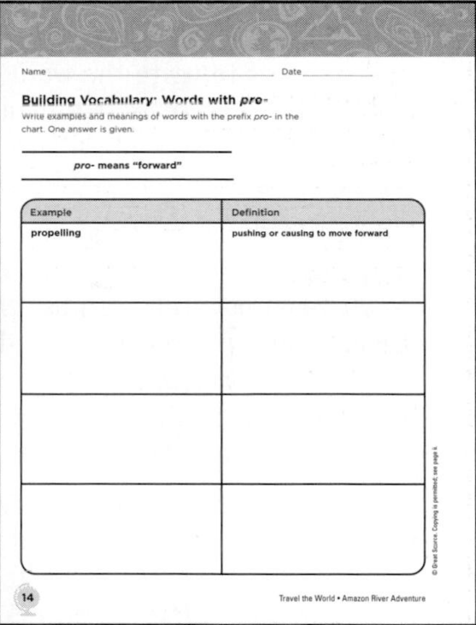

Name____________________ Date__________

Building Vocabulary: Words with *pro-*

Write examples and meanings of words with the prefix *pro-* in the chart. One answer is given.

pro- means "forward"

Example	Definition
propelling	pushing or causing to move forward

© Great Source. Copying is permitted; see page ii.

14 Travel the World • Amazon River Adventure

Writing Notes for Visualizing

Ask students which part of the article they were able to visualize best. Encourage students to picture that part in their minds, using as many details from the text as they can. Then have students write a description of that part and draw it on the visualizing activity on *Student Journal* page 13.

Vocabulary Prefix *pro-*

Display the word *propelling.* Ask: *What do you know about the word* propelling*?* Remind students that in the article, *propelling* refers to something that is pushing forward. Explain that the meaning of *pro-* is "forward." Brainstorm a list of words with the prefix *pro-*. Then have partners complete the prefix activity on *Student Journal* page 14.

Phonics/Word Study

Vowel Alternations

Display and read aloud the words *impose* and *imposition*. Ask students what sound the *o* has in *impose*. (long *o* sound) Then ask what sound the *o* in *imposition* has. (schwa) Point out that if students remember how to spell *impose*, it will help them spell *imposition*. Now, work with students to complete the in-depth vowel alternations activity on TE page 38.

Phonics/Word Study

Vowel Alternations: Long to Schwa

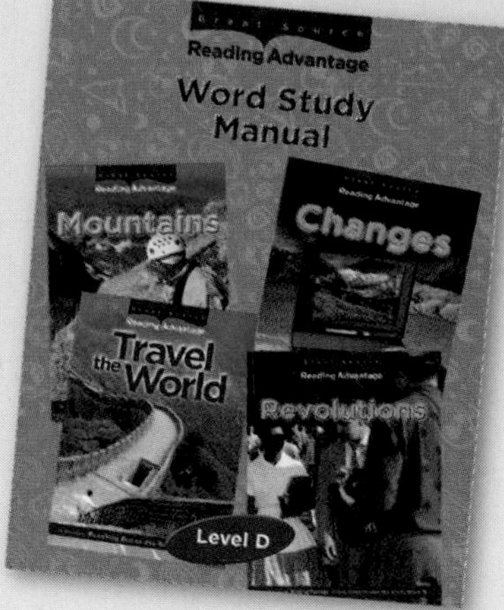

Just as consonants can sound different in related words, so can vowels. Consider the word *opposition*. It is regularly misspelled, and the feature that is most often misrepresented is the schwa sound. The schwa in *opposition* is the *o* in the second syllable: *opp**o**sition*. Often, students rely on what they hear in the word, and a schwa is, by definition, an unstressed vowel. Identifying the correct vowel is difficult. If students are aware of the spelling-meaning connection, they can access the base word *oppose*. Knowing that, students can recall the original sound of the vowel, which is clearly a long *o* in *oppose*. The schwa, then, becomes clear.

- Ask students to write the word *opposition* in their notebooks. Ask students to name the vowel they included in the second syllable. Point out that the wrong vowel is often used in this part of the word.
- Explain to students the spelling-meaning connection and the importance of the base word. Then explain to students how they can use the base word to help them ascertain the correct spelling. For practice, use the word *description* to see if students are able to come up with the word *describe* to illuminate the spelling of *description*.
- Provide students with a list of vowel alternation words and ask them to generate the base word and identify the correct vowel in the schwa position. (See *Word Study Manual* page 37.) Point out that it may not always be in the second syllable.

Answers for *Word Study Manual* page 37 include *competition, compete; confidence, confide; deposition, deposit; proposition, propose; verification, verify; implication, imply; definition, define; genetic, gene; description, describe; supposition, suppose; classification, classify; certification, certify; opposition, oppose; imposition, impose; innovation, innovate; notification, notify; identification, identify; purification, purify; resident, reside; repetition, repeat; position, pose; application, apply; multiplication, multiply;* and *modification, modify.*

For more information on word sorts and spelling stages, see pages 5–31 in the *Word Study Manual.*

Focus on . . .

Use one or more activities in this section to focus on a particular area of need in your students.

Comprehension Strategy Support

To help those students who need more practice using the strategies covered in this lesson, work one-on-one or in small groups to apply the strategy prompts below. Apply the prompts to a *Reading Advantage* paperback, a classroom library book, or a new or familiar selection in the magazine. Always model your own thinking first.

Making Connections

- What does this story (article, passage) remind me of?
- What do I already know about this topic?
- Where have I heard about this topic before?
- What do I have in common with the characters, people, or situations in the text?
- What other books, stories, articles, movies, or TV shows does this text make me think about?

Monitor Understanding

- Do I understand what I'm reading? If not, what part is confusing to me?
- What fix-up strategies can I use to solve the problem? (See During Reading for fix-up strategies.)
- Why did a character say (do, think, ask) that?
- What images do I visualize from the text? What parts can't I visualize?
- Why did the author include (or not include) those details?

Writing Journal Entry

Have students recall a trip they have taken. Ask for volunteers to share some ideas. Then have students write a journal entry that focuses on one particular day of the trip. Before students begin to write, have them create a list of things they did on that particular day, and then number the events in the order in which they occurred. Now they can use the sequence of events to write about their day, from beginning to end. Have students label their entries with the date and place.

For instruction and practice writing sequence paragraphs, see lessons in *Writing Advantage,* pages 114–151.

Fluency: Expression

After students have read the selection at least once, have them choose one journal entry to practice for fluent reading. First, have students read the entry silently. Then, divide them into small groups or pairs and have students read their entry aloud. Encourage students to use expression to convey the feelings of the writer.

As you listen to students read, use these prompts to guide them.

- Think how the writer might feel and sound. Convey those feelings in your reading.
- Punctuation, such as exclamation points, will help guide your expression.
- Commas and periods will help guide the pacing of your reading.

When students read aloud, do they—

✓ reflect an understanding of the text?
✓ demonstrate appropriate timing, stress, and intonation?
✓ incorporate appropriate speed and phrasing?

English Language Learners

To support students' comprehension of "Amazon River Adventure," review multiple meaning words found in the selection: page 22: *passes;* page 23: *course, break;* page 24: *roll, note, leaves;* page 25: *well;* and page 26: *due, mouth, trip.*

1. Write each word and its definition on chart paper, and discuss its meaning in the context of the selection.
2. Have partners write sentences using the words and their multiple meanings.
3. Have students illustrate their sentences and share them with the class.

Independent Activity Options

While you work with individuals or small groups, others can work independently on one or more of the following options.

- Level D paperback books, see TE pages 367–372
- Level D *eZines*
- Repeat word sorts from this lesson
- *Student Journal* pages for this lesson
- *Writing Advantage* independent lessons

Assessment

Strategy Assessment

To help you and your students assess their use of comprehension strategies, ask the following questions. Students can complete a written response or provide verbal answers in a one-on-one reading conference.

1. **Making Connections** As you read the article, what connections did you make? (Answers will vary. Students may mention that the article reminded them of information they already knew, provided new information, or raised questions.)
2. **Monitor Understanding** As you think back about the selection, what images do you picture in your mind? Why? (Answers will vary, but students should be able to explain why the images they picture are so strong, such as words that helped them.)

For ongoing informal assessment, use the checklists on pages 61–64 of *Level D Assessment*.

Word Study Assessment

Use these steps to help you and your students assess their understanding of vowel alternations.

1. Write the following words on the board or on word cards: *competition, exposition,* and *notification*.
2. Ask students to write on their own papers the base word for each word and to underline the vowel in the schwa position.

Word	Base Word
competition	compete
exposition	expose
notification	notify

LESSON **5**

Sacagawea: Native American . . .

Travel the World, pages 28–31

SUMMARY

This **biographical sketch** focuses on the contributions Sacagawea made to the successful expedition of Lewis and Clark.

COMPREHENSION STRATEGY

Inferential Thinking

WRITING

Biographical Sketch

VOCABULARY

Suffix *-ible/-able*

PHONICS/WORD STUDY

Vowel Alternations: Long to Short

Lesson Vocabulary

expedition	edible
surveying	documented
translators	

MATERIALS

Travel the World, pp. 28–31
Student Journal, pp. 15–18
Word Study Manual, p. 38
Writing Advantage, pp. 114–151

Sacagawea Native American Navigator

A Map of LEWIS AND CLARK'S TRACK, Across the Western Portion of North America From the MISSISSIPPI TO THE PACIFIC OCEAN; By Order of the Executive of the UNITED STATES.

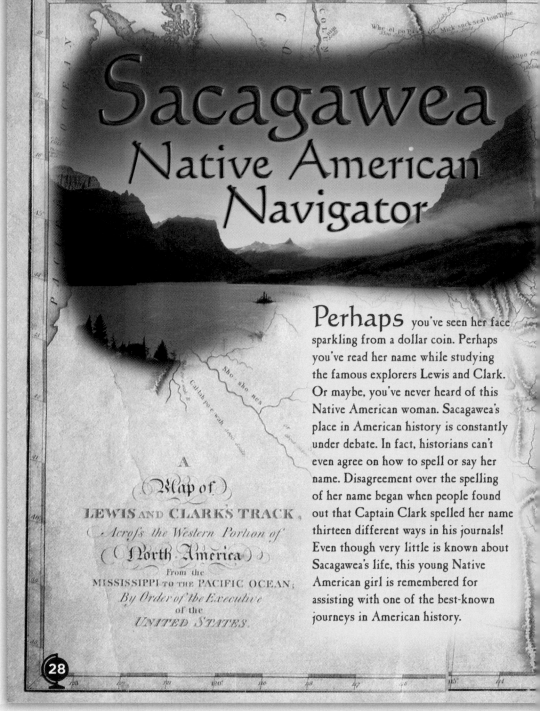

Perhaps you've seen her face sparkling from a dollar coin. Perhaps you've read her name while studying the famous explorers Lewis and Clark. Or maybe, you've never heard of this Native American woman. Sacagawea's place in American history is constantly under debate. In fact, historians can't even agree on how to spell or say her name. Disagreement over the spelling of her name began when people found out that Captain Clark spelled her name thirteen different ways in his journals! Even though very little is known about Sacagawea's life, this young Native American girl is remembered for assisting with one of the best-known journeys in American history.

28

Before Reading

Use one or more activities.

Anticipation Guide

Create an anticipation guide for students. (See TE page 389 for an anticipation guide BLM.) Ask students to read the statements and decide whether they agree or disagree with each one. As students make their decisions, they can place a check in the AGREE or DISAGREE box before each statement. Then discuss the responses. (See top of right column on page 41.)

Vocabulary Preview

List and say the vocabulary words. Have students choose a familiar word to start the word map on *Student Journal* page 15. Have them write the word and its definition. Tell students they will complete the page after reading. Use the word *expedition* to model.

Preview the Selection

Have students preview pages 28–31 in the magazine, taking special notice of the headings.

Make Predictions/ Set Purpose

Using the information they gathered in previewing the selection, students should make predictions about what they will learn. If students have trouble generating a purpose for reading, suggest that they read to find out how Sacagawea contributed to the Lewis and Clark expedition.

Early Years

Sacagawea (sak uh juh WEE uh) was born around 1788 in what is now the state of Idaho. She was a member of the Lemhi Shoshone (sho SHO nee) Native American tribe. Her name means "bird woman." During the fall of 1800 the Lemhi Indians moved to the three forks in the Missouri River to spend the winter. The weather was milder there, and food was more available. However, another tribe of Native Americans attacked them. The attackers took many Lemhi Indians as prisoners. Sacagawea was one of the prisoners. After three or four years as a prisoner, she was sold as a slave to a French fur trader. His name was Toussaint Charbonneau (too SAHNT shar bohn O). He took Sacagawea as one of his many wives. When Sacagawea was only fourteen or fifteen years old, she gave birth to a son, Jean-Baptiste.

Adventures with Lewis and Clark

Soon after Sacagawea's son was born, two English explorers named Lewis and Clark arrived at Charbonneau and Sacagawea's home. Lewis and Clark were on an important expedition, or journey, exploring the western United States. Their expedition was both military and scientific. Mainly, they were surveying western America: measuring and studying the land, taking notes about the natives, and describing the plants and animals they found. However, Lewis and Clark needed someone who could speak and understand Native American languages and translate, or change, them into English. So, Lewis and Clark hired Charbonneau and Sacagawea as translators. Together, the expedition headed west. At that time, no one on the expedition, not even Lewis or Clark, could have known how much help Sacagawea would be on the journey.

29

DIFFERENTIATED INSTRUCTION

ANTICIPATION GUIDE

Here is an example:

AGREE	DISAGREE	
		1. Sacagawea was a Native American woman.
		2. Sacagawea was part of the Lewis and Clark expedition.
		3. Sacagawea had little experience with the land and plants.

Student Journal page 15

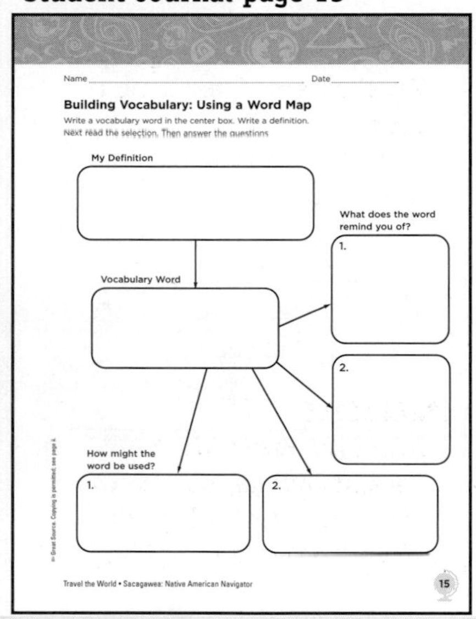
Name ______ Date ______

Building Vocabulary: Using a Word Map

Write a vocabulary word in the center box. Write a definition. Next read the selection. Then answer the questions.

My Definition

What does the word remind you of?

1.

2.

Vocabulary Word

How might the word be used?

1.

2.

Travel the World • Sacagawea: Native American Navigator

15

During Reading

Comprehension

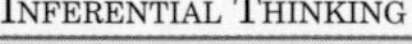
INFERENTIAL THINKING

Use the questions to model for students how to make inferences about Sacagawea. Then have students make inferences of their own.

- What does the text tell me about Sacagawea?
- What ideas can I infer that the author does not state directly?

Teacher Think Aloud

I infer that Sacagawea was courageous and caring, despite her early experiences. It says she was only a teenager when she joined the trip, so it must have taken courage to go away with strangers. Also, she shared her knowledge with the explorers, showing them how to find edible plants and berries. This shows she cared about the explorers.

Fix-Up Strategies

Offer these strategies to help students read independently.

If you don't understand what you're reading:

- Reread the difficult section to look for clues to help you comprehend.
- Read ahead to find clues to help you comprehend.
- Retell, or say in your own words, what you've read.
- Visualize, or form mental pictures of, what you've read.

DIFFERENTIATED INSTRUCTION

SMALL GROUP

Comprehension

INFERENTIAL THINKING

To help students draw a conclusion from a section of text, have them reread "The Mystery of Her Death" on page 31. Then ask:

1. Was there a written record of Sacagawea's death? (No.)
2. Is there more than one idea about when she may have died? Explain. (Yes. She may have died in 1812 or 1884.)
3. What conclusion about Sacagawea's death can you draw from this information? (We don't know when she died.)

Student Journal pages 16–17

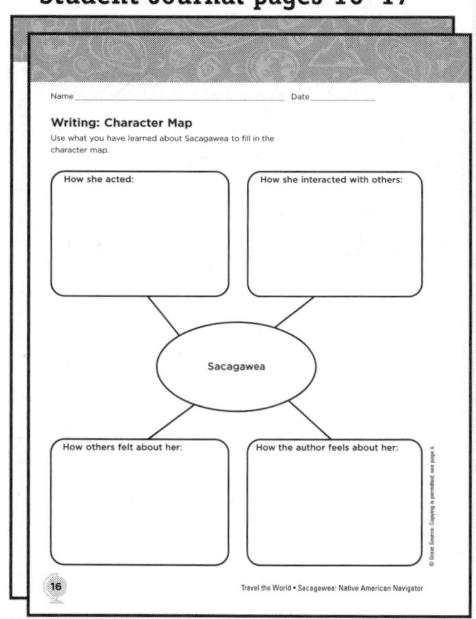

Name________ Date________

Writing: Character Map

Use what you have learned about Sacagawea to fill in the character map.

How she acted:

How she interacted with others:

Sacagawea

How others felt about her:

How the author feels about her:

16 Travel the World • Sacagawea: Native American Navigator

How Sacagawea Helped the Expedition

The explorers and their helpers began their two-year-long trip in St. Louis, Missouri. They followed the Missouri River past Iowa, through North and South Dakota, and into Montana. They crossed the Rocky Mountains and reached the Columbia River, which, in turn, led to the Pacific Ocean. They were lucky that they brought Sacagawea with them. On their journey they came across a tribe of Lemhi Indians led by Sacagawea's oldest brother. Because they were family, she was able to get food, horses, and guides for the expedition. The Lemhi also provided advice on how to cross the Rockies. Without these supplies and advice, there is a good chance that the expedition wouldn't have been able to continue.

Next, Sacajawea shared her knowledge of how to find food with the explorers. She taught them how to find edible plants. Lewis and Clark wrote in their journals about how Sacagawea dug up roots, onions, and other wild plants for everyone to eat. Some of the plants that she brought for the explorers to eat were new to them. By carefully describing them, Lewis won scientific credit for finding new kinds of plants.

Sacagawea also found and picked different berries for them to eat. She showed the explorers where to find the berries and which ones were not poisonous. She also showed them how and where to find animals like sheep and bison.

Sacagawea helped the explorers by having a calm, cool personality. Two times in his journals, Lewis described Sacagawea's calmness. Once, when the explorers' boats overturned, only Sacagawea set to work collecting the things that had washed overboard. One of those items was very important—notes that Lewis and Clark had written.

Perhaps most importantly, Sacagawea and her baby boy acted as a symbol of peace. The expedition of Lewis and Clark brought white men into areas that were not friendly to them. Because of Sacagawea and her baby, the Native American tribes greeted the explorers with wonder and not anger.

A statue in Portland, Oregon, shows Sacagawea holding her son and pointing west.

30

After Reading

Use one or more activities.

Check Purpose

Have students decide if their purpose was met. Did they discover what kind of life Sacagawea led? Did they learn how she helped Lewis and Clark?

Discussion Questions

Continue the group discussion with the following questions.

1. What are some events that occurred in Sacagawea's life before she met Lewis and Clark? Tell about those events in order. (Sequence)
2. How was Sacagawea's life as a Native American important to the success of the expedition? (Draw Conclusions)
3. What do you understand now about Sacagawea that you didn't understand before? (Making Connections)

Revisit: Anticipation Guide

Look back with students at the anticipation guide. How accurate were their responses? Which would they like to adjust?

Revisit: Word Map

Have students return to the word map on *Student Journal* page 15. Have students review the original definition of their selected vocabulary word and adjust it as needed. Then have them answer the questions.

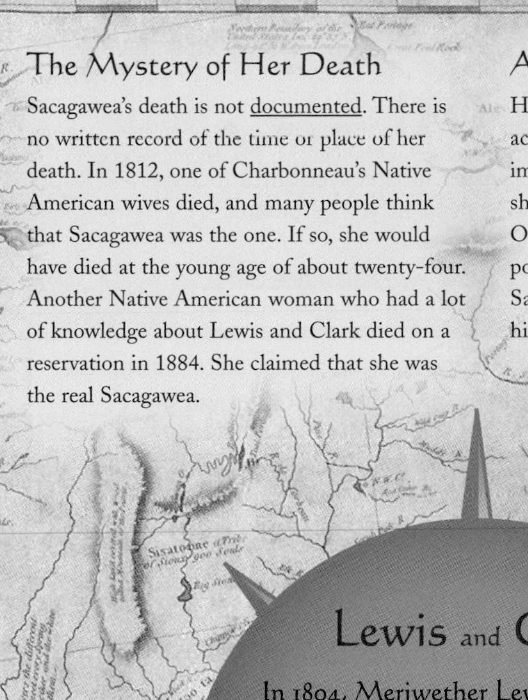

The Mystery of Her Death

Sacagawea's death is not documented. There is no written record of the time or place of her death. In 1812, one of Charbonneau's Native American wives died, and many people think that Sacagawea was the one. If so, she would have died at the young age of about twenty-four. Another Native American woman who had a lot of knowledge about Lewis and Clark died on a reservation in 1884. She claimed that she was the real Sacagawea.

A Place in History

Historians argue about how much Sacagawea actually helped Lewis and Clark and about the importance of her place in history. Some feel that she saved the expedition from many disasters. Others feel that her role is blown out of proportion. Nevertheless, one thing is sure: Sacagawea has earned a solid place in American history and folklore. ◆

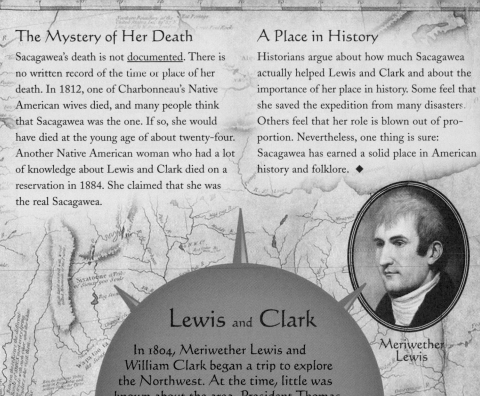

Lewis and Clark

In 1804, Meriwether Lewis and William Clark began a trip to explore the Northwest. At the time, little was known about the area. President Thomas Jefferson wanted to learn more about it and to establish contact with the Native Americans who lived there. He also hoped that there would be a good land route between the Atlantic and Pacific oceans. Lewis and Clark arrived home in 1806, having decided that there was no easy east-west land route.

Meriwether Lewis

William Clark

31

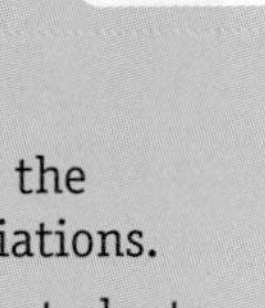

DIFFERENTIATED INSTRUCTION

Vocabulary

Suffix *-ible/-able*

Help students understand the meaning of the suffix variations.

1. Display *breakable*. Tell students it means "able to be broken" and that *-able* is a suffix added to the end of a word to change the word's meaning. Adding *-able* changes the meaning to include "able to be."
2. Now display *horrible* and explain that *-ible* is a variant of *-able* with the same meaning. Then have students tell what they think each of the four words means.

Possible answers to **Student Journal page 18** are *incredible*, *reliable*, *acceptable*, and *visible*.

Name ______ Date ______

Building Vocabulary: Suffix *-ible/-able*

Write words you know that contain the suffix -ible/-able. Write a definition for each word. Use a dictionary to help you, if you wish.

-ible/-able means "able to, having the ability to"

Words	Definitions
edible	able to be eaten

18 Travel the World • Sacagawea: Native American Navigator

Writing Biographical Sketch

Have students discuss what they know about Sacagawea. Write their ideas on the board or on a chart. Next, have students use their discussion to help them complete the character map on *Student Journal* page 16. Then have students use their character maps as guides to write their own biographical sketch of Sacagawea, on *Student Journal* page 17.

Vocabulary Suffix *-ible/-able*

Have students find the word *edible* on page 30. Ask: *What do you know about this word? What context clues lead you to its meaning?*

Identify the suffix *-ible* as a word part that means "able to, having the ability to." Note that the root *ed-* means "to eat." Ask volunteers to use the two word parts to define *edible*. (able to be eaten) Then have students complete *Student Journal* page 18. (See Differentiated Instruction.)

Phonics/Word Study

Vowel Alternations

Display and read aloud the words *recite* and *recitation*. Ask students what sound the *i* has in *recite*. (long *i* sound) Then ask what sound the first *i* in *recitation* has. (short *i* sound) Point out that if students remember how to spell *recite*, it will help them spell the related word *recitation*. Now, work with students to complete the in-depth vowel alternations activity on TE page 44.

Phonics/Word Study

Vowel Alternations: Long to Short

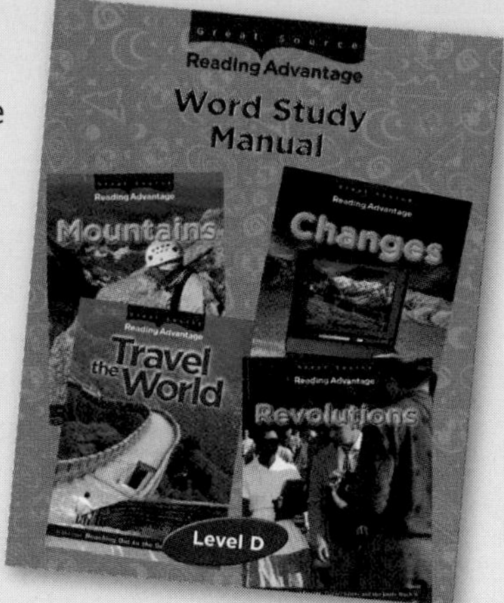

There are different kinds of vowel alternations; the long-to-schwa was one of them. There are also long-to-short changes that occur. Consider the word *crime*. When the word changes to *criminal*, what happens to that long *i* in *crime*? The long *i* shifts to a short *i*. While this is more obvious to the ear than the long-to-schwa change, it still is worth pointing out to students.

- Ask students to look at the long *i* in *crime* and how it changes to a short *i* in *criminal*. This is not uncommon, and it happens across all the vowels.
- Explain to students the spelling-meaning connection and the importance of the base word. Then explain to them how they can use the base word to help ascertain the correct spelling. Further reinforce this by using the word *ignition* to see if students are able to come up with the base word (*ignite*) and then use it to illuminate the spelling of *ignition*. In this case, they can depend on their knowledge of short vowels as well as the base word to figure it out.
- Provide students with a list of vowel alternation words and ask them to generate the base word and identify the vowel that has shifted. (See *Word Study Manual* page 38.)

Vowel Alternations Sort Two: Long to Short			
criminal crime	ignition ignite	humanity humane	sufficient suffice
recitation recite	cavity cave	gravity grave	natural nature
volcanic volcano	wisdom wise	telescopic telescope	production produce
assumption assume	prescription prescribe	division divide	pleasant please
convention convene	microscopic microscope	national nation	dreamt dream
health heal	parasitic parasite	consumption consume	extremity extreme

For more information on word sorts and spelling stages, see pages 5–31 in the *Word Study Manual*.

Focus on . . .

Use one or more activities in this section to focus on a particular area of need in your students.

Comprehension STRATEGY SUPPORT

To help those students who need more practice using the strategies covered in this lesson, work one-on-one or in small groups to apply the strategy prompts below. Apply the prompts to a *Reading Advantage* paperback, a classroom library book, or a new or familiar selection in the magazine. Always model your own thinking first.

Inferential Thinking

- What are the causes or effects of this event?
- What do I learn from the character or person's thoughts, words, or actions?
- What do I know (or infer) from the text that the author hasn't stated directly?
- What conclusions can I draw?

Writing **Biographical Sketch**

Have students write a biographical sketch of a friend or relative. To help them plan what they will write, provide a blank character map for each student. (See TE page 391.) Students can use the character maps to write their biographical sketches.

For instruction and practice writing informational paragraphs, see lessons in *Writing Advantage,* pages 114–151.

Fluency: Pacing

After they have read the article at least once, have partners alternate reading aloud the two sections of text at the top of page 31. Use the special feature on Lewis and Clark on the same page to model reading smoothly and at an even pace.

As you listen to students read, use these prompts to guide them.

- Read the words smoothly. Try not to hesitate or repeat words.
- Try previewing the paragraph to look for any difficult or unfamiliar words. Previewing will also help you see in advance how groups of words naturally go together.
- Let the punctuation guide your reading. Pause at commas and at the end of each sentence.

When students read aloud, do they—

✓ demonstrate a smooth pace, not too fast or too slow?

✓ incorporate well-timed pauses between words and phrases?

✓ reflect an awareness and understanding of punctuation?

English Language Learners

Review with students the concept of adjectives. During the activity, students may use a thesaurus to help them.

1. Have partners brainstorm a list of adjectives that describe Sacagawea.
2. Compile the lists and display them. Discuss the meanings of the words.
3. Ask students to pick four new adjectives, write each word in a sentence, and share sentences.

Independent Activity Options

While you work with individuals or small groups, others can work independently on one or more of the following options.

- Level D paperback books, see TE pages 367–372
- Level D *eZines*
- Repeat word sorts from this lesson
- *Student Journal* pages for this lesson
- *Writing Advantage* independent lessons

Assessment

Strategy Assessment

To help you and your students assess their use of comprehension strategies, ask the following questions. Students can complete a written response or provide verbal answers in a one-on-one reading conference.

- **Inferential Thinking** What conclusions can you draw about the relationship between Lewis and Clark and the Native American tribes the explorers encountered? Why? (Answers will vary. Students may infer that without Sacagawea, there may have been fights between the tribes, and Lewis and Clark, and that the explorers may not have been able to finish their expedition. The text supports these inferences by saying that Sacagawea and her baby "acted as a symbol of peace" and that the tribes "greeted the explorers with wonder and not anger.")

For ongoing informal assessment, use the checklists on pages 61–64 of *Level D Assessment*.

Word Study Assessment

Use these steps to help you and your students assess their understanding of vowel alternations.

1. Write the following words on the board or on word cards: *telescopic*, *convention*, *division*, and *prescription*.
2. Ask students to write the base word for each word and to underline the vowel that shifts from a long-to-short sound.

Word	Base Word
telescopic	telescope
convention	convene
division	divide
prescription	prescribe

LESSON **6**

Brotherly Love *and* End of Summer

Travel the World, pages 32–37

SUMMARY

The **short story** tells about a sixteen-year-old boy who feels overshadowed by his older brother. The **poem** that follows the story is about two siblings bidding good-bye to the last day of summer.

COMPREHENSION STRATEGIES

Making Connections
Understanding Text Structure

WRITING

Journal Entries

VOCABULARY

Multiple Meanings

PHONICS/WORD STUDY

Vowel Alternations: Short to Schwa

Lesson Vocabulary

palpable prospect

MATERIALS

Travel the World, pp. 32–37
Student Journal, pp. 19–21
Word Study Manual, p. 39
Writing Advantage, pp. 30–56

Brother

"Breakfast is ready!"

"None for me, Mom. We have a soccer meeting before school today. I've got to get going."

"Here, Luis, at least take this banana."

"You know, Mom, if I had a car of my own … "

"Not this early in the morning," Luis's father said, slapping the newspaper down on the table.

"Gotta go." Luis was outside the door, only catching a glimpse of his older brother, Tomas, as the screen door squeaked shut behind him. In seconds he was on his bicycle rolling past his brother's '76 Chevy. It's so unfair that Tomas has a car and I don't, Luis thought. I don't care that he's a year older than I am.

How am I supposed to have a life as a sixteen-year old without a car?

- - - - - - - -

The final bell of the day rang out. Luis stretched his long legs from beneath the cramped desk in chemistry class and headed to the locker room.

"Hey, Luis, wait up. I've got a question for you."

"Charles, I'm going to be late for the game."

"No problem. I'll walk with you. So, have you heard about the party at Shanelle's Friday night? We've got to go, man. Everyone is gonna be there."

"You'll have to pick me up or something."

"Can't you use Tomas's car this once?"

"I could ask, but … "

"Great. See you tomorrow night." Before Luis could finish, Charles had turned the corner and was gone.

- - - - - - - -

"I'm open!" Luis's heart was pounding as he dashed toward the goal. He could feel the thin layer of sweat on his skin and taste the salt crusting on the edges of his lips. "I'm open, I have a shot!"

Tomas glanced at his brother.

32

Before Reading

WHOLE CLASS Use one or more activities.

Create a List

Start a discussion with students about siblings. Ask:

- What is it like to have an older brother or sister? To be an older brother or sister?
- What is it like to have a younger brother or sister? To be a younger brother or sister?
- What is it like to be an only child?

Write students' thoughts in a list. Revisit the list after students finish reading the story.

1. Sometimes I like having an older sister, but sometimes I don't.
2. I don't like when my younger brother gets to do things that I never could.
3. I wish I had an older brother who could play sports with me.

Vocabulary Preview

Write the two vocabulary words on the board and read them aloud to make sure students understand the pronunciation of each word. Then have students complete the associations activity on *Student Journal* page 19. Model the process with one of the words.

ly Love

But instead of passing the ball to Luis, he passed it to Roger, who shot and scored the winning goal. Luis slowed down to a jog and then a walk. The referee's whistle blew. Hands on hips and breathing hard, Luis got right in Tomas's face. "What's the big idea? I was open."

"No sweat. Roger scored."

"That's not the point. The point is I was open." Luis's chest pushed against his brother's.

"Enough, boys," the coach chimed in. "The play was fine. Have a seat. Let's talk about the starting lineup for tomorrow's game." While the coach talked, Luis went over and over the play in his head. Tomas didn't pass me that ball to spite me, he thought.

33

DIFFERENTIATED INSTRUCTION

SMALL GROUP

Make Predictions/ Set Purpose

Use the following steps to help students make predictions:

1. Explain that when you make predictions, you use the information you already know to predict what will happen next.
2. Have a student read the first column on page 32. Then ask: *What is going on here? What problems do you predict Luis will have in this story, judging from his comments about a car and his reaction to his brother?*
3. Tell students that periodically stopping to predict what will happen next will help them better understand what they read.

Student Journal page 19

Name ________________ Date ________

Building Vocabulary: Making Associations

Think about what you already know about the two words listed. Then answer the questions for each word.

Word palpable

What do you think about when you read this word? ________

What does the word remind you of? ________

What do you already know about this word? ________

Word prospect

What do you think about when you read this word? ________

What does the word remind you of? ________

What do you already know about this word? ________

Now watch for these words in the magazine selection. Were you on the right track?

Travel the World • Brotherly Love 19

Preview the Selection

Have students read the title and look at the pictures on pages 32–36. Use these prompts to orient students to the story.

- What do the title and the illustrations tell you about the story?
- What do you think this story will be about?
- Why do you think the author supplies factual information about soccer?
- Do you think this story is fiction or nonfiction? How can you tell?

Teacher Think Aloud

I think this selection is fiction because I see a lot of dialogue, or words in quotation marks that characters are saying. The title makes me think the story might be about how one brother helps another. There are a lot of soccer images, so I think the game has something to do with the story. I also see a car and fruit. I wonder what happens in this story.

Make Predictions/ Set Purpose

Using the information they gathered in previewing the selection, students should make predictions about what they will learn. If students have trouble generating a purpose for reading, suggest that they read to find out why the story is called "Brotherly Love." (See Differentiated Instruction.)

DIFFERENTIATED INSTRUCTION

Comprehension

MAKING CONNECTIONS

Help students make connections with the text by doing the following activity.

1. Ask: *Do you agree with Luis that the reason Tomas didn't pass him the ball was to spite him? Why or why not?*
2. Have students discuss the question with a partner. Remind them to draw on what they've learned about Tomas from the story, as well as their own experiences.
3. Ask pairs to share their responses.

At dinner that night, neither Tomas nor Luis spoke unless spoken to. By dessert the tension was so palpable, you could almost reach out over the fruit bowl and touch it. "I'm not eating like this again," Mr. Martinez declared. "After a long day, I deserve a pleasurable dinner. What is going on here?"

"Junior is just mad because I didn't pass the ball to him in the soccer game."

"Yeah, right," Luis snorted sarcastically.

"Well, then, what is it?" Mr. Martinez pressed. And Luis let it all out.

"Sure, Tomas didn't pass me the ball today. I was open, he saw me. But you know what? In this house, it's always Tomas this, Tomas that. He has a car. He has a girlfriend. He's going to Spain this summer. He's on the student council. He has the bigger bedroom. Should I continue?"

"Get over it, Luis." Tomas pushed his chair back from the table, lifted his plate, and disappeared into the kitchen.

"It's so unfair." Luis stood and vanished up the stairs. The sound of a door slamming shut echoed across the dining room table.

In the car on the way to school the next morning, Luis stared straight out the window. School would be finished next week. Tonight was Shanelle's end-of-year party. How was he going to ask Tomas for the car after the scene he made last night? Blew it again, jerk, he thought to himself. But a smirk crept across his face as he thought of the prospect of driving his friends to a party.

Maybe it was a possibility. "Hey, Tomas?"

"Yeh?"

"What are you doing tonight after the game?"

"I was just planning on hanging out with Kate. Maybe renting a movie. Why?"

"Uh, well, Charles mentioned this thing tonight."

"What thing?"

Soccer Around the World

Soccer is truly an international sport. The Fédération Internationale de Football Association (FIFA) sponsors World Cup™ soccer. The first tournament was played in Uruguay in 1930. Except for a twelve-year break for World War II, the tournament has been played every four years. Since 1958, the location of the games has switched back and forth between Europe and the Americas. However, Korea and Japan were the co-hosts in 2002. Soccer is extremely popular. Over 37 billion people watched the World Cup™ games in France in 1998.

34

During Reading

Comprehension

MAKING CONNECTIONS

Use these questions to model making connections with the text. Then have students share some of the connections they made.

- What does this story remind me of?
- Have I had similar experiences?
- With which character do I identify the most?

(See Differentiated Instruction.)

Teacher Think Aloud

This story reminds me of times when my sister and I weren't speaking, and it would be very quiet at the dinner table. I was the oldest, and my sister thought I had all the fun. Reading this story from Luis's point of view helps me understand why she felt that way. I was allowed to do things that she wanted to do, but couldn't. I guess I wouldn't have liked that either.

Comprehension

UNDERSTANDING TEXT STRUCTURE

Use these questions to model understanding the conflict and the resolution in a piece of fiction. Then have students identify and explain the story elements (characters, setting, conflict, plot, resolution).

- Which character has a problem in the story?
- What is the problem, or conflict?
- How is the conflict resolved?

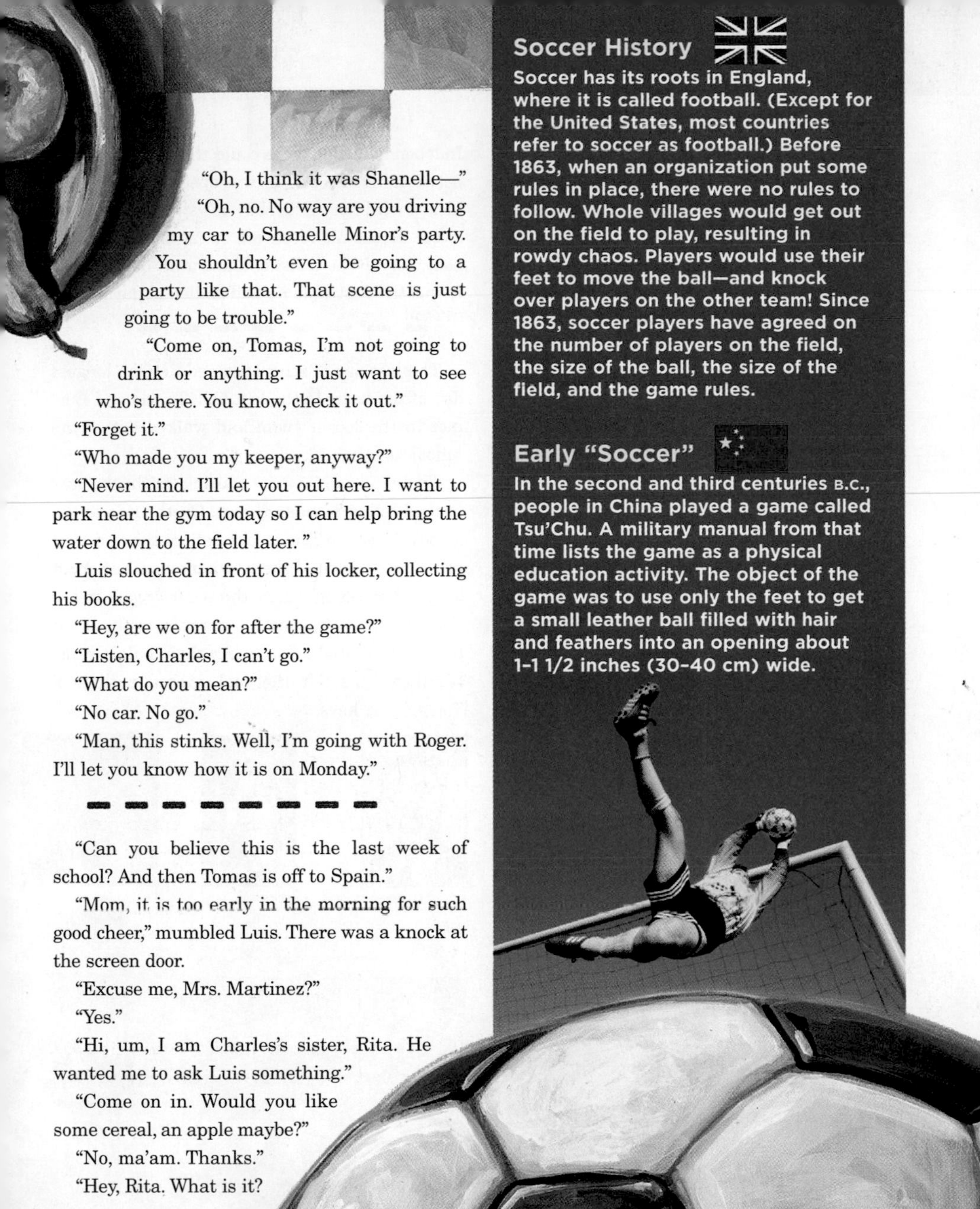

"Oh, I think it was Shanelle—"

"Oh, no. No way are you driving my car to Shanelle Minor's party. You shouldn't even be going to a party like that. That scene is just going to be trouble."

"Come on, Tomas, I'm not going to drink or anything. I just want to see who's there. You know, check it out."

"Forget it."

"Who made you my keeper, anyway?"

"Never mind. I'll let you out here. I want to park near the gym today so I can help bring the water down to the field later. "

Luis slouched in front of his locker, collecting his books.

"Hey, are we on for after the game?"

"Listen, Charles, I can't go."

"What do you mean?"

"No car. No go."

"Man, this stinks. Well, I'm going with Roger. I'll let you know how it is on Monday."

"Can you believe this is the last week of school? And then Tomas is off to Spain."

"Mom, it is too early in the morning for such good cheer," mumbled Luis. There was a knock at the screen door.

"Excuse me, Mrs. Martinez?"

"Yes."

"Hi, um, I am Charles's sister, Rita. He wanted me to ask Luis something."

"Come on in. Would you like some cereal, an apple maybe?"

"No, ma'am. Thanks."

"Hey, Rita. What is it?

Soccer History

Soccer has its roots in England, where it is called football. (Except for the United States, most countries refer to soccer as football.) Before 1863, when an organization put some rules in place, there were no rules to follow. Whole villages would get out on the field to play, resulting in rowdy chaos. Players would use their feet to move the ball—and knock over players on the other team! Since 1863, soccer players have agreed on the number of players on the field, the size of the ball, the size of the field, and the game rules.

Early "Soccer"

In the second and third centuries B.C., people in China played a game called Tsu'Chu. A military manual from that time lists the game as a physical education activity. The object of the game was to use only the feet to get a small leather ball filled with hair and feathers into an opening about 1-1 1/2 inches (30-40 cm) wide.

35

Teacher Think Aloud

I discovered right away that Luis has a problem. He wants to have his own car. In fact, he wants everything his brother Tomas has, but especially a car. Luis tries to solve his problem by borrowing his brother's car to go to a party. Tomas refuses, and Luis is upset. The solution to Luis's car problem comes as a big surprise to him. When Tomas leaves to visit Spain, he gives Luis the car keys.

Fix-Up Strategies

Offer these strategies to help students read independently.

If you don't understand what you're reading:

- Reread the difficult section to look for clues to help you comprehend.
- Read ahead to find clues to help you comprehend.
- Retell, or say in your own words, what you've read.
- Visualize, or form mental pictures of, what you've read.

If you don't understand a word:

- Reread the sentence. Look for ideas and words that provide meaning clues.
- Find clues by reading a few sentences before and after the confusing word.
- Look for the base or root word and think about its meaning.
- Think about the topic or plot at this point to see if either offers meaning clues.

DIFFERENTIATED INSTRUCTION

SMALL GROUP

Writing Journal Entries

Use these strategies to help students write their journal entries.

1. Discuss with students the importance of making good decisions. Point out that decisions sometimes have critical consequences.
2. Ask: *Why do you think Roger decided to take his brother's car without asking? How might he have felt about his decision the next day?*
3. Then ask students: *How did Luis feel when his brother refused to let him take the car? Why do you think he decided not to go to the party? How do you think he felt about his decision on Monday?*

Student Journal page 20

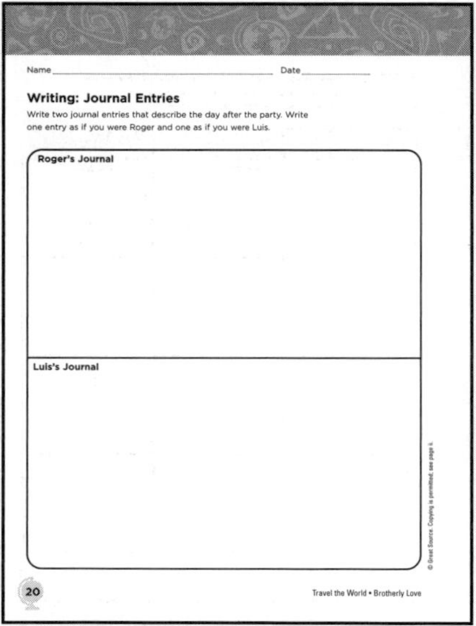
Name ______ Date ______

Writing: Journal Entries

Write two journal entries that describe the day after the party. Write one entry as if you were Roger and one as if you were Luis.

Roger's Journal

Luis's Journal

20 Travel the World • Brotherly Love

Where's Charles?"

"Charles wanted to know if you could get his yearbook signed for him today, Luis. He won't be in school."

"Why not?" Luis had thought it was weird that Charles hadn't called him over the weekend. But he didn't think it was that weird.

"The police were called to the party. A neighbor had reported loud noise from the party. When the police were walking up the driveway, they noticed a car that had been reported stolen. It was Roger's. Roger had taken his brother's car without asking, and his brother reported it stolen. The cops gave Roger a warning and lectured everyone else about making too much noise. The police scared everyone pretty badly. Mom and Dad are really angry." She held out Charles's yearbook. Tomas stepped up to Rita because Luis stood there, stunned.

"Sure no problem, Rita. Luis will do it." Tomas reached out and took the yearbook. He shoved it toward Luis's chest.

"Thanks," Luis said, unsure if he was talking to Rita or Tomas. "Thanks."

That afternoon, Luis was in the middle of a game, running. Running was the only thing that made him feel free. He could feel his quads tightening as he ran, as his cleats banged down the grassy field. When he sprinted, he felt like he could run forever. Run away. Someplace where he was Luis, not Tomas's little brother, not Mr. Martinez's son. Just Luis. Fast. Strong. Independent. Before he could think, the ball was between his feet, and he was open for a shot. Luis kicked with his whole body; his sweaty black hair swept across his forehead, sweat spurted off his body. Score! The whistle. The crowd. Luis smiled. It was the first time he had smiled in days.

The last day of school seemed like the longest day of the year. At the last bell, Tomas and Luis met in the locker room and walked out of the school together.

Their parents were waiting with the car packed full of Tomas's things. On the ride to the airport Luis and Tomas joked about the assistant principal's hair and their father's new hat. They laughed and laughed. At the security gate in the airport, Tomas hugged his parents. He held out his hand to shake Luis's. As their palms came together, Luis felt the cool, jagged outline of Tomas's car keys. ◆

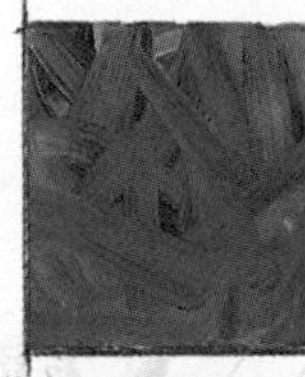

36

After Reading

WHOLE CLASS

Use one or more activities.

Check Purpose

Have students decide if their purpose was met. Did they learn more about trusting others and making good decisions?

Discussion Questions

Continue the group discussion with the following questions.

1. What happened as a result of Tomas's refusal to let Luis use the car? (Cause-Effect)
2. Did you predict that Tomas would give the car keys to Luis, or were you surprised? Explain. (Predict)
3. What was your favorite part of the story? Why? (Making Connections)

Revisit: Sibling List

Have partners discuss the range of feelings Luis has toward his older brother. Compare Luis's feelings to the list.

Revisit: Associations Activity

Encourage students to revisit the associations activity on *Student Journal* page 19. Do they need to revise or add to any answers?

END OF SUMMER

This morning my family is leaving
the ocean, packing the backseat
of the car, driving home.
My brother and I sneak out
by the garage door and walk
down the gravel rolling hill road
to the bay for the last time this summer.

My brother bends to the tide
and combs his fingers through
the pooling water. I stand barefoot
beside him, sandals in hand.
It is barely morning
and this day seems full of possibilities.

I have no way of knowing
this is the last time
I will look at that horizon
with these eyes.

37

Poem: End of Summer

Have students read the poem silently. Then read the poem aloud to them. Point out that the first two stanzas describe a situation and the third stanza tells the poet's response to a situation. Discuss the situation and the response. If needed, use these prompts to guide students.

- What is the situation that the poet describes?
- What is the poet's response to the situation?
- What do you think the poet's message is?

Possible answers to **Student Journal page 21** include *spoke, bowl, mad, right, ball, saw, back,* and *plate.*

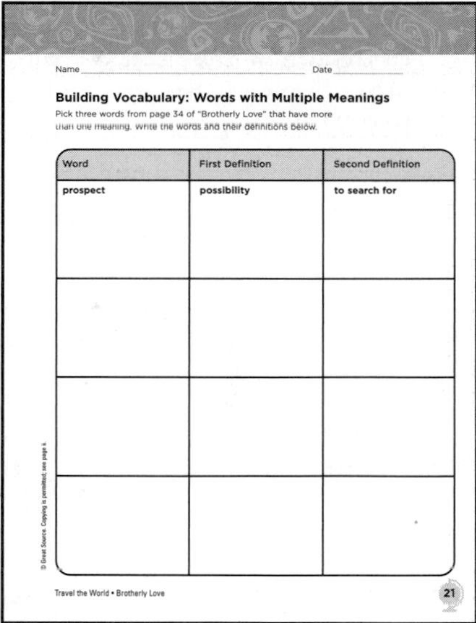

Name ______ Date ______

Building Vocabulary: Words with Multiple Meanings

Pick three words from page 34 of "Brotherly Love" that have more than one meaning. Write the words and their definitions below.

Word	First Definition	Second Definition
prospect	possibility	to search for

Travel the World • Brotherly Love 21

Writing Journal Entries

Tell students that they will write two journal entries, one as if they were Roger; the other, Luis. Before they write, engage students in a brief discussion about the decisions the boys made on the day of the party and how they felt about them the following day (or on Monday). Make a list of students' ideas. Encourage students to refer to the list as they complete the journal entries on *Student Journal* page 20. (See Differentiated Instruction.)

Vocabulary

Multiple Meanings

Discuss with students that many words have multiple meanings. Draw students' attention to the word *prospect* on page 34. Ask students what *prospect* means in that sentence. (possibility) Then ask students to figure out the meaning of *prospect* in this sentence: *The miners went to* prospect *gold in the hills of Montana.* (to search for) Have students pick three words from page 34 to use in the chart on *Student Journal* page 21.

Phonics/Word Study

Vowel Alternations

Display and read aloud the words *system* and *systemic*. Ask students what sound the *e* has in *system*. (short *e* sound) Then ask what sound the *e* has in *systemic* (schwa). Note that if students recognize that *system* is the base word for *systemic*, it will help them remember how to spell the longer word. Now, work with students to complete the in-depth vowel alternations activity on TE page 52.

Phonics/Word Study

More Vowel Alternations: Short to Schwa

There are three different kinds of vowel alternations. The long-to-schwa and the long-to-short alternations have been examined. The final one is the short-to-schwa alternation. Consider the word *adapt*. When the word changes to *adaptation*, what happens to the short *a* that is so obvious in *adapt*? It shifts to a schwa. While this change is more obvious to the ear when it is a long-to-schwa change, having students focus their attention to the short-to-schwa will help them make this spelling-meaning connection. Knowing that *adapt* has a short *a* will help them preserve that vowel in this new iteration (*adaptation*).

- Ask students to examine the short *a* in *adapt* and how it changes to a schwa in *adaptation*. This is not uncommon, and it happens across all the vowels. What they need to remember is that other forms of the word can yield clues to the reduced vowel (schwa).
- Explain to students the spelling-meaning connection and the importance of the base word. Explain to them how they can use the base word and/or other forms of the word to help them determine the correct spelling. Further reinforce this by using the word *metal* to see if students are able to come up with another form of the word (*metallic*) and to see how they can use the new form to help spell the schwa in *metal*. In this case, they can depend on their knowledge of short vowels as well as the base word to figure it out.
- Provide students with a list of base words and ask them to generate the vowel alternation word and identify the correct vowel in the schwa position. Point out that it is not always in the second syllable. It could be in the third syllable as well.
- On *Word Study Manual* page 39, you can find lists of related words.

Short to Schwa		
locality	local	localize
adapt	adaptation	
excel	excellent	
legality	legal	legalize

For more information on word sorts and spelling stages, see pages 5–31 in the *Word Study Manual*.

Focus on . . .

Use one or more activities in this section to focus on a particular area of need in your students.

Comprehension STRATEGY SUPPORT

To help those students who need more practice using the strategies covered in this lesson, work one-on-one or in small groups to apply the strategy prompts below. Apply the prompts to a *Reading Advantage* paperback, a classroom library book, or a new or familiar selection in the magazine. Always model your own thinking first.

Making Connections

- What does this story (article, passage) remind me of?
- What do I already know about this topic?
- Where have I heard about this topic before?
- What do I have in common with the characters, people, or situations in the text?
- What other books, stories, articles, movies, or TV shows does this text make me think about?

Understanding Text Structure

- What kind of text is this? (book, story, article, guidebook, play, manual)
- How does the author organize the text? (cause-effect, problem-solution, chronological order, description, question-answer, comparison-contrast)
- What details support my thoughts about the text structure?
- What is the cause (effect, problem, solution, order, question, answer)?
- If fiction, who are the characters? What is the setting, plot, conflict, and resolution?

Writing Letter to Luis

Have students write a letter to Luis. They can give him advice about how to handle being a younger brother, or explain how they can relate to his experiences, or both. Model for students how to use the conventions of a letter (greeting, date, body, closing, signature).

To instruct students on how to use strong verbs in their writing, see lessons in *Writing Advantage*, pages 30–55.

Fluency: Expression

After students have read the poem "End of Summer" at least once silently, have partners read the poem aloud chorally. Explain to students that to read the poem expressively, they must first understand the mood that the poet sets. Discuss with students the mood of the poem. (sad, mournful)

As you listen to students read, use these prompts to guide them in reading expressively.

- Use punctuation marks and stanza breaks to help you read expressively. Make sure not to stop at the end of each line, but rather, use the commas and periods for indications where to pause.
- Match your tone of voice to the mood.

When students read aloud, do they—

✓ reflect an understanding of the text?

✓ demonstrate appropriate timing, stress, and intonation?

✓ incorporate appropriate speed and phrasing?

English Language Learners

To support students' comprehension of "Brotherly Love," review the meaning of *cause and effect*. First, define *cause* and then define *effect*. Give at least one example. Then, ask: *Why didn't Luis have time to eat breakfast? Why was Luis upset with Tomas after the game? What effect did the police have on the people at the party?*

Have partners discuss the answers and then list the cause and effect for each question. They should be able to find support for their answers in the text.

Independent Activity Options

While you work with individuals or small groups, others can work independently on one or more of the following options.

- Level D paperback books, see TE pages 367–372
- Level D *eZines*
- Repeat word sorts from this lesson
- *Student Journal* pages for this lesson
- *Writing Advantage* independent lessons

Assessment

Strategy Assessment

To help you and your students assess their use of comprehension strategies, ask the following questions. Students can complete a written response or provide verbal answers in a one-on-one reading conference.

1. **Making Connections** What in your own life did this story make you think of? Explain. (Answers will vary.)
2. **Understanding Text Structure** Fiction may include a lot of dialogue, as in this story. Why might authors include dialogue? (Answers will vary. Students may say that dialogue makes a story seem more real and helps the reader better know the characters, or that unrealistic dialogue detracts from a story.)

See *Level D Assessment* page 10 for formal assessment to go with *Travel the World*.

Word Study Assessment

Use these steps to help you and your students assess their understanding of vowel alternations.

1. Write the following base words on the board or on word cards: *inform, habit, critic, edit,* and *excel.*
2. Ask students to provide a vowel alternation word for each one, and to tell which vowel shifts from a short to a schwa sound.

Base Word	Related Word	Changed Vowel Sound
inform	information	*o*
habit	habitat	*i*
critic	criticize	2nd *i*
edit	editor	*i*
excel	excellent	*e*

LESSON 7

The Grizzlies of Yellowstone

Travel the World, pages 38–43

SUMMARY

This **radio play** about campers watching grizzly bears come out of hibernation in Yellowstone National Park offers sound advice about safe bear encounters.

COMPREHENSION STRATEGIES

Making Connections
Monitor Understanding

WRITING

Play Scene

VOCABULARY

Denotation and Connotation

PHONICS/WORD STUDY

Vowel Alternations Review

Lesson Vocabulary

sanctuary	provokes
varied	wily
menace	authenticity

MATERIALS

Travel the World, pp. 38–43
Student Journal, pp. 22–25
Word Study Manual, p. 40
Writing Advantage, pp. 170–181

THE GRIZZLIES OF YELLOWSTONE

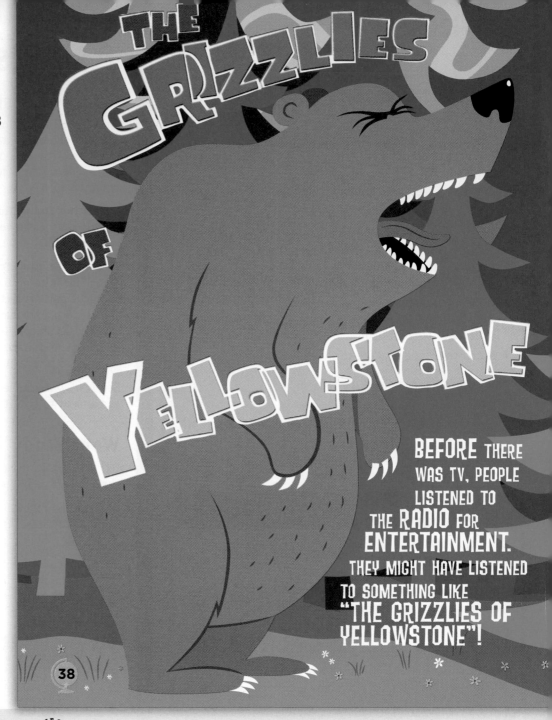

BEFORE THERE WAS TV, PEOPLE LISTENED TO THE RADIO FOR ENTERTAINMENT. THEY MIGHT HAVE LISTENED TO SOMETHING LIKE "THE GRIZZLIES OF YELLOWSTONE"!

38

Before Reading  Use one or more activities.

Anticipation Guide

Create an anticipation guide for students. (See TE page 389 for a BLM.) Ask students to read the statements and place a check in the AGREE or DISAGREE box before each statement. Tell students that they will have the chance to review the anticipation guide after they read the selection.

AGREE	DISAGREE	
		1. You should run when you come across a bear.
		2. Bears like to eat peanut butter and potato chips.
		3. If you come across a bear, you should make a lot of noise.
		4. In bear country, people should not travel together.

Vocabulary Preview

With students, review the vocabulary list and clarify pronunciations. Have students begin the chart on *Student Journal* page 22, filling in only the prediction column before reading the article. Students will complete the chart after they have finished the article.

John
Beau
Sheri
Sponsor
Ranger

As the scene opens, Beau and Sheri are sitting around a campfire, warming their hands and talking. John is narrating the action for the radio audience.

JOHN: *(in a soft voice, so as not to disturb the campers and bears)* Welcome, viewers, to scenic Yellowstone Park. It's just before sunrise here among these 2.2 million acres of wilderness, and we are waiting for some campers observe grizzly bears as they come out of hibernation. This park is a sanctuary, a place in which grizzlies can feel safe. So that we can hear what happens, microphones have been set up around the campsite and near the bear den. These amazing bears haven't ventured out of their caves since the first heavy snow of winter. We'll see if they do today.

BEAU: Seriously, I heard that grizzly bears are starving after months of hibernation. You know, come to think of it, I'm pretty hungry myself. Those energy bars didn't quite fill me up. I could eat a bear . . . heh, heh, heh.

SHERI: Beau, don't even joke like that. But I know how you feel. I wish we had some food, and I wish I could bathe in the winter sun all afternoon like a bear does when it comes out of hibernation. I don't see why those scientists have told all the tourists to stay away. How can a bear coming out of hibernation be *that* dangerous?

BEAU: The scientists made that warning because the bears are very dangerous when they come out of hibernation. Like us right now, they are starved because they haven't eaten for months. Campers and hikers tend to leave around potato chips and peanut butter sandwiches, which attract the bears. Bears go wild for that stuff.

SHERI: I thought that when bears come out of hibernation, they eat winterkill. You know, carcasses of animals that are lying in the melting snow. Elk and bison, right?

JOHN: And there you have it—a real life discussion between campers during the first thaw at Yellowstone. Dead animals don't seem like a hearty meal to me, especially after not eating or drinking all winter. We'll be back after a word from our sponsor.

SPONSOR: Tired of sleepless nights? Just can't get comfortable in your own bed? Try our new Bear Bunk, available at all top-of-the-line furniture stores. Say good-bye to restless nights. We guarantee you'll be sleeping like a bear.

JOHN: And now, back to the campers and bears.

39

DIFFERENTIATED INSTRUCTION 

Preview the Selection

To help students understand the characteristics of a radio play, use the following steps:

1. List these script features: cast of characters, dialogue, scenes.
2. Explain each feature. The cast of a play refers to the different characters in the story. For example, in this radio play, there are five characters. The dialogue is what each character says. The scenes are the different sections of the drama.
3. Have students talk about plays they have seen performed or read. Discuss how readers can learn about characters, setting, and plot through dialogue.

Student Journal page 22

Name ________________ Date ________

Building Vocabulary: Predictions

How do you think these words will be used in "The Grizzlies of Yellowstone Park"? Write your answers in the second column. Next, read the article. Then, clarify your answers in the third column.

Word	My prediction for how the word will be used	How the word was actually used
sanctuary		
varied		
menace		
provokes		
wily		
authenticity		

© Great Source. Copying is permitted; see page ii.

22 Travel the World • The Grizzlies of Yellowstone

Preview the Selection

Have students look through the six pages of the radio play, pages 38–43 in the magazine. Use these or similar prompts to guide students to notice the important features of the text.

- What form of writing will you read? How do you know?
- What do you think the selection is about?
- Do you think the selection is fiction or nonfiction? Why? Could it be both?

(See Differentiated Instruction.)

Teacher Think Aloud

When I looked at the title and the picture of the bear, I thought this selection would be an informative article about bears in Yellowstone Park. But as I turn the pages, I see that it is a play. There's a cast list and what looks like a script, with the speaker's name next to his or her lines. A play is probably fiction, but it might give some facts about grizzly bears, too.

Make Predictions/ Set Purpose

Using the information they gathered in previewing the selection, students should make predictions about what they will learn. If students have trouble generating a purpose for reading, suggest that they read to see if they were correct in their anticipation guide, as well as read to learn what to do if they meet a grizzly bear.

DIFFERENTIATED INSTRUCTION 

Comprehension

MAKING CONNECTIONS

To help students make connections with the radio play, discuss their experiences with national parks.

1. What do you know about America's national parks and the wildlife in them?
2. Have you ever visited a national park? If so, what was it like?
3. If you were hiking in Yellowstone, what sorts of questions would you ask a park ranger?

BEAU: Hey, Sheri, come here behind this tree. It looks like the bears are awake. They seem dazed.

SHERI: Well, wouldn't you be after months of not eating or drinking? During hibernation, a bear's body systems slow way down. I think that a female bear loses nearly 40% of her body weight while she hibernates. That must be quite a shock to the system. Hey, how do we know these are grizzlies and not black bears?

BEAU: Well, black bears don't have that hump on their backs. Their foreheads are flat, and their ears are pretty small.

SHERI: Is it true that black bears can run very fast? Up to 25 miles per hour?

BEAU: That's true, black bears are fast, but grizzlies have size. A female grizzly grows to about three feet tall at the shoulders, which is when she is on all fours. That young male over there probably already weighs 600 pounds. I bet that baby girl is close to 350. Male grizzlies can reach 715 pounds by adulthood. Pretty impressive, considering I weigh 175 pounds.

JOHN: I can confirm that grizzlies have very large claws. The park ranger told me their claws point out about two inches and are seriously sharp. We'll be back to see how the bears hunt after a word from our sponsor.

YELLOWSTONE NATIONAL PARK

Yellowstone National Park reaches into three states: Idaho, Montana, and Wyoming. One of the most popular tourist spots in the park is Old Faithful. Old Faithful is a geyser. A geyser is like a volcano, except that instead of erupting lava, it gushes water. It got its name because it erupts like clockwork every 45 to 100 minutes. Each eruption lasts from 1 1/2 to 5 minutes and shoots boiling water 106–184 feet (30–50 meters) into the air. Each time Old Faithful erupts, anywhere from 3,700 to 8,400 gallons (14,000 to 32,000 liters) of water burst out of the ground. For more about Yellowstone National Park, you can visit the National Park Service web site at www.nps.gov/yell/.

40

During Reading

Comprehension 

MAKING CONNECTIONS

Use these questions to model making connections with the text. Then have students tell about connections they made.

- Does this remind me of anything I've read or heard about?
- Will this information help me in any way? Explain.
- Have I ever had a similar experience?

(See Differentiated Instruction.)

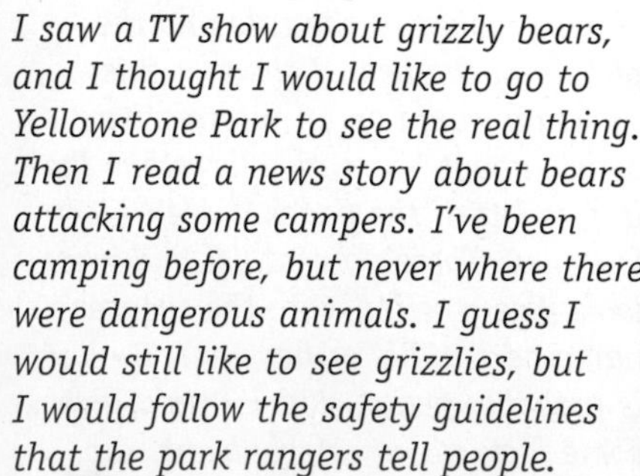

Teacher Think Aloud

I saw a TV show about grizzly bears, and I thought I would like to go to Yellowstone Park to see the real thing. Then I read a news story about bears attacking some campers. I've been camping before, but never where there were dangerous animals. I guess I would still like to see grizzlies, but I would follow the safety guidelines that the park rangers tell people.

Comprehension 

MONITOR UNDERSTANDING

Use these questions to model monitoring understanding by asking questions. Then have students ask questions of their own and try to resolve any confusion.

- What is going on here?
- Why did that character say that?
- What fix-up strategy can I try to fix my confusion?

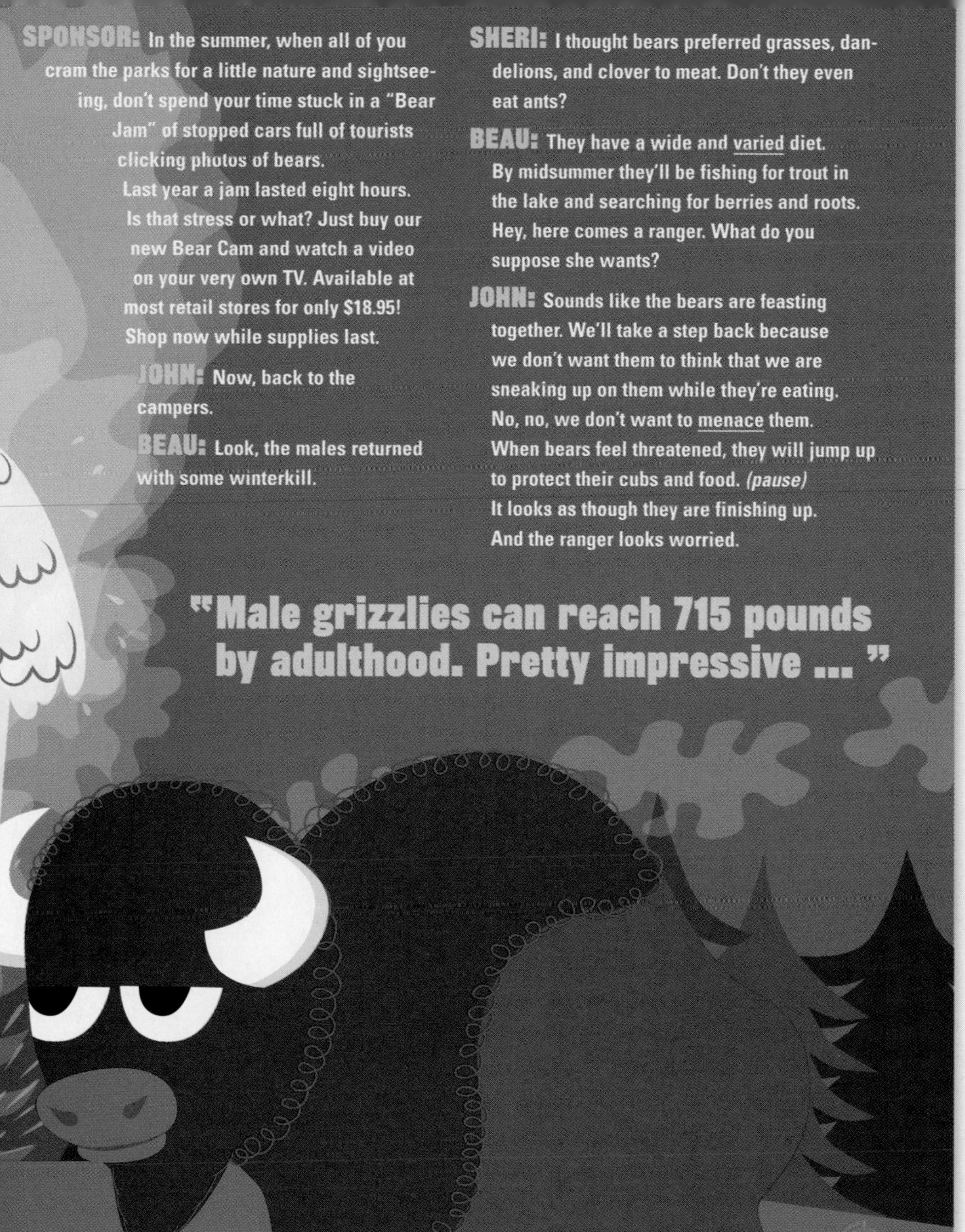

SPONSOR: In the summer, when all of you cram the parks for a little nature and sightseeing, don't spend your time stuck in a "Bear Jam" of stopped cars full of tourists clicking photos of bears. Last year a jam lasted eight hours. Is that stress or what? Just buy our new Bear Cam and watch a video on your very own TV. Available at most retail stores for only $18.95! Shop now while supplies last.

JOHN: Now, back to the campers.

BEAU: Look, the males returned with some winterkill.

SHERI: I thought bears preferred grasses, dandelions, and clover to meat. Don't they even eat ants?

BEAU: They have a wide and varied diet. By midsummer they'll be fishing for trout in the lake and searching for berries and roots. Hey, here comes a ranger. What do you suppose she wants?

JOHN: Sounds like the bears are feasting together. We'll take a step back because we don't want them to think that we are sneaking up on them while they're eating. No, no, we don't want to menace them. When bears feel threatened, they will jump up to protect their cubs and food. *(pause)* It looks as though they are finishing up. And the ranger looks worried.

"Male grizzlies can reach 715 pounds by adulthood. Pretty impressive ... "

41

Teacher Think Aloud

I got confused when I read the sponsor's speech on page 39. Since I had been reading facts about bears, I thought a Bear Bunk was a real thing—a way to sleep protected from bears. Then when I read on, I realized that it was just a joke. The sponsor's message was supposed to sound like a commercial on radio or TV. So when the next sponsor's message appeared, I was ready.

Fix-Up Strategies

Offer these strategies to help students read independently.

If you don't understand what you're reading:

- Reread the difficult section to look for clues to help you comprehend.
- Read ahead to find clues to help you comprehend.
- Retell, or say in your own words, what you've read.
- Visualize, or form mental pictures of, what you've read.

If you don't understand a word:

- Reread the sentence. Look for ideas and words that provide meaning clues.
- Find clues by reading a few sentences before and after the confusing word.
- Look for the base or root word and think about its meaning.
- Think about the topic or plot at this point to see if either offers meaning clues.

DIFFERENTIATED INSTRUCTION (SMALL GROUP)

Vocabulary Denotation and Connotation

Help students with *Student Journal* page 25 by explaining more about denotation and connotation.

- Note that *menace* can be a noun meaning "something that threatens," or a verb meaning "to threaten." Explain to students that this is the denotation, or definition, of the word.
- Explain that the connotation is a personal association someone might have for the word *menace*. The main character in the *Dennis the Menace* comic strip is an example. In this case, *menace* connotes "someone who pesters you."

Student Journal pages 23–24

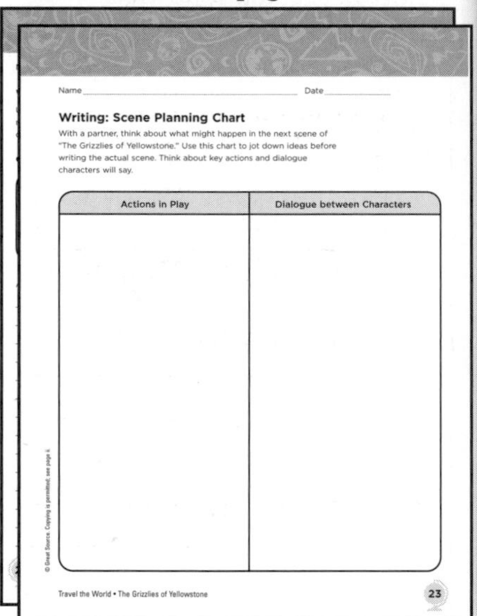

Name________________ Date__________

Writing: Scene Planning Chart

With a partner, think about what might happen in the next scene of "The Grizzlies of Yellowstone." Use this chart to jot down ideas before writing the actual scene. Think about key actions and dialogue characters will say.

Actions in Play	Dialogue between Characters

© Great Source. Copying is permitted; see page ii.

Travel the World • The Grizzlies of Yellowstone 23

RANGER: Okay, you two, gather around this campfire and let's review what you know about bear safety. What do you do when you are hiking and you come across a bear?

SHERI: Make a lot of noise?

RANGER: That's right. But what is wrong with the camping situation you two have going right here?

BEAU: Well, we are supposed to travel in a larger group. A large group crowded together confuses the bear. It can't tell how many humans there actually are. Three or four little people can look like one big person.

RANGER: That's right. You should practice what you preach. Should you ever run when you come across a bear?

SHERI: This I know from watching too much TV. No. Never run. Running provokes the bears and makes them want to run after you. Even if you think you can climb high up in a tree—most likely, you can't get high enough to get out of a bear's way!

BEAU: I'd hold my ground and then back away from the bear. I read that a very wily camper tricked a bear by dropping his hat as he backed away from it. The bear was so interested in the hat that he stopped to sniff it and play with it. Those extra seconds gave that clever camper time to get out of the way!

RANGER: I've heard that story, too, but I don't know if it's true. No one can prove its authenticity. What are you going to do with your garbage?

SHERI: We'll take it with us. We stored our food far away from the tent last night just to be safe. I remember seeing pictures back in the 1970s of those open garbage dumps where people dumped leftovers from the restaurants and hotels.

RANGER: Yes, they became bear playgrounds. Those dumps were covered up and closed a long time ago. Why are the bears so tired and sluggish right now?

42

After Reading (WHOLE CLASS)

Use one or more activities.

Check Purpose

Have students decide if their purpose was met. Did students learn what they should do if they meet a grizzly bear?

Discussion Questions

Continue the group discussion with the following questions.

1. Why do you think the sponsors chose to talk about "bear bunks" and "bear cams" during this radio play? (Make Inferences)
2. What is the effect of leaving trash around a campsite? (Cause-Effect)
3. Did you enjoy reading this radio play? Why or why not? (Making Connections)

Revisit: Anticipation Guide

Have students look back at their responses to the anticipation guide. Do they agree with their original choices? Would they like to revise any choices?

Revisit: Predictions Chart

Have students complete the third column in the predictions chart on *Student Journal* page 22. How were the words actually used?

"Running provokes the bears and makes them want to run after you. Even if you think you can climb high up in a tree—most likely, you can't get high enough ... "

BEAU: When bears hibernate, their heart rates drop from near seventy to twelve beats per minute. If that happened to me, I'd faint!

RANGER: You two know your stuff! I just wish that you would put all that knowledge into practice. You've been lucky so far today, but that doesn't mean you'll be lucky later. If you don't mind, I'll guide you back to the lodge.

SHERI: If you insist. But isn't the lodge still on part of the bear's home range? I mean, don't bears search for food in a huge area? More than 200 square miles?

RANGER: Yes, and they share land with other bears. However, the lodge's concrete walls provide much more protection than that canvas tent. Let's clean up this campsite, make sure the campfire is out, and get moving before these grizzlies do.

JOHN: There you have it: campers watching grizzly bears come out of hibernation in Yellowstone National Park. We hope you enjoyed our show today. Join us next week when we interview a family of sushi chefs about blowfish and ask, "Are they really that poisonous, or are you just blowing things out of proportion?" ◆

WILDLIFE IN YELLOWSTONE

Scientists brought gray wolves back into Yellowstone Park in 1995 after most of them had been hunted and trapped for their fur. Now, there are over 110 wolves roaming the park. Usually, wolves won't attack people. Even so, don't go near a wolf. Wolves are wild animals, and it is impossible to predict how any one wolf will act.

43

DIFFERENTIATED INSTRUCTION

Writing Play Scene

Use these strategies to help students prepare for their writing.

1. Have students suggest events that might happen in a new scene. Suggest that they identify at least three events. Jot them down on the board.
2. For each event, have students suggest what the main characters, Beau and Sheri, might say. Write the ideas for dialogue beside the corresponding event.

Student Journal page 25

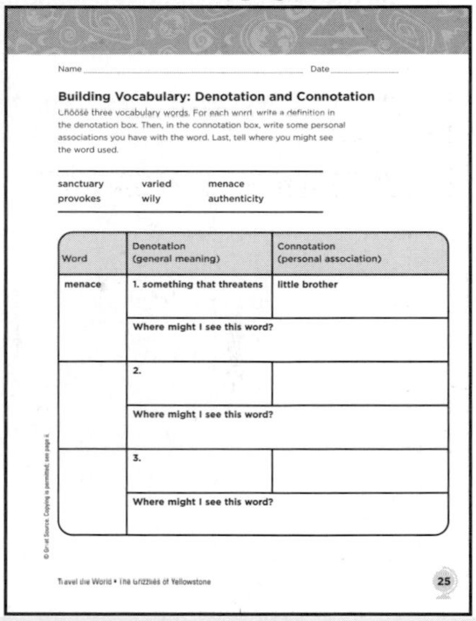

Name ______ Date ______

Building Vocabulary: Denotation and Connotation

Choose three vocabulary words. For each word, write a definition in the denotation box. Then, in the connotation box, write some personal associations you have with the word. Last, tell where you might see the word used.

sanctuary varied menace
provokes wily authenticity

Word	Denotation (general meaning)	Connotation (personal association)
menace	1. something that threatens	little brother
	Where might I see this word?	
	2.	
	Where might I see this word?	
	3.	
	Where might I see this word?	

Writing Play Scene

Have partners write a second scene for the radio play. Before they write, briefly discuss what might happen in the next scene. Remind students to continue the same text format, paying close attention to the dialogue between characters, and the narration that John provides. Have students use the chart on *Student Journal* page 23 as a planning guide before writing their scene on *Student Journal* page 24. (See Differentiated Instruction.)

Vocabulary Denotation and Connotation

Display *menace* and ask: *What is the definition of this word? What associations do you make when you see or hear the word* menace?

Tell students that words have denotations (general meanings) and connotations (personal associations). Have partners complete *Student Journal* page 25. (See Differentiated Instruction.)

Phonics/Word Study

Vowel Alternations Review

Display the following pairs of words, with the vowels underlined as shown: *cave, cavity; pose, position; locality, local.* Say the words in each pair and point out the underlined vowels. Ask students whether the vowel alternation in each is long-to-schwa, long-to-short, or short-to-schwa. (long-to-short, long-to-schwa, short-to-schwa) Now, work with students to complete the in-depth activity on TE page 60.

Vowel Alternations Review

There are three kinds of vowel alternations: long-to-schwa, long-to-short, and short-to-schwa. The more students are exposed to each of them, the more likely students will be able to remember how to spell the word changes correctly. Try the following steps.

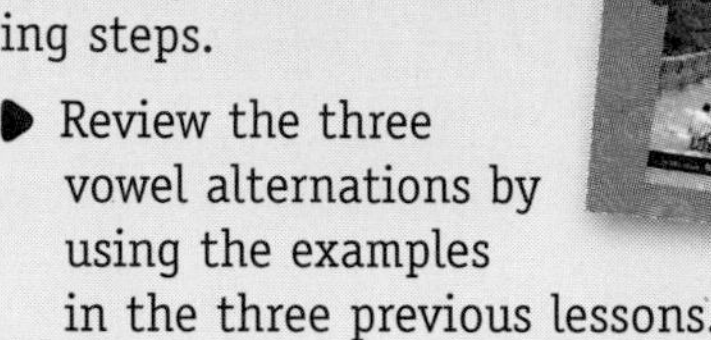

- Review the three vowel alternations by using the examples in the three previous lessons.

- Create a sort with the following heads and examples (see below).
- Have students sort in pairs, making sure that each word is said out loud.
- Once the sort is completed, double-check students' work.

Vowel Alternations Review Sort: Headings

Long-to-Schwa:	Long-to-Short:	Short-to-Schwa:
impose/imposition	divine/divinity	locality/local
suppose/supposition	nation/national	metallic/metal
compete/competition	cave/cavity	fatality/fatal
pose/position	volcano/volcanic	hospitality/hospital
	parasite/parasitic	prohibit/prohibition
	recite/recitation	hypocrisy/hypocrite
	apply/application	
	classify/classification	

For more information on word sorts and spelling stages, see pages 5–31 in the *Word Study Manual.*

Focus on . . .

Use one or more activities in this section to focus on a particular area of need in your students.

Comprehension STRATEGY SUPPORT

To help those students who need more practice using the strategies covered in this lesson, work one-on-one or in small groups to apply the strategy prompts below. Apply the prompts to a *Reading Advantage* paperback, a classroom library book, or a new or familiar selection in the magazine. Always model your own thinking first.

Making Connections

- What does this story (article, passage) remind me of?
- What do I already know about this topic?
- Where have I heard about this topic before?
- What do I have in common with the characters, people, or situations in the text?
- What other books, stories, articles, movies, or TV shows does this text make me think about?

Monitor Understanding

- Do I understand what I'm reading? If not, what part is confusing to me?
- What fix-up strategies can I use to solve the problem? (See During Reading for fix-up strategies.)
- Why did a character say (do, think, ask) that?
- What images do I visulize from the text? What parts can't I visualize?
- Why did the author include (or not include) those details?

Writing Safety Pamphlet

Have students write a bear safety pamphlet for Yellowstone National Park. The pamphlets should describe the necessary precautions park visitors should take to prevent close encounters with grizzlies. Before students begin to write, have them look back at "The Grizzlies of Yellowstone" to jot down safety tips they can find in the text. Encourage students to include visual aids in their pamphlets.

If your students need more practice or further instruction on taking notes, see lessons in *Writing Advantage*, pages 170–181.

Fluency: Expression

After students have read the selection at least once, have students form small groups to read the radio play aloud as a Readers Theater.

As you listen to groups read, use these prompts to guide them.

- Read with expression. Put yourself in the situation of the character. How would a sponsor sound? How would an expert on bear safety sound?
- Preview what you will read. Notice the different punctuation marks and what these signal to you. Pause at commas and periods. Let your voice rise at the end of sentences marked with a question mark.

When students read aloud, do they—

✓ reflect an understanding of the text?

✓ demonstrate appropriate timing, stress, and intonation?

✓ incorporate appropriate speed and phrasing?

English Language Learners

To support fluency skills, practice appropriate pacing, intonation, and expression.

1. Have students work in groups of five to read "The Grizzlies of Yellowstone" aloud.
2. Assign each group member one of the roles in the play. Allow groups to add sound effects to their performances.
3. While students read, spend time listening to each group read aloud. As much as possible, provide feedback and tips for improving their pacing, intonation and expression.

Independent Activity Options

While you work with individuals or small groups, others can work independently on one or more of the following options.

- Level D paperback books, see TE pages 367–372
- Level D *eZines*
- Repeat word sorts from this lesson
- *Student Journal* pages for this lesson
- *Writing Advantage* independent lessons

Assessment

Strategy Assessment

To help you and your students assess their use of comprehension strategies, ask the following questions. Students can complete a written response or provide verbal answers in a one-on-one reading conference.

1. **Making Connections** What in your own life or in the world today did you think of as you were reading the radio play? (Answers will vary. Students may mention wilderness experiences they've had and wildlife they've seen, information they've read or heard about the national parks, facts about bears, and so on.)
2. **Monitor Understanding** If you could ask the author a question about the play to help you better understand it, what would it be? (Answers will vary. Students may have questions about why the author included certain information, what message the author was trying to convey, and so on.)

For ongoing informal assessment, use the checklists on pages 61–64 of *Level D Assessment*.

Word Study Assessment

To help you and your students review and assess their understanding of vowel alternations, use the examples given in the three previous lessons. Then use these steps.

1. Write each pair of words on the board or on word cards. Word pairs are *recite, recitation; systemic, system; impose, imposition.*
2. Ask students to tell which vowel makes the alternation, and whether it is a long-to-schwa, long-to-short, or short-to-schwa alternation.

Word	Related word	Vowel	Sound change
recite	recitation	*i*	long-to-short
systemic	system	*e*	short-to-schwa
impose	imposition	*o*	long-to-schwa

LESSON **8**
When in Rome
Travel the World, pages 44–49

SUMMARY

This **narrative** tells about the daily life of a middle-class man who lived in ancient Rome.

COMPREHENSION STRATEGIES

Understanding Text Structure
Inferential Thinking

WRITING

Compare-Contrast

VOCABULARY

Concept Ladder

PHONICS/WORD STUDY

Greek Roots

Lesson Vocabulary

accommodate	orating
lavish	siesta
aqueduct	spectacle
gradient	

MATERIALS

Travel the World, pp. 44–49
Student Journal, pp. 26–28
Word Study Manual, p. 41
Writing Advantage, pp. 114–151

WHEN IN ROME

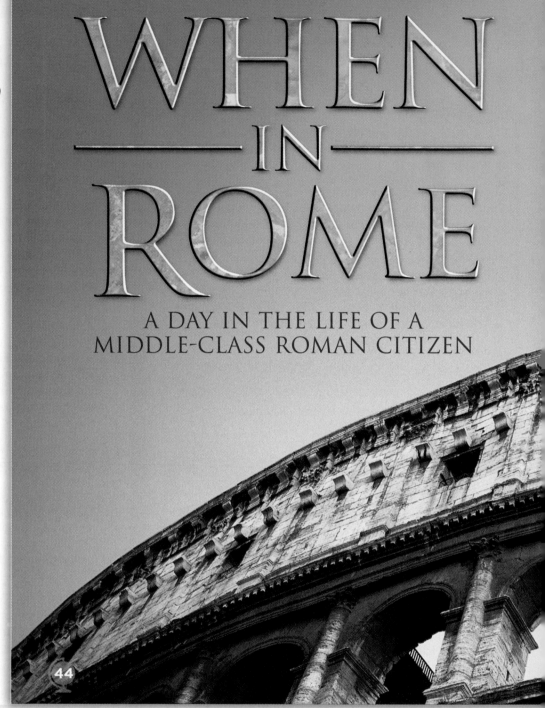

A DAY IN THE LIFE OF A MIDDLE-CLASS ROMAN CITIZEN

44

Before Reading 

Use one or more activities.

Make a K-W-L Chart

Create a K-W-L chart to help students both identify their knowledge of the city of Rome and formulate questions about what they would like to learn about Rome. Suggest that students read to find the answers to their questions. Revisit the chart after students have read the narrative. (See Differentiated Instruction.)

Rome		
What I Know	What I Want to Learn	What I Learned
Rome is in Italy.	What is special about Rome?	
People speak Italian in Rome.	Was pizza invented in Italy?	

Vocabulary Preview

Read the vocabulary words aloud or write them on the board for students to see. Encourage students to locate each word in the text and use the words and sentences around the word to help discover its meaning. Then have students choose a vocabulary word for the word map on *Student Journal* page 26. Students can write the definition before reading the selection. After they finish reading, they can answer the two questions. Model the process for students.

you visit Rome, Italy, today, you will see signs of its glorious past. Two thousand years ago, Rome was a great and powerful city. The city was ruled by an emperor, and there were slaves. In between were the members of the middle class. A middle-class Roman man might work as a shopkeeper. Shopkeepers often lived in apartments over their stores so that they had some flexibility in their schedules. Or a middle-class Roman might be a builder. Romans built many roads, aqueducts, temples, and buildings. The account on the next page tells about a middle-class Roman man who might have lived during the Imperial Age, which lasted from about the first-century to about A.D. 500.

DIFFERENTIATED INSTRUCTION

SMALL GROUP

MAKE A K-W-L CHART

To introduce students to ancient Rome, use the steps below:

1. Using a map or globe, point out Rome's exact location.
2. Explain that Rome is the capital of Italy and has been an important center of civilization for over two thousand years. Note that Rome was the imperial power of Europe, northern Africa, and western Asia for hundreds of years. In addition to beautiful churches, temples, palaces, gardens, and landmarks such as the Colosseum, Rome is home to many priceless art collections, which include the works of Michelangelo, Leonardo da Vinci, and Raphael.

Student Journal page 26

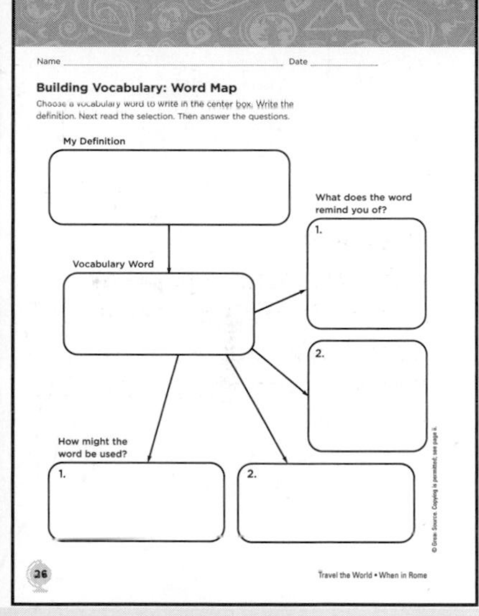

Name ______ Date ______

Building Vocabulary: Word Map

Choose a vocabulary word to write in the center box. Write the definition. Next read the selection. Then answer the questions.

My Definition

Vocabulary Word

What does the word remind you of?

1.

2.

How might the word be used?

1.

2.

26

Travel the World • When in Rome

© Great Source. Copying is permitted; see page ii.

Preview the Selection

Have students look through the six pages of the article. Use these prompts to guide students to notice the important features of the text.

- What kinds of visual aids does the selection provide?
- What do you think you will learn about as you read?

Point out to students that the selection is written in the first person.

Teacher Think Aloud

By the photographs, I could tell that this selection is about ancient times. The title tells me that it is about Rome. I was thinking that it would be all historical facts, until I read the first sentence on page 46: "My name is Horace . . ." That was a surprise! Horace is going to tell us what his life in ancient Rome is like. I think that will be more interesting than straight facts.

Make Predictions/ Set Purpose

Using the information they gathered in previewing the selection, students should make predictions about what they will learn. If students have trouble generating a purpose for reading, suggest that they read to learn about the daily life of a middle-class man in ancient Rome.

DIFFERENTIATED INSTRUCTION SMALL GROUP

Comprehension

UNDERSTANDING TEXT STRUCTURE

Follow these steps to help students understand the organization of information.

1. List on the board some different ways in which an author can organize ideas: cause-effect, problem-solution, chronological order, description, question-answer, comparison-contrast.
2. Discuss with students each kind of structure.
3. Ask students how the ideas in "When in Rome" are organized. (by different descriptions of Horace's life)

MY name is Horace, and I am what you would consider a middle-class Roman citizen. I own a shop and live with my wife, Penelope, and our two children, Anthony and Maria.

Living in Ancient Rome is like living in any other big city. I have to accommodate, or put up with, crowds, noise, smoke, and dust. Soldiers constantly march in the streets, parading in their leather armor. But when I lift my eyes up from the road, the magnificent temples and public buildings along the streets calm me. Just this morning as I took my daily walk up and down one of the seven hills, I saw the most lavish home: the main atrium opened up into a large courtyard with a fountain and statues.

My family and I live in an apartment, as do many middle-class citizens. We have running water from the aqueduct, a pipelike system that brings water from the natural springs in the countryside to town. My father was an aqueduct builder. He used to say that the most challenging thing about the building of an aqueduct was getting it in the right position. Since Romans do not use pumps to move their water, the aqueducts must be on a constant gradient, or slope. The only complaint I have about our apartment is that we don't have a toilet. We use the public one down the street.

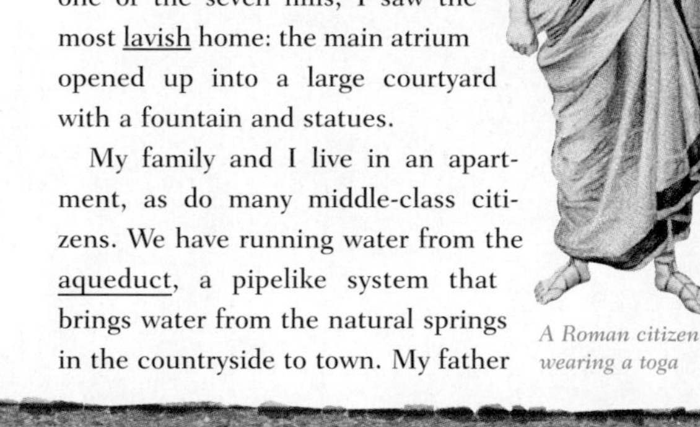

A Roman citizen wearing a toga

Our apartment is on the second floor of a building, directly over the shop that my family owns. We sell fresh fruits and vegetables and are open for a few hours in the morning and for a few hours in the afternoon. When I am out or not able to run the shop, Penelope (pen EL uh pee) manages things.

Penelope and I were married when I was fifteen and she was thirteen. We would have been punished if we had married later than age sixteen. In Rome, citizens can't marry a relative who is four or fewer times removed. I bought my wife a ring that she wears on the third finger of her left hand. The veins in that finger run directly to her heart.

46

During Reading

Comprehension

UNDERSTANDING TEXT STRUCTURE

Use these questions to model determining the text structure of the selection. Then have students tell how the text structure helps them understand the information.

- What is the text structure?
- How does the text structure help me understand the information?

(See Differentiated Instruction.)

Teacher Think Aloud

This text is written as if a Roman man from the Middle Ages were speaking to me. I find this a very good way to learn about history. It's like reading a story, but it contains lots of facts. Also, rather than talking about major historical events, it tells how everyday people live. I think that maybe the author chose this structure to make the information easy to understand and remember.

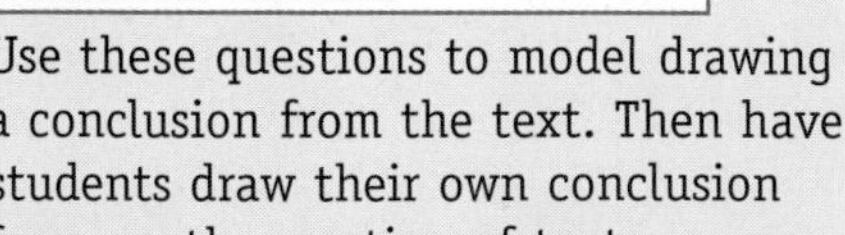

Comprehension

INFERENTIAL THINKING

Use these questions to model drawing a conclusion from the text. Then have students draw their own conclusion from another section of text.

- What information does Horace give me?
- What do I know, or infer, from that information that Horace doesn't state directly?

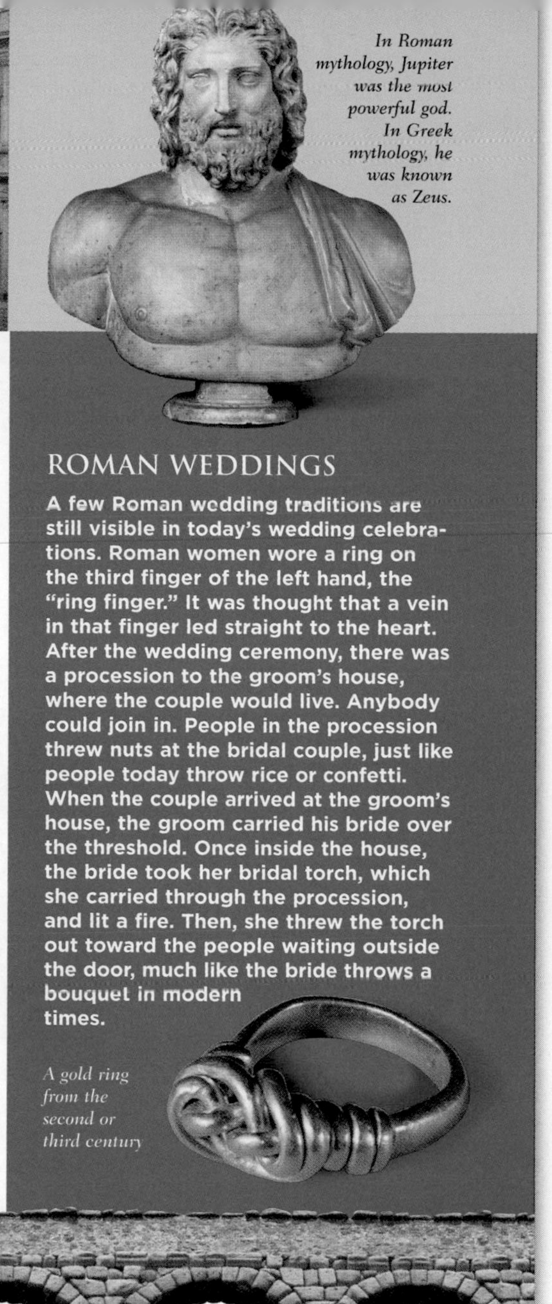

In Roman mythology, Jupiter was the most powerful god. In Greek mythology, he was known as Zeus.

Left: *The Roman Forum was the center of religion, politics, and business.*
Center: *The Via Appia in Rome was completed in 312 B.C.*
Right: *Artist's version of what the Roman Forum looked like*

ON the night before the wedding, my wife cried. She gave her birth locket to her father and gave away all of her toys. A birth locket is a special locket all children of Rome are given when born. It contains an amulet, or charm, that protects the wearer from evil. The morning of our wedding, Penelope's mother dressed her in a long gown and tied a belt called the knot of Hercules around her waist. Hercules is the protector of married life. The knot symbolized the fact that my wife would be safe.

The wedding ceremony was simple. Penelope and I held hands as we stood before the priest. Then, we sat on stools facing an altar and made an offering to the leader of the gods, Jupiter. After dinner all the guests joined the bridal march to my house. Many strangers joined in, too. There were torchbearers and flutists and people throwing nuts at us. At the doorway, I carried my wife over the threshold.

ROMAN WEDDINGS

A few Roman wedding traditions are still visible in today's wedding celebrations. Roman women wore a ring on the third finger of the left hand, the "ring finger." It was thought that a vein in that finger led straight to the heart. After the wedding ceremony, there was a procession to the groom's house, where the couple would live. Anybody could join in. People in the procession threw nuts at the bridal couple, just like people today throw rice or confetti. When the couple arrived at the groom's house, the groom carried his bride over the threshold. Once inside the house, the bride took her bridal torch, which she carried through the procession, and lit a fire. Then, she threw the torch out toward the people waiting outside the door, much like the bride throws a bouquet in modern times.

A gold ring from the second or third century

A Roman aqueduct

47

Teacher Think Aloud

On page 46, Horace tells me that he and his wife were married when he was fifteen and she was thirteen. Then I read this on page 47: "On the night before the wedding, my wife cried. She gave her birth locket to her father and gave away all of her toys." Although Horace doesn't say so, I think his wife was unhappy to get married so young, even though it was the custom.

Fix-Up Strategies

Offer these strategies to help students read independently.

If you don't understand what you're reading:

- Reread the difficult section to look for clues to help you comprehend.
- Read ahead to find clues to help you comprehend.
- Retell, or say in your own words, what you've read.
- Visualize, or form mental pictures of, what you've read.

If you don't understand a word:

- Reread the sentence. Look for ideas and words that provide meaning clues.
- Find clues by reading a few sentences before and after the confusing word.
- Look for the base or root word and think about its meaning.
- Think about the topic or plot at this point to see if either offers meaning clues.

ROMAN FACTS

- Rome was founded in 753 B.C., according to legend.
- Rome is located along the Tiber River, about 15 miles inland from the Mediterranean Sea.
- Latin, the language of ancient Rome, is the basis of French, Italian, and Spanish.
- Rome is the capital of Italy.

Above: *This third-century Roman grave marker shows a market scene with two little monkeys to attract customers.*

I'm getting off the subject. Daily life in Rome is never boring. Some people, though, might think that my days are routine. I start with a small breakfast of bread, wine, olives, and cheese. The rich eat fish, fruit and meats for breakfast. They never cook their own food or clean up.

Before I go out in the morning I make sure that my hair is neat and short and that I am clean-shaven. I put on my toga, although it is uncomfortable. The cold seeps right up onto my legs. I am thinking of buying a tunic this afternoon. A tunic, which looks more like a long shirt, is worn with stockings.

After getting dressed, I walk down to the forum, where I do my shopping, trading, and banking. Court seems to always be in session in the forum, and sometimes I stay to listen to the senators speak and argue. Even early in the morning, someone is usually out in the forum orating—we Romans are great arguers.

A second-century grave marker shows a father holding his daughter's hand.

Next, it's off to the baths. I try to bathe at least once a day. In Rome, there are separate baths for men and women. There is nothing like slipping into a hot pool and then lying in the steam room or sauna. When I'm feeling up to it, I go to the exercise room, which is also located in the baths. The only problem with the baths is that they are packed with Roman citizens. I think that there are nearly 900 public baths in Rome. The one I go to holds about 300 people, but there is a bath by the arena that holds nearly 1,500!

For lunch I usually treat myself and my family to cold

Student Journal page 27

Name________________ Date________

Writing: Compare and Contrast

Compare and contrast your life with the life of a citizen in ancient Rome. Make sure you answer these two questions: How is my life similar to the life of a citizen in ancient Rome? How is my life different from the life of a citizen in ancient Rome?

Travel the World • When in Rome 27

After Reading

WHOLE CLASS Use one or more activities.

Check Purpose

Have students decide if their purpose was met. What did they learn about the daily life of a middle-class man in ancient Rome?

Discussion Questions

Continue the group discussion with the following questions.

1. What do you think Horace was most proud of in his life and about Rome? (Inferential Thinking)
2. How do you think Horace's lifestyle was different from that of a wealthy Roman? (Compare-Contrast)
3. What did you find most interesting about life in ancient Rome? (Making Connections)

Revisit: K-W-L Chart

Revisit the K-W-L chart about Rome. Have students fill in the third column of the chart.

ROMAN FUNERALS

When a Roman citizen died, his body was washed and a coin was placed in his mouth. The coin paid Charon, the ferryman who carried the dead across the river Styx to the underworld. Many Romans belonged to *collegia*, or funeral societies. They paid monthly dues to guarantee that they would have a proper funeral.

Above: Carving on a third-century stone coffin shows Charon rowing souls across the Styx.

meat with olives, cheese, salad, and fruit. My children come home from school for lunch, and we eat together. Then it is time for my siesta, my midday nap. All the citizens of Rome take a siesta. Children have a two or three hour break from their studies but return to school after siesta to finish their classes.

AT dinner the whole family sits around the table for the main meal of the day. After dinner, we choose our evening entertainment. My favorite spectacle to watch is the open-air theater. My son prefers the gladiator battles at the Coliseum and being among the masses—sometimes nearly 45,000 people. My wife prefers the Circus Maximus and the chariot races, while my daughter loves to go to the Campus to watch the track and field games. The fabulous thing is all these events are free to Roman citizens.

After all these years, I can truly say that I am proud to be a Roman citizen. We Romans see things for what they are. Take a walk through any square in the city and you will see what I mean. Some sculptors shape men's bodies to look perfect, without a flaw, but a Roman artist won't even spare an emperor. If the emperor has a huge nose, his statue has a huge nose. Furthermore, we Romans build roads that connect to one another. All roads built by the Romans lead here, to the great city of Rome, the heart of our empire. ◆

Emperor Trajan ruled Rome from A.D. 98–117.

49

DIFFERENTIATED INSTRUCTION

Writing

Compare-Contrast

To help students complete this activity, use these steps:

1. Ask students: *What aspects of his daily life does Horace describe?* Display students' responses. (Topics should include where he lives, how he bathes, how he gets running water, what he eats at meals, customs of marriage, and forms of entertainment.)
2. Students should use the topics on the board to help them compare and contrast their lives with that of Horace.

Student Journal page 28

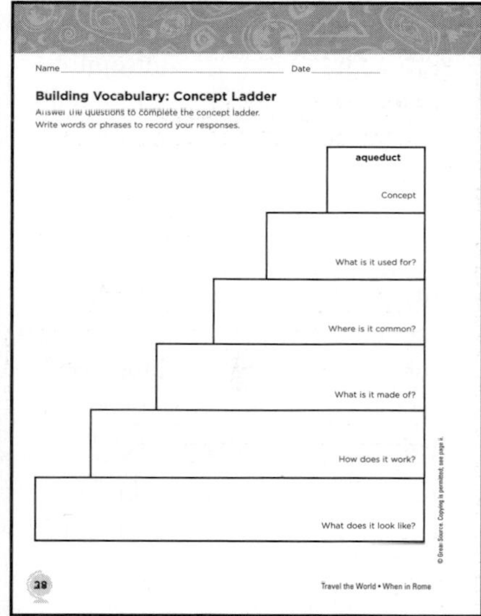

Name ______ Date ______

Building Vocabulary: Concept Ladder

Answer the questions to complete the concept ladder.
Write words or phrases to record your responses.

aqueduct
Concept
What is it used for?
Where is it common?
What is it made of?
How does it work?
What does it look like?

28 Travel the World • When in Rome

Writing Compare-Contrast

Have students compare and contrast their lives with the life of an average citizen in ancient Rome. Help students organize their thoughts by making a class chart. Show two columns: one for "compare" and one for "contrast." Ask volunteers to suggest ideas for the chart. Then have students use the class chart to write a brief compare-contrast essay on *Student Journal* page 27. (See Differentiated Instruction.)

Vocabulary Concept Ladder

Display the word *spectacle* and ask the following questions to help students build a concept ladder for the word.

- What is a *spectacle*? (something unusual to watch)
- Where might someone see a *spectacle*?
- What are different kinds of *spectacles*?

After building a concept ladder for *spectacle*, have partners complete the concept ladder on *Student Journal* page 28 for the word *aqueduct*.

Phonics/Word Study

Greek Roots

Tell students that many English words have Greek or Latin "roots." Write the root *auto* on the board, telling students that it means "self." Ask them to think of words that begin with *auto* and explain how each word relates to "self." (For example, an *autobiography* is a book about oneself.) Now, work with students to complete the in-depth roots activity on TE page 68.

Phonics/Word Study

Greek Roots

1. Introduce the root that you are teaching, offering a few words that contain the same root. Discuss the words to see if students can define them. Discussion of each word should trigger some ideas as to what the root means.
2. Ask students what the words have in common. Through the processes of deduction and association, students should discover the meaning of the root.
3. Ask students to identify other words with the same root. Word sorts can be found in the Word Study Manual. (See Word Study Manual page 41.)
4. Have students create a roots section in their Word Study notebooks. They should begin collecting words with each root they study.

aster/astr **(star)**

astronomy, astrology, asterisk
astronomical, astral

auto **(self)**

autobiography, autopilot, autoclave
autocracy, automobile, automatic
automaton, autonomy, autopsy

bio **(life)**

biology, biome, biotic
antibiotic, biopsy, biography
bioengineering, biochemical, biosphere
biological warfare, biodegradable

gram **(thing written)**

diagram, telegram, cardiogram
monogram, program, anagram
cryptogram, epigram, hologram
parallelogram

Discovering the Roots

aster/astr	*auto*	*bio*	*gram*
asteroid	automobile	biology	anagram
astral	autonomy	biosphere	monogram
astronomy	autocracy	biography	cryptogram
astronaut	autobiography	biodegradable	epigram
astrology	autopsy	biochemical	cardiogram

For more information on word sorts and spelling stages, see pages 5–31 in the *Word Study Manual.*

Focus on . . .

Use one or more activities in this section to focus on a particular area of need in your students.

Comprehension STRATEGY SUPPORT

To help those students who need more practice using the strategies covered in this lesson, work one-on-one or in small groups to apply the strategy prompts below. Apply the prompts to a *Reading Advantage* paperback, a classroom library book, or a new or familiar selection in the magazine. Always model your own thinking first.

Understanding Text Structure

- What kind of text is this? (book, story, article, guidebook, play, manual)
- How does the author organize the text? (cause-effect, problem-solution, chronological order, description, question-answer, comparison-contrast)
- What details support my thoughts about the text structure?
- What is the cause (effect, problem, solution, order, question, answer)?
- If fiction, who are the characters? What is the setting, plot, conflict, and resolution?

Inferential Thinking

- What are the causes or effects of this event?
- What do I learn from the character or person's thoughts, words, or actions?
- What do I know (or infer) from the text that the author hasn't stated directly?
- What conclusions can I draw?

Writing Description

Have students write a brief descriptive essay of a typical day in their own life. Make sure students understand the text structure (description) that was used in "When in Rome." Have students use this structure as a guide for writing their essays. Encourage students to use a chart like the one below to organize their thoughts.

Part of Day	What I Do
Morning	
Afternoon	
Evening	

For more instruction on writing descriptive paragraphs, see lessons in *Writing Advantage*, pages 114–151.

Fluency: Pacing

After students have read the selection at least once, they can use a portion of it to practice fluent reading. Have students choose a favorite section. Then have them read it silently a few times to become comfortable with the text. Then have partners read their favorite section aloud to each other.

As you listen to students read, use these prompts to guide them.

- Read at an even pace, not too fast and not too slowly. An even pace will keep your partner's attention.
- Try to make your reading sound natural, as if you are telling about your own life.

When students read aloud, do they—

- ✓ demonstrate a smooth pace, not too fast or too slow?
- ✓ incorporate well-timed pauses between words and phrases?
- ✓ reflect an awareness and understanding of punctuation?

English Language Learners

To support students as they develop the skill of comparing and contrasting, use a Venn diagram and examine the lifestyles of Horace and a wealthy Roman citizen as described in "When in Rome."

1. Model how to draw, label, and complete a Venn diagram.
2. Have partners make a list describing the lifestyles of Horace and a wealthy Roman citizen.
3. Have students complete the appropriate sections of their Venn diagram. Then share with the groups and compare.

Independent Activity Options

While you work with individuals or small groups, others can work independently on one or more of the following options.

- Level D paperback books, see TE pages 367–372
- Level D *eZines*
- Repeat word sorts from this lesson
- *Student Journal* pages for this lesson
- *Writing Advantage* independent lessons

Assessment

Strategy Assessment

To help you and your students assess their use of comprehension strategies, ask the following questions. Students can complete a written response or provide verbal answers in a one-on-one reading conference.

1. **Understanding Text Structure** Besides the narrative about Horace, the text has several sidebars that tell different facts about Rome. How did these sidebars help your understanding? (Answers will vary. Students may say, for example, that the features answered questions they were wondering about as they read.)
2. **Inferential Thinking** Did you conclude from the text that Horace was proud to live in Rome? Explain. (Answers will vary, but students should cite passages in the text that indicate Horace's pride.)

For ongoing informal assessment, use the checklists on pages 61–64 of *Level D Assessment*.

Word Study Assessment

Use these steps to help you and your students assess their understanding of Greek and Latin influences on spelling.

1. Write the following words on the board or on word cards: *autograph, asteroid, diagram, biography*. Each word contains one of the roots students have just studied.
2. Ask students to find the root in each word and give its meaning. Then ask them to define the word. They can use a dictionary, as necessary, but they should explain the root's connection to the word's meaning.

Word	Base Word	Root Meaning
autograph	*auto*	self
asteroid	*aster/astr*	star
diagram	*gram*	thing written
biography	*bio*	life

LESSON **9**

On Safari

Travel the World, pages 50–55

SUMMARY

This **journal** by an American high school student describes a four-day safari in South Africa.

COMPREHENSION STRATEGIES

Monitor Understanding
Understanding Text Structure

WRITING

Timeline

VOCABULARY

Multiple Meanings

PHONICS/WORD STUDY

Greek Roots

Lesson Vocabulary

diversity	slathering
moronic	apartheid
pride	secretes

MATERIALS

Travel the World, pp. 50–55
Student Journal, pp. 29–31
Word Study Manual, p. 42
Writing Advantage, pp. 30–56

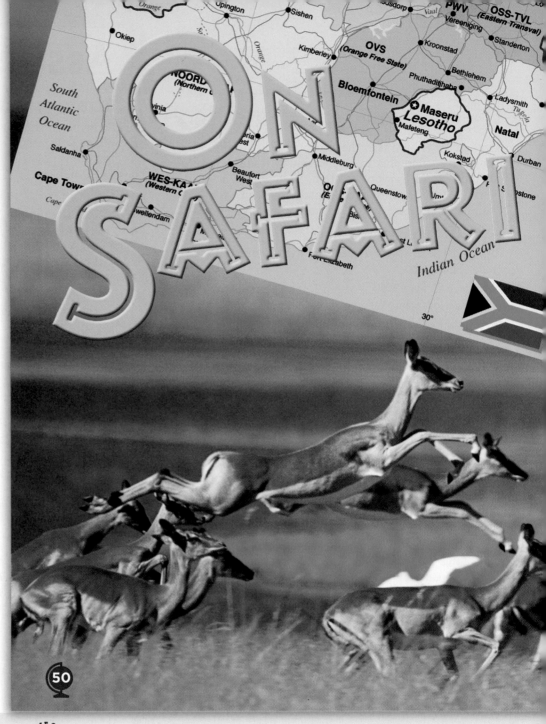

Before Reading

Use one or more activities.

Make a List

Draw students' attention to the title of the journal, "On Safari." Begin a brief discussion of what students know about safaris. As students respond, write the information in a list. Tell students that they will revisit the list to add any new information they learned after reading the selection. (See Differentiated Instruction.)

What is a *safari*?

1. a group trip
2. a trip where people hunt or photograph animals
3. takes place in Africa, India, Tibet
4.

Vocabulary Preview

Have students choose one of the vocabulary words to begin the word web on *Student Journal* page 29. Have students look for context clues to help them define the word. Then, in the box underneath the web, students should write a definition for the word. After students finish reading the selection, they can add details around the web to help define the word. Model the process with the word *diversity*.

DAY 1

Dear Journal,

This morning my cousin, Tamika, and I landed in Cape Town, the oldest city in South Africa. Reading the tour book on the plane, I learned that South Africa is called the "rainbow nation" because of its cultural diversity. There is a wide variety of people here: Blacks, Whites, Afrikaners, and Colored people. And the languages! In South Africa, they speak English, Zulu, Swazi, Afrikaans, and other languages. I hope that most people on our tour group speak English.

Tamika and I have been planning this safari since we started high school. This is our senior summer adventure. So we don't feel like moronic tourists who just fumble about like fools, we've been practicing some words used in South Africa. Here is what I remember: Hello is *Howzit*, your friend is your *mate* (just like in Australia). An apartment is a *flat*—which I know is what they call apartments in England because my brother studied in London last year. Every time he phoned he went on and on about his cool flat. I've also learned a little Zulu: Yes is *Yebo* and no is *Ca*. Pretty basic, I know, but it's a start.

DIFFERENTIATED INSTRUCTION

SMALL GROUP

MAKE A LIST

Provide background information for students by explaining that a safari is a group trip taken to photograph or observe wild animals. People usually go on safari in Africa, where they can find animals such as lions, leopards, and elephants. A number of vehicles often travel together. Most safaris are about two weeks long.

Student Journal page 29

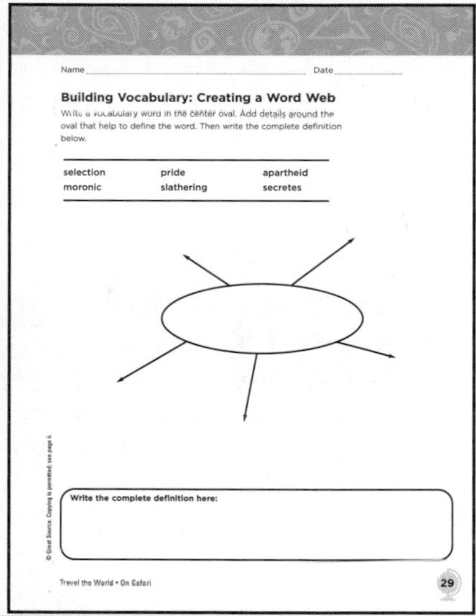

Name ______ Date ______

Building Vocabulary: Creating a Word Web

Write a vocabulary word in the center oval. Add details around the oval that help to define the word. Then write the complete definition below.

selection	pride	apartheid
moronic	slathering	secretes

Write the complete definition here:

Travel the World • On Safari

29

Preview the Selection

Have students read the title and look at the photographs on pages 50–55. Use these or similar prompts to guide students to notice the important features of the text.

- What does the title tell you about the selection?
- How is the information organized?
- What do you know about the items in the photographs?

Teacher Think Aloud

The title of this selection is "On Safari." I think safaris used to be trips that people took to hunt wild animals, but today people go on safaris to look at the animals and take pictures. The text looks like journal entries, so I think that this is about a real safari the author took. I want to find out what going on a safari is really like.

Make Predictions/ Set Purpose

Using the information they gathered in previewing the selection, students should make predictions about what they will learn. If students have trouble generating a purpose for reading, suggest that they read to learn what happens on a safari.

DIFFERENTIATED INSTRUCTION

Comprehension

MONITOR UNDERSTANDING

To help students practice visualizing, follow these steps:

1. Have students close their eyes as you read aloud the description of the white rhino on page 54. Tell students to picture in their minds what the rhino looks like.
2. Afterward, have students look at the photograph of the rhino on page 54. Discuss how their mental images were the same as or different from the photograph. Which details in the text helped them the most?

Cape Town: View of Table Mountain

It's our summer break, but it's winter in South Africa. We packed for cool days, but, hopefully, it shouldn't get much colder than freezing. The time here is seven hours ahead of home. When we call our parents in Philadelphia at 7 P.M., they will be having lunch! Before we left the United States, Tamika changed some of our American money to South African money, which is called *rand*. One rand equals one hundred cents, just like our dollar equals one hundred pennies.

Here's what we saw in Cape Town today:

First we went to this amazing mountain called Table Mountain. We climbed it because we'd been sitting on the plane for hours and hours, and I didn't want to ride in the cable car. Now, I'm a little sorry because my calf muscles are so sore from hiking up 1,086 meters (3,562 feet)! When we got to the top, Tamika said she felt like she was on the top of the world. After some ice cream, we wandered on one of the many walking paths. We saw a dassie, which is this animal that looks like a giant guinea pig. It was harmless and just lazed about, sunbathing on the rocks.

After riding the cable car down the mountain, we strolled along the waterfront and window-shopped. Soon, jet lag caught up with us. So we got a small bite to eat—Tamika had smoked crocodile, which I think is totally gross. I had chicken and shrimp curry.

And, now I am getting ready to conk out for the night. I can't wait until tomorrow!

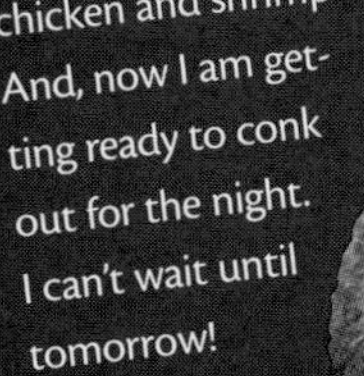

A dassie suns itself on a rock.

52

During Reading

Comprehension

MONITOR UNDERSTANDING

Use these questions to model visualizing the text. Then have students tell about a part they visualized and how their mental images helped them better understand the text.

- Can I picture what the author is talking about?
- What details help me create a strong mental image?

(See Differentiated Instruction.)

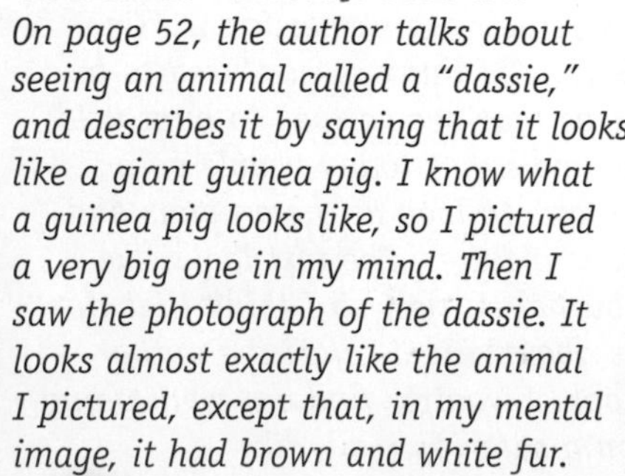

Teacher Think Aloud

On page 52, the author talks about seeing an animal called a "dassie," and describes it by saying that it looks like a giant guinea pig. I know what a guinea pig looks like, so I pictured a very big one in my mind. Then I saw the photograph of the dassie. It looks almost exactly like the animal I pictured, except that, in my mental image, it had brown and white fur.

Comprehension

UNDERSTANDING TEXT STRUCTURE

Use these questions to model determining the organization of the text. Then have students tell what they notice about the text structure.

- What is the text structure?
- How are the ideas organized within the structure?
- How does this text structure help me understand the material?

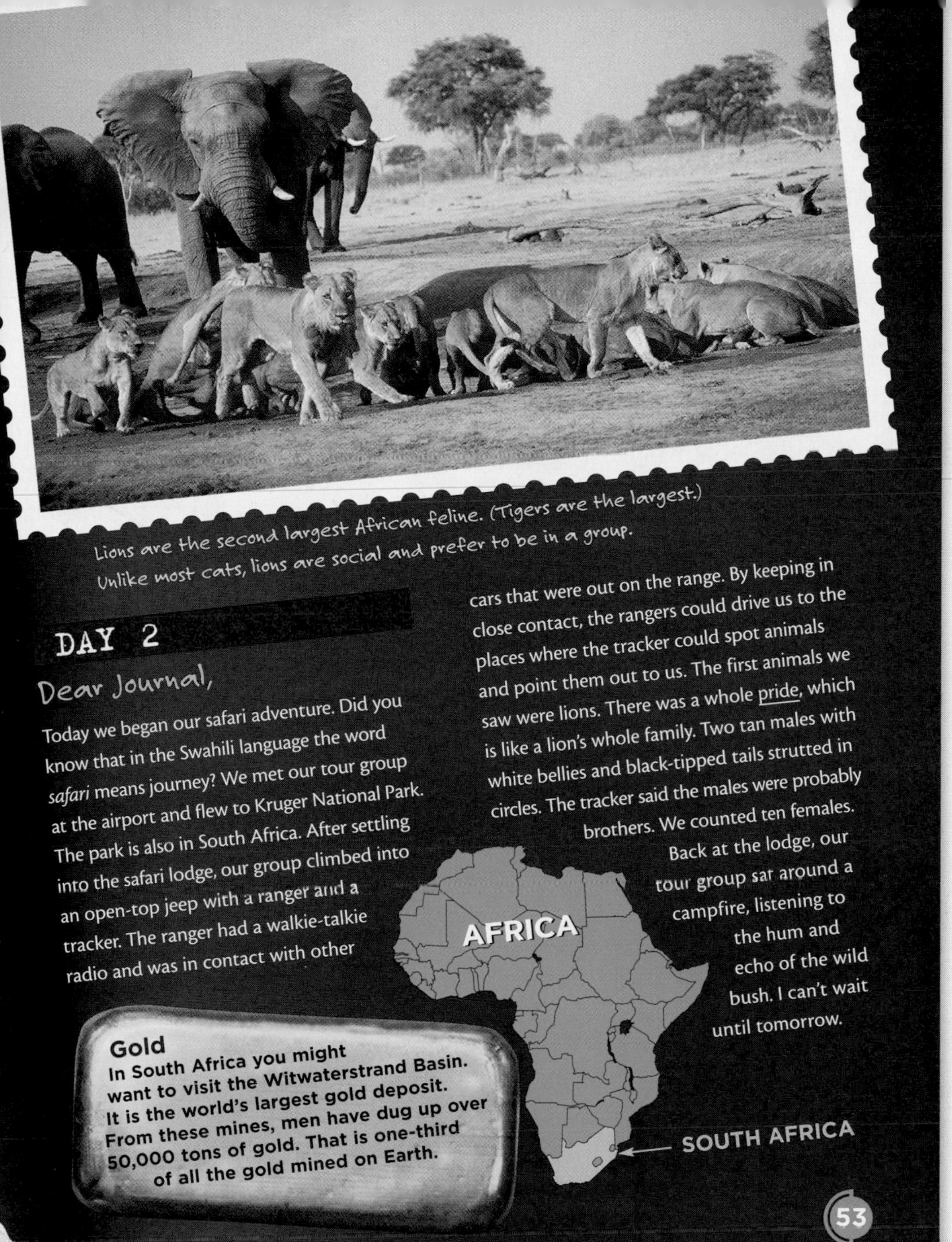

Lions are the second largest African feline. (Tigers are the largest.) Unlike most cats, lions are social and prefer to be in a group.

DAY 2

Dear Journal,

Today we began our safari adventure. Did you know that in the Swahili language the word *safari* means journey? We met our tour group at the airport and flew to Kruger National Park. The park is also in South Africa. After settling into the safari lodge, our group climbed into an open-top jeep with a ranger and a tracker. The ranger had a walkie-talkie radio and was in contact with other cars that were out on the range. By keeping in close contact, the rangers could drive us to the places where the tracker could spot animals and point them out to us. The first animals we saw were lions. There was a whole pride, which is like a lion's whole family. Two tan males with white bellies and black-tipped tails strutted in circles. The tracker said the males were probably brothers. We counted ten females. Back at the lodge, our tour group sat around a campfire, listening to the hum and echo of the wild bush. I can't wait until tomorrow.

Gold
In South Africa you might want to visit the Witwaterstrand Basin. It is the world's largest gold deposit. From these mines, men have dug up over 50,000 tons of gold. That is one-third of all the gold mined on Earth.

53

Teacher Think Aloud

As I look through this selection, I see that the heads are structured like a journal with daily entries. The entries are labeled Day 1, Day 2, and so on. Each entry begins with the words Dear Journal. *Within this structure, I believe the ideas are ordered chronologically. Each event is told in the order in which it occurred.*

Fix-Up Strategies

Offer these strategies to help students read independently.

If you don't understand what you're reading:

- Reread the difficult section to look for clues to help you comprehend.
- Read ahead to find clues to help you comprehend.
- Retell, or say in your own words, what you've read.
- Visualize, or form mental pictures of, what you've read.

If you don't understand a word:

- Reread the sentence. Look for ideas and words that provide meaning clues.
- Find clues by reading a few sentences before and after the confusing word.
- Look for the base or root word and think about its meaning.
- Think about the topic or plot at this point to see if either offers meaning clues.

Student Journal page 30

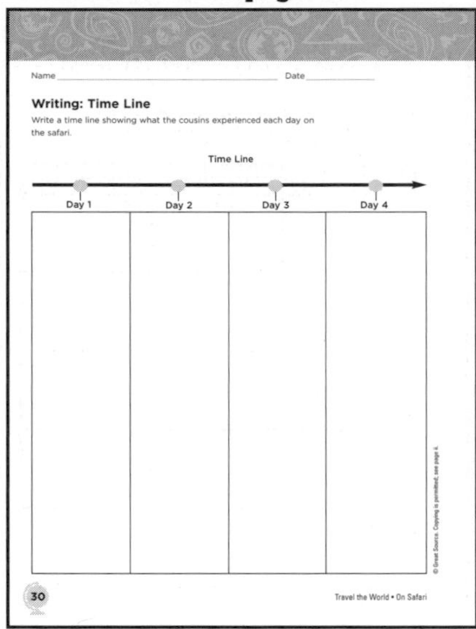
Name ______ Date ______

Writing: Time Line

Write a time line showing what the cousins experienced each day on the safari.

Time Line

Day 1	Day 2	Day 3	Day 4

30 Travel the World • On Safari

DAY 3

Dear Journal,

We were out on the range again at about ten this morning. After driving for what seemed like hours and slathering on the insect repellent, our group came across a rhinoceros at a watering hole. Was it ever ugly! The tracker said that all the rhinos are endangered because people have hunted them too much. This was a white rhino. He had three toes on each foot and his skin was thick and gray, not white at all. He probably weighed over two tons. All that weight from eating just grasses and leaves. Amazing!

Back at the lodge, Tamika and I called our parents to let them know we were having a great time.

South African Flag

When apartheid, a political system that was unfair to minorities, ended in South Africa in the early 1990s, the country raised a new flag. The flag has six colors. Each color represents a different culture in South Africa. The Y-shaped sign is a symbol. It stands for joining history with the present day to make a united future.

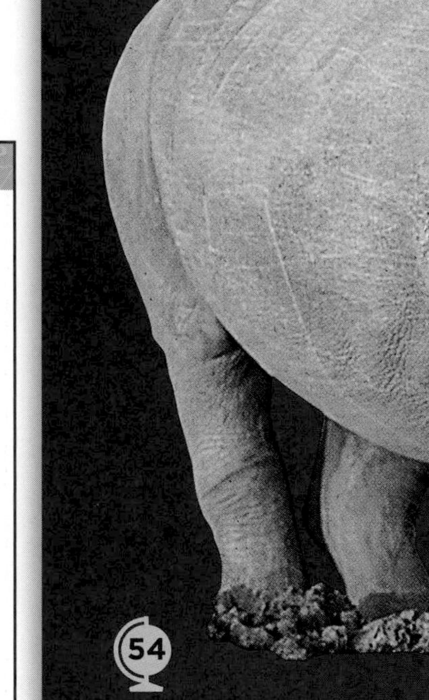

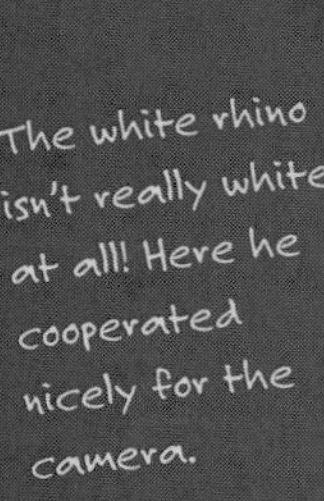
The white rhino isn't really white at all! Here he cooperated nicely for the camera.

54

After Reading

Use one or more activities.

Check Purpose

Have students decide if their purpose was met. Did they learn more about what happens on a safari?

Discussion Questions

Continue the group discussion with the following questions.

1. Why do you think the author of this selection chose to write in journal form? (Inferential Thinking)
2. How is this journal similar to and different from a short story? (Compare-Contrast)
3. Did the selection change your thinking about a safari? Why or why not? (Making Connections)

Revisit: List

Revisit the list that students made at the beginning of the lesson. Ask: *What did you learn? What information surprised you?* Then, as a group, add more items to the list.

Revisit: Word Web

Revisit the word web on *Student Journal* page 29. Students should add new details and adjust their definition as needed.

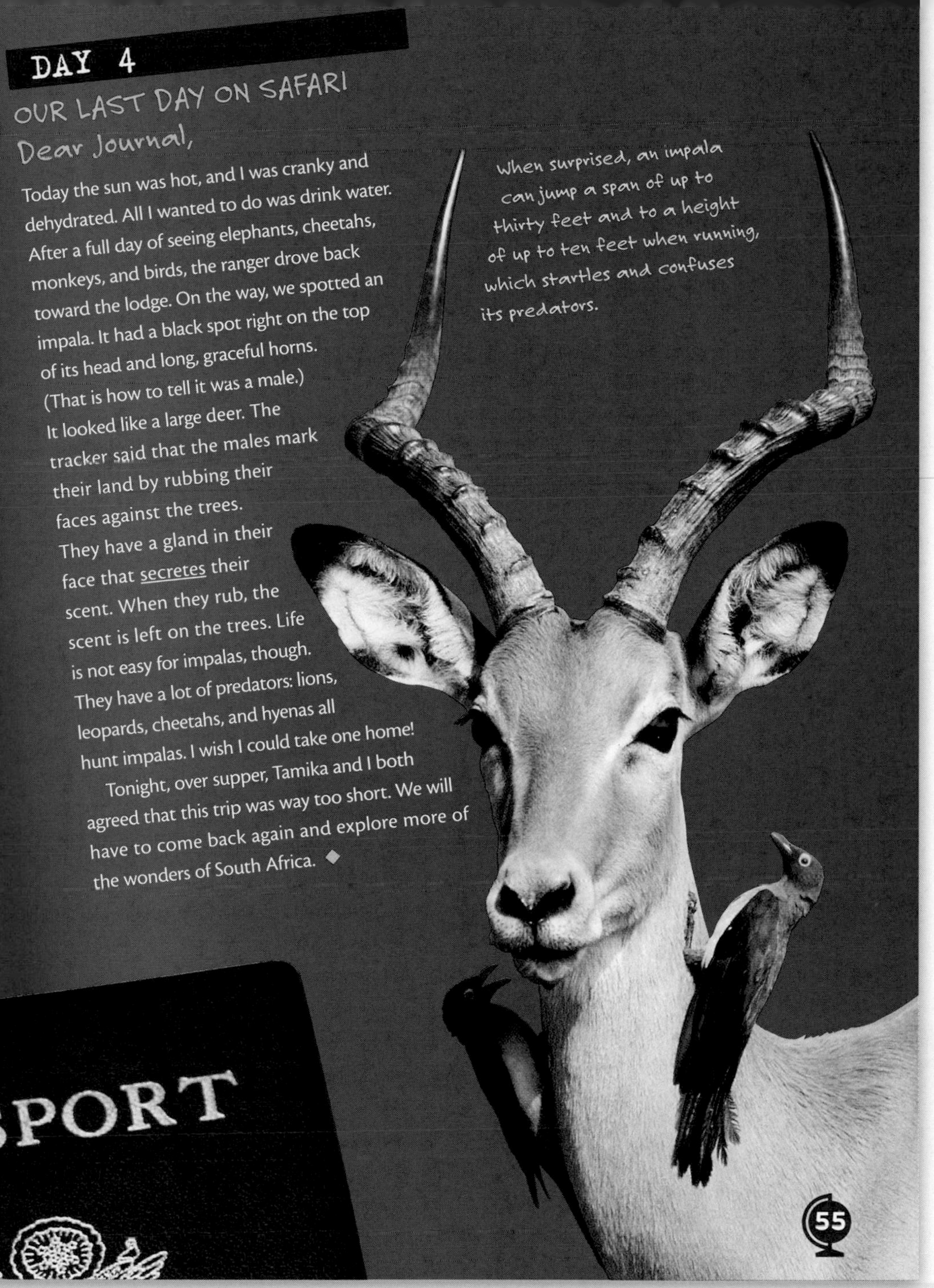

DAY 4

OUR LAST DAY ON SAFARI

Dear Journal,

Today the sun was hot, and I was cranky and dehydrated. All I wanted to do was drink water. After a full day of seeing elephants, cheetahs, monkeys, and birds, the ranger drove back toward the lodge. On the way, we spotted an impala. It had a black spot right on the top of its head and long, graceful horns. (That is how to tell it was a male.) It looked like a large deer. The tracker said that the males mark their land by rubbing their faces against the trees. They have a gland in their face that secretes their scent. When they rub, the scent is left on the trees. Life is not easy for impalas, though. They have a lot of predators: lions, leopards, cheetahs, and hyenas all hunt impalas. I wish I could take one home!

Tonight, over supper, Tamika and I both agreed that this trip was way too short. We will have to come back again and explore more of the wonders of South Africa. ◆

When surprised, an impala can jump a span of up to thirty feet and to a height of up to ten feet when running, which startles and confuses its predators.

55

Student Journal page 31

Name _______________ Date _______

Building Vocabulary: Words with Multiple Meanings

Pick four words from page 31 of the selection that have more than one meaning. Write the words and the definitions below.

Word	First Definition	Second Definition
pride	a group of lions	self-respect

Travel the World • On Safari 31

Writing Timeline

Tell students that a timeline shows the order in which events happen. A reader can see at a glance what the key events are and when they occur. Have students write on *Student Journal* page 30 a timeline of the safari's key events. Before students begin their timeline, have partners discuss what the cousins experienced on each day of the safari.

Vocabulary Multiple Meanings

Discuss with students that many words have more than one meaning. Give the word *pride* as an example, used in a sentence on page 53. Ask students what the word means. (the name given to a group of lions living together) Then ask for another meaning. (self-respect) Have students find three other words in the selection that have multiple meanings. Students should now complete the multiple meanings chart on *Student Journal* page 31.

Phonics/Word Study

Greek Roots

Display the following Greek roots and their meanings: *tele* (far, distant), *photo* (light), *therm* (heat), and *micro* (small). Challenge students to think of a word that begins with each root and to explain how the meaning of the word relates. (Examples: *telescope*, *telephone*; *photograph*, *photocopier*; *thermostat*, *thermos*; *microchip*, *microscope*). Now, work with students to complete the in-depth roots activity on TE page 76.

Phonics/Word Study

Greek Roots

For instruction to introduce a root, see TE page 68. Work with students to discover the meaning of each root. See *Word Study Manual* page 42 for a related word sort.

tele **(far, distant)**

telegraph	telethon
telephone	television
telephoto	telecommunications
telescope	teleconference

therm **(heat)**

thermal	thermonuclear
geothermal	thermos
thermometer	thermostat

photo **(light)**

photocell	photograph
telephoto	photojournalism
photocopier	photosynthesis

micro **(small)**

microscope	microchip
microfilm	microcomputer
microphones	microorganism
microwave	

Discovering the Roots

micro	*therm*	*photo*	*tele*
microchip	thermal	photosynthesis	telephoto
microcomputer	thermometer	telephoto	telephone
microwave	thermos	photograph	telegraph
microscope	thermostat	photocopier	television
microphone	geothermal	photocell	telescope

For more information on word sorts and spelling stages, see pages 5–31 in the *Word Study Manual*.

Focus on . . .

Use one or more activities in this section to focus on a particular area of need in your students.

Comprehension STRATEGY SUPPORT

To help those students who need more practice using the strategies covered in this lesson, work one-on-one or in small groups to apply the strategy prompts below. Apply the prompts to a *Reading Advantage* paperback, a classroom library book, or a new or familiar selection in the magazine. Always model your own thinking first.

Monitor Understanding

- Do I understand what I'm reading? If not, what part is confusing to me?
- What fix-up strategies can I use to solve the problem? (See During Reading for fix-up strategies.)
- Why did a character say (do, think, ask) that?
- What images do I visualize from the text? What parts can't I visualize?
- Why did the author include (or not include) those details?

Understanding Text Structure

- What kind of text is this? (book, story, article, guidebook, play, manual)
- How does the author organize the text? (cause-effect, problem-solution, chronological order, description, question-answer, comparison-contrast)
- What details support my thoughts about the text structure?
- What is the cause (effect, problem, solution, order, question, answer)?
- If fiction, who are the characters? What is the setting, plot, conflict, and resolution?

Writing Journal Entry

Brainstorm with students about trips they'd like to take. Ask: *What places would you like to visit? What would you like to see? Why?* Write students' ideas on a chart. Then have students choose a destination, think about things to do there, and write a journal entry describing the first whole day of their trip. Students can share their journal entries with a partner.

To help students use strong verbs and specific nouns, see lessons in *Writing Advantage*, pages 30–56.

Fluency: Expression

After students have read the selection at least once, have them choose one journal entry to practice for fluency. Students should first read their entry silently, several times, to become comfortable with the text. Then discuss as a group how to add expression and inflection to one's voice when reading aloud. Assign partners to read their journal entries to each other.

As you listen to students read, use these prompts to guide them in reading expressively.

- Think about the writer's attitude.
- Think about when you were in a new and exciting situation. How did you sound?
- Emphasize strong feelings when they appear. For example, "First, we went to this amazing mountain called Table Mountain." Emphasize the word *amazing*.
- Let your own life experience be your guide for adding expression to your voice.

When students read aloud, do they—

✓ reflect an understanding of the text?

✓ demonstrate appropriate timing, stress, and intonation?

✓ incorporate appropriate speed and phrasing?

English Language Learners

To support students as they complete the timeline activity on *Student Journal* page 30, provide students with background knowledge.

1. Discuss the concept of timelines.
2. Have students complete a timeline that represents their own lives. Each timeline should include five or six entries, each about a key event in the student's life.
3. Have students share their timelines with the class.

Independent Activity Options

While you work with individuals or small groups, others can work independently on one or more of the following options.

- Level D paperback books, see TE pages 367–372
- Level D *eZines*
- Repeat word sorts from this lesson
- *Student Journal* pages for this lesson
- *Writing Advantage* independent lessons

Assessment

Strategy Assessment

To help you and your students assess their use of comprehension strategies, ask the following questions. Students can complete a written response or provide verbal answers in a one-on-one reading conference.

1. **Monitor Understanding** Tell about a part of the text, without any accompanying photograph, that you pictured in your mind. What details or personal knowledge helped you visualize that part? (Answers will vary. Images students might mention include the hike up the mountain, the cable car ride, the two male lions, or the campfire.)
2. **Understanding Text Structure** In what ways did the structure of the text help you understand what you were reading? (Answers will vary. Students may have found the breakdown by days and the chronological order of events helpful.)

For ongoing informal assessment, use the checklists on pages 61–64 of *Level D Assessment*.

Word Study Assessment

Use these steps to help you and your students assess their understanding of Greek influences on spelling.

1. Write the following words on the board or on word cards: *microphone, television, thermal, photosynthesis*. Each word contains one of the roots students have just studied.
2. Ask students to find the root in each word and give its meaning.
3. Then ask students to define the word. They can use a dictionary, as necessary, but they should explain the root's connection to the word's meaning.

Word	Root	Root Meaning
microphone	*micro*	small
television	*tele*	far, distant
thermal	*therm*	heat
photosynthesis	*photo*	light

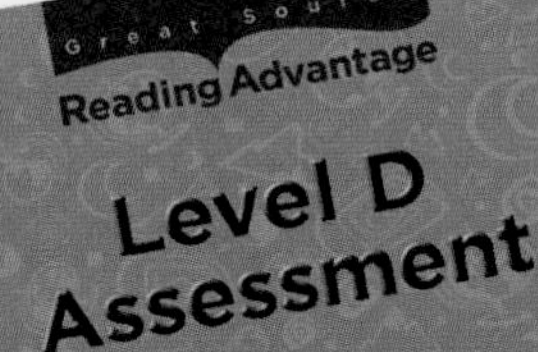

LESSON **10**

The Beautiful Girl on Whose Lips Bloom Roses

Travel the World, pages 56–61

SUMMARY

This **folktale** tells about a young girl with a unique gift.

COMPREHENSION STRATEGIES

Making Connections
Understanding Text Structure

WRITING

Story Map/Summary

VOCABULARY

Synonyms

PHONICS/WORD STUDY

Greek Roots

Lesson Vocabulary

entourage	transaction
envious	intently
parched	relinquished
sneered	

MATERIALS

Travel the World, pp. 56–61
Student Journal, pp. 32–35
Word Study Manual, p. 43
Writing Advantage, pp. 30–56

THE BEAUTIFUL GIRL ON WHOSE LIPS BLOOM ROSES

A BULGARIAN FOLKTALE, RETOLD

56

Before Reading  Use one or more activities.

Folktale Features Chart

Encourage students to name and talk briefly about folktales they know. Then have them use their discussion to help you complete a features chart. Ask:

- Where do folktales often take place?
- When do they take place?
- What kinds of characters are in folktales?
- What kinds of events happen?
- How do folktales end?

(See Differentiated Instruction.)

Folktale Features	
Settings	in the woods, in a castle, in a small village; once upon a time, long ago
Characters	kings and queens, villagers, animals that behave like people, people with special powers or gifts
Plots	save someone, get back something taken, reveal true identity; repetition of events
Endings	happily ever after; problems solved; bad characters punished

Vocabulary Preview

List and say the vocabulary words. Encourage volunteers to share what they know about specific words. Have students find each word in the story and use context clues to help them discover the meaning. Then have students begin the knowledge rating chart on *Student Journal* page 32. Students should fill in as many boxes as possible. They will return to the chart after they finish reading the selection.

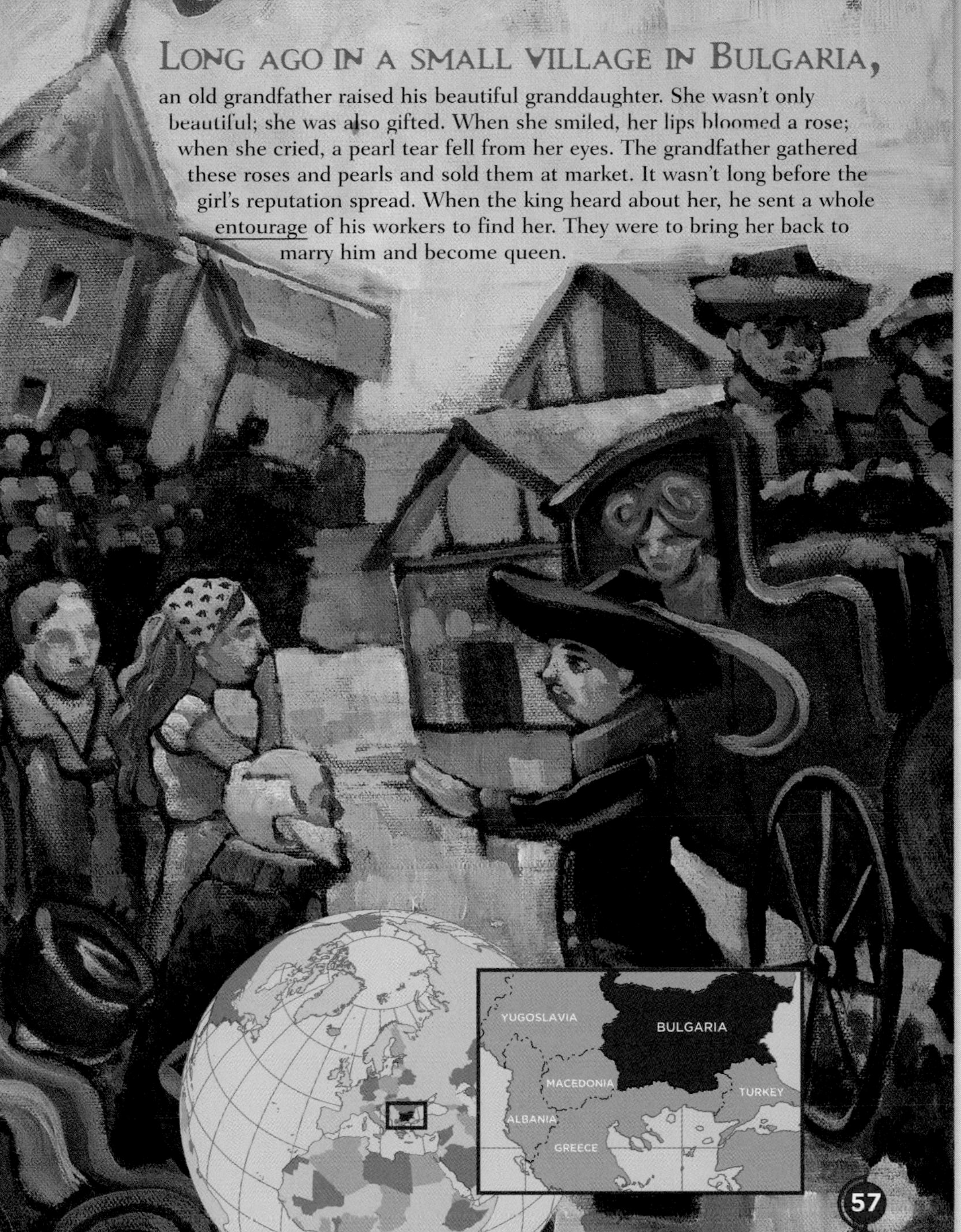

LONG AGO IN A SMALL VILLAGE IN BULGARIA, an old grandfather raised his beautiful granddaughter. She wasn't only beautiful; she was also gifted. When she smiled, her lips bloomed a rose; when she cried, a pearl tear fell from her eyes. The grandfather gathered these roses and pearls and sold them at market. It wasn't long before the girl's reputation spread. When the king heard about her, he sent a whole entourage of his workers to find her. They were to bring her back to marry him and become queen.

57

DIFFERENTIATED INSTRUCTION

FOLKTALE FEATURES CHART

SMALL GROUP

Help students recognize the characteristics of a folktale:

1. First, explain that a folktale is a story that is told among a group of people. Usually, folktales have a message. Because the stories have been passed down for many years, often unwritten, folktales can have different versions.
2. Give students examples of folktales with which they may be familiar. Examples might be African stories about Anansi the spider, American tales about Paul Bunyan, Aesop's fables, or fairy tales such as "Cinderella."

Student Journal page 32

Name ________________ Date ________

Building Vocabulary: Knowledge Rating Chart

Show your knowledge of each word by filling in the other boxes in the row.

Word	Define or Use in a Sentence	Where Have I Seen or Heard It?	How Is It Used in the Selection?	Looks Like (Words or Sketch)
entourage				
envious				
parched				
sneered				
transaction				
intently				
relinquished				

32 Travel the World • The Beautiful Girl on Whose Lips Bloom Roses

Preview the Selection

Have students look through the six pages of the folktale. Use these prompts to guide students to notice the important features of the text.

- Do you think this selection is fiction or nonfiction? What clues tell you?
- What do you know about the main character, just from the title?
- What events do the pictures suggest?

Teacher Think Aloud

The subtitle says that this selection is a folktale, so I know it is fiction. Usually, something unusual or magical happens in a folktale. I think it will happen to the girl in the title, and it will have to do with roses. When I look at the pictures, the important characters seem to be the girl, a dark-haired woman, and an old man. I am really interested to read what happens.

Make Predictions/ Set Purpose

Using the information they gathered in previewing the selection, students should make predictions about what they will learn. If students have trouble generating a purpose for reading, suggest that they read to find out what happens to the beautiful girl in the story.

DIFFERENTIATED INSTRUCTION 

Comprehension

UNDERSTANDING TEXT STRUCTURE

To help students understand the folktale genre, follow these steps.

1. Have students review the folktale features chart they created before reading. Ask: *What is the setting of this story? Who are the characters?*
2. Make a new chart similar to the folktale features chart. Title the new chart "Features of 'The Beautiful Girl on Whose Lips Bloom Roses.'" As a group, fill in the new chart.

When the king's entourage reached the village, they explained the king's wishes to the grandfather. After many nights of thinking, the grandfather finally allowed them to take his granddaughter. There wasn't enough room to ride in the carriage, however, so the girl walked beside it. Soon she became very thirsty. Among the messengers and soldiers, there was a girl who wanted what others had. This girl wanted to marry the king. When the beautiful girl complained of thirst, the envious one said, "I will give you some water if you give me one of your eyes." The girl's throat was so parched that she was dizzy and couldn't think straight. She agreed, popped out her eye, and traded it for some water. The envious one secretly placed the eye in a velvet box.

The king's party continued traveling through the heat of midday, and the one-eyed girl continued walking beside the carriage. She became terribly thirsty again. The envious one whispered, "If you give me your other eye, I'll give you some cold water to drink." The girl, dizzy from thirst, popped out her other eye and traded it for a drink. The envious one placed the second eye in a velvet box.

Soon the girl was stumbling beside the carriage because she was blind. The envious one raised her eyebrow and said, "Why would the king want a blind girl for a queen? Let's leave her here in the forest." They left the poor girl alone in the forest.

58

During Reading

Comprehension 

MAKING CONNECTIONS

Use these questions to model making connections with the text. Then have students make their own connections.

- What does this story remind me of?
- Do I have anything in common with any of the characters?

Teacher Think Aloud

I'm not exactly like any of the characters, but I'm a little like a few of them. I'd like to think that I would've helped the blind girl if I had found her in the woods, as the old man did. And I'm a little like the queen. I'd like to have money and jewels, but I don't think I could lie just to get them.

Comprehension 

UNDERSTANDING TEXT STRUCTURE

Use these questions to model understanding the text structure of a folktale. Then have students identify and describe the story elements (characters, setting, conflict, plot, resolution).

- What elements of folktales do I notice?
- How does recognizing these elements help my understanding of the story?

(See Differentiated Instruction.)

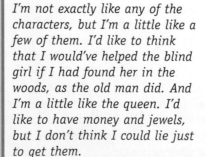

The king's entourage soon arrived at the palace. They introduced the envious girl to the king and told him that she was the famous one. The next day the king married her in a fancy ceremony with white horses, lilies, and sweet wedding cake. Time passed and the king waited for his wife to smile or cry, but she did neither. All she did was pace the palace halls, day in and day out.

Meanwhile, an old man found the beautiful girl in the woods. He reminded the girl of her own much-loved grandfather. He took her to his home and cared for her. He washed her bloodstained cheeks. He fed her fresh fruits and healing teas. One evening the old man sneezed and blew his nose so loudly that the girl laughed out loud. A rose dropped from her lips. She scooped it up and gave it to the old man. She said, "Take this rose to the city and cry out, 'I sell a rose for an eye!' Only give the rose to the one who gives you an eye!"

The old man thought this was a strange request. But because he loved the girl, he took the rose and went to the city yelling, "A rose for an eye!" The townspeople looked at him as if he were mad. At the last light of day, he passed by the palace where the queen sat on her balcony. "What are you yelling, old man?" she sneered.

"I sell a rose for an eye!" he cried, not recognizing the queen.

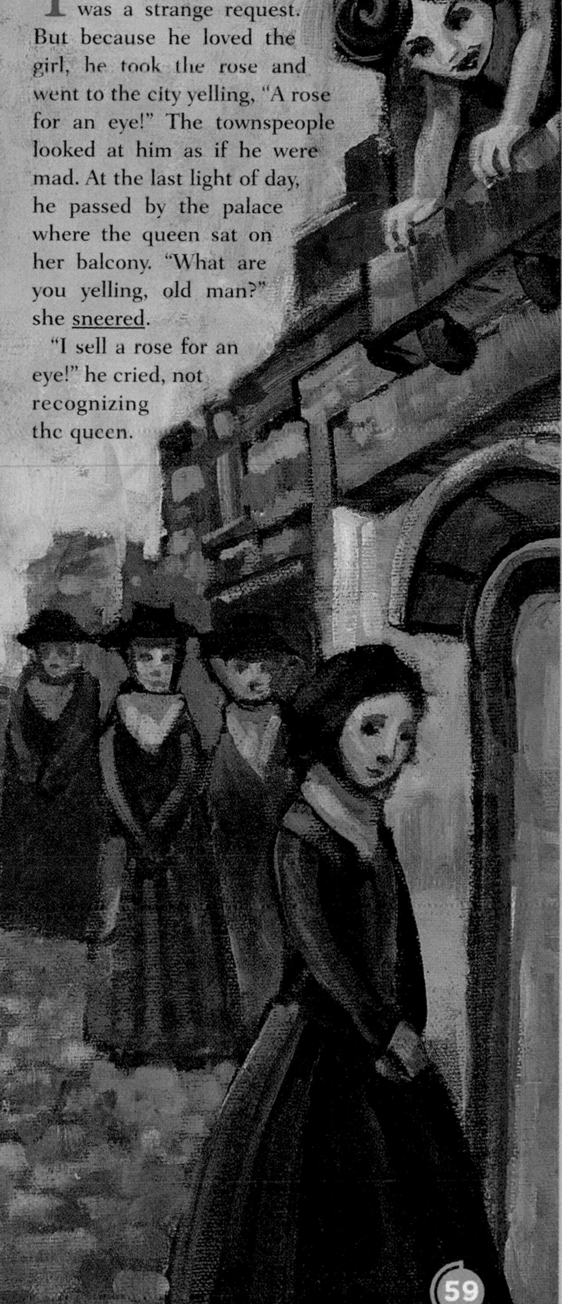

Teacher Think Aloud

I find many common elements of folktales in this story. The story takes place "long ago" and in a faraway land. It involves a beautiful girl who has unique gifts, and a king who wants to marry the girl. Some events happen in a forest. And there is the use of repetition. The girl asked for water twice, and twice her rival took one of her eyes.

Fix-Up Strategies

Offer these strategies to help students read independently.

If you don't understand what you're reading:

- Reread the difficult section to look for clues to help you comprehend.
- Read ahead to find clues to help you comprehend.
- Retell, or say in your own words, what you've read.
- Visualize, or form mental pictures of, what you've read.

If you don't understand a word:

- Reread the sentence. Look for ideas and words that provide meaning clues.
- Find clues by reading a few sentences before and after the confusing word.
- Look for the base or root word and think about its meaning.
- Think about the topic or plot at this point to see if either offers meaning clues.

"I'll take it!" The queen jumped up, grabbed the velvet box from beneath the bed and gave the old man an eye. In return, he gave her the rose.

A few days later, the old man made the girl laugh again. Another rose dropped from her lips. She gave the old man the same directions, and again he went to the city selling a rose for an eye. The townspeople shooed him away. Yet, when the old man passed by the palace, the same woman on the balcony was ready to trade an eye for his rose. The old man took the eye back to the girl. She put both of her eyes back in place.

All of this excitement made the girl cry. As she cried, pearls dropped from her eyes. She gave them to the old man and told him to go to the city and sell them. The queen eagerly bought them from the old man.

With the roses and pearls, the queen decided she would fool the king. At dinner that night, she laughed for the first time. The queen opened her mouth and showed him the rose hidden inside. The next morning, after hiding some pearls on her pillow, she began to cry. When the king turned to comfort her, he caught pearls rolling off her pillow.

Many times the old man returned to the city to sell the queen fresh roses and shiny pearls. One day a messenger of the king spotted the queen making her transaction with this strange old man. He reported to the king that the queen was making a deal with an old man for roses and pearls. The king decided to test the queen. That night he sent out invitations for a singing competition at the palace. He invited all girls, rich and poor.

Student Journal pages 33–34

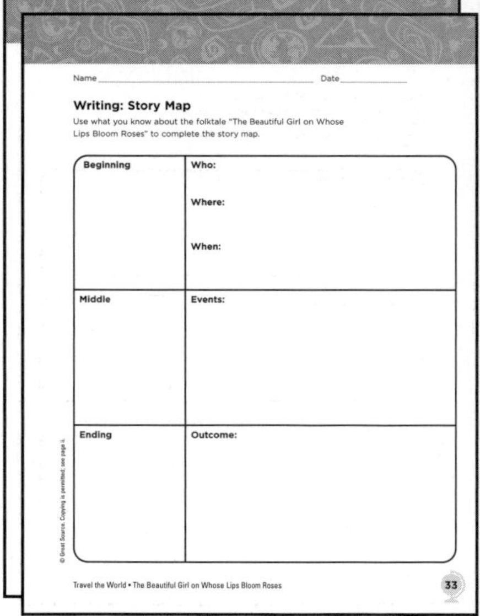

Name ______________________ Date __________

Writing: Story Map

Use what you know about the folktale "The Beautiful Girl on Whose Lips Bloom Roses" to complete the story map.

Beginning	**Who:** **Where:** **When:**
Middle	**Events:**
Ending	**Outcome:**

© Great Source. Copying is permitted; see page ii.

Travel the World • The Beautiful Girl on Whose Lips Bloom Roses 33

After Reading

Use one or more activities.

Check Purpose

Have students evaluate their predictions. Did the story happen as they thought it would? Did they find out what happened to the girl at the end of the story?

Discussion Questions

Continue the group discussion with the following questions.

1. From whose point of view is the folktale told? (Inferential Thinking)
2. How is the beautiful girl's problem solved? (Problem-Solution)
3. Do the characters and events of this folktale remind you of any other stories you have read? Which one or ones? (Making Connections)

Revisit: Folktale Features Chart

Look back with students at the folktale features chart. How does this Bulgarian folktale fit into the folktale genre?

Revisit: Knowledge Rating Chart

Have students return to the knowledge rating chart on *Student Journal* page 32. Have them complete any unfinished boxes. Encourage students to share their responses with a partner.

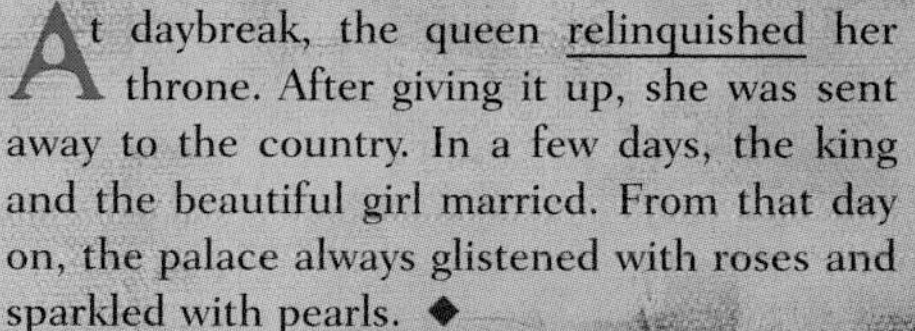

The night of the competition, all the girls from the city and the country came to the palace. The beautiful girl came, too. They sat around the king's throne and sang. The king listened intently. When the beautiful girl stood up to sing, she said, "I will not sing tonight. Instead I will tell you a story. There was once a girl whose lips bloomed with roses and whose eyes cried pearls. . . ." The girl went on with the story of how she was badly treated. When she finished, the king stood and lifted her veil. Before him stood the most beautiful girl he had ever seen. She smiled up at the kind king. Before the roses bloomed on her lips, he knew that this girl was his true wife.

At daybreak, the queen relinquished her throne. After giving it up, she was sent away to the country. In a few days, the king and the beautiful girl married. From that day on, the palace always glistened with roses and sparkled with pearls. ◆

61

Possible answers for **Student Journal page 35** include *entourage*: *group, groupies, following, train; relinquish*: *give up, surrender, yield, hand over.*

Name ______________________ Date __________

Building Vocabulary: Synonyms

What other words could you use in place of the two vocabulary words below? Think of and write two or three synonyms for each word. Then choose another word from the story and write two or three synonyms for it.

Synonyms for *entourage*

1. following
2.
3.

Synonyms for *relinquished*

1. surrendered
2.
3.

Synonyms for ____________

1.
2.
3.

Travel the World • The Beautiful Girl on Whose Lips Bloom Roses 35

Writing Story Map/Summary

Have students discuss the setting, characters, events, and ending of the folktale while you jot down notes on the board. Then have students complete the story map on *Student Journal* page 33. Have students use the story maps to write a summary of the folktale on *Student Journal* page 34. Ask students to end their summary with an explanation of the lesson they think the folktale teaches.

Vocabulary Synonyms

Write *parched* and have students find the word on page 58. Ask students:

- What is the meaning of the word? (dry, thirsty)
- What context clues help you know?
- What is a word you could use in place of *parched*? (*dry*)

Work with students to complete *Student Journal* page 35, on which they will write synonyms for *entourage* and *relinquish*.

Phonics/Word Study

Greek Roots

Write the following roots and their meanings on the board: *centr* (center), *cosm* (universe, world), *derm* (skin), and *geo* (the earth). Ask students to list any words that have those roots. (*egocentric, cosmic, pachyderm,* and *geology*). Discuss the meaning of each word and how it relates to the meaning of its root. Now, work with students to complete the in-depth Greek roots activity on TE page 84.

Phonics/Word Study

Greek Roots

For instruction to introduce a root, see TE page 68. Work with students to discover the meaning of each root. See *Word Study Manual* page 42 for a related word sort.

centr **(center)**

center	eccentric
centrifugal	egocentric
concentrate	ethnocentric
concentric	centrist

cosm **(universe, world)**

cosmic	cosmopolitan
cosmonaut	microcosm

derm **(skin)**

dermatology	pachyderm
epidermis	taxidermy
hypodermic	

geo **(the earth)**

geode	geology
geocentric	geophysics
geographic	geothermal

Discovering the Roots

centr	*cosm*	*derm*	*geo*
egocentric	cosmic	dermatology	geode
centrist	cosmos	epidermis	geology
centrifugal	cosmonaut	hypodermic	geophysics
ethnocentric	cosmopolitan	pachyderm	geographic
concentric	microcosm	taxidermy	geothermal

For more information on word sorts and spelling stages, see pages 5–31 in the *Word Study Manual.*

Focus on . . .

Use one or more activities in this section to focus on a particular area of need in your students.

Comprehension STRATEGY SUPPORT

To help those students who need more practice using the strategies covered in this lesson, work one-on-one or in small groups to apply the strategy prompts below. Apply the prompts to a *Reading Advantage* paperback, a classroom library book, or a new or familiar selection in the magazine. Always model your own thinking first.

Understanding Text Structure

- What kind of text is this? (book, story, article, guidebook, play, manual)
- How does the author organize the text? (cause-effect, problem-solution, chronological order, description, question-answer, comparison-contrast)
- What details support my thoughts about the text structure?
- What is the cause (effect, problem, solution, order, question, answer)?
- If fiction, who are the characters? What is the setting, plot, conflict, and resolution?

Making Connections

- What does this story (article, passage) remind me of?
- What do I already know about this topic?
- Where have I heard about this topic before?
- What do I have in common with the characters, people, or situations in the text?
- What other books, stories, articles, movies, or TV shows does this text make me think about?

Writing Point of View

Help students identify from whose point of view the folktale is told. (a narrator—someone outside the story action) Have students write to retell the folktale from a different point of view, that of one of the characters. Encourage students in small groups to brainstorm ideas before they begin to write individually. Have them think about how each character's version of the story would differ.

To help students *show* rather than *tell* in their writing, see lessons in *Writing Advantage*, pages 30–56.

Fluency: Pacing

After students have read the folktale at least once, have them listen as you model how to read one page at a smooth and even pace. Point out that reading too quickly, too slowly, or in a stumbling way can make it difficult for listeners to understand the story. Then have partners choose a page and take turns reading aloud to each other.

As you listen to students read, use these prompts to guide them.

- Use the punctuation as a guide to pacing. Think about what each mark signals.
- Keep your eyes on the text as you read so that you don't lose your place.
- Use your voice to create interest and hold the audience's attention. Remember that folktales originated as oral stories.

When students read aloud, do they—

✓ demonstrate a smooth pace, not too fast or too slow?

✓ incorporate well-timed pauses between words and phrases?

✓ reflect an awareness and understanding of punctuation?

English Language Learners

Help students deepen their understanding of folktales.

1. Ask students to work with a partner and read another familiar folktale. If necessary, suggest additional titles.
2. Have students remember the folktale of *The Beautiful Girl on Whose Lips Bloom Roses*. Ask each pair to discuss the similarities and differences shared by the two folktales.
3. Encourage students to share folktales from their own cultures.

Independent Activity Options

While you work with individuals or small groups, others can work independently on one or more of the following options.

- Level D paperback books, see TE pages 367–372
- Level D *eZines*
- Repeat word sorts from this lesson
- *Student Journal* pages for this lesson
- *Writing Advantage* independent lessons

Assessment

Strategy Assessment

To help you and your students assess their use of comprehension strategies, ask the following questions. Students can complete a written response or provide verbal answers in a one-on-one reading conference.

1. **Making Connections** How is this folktale similar to "Cinderella"? (Answers will vary. Students should mention that, in both cases, people were mean to the main character, there were magical elements in both, both women married royal men, and both endings were happy ones.)
2. **Understanding Text Structure** Which character did you like best in this folktale? Why? (Answers will vary.)

For ongoing informal assessment, use the checklists on pages 61–64 of *Level D Assessment*.

Word Study Assessment

Use these steps to help you and your students assess their understanding of Greek influences on spelling.

1. Write the following words on the board or on word cards: *epidermis, geode, concentric, microcosm*. Each word contains one of the roots students have just studied.
2. Ask students to find the root in each word and give its meaning. Then ask them to define the word. They can use a dictionary, as necessary, but they should explain the root's connection to the word's meaning.

Word	Root	Root Meaning
epidermis	*derm*	skin
geode	*geo*	the Earth
concentric	*centr*	center
microcosm	*cosm*	universe, world

LESSON **11**

The Great Wall of China *and* The World . . .

Travel the World, pages 62–end

SUMMARY

The first **article** provides a brief history of the construction of the Great Wall of China. The second **article** is a short feature.

COMPREHENSION STRATEGY

Determining Importance

WRITING

Notes for Visualizing

VOCABULARY

Context

PHONICS/WORD STUDY

Greek Roots *graph, homo, morph, phone*

Lesson Vocabulary

itinerary	disrepair
meandering	restoration
fortification	elaborate
persistence	

MATERIALS

Travel the World, pp. 62–end
Student Journal, pp. 36–39
Word Study Manual, p. 44
Writing Advantage, pp. 56–93

The Great Wall of China

China

Built over 2,000 years ago to keep enemies out, the Great Wall of China is now a major tourist attraction.

If you're thinking about a trip to China, be sure to put the Great Wall on the itinerary. This ancient wonder spans thousands of miles, through rugged mountains, arid desert, and frozen plains. No one has ever measured the Great Wall, but estimates are that it is more than 4,000 miles long. If you could transport it to North America, the Great Wall would stretch all the way from the North Pole to Miami, Florida!

It took more than two thousand years to build the Great Wall. Close to a million people worked on the meandering fortification. They labored without power tools or electric equipment of any kind. For each mile of the wall, workers had to hand cut thousands of granite stones. This amazing accomplishment stands as a symbol of the strength and persistence of the Chinese people. Its story reflects the rich history of a country whose civilization dates back thousands of years.

The ancient Chinese developed a sophisticated culture. They had one of the earliest written languages. They also invented paper, porcelain, and silk cloth. The ancient Chinese built great cities and had a well-organized government. Scholars believe that the ancient Chinese were so proud of their culture that they worked hard to protect it from less developed peoples. In order to remain separate from outsiders, the Chinese built walls around their villages.

The first emperor of China, Qin [chin] Shi Huang, oversaw the first phase of the Great Wall. Beginning in 221 B.C., Qin Shi Huang ordered workers to repair old sections of wall and link them to new walls. Qin's builders used local materials. While much of the Qin wall was made with native stone, in places where stone was unavailable, workers used layers of packed earth. Qin died eleven years after he had become emperor. By that time, workers had completed 3,000 miles of wall designed to protect China's northern frontiers from invasion.

During the Han Dynasty, (206 B.C.– A.D. 220), the Great Wall was expanded. Emperor Wu Di, considered the greatest of the Han rulers, oversaw the second great period

62

Before Reading

Use one or more activities.

Make a Category Chart

Ask students the following question: *What do you know about the Great Wall of China?* Have students write their answers on self-stick notes, one thought per note. Then read the notes as a group. Work together to organize the notes into possible categories. (Categories may include tourism, length, construction, defense.) Students will revisit the chart later.

Vocabulary Preview

Display the vocabulary and read the words aloud. Ask: *Have you seen this word before? Can you use it in a sentence? Does it remind you of something?* Have students begin the knowledge rating chart on *Student Journal* page 36.

Preview the Selection

Have students look over pages 62–63 in the magazine. Discuss the important elements of the article.

Make Predictions/ Set Purpose

Using the information they gathered in previewing the selection, students should make predictions about what they will learn. If students have trouble generating a purpose for reading, suggest that they read to discover why the Great Wall is a major tourist attraction today.

of construction. During his reign, workers built more than 300 miles of wall across the Gobi desert. During this period, safe caravan routes, known as the Silk Roads, were created. These routes opened China to the Western world. Traders from Alexandria, Antioch, Baghdad, and Rome passed through the Great Wall to trade their wares for jade, gold, spices, precious gems, and silk. Market towns formed at various gates along the Great Wall to provide goods for the traders.

The Han empire collapsed in A.D. 220 By that time, the wall had fallen into disrepair. Barbarian tribes took control of China. Although some barbarian emperors oversaw construction of new wall, the importance of the Great Wall faded. Beginning in 618, the Tang dynasty led an offensive military strategy that did not depend on the Great Wall for defending the country.

The next major phase of construction did not begin for another four hundred years. When the Ming dynasty came to power in 1368, the Great Wall was in desperate need of repair. A series of nearly a dozen emperors oversaw a major restoration program. It took two hundred years, but the Ming rulers built more wall than any other dynasty. The wall that they constructed was bigger, longer, and more ornate than previous efforts. Workers used bricks and a variety of wood to create elaborate watchtowers, gates, and thick walls. Small temples and teahouses were built along the path of the wall.

During the Ming era, China became a world power. Chinese trade ships sailed to ports in India, Japan, the Persian Gulf, and the South Pacific. During this time, soldiers were positioned in watchtowers along the Great Wall. Border guards lived in so-called castles along the wall. When the Ming dynasty ended in 1620, barbarians took over for almost three hundred years. The Great Wall no longer kept out invading forces, and over time, the beautiful structure decayed.

It wasn't until the 1980s, when Deng Xiaoping (deng shou PING) came to power, that workers began to repair parts of the Great Wall. If you travel to China, make sure you walk along the restored parts of the wall. This sleeping dragon tells the history of an ancient civilization that went to amazing lengths to protect itself from outside forces. ◆

Qin Shi Huang was a tyrant who banned free thought and free speech.

Facts on the Wall

- The Great Wall is sometimes called "the longest cemetery on earth." When workers died on the job, they were buried in the wall.
- The Great Wall is not one long wall. It is a series of many walls.
- Hundreds of miles of the wall were torn down in the 1960s after Mao Zedong ordered anything ancient to be destroyed.
- In 1984, Deng Xiaoping, leader of the Communist Party, oversaw the restoration of the Great Wall.

63

DIFFERENTIATED INSTRUCTION

Comprehension

DETERMINING IMPORTANCE

Help students determine the importance of ideas on the basis of a purpose for reading that you provide.

1. Say: *Suppose that you are reading this article because you will be taking a trip to China and visiting the Great Wall. Which of the three sentences in the last paragraph on page 63 would be the most important one to remember?* (The middle one: "If you travel to China . . . ")
2. Ask students to explain why that information is the most important.

Student Journal page 36

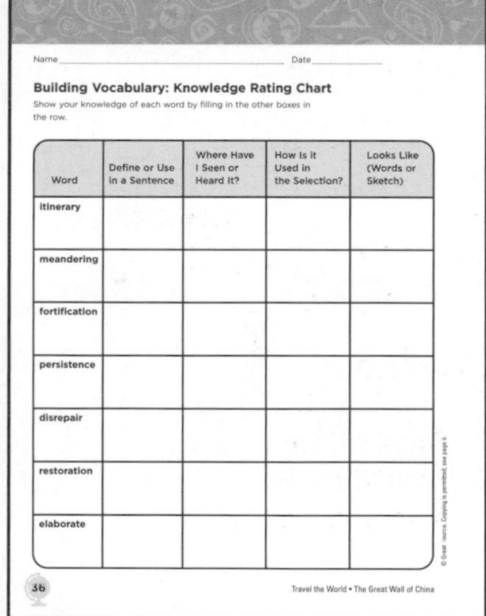

Name ______________ Date ________

Building Vocabulary: Knowledge Rating Chart

Show your knowledge of each word by filling in the other boxes in the row.

Word	Define or Use in a Sentence	Where Have I Seen or Heard It?	How Is it Used in the Selection?	Looks Like (Words or Sketch)
itinerary				
meandering				
fortification				
persistence				
disrepair				
restoration				
elaborate				

36 Travel the World • The Great Wall of China

© Great Source. Copying is permitted; see page ii.

During Reading

Comprehension

DETERMINING IMPORTANCE

SMALL GROUP

Use these questions to model determining the importance of information within the text. Then have students read a paragraph and state what they think are the most important ideas.

- What big ideas does the author want me to understand?
- What are the important details?

(See Differentiated Instruction.)

Teacher Think Aloud

This text contains a lot of details—too many for me to remember! It helps to think about what the author really wants me to understand. I think that the author wants me to know how impressive the wall is, and why I might want to visit it. On the first page, the important details are that the wall was very hard to build and that it was first built to protect Chinese culture, but was later used for defense.

Fix-Up Strategies

Offer these strategies to help students read independently.

If you don't understand what you're reading:

- Reread the difficult section to look for clues to help you comprehend.
- Read ahead to find clues to help you comprehend.
- Retell, or say in your own words, what you've read.
- Visualize, or form mental pictures of, what you've read.

Answers for Student Journal page 39

						1										
						F										
	3			2	F	O	R	T	I	F	Y					
	R					R		5								
4 P	E	R	S	I	S	T		I								
	S		6			I		T		7				8		
	T		D			F		I		P				M		
	O		I			I		N		E				E		
	R		S			C		E		R				A		
	A	9	R	E	P	A	I	R		S				N		
	T		E			T		A		I				D		
	I		P			I	10	R	E	S	T	O	R	E		
	O		A			O		Y		T				R		
	N		I			N				E						
			R			11	M	E	A	N	D	E	R	I	N	G
										C						
	12	E	L	A	B	O	R	A	T	E						

Student Journal page 37

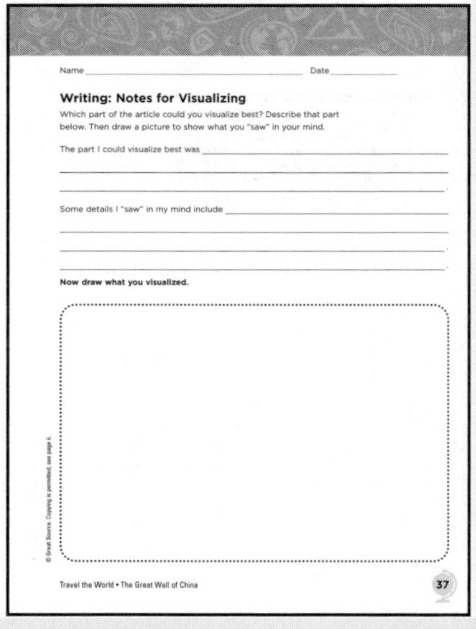
Name ______________________ Date ________

Writing: Notes for Visualizing

Which part of the article could you visualize best? Describe that part below. Then draw a picture to show what you "saw" in your mind.

The part I could visualize best was ______________________

____

Some details I "saw" in my mind include ______________________

____

Now draw what you visualized.

CREDITS

Program Authors
Laura Robb
James F. Baumann
Carol J. Fuhler

Editorial Board
Avon Cowell
Joan Kindig
Craig Roney
Jo Worthy

Magazine Writers
Anina Robb
Lauren Kaufmann

Design and Production
Preface, Inc.

Photography:
Inside front cover, l © Gamma/SuperStock; cl © Steve Lewis/Getty Images; cr © JH Pete Carmichael/Getty Images; r © Fredde Lieberman/Index Stock; l © Rowan Beste/Animals Animals; p. 1 © Corbis; p. 3 © Yves Lanceau/NHPA Limited registered in England no. 4677644 VAT no. GB 807968582; p. 4bl © Fritz Prenzel/Animals Animals; br © Reuters NewMedia Inc./Corbis; p. 5t © Siede Preis/Getty Images; © Rowan Beste/ Animals Animals; p. 6t © Paddy Ryan/ Animals Animals; b © Bill Bachman/Photo Researchers, Inc.; pp. 8–9 © Adam Woolfitt/Corbis; p. 10 © Charles & Josette Lenars/Corbis; p. 11t © Gamma/SuperStock; c © SuperStock; b © Charles & Josette Lenars/Corbis; p. 12 © Robert Harding World Imagery/Alamy; p. 13b © Annebicque Bernard/Corbis; p. 13t, p. 14t © Gianni Dagli Orti/Corbis; p. 14bl © Gianni Dagli Orti/The Art Archive; br © Wayne Lawler; Ecoscene/Corbis; p. 15 © Bruce Dale/National Geographic Collection; p. 16bl © Robert Harding World Imagery/Alamy; pp. 16–17bkgd © Kevin Schafer/Getty Images; p. 17t © Steve Bloom Images/Alamy; pp. 18–19bkgd © Richard Elliot/Getty Images; p. 19t © Norbert Rosing/National Geographic Collection; c © Jonathan and Angela/Getty Images; pp. 20–21bkgd © Kim Heacox/Getty Images; p. 20b © Galen Rowell/Corbis; p. 21t © Hulton-Deutsch Collection/Corbis; b © Galen Rowell/Peter Arnold, Inc.; p. 22bkgd © J. P. Fruchet/Getty Images; bl © JH Pete Carmichael/Getty Images; p. 23t © Charles & Josette Lenars/Corbis; bl © Paul Grebliunas/Getty Images; br © Timothy O'Keefe/Index Stock; p. 24l © Michael & Patricia Fogden/Corbis; r © Gregory Ochocki/Photo Researchers, Inc.; p. 25t © Brian Kenney/Getty Images; bl © Davies + Starr/Getty Images; br © Brian Hagiwara/FoodPix; p. 26tl © Kevin Schafer/Corbis; tr © Michael Doolittle/Peter Arnold, Inc.; b © David A. Harvey/ National Geographic Collection; p. 27t © Digital Vision; b © Mark Edwards/Peter Arnold, Inc.; p. 28t © Darrell Gulin/ Corbis; pp. 28–29bkgd © Corbis; p. 29tl © Fredde Lieberman/ Index Stock; p. 29tr, pp. 30–31bkgd © Corbis; p. 30b © AP Photo/Don Ryan; p. 31t, b © Bettmann/Corbis; p. 35 © TempSport/Corbis; p. 37 © Richard Hamilton Smith/ Corbis; p. 40 © Ralph A. Clevenger/Corbis; p. 43 © Lynn Rogers/Peter Arnold, Inc.; pp. 44–45bkgd © Corbis; p. 46tl © Robert Harding World Imagery/Alamy; tr © Scala/Art Resource; c © Historical Picture Archive/Corbis; b © Vanni Archive/Corbis; p. 47tl © Scala/Art Resource; tr © Araldo de Luca/Corbis; b © Vanni Archive/Corbis; p. 47c, p. 48c © Erich Lessing/Art Resource, NY; p. 48b © Vanni Archive/Corbis; pp. 48–49t © Erich Lessing/Art Resource, NY; p. 49tr © Erich Lessing/Art Resource; c © Araldo de Luca/Corbis; b © Vanni Archive/Corbis; p. 50t © MAPS.com/Corbis; t © Robert Harding World Imagery/Alamy; pp. 50–51b © Stephen Wilkes/Getty Images; p. 52t © Walter Bibikow/Getty Images; b © Joe McDonald/Corbis; p. 53t © Martin Harvey/Peter Arnold, Inc.; p. 54l © Nigel J. Dennis/Peter Arnold, Inc.; pp. 54–55r © C. Sherburne/PhotoLink/Getty Images; p. 55r © Theo Allofs/Getty Images; pp. 62–63bkgd © Eric Meola/Getty Images; p. 63t © Giraudon/Art Resource, NY; p. 64t © Fredde Lieberman/Index Stock; b © JH Pete Carmichael/Getty Images; p. 65tl © Timothy McCarthy/Art Resource NY; tr © Eric Meola/Getty Images; cl © Nigel J. Dennis/Peter Arnold, Inc.; cr © Rowan Beste/Animals Animals; b © Richard Elliot/Getty Images

Illustration
Inside front cover, Tom Foty, John Coulter, Aaron Jasinski; pp. 5, 9, 16, 17, 26, Preface, Inc.; pp. 32–36, Tom Foty; p. 40, Preface, Inc.; pp. 38–43, John Coulter/Lilla Rogers Studio; pp. 43, 45–49, 53, 57, Preface, Inc.; pp. 56–61, Aaron Jasinski; pp. 62–inside back cover, Preface, Inc.

The World at Your Feet

NORTH AMERICA

The Coin Act of 1997 authorized the government to issue a new dollar coin. A committee chose to honor Sacagawea, the Shoshone woman who acted as interpreter and guide for Lewis and Clark.

SOUTH

Macaws, along with herons, anacondas, monkeys, and river dolphins, live in and along the banks of the Amazon River, the second longest river in the world.

ANTARCTICA

After Reading

Use one or more activities.

Check Purpose

Have students decide if their purpose was met. Why might tourists want to go to the Great Wall of China?

Discussion Questions

Start a group discussion with the following questions.

1. What did you learn about the Great Wall of China? (Details)
2. What part of the article were you best able to visualize? Retell this part. (Monitor Understanding)
3. Do you think you would like to visit the Great Wall of China? Why or why not? (Making Connections)

Revisit: Category Chart

Revisit the category chart to see if students want to change or add any information. Is there another category they may want to add, such as influential people or important dates?

Revisit: Knowledge Rating Chart

Have students revisit the knowledge rating chart on *Student Journal* page 36. Students can complete any empty boxes or change any meanings, as necessary.

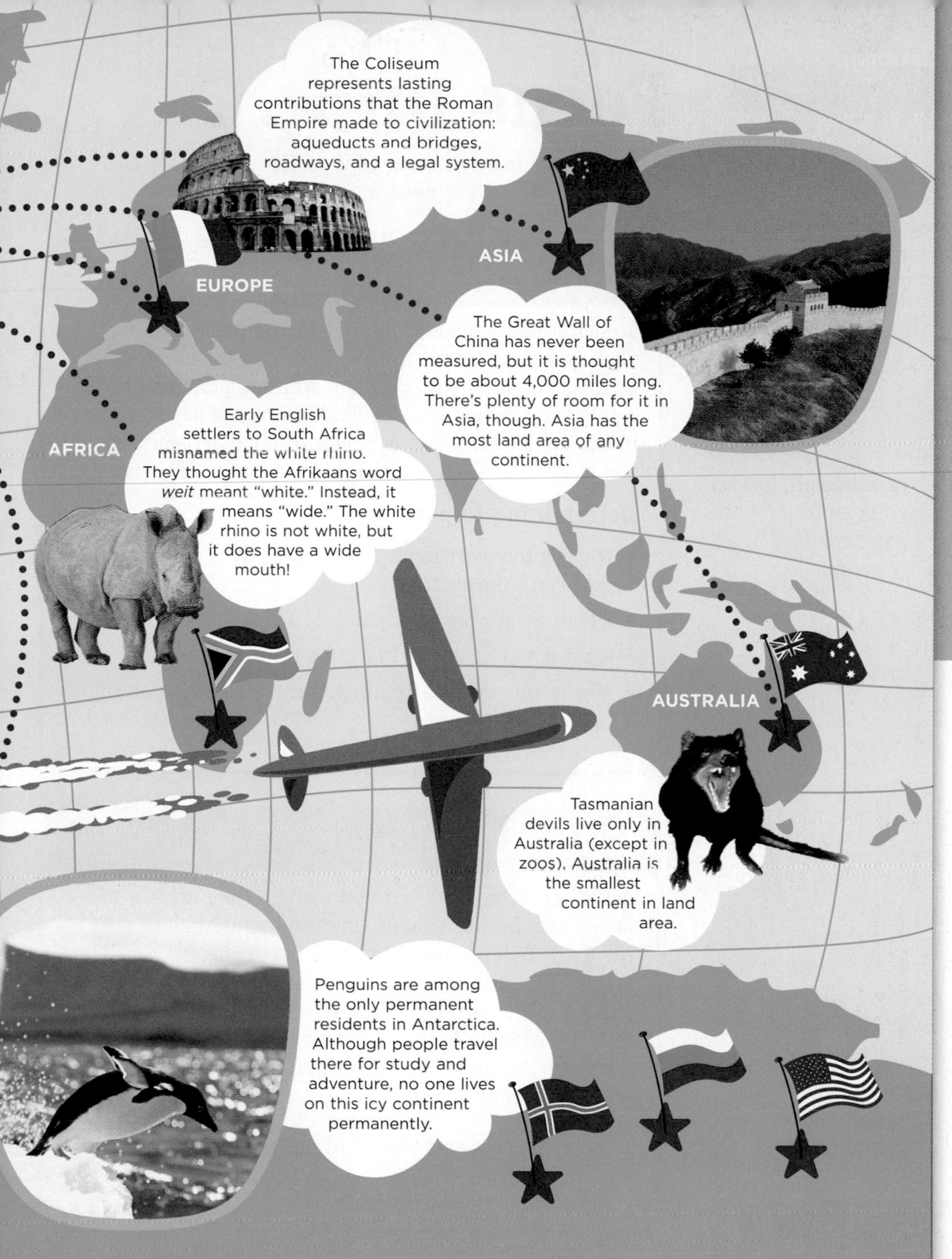

The Coliseum represents lasting contributions that the Roman Empire made to civilization: aqueducts and bridges, roadways, and a legal system.
ASIA
EUROPE
The Great Wall of China has never been measured, but it is thought to be about 4,000 miles long. There's plenty of room for it in Asia, though. Asia has the most land area of any continent.
AFRICA
Early English settlers to South Africa misnamed the white rhino. They thought the Afrikaans word *weit* meant "white." Instead, it means "wide." The white rhino is not white, but it does have a wide mouth!
AUSTRALIA
Tasmanian devils live only in Australia (except in zoos). Australia is the smallest continent in land area.
Penguins are among the only permanent residents in Antarctica. Although people travel there for study and adventure, no one lives on this icy continent permanently.

Short Feature: The World at Your Feet

Briefly preview the feature "The World at Your Feet" with students.

- What do you notice first about this feature?
- What pictures do you recognize? What do the pictures show?

Lead students to see that this magazine feature helps to conclude the magazine by highlighting some of the things they have read about. Read the feature aloud with students, calling on volunteers to choose a caption and read it aloud. Encourage students to add one or two more facts they learned about each continent in *Travel the World*.

Student Journal pages 38–39

Name ______ Date ______

Building Vocabulary: Using Context to Understand a Word

Select a vocabulary word you defined from the context. Complete the statements and answer the questions about your word.

itinerary meandering fortification persistence
disrepair restoration elaborate

My Word in Context:

I think this word means ______

because ______

My word is ______

My word is not ______

Where else might I find this word? ______

What makes this an important word to know? ______

38 Travel the World • The Great Wall of China

© Great Source. Copying is permitted; see page ii.

Writing Notes for Visualizing

Ask students which parts of the article they could visualize best. List their responses on the board. Next, have volunteers describe the pictures they "saw" in their minds. Then have students complete the visualizing activity on *Student Journal* page 37.

Vocabulary Context

Have students locate the word *restoration* on page 63. Explain to students that the context will help them figure out what *restoration* means. (the act of bringing back into a prior condition or use)

Have students complete *Student Journal* page 38. You may also want to have students complete *Student Journal* page 39.

Phonics/Word Study

Greek Roots

Write the root *graph* on the board and tell students it means "to write." Ask them to think of words that end with *graph*(y) and to explain how the words relate to writing. (For example, a *paragraph* is a short piece of writing. Other words: *autograph, telegraph, biography, calligraphy*.) Now, work with students to complete the in-depth Greek roots activity on TE page 90.

Phonics/Word Study

Greek Roots

For instruction to introduce a root, see TE page 68. Work with students to discover the meaning of each root. See Word Study Manual page 44 for a related word sort.

The final Greek roots to be examined are *graph* (to write), *homo* (same), *morph* (having a form), and *phone* (sound).

***graph* (to write)**

autograph	epigraph	phonograph
biography	seismograph	polygraph
calligraphy	graphics	geography
cartographer	homograph	telegraph
choreographer	oceanography	
digraph	paragraph	

***homo* (same)**

homograph	homogenize
homophone	homochromatic
homogeneous	homocentric

***morph* (having a form)**

animorphs	morpheme
amorphous	morphology
metamorphosis	morphosis

***phone* (sound)**

cacophony	microphone	saxophone
earphone	phoneme	stereophonic
headphone	phonics	symphony
homophone	phonograph	telephone
megaphone	polyphonic	xylophone

Discovering the Roots

graph	*homo*	*morph*	*phone*
autograph	homograph	animorphs	telephone
biography	homophone	amorphous	phonics
polygraph	homochromatic	metamorphosis	megaphone
geography	homogeneous	morpheme	cacophony
telegraph	homogenize	morphology	headphone

For more information on word sorts and spelling stages, see pages 5–31 in the *Word Study Manual*.

Focus on . . .

Use one or more activities in this section to focus on a particular area of need in your students.

Comprehension STRATEGY SUPPORT

To help those students who need more practice using the strategies covered in this lesson, work one-on-one or in small groups to apply the strategy prompts below. Apply the prompts to a *Reading Advantage* paperback, a classroom library book, or a new or familiar selection in the magazine. Always model your own thinking first.

Determining Importance

- What is the most important idea in the paragraph? How can I prove it?
- Which details are unimportant? Why?
- What does the author want me to understand?
- Why is this information important (or not important) to me?

Writing Friendly Letter

Ask students to write letters in which they explain to family members or friends why they would like to visit the Great Wall of China. Before students begin, have them brainstorm a list of facts about the wall that they might include in the letter. Then review with students the format of a friendly letter—heading, greeting, body, closing, signature. Invite students to share their finished letters with the group.

To help students edit their writing, see lessons in *Writing Advantage*, pages 56–93.

Fluency: Pacing

After students have read the article at least once, have them read it aloud with partners to practice fluent reading. Suggest that partners each read one page of the article.

As students read, caution them against reading too fast, too slow, or in a halting manner—actions that can make it difficult for listeners to grasp a sense of the words. Model the difference between evenly paced reading and unevenly paced reading. Then circulate among pairs as they read, offering prompts such as the following:

- Listen to me read. Then read it just as I did.
- Reread this sentence a little bit faster, or a little more slowly.
- Practice saying unfamiliar words or names. Then you won't stumble over them when you read.

When students read aloud, do they—

- ✓ demonstrate a smooth pace, not too fast or too slow?
- ✓ incorporate well-timed pauses between words and phrases?
- ✓ reflect an awareness and understanding of punctuation?

English Language Learners

To support students in preparation for making the category chart on TE page 86, provide them with background knowledge and review the skill.

1. Select a topic that you expect is familiar to most students (food, sports, animals).
2. Have students brainstorm a list of thirty words associated with the topic. Then, have partners organize the words into five categories.
3. Have pairs share with the class.

Independent Activity Options

While you work with individuals or small groups, others can work independently on one or more of the following options.

- Level D paperback books, see TE pages 367–372
- Level D *eZines*
- Repeat word sorts from this lesson
- *Student Journal* pages for this lesson
- *Writing Advantage* independent lessons

Assessment

Strategy Assessment

To help you and your students assess their use of comprehension strategies, ask the following question. Students can complete a written response or provide verbal answers in a one-on-one reading conference.

- **Determining Importance** Why do you think the information in the article is important to know, whether or not you ever visit the Great Wall? (Answers will vary but may include that China is a great power in the world today, and that learning about the country is important in promoting understanding between our peoples.)

See *Level D Assessment* page 14 for formal assessment to go with *Travel the World*.

Word Study Assessment

Use these steps to help you and your students assess their understanding of Greek and Latin influences on spelling.

1. Write the following words on the board or on word cards: *homogeneous, saxophone, epigraph, amorphous*. Each word contains one of the roots students have just studied.
2. Ask students to find the root in each word and give its meaning. Then ask them to define the word. They can use a dictionary, as necessary, but they should explain the root's connection to the word's meaning.

Word	Root	Root Meaning
homogeneous	*homo*	same
saxophone	*phone*	sound
epigraph	*graph*	to write
amorphous	*morph*	having a form

Level D, Magazine 2

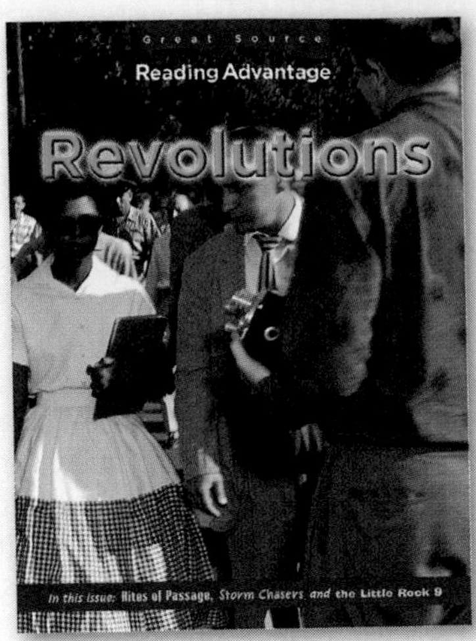

Revolutions

Magazine Summary

Revolutions magazine contains a variety of literature, including a play, a memoir, an interview, a short story, poetry, and several articles. Each selection takes a different look at the concept of revolution. By reading the various pieces, students will gain a clearer understanding of the many ways in which this word can be defined.

Content–Area Connection: social studies
Lexile measure: 850L

Revolutions Lesson Planner

LESSON	BEFORE READING	DURING READING	AFTER READING
LESSON 12 **Revolutions Big & Small** (article and poem) page 96	Make a List Vocabulary Preview Preview the Selection Make Predictions/Set Purpose	Making Connections Monitor Understanding	Check Purpose Discussion Questions Writing: personal response Vocabulary: suffixes *-able*/*-ible* Phonics/Word Study: Latin roots
LESSON 13 **Letters of Revolution** *and* **At a Surrealist Show** (guide) page 104	Three Concept Webs Vocabulary Preview Preview the Selection Make Predictions/Set Purpose	Inferential Thinking Making Connections	Check Purpose Discussion Questions Writing: letter Vocabulary: context Phonics/Word Study: Latin roots
LESSON 14 **Rites of Passage: from Birth to Death** (article) page 112	Anticipation Guide Vocabulary Preview Preview the Selection Make Predictions/Set Purpose	Determining Importance Making Connections	Check Purpose Discussion Questions Writing: compare-contrast Vocabulary: related words Phonics/Word Study: Latin roots
LESSON 15 **The 1960s Music Scene: A Revolution Inside a Revolution** (interview) page 120	Begin a List Vocabulary Preview Preview the Selection Make Predictions/Set Purpose	Understanding Text Structure	Check Purpose Discussion Questions Writing: outline and essay Vocabulary: compound words Phonics/Word Study: Latin roots

Overview

Preview the Magazine

Give students plenty of time to preview the magazine. Have them read selection titles and look at the photographs and illustrations. Make sure that students look at the artwork on the front and back covers. Tell students that the magazine offers a variety of literature, all focused on the concept of revolution. Then have students compile a class list about revolution.

A revolution can be...
1. a big battle between countries
2. a big battle within a country
3. a major change in a culture
4.

PHONICS/ WORD STUDY	FOCUS ON	ASSESSMENT	HIGHER-ORDER THINKING QUESTIONS
Latin Roots	Writing: double-entry journal Fluency: punctuation English Language Learners Independent Activity Options	Making Connections Monitor Understanding Latin Roots	Compare two "revolutions" students discover in interviewing their relatives. Use information and specific details from the play to support your answer. What benefits did Lattice's grandmother receive from the invention of frozen dinners? Use information and specific details from the play to support your answer.
Latin Roots	Writing: report Fluency: expression English Language Learners Independent Activity Options	Inferential Thinking Making Connections Latin Roots	The Portuguese who settled Sri Lanka took what revolutionary action? Were there consequences? Use information and specific details from the letter to support your answer. Why was the Selma March revolutionary? What changes occurred because of it? Use information and specific details from the letter to support your answer.
Latin Roots	Writing: opinion paragraph Fluency: expression English Language Learners Independent Activity Options	Determining Importance Making Connections Latin Roots	Compare and contrast two of the coming of age rituals described in the article (Quinceanera, Bat Mitzvah, Bar Mitzvah, or Apache Sunrise). Use information and specific details from the article to support your answer. Imagine you could visit Japan for a kindergarten graduation. What would you particularly look for at the event? Use information and specific details from the article to support your answer.
Latin Roots	Writing: interview Fluency: pacing English Language Learners Independent Activity Options	Understanding Text Structure Latin Roots	What factors led to the influence of popular music in the 1960s? Use information and specific details from the article to support your answer. What characteristics of folk music made it popular during the 1960s? Use information and specific details from the article to support your answer.

Revolutions Lesson Planner

LESSON	BEFORE READING	DURING READING	AFTER READING
LESSON 16 **A Revolution in Industry** (memoir) page 126	Anticipation Guide Vocabulary Preview Preview the Selection Make Predictions/Set Purpose	Monitor Understanding Inferential Thinking	Check Purpose Discussion Questions Writing: letter Vocabulary: synonyms and antonyms Phonics/Word Study: Latin roots
LESSON 17 **Sophie Germain: A Revolutionary Thinker** (biographical sketch) page 134	Make a Chart Vocabulary Preview Preview the Selection Make Predictions/ Set Purpose	Understanding Text Structure	Check Purpose Discussion Questions Writing: biographical sketch Vocabulary: context Phonics/Word Study: Latin roots
LESSON 18 **Senior Year** *and* **An Unexpected Revolution** (poem and short story) page 141	Poem: Senior Year Make a List Vocabulary Preview Preview the Selection Make Predictions/Set Purpose	Making Connections Understanding Text Structure	Check Purpose Discussion Questions Writing: book jacket Vocabulary: denotation and connotation Phonics/Word Study: Latin roots
LESSON 19 **On the Chase** (first-person account) page 152	Association Web Vocabulary Preview Preview the Selection Make Predictions/Set Purpose	Determining Importance Monitor Understanding	Check Purpose Discussion Questions Writing: journal entry Vocabulary: word relationships Phonics/Word Study: Latin roots
LESSON 20 **Revolutions in Style: Fashion Through the Ages** (article) page 160	Make a List Vocabulary Preview Preview the Selection Make Predictions/Set Purpose	Monitor Understanding Inferential Thinking	Check Purpose Discussion Questions Writing: comparison chart Vocabulary: prefixes Phonics/Word Study: Latin roots
LESSON 21 **The Little Rock Nine, 1957** (radio play) page 168	Concept Web Vocabulary Preview Preview the Selection Make Predictions/Set Purpose	Understanding Text Structure	Check Purpose Discussion Questions Writing: journal entry Vocabulary: context clues Phonics/Word Study: Latin roots
LESSON 22 **The Wheel: A Revolutionary Revolution** *and* **Freedom of Speech** (article and poem) page 174	Make a List Vocabulary Preview Preview the Selection Make Predictions/Set Purpose	Monitor Understanding Inferential Thinking	Check Purpose Discussion Questions Writing: notes for visualizing Vocabulary: concept ladder Phonics/Word Study: Latin roots

PHONICS/ WORD STUDY	FOCUS ON	ASSESSMENT	HIGHER-ORDER THINKING QUESTIONS
Latin Roots	Writing: chart Fluency: phrasing English Language Learners Independent Activity Options	Monitor Understanding Inferential Thinking Latin Roots	What image does Bill Miller convey about life in the factory for a child worker? Use information and specific details from the article to support your answer. Imagine you were Bill Miller. How would you persuade your aunt to keep a cousin down on the farm, instead of sending him to the city to live and work with you? Use information and specific details from the article to support your answer.
Latin Roots	Writing: obituary Fluency: pacing English Language Learners Independent Activity Options	Understanding Text Structure Latin Roots	What factors created problems for Sophie Germain's desire to study mathematics? Use information and specific details from the article to support your answer. What evidence does the author give to support the idea that Sophie Germain would study mathematics, no matter what? Use information and specific details from the article to support your answer.
Latin Roots	Writing: character portrait Fluency: expression English Language Learners Independent Activity Options	Making Connections Understanding Text Structure Latin Roots	Compare and contrast the choices facing Naomi and the poet in "Senior Year." Use information and specific details from the story and poem to support your answer. What conflicts does the author face in "An Unexpected Revolution"? Use information and specific details from the story and poem to support your answer.
Latin Roots	Writing: news story Fluency: expression English Language Learners Independent Activity Options	Determining Importance Monitor Understanding Latin Roots	What would you say to a friend to persuade him/her to chase a severe storm with you? Use information and specific details from the article to support your answer. How does the author's storm chasing equipment help his work as a storm spotter? Use information and specific details from the article to support your answer.
Latin Roots	Writing: persuasive paragraph Fluency: pacing English Language Learners Independent Activity Options	Monitor Understanding Inferential Thinking Latin Roots	Why have fashions changed through the ages? Use information and specific details from the article to support your answer. Compare the fashions of the middle ages and the 1800s. How are they similar? How are they different? Use information and specific details from the article to support your answer.
Latin Roots	Writing: short essay Fluency: expression English Language Learners Independent Activity Options	Understanding Text Structure Latin Roots	In 1957, what circumstances led to the integration of Little Rock High School? Use information and specific details from the article to support your answer. What evidence does the author supply that there was danger facing the Little Rock Nine? Use information and specific details from the article to support your answer.
Latin Roots	Writing: short essay Fluency: pacing English Language Learners Independent Activity Options	Monitor Understanding Inferential Thinking Latin Roots	Imagine you are a Segway sales person. How would you persuade a customer to make the purchase? Use information and specific details from the article to support your answer. What evidence does the author suggest to support the idea that life, as we know it, would not exist without the invention of the wheel? Use information and specific details from the article to support your answer.

LESSON **12**

Revolutions Big & Small

Revolutions, pages 2–7

SUMMARY

This is a **play** about how seemingly ordinary events or developments can have revolutionary effects on people's lives.

COMPREHENSION STRATEGIES

Making Connections
Monitor Understanding

WRITING

Personal Response

VOCABULARY

Suffix *-able/-ible*

PHONICS/WORD STUDY

Latin Roots *tract, spect/spec/spic, port*

Lesson Vocabulary

Communists	coup
hullabaloo	minimum
disposable	

MATERIALS

Revolutions, pp. 2–7
Student Journal, pp. 40–42
Word Study Manual, p. 45
Writing Advantage, pp. 170–181

Before Reading

Use one or more activities.

Make a List

Introduce the subject of revolutions. Tell students that revolutions are not solely wars. A revolution can be a change that affects how we live our lives. Ask students what recent events or objects have made a difference in the way people live today. Record their responses in a list. You can start the list by writing *laptop computers,* which make it possible for people to work just about anywhere. Add students' suggestions to the list.

Everyday Revolutions
1. laptop computers
2. microwave ovens
3.

Vocabulary Preview

List the selection vocabulary on an overhead transparency or on the board. Assess prior knowledge by asking students to begin the predictions chart on *Student Journal* page 40. Model the process of predicting, using the word *Communist.* Students will finish the chart after reading.

CAST

Joan

Latrice

Jamal

Salvador

Mr. Washington, history teacher

Grandma, Latrice's grandmother

Grandpa, Jamal's great-grandfather

SCENE I

Busy school hallway. Students gather around their lockers before the last class on the first day of school.

(Lights come up on two senior girls.)

JOAN: How was your morning, Latrice?

LATRICE: Okay, I guess. We spent so much time in homeroom, though, that the rest of the day went by in a blur.

JOAN: I'm just glad we have late lunch this year. One class after lunch, and then we're out. Here come Jamal and Salvador.

JAMAL: I can't believe you guys haven't been in any of my classes.

LATRICE: Well, we all have this last class together.

SALVADOR: What a stupid class—twentieth-century revolutions. Can't these teachers be more inspired?

JOAN: It might be fun. Anyway, at least we have Mr. Washington and not Ms. Ellis.

JAMAL: Amen.

(The bell rings, and the students walk into the classroom.)

MR. WASHINGTON: Good afternoon. Everyone, take a seat and we'll get started. I'm passing around a class outline. Make sure you get a copy. Yes, Salvador?

SALVADOR: *(putting his hand down, staring at the outline)* You mean we have to give a presentation *tomorrow?*

MR. WASHINGTON: You've skipped ahead. But, yes. Don't worry. It's just a first draft interview that you'll conduct with an older family member or friend.

JAMAL: I thought this class was about revolutions.

MR. WASHINGTON: It is. I want you to get a first-hand account of a revolution that touched an older relative or friend.

LATRICE: Nobody in my family was ever in a war.

MR. WASHINGTON: That's OK, Latrice. I want to broaden your idea of what makes a revolution. Sure, a revolution can be a war, but it can also be other things. I guarantee—if you take half an hour to sit down with an older person, you'll hear about a revolution. Questions?

(Classroom darkens. Students slump in their seats, and Mr. Washington's voice fades.)

DIFFERENTIATED INSTRUCTION SMALL GROUP

Preview the Selection

Use these strategies to familiarize students with the genre of this selection.

1. Ask students if they have ever acted in or seen a play. Explain that in a drama, the story is told through dialogue, or what people say to each other.
2. Discuss the stage directions. Model the way these directions help you visualize, or picture in your mind, the way the drama might look on a stage.
3. You may want to compare the scenes of a play with the chapters of a book; scenes divide the play into sections.

Student Journal page 40

Name ______________ Date ________

Building Vocabulary: Predictions

How do you think these words will be used in "Revolutions: Big and Small"? Write your answers in the second column. Next, read the article. Then, clarify your answers in the third column.

Word	My prediction for how the word will be used	How the word was actually used
Communist		
hullabaloo		
disposable		
coup		
minimum		

© Great Source. Copying is permitted; see page ii.

40 Revolutions • Revolutions: Big and Small

Preview the Selection

Have students look through the six pages of the play, pages 2–7 in the magazine. Use these or similar prompts to guide students to notice the important features of the text.

- What did you notice first about the arrangement of the selection text?
- What do you think the selection will be about?
- Do you think the selection is fiction or nonfiction? Why?

(See Differentiated Instruction.)

Teacher Think Aloud

I know that revolutions are usually major events. I wonder what a small revolution would be. As I flip through the play, I see pictures of both a TV dinner and a man at a typewriter. What do they have to do with revolutions? I'll read the play to find out.

Make Predictions/ Set Purpose

Students should use the information gathered in previewing the selection to make some predictions about what will happen in the play. To help students set a purpose, suggest that they read to learn more about revolutions and how they affect people's lives.

DIFFERENTIATED INSTRUCTION

Comprehension

MAKING CONNECTIONS

Use the following examples to make connections.

1. Say: *Does any of this sound familiar to me? Yes. I remember my great-aunt talking about the Depression in the 1930s. She would talk about all the people who had no jobs. Those were pretty bad days.*
2. Ask volunteers to respond to the same question.

SCENE II

Latrice's kitchen after dinner. She's sitting at the table, staring at a blank sheet of paper.

LATRICE: How am I ever going to start this project? *(She taps her pencil, gets up, opens the refrigerator, closes it. Looks out the window. Sits back down.)* Mom! I'm calling Grandma. *(Latrice picks up the telephone and calls her grandmother.)* Grandma? Hi, it's me, Latrice.

(Lights come up on another corner of the stage. Latrice's grandmother is seated, holding the phone to her ear.)

GRANDMA: Hello, dear. Is everything all right?

LATRICE: Yes. I'm just calling because I have this school project, and I'm supposed to ask you a question.

GRANDMA: Splendid. I hope I have the right answer. Go ahead, dear.

LATRICE: Well...uh...so, what was a revolution in your life?

GRANDMA: In what sense?

LATRICE: I don't know, Grandma. That's the question.

GRANDMA: That's a wide-open question, isn't it? Hmmm . . . I'd have to say that the frozen dinner was a revolution in my life.

LATRICE: What? Can't you think of something else?

GRANDMA: Oh, I remember it well. It was the mid-1950s. Your grandfather and I both worked. I'd rush home from the drugstore every night to try to get a meal on the table by 6:30. That wasn't easy. So, I would buy frozen dinners: turkey, cornbread dressing and gravy, butter peas, and sweet potatoes. When I was tired or late, those meals saved the day. Plus, the food was packaged on an aluminum tray. I could heat and serve the meals right in the trays. No dishes to clean! It really revolutionized my life, sweetheart.

LATRICE: But how?

GRANDMA: Think about it, Latrice. I was no longer a slave to the grocery store, the kitchen, or my husband's stomach. I could work later, earn extra money, and have energy after dinner to read or go out. Frozen food really changed women's lives.

LATRICE: Thanks, Grandma.

GRANDMA: Sure, dear. Let me know how the project goes.

(Lights dim on Latrice as she starts writing.)

During Reading

Comprehension

MAKING CONNECTIONS

Use these questions to model making connections. Then have students make their own connections with the text.

- What does the play remind me of?
- Have I had any similar experiences?
- Does it remind me of anything else I have read?

(See Differentiated Instruction.)

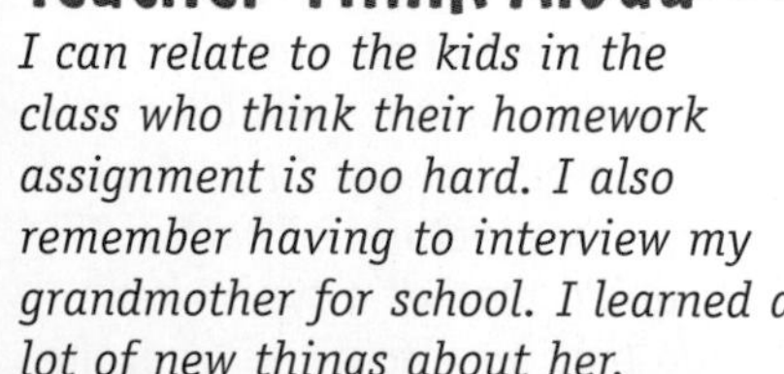

Teacher Think Aloud

I can relate to the kids in the class who think their homework assignment is too hard. I also remember having to interview my grandmother for school. I learned a lot of new things about her.

Comprehension

MONITOR UNDERSTANDING

Use these questions to model for students how to visualize what they read. Then have students tell about a part they visualized.

- What happens in each scene?
- Which revolution can I visualize the best?
- What strong images do I "see?"

SCENE III

Lights rise on Jamal at home in his room.

JAMAL: I don't know how I'm going to do this project. My grandparents weren't revolutionary at all. *(Jamal walks down the hall and knocks on his great grandfather's bedroom door.)* Grandpa, may I come in?

GRANDPA: Sure, Jamal. Switch on the light.

JAMAL: I didn't mean to wake you...

GRANDPA: No, no. I was just resting my eyes. I've been reading *Native Son.* Have you ever read that book?

JAMAL: Uh, no. Gramps? I have this project for school, and it's really stupid. I'm supposed to ask you about a revolution in your life.

(Grandpa smiles, takes off his glasses and rubs his eyes.)

GRANDPA: Sit down. Let me see. I was living in Arizona, and I think the year was 1938. Those were tough times. The country was in the middle of the Great Depression. Like everyone else, I was having a hard time finding work. I wanted to marry your great-grandmother, but I was too embarrassed to ask. You see, I couldn't support her. That's when I heard about the WPA.

JAMAL: What's that?

GRANDPA: President Franklin Delano Roosevelt had this great idea to start a program that would put people to work. It was called the Works Project Administration, or WPA. Out-of-work people began building skyscrapers, bridges, and stadiums. Roosevelt's plan also helped the more creative types. Part of the WPA was the Federal Writer's Project, or the FWP. When I heard about the FWP, I went to the office and was hired as one of the Arizona Guide Book writers. My job was to document all kinds of information about Arizona—travel, place names, folklore, and zoology. Why, there's a copy of my book downstairs. Have you ever looked through it?

JAMAL: Sorry, Gramps. I didn't know you were a writer. I thought you were an accountant.

GRANDPA: Oh, I was. But before that, the FWP gave me a chance to travel around the state. And do you know, it paid over 6,700 writers? It started the careers of some famous writers—people like Zora Neale Hurston, Saul Bellow, and Richard Wright. He's the gentleman who wrote that book I was reading before you came in.

Teacher Think Aloud

In my mind, I can see a TV dinner like the one Latrice's grandmother talked about. I ate them when I was young, and I remember the shiny aluminum trays. Now, frozen dinners usually come in plastic trays because you can't put aluminum in the microwave. Microwave ovens weren't around in the 1950s.

Fix-Up Strategies

Offer these strategies to help students read independently.

If you don't understand what you're reading:

- Reread the difficult section to look for clues to help you comprehend.
- Read ahead to find clues to help you comprehend.
- Retell, or say in your own words, what you've read.
- Visualize, or form mental pictures of, what you've read.

If you don't understand a word:

- Reread the sentence. Look for ideas and words that provide meaning clues.
- Find clues by reading a few sentences before and after the confusing word.
- Look for the base or root word and think about its meaning.
- Think about the topic or plot at this point to see if either offers meaning clues.

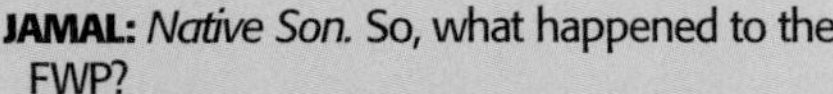

DIFFERENTIATED INSTRUCTION SMALL GROUP

Vocabulary Suffix

-able/-ible

Use these strategies to help students understand variations of the suffix.

1. Display the word *lovable*. Tell students it means "able to be loved." Explain that *-able* is a suffix, or word part added to the end of a word to change its meaning. Adding *-able* changes the meaning to include "able to be."
2. Now write *shrinkable, scratchable, believable,* and *edible*. Ask volunteers to define the first three words. Point to *edible* and explain that *-ible* and *-able* have the same meaning.

Student Journal page 41

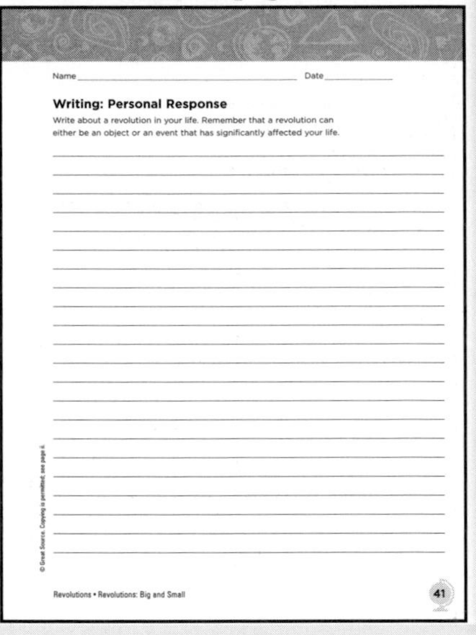

Name ______________ Date ______

Writing: Personal Response

Write about a revolution in your life. Remember that a revolution can either be an object or an event that has significantly affected your life.

© Great Source. Copying is permitted; see page ii.

Revolutions • Revolutions: Big and Small 41

JAMAL: *Native Son.* So, what happened to the FWP?

GRANDPA: It was an odd time in America, Jamal. I suppose because the project was so successful, people became jealous and suspicious and accused us of being Communists. Soon, no one would take part in my interviews. For a long time, I wouldn't admit that I ever worked for the FWP because of the hullabaloo. I rarely bring it up now.

JAMAL: But the WPA and FWP gave a lot of people jobs?

GRANDPA: Oh, yes. It truly was a revolution for workers. It gave millions of people jobs and helped the country get out of the Depression.

JAMAL: Cool. I never knew you were part of something so important.

SCENE IV

Mr. Washington's classroom, before class.

LATRICE: Guys, you are not going to believe what my grandmother said!

JAMAL: I will. I had no idea my great-grandfather was so cool.

JOAN: My great-uncle went on and on about plastics and how we use them to keep food fresh, how medicine has improved with disposable needles and blood bags, how plastic bottles are so much safer than the old glass ones.

LATRICE: I never thought about that. A lot of the parts inside of a car are made out of plastic, not to mention your football equipment, right, Salvador?

SALVADOR: True. Plastics must have really transformed the world. My grandfather talked about the coup in Argentina against the dictator, Ramon Castillo, in the 1940s. Until then, a strict government had ruled Argentina. The people had no voice. Then the army took over, but the new government was just as bad as the old one. It wasn't until Juan Peron rose to power that Argentina changed. Peron believed in unions, minimum wages, and fair treatment of workers.

LATRICE: Like in the movie *Evita*, right?

SALVADOR: Yes, Evita was his wife. Grandpa said Peron improved life in Argentina. The economy grew, and for the first time, everyone got paid vacations and free medical care. They built orphanages, schools, and homes for the elderly. Life improved 100 percent. It was during this time that Grandpa and his brother raised enough money to come to America.

MR. WASHINGTON: Class, let's begin. The twentieth century was a time of change. Perhaps no other century has seen so many advances...

(Lights fade on class taking notes.) ◆

After Reading

WHOLE CLASS Use one or more activities.

Check Purpose

Have students decide if their purpose was met. Did students learn about revolutions and how they affect people's lives?

Discussion Questions

Continue the group discussion with the following questions.

1. What do you think is the author's purpose in "Revolutions Big & Small"? (Inferential Thinking)
2. How does plastic affect your life? (Making Connections)
3. What led to the development of frozen dinners? (Monitor Understanding)

Revisit: Predictions Chart

Have students return to the predictions chart on *Student Journal* page 40. Students should complete the third column of the chart. How were the words actually used?

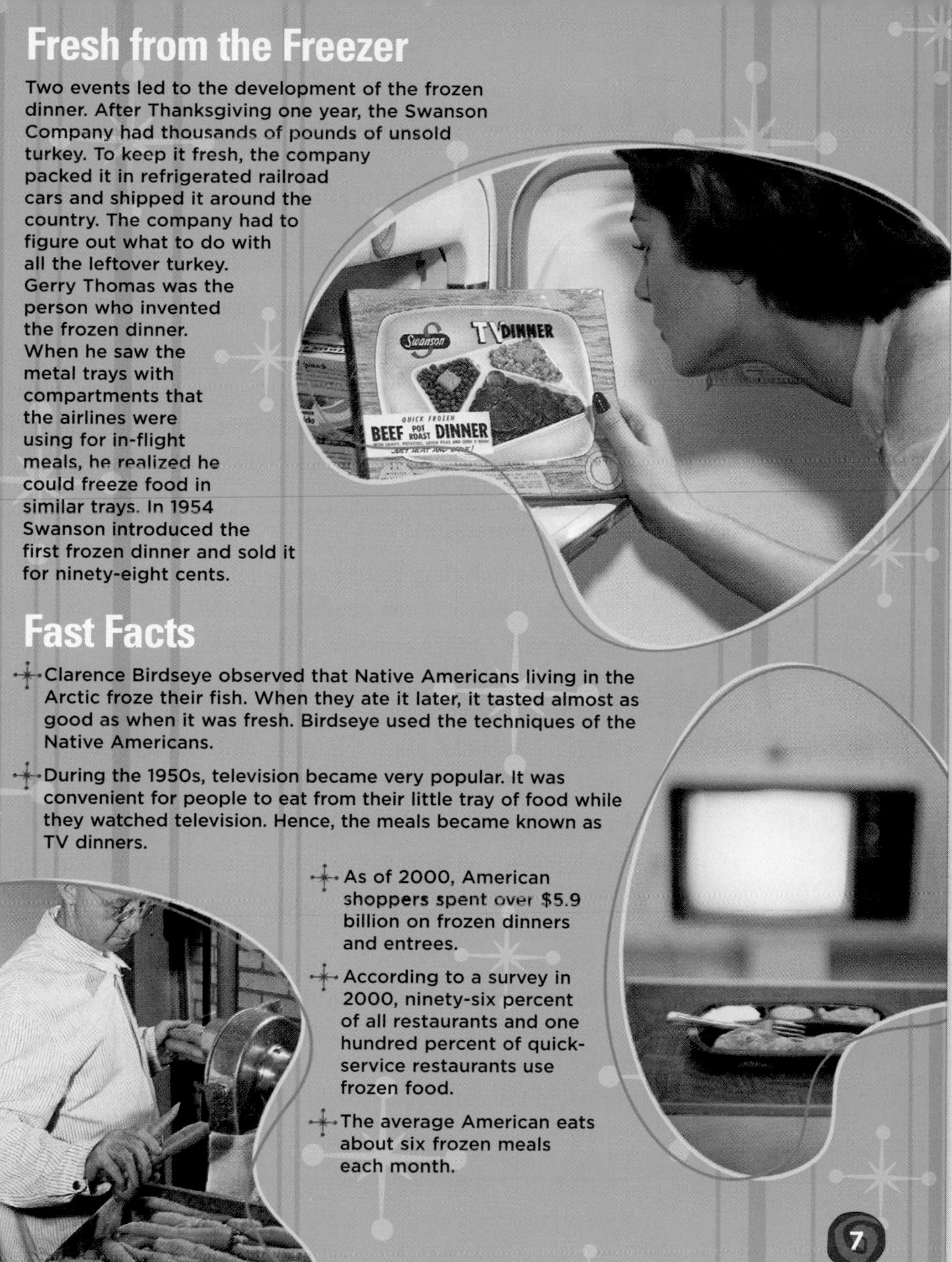

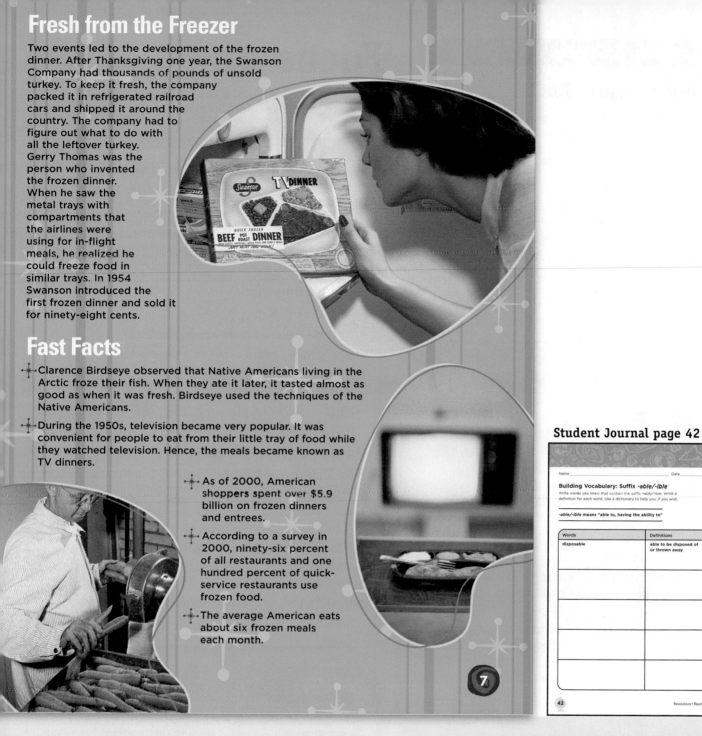

Fresh from the Freezer

Two events led to the development of the frozen dinner. After Thanksgiving one year, the Swanson Company had thousands of pounds of unsold turkey. To keep it fresh, the company packed it in refrigerated railroad cars and shipped it around the country. The company had to figure out what to do with all the leftover turkey. Gerry Thomas was the person who invented the frozen dinner. When he saw the metal trays with compartments that the airlines were using for in-flight meals, he realized he could freeze food in similar trays. In 1954 Swanson introduced the first frozen dinner and sold it for ninety-eight cents.

Fast Facts

- Clarence Birdseye observed that Native Americans living in the Arctic froze their fish. When they ate it later, it tasted almost as good as when it was fresh. Birdseye used the techniques of the Native Americans.
- During the 1950s, television became very popular. It was convenient for people to eat from their little tray of food while they watched television. Hence, the meals became known as TV dinners.
- As of 2000, American shoppers spent over $5.9 billion on frozen dinners and entrees.
- According to a survey in 2000, ninety-six percent of all restaurants and one hundred percent of quick-service restaurants use frozen food.
- The average American eats about six frozen meals each month.

7

Student Journal page 42

Name ______ Date ______

Building Vocabulary: Suffix *-able/-ible*

Write words you know that contain the suffix *-able/-ible*. Write a definition for each word. Use a dictionary to help you, if you wish.

***-able/-ible* means "able to, having the ability to"**

Words	Definitions
disposable	able to be disposed of or thrown away

42 Revolutions • Revolutions: Big and Small

Writing Personal Response

Tell students that they will each write about a revolution in their life. Before they write, have them brainstorm a list of things or events that have made a significant difference in their life, and share their lists in small groups. Then have students complete the personal response writing activity on *Student Journal* page 41.

Vocabulary Suffix *-able/-ible*

Ask: *What are* disposable *things*? Explain that the word *disposable* is made up of the word *dispose* and the suffix *-able*. The suffix *-able* and its variant form *-ible* mean "able to, having the ability to." *Dispose* means "throw away, put away," so *disposable* means "able to be disposed of, or thrown away."

Have partners work to complete the suffix chart on *Student Journal* page 42. (See Differentiated Instruction.)

Phonics/Word Study

Latin Roots

Write these words on the board: *script, describe, scribble*. Ask partners to discuss what these words have in common. (a syllable or root) Then write the Latin root *scrip, scrib* on the board. Explain that the root means "to write." Ask volunteers to explain how the meaning of each word is related to the Latin. Now, work with students to complete the in-depth Latin roots activity on TE page 102.

Phonics/Word Study

Introducing Latin Roots

- Introduce the root that you are teaching by offering a few words that contain that root. Discuss the words to see if students can define them. Discussion of each word should trigger some ideas as to what the root means.
- Ask what the words have in common. Through the processes of deduction and association, students should discover the meaning of the root.
- Ask students to identify other words with the same root. You can find word sorts in the *Word Study Manual* that will help students "see" the connections. (See *Word Study Manual* page 45 for a sort with *tract*, *spect/spec/spic*, and *port*.)
- Have students create a roots section in their Word Study notebooks. They should begin collecting words with each root they study.

tract **(to pull)**

Use the directions above to explore this root with students. Have students consider the word *tractor*.

abstract	subtract	distract
attract	traction	detract
extract	tractor	retract
protract	contract	

spect/spec/spic **(to see)**

Explain that the prefix *retro-* means "backward." The phrase *in retrospect* means "a look backward."

aspect	inspector	prospect	respect
circumspect	introspection	retrospect	specimen
suspect	perspective	spectacle	spectator

port **(to carry)**

export	important	transport
import	portable	report
deport	porter	deportment

Discovering the Roots

tract	*spect*	*port*
attract	spectacles	portable
extract	inspect	transport
retract	respect	portage
subtract	perspective	import
tractor	suspect	export

For more information on word sorts and spelling stages, see pages 5–31 in the *Word Study Manual*.

Focus on . . .

Use one or more activities in this section to focus on a particular area of need in your students.

Comprehension STRATEGY SUPPORT

To help those students who need more practice using the strategies covered in this lesson, work one-on-one or in small groups to apply the strategy prompts below. Apply the prompts to a *Reading Advantage* paperback, a classroom library book, or a new or familiar selection in the magazine. Always model your own thinking first.

Making Connections

- What does this story (article, passage) remind me of?
- What do I already know about this topic?
- Where have I heard about this topic before?
- What do I have in common with the characters, people, or situations in the text?
- What other books, stories, articles, movies, or TV shows does this text make me think about?

Monitor Understanding

- Do I understand what I'm reading? If not, what part is confusing to me?
- What fix-up strategies can I use to solve the problem? (See During Reading for fix-up strategies.)
- Why did a character say (do, think, ask) that?
- What images do I visualize from the text? What parts can't I visualize?
- Why did the author include (or not include) those details?

Writing Double-Entry Journal

Have students make double-entry journal notes about "Revolutions Big & Small." Display the headings for a double-entry journal chart. Have students look back through the article to find passages and big ideas that were interesting or important to them. In the first column, students should write quotations from the article and in the second column, why each entry is important to them personally. (See TE page 380 for a double-entry journal BLM.)

Double-Entry Journal

Quotations	My Thoughts and Feelings

For more instruction on looking back to the text and taking notes, see lessons in *Writing Advantage*, pages 170–181.

Fluency: Punctuation

After students have read the selection at least once, have them form groups to read aloud parts of the play. As you listen to students read, use these prompts to guide them.

- Preview what you will read. Notice the different punctuation marks and what they signal to you. Pause at commas and periods. Let your voice rise at the end of sentences marked with a question mark. Put excitement in your voice when exclamation marks are present.
- Read with expression. Put yourself in the situation of the character. How would a frustrated teenager sound? How would reminiscent grandparents sound? Point out the stage direction instructions for each character.

When students read aloud, do they—

✓ demonstrate appropriate meaning and usage of punctuation marks?

✓ incorporate appropriate timing, stress, and intonation?

✓ exhibit well-timed pauses between words and phrases?

English Language Learners

To support students' understanding of word formation, examine the effect of adding the prefix *un-* to words containing the suffix *-able/-ible*.

1. Remind students that adding *-able/-ible* to a word changes the meaning to include the notion of "able to be" or that "it can be."
2. Explain that adding the prefix *un-* to a word changes the meaning to include the notion of "not."
3. Brainstorm several examples with the group (*unlovable, unobtainable*). Discuss each word.

Independent Activity Options

While you work with individuals or small groups, others can work independently on one or more of the following options.

- Level D paperback books, see TE pages 367–372
- Level D *eZines*
- Repeat word sorts from this lesson
- *Student Journal* pages for this lesson
- *Writing Advantage* independent lessons

Assessment

Strategy Assessment

To help you and your students assess their use of comprehension strategies, ask the following questions. Students can complete a written response or provide verbal answers in a one-on-one reading conference.

1. **Making Connections** In what ways did you make connections with this play? Explain. (Answers will vary, but possible connections include having to interview someone for an assignment, eating a TV dinner, reading an article about the Great Depression, using plastic items.)
2. **Monitor Understanding** What parts of the play did you visualize well? (Answers will vary.)

For ongoing informal assessment, use the checklists on pages 61–64 of *Level D Assessment*.

Word Study Assessment

Use these steps to help you and your students assess their understanding of Latin roots.

1. Present the chart below. Read the roots and words aloud.
2. Have students explain how the meaning of each word is related to the root.

tract "to pull"	*spect/spec/spic* "to see"	*port* "to carry"
tractor	inspector	portable
extract	spectacle	transport
subtract	spectator	important

LESSON **13**

Letters of Revolution *and* At a Surrealist Show

Revolutions, pages 8–13

SUMMARY

Three **letters** tell about revolutions. A **poem** follows.

COMPREHENSION STRATEGIES

Inferential Thinking
Making Connections

WRITING

Letter

VOCABULARY

Context

PHONICS/WORD STUDY

Latin Roots *dict, rupt, scrib/script*

Lesson Vocabulary

eligible, accurate, disperse, contradicted, coerced

MATERIALS

Revolutions, pp. 8–13
Student Journal, pp. 43–45
Word Study Manual, p. 46
Writing Advantage, pp. 8–12

Letters of Revolution

It takes vision and bravery to try to make changes in society. The following letters record the thoughts and actions of three people who prompted changes in politics, science, and culture.

Marion, Alabama
March 10, 1965

Dear Uncle Charles,

I don't know when this letter will reach you in Chicago, but I feel as if I need to write you now. Perhaps you've heard about the sit-ins at the lunch counters in Nashville and Greensboro, North Carolina. College students, led by James Lawson and Diane Nash, are strong-minded. After the sit-ins, the mayor of Nashville even admitted that segregation—separating different races of people—was wrong. Those lunch counters began to serve both black and white people. I thought that event was the beginning of change, but what happened this past Sunday really shocked me.

All winter I volunteered for a group trying to register blacks to vote. I worked for no money, and it was a dangerous job. Some volunteers were arrested and jailed; some disappeared. But everything exploded when a police officer killed a peaceful demonstrator here in Marion. The people in town held a meeting and decided to march on Sunday, March 7, from Selma, Alabama, to Montgomery, Alabama, to protest the violence. At the state capital, we planned to meet Governor George Wallace to tell him that we were upset and we wanted to register blacks to vote.

8

Before Reading  Use one or more activities.

Begin Three Concept Webs

Write the words *civil rights*, *Galileo*, and *Sri Lanka* in three different ovals on the board. Then begin a brief discussion about what students know about these subjects. Add notes to the webs as students respond. Tell students that after reading the letters, they will come back to the webs to add any new information they learn while reading. (See Differentiated Instruction.)

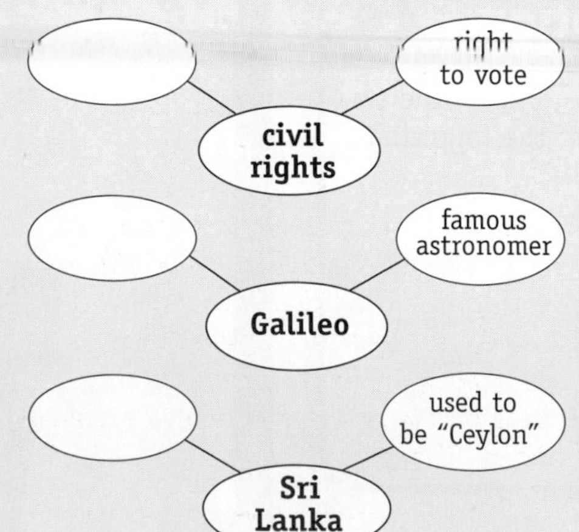

Vocabulary Preview

Display the selection vocabulary. Discuss any associations students have with the words. What do students know about the words? Where have they heard them used before? Students can write their thoughts in the associations activity on *Student Journal* page 43. Model the process using the word *disperse*.

The Right to Vote

In 1965, 15,000 African Americans were eligible to vote in Selma, Alabama, but only 355 were registered. Southern blacks faced many difficulties:

- They were often told that they could not register.
- Voter registration offices were open only a few hours each month.
- Only a small number of applications would be sorted each month.
- When blacks came to register, office workers took lunch breaks and refused to return to work.

Dr. Martin Luther King, Jr., agreed to lead our protest march. Governor Wallace refused to let us march. Dr. King went to Washington to talk to President Johnson. He told us not to march until he returned. People were too upset to listen, though, and the march went on as planned. I was nervous, but I joined in.

At the bridge marking the Selma city line, a large group of state police was waiting for us. They yelled at us to disperse. But they didn't give us any time to leave. Instead, they sprayed us with tear gas and hit us with sticks. Then they chased us to a housing project, where they kept on beating us. They even beat people who lived in the project and hadn't even been marching!

Dr. King announced that he would lead another march approved by President Johnson on March 25. But Uncle Charles, many people are hurt and in jail. They didn't do anything wrong. I don't understand why they ended up behind bars. It's so unfair. This was the bloodiest Sunday you could ever imagine.

Your niece,

Deborah

Bloody Sunday

African Americans were angry because they couldn't register to vote. Their anger led to protest marches in the South. One particularly violent march occurred on March 7, 1965, in Selma, Alabama. This date became known as Bloody Sunday because of the many injuries suffered by the marchers. The news media picked up the story of the Selma march. President Lyndon Johnson was deeply moved by the situation. He gave a speech to Congress expressing his strong support for civil rights. This speech convinced Congress to pass the Voting Rights Act, which eased the difficulties southern blacks had faced in registering to vote.

9

DIFFERENTIATED INSTRUCTION

BEGIN THREE CONCEPT WEBS

To help students get started on the concept webs, discuss the following information.

1. Civil rights are privileges that American citizens have by law—for example, the right to vote.
2. Galileo was an astronomer who improved the telescope.
3. Sri Lanka is an island country near the coast of southern India. It used to be called Ceylon.

Student Journal page 43

Name ______ Date ______

Building Vocabulary: Making Associations

Pick two words from the vocabulary list below. Think about what you already know about each word. Then answer the following questions for each word.

eligible coerced contradicted
disperse accurate

Word ______

What do you think about when you read this word? ______

Who might use this word? ______

What do you already know about this word? ______

Word ______

What do you think about when you read this word? ______

Who might use this word? ______

What do you already know about this word? ______

Now watch for these words in the magazine selection. Were you on the right track?

© Great Source. Copying is permitted; see page ii.

Revolutions • Letters of Revolution 43

Preview the Selection

Have students read the title. Ask a volunteer to read the head note. Have students skim the letters on pages 8–11. Use these or similar prompts to orient students.

- What information does the title give you?
- What does the head note tell you?
- How is the selection organized?

Teacher Think Aloud

As I scan the selection, I see what look like friendly letters. I love to read letters! I wonder who's writing these letters, and what they have to say about revolutions. When I read the blurb under the title, I see that I will read letters by three different people. I wonder if I will have heard of any of these people or the events they write about. I'll read to find out.

Make Predictions/ Set Purpose

Students should use the information gathered in previewing the selection to make some predictions about what they will learn from the letters. To help students set a purpose for reading, suggest that they read to learn more about the way revolutions changed people's thinking and lives.

DIFFERENTIATED INSTRUCTION 

Comprehension

INFERENTIAL THINKING

To help students understand how to make inferences, use the following questions about the second letter.

- What did Galileo say about the earth and the sun? (He said the earth revolved around the sun.)
- How did the Catholic Church feel about Galileo? (The Church thought his idea was against their religion.)
- What can you say about science and religion during the time of Galileo? (Answers will vary.)

Florence, Italy 1633

My Dear Friend,

First, I would like to thank you for your kind words about the telescope that I built. It was quite a thrill for me to discover the four moons of Jupiter. I know the sights of the sky will amaze you, too.

Perhaps you are confused as to why I am writing you from Florence and not Rome. I'm afraid that I have upsetting news to share. I'm in deep trouble with the Catholic Church. It has found me guilty of heresy, of opposing church beliefs. They've banished me from Rome to my home in Florence. Here, I am under house arrest for the rest of my life. I suppose I am lucky, for this was a light sentence. I could have been tortured or even put to death. Thank God I am alive! The trouble began when I said that I believed in the Copernican system. According to this system, the Sun is the center of our solar system, not Earth. The church doesn't like this theory and considers it heretical, or an insult to the religion. I have been coerced, or forced, into softening my support for the Copernican system. What else can I do under this kind of pressure?

I'm afraid that my eyesight is failing, and I will become totally blind. Therefore, this will probably be my last letter.

Yours truly,
Galileo Galilei

Galileo

Galileo Galilei (1564-1642) was an Italian astronomer and physicist. During his career as a university professor, Galileo taught astronomy courses. To prepare for his teaching, Galileo studied Greek astronomer Ptolemy's theory that the Sun and planets revolved around Earth. As he studied, Galileo began to question this theory. He became convinced that a Polish astronomer, Copernicus, had a more accurate theory. Copernicus thought that Earth and the other planets revolved around the Sun. This was different from what people had believed for many years. It was, truly, a revolutionary idea. Galileo's work with telescopes—building and improving them—helped him support this theory. When he published his ideas, the Catholic Church was not pleased. The church felt that the Copernican theory contradicted church teachings.

10

During Reading

Comprehension

INFERENTIAL THINKING

Use these questions to model how to think inferentially. Then have students make their own inferences.

- What do I learn about the writers of the letters?
- In what ways are the writers similar to each other?
- What conclusions can I draw about the events in each letter?

(See Differentiated Instruction.)

Teacher Think Aloud

When I read the first letter, I think about the writer, Deborah, and what kind of person she is. I learn that she worked hard to get blacks to register to vote. This was a dangerous job, and she did it for no money. Deborah must be a very brave person who believes strongly in the right of all citizens to vote. She is willing to work for a cause that she thinks is right.

Comprehension 

MAKING CONNECTIONS

Use these questions to model making connections. Then have students make their own connections to the text.

- What letters do I like the best? Why?
- Do I already know anything about the information in the letters?
- What do I think of people who take stands on issues?

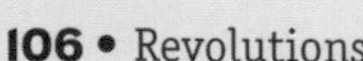

Colombo, 1557

Dear Uncle,

I am writing to update you on the next shipment of spices. First, let me reassure you that the Portuguese people who have settled in Colombo are doing quite well. Since there are more Portuguese men traveling here than women, many of my brothers have married Asian women from this island. We are all very excited at the hope of forming a new, large Portuguese country. After all, Portugal is so small. The intermarriage experience seems to be a success so far: the children of these marriages speak Portuguese, are Catholic, and adjust easily to the steamy, tropical conditions here.

I often heard my grandfather tell me stories of when you and he arrived in Sri Lanka in 1505 with the first group of ships. How exciting it must have been to sail with Vasco De Gama! You and your fellow sailors made a clever decision. By moving beyond the spice trade and helping the local kings, we Portuguese set ourselves up as rulers. We were able to take control of the coast after agreeing to help the kings. It wasn't hard for our trained sailors to protect Sri Lanka from hostile, unfriendly attackers. And all in exchange for some spices!

In the next shipment, please look for a large supply of cinnamon, ginger, nutmeg, and pepper. You should be able to sell the spices for plenty of money.

Your great nephew,
Marcus

Sri Lanka

King Manuel I of Portugal sent a fleet of ships led by Vasco de Gama around the tip of Africa to find India. The king wanted to control a sea route to India so he could import spices cheaply. (He would later sell the spices for a higher price.) As a result, the Portuguese ruled the island now known as Sri Lanka from the end of the 1500s until the Dutch took control in 1656. In 1796, British forces captured the island. They made the island the crown colony of Ceylon in 1802. After 450 years of European rule, Ceylon became an independent nation in 1948. Cinnamon and pepper are still chief products of Sri Lanka, just as they were more than 400 years ago. Sri Lanka is also the third largest grower of tea (after China and India). Colombo is the capital of modern-day Sri Lanka.

11

Teacher Think Aloud

I liked the letter about civil rights the best. I related most to the writer—I thought she was a really strong person, and I think I'm a strong person. I also know more about the civil rights movement than I do about Galileo or Sri Lanka, so that first letter was the most meaningful to me.

Fix-Up Strategies

Offer these strategies to help students read independently.

If you don't understand what you're reading:

- Reread the difficult section to look for clues to help you comprehend.
- Read ahead to find clues to help you comprehend.
- Retell, or say in your own words, what you've read.
- Visualize, or form mental pictures of, what you've read.

If you don't understand a word:

- Reread the sentence. Look for ideas and words that provide meaning clues.
- Find clues by reading a few sentences before and after the confusing word.
- Look for the base or root word and think about its meaning.
- Think about the topic or plot at this point to see if either offers meaning clues.

DIFFERENTIATED INSTRUCTION
DISCUSSION QUESTIONS

To provide help with Discussion Question 1, guide students with the following information.

- A letter writer might write his or her opinions about the event. A journalist would strive to be objective.
- A letter writer might write about what he or she saw or experienced. A journalist might interview several witnesses to or participants in the event.

Student Journal page 44

Name________________ Date__________

Writing: Letter from Uncle Charles

Write a letter that Uncle Charles might write to Deborah, addressing her feelings about unfairness. Be sure to include the date, the place he is writing from, a salutation, a body, and a closing.

44 Revolutions • Letters of Revolution

after Paysage Catalan
(Le Chasseur, 1923) by Joan Miró

Beetle people bare down
to feel their insides itching.
They cry *eeee* until their lips stiffen,
straighten into charcoal lines
as thin as their legs – (they only have two).

Black holes pop up, circled
by a yellow brighter than a bumblebee's.
No one worries.
Right now it's key to focus
above their heads, where
hairs drip oil into new eyes,
watery cells, tinted iris-violet.

And soon, with two more pupils,
you will be able to see this all more clearly.

After Reading

Use one or more activities.

Check Purpose

Have students decide if their purpose was met. Did they learn more about how revolutions changed people's thinking and lives? Were they able to learn more about civil rights, Galileo, and Sri Lanka?

Discussion Questions

Continue the group discussion with the following questions.

1. How might a letter writer and a newspaper journalist write about the same public event? (Inferential Thinking)
2. Do you think it's ever right to break the law? (Making Connections)
3. How was each letter writer brave? (Compare-Contrast)

(See Differentiated Instruction.)

Revisit: Concept Webs

Revisit the concept webs that students began before reading the selection. What new information can students add to each web?

Revisit: Associations Activity

Return to the associations activity on *Student Journal* page 43. Have students add or revise any information they wish. Ask for volunteers to share some of their responses.

ealist
Show

Surrealism was a revolutionary movement in art that took place between World War I and World War II. It was a reaction against art that showed things in a realistic way. Some called Surrealism "anti-art." Many Surrealist painters played with colors and shapes, and placed objects together in new, unexpected ways. The Surrealists used their art to show feelings and images found in dreams.

13

Poem: At a Surrealist Show

Explain to students that the title of the poem "At a Surrealist Show" may refer to a gallery or museum exhibit of surrealist paintings. Have students read the poem silently. Then read the poem aloud as students follow along. If needed, use these prompts to guide students.

- What is "surrealism"?
- What does the poem make you visualize?
- What does the poem "say" to you?
- Do you like or dislike the poem? Why?

Student Journal page 45

Name ______ Date ______

Building Vocabulary: Context

Use your knowledge of the word *eligible* to answer the questions below. Ask a friend or consult the internet if you need more information.

eligible (adjective) means "qualified to be chosen or to participate"

1. Who is eligible to get a driver's license in the United States? ______
2. Who is eligible to vote in the United States? ______
3. Who is eligible to go to college in the United States? ______
4. Who is eligible to become President of the United States? ______
5. Who is eligible to be on a trial jury in your state? ______

Revolutions • Letters of Revolution 45

Writing Letter

Read these sentences from Deborah's letter: *But Uncle Charles, many people are hurt and in jail. They didn't do anything wrong. I don't understand why they ended up behind bars. It's so unfair.* Discuss what Deborah is feeling (anger and dismay) and how her Uncle Charles might respond. Make a list of students' ideas. Then have students write a letter from Uncle Charles to Deborah addressing her feelings. Have students complete the letter on *Student Journal* page 44.

Vocabulary Context

Display and discuss the word *eligible.* Ask:

- How is this word used in the selection? (*In 1965, 15,000 African Americans were eligible to vote . . .*)
- What is the meaning of the word? (qualified to participate)
- What else do you know about the word? Where else might it be used?

Have students complete *Student Journal* page 45.

Phonics/Word Study

Latin Roots

Write the word *predict* on the board and tell students that it contains the Latin root *dict*, which means "to say" or "to speak." Ask how the meaning of *predict* relates to its root (to *predict* means "to say something in advance"). Ask students to name other words that contain the root *dict*. List their answers on the board. Now, work with students to complete the in-depth Latin roots activity on TE page 110.

Phonics/Word Study

More Latin Roots

For instruction to introduce a root, see TE page 102. Work with students to discover the meaning of each root. See *Word Study Manual* page 46 for a related word sort.

dict **(to speak)**

Although the sound of the root changes in the words *edict* and *indict*, the meaning stays the same. Demonstrate for students how knowing the meanings of a prefix and a root can help them unlock the meaning of a word that may seem unfamiliar at first. Display the prefix *contra-* and ask students what they think it means. Provide example words such as *contrast*. Students should recognize that *contra-* means "against." Then write *dict*. Encourage students to tell what they think the root means. Give *contradict* as an example. Students should realize that *contradict* means "against what was said."

edict predict dictionary
indict verdict diction
dictate contradict

rupt **(to break)**

Have students think about the word *erupt*. Ask them to use *erupt* to understand *rupt*.

abrupt corrupt disrupt
bankrupt erupt
rupture interrupt

scrib/script **(to write)**

Ask students to consider the word *scribble*. When the root word *scrib*, used in verbs, is changed to a noun, it is modified to *script*. The first four examples below follow this predictable change.

describe description nondescript
prescribe prescription postscript
inscribe inscription scribble
subscribe subscription script

Discovering the Roots

dict	*rupt*	*scrib/script*
diction	eruption	postscript
dictate	rupture	prescribe
contradict	corrupt	scribble
verdict	interrupt	script
predict	disrupt	inscription

For more information on word sorts and spelling stages, see pages 5–31 in the *Word Study Manual.*

Focus on . . .

Use one or more activities in this section to focus on a particular area of need in your students.

Comprehension STRATEGY SUPPORT

To help those students who need more practice using the strategies covered in this lesson, work one-on-one or in small groups to apply the strategy prompts below. Apply the prompts to a *Reading Advantage* paperback, a classroom library book, or a new or familiar selection in the magazine. Always model your own thinking first.

Inferential Thinking

- What are the causes or effects of this event?
- What do I learn from the character or person's thoughts, words, or actions?
- What do I know (or infer) from the text that the author hasn't stated directly?
- What conclusions can I draw?

Making Connections

- What does this story (article, passage) remind me of?
- What do I already know about this topic?
- Where have I heard about this topic before?
- What do I have in common with the characters, people, or situations in the text?
- What other books, stories, articles, movies, or TV shows does this text make me think about?

Writing Report

Explain to students that in earlier times, letters were a mainstay of communication. Today, there are many forms of communication. Ask students to write a brief report about recent technological revolutions in communications. First, brainstorm with students and list recent technologies. Possibilities include personal computers, the Internet, DVDs, cellular phones, video cameras, and communication satellites. Ask students how this technology has changed family and work life? Have students share their ideas before they begin.

For more practice on the art of brainstorming, see lessons in *Writing Advantage,* pages 8–12.

Fluency: Expression

After students have read the poem "At a Surrealist Show" at least once, explain to students that to read it aloud expressively, they must first "see" the images that the poet describes. Have partners read the poem to each other and tell what they visualize.

As you listen to students read, use these prompts to guide them in reading expressively.

- Picture the images as you read.
- Read a bit slowly to give your listeners time to "see" the images.
- Say each word clearly.

When students read aloud, do they—

✓ reflect an understanding of the text?

✓ demonstrate appropriate timing, stress, and intonation?

✓ incorporate appropriate speed and phrasing?

English Language Learners

To support students' understanding of the lesson's topic, explore with students the different ways in which they can express thoughts about revolution and change.

1. Have students work with a partner to discuss what they wish they could change about their school, their community, and their world.
2. Model the sentences for students:
   - *If I could, I would change…*
   - *I would like to change…*
   - *I wish I could change…*
3. Share the responses with the whole class.

Independent Activity Options

While you work with individuals or small groups, others can work independently on one or more of the following options.

- Level D paperback books, see TE pages 367–372
- Level D *eZines*
- Repeat word sorts from this lesson
- *Student Journal* pages for this lesson
- *Writing Advantage* independent lessons

Assessment

Strategy Assessment

To help you and your students assess their use of comprehension strategies, ask the following questions. Students can complete a written response or provide verbal answers in a one-on-one reading conference.

1. **Inferential Thinking** Choose two of the letters in this selection. How are the writers similar and different? (Answers will vary. Possible responses include that Deborah and Galileo are both brave people who stand up against society's beliefs. Deborah continues her fight, whereas Galileo is forced to soften his statements to avoid punishment.)
2. **Making Connections** How would you feel and respond if you received one of the letters in this selection? (Answers will vary.)

For ongoing informal assessment, use the checklists on pages 61–64 of *Level D Assessment*.

Word Study Assessment

Use these steps to help you and your students assess their understanding of Latin roots.

1. Present the chart below. Read the roots and words aloud.
2. Have students explain how the meaning of each word is related to the root.

dict "to speak"	*rupt* "to break"	*scrib, script* "to write"
predict	rupture	script
contradict	corrupt	prescribe
dictate	disrupt	inscription

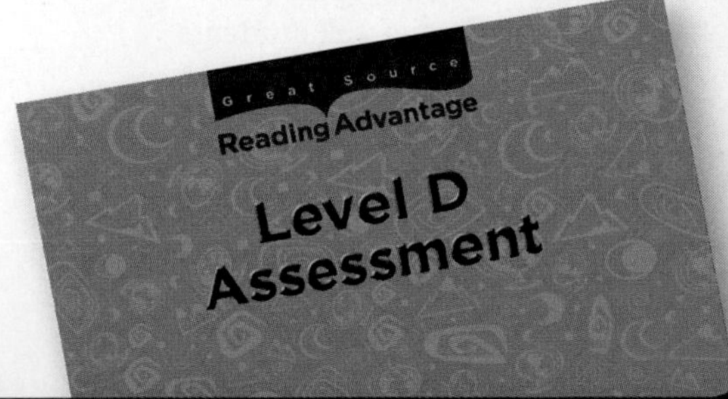

LESSON **14**

Rites of Passage: From Birth to Death

Revolutions, pages 14–19

SUMMARY

This **article** explores several rites of passage, both religious and social, from different cultures.

COMPREHENSION STRATEGIES

Determining Importance
Making Connections

WRITING

Compare-Contrast

VOCABULARY

Related Words

PHONICS/WORD STUDY

Latin Roots *aud, cred, equa/equi*

Lesson Vocabulary

disciplined
fortitude
obligations
aspects
attainments

MATERIALS

Revolutions, pp. 14–19
Student Journal, pp. 46–49
Word Study Manual, p. 49
Writing Advantage, pp. 152–169

Rites of Passage
From Birth to Death

Ghana funeral dance

14

Before Reading

Use one or more activities.

Anticipation Guide

Introduce the phrase *rite of passage,* inviting students to share what they think it means. Then display an anticipation guide and ask students or pairs to read the statements and to check the AGREE or DISAGREE box. (See TE page 389 for an anticipation guide BLM.) Discuss the responses as a group. Explain that students will revisit the guide, after reading, to see if any of their opinions have changed. (See Differentiated Instruction.)

Anticipation Guide

AGREE	DISAGREE	
		1. A rite of passage is a tradition that marks a stage of a person's life.
		2. A rite of passage is always religious.
		3. All cultures have rites of passage.
		4. Modern societies have no rites of passage.

Vocabulary Preview

Display the selection vocabulary. Have students find each word in the text and use the context to discover the meaning. Assess prior knowledge by asking students to choose a familiar word to use for the word map on *Student Journal* page 46. Before students read the article, model how to fill in the definition box. Students will complete the word map after they read the article.

Cultures from around the world have created different traditions to mark the stages of a person's life.

Japanese children at kindergarten graduation

Early Years: Kindergarten Graduation in Japan

People around the world celebrate important dates, such as birthdays, weddings, and funerals. But many cultures also celebrate other rights of passage that are unique to their part of the world. In the west, when we hear the word *graduation*, we think of high school or college. However, in Japan, graduation from kindergarten is an important rite of passage called the "Great Transformation." The ceremony is held in the spring. The four- and five-year-olds leave the wild world of youngsters and become disciplined, obedient, and respectful school children. Most kindergarten graduations are carefully planned and practiced. Often, the children, standing tall, file into an auditorium or theater. Sometimes their hands are glued to their sides to remind them not to fidget. The students line up in front of their chairs, bow to the audience, and sit. They are expected not to wiggle or throw temper tantrums. They must sit quietly through the long ceremony. Family and friends stand and make speeches in honor of the students. The dean or principal gives a speech to the children full of advice about life's lessons. At the end, the dean awards each student with a diploma or certificate.

15

DIFFERENTIATED INSTRUCTION

SMALL GROUP

ANTICIPATION GUIDE

Before students begin work on the anticipation guide, explain the following:

1. An anticipation guide is a series of statements that students respond to before reading a selection. It is not meant to quiz students, but rather to prompt discussion, build background, and set purposes for reading.
2. Tell students that after they finish reading the selection, they will revise their responses.

Student Journal page 46

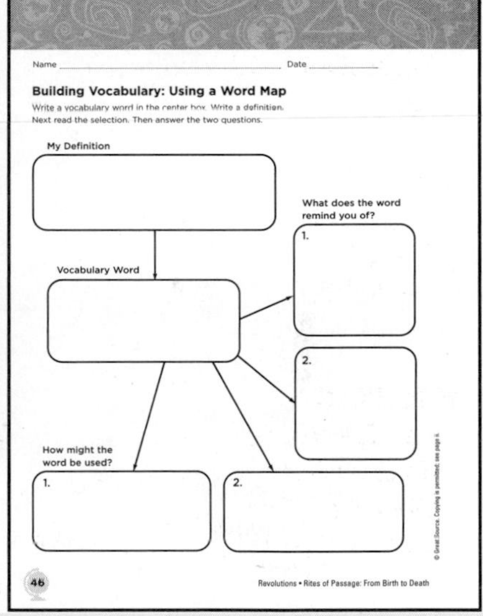

Name ______ Date ______

Building Vocabulary: Using a Word Map

Write a vocabulary word in the center box. Write a definition. Next read the selection. Then answer the two questions.

My Definition

Vocabulary Word

What does the word remind you of?

1.

2.

How might the word be used?

1.

2.

Preview the Selection

Have students skim the selection, pages 14–19 in the magazine. Use these or similar prompts to guide students to notice important features of the text.

- What do you notice about the way the article is organized?
- Do you think the article is fiction or nonfiction? Why do you think that?
- What do the section headings tell you about the rites of passage you will be reading about?

Teacher Think Aloud

The title of this article tells me that it is about rites of passage "from birth to death." I know that birth and death are important parts of the human life cycle. So is graduating from high school. I wonder what other rites of passage there are and how they are celebrated. I'll read to find out.

Make Predictions/ Set Purpose

To set their own purposes for reading, ask students to choose a statement from the anticipation guide that they hope to prove or disprove. To help students set a purpose, suggest that they read to learn about rites of passage in different cultures.

DIFFERENTIATED INSTRUCTION 

Comprehension

MAKING CONNECTIONS

Use the following prompts to help students make connections with the text.

- What important milestones in life have you experienced? What important life events do you expect to experience in the future? (Responses may include being born, reaching an important birthday, graduating from high school, getting married, having children.)
- How do your experiences marking life's milestones compare with the rites of passage in the selection? (Answers will vary.)

Painted moment at the Apache Sunrise Ceremony

Middle Years: The Apache Sunrise Ceremony

The Sunrise Ceremony is a rite of passage practiced by the Apache Indians. It marks the change from girl to woman. The ceremony, which lasts four days, takes place the summer after a girl has her first menstrual cycle.

Day 1: Preparations

Before sunrise, the girl's godmother and godfather dance into camp. The godmother dresses the young girl. A medicine man gives an opening speech about the importance of customs, charity, and prayer. Next comes the Dressing Ceremony. During this ceremony, the young girl's clothes are decorated with feathers, scarves, beads, and shells. Finally, an eagle's feather is placed in her hair. Apaches believe that the Creator can communicate through this feather. Many say they've seen the eagle's feather "stand up on its own" or "dance atop the girl's head."

Day 2: Day of Dance

The next day's rituals also begin before sunrise and form a Day of Dance. The girl dances for over six hours. She dances with a special walking stick that she will use again as an old woman. After the long sunrise dance, the girl is usually very tired, but she must go to a get-together for guests and visitors. The parents give the girl a "burden basket." She must give away the items in this basket—usually candy and fruit. This symbolizes how generous she will always be. This long day is supposed to help make the girl a stronger person.

Days 3 and 4: Prayer and Dance

The third morning is full of special prayers. The girl's godfather paints the girl's face with clay and corn. Then they dance together for four more hours. After this dance, the girl rests until the last day of prayers.

Coping with Adult Life

The Apache believe this physically and emotionally challenging ceremony helps young girls find the courage they will need to face the many challenges of adult life. This rite shows the girls the fortitude, or strength, they have inside.

16

During Reading

Comprehension 

DETERMINING IMPORTANCE

Use these questions to model determining the importance of details in the section on page 15. Then have students determine the importance of details on page 16.

- What big ideas does the author want me to understand?
- What details support my beliefs?

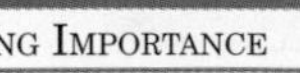

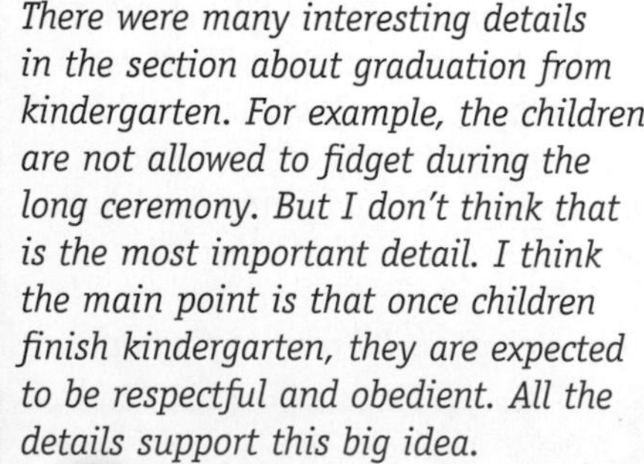

Teacher Think Aloud

There were many interesting details in the section about graduation from kindergarten. For example, the children are not allowed to fidget during the long ceremony. But I don't think that is the most important detail. I think the main point is that once children finish kindergarten, they are expected to be respectful and obedient. All the details support this big idea.

Comprehension 

MAKING CONNECTIONS

Use these questions to model making connections. Then have students make their own connections.

- Have I seen, heard, or read about something like this before?
- How do my experiences help me understand the rites of passage in the selection?

(See Differentiated Instruction.)

Bar Mitzvah and Bat Mitzvah

When Jewish boys and girls reach the age of thirteen, they are considered mature enough to carry out the obligations, or duties, of their religion. Many of these obligations are set out in the commandment of the *Torah*, the Jewish bible. In fact, *Bar Mitzvah* and *Bat Mitzvah* literally mean "Son of the Commandment" and "Daughter of the Commandment."

Although a Jewish child automatically becomes a Bar or Bat Mitzvah upon reaching the age of thirteen (sometimes twelve), it became customary to mark the occasion with a ceremony. Jewish boys and girls prepare for many months for this ceremony. They study Jewish traditions, history, and beliefs. A lot of hard work is necessary to learn everything.

During the ceremony, the child recites a blessing over the Torah. Then he or she chants a portion of the Torah in Hebrew and gives a speech explaining how the Torah portion applies to his or her life. After the ceremony, there is often a reception, with food, music, and dancing.

Being a Bar or Bat Mitzvah is not the same as being considered an adult; the ceremony does not imply that a Jewish person is now ready to go out on one's own or to marry and raise children. Nor is it a graduation marking the end point of one's Jewish education. Being a Bar Mitzvah or Bat Mitzvah simply means that a child is ready to be held responsible for his or her actions.

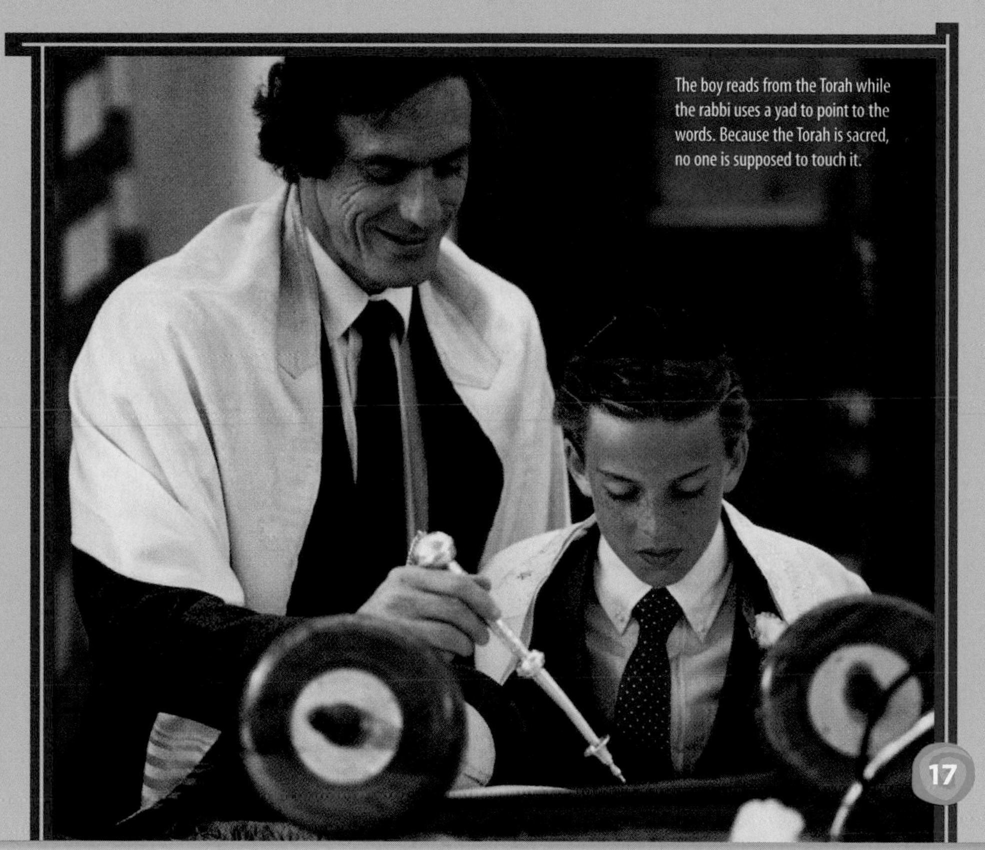

The boy reads from the Torah while the rabbi uses a yad to point to the words. Because the Torah is sacred, no one is supposed to touch it.

17

Teacher Think Aloud

When I read the section about Quinceañera, I remember the "Sweet Sixteen" parties I went to as a teenager. When a girl turned sixteen, she often had a party with music, dancing, and snacks. I can relate my own experiences to the Quinceañera celebrations.

Fix-Up Strategies

Offer these strategies to help students read independently.

If you don't understand what you're reading:

- Reread the difficult section to look for clues to help you comprehend.
- Read ahead to find clues to help you comprehend.
- Retell, or say in your own words, what you've read.
- Visualize, or form mental pictures of, what you've read.

If you don't understand a word:

- Reread the sentence. Look for ideas and words that provide meaning clues.
- Find clues by reading a few sentences before and after the confusing word.
- Look for the base or root word and think about its meaning.
- Think about the topic or plot at this point to see if either offers meaning clues.

DIFFERENTIATED INSTRUCTION

SMALL GROUP

Writing

Compare-Contrast

To help students complete a compare-contrast T-chart, have them follow these steps:

1. Make a T-chart and label the columns with the two events you are going to compare.
2. In the left-hand column, list facts and details for one event.
3. In the right-hand column, next to each fact and detail listed, tell how the second event is the same or different.

The seven chambelanes gather around the Quinceañera to celebrate her coming of age.

Quinceañera

On a Hispanic girl's fifteenth birthday, she celebrates a Quinceañera. The word *Quinceañera* comes from the Spanish words *quince*, which means "fifteen," and *años*, which means "years." The Quinceañera ceremony marks a Hispanic girl's passage toward womanhood. Originally, the Quinceañera symbolized that a girl was ready to marry and become a wife. Today, it symbolizes that a girl is ready to date, get an after-school job, or do volunteer work.

There are two aspects of a Quinceañera: religious and social. The day begins with the religious portion of the event. Traditionally, none of the guests see the girl before she enters the church for Mass. The church service is usually only for relatives and a few close friends. During the service, a priest blesses the girl and talks to her about becoming a woman. Often, a close girlfriend places a crown on the birthday girl's head, and the girl may present flowers to the Virgin Mary.

After the religious ceremony, it is time for the long-planned-for party. Some of the parties are as fancy as weddings, with gowns, limousines, photographers, catered meals, live music, and flowers. The Quinceañera selects a "court" consisting of fourteen friends, usually seven girls, called "damas," and seven boys, called "chambelanes" or "galanes." The girl and her friends dress up in gowns and tuxedoes, and perform dances that they have rehearsed. The dancing continues, sometimes long into the night.

The Quinceañera celebration honors a girl's spiritual and social attainments through religious observance, music, and dance. It also provides an opportunity for her friends and family to wish her well as she takes on the growing responsibilities of becoming a woman.

Student Journal pages 47–48

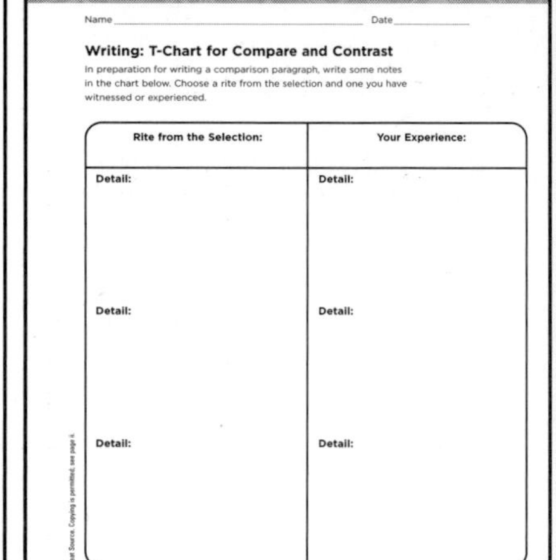

Name ______________ Date ________

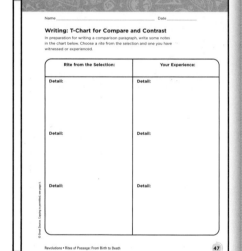

Writing: T-Chart for Compare and Contrast

In preparation for writing a comparison paragraph, write some notes in the chart below. Choose a rite from the selection and one you have witnessed or experienced.

Rite from the Selection:	Your Experience:
Detail:	Detail:
Detail:	Detail:
Detail:	Detail:

© Great Source. Copying is permitted; see page ii.

Revolutions • Rites of Passage: From Birth to Death 47

After Reading

WHOLE CLASS

Use one or more activities.

Check Purpose

Have students decide if their purpose was met. Were they able to find information to prove or disprove the statement they chose? What were some rites of passage they read about?

Discussion Questions

Continue the group discussion with the following questions.

1. What is a rite of passage? (Monitor Understanding)
2. Why do you think cultures have traditions to mark the stages in a person's life? (Inferential Thinking)
3. What other traditions have you heard of? (Making Connections)

Revisit: Anticipation Guide

Revisit the anticipation guide and poll students to see if they agree or disagree with the statements.

Revisit: Word Map

Have students finish the word map activity on *Student Journal* page 46. Have students who chose similar words meet to discuss the two questions on the page. Then review the activity with the whole group.

Later Years:
Death—A Continuation of Life

In Ghana, death is a rite of passage for the soul into the next world. In many African cultures, there is a second burial ceremony forty days after the first. These forty days give the family time to raise money, prepare for the ceremony, and await the arrival of relatives.

While many see death as the end of life, some Africans view death as another part of the journey. Artists design objects to represent, or stand for, this journey.

The Akan people of Ghana create a pottery vase called the "family pot." An artist shapes the handle of the lid into a human head with a snake slithering around the lid. The snake symbolizes the death that will surround all people. At the second burial ceremony, family members fill the pot with trimmings of the dead person's hair and nails. Hair and nails grow all through life, and they symbolize that the dead person will continue to grow and live in the afterlife. The family carries the vessel to the cemetery, along with food and wine, as an offering to their dead family member. The Akan people believe that the soul lives on after death.

Ghana funeral dance

19

DIFFERENTIATED INSTRUCTION

Vocabulary

Related Words

Related-Words Chart

Key Word: *fortitude*		
Related Word	**Part of Speech**	**Definition**
fortify	verb	to make strong
fortified	adjective	enriched; made stronger
fortissimo	adverb	(music) loudly; with force
fort	noun	a stronghold
fortification	noun	something that strengthens

Student Journal page 49

Name ______ Date ______

Building Vocabulary: Related Words

Pick a word you are familiar with as the key word. Then write three or four words that are related to the key word. Write the part of speech and the definition of each related word. Use a dictionary for help, if you wish.

Key Word: ______

Related Words	Part of Speech	Definition

Hévolutions • Rites of Passage: From Birth to Death 49

Writing Compare-Contrast

Ask students which rites of passage from the selection remind them of experiences they have had or have witnessed. Ask students to choose one of the rites of passage to compare with their own experiences. Have students complete the T-chart on *Student Journal* page 47 to organize their thoughts for writing a compare-contrast paragraph. Students can write their paragraphs on *Student Journal* page 48. (See Differentiated Instruction.)

Vocabulary Related Words

Knowing the meaning of one word can help students figure out the meanings of other related words. Read aloud the last sentence on page 16. Ask:

- What does *fortitude* mean?
- What part of speech is *fortitude*?
- What words are related to *fortitude*?

Draw a chart with related words listed as shown. Have students complete *Student Journal* page 49. (See Differentiated Instruction.)

Phonics/Word Study

Latin Roots

Write the phrase *That's incredible!* on the board. Have pairs of students analyze the word *incredible* by breaking it into syllables and trying to find the meaning of each part. (*In-* means "not," *cred* means "to believe," and *-ible* means "able to." So the word *incredible* means "not able to believe.") Now, work with students to complete the in-depth Latin roots activity on TE page 118.

Phonics/Word Study

Latin Roots

For instruction to introduce a root, see TE page 102. Work with students to discover the meaning of each root. See *Word Study Manual* page 49 for a related word sort.

aud **(to hear)**

audible
audience
audio
audiology
audit
auditorium
auditory
audiovisual
inaudible
audiometer

cred **(to trust, believe)**

A *credo* is something a person believes in. With that in mind, have students think about how *credentials* and *credo* are related. To help them, have students name different kinds of credentials—driver's license, passport, birth certificate, school ID.

credence
credentials
credible
credulous
credo
credit
discredit
incredible
incredulous

equa/equi **(even)**

Equal is a concept students have known since they were very young. Siblings expect *equal* treatment from their parents. Students in the workplace expect *equitable* treatment from their employers. Students expect that their teachers are giving *equal* amounts of homework to their classes. Students know the concept, but the following words will enlarge their understanding of it.

equality
equitable
equation
equator
equidistant
equilateral
equinox
equity
equilibrium

Discovering the Roots

aud	*cred*	*equa/equi*
audio	incredible	equinox
audible	credit	equal
audience	discredit	equation
auditorium	credence	equality
audiovisual	credentials	equidistant

For more information on word sorts and spelling stages, see pages 5–31 in the *Word Study Manual*.

Focus on . . .

Use one or more activities in this section to focus on a particular area of need in your students.

Comprehension Strategy Support

To help those students who need more practice using the strategies covered in this lesson, work one-on-one or in small groups to apply the strategy prompts below. Apply the prompts to a *Reading Advantage* paperback, a classroom library book, or a new or familiar selection in the magazine. Always model your own thinking first.

Determining Importance

- What is the most important idea in the paragraph? How can I prove it?
- Which details are unimportant? Why?
- What does the author want me to understand?
- Why is this information important (or not important) to me?

Making Connections

- What does this story (article, passage) remind me of?
- What do I already know about this topic?
- Where have I heard about this topic before?
- What do I have in common with the characters, people, or situations in the text?
- What other books, stories, articles, movies, or TV shows does this text make me think about?

Writing Opinion Graph

Ask students whether rites of passage are important. Allow time for students to share their ideas. Then have students write a paragraph supporting their viewpoint. Tell students that their paragraphs should state a viewpoint, give three reasons to support that viewpoint, and end with a conclusion. Have students use the following organizer to plan their paragraphs. (The main idea BLM on TE page 385 can be used here.)

Viewpoint:		
Reason 1:	Reason 2:	Reason 3:
Concluding statement:		

To give students more practice with writing persuasive essays, see lessons in *Writing Advantage*, pages 152–169.

Fluency: Expression

After students have read the selection at least once, have them choose one of the rites to read aloud. Discuss with students that although the passages are nonfiction, the author uses a friendly, conversational tone to relay the information. Encourage students to try to convey this feeling by reading expressively.

Use prompts such as the following to help students read expressively.

- Notice the punctuation. Remember to pause for commas and stop for periods.
- Words that are in special type should be read with emphasis or stress.
- Quotation marks are often used to set off titles or special phrases. Make sure you read these words together.

When students read aloud, do they—

✓ reflect an understanding of the text?
✓ demonstrate appropriate timing, stress, and intonation?
✓ incorporate appropriate speed and phrasing?

English Language Learners

Use these steps to support students as they learn to understand and describe the main ideas and details of a story.

1. Use the Teacher Think Aloud on TE page 114 to model the activity.
2. Work with students to determine the main idea and significant details of the section called "Quinceañera." Show students the parts of the text that help identify the main idea and significant details.

Independent Activity Options

While you work with individuals or small groups, others can work independently on one or more of the following options.

- Level D paperback books, see TE pages 367–372
- Level D *eZines*
- Repeat word sorts from this lesson
- *Student Journal* pages for this lesson
- *Writing Advantage* independent lessons

Assessment

Strategy Assessment

To help you and your students assess their use of comprehension strategies, ask the following questions. Students can complete a written response or provide verbal answers in a one-on-one reading conference.

1. **Determining Importance** What are some of the most important ideas you learned from this selection? Why are these ideas important? (Answers will vary. Possible answers are that many cultures celebrate rites of passage. Often, these mark the change from childhood to a more mature, responsible age.)
2. **Making Connections** In what ways did you connect to this selection? Explain. (Answers will vary. Accept related responses.)

For ongoing informal assessment, use the checklists on pages 61–64 of *Level D Assessment*.

Word Study Assessment

Use these steps to help you and your students assess their understanding of Latin roots.

1. Present the chart below. Read the roots and words aloud.
2. Have students explain how the meaning of each word is related to the root.

aud "to hear"	*cred* "to trust or believe"	*equa, equi* "even"
inaudible	credible	equality
auditorium	incredulous	equation
audiovisual	credit	equidistant

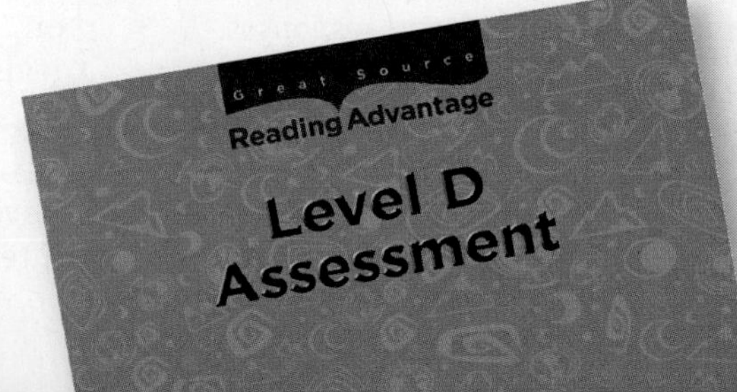

LESSON **15**

The 1960s Music Scene: A Revolution . . .

Revolutions, pages 20–23

SUMMARY

This **interview** tells how popular music in the 1960s both reflected and influenced cultural changes.

COMPREHENSION STRATEGY

Understanding Text Structure

WRITING

Outline and Essay

VOCABULARY

Compound Words

PHONICS/WORD STUDY

Latin Roots *flect/flex, form, hos*

Lesson Vocabulary

prosperity	censors
lyrics	blacklisted
epitomized	burgeoning

MATERIALS

Revolutions, pp. 20–23
Student Journal, pp. 50–53
Word Study Manual, p. 50
Writing Advantage, pp. 13–29

THE 1960s MUSIC SCENE

A REVOLUTION INSIDE A REVOLUTION

The 1960s was a decade of change for the United States. The civil rights, women's rights, and anti-war movements all brought about great change.

20

Before Reading 

Use one or more activities.

Make a List

Have students examine the photographs and captions in the selection. Ask students what they know about 1960s music. Record students' responses. Tell students that, after reading the interview, they will revisit the list.

1960s Music

1. loud guitars
2. British (The Beatles, The Who)
3. folk music-protest songs

Vocabulary Preview

Display the selection vocabulary. To assess prior knowledge, ask students to begin the knowledge rating chart on *Student Journal* page 50. They will revisit the chart later.

Preview the Selection

Have students look through the interview. Discuss what they notice.

Make Predictions/ Set Purpose

Students should use the information gathered in the selection preview to make predictions about what they will learn from the interview. To help students set a purpose, suggest that they read to learn how music can reflect or cause change in the world.

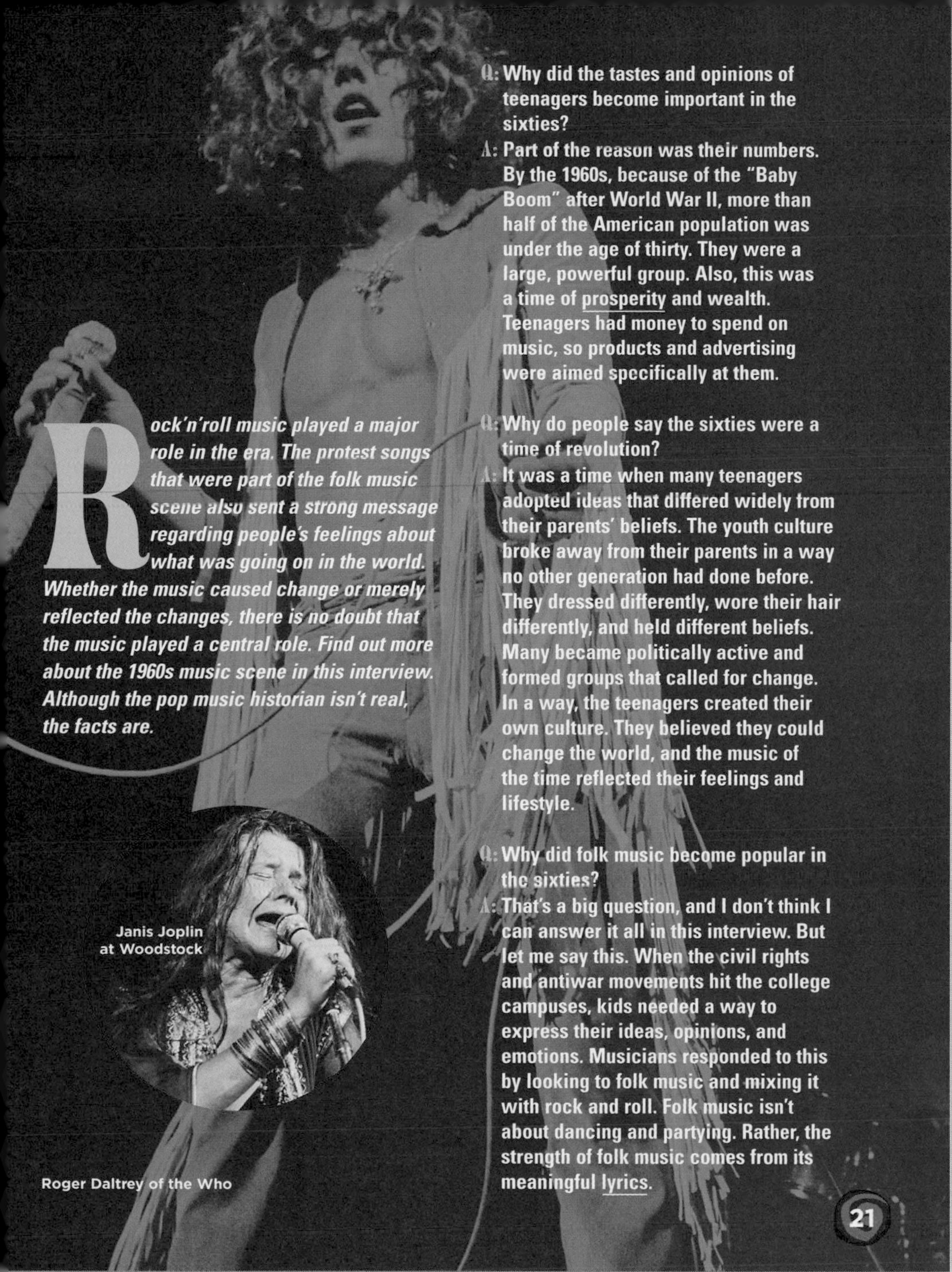

Q: Why did the tastes and opinions of teenagers become important in the sixties?

A: Part of the reason was their numbers. By the 1960s, because of the "Baby Boom" after World War II, more than half of the American population was under the age of thirty. They were a large, powerful group. Also, this was a time of prosperity and wealth. Teenagers had money to spend on music, so products and advertising were aimed specifically at them.

Rock'n'roll music played a major role in the era. The protest songs that were part of the folk music scene also sent a strong message regarding people's feelings about what was going on in the world. Whether the music caused change or merely reflected the changes, there is no doubt that the music played a central role. Find out more about the 1960s music scene in this interview. Although the pop music historian isn't real, the facts are.

Q: Why do people say the sixties were a time of revolution?

A: It was a time when many teenagers adopted ideas that differed widely from their parents' beliefs. The youth culture broke away from their parents in a way no other generation had done before. They dressed differently, wore their hair differently, and held different beliefs. Many became politically active and formed groups that called for change. In a way, the teenagers created their own culture. They believed they could change the world, and the music of the time reflected their feelings and lifestyle.

Q: Why did folk music become popular in the sixties?

A: That's a big question, and I don't think I can answer it all in this interview. But let me say this. When the civil rights and antiwar movements hit the college campuses, kids needed a way to express their ideas, opinions, and emotions. Musicians responded to this by looking to folk music and mixing it with rock and roll. Folk music isn't about dancing and partying. Rather, the strength of folk music comes from its meaningful lyrics.

Janis Joplin at Woodstock

Roger Daltrey of the Who

21

DIFFERENTIATED INSTRUCTION

Comprehension

UNDERSTANDING TEXT STRUCTURE

To help students understand the structure of an interview, use the following steps.

1. Explain that an interview is a meeting or conversation in which a person asks another person questions about personal opinions, experiences, or an area of expertise.
2. In a printed interview, the interviewer and interviewee may be identified by their names, or by the letters *Q* for *question* and *A* for *answer*.

Student Journal page 50

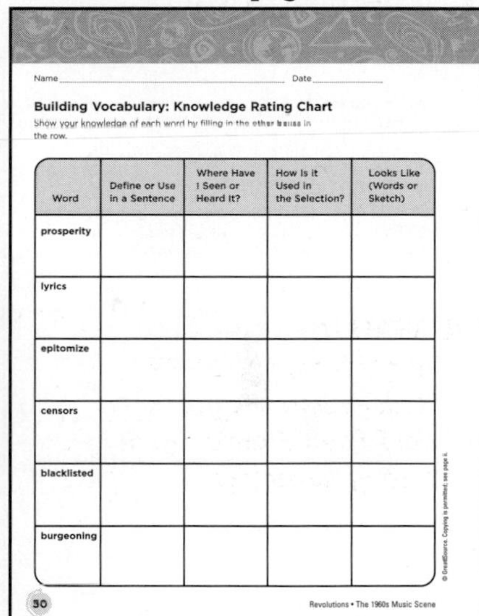

Name______________ Date__________

Building Vocabulary: Knowledge Rating Chart

Show your knowledge of each word by filling in the other boxes in the row.

Word	Define or Use in a Sentence	Where Have I Seen or Heard It?	How Is It Used in the Selection?	Looks Like (Words or Sketch)
prosperity				
lyrics				
epitomize				
censors				
blacklisted				
burgeoning				

30 Revolutions • The 1960s Music Scene

During Reading

Comprehension

SMALL GROUP

UNDERSTANDING TEXT STRUCTURE

Use these questions to model how to identify the text structure of an interview. Then have students explain how the text structure helps them understand the selection.

- How can I tell this is an interview?
- Who is being interviewed? By whom?
- Why is an interview a good way to convey information?

(See Differentiated Instruction.)

Teacher Think Aloud

When I see Q: and A:, I know that I'm reading an interview. The Q *stands for* question *and the* A *stands for* answer. *This structure helps me tell what was important to the author because the author decided what questions to ask.*

Fix-Up Strategies

Offer these strategies to help students read independently.

If you don't understand what you're reading:

- Reread the difficult section to look for clues to help you comprehend.
- Read ahead to find clues to help you comprehend.
- Retell, or say in your own words, what you've read.
- Visualize, or form mental pictures of, what you've read.

Bob Dylan

Q: How did the hippie culture of the sixties influence music?

A: Hippies believed in love and peace, and they rejected many of the accepted standards of society. Music was very important to them. The musicians of the time wrote songs that reflected the hippies' beliefs. Groups like The Grateful Dead epitomized hippie culture; they were the typical hippie band. And don't forget Woodstock—the three-day music festival held in a meadow in New York. It brought people and music together in a way that is still talked about today.

Q: Did the government try to stop this music?

A: Music censors had tried to edit Elvis back in the 1950s, because they thought his dancing was too sexy. In the 1960s, when lyrics supported integration of blacks and whites, peace, and freedom, the censors began to worry. In the 1960s, a TV show called *Hootenanny* featured folk music. Cameras taped a studio full of young adults sitting around listening to folk singers. However, Pete Seeger, the unofficial "father" of the folk revival, was banned from the show in 1963. The House Committee on Un-American Activities had blacklisted him, saying that his beliefs were radical and un-American. Because Seeger was censored, well-known musicians like Bob Dylan and Joan Baez refused to perform on the show.

Q: What did pop music have to do with the war in Vietnam?

A: There was a huge antiwar movement in the United States. Many people opposed the Vietnam War. They didn't believe that American men and women should have to fight a war they didn't believe in. Music was the heart and soul of the antiwar movement. Soldiers listened to the music on their radios, while young people at home played the songs as a protest. Perhaps you've heard "Give Peace a Chance" by John Lennon. Some of the lyrics are, "All we are saying is give peace a chance." The song reflects the desire for a peaceful end to the Vietnam War.

Q: Can you name the best-known protest song?

A: I'd have to say "Blowin' in the Wind" by Bob Dylan. It was in response to the burgeoning, ever-growing, civil rights movement. The song asks when the times will change, when life will be fair. Sadly, the refrain answers: *The answer is blowin' in the wind.* The song expresses the hopelessness that many young people were feeling at the time.

Q: Did the music really make a difference?

A: It's hard to say how much influence or power the music actually had. However, it did give many young people a way to express their concerns and feelings. It acted as a unifying force for an entire generation of young people, whose shared hopes and ideals were captured by the music. Much of the music from the 60s is still played on the radio, sold in stores, and held near to the heart of a generation. ◆

22

Student Journal pages 51–52

Name______________________ Date__________

Writing: Outline

Complete the outline. Use your personal experience and information from the selection to help you.

Essay Topic: Power of Music

Subtopic 1: Ways music influences people

Main idea statement: ______________________

Details: ______________________

Subtopic 2: Role of music today vs. role in 1960s

Main idea statement: ______________________

Details: ______________________

Revolutions • The 1960s Music Scene 51

After Reading

Use one or more activities.

Check Purpose

Have students decide if their purpose was met. Did they learn more about how music can reflect or cause change in the world?

Discussion Questions

Continue the group discussion with the following questions.

1. Are the pop music historian's answers fact or opinion? Explain. (Fact-Opinion)
2. Do you think the 1960s music made a difference? Explain. (Draw Conclusions)
3. Do you wish you lived in the 1960s? Why or why not? (Making Connections)

Revisit: List

Revisit the list about music in the 1960s. Ask students what they learned about the singers and their music. Add students' responses to the list.

Revisit: Knowledge Rating Chart

Revisit the chart on *Student Journal* page 50. Tell students they can make adjustments or changes and complete any empty boxes. Encourage volunteers to share some responses.

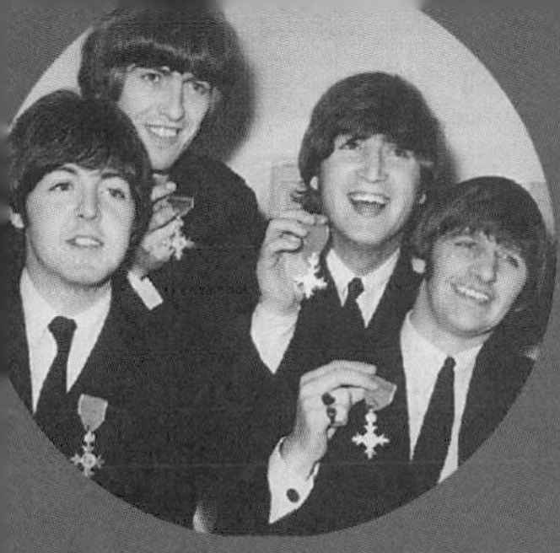

The Beatles

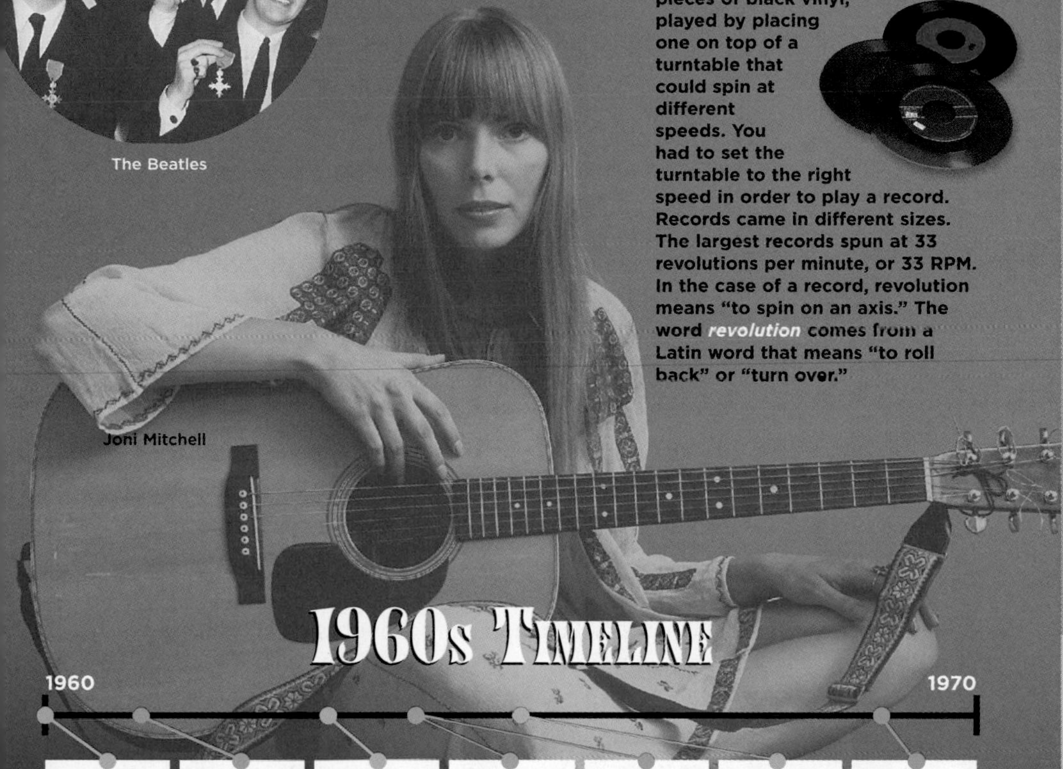

Life Before CDs

Before CDs, there were cassette tapes. Before tapes, there were records. Records were flat, round pieces of black vinyl, played by placing one on top of a turntable that could spin at different speeds. You had to set the turntable to the right speed in order to play a record. Records came in different sizes. The largest records spun at 33 revolutions per minute, or 33 RPM. In the case of a record, revolution means "to spin on an axis." The word **revolution** comes from a Latin word that means "to roll back" or "turn over."

Joni Mitchell

1960s Timeline

1960 — 1970

1960	1961	1963	1964	1964	1965	1969
John F. Kennedy was elected president, the youngest person ever to become president, and the first Catholic.	John Glenn became the first American to orbit Earth.	President Kennedy was assassinated. Vice president Lyndon B. Johnson became president.	The Civil Rights Act of 1964 was passed. The law meant that no one could discriminate against another person on the basis of color, race, national origin, religion, or sex.	The Beatles toured the United States, creating a sensation.	President Johnson sent the Marines, the first ground troops, into the Vietnam War.	Neil Armstrong and Buzz Aldrin landed on the moon, becoming the first people ever to set foot on the moon.

23

DIFFERENTIATED INSTRUCTION

Vocabulary

Compound Words

To increase students' understanding of compound words, use the following strategies.

1. Explain to students that a compound word is made up of component words that contribute to its meaning.
2. Ask students to name compound words that have the word *sea* as one of their components. Examples include *seacoast*, *seafood*, *seagull*, *seaport*, *seashell*, *seaside*, and *seaweed*. Then help students brainstorm a list of common compound words, such as *carpool*, *playground*, and *airport*.

Student Journal page 53

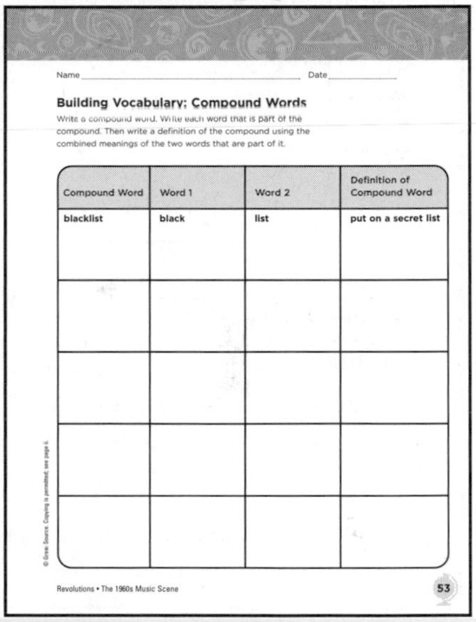

Name ____________ Date ______

Building Vocabulary: Compound Words

Write a compound word. Write each word that is part of the compound. Then write a definition of the compound using the combined meanings of the two words that are part of it.

Compound Word	Word 1	Word 2	Definition of Compound Word
blacklist	black	list	put on a secret list

Revolutions • The 1960s Music Scene 53

Writing Outline and Essay

Discuss the ways in which music influences people. Suggest some ideas to get students thinking. (Music can energize or calm people. It can mirror or take away from people's lives.) Write ideas on the board. Guide students in comparing the influence music has now with the influence it had in the 1960s. Have students use the discussion and notes on the board to complete *Student Journal* pages 51 and 52.

Vocabulary Compound Words

Display the word *blacklist*. Identify it as a compound word, or a word made up of two smaller words. Explain that *black* can mean "secret." *List* means "a series of names or items." Combined, the two words mean "to put on a secret list." Ask students to find two more compound words in the interview (*teenagers* and *lifestyle*) and then to think of two other compound words they know. Have them complete *Student Journal* page 53. (See Differentiated Instruction.)

Phonics/Word Study

Latin Roots

Display the words *conform, formation, deform*. Ask partners to discuss what these words have in common. Then display the Latin root *form,* explaining that it means "shape." Ask students how the meaning of each of the three words is related to the Latin root. Now, work with students to complete the in-depth Latin roots activity on TE page 124.

Phonics/Word Study

More Latin Roots

For instruction to introduce a root, see TE page 102. Work with students to discover the meaning of each root. See *Word Study Manual* page 50 for a related word sort.

flect/flex **(to bend, curve)**

Remind students that the word *flexible* means "an ability to change easily." It can also mean "the ability to easily maneuver physically."

deflect
flex
flexible
genuflect
inflection
reflect
inflexible

form **(a shape)**

conform
reform
uniform
platform
format
deform
formulate
informal
formation
malformed
transform

hos **(host)**

host/hostess
hostel
hospitality
hostage
hospice
hospital

Discovering the Roots

flect, flex	*form*	*hos*
reflect	formulate	host
deflect	conform	hospital
genuflect	reform	hostel
flexible	malformed	hospice
inflection	deform	hospitality

For more information on word sorts and spelling stages, see pages 5–31 in the *Word Study Manual.*

Focus on . . .

Use one or more activities in this section to focus on a particular area of need in your students.

Comprehension STRATEGY SUPPORT

To help those students who need more practice using the strategies covered in this lesson, work one-on-one or in small groups to apply the strategy prompts below. Apply the prompts to a *Reading Advantage* paperback, a classroom library book, or a new or familiar selection in the magazine. Always model your own thinking first.

Understanding Text Structure

- What kind of text is this? (book, story, article, guidebook, play, manual)
- How does the author organize the text? (cause-effect, problem-solution, chronological order, description, question-answer, comparison-contrast)
- What details support my thoughts about the text structure?
- What is the cause (effect, problem, solution, order, question, answer)?
- If fiction, who are the characters? What is the setting, plot, conflict, and resolution?

Writing Interview

Have students interview each other about the ways in which today's music may or may not be revolutionary. First discuss today's music with students. You may want to ask if it has introduced new instrumentation, rhythms, singing styles, melodies, and lyrics. Work together as a group to formulate some interview questions. Students can choose three questions to ask a partner. Have students record the answers in a form similar to the selection.

When the interviews are finished, have students write an introductory paragraph to provide background for their audience. To provide instruction on introductory paragraphs, see lessons in *Writing Advantage*, pages 13–29.

Fluency: Pacing

After students have read the interview at least once, have partners read the interview to each other. Suggest that they alternate being the interviewer and historian. Explain to students that in order for the questions and answers of an interview to be clearly understood, they must be read at an even pace, not too quickly or too slowly.

As you listen to students read, use these prompts to guide them to read at an even pace.

- Pause slightly between the questions and answers.
- Use punctuation clues, such as commas and periods, to tell you where to pause and stop.
- Read conversationally, or the way you talk.

When students read aloud, do they—

- ✓ demonstrate a smooth pace, not too fast or too slow?
- ✓ incorporate well-timed pauses between words and phrases?
- ✓ reflect an awareness and understanding of punctuation?

English Language Learners

To support students as they develop their understanding of fact and opinion, extend the discussion about facts and opinions in the After Reading section on TE page 122.

1. Review the concept of facts and opinion.
2. With the whole class, discuss whether the pop music historian's answers in the interview are fact or opinion.
3. Have students work in pairs to find three more facts and three more opinions in the text. Have pairs discuss their findings with the class.

Independent Activity Options

While you work with individuals or small groups, others can work independently on one or more of the following options.

- Level D paperback books, see TE pages 367–372
- Level D *eZines*
- Repeat word sorts from this lesson
- *Student Journal* pages for this lesson
- *Writing Advantage* independent lessons

Assessment

Strategy Assessment

To help you and your students assess their use of comprehension strategies, ask the following question. Students can complete a written response or provide verbal answers in a one-on-one reading conference.

- **Understanding Text Structure** Why do you think the author chose to use an interview text structure for this selection? (Answers will vary. A possible response may be that the author wanted to share her conversation with a music history expert in an informal, conversational way. She wanted to highlight the answers of the interviewee.)

For ongoing informal assessment, use the checklists on pages 61–64 of *Level D Assessment*.

Word Study Assessment

Use these steps to help you and your students assess their understanding of Latin roots.

1. Present the chart below. Read the roots and words aloud.
2. Have students explain how the meaning of each word is related to the root.

flect, flex "to bend, curve"	*form* "a shape"	*hos* "host"
flexible	uniform	hospital
reflect	format	host
flex	reform	hostage

LESSON **16**

A Revolution in Industry

Revolutions, pages 24–29

SUMMARY

In this **memoir**, Bill Miller describes the hardships he endured as a child laborer during the Industrial Revolution.

COMPREHENSION STRATEGIES

Monitor Understanding
Inferential Thinking

WRITING

Letter

VOCABULARY

Synonyms and Antonyms

PHONICS/WORD STUDY

Latin Roots *langu/lingu, liber, man*

Lesson Vocabulary

industrial	meager
employed	scavenger
urban	quota
flat	

MATERIALS

Revolutions, pp. 24–29
Student Journal, pp. 54–57
Word Study Manual, p. 51
Writing Advantage, pp. 30–56

A Revolution in INDUSTRY

24

Before Reading  Use one or more activities.

Anticipation Guide

Create an anticipation guide for students. (See TE page 389 for a BLM anticipation guide.) Ask students to read the statements and place a check in the AGREE or DISAGREE box before each statement.

Anticipation Guide

AGREE	DISAGREE	
		1. Children would work in factories for twelve hours.
		2. Although work was hard, factories were very clean.
		3. Many children lost body parts working in factories.
		4. Factory workers were fed three healthy meals a day.

Vocabulary Preview

Display the selection vocabulary. Assess prior knowledge by asking students to complete the word sort on *Student Journal* page 54. Use *scavenger* to model the sorting process. Have students sort each vocabulary word by predicting how it will be used in the memoir. As needed, review the parts of speech. Students will revise the sorting chart after they have finished the selection.

The *Industrial Revolution began in England during the nineteenth century. At the start of the revolution, there were no laws protecting workers' rights. The growing factories needed a work force. However, factory owners didn't want to spend a lot of money to pay workers. The owners employed children because they did not have to pay them high wages. Because most children weren't educated enough to complain, they were easy for factory owners to handle. The following is an imagined memoir of a boy's experience working in a cotton mill.*

My Year in the Mills

I know I might seem young to be writing a memoir. After all, I'm only twenty-three. However, because my life is likely to be cut short by the hardships of working in a factory, I had better get started.

My name is Bill Miller. My family moved to London from our farm in 1823 because my father thought we could make a better life for ourselves in the city. My brother, James, and I were all for the move, because we were tired of waking up early to milk cows and clean the stables. Farm life was hard work. How hard could life in the city be, we thought? In the city there were machines and big buildings, not cows. We didn't appreciate how great life was on the farm—mother always had a hot meal on the table, and there was always clean hay to sleep on at night. We had no idea that the city would turn out to be an urban nightmare.

The Industrial Revolution

The period in the 1700s and 1800s is known as the Industrial Revolution. Before that time, most people lived in small villages, grew their own food, and made most of what they needed at home (for example, clothing and furniture). As the nineteenth century progressed, many machines were invented that made products faster and cheaper. With more factories, more workers were needed to run the machines. People moved from villages to cities to work in the factories. Factory owners employed children, because they were cheap labor. Until the late 1800s, there were no child labor laws to protect children from harsh working conditions and long hours.

25

DIFFERENTIATED INSTRUCTION — SMALL GROUP

Preview the Selection

To help students understand the genre, or type of literature, of this selection, give the following characteristics of a memoir:

1. A memoir is a written record of a person's life and experiences.
2. Memoirs are less structured than formal autobiographies and tell about a part of a person's life—often a public part, rather than his or her entire life.
3. The purpose of a memoir is to provide information about someone's life.

Student Journal page 54

Name ____________ Date ________

Building Vocabulary: Parts of Speech Word Sort

Based upon what you already know about the words, how do you think each one will be used in "A Revolution in Industry"? Sort each word into the proper category below. After you have read the selection, confirm or move the word to the correct category.

industrial employed urban flat
meager quote scavenger

Noun			Verb	Adjective
Person	Place	Thing		

54 Revolutions • A Revolution in Industry

Preview the Selection

Have students look through the six pages of the memoir, pages 24–29 in the magazine. Use these or similar prompts to orient students to the selection.

- What do you notice first?
- What form of writing do you think you will read? How do you know?
- What do you think the author's purpose is?

(See Differentiated Instruction.)

Teacher Think Aloud

As I flip through the selection, I see pictures of factories and young boys. The boys don't look very happy. I wonder if they work in the factories. I hope the article tells me about the boys' lives because that's what I'm curious about. I don't know if this selection will be fiction or nonfiction. I'll read to find out.

Make Predictions/ Set Purpose

Students should use the information gathered in the selection preview to make predictions about what they will learn from the selection. To help students set a purpose, suggest that they read to see if they were correct in their anticipation guide, and to learn how the Industrial Revolution affected children.

DIFFERENTIATED INSTRUCTION

Comprehension

MONITOR UNDERSTANDING

To help students visualize, use these steps.

1. Read aloud a detailed section of the text, for example, "*. . . To make matters worse . . . a thin layer of dust and grime from the machines covered the food.*"
2. Ask: *What words or phrases from the passage help you imagine what the scene was like?* You might explain that the phrase "a thin layer of dust and grime from the machines covered the food" helps you "see" a gross, dirty plate of food in front of you. That image helps you better understand the boys' horrific working conditions.

I was just six when we moved into that one-room flat in London. It was the end of November and the city was cold and dark. The day after we arrived, my whole family went to work. My father took my brother and me to the cotton mills. My mother found a job in a sewing factory. She was so busy sewing for other people that she had no time left to fix holes in our socks, let alone knit us a sweater for winter. You might wonder why we weren't in school. Well, in the early 1800s, school was not required. My parents couldn't afford to send my brother and me to school. We needed all the money we earned, even if it was a meager three pence per day.

Because I was so young, I worked as a scavenger at the mill. My job was to pick up the loose cotton from under the machines. The job wasn't too hard and took no thought at all, but it turned out to be quite dangerous. The machines were never turned off, and we were expected to pick up the cotton while the machines were running. Many of the boys I worked with lost fingers or parts of their arms. Back on the farm, I could cut off a chicken's head any day, but human blood still makes me sick to my stomach.

We left home for the factory at 5:30 A.M. and began work by 6. It became all too clear that my days were no longer going to be full of blue sky and rolling hills. The factory was dirty, and its roof was low, which made the inside dark and stuffy. There was no sink for washing, no privacy for changing clothes, and no toilets for relieving yourself. The summer I was stuck in that factory must have been the hottest summer ever in London. On the days when it was warm outside and all the machines were going, the temperature in the factory must have hit a hundred

26

During Reading

Comprehension

MONITOR UNDERSTANDING

Use these questions to model visualizing. Then have students tell about a part they visualized.

- Can I picture what is happening?
- How do the pictures help me better understand the text?
- Can I tell in my own words what I've read so far?

(See Differentiated Instruction.)

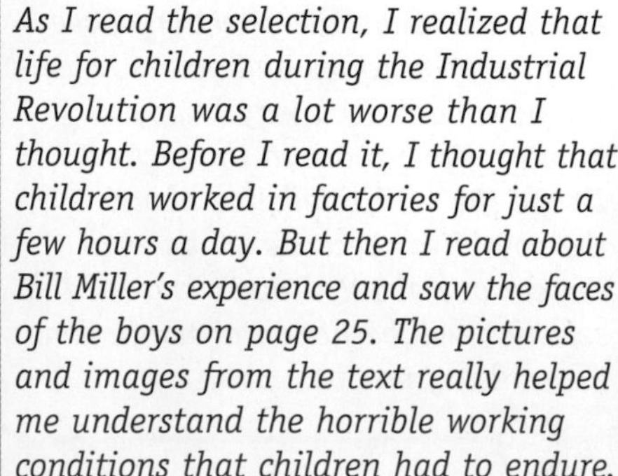

Teacher Think Aloud

As I read the selection, I realized that life for children during the Industrial Revolution was a lot worse than I thought. Before I read it, I thought that children worked in factories for just a few hours a day. But then I read about Bill Miller's experience and saw the faces of the boys on page 25. The pictures and images from the text really helped me understand the horrible working conditions that children had to endure.

Comprehension

INFERENTIAL THINKING

Use these questions to model for students how to think inferentially. Then have students make their own inferences based on the text.

- What do I learn about the boy?
- What effects do the working conditions have on the children?
- What conclusions can I draw about the Industrial Revolution?

degrees. It was hard to breathe. Dust from the cotton flew around in clouds of dirt. We all breathed in the cotton dust. To this day, I suffer from a deep cough. I'm sure it must be related to all that bad air.

As far as working hard, the factory was much worse than the farm. A typical day lasted about twelve hours. I remember hearing rumblings from the workers about a man named Sadler who introduced a law in Parliament to limit children to working ten hours, but Parliament didn't pass it. Or if they did, the owner of our factory didn't pay attention. On the farm, we always took a break for lunch when the sun was high in the sky. In the factory, the owner was supposed to feed us, and I can't say that he didn't—if you have a strange definition of food. The slop slapped on our plates tasted terrible. Worse than terrible! It had no taste at all. To make matters worse, we were expected to work and eat at the same time. That meant that a thin layer of dust and grime from the machines covered the food. I lost ten pounds that year.

I discovered that I didn't like having a boss. On the farm, after father gave me directions, I was pretty much my own boss all day. In the factory, the overseers never took their eyes off me. For example, if I was late for work, they took money from my paycheck. The first time I was late, I tried to explain that my family couldn't afford a clock. We told time by the church bells as best we could. The overseer didn't care, and he beat me. I became discouraged because even if I could afford a watch, our factory banned workers from wearing watches. I overheard the older men saying that they thought the owners made this rule so they didn't have to pay us for all the time we worked.

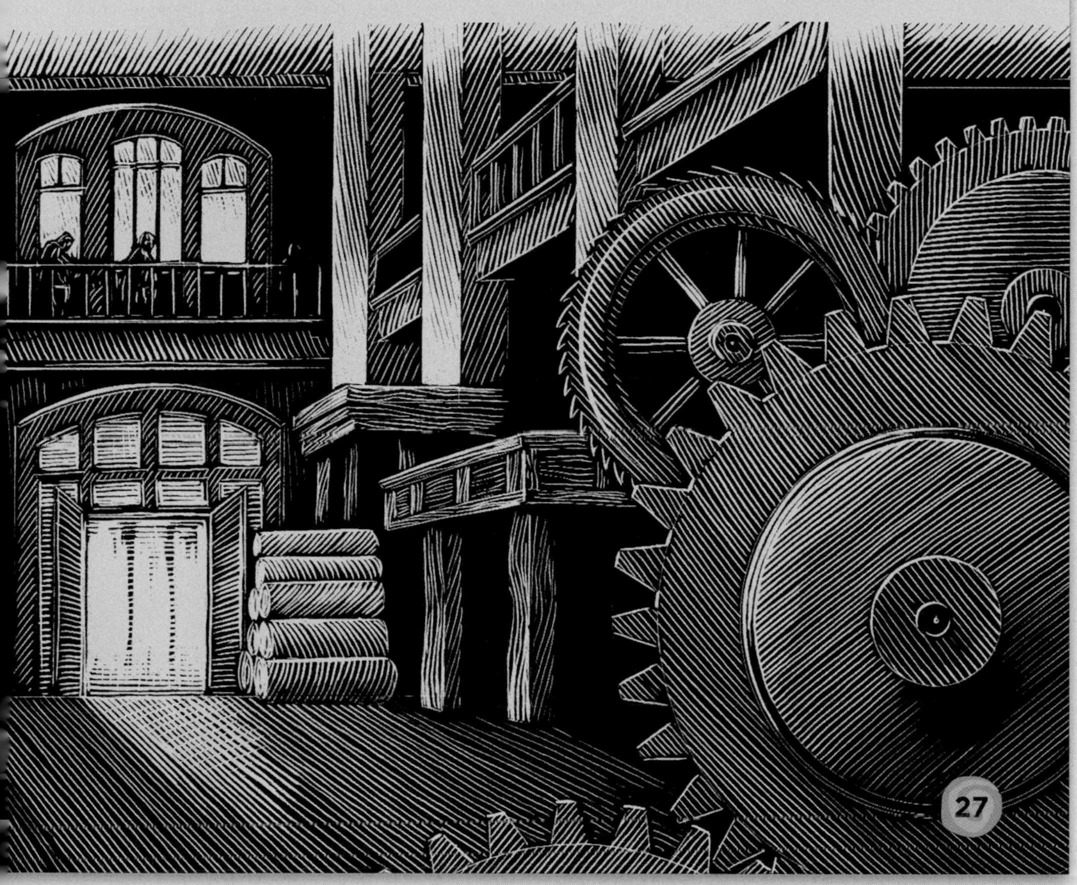

27

Teacher Think Aloud

I always think about the Industrial Revolution as a time that was good for people. New products were mass-produced, and people could buy goods more cheaply. But from this text, I see another side of the story. I can conclude that although this was a time of progress, it was also a time of great difficulty for poor workers and children who were abused by factory owners.

Fix-Up Strategies

Offer these strategies to help students read independently.

If you don't understand what you're reading:

- Reread the difficult section to look for clues to help you comprehend.
- Read ahead to find clues to help you comprehend.
- Retell, or say in your own words, what you've read.
- Visualize, or form mental pictures of, what you've read.

If you don't understand a word:

- Reread the sentence. Look for ideas and words that provide meaning clues.
- Find clues by reading a few sentences before and after the confusing word.
- Look for the base or root word and think about its meaning.
- Think about the topic or plot at this point to see if either offers meaning clues.

Student Journal pages 55–56

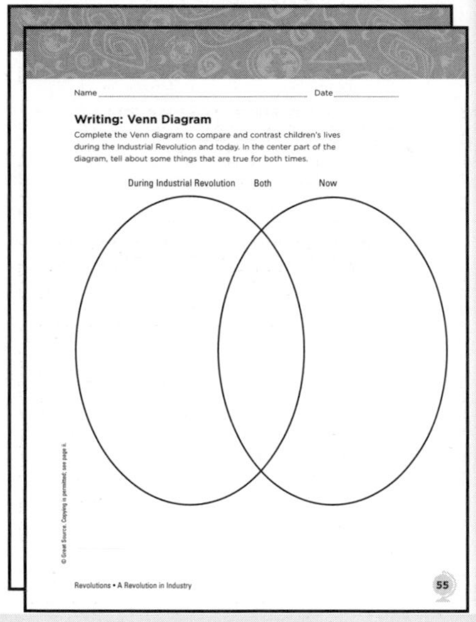

Name ______________________ Date __________

Writing: Venn Diagram

Complete the Venn diagram to compare and contrast children's lives during the Industrial Revolution and today. In the center part of the diagram, tell about some things that are true for both times.

During Industrial Revolution Both Now

© Great Source. Copying is permitted; see page ii.

Revolutions • A Revolution in Industry 55

The work was boring, and being on my feet all day was exhausting. I found it hard to work quickly, so that I could collect my share of cotton and meet my quota. But if I slowed down, even just a bit, the overseer hit me with a leather strap or dunked my head in the water tank.

Those punishments usually scared me awake, and I could work until I finished my shift. However, I remember one day when I hadn't collected my share of cotton. My punishment was to be weighted. The overseer tied a weight (it must have been twenty or thirty pounds) around my neck and made me walk up and down the factory aisles for what seemed like an hour. I was supposed to be an example for the others. I guess the overseer thought that after watching me, the others would work hard to avoid the same punishment. Believe me, I never missed my quota again, even if I had to steal cotton from someone else's bag. Luckily, I didn't suffer any long-term injuries from being weighted, although I do have a stiff neck when it rains.

Luckily, a week after walking with the weight, my mother got a letter from her sister, Jane. She lived with her husband on a farm in southern England. They needed extra help and were wondering if my brother and I could come. They'd give us food and beds, although they couldn't afford to pay us. We didn't stop to think about it but said yes right away. The next day my brother and I were on the train, and in a few hours, we were running barefoot across a green, fresh meadow! ◆

After Reading

Use one or more activities.

Check Purpose

Have students decide if their purpose was met. Were their responses correct in their anticipation guide? Did students learn how the Industrial Revolution changed children's lives?

Discussion Questions

Continue the group discussion with the following questions.

1. Compare the urban life and the farm life Bill describes. (Compare-Contrast)
2. What effect do you think Bill's punishment had on the other factory workers? (Cause-Effect)
3. If you were a child laborer, how would you cope with factory work? (Making Connections)

Revisit: Word Sort Chart

Have students revisit the word sort chart on *Student Journal* page 54. Have them discuss how they categorized initially. If their predicted sort for a word is incorrect, have them now write the correct part of speech in the chart.

Documenting the Horrors of the Time

Some writers who lived during the Industrial Revolution wrote about the awful conditions of the factories. Perhaps the most famous English writer from this time is Charles Dickens. You might have read or seen a film version of Dickens's A Christmas Carol. When Dickens was twelve, his family was in debt, and he was forced to work in a factory. His time in the factory haunted him his whole life. The scars from this experience show up in the dark themes of his books, including Great Expectations, Oliver Twist, and David Copperfield.

29

DIFFERENTIATED INSTRUCTION

SMALL GROUP

Vocabulary Synonyms and Antonyms

Review the terms *synonyms* and *antonyms.*

1. Display the words *child* and *labor.* Ask volunteers to suggest synonyms for *child.* (*kid, youngster, girl, boy*) Then ask for antonyms. (*adult, grownup*)
2. Ask volunteers to suggest synonyms and antonyms for the word *labor.* (synonyms: *work, pain*; antonyms: *relax, inactivity*)
3. Model how to use a thesaurus to find synonyms and antonyms.

Student Journal page 57

Name ______________________ Date __________

Vocabulary Building: Synonym and Antonym Chart

Choose three vocabulary words. For each word, think of a word or phrase that is a synonym (similar in meaning). Then think of a word or phrase that is an antonym (opposite in meaning). Use a thesaurus to help you, if you wish. Then answer the questions.

industrial employed urban flat
meager quote scavenger

Vocabulary Word	Synonyms	Antonyms
urban	city-like	rural

What are some present-day industries that you know about? ______________________

What vegetable would you like a meager portion of? ______________________

Where do you hope to be employed someday? ______________________

© Great Source. Copying is permitted; see page ii.

Revolutions • A Revolution in Industry 57

Writing Letter

Have students write a letter to Bill Miller telling him how life for children has changed since the Industrial Revolution. Before students write independently, brainstorm a list of differences between how children lived back then and now. Ask students to use the discussion list to complete the Venn diagram on *Student Journal* page 55. Then have them complete the letter-writing activity on *Student Journal* page 56.

Vocabulary Synonyms and Antonyms

Display the word *urban*. Ask: *What is the definition of* urban? *What other words come to mind when you hear or see* urban? Point out any synonyms or antonyms that students named. For example, *city* could be considered a synonym. Ask a volunteer for an antonym. (*rural* or *farmlike*) Now, have students complete *Student Journal* page 57. (See Differentiated Instruction.)

Phonics/Word Study Latin Roots

Ask: *Is anyone in this class bilingual? Does anyone know someone who is bilingual?* Then ask what *bilingual* means (speaking two languages). Note that the root *langu, lingu* means "tongue," or "language." Ask volunteers to name other words that contain this root, and list them on the board. Now, work with students to complete the in-depth Latin roots activity on TE page 132.

Phonics/Word Study

More Latin Roots

For instruction to introduce a root, see TE page 102. Work with students to discover the meaning of each root. See *Word Study Manual* page 59 for a related word sort.

langu/lingu
(the tongue)

language
lingo
bilingual
linguist
linguistics
multilingual

liber **(free)**

liberty
liberal
liberalism
liberate
libertine

man **(hand)**

manacle
manage
mandate
maneuver
manipulate
manner
manual
manufacture
manuscript
manicure

Discovering the Roots

langu/lingu	*liber*	*man*
language	liberty	manacle
linguist	liberal	manipulate
bilingual	liberate	manufacture
multilingual	libertine	manicure
lingo	liberalism	manual

For more information on word sorts and spelling stages, see pages 5–31 in the *Word Study Manual.*

Focus on . . .

Use one or more activities in this section to focus on a particular area of need in your students.

Comprehension STRATEGY SUPPORT

To help those students who need more practice using the strategies covered in this lesson, work one-on-one or in small groups to apply the strategy prompts below. Apply the prompts to a *Reading Advantage* paperback, a classroom library book, or a new or familiar selection in the magazine. Always model your own thinking first.

Monitor Understanding

- Do I understand what I'm reading? If not, what part is confusing to me?
- What fix-up strategies can I use to solve the problem? (See During Reading for fix-up strategies.)
- Why did a character say (do, think, ask) that?
- What images do I visualize from the text? What parts can't I visualize?
- Why did the author include (or not include) those details?

Inferential Thinking

- What are the causes or effects of this event?
- What do I learn from the character or person's thoughts, words, or actions?
- What do I know (or infer) from the text that the author hasn't stated directly?
- What conclusions can I draw?

Writing Chart

Show students how to create a T-chart about the benefits and drawbacks of the Industrial Revolution. First, discuss possible answers as a group. Then, have partners work together to create their own chart. Encourage students to look back into "A Revolution in Industry" to find drawbacks. They may need to infer benefits. Encourage students to use strong verbs and specific nouns in their charts.

Industrial Revolution	
Benefits	Drawbacks

For instruction on how to use strong verbs and specific nouns, see *Writing Advantage,* pages 30–55.

Fluency: Phrasing

After students have read the selection at least once silently, have student pairs choose two paragraphs to alternate reading aloud to each other.

As you listen to students read, use these prompts to guide them.

- Preview what you will read. Notice the different punctuation marks and what these signal to you. Pause at commas and periods. Put excitement into your voice when you see an exclamation point.
- Look for groups of words that naturally go together. Many times, words are held together or "chunked" with commas. Reading these words in "chunks" will help you sound natural.

When students read aloud, do they—

✓ demonstrate quick recognition of words and phrases?
✓ exhibit an understanding of phrasal construction?
✓ incorporate appropriate timing, stress, and intonation?

English Language Learners

To support students in preparation for the vocabulary activity on page 131, work with students to build background knowledge about urban, suburban, and rural areas.

1. Gather pictures of urban, suburban, and rural areas.
2. Have students work with a partner to discuss what they notice about the pictures. Ask them to describe what they see.
3. As a group, brainstorm synonyms and antonyms associated with each of the areas.

Independent Activity Options

While you work with individuals or small groups, others can work independently on one or more of the following options.

- Level D paperback books, see TE pages 367–372
- Level D *eZines*
- Repeat word sorts from this lesson
- *Student Journal* pages for this lesson
- *Writing Advantage* independent lessons

Assessment

Strategy Assessment

To help you and your students assess their use of comprehension strategies, ask the following questions. Students can complete a written response or provide verbal answers in a one-on-one reading conference.

1. **Monitor Understanding** What part of this selection did you visualize the best? Describe what you "saw." (Answers will vary. Possible response: I imagine the smoky, dirty, dark factory rooms with low ceilings.)
2. **Inferential Thinking** With the information in this selection, how would you compare life on a farm with life in a factory? (Answers will vary. Possible responses may include that both types of work were difficult and involved long hours. Working on a farm involved fresh air, some freedom of movement, and breaks for good meals. Working in a factory was dirty and abusive, there were no breaks, and bosses kept an eye on workers, punishing them if they did not work fast enough.)

For ongoing informal assessment, use the checklists on pages 61–64 of *Level D Assessment*.

Word Study Assessment

Use these steps to help you and your students assess their understanding of Latin roots.

1. Present the chart below. Read the roots and words aloud.
2. Have students explain how the meaning of each word is related to the root.

man "hand"	*langu, lingu* "tongue"	*liber* "free"
manual	language	liberty
manicure	linguist	liberate
manufacture	multilingual	liberal

LESSON **17**

Sophie Germain: A Revolutionary Thinker

Revolutions, pages 30–34

SUMMARY

This **biographical sketch** of Sophie Germain tells how she overcame social prejudices to become a respected mathematician.

COMPREHENSION STRATEGY

Understanding Text Structure

WRITING

Biographical Sketch

VOCABULARY

Context

PHONICS/WORD STUDY

Latin Roots *medi/medio, mem, mob/mot*

Lesson Vocabulary

embodies	engrossed
prominent	pseudonym
baffled	innovative
extensive	indignity

SUMMARY

Revolutions, pp. 30–34
Student Journal, pp. 58–61
Word Study Manual, p. 52
Writing Advantage, pp. 56–93

Sophie Germain: A Revolutionary Thinker

SOPHIE GERMAIN HAD REVOLUTIONARY IDEAS FOR A MATHEMATICIAN—AND FOR A WOMAN. IN A TIME WHEN MOST WOMEN WERE PREVENTED FROM LEARNING MATHEMATICS, GERMAIN IMPRESSED MALE MATHEMATICIANS WITH HER FRESH IDEAS ABOUT NUMBERS.

Sophie Germain was born in Paris, France, in 1776. Germain's life embodies the word *revolutionary.* Her ideas about mathematics became prominent because of her fighting spirit. Germain was intelligent, brave, and stubborn, and she solved math problems that had left male mathematicians baffled.

As the middle child of a wealthy family, Germain grew up in a home filled with books, ideas, and conversation. In 1789, as the French Revolution shook the streets of Paris, Germain turned thirteen. Because of the danger on the streets, Germain was not allowed to leave the house or play outside. On one particularly boring day, Germain crept into her father's extensive, well-stocked library. There, as she sat reading, she came across the story of Archimedes, known as the "father of calculus."

Archimedes (287-212 B.C.) was a Greek mathematician who lived for a time on the island of Sicily. After the Romans invaded Sicily, they held Archimedes prisoner. One day, while he was working on a math problem, a Roman guard who didn't know Archimedes began questioning him. Archimedes was so involved in solving the problem that he didn't hear or answer the guard. The guard became fed up and ended up killing Archimedes. After reading the story of Archimedes, Germain thought that anyone who became so engrossed in a topic that he didn't hear an armed guard must be studying something interesting. As legend has it, from then on, Germain studied math.

Before Reading

Use one or more activities.

Make a Chart

Ask: *Who are some people who might be considered revolutionary thinkers?* Record students' thoughts in a chart such as this one:

Revolutionary Thinkers
1. Martin Luther King, Jr.: Nonviolent protests brought social reform.
2. Galileo Galilei: Ideas about solar system went against the church.

Vocabulary Preview

Display the selection vocabulary. Ask students to complete the word associations activity on *Student Journal* page 58.

Preview the Selection

Have students skim the selection. Discuss what students notice. Can they tell that it's a biography? Why?

Make Predictions/ Set Purpose

Students should use the information gathered in the selection preview to make predictions about what they will learn about Sophie Germain. To help students set a purpose, suggest that they read to discover how a woman changed the field of mathematics.

DIFFERENTIATED INSTRUCTION 

Comprehension

UNDERSTANDING TEXT STRUCTURE

To help students become familiar with the chronological, or time-order, text structure, have them create a timeline as they read, using the dates and events from the text. Then have them work in pairs to retell the order of events in Sophie Germain's life.

Student Journal page 58

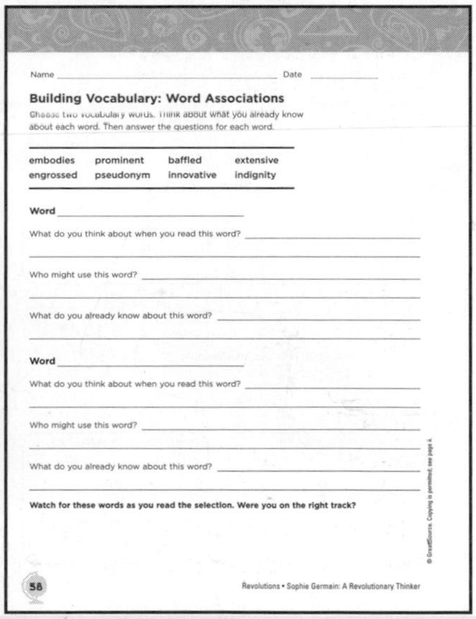

Name ______________________ Date __________

Building Vocabulary: Word Associations

Choose two vocabulary words. Think about what you already know about each word. Then answer the questions for each word.

embodies	prominent	baffled	extensive
engrossed	pseudonym	innovative	indignity

Word ______________________

What do you think about when you read this word? ______________________

Who might use this word? ______________________

What do you already know about this word? ______________________

Word ______________________

What do you think about when you read this word? ______________________

Who might use this word? ______________________

What do you already know about this word? ______________________

Watch for these words as you read the selection. Were you on the right track?

© Great Source. Copying is permitted; see page ii.

58 Revolutions • Sophie Germain: A Revolutionary Thinker

During Reading

Comprehension

SMALL GROUP

UNDERSTANDING TEXT STRUCTURE

Use these questions to model how to identify the chronological, or time-order, text structure of the biographical sketch. Then have students identify parts of the text that help them recognize the text structure.

- How is this selection structured?
- What clue words help me follow the structure of the text?

(See Differentiated Instruction.)

Teacher Think Aloud

This selection tells me the story of Sophie Germain's life. In the first sentence, I see a date: 1776. In the next paragraph, I see another date: 1789. As I continue to read, I see more dates. These dates go in time-order. I am reading about the events of Sophie's life in the order they occurred. Knowing the order of events helps me keep track of the information.

Fix-Up Strategies

Offer these strategies to help students read independently.

If you don't understand what you're reading:

- Reread the difficult section to look for clues to help you comprehend.
- Read ahead to find clues to help you comprehend.
- Retell, or say in your own words, what you've read.
- Visualize, or form mental pictures of, what you've read.

During this time, it wasn't proper for a young, upper-class girl to study math. It was, however, acceptable for girls to know something about math in case the subject came up at a party. Although Germain's mother and father tried to stop it, Germain's desire for knowledge continued. Using the books in her father's library, Germain taught herself math. To avoid her parents' disapproval, Germain studied at night after they went to sleep. When they found out what she was doing, Germain's parents refused to make fires or light candles in her room at night so she would be forced to stay in bed. Finally, her parents realized that they couldn't stop her.

In 1794, when Germain was eighteen, a new math school opened in Paris. Germain wasn't allowed to sign up for classes because she was a woman. However, she found a way to get the notes from the classes, and she studied them on her own. During this time, Germain became interested in the ideas of a man named J. L. Lagrange. At the end of the semester, using the fake male name M. LeBlanc, Germain turned in a paper to Lagrange. The paper impressed him so much that he wanted to meet the student who had written it. Lagrange was amazed that the author of the paper was a woman, and he agreed to teach Germain. With the support of Lagrange, Germain gained access to the world of mathematics.

In 1804, a German mathematician named Gauss caught Germain's interest. She wrote to him, again using her fake name, or pseudonym (SUE duh nim). Gauss didn't find out for three years that his pen pal was a woman. When he found out, he was thrilled. Gauss and Germain wrote letters back and forth, sharing innovative ideas about number theory. These exchanges of new ideas led Germain to her most important ideas about math. Unfortunately, Gauss took a job teaching science at a university. Once out of the field of mathematics, Gauss stopped writing to Germain.

Germain thought she needed a new teacher. At this time, the French Academy announced a contest that would last two years. For the contest, mathematicians had to write papers explaining a complicated mathematical idea. Germain worked hard on her paper. Although Germain's was the only paper in the contest, she didn't win the prize. It was clear to the judges that the author of the paper had not attended college. Her theory was good, but there were basic errors. To allow more entries, the contest deadline was pushed back two years.

Student Journal pages 59–60

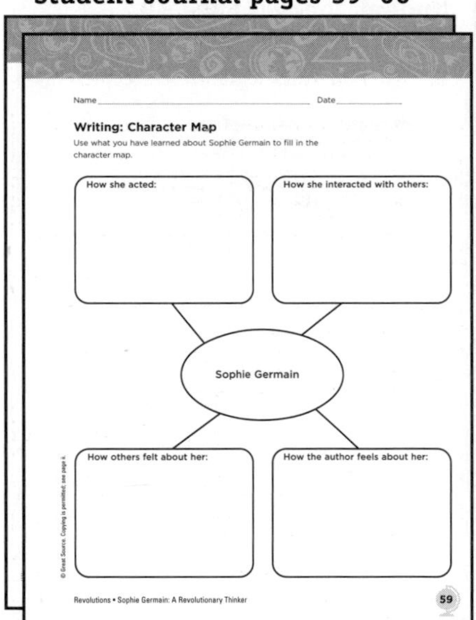

Name ________________ Date ________

Writing: Character Map

Use what you have learned about Sophie Germain to fill in the character map.

How she acted:

How she interacted with others:

Sophie Germain

How others felt about her:

How the author feels about her:

Revolutions • Sophie Germain: A Revolutionary Thinker 59

After Reading  Use one or more activities.

Check Purpose

Have students decide if their purpose was met. Can students explain how Germain was able to change the field of mathematics?

Discussion Questions

Continue the group discussion with the following questions.

1. What obstacles did Sophie Germain have to overcome to achieve her goal? (Details)
2. What do you think of Germain? If you could ask her one question, what would it be? (Making Connections)
3. What features does the selection have that make it a biography? (Understanding Text Structure)

Revisit: Chart

Revisit the revolutionary thinkers chart students began in Before Reading. Do students think Sophie Germain's name should be added to the chart? Do they think Sofia Kovalevsky's name should be added to the chart? Why or why not?

Revisit: Word Associations

Ask students to share what they wrote for the word associations activity on *Student Journal* page 58. Were they on the right track?

Another Great Female Thinker

Sofia Kovalevsky (1850-1891) was the first woman to receive a Ph.D. in mathematics. As a young woman, Sofia showed great promise, but the universities in her native Russia would not allow women to attend classes. Sofia decided to leave Russia in order to study mathematics. At the time, women couldn't travel alone, so Sofia married Vladimir Kovalevsky and then moved to Switzerland, where she studied for a year with a famous mathematician. She went on to spend four years studying in Berlin, Germany, and earned her Ph.D. in 1874. Because of strict policies against hiring female professors, Sofia couldn't get a job. In 1883, Sofia was hired as a lecturer at the University of Stockholm in Sweden. Despite facing many obstacles, Sofia persisted in her quest for knowledge and recognition. Every year since 1985, high schools and colleges in the United States have observed Sofia Kovalevsky Day. The day both honors Sofia and encourages young women to study mathematics.

33

DIFFERENTIATED INSTRUCTION

Writing

Biographical Sketch

To help students understand a character map, use these strategies:

1. Explain that a character map is a tool for keeping track of information about the main character in a biographical sketch.
2. Work with students to identify kinds of information they would expect in a biographical sketch (what the person says and does; how others feel about her).
3. Have students skim page 30 to find as much as they can about Sophie Germain. Help them categorize their findings.

Student Journal page 61

Name ______ Date ______

Building Vocabulary: Using Context to Understand a Word

Select a vocabulary word you defined from the context. Complete the statements and answer the questions about your word.

embodies	prominent	baffled	extensive
engrossed	pseudonym	innovative	indignity

My Word in Context:

I think this word means ______

because ______

My word is ______

My word is not ______

Where else might I find this word? ______

What makes this an important word to know? ______

Revolutions • Sophie Germain: A Revolutionary Thinker 61

Writing Biographical Sketch

Have students review what they learned about Sophie Germain. Discuss these points: how she acted, how she interacted with others, how others felt about her, and how the author feels about her. Record students' responses and have students refer to these notes as they complete the character map on *Student Journal* page 59. Then have students write their own biographical sketches of Germain, on *Student Journal* page 60. (See Differentiated Instruction.)

Vocabulary Context

Write these sentences, underlining the word *innovative*: "*Gauss and Germain wrote letters back and forth, sharing* innovative *ideas about number theory. These exchanges of new ideas led Germain to her most important ideas about math.*" Have students read the sentences. Then point out that the second sentence provides the context needed to figure out what *innovative* means. (new) Have students complete *Student Journal* page 61.

Phonics/Word Study

Latin Roots

Display these words: *memory, remember, memoir*. Ask partners to discuss what these words have in common. (a syllable or root) Then write the Latin root *mem* on the board. Explain that the root means "remembering." Ask students how the meaning of each of the three words is related to the Latin root. Now, work with students to complete the in-depth Latin roots activity on TE page 139.

Germain wrote her old mentor, Lagrange, and he helped her correct her mistakes. Two years later, Germain turned in her improved paper. She won an honorable mention. The contest continued. Germain worked on the paper for two more years and turned it in again. On the third try, she won first place. Her paper, called "Memoir on the Vibrations of Elastic Plates," was an important contribution to the field of the elasticity of metals. The ideas behind her paper, which she worked on for six years, became her life's work. Germain spent most of her career working and reworking the ideas in this paper.

Winning the prize from the French Academy opened doors for Sophie Germain. She became known as a distinguished mathematician. She became the first woman to attend lectures and classes at the French Academy of Science. Germain knew that her achievements were important for all women.

At the age of fifty-five, Sophie Germain died of breast cancer. On her death certificate in the space marked *profession,* she was identified as a "property owner," not a mathematician. Despite this final indignity, Germain's long-lasting reputation is as a groundbreaking female mathematician. ◆

Making Math Fun

Theoni Pappas (born 1944) wants to make math fun. She knows from her many years as a high school math teacher that many people are afraid of numbers. In the late 1970s, Pappas and her business partner started a company that makes fun things, such as T-shirts and calendars, which contain mathematical shapes, theories, or concepts. On the math calendar, each day has a problem. The answer to the problem is the date! Pappas wants to combine math and humor in order to break down people's fears about math. She has even published a book of poetry about mathematical topics.

34

Phonics/Word Study

More Latin Roots

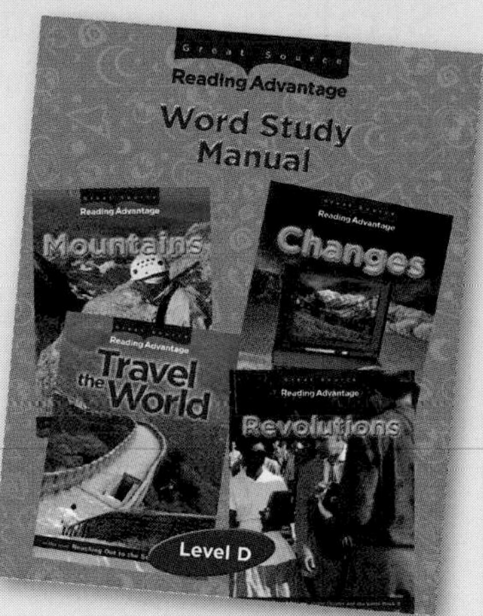

For instruction to introduce a root, see TE page 102. Work with students to discover the meaning of each root. See *Word Study Manual* page 52 for a related word sort.

medi/medio **(middle)**

intermediate mediocre
medial Mediterranean
median medium
mediate medieval

mem **(mindful, remembering)**

Discuss the concepts of *memoir* and *memorabilia*. Many students may be unfamiliar with the words.

memory commemorate
memorize memo
memoir remembrance
memorial memento
memorabilia

mob/mot **(to move)**

automobile mob
bookmobile motel
immobile motion
mobile motor
mobility remote
locomotion promote

Discovering the Roots

medi/medio	*mem*	*mob/mot*
medial	memory	mobility
mediocre	memorial	automobile
medium	commemorate	bookmobile
median	memo	motel
mediate	remembrance	locomotion

For more information on word sorts and spelling stages, see pages 5–31 in the *Word Study Manual.*

Focus on . . .

Use one or more activities in this section to focus on a particular area of need in your students.

Comprehension STRATEGY SUPPORT

To help those students who need more practice using the strategies covered in this lesson, work one-on-one or in small groups to apply the strategy prompts below. Apply the prompts to a *Reading Advantage* paperback, a classroom library book, or a new or familiar selection in the magazine. Always model your own thinking first.

Understanding Text Structure

- What kind of text is this? (book, story, article, guidebook, play, manual)
- How does the author organize the text? (cause-effect, problem-solution, chronological order, description, question-answer, comparison-contrast)
- What details support my thoughts about the text structure?
- What is the cause (effect, problem, solution, order, question, answer)?
- If fiction, who are the characters? What is the setting, plot, conflict, and resolution?

Writing Obituary

Invite students to correct the final indignity shown on Sophie Germain's death certificate by writing an obituary worthy of a distinguished mathematician. Before beginning, brainstorm a list of information that is usually included in an obituary, or death notice. (date of death, birth; family members, accomplishments) If possible, provide obituaries for students to use as models.

If you'd like students to edit their writing, see lessons in *Writing Advantage*, pages 56–93, for different kinds of editing instruction.

Fluency: Pacing

After students have read the selection at least once, they can select two or three paragraphs to practice fluent reading. Students can read aloud to a partner. Circulate among students as they read, using these prompts to help them read at an even pace.

- Listen to me read. Then read it just like I did.
- Read a little bit faster (or slower) so readers can make sense of the words.
- Practice saying the words and names you are unfamiliar with. That way you won't hesitate or stumble over the words when you read.

When students read aloud, do they—

✓ demonstrate a smooth pace, not too fast or too slow?
✓ incorporate well-timed pauses between words and phrases?
✓ reflect an awareness and understanding of punctuation?

English Language Learners

Practice with students the skill of making connections.

1. Display *perseverance* and *determination*. Discuss the words' meanings and explain that they are synonyms.
2. Ask students to think about a time when they demonstrated these qualities, and have them share.
3. Have students make connections with the story and relate their perseverance and determination with that of Sophie.

Independent Activity Options

While you work with individuals or small groups, others can work independently on one or more of the following options.

- Level D paperback books, see TE pages 367–372
- Level D *eZines*
- Repeat word sorts from this lesson
- *Student Journal* pages for this lesson
- *Writing Advantage* independent lessons

Assessment

Strategy Assessment

To help you and your students assess their use of comprehension strategies, ask the following question. Students can complete a written response or provide verbal answers in a one-on-one reading conference.

- **Understanding Text Structure** How did the text structure help you understand the text? (Answers will vary. Possible responses may include that the story was told in time-order, which made it easy to follow Sophie's accomplishments.)

See *Level D Assessment* page 22 for formal assessment to go with *Revolutions*.

Word Study Assessment

Use these steps to help you and your students assess their understanding of Latin roots.

1. Present the chart below. Read the roots and words aloud.
2. Have students explain how the meaning of each word is related to the root.

medi/medio "middle"	*mem* "mindful, remembering"	*mob/mot* "to move"
mediocre	commemorate	mobility
median	memorial	automobile
medium	memory	locomotion

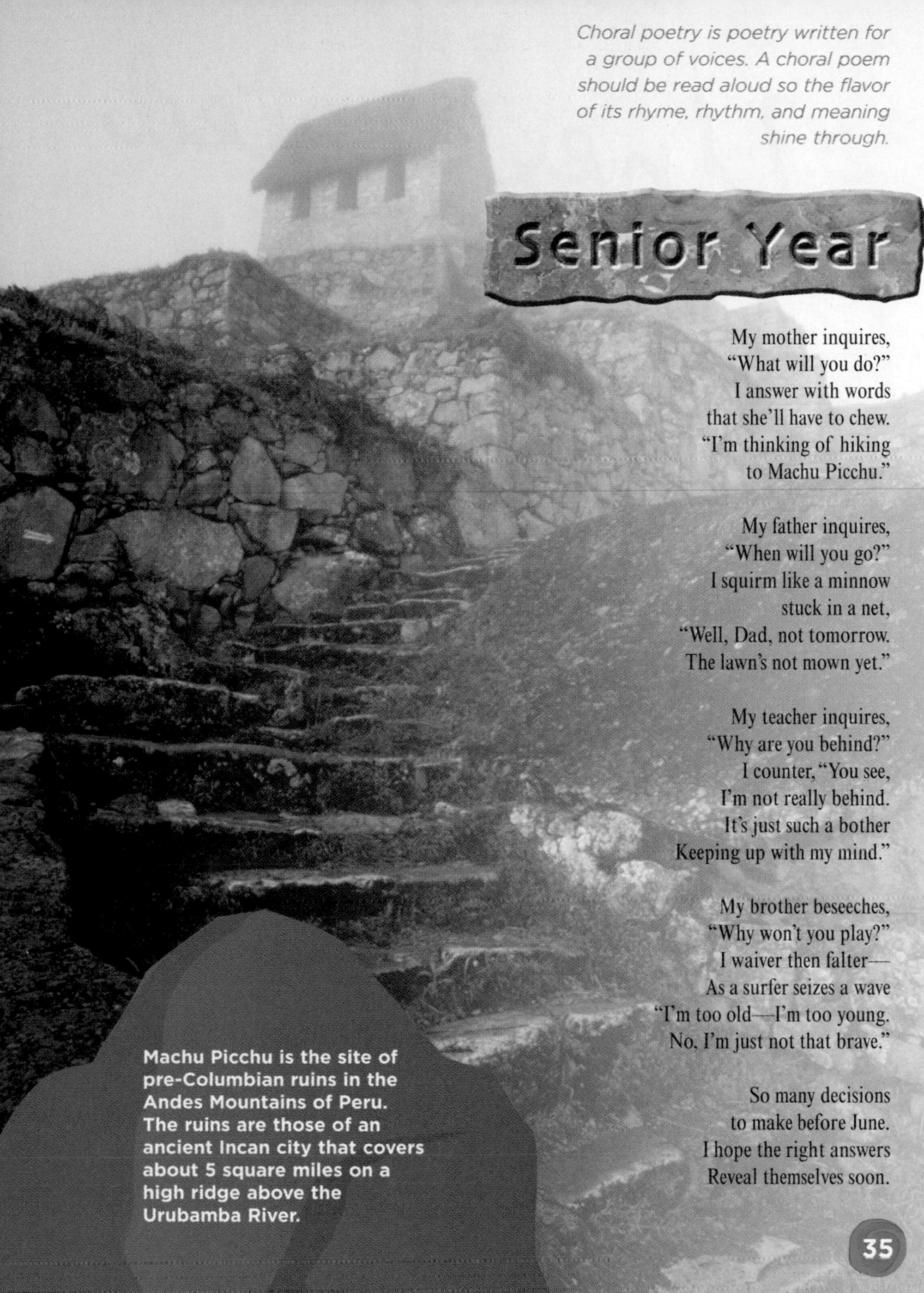

Choral poetry is poetry written for a group of voices. A choral poem should be read aloud so the flavor of its rhyme, rhythm, and meaning shine through.

Senior Year

My mother inquires,
"What will you do?"
I answer with words
that she'll have to chew.
"I'm thinking of hiking
to Machu Picchu."

My father inquires,
"When will you go?"
I squirm like a minnow
stuck in a net,
"Well, Dad, not tomorrow.
The lawn's not mown yet."

My teacher inquires,
"Why are you behind?"
I counter, "You see,
I'm not really behind.
It's just such a bother
Keeping up with my mind."

My brother beseeches,
"Why won't you play?"
I waiver then falter—
As a surfer seizes a wave
"I'm too old—I'm too young.
No, I'm just not that brave."

So many decisions
to make before June.
I hope the right answers
Reveal themselves soon.

Machu Picchu is the site of pre-Columbian ruins in the Andes Mountains of Peru. The ruins are those of an ancient Incan city that covers about 5 square miles on a high ridge above the Urubamba River.

35

LESSON **18**

Senior Year *and* An Unexpected Revolution

Revolutions, pages 35–43

SUMMARY

The **poem** and **short story** both deal with decisions and consequences.

COMPREHENSION STRATEGIES

Making Connections
Understanding Text Structure

WRITING

Book Jacket

VOCABULARY

Denotation and Connotation

PHONICS/WORD STUDY

Latin Roots *mort, numer, pater/pat*

Lesson Vocabulary

tentatively	insensitive
elapsed	defiant
JV	exercising

MATERIALS

Revolutions, pp. 35–43
Student Journal, pp. 62–65
Word Study Manual, p. 53
Writing Advantage, pp. 94–113

Before Reading

WHOLE CLASS Use one or more activities.

Read "Senior Year"

Ask: *What is revolutionary?* Have students read the poem, and discuss.

Make a List

Brainstorm with students a list of school sports. Divide the list into team-oriented and individually oriented sports.

School Sports	
Team	Individual
Baseball	Tennis
Soccer	Track

Vocabulary Preview

Display the selection vocabulary. Assess prior knowledge by asking students to begin the predictions chart on *Student Journal* page 62. They will finish it later.

Preview the Selection

Have students survey the eight pages of the story. Discuss students' observations of important text features.

Make Predictions/Set Purpose

Students should use the information gathered in the selection preview to make predictions about what they will learn about the characters and plot. To help students set a purpose, suggest that they read to discover why the story is titled "An Unexpected Revolution."

DIFFERENTIATED INSTRUCTION

Comprehension

MAKING CONNECTIONS

Prompt students to make connections with the text by asking these questions:

- Have I ever read anything about a female who joined an all-male sport or career? How was that person like Naomi?
- How is Naomi's family similar to other families I know?
- How are the students in Naomi's school like students I know?

Student Journal page 62

Name ______ Date ______

Building Vocabulary: Predictions

How do you think these words will be used in "An Unexpected Revolution"? Write your answers in the second column. Next, read the article. Then, clarify your answers in the third column.

Word	My prediction for how the word will be used	How the word was actually used
tentatively		
elapsed		
JV		
insensitive		
defiant		
exercising		

62 Revolutions • An Unexpected Revolution

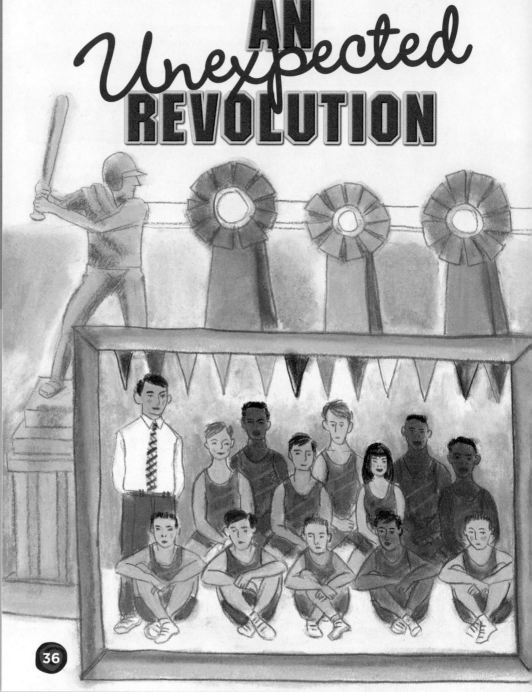

AN *Unexpected* REVOLUTION

36

During Reading

Comprehension

MAKING CONNECTIONS

Use these questions to model making connections to a text. Then have students make their own connections to the text.

- What do I know about school sports teams?
- Has anyone I know tried to join a team in the same way Naomi did?

(See Differentiated Instruction.)

Teacher Think Aloud

At my school, there are separate teams for boys and girls. If a girl wants to play basketball, for example, she has to try out for the girls' team. Even if she is better than all the boys on the boys' team, I don't think she'd be allowed to play on the boys' team. But there's only a boys' hockey team, no girls' team. I wonder what would happen if a girl tried out for the hockey team.

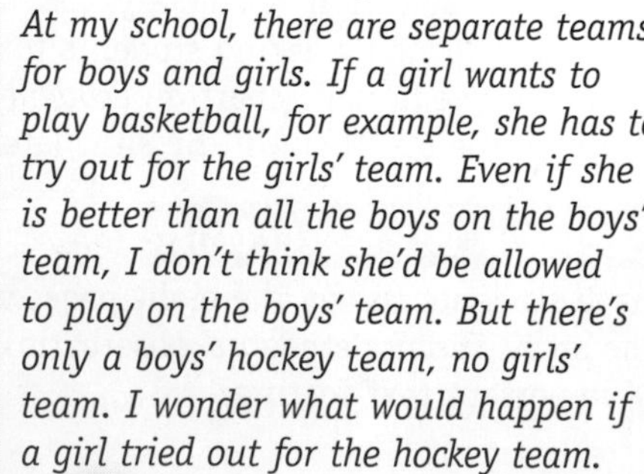

Comprehension

UNDERSTANDING TEXT STRUCTURE

Use these questions to model how to understand the structure of realistic fiction. Then have students identify and describe the story elements.

- Who is the main character? What problem or conflict does she face?
- What is the setting of the story?
- How do I know it is realistic fiction?

(See Differentiated Instruction.)

"**See** you tomorrow, Mrs. Hashimi."

"Didn't you say you were trying out for the team tomorrow?"

"I was going to, but I'm having second thoughts. Maybe it isn't such a good idea for a girl to be on the wrestling team, anyway."

"I don't see why not. We women wrestle with as many things in life as men do."

"In a way, maybe you're right. But I'm nervous about my physical condition."

"You are the fittest young person I know, Naomi."

Naomi blushed. She was fit and proud of the effort she put into getting in shape: running three miles before school and lifting weights at the gym on the weekends. When most kids in her class were vegging-out in front of the TV, Naomi was active.

"I'll let you know what I decide. Bye." Naomi quietly closed the door to Mrs. Hashimi's room and headed toward the front door of the nursing home, waving to Mr. Hart and Mr. Bass. As she stepped outside, she took a deep breath of the cool, fall air. She could smell the earthy scent of autumn leaves and the hint of apples in the air. Fall was a big joker, she thought to herself as she headed home: one last burst of color, full of hope, and then months of gray.

"Hi, Sweetie. Do you want a snack?"

"No, thanks, Mom. I can wait 'til dinner. I'm going upstairs to start on my homework." Naomi brushed a quick kiss on her mother's cheek and started for her room. At the top of the stairs, she noticed her shoulders were tense. She took a deep breath and exhaled. *What am I going to do?* she thought.

Naomi shut the door to her bedroom. The thought still seemed odd to her. After all, it just became *her* room a year ago. Before then, she had shared the room with her twin brother, Nate. They had shared so many things. Nate and Naomi: they finished each other's sentences; they liked the same foods, colors, music; they both dreamed of traveling the world.

Naomi slumped into her desk chair. She had convinced her parents to keep Nate's bed in the room, arguing that she'd be having girlfriends over, and they could sleep on the bed. Naomi opened her chemistry book and started working on equations. Her eyes were tired from reading to Mrs. Hashimi. She closed them for a moment and drifted off.

A hush came over the gym. Naomi could feel the hard metal bleachers through her jeans, and held her father's hands to warm her own. On the mat, Nate jumped around like a boxer. He was quite small for his age, wrestling at 98 pounds as a freshman. He was twelve pounds lighter than Naomi. Blue and white streamers whirred from the fans. This was the regional meet, and winners would qualify for the state meet. As a first-year wrestler, Nate had gone further than anyone imagined. He'd wanted to wrestle ever since studying Greek and Roman history in the fifth grade. He traced the pictures of the wrestlers from his textbook and hung them above his desk. Naomi thought their outfits were silly, but Nate was hooked.

37

DIFFERENTIATED INSTRUCTION

Comprehension

UNDERSTANDING TEXT STRUCTURE

Remind students of the basic elements of realistic fiction:

- a believable main character who faces a realistic conflict, or problem
- a real-life setting taking place in the present or near past
- a plot, or sequence of events, that is believable, moves the story forward, and shows how the conflict is resolved
- a theme, big idea, or message, that the author wants you to learn from the story

Teacher Think Aloud

The characters and plot in this selection are very believable. I think what happens in this story could happen in real life. This shows me the story can be considered realistic fiction.

Fix-Up Strategies

Offer these strategies to help students read independently.

If you don't understand what you're reading:

- Reread the difficult section to look for clues to help you comprehend.
- Read ahead to find clues to help you comprehend.
- Retell, or say in your own words, what you've read.
- Visualize, or form mental pictures of, what you've read.

If you don't understand a word:

- Reread the sentence. Look for ideas and words that provide meaning clues.
- Find clues by reading a few sentences before and after the confusing word.
- Look for the base or root word and think about its meaning.
- Think about the topic or plot at this point to see if either offers meaning clues.

DIFFERENTIATED INSTRUCTION

Writing Book Jacket

To help students complete the plot diagram on *Student Journal* page 63, help them define the following:

1. Exposition: The author introduces the setting, the main characters, and the background information.
2. Rising Action: The author presents a series of conflicts or struggles that a main character goes through.
3. Climax: This is the turning point of the story. It is usually the most intense point.
4. Falling Action: The conflict begins to resolve.
5. Resolution: This is the ending that brings the story to a close.

Student Journal pages 63–64

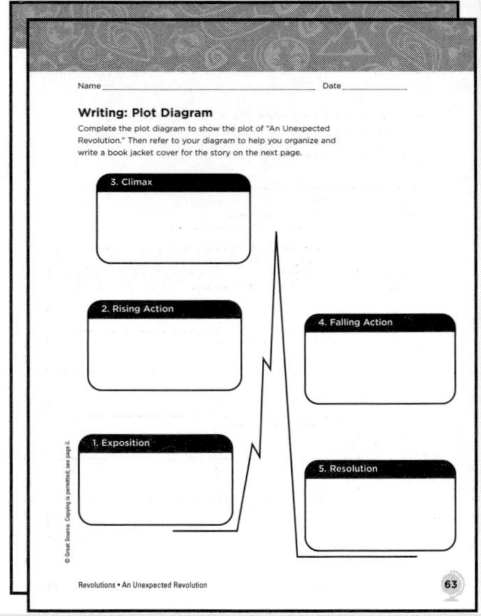

Name ____________ Date ________

Writing: Plot Diagram

Complete the plot diagram to show the plot of "An Unexpected Revolution." Then refer to your diagram to help you organize and write a book jacket cover for the story on the next page.

3. Climax

2. Rising Action

4. Falling Action

1. Exposition

5. Resolution

Revolutions • An Unexpected Revolution 63

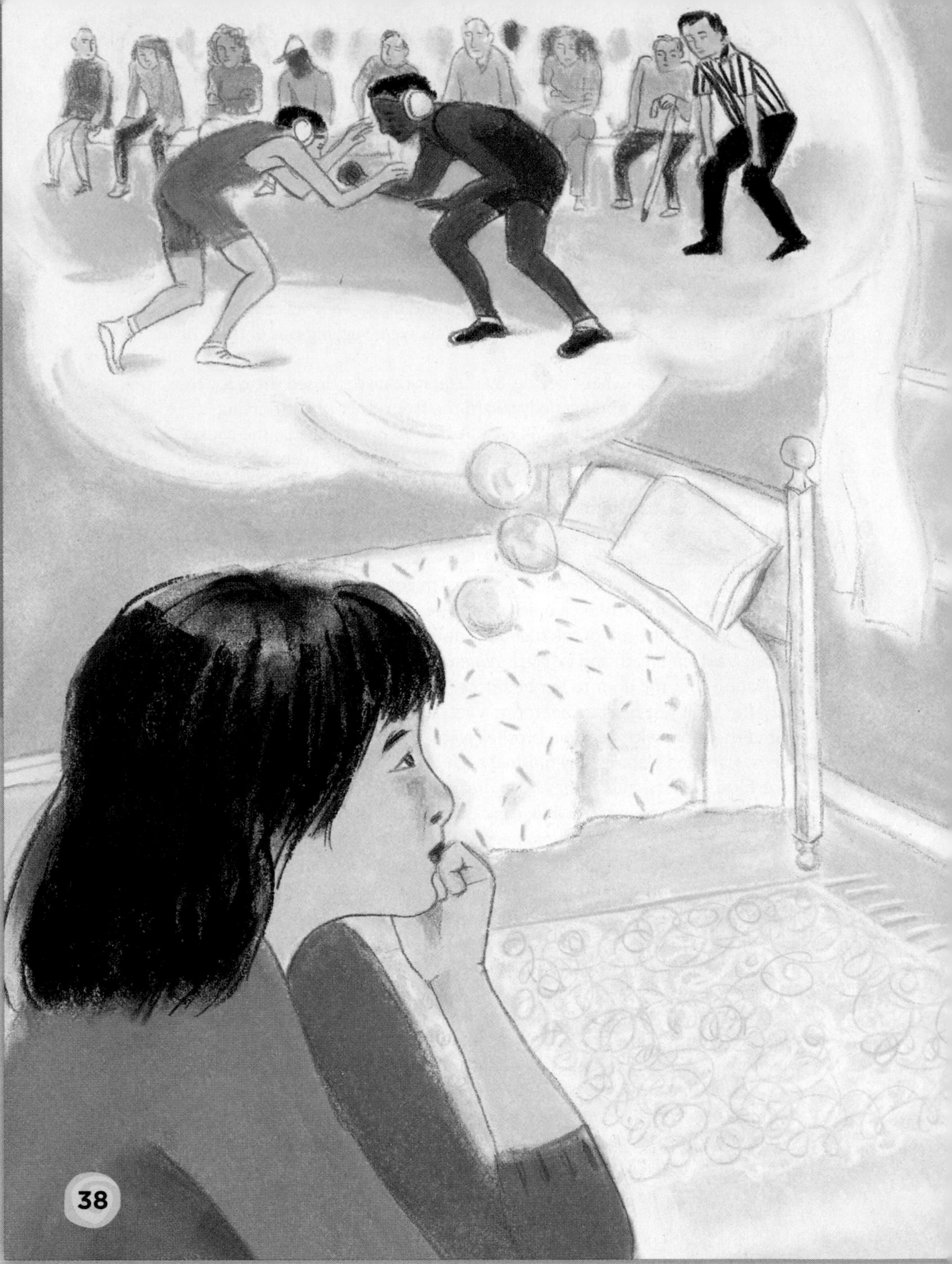

After Reading

Use one or more activities.

Check Purpose

Have students decide if their purpose was met. Were students able to predict what would happen if a girl tried to join the school wrestling team? Did they figure out why the story was titled "An Unexpected Revolution"?

Discussion Questions

Continue the group discussion.

1. Would you recommend this story to a friend? Why? (Making Connections)
2. Do you think this story is a good example of realistic fiction? Why? (Understanding Text Structure)
3. Why do you think the author chose this title? Do you agree with the author's choice? Explain your thinking. (Inferential Thinking)

Revisit: List

Ask students to look at the lists they created in Before Reading. If wrestling is not there, add it at this time and discuss how individualized sports can benefit from a team approach.

Revisit: Predictions Chart

Have students use context from the story to complete the predictions chart on *Student Journal* page 62. How were the words actually used?

Now, Nate was on his way to a medal and maybe even a trophy. The referee signaled for the two lightweights to enter the circle. Nate and his opponent faced off. Naomi giggled to herself. It always seemed like wrestlers danced together during the first few moments of a match. Nate had explained to her many times that he was getting a feeling for his opponent's moves, his center of gravity, and his level of concentration. Just then, Nathan's skin slapped against the mat, and in an instant, his head whipped back off the mat, slamming into the unpadded floor. A motionless body . . . Naomi's father standing . . .

"Naomi, supper!" Shaking off her dream, Naomi turned to the door. Her father stood, smiling.

"Be down in a minute, Dad."

"Hurry, we're having teriyaki tonight!"

Walking into school the next morning, Naomi couldn't escape the posters:

Wrestling Team Tryouts After School Today!

"Hey, Naomi."

"Hi, Shanelle. What's up?"

"Do you want to go to the mall after school? I need shoes for the dance tomorrow night."

"I'm not sure. I might be busy." Naomi's voice trailed off.

"That's OK. I'll catch you sixth period, and you can tell me then."

"No—I mean . . . let's just say . . . no. I'm pretty sure I won't make it."

"Well, you are going to the dance, aren't you?"

"Yeah, I guess so." Satisfied, Shanelle trotted off down the hall. Naomi slipped into English class.

"That's it. Class dismissed." Naomi jumped, startled by the bell and her English teacher's hand on her shoulder. "Are you all right, Naomi? You seem to be in another world today."

"I'm sorry, Mrs. Hathaway. I have a lot on my mind today."

"Well, don't make a habit of it. You are a terrific English student, and I don't want you to forget how important your junior year grades are to colleges."

"Yes, ma'am." Naomi crept, head down, into the hallway. *This is it*, she thought, as she watched students load up their backpacks at their lockers.

Naomi headed to the locker room, slipped out of her school clothes and into her blue and white uniform. Windows cracked for fresh air left her skin shivering with goose bumps. She crept into the gym as tentatively as a mouse. Boys were already seated on the first row of bleachers, and Coach Manuel paced in front of them, clipboard in hand, silver whistle dangling around his neck. It seemed to Naomi, as she stepped closer, that the huge room suddenly went silent.

"Well, Ms. Shaw, what can I do for you?" Coach Manuel smiled and checked his watch.

"I'm here to try out for the team." Naomi's voice sounded strange, as if it had suddenly gotten very high. A few boys laughed out loud, and others shifted uncomfortably on the bleachers. *How many minutes are going to pass before someone says something?* Naomi thought, although only a few seconds had elapsed.

"I see," Coach frowned. "We don't have any girls on the team, Ms. Shaw."

"I know, Coach. I'll wrestle boys."

Unsure of how to respond, Coach Manuel said, "Have a seat then."

"I'm not wrestling a girl," Jim Vance said and stood up.

"Sit down, Jim," Coach said. "Since this is tryouts for the JV team, and none of you have wrestled before, this tryout will consist mostly of physical fitness tests. Show me you have what it takes to train to be a wrestler, and I'll show you how to wrestle." Naomi smiled to herself. Physical fitness she could do.

That afternoon, Naomi outran all the boys in the two-mile race, did more sit-ups in a minute than all of them and more push-ups in a minute than all but one of them. After an hour of different tests, Naomi was pleased with her performance.

"That's it for today, guys. I mean, you all," Coach said. "Team lists will be posted by three o'clock tomorrow on my office door. Good work this afternoon."

39

Student Journal page 65

Name ________ Date ________

Building Vocabulary: Denotations and Connotations

Choose three vocabulary words. For each word, write a definition in the Denotation box. Then, in the Connotation box, write to tell what personal associations you have with the word. Last, tell where you might see the word used.

tentatively elapsed JV
insensitive defiant exercising

Word	Denotation (general meaning)	Connotation (personal association)
	1.	
	Where might I see this word?	
	2.	
	Where might I see this word?	
	3.	
	Where might I see this word?	

Revolutions • An Unexpected Revolution 65

Writing Book Jacket

Have students work in pairs to complete the plot diagram on *Student Journal* page 63. Then they can use their ideas to write a synopsis of the story on *Student Journal* page 64. Remind students that the text on a book jacket tells what a story is about—without giving away the ending. Share with students several book jackets so they can read some existing synopses. (See Differentiated Instruction.)

Vocabulary Denotation and Connotation

Remind students that words have denotations (general meanings) and connotations (personal associations). Point out that *tentatively* denotes "with uncertainty:" *We tentatively made plans to meet on Saturday*. Explain that a connotation for *tentatively* might deal with a shy person, or one who lacks confidence: *The new student tentatively entered the crowded classroom*. Have partners complete *Student Journal* page 65.

Phonics/Word Study Latin Roots

Display these words: *mortal*, *mortified*. Ask students what the words mean. Have students use a dictionary, if necessary. Then write the Latin root *mort* (death) on the board. Discuss the words in relation to the root. Now, work with students to complete the in-depth Latin roots activity on TE page 150.

The boys headed to their locker room and Naomi turned to go. "Ms. Shaw, may I have a word with you?"

"Yes, Coach."

"That was quite a performance you put on this afternoon. Now tell me you aren't serious."

"I can't do that, Coach. I really want to be on the team."

"But, Naomi, there are no other girls in the league."

"I don't mind, Coach. I'll wrestle anyone who is at my weight. That's fair, right?"

"You know that you are going to cause a lot of problems. But I don't see how I can keep you off the team. You're in better shape than any of the boys."

"Thanks, Coach."

"Don't thank me, yet."

✲ ✲ ✲ ✲ ✲ ✲ ✲ ✲ ✲ ✲

"I did it, Mrs. Hashimi."

"Oh, I knew you would. I'm so proud of you, Naomi."

"I don't know if I have time to read today, but I'll be back Monday after school, okay?"

"Not tomorrow?"

"Well, there's a dance tomorrow night . . . "

"Don't say another word. Hurry home, and tell your parents."

Naomi dashed out of the nursing home, waving in a flurry to Mr. Hart and Mr. Bass. She hadn't stopped to think that her parents would be anything but happy until she grasped the screen door handle. Opening it, she saw her mother and father seated at the kitchen table. Naomi slinked in.

"Mrs. Vance just called me."

"Uh-huh."

"Jim said you were at wrestling tryouts?"

"Yes, I . . . "

"I don't want to hear it." Her mother stood and ran out of the kitchen, holding her hand over her mouth.

"How could you be so insensitive to your mother's feelings, Naomi?"

"What do you mean, Dad? I just thought . . . "

"No, you *didn't* think. That's the problem. Your brother *died* wrestling, Naomi. Why would you even think of doing it?"

"I didn't, I mean, it's not . . . " Naomi couldn't organize her thoughts to speak. She wanted to tell her father that Nate loved wrestling. He was happiest when he was training with his teammates. He was never afraid. And wrestling made Naomi feel closer to him, connected in a way. She knew Nate wouldn't mind. He would want her to love wrestling as much as he did. But Naomi couldn't speak. She couldn't face the pain in her father's eyes.

"Just go to your room. Leave your mother alone. She's very upset. And, you are *not* going to wrestle." Naomi didn't argue, even though part of her felt defiant, as if she had to stand up for what she believed in. Her parents had never forbidden her from doing anything before.

In her room, exhausted from tryouts, Naomi collapsed on the bed and slept straight through dinner. The next morning, she slipped out of the house before her parents awoke.

"I can't believe you went to wrestling tryouts!" Shanelle snuck up behind Naomi at her locker. "Everyone's talking about you. It's like you started some female revolution. Everyone is saying you really shamed those guys, Naomi. Just wait until you beat them in matches!"

"I'm not going to be on the team, Shanelle."

"What? You have to be! You have no idea what you started. Missy Toan is writing a letter to the school newspaper about how many extracurricular activities exclude girls and how the student council is going to ask the principal to make some changes."

"Listen, I didn't ask to be a spokesperson for all the girls in school."

"There's a sit-in happening right now in the commons, and all the girls want you to speak." Naomi noticed a group of teachers heading toward the commons area along with a cluster of girls holding signs. As she turned to go, she saw her parents walk into school.

"Mom? Dad? What are you doing here?"

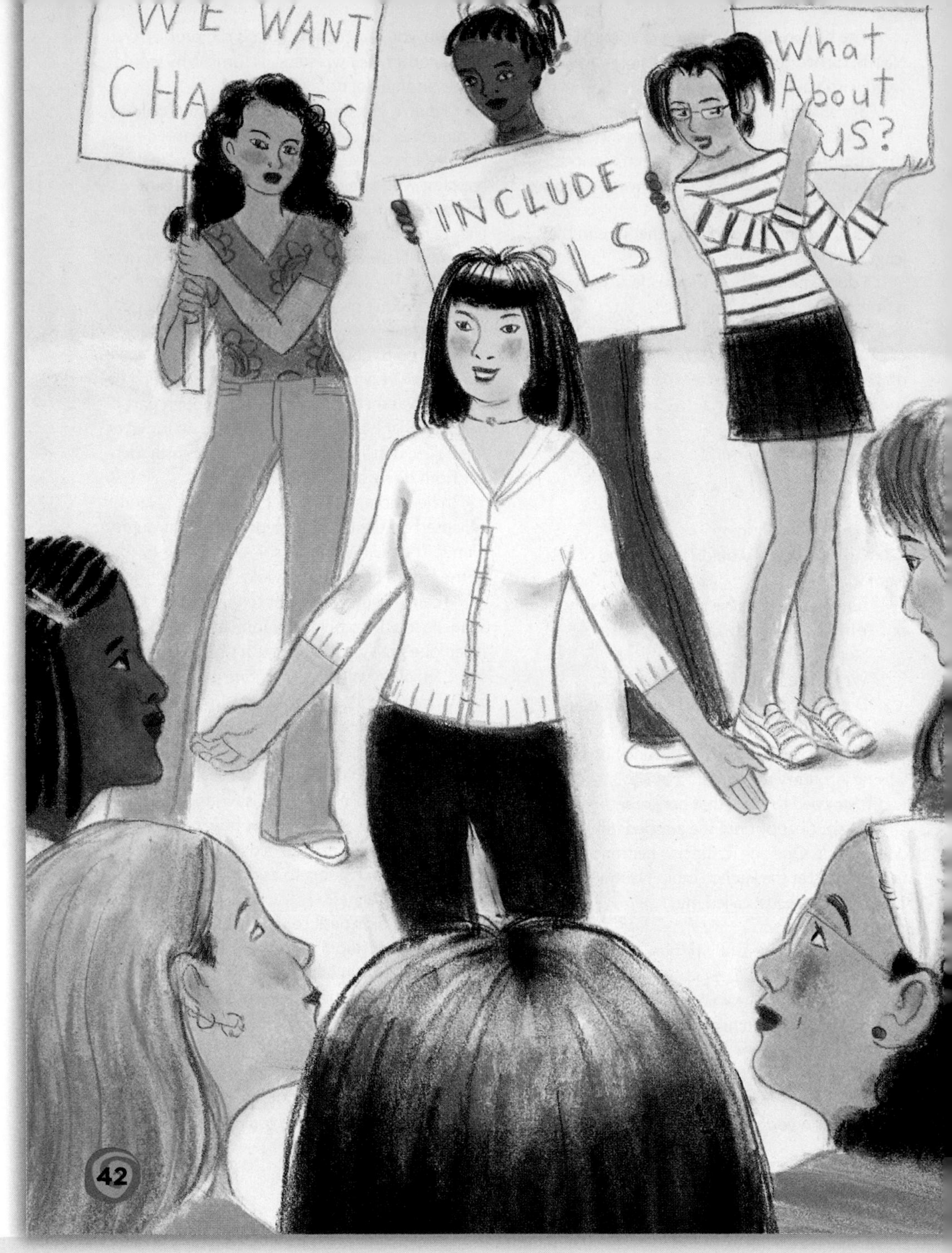
WE WANT
INCLUDE
What
About
US?
42

"We just got a call from the principal, saying he needed to speak to us immediately." In a daze, Naomi, steered by Shanelle, made her way to the commons. There, a whole group of girls cheered her. Across the way, her parents stood beside the principal, their faces blank.

Missy Toan stood up. "We are exercising our rights in a peaceful way this morning. Yesterday, Naomi Shaw stood up for all the girls in this school." A cheer rose up and then the chant: "Speech! Speech!" Reluctantly, Naomi stepped into the middle of the circle.

"I didn't mean to start a whole thing," Naomi blushed. "I tried out for the team because I wanted to do something every day that would remind me of my brother, Nate. But if what I did—I mean what his memory did—was to get everyone thinking about what's fair and what's not, then I'm glad. I think that everyone, regardless of gender or race or age, should have the same chances. After all, this is a *public* school." Naomi looked over to her parents. Her mother took her father's hand and smiled slowly. Naomi could see her brother in her mother's face, and she knew that she would be learning how to wrestle that afternoon. ◆

FEMALE WRESTLING ON THE RISE

Women are gaining acceptance as sumo wrestlers. Although men have dominated this popular Japanese sport for many years, there are now many women-only international sumo contests. Because sumo wrestling requires mental strategy, not brute strength, women are well-suited to the sport. The goal of a match is to push your partner outside of the ring or to make him or her touch the ground with any part of the body, except for the soles of their feet. Sumo wrestling is a great cardiovascular workout, making it ideal for anyone who wants to get into shape!

WOMEN IN THE BOSTON MARATHON

In 1967 women could not enter the Boston Marathon officially. Because she entered as K. Switzer, no one realized that Kathrine Switzer was a woman until after the race began. One official tried to rip her number off as she ran by, but he was pushed out of the way by a male runner, who later married Kathy. In 1972 women were finally allowed to participate in the Boston Marathon. For many years, men had kept women out of marathons because of the mistaken belief that women's bodies couldn't handle the tough training and competition.

43

Phonics/Word Study

More Latin Roots

For instruction to introduce a root, see TE page 102. Work with students to discover the meaning of each root. See *Word Study Manual* page 53 for a related word sort.

mort **(death)**

Students may be surprised to know that *mortgage* and *rigor mortis* have the same root. Have students tell what they know about each word.

mortal	postmortem
immortal	mortified
mortuary	rigor mortis
mortgage	

numer **(number)**

number	numerical
numeral	numerous
numerator	enumerate

pater/pat **(father)**

Help students notice the pattern: *patron/matron, patriarch/matriarch*, and *paternal/maternal.*

paternal	patronize
patriarch	expatriate
patron	repatriated

Discovering the Roots

mort	*numer*	*pater/pat*
postmortem	number	paternal
mortified	numeral	patricide
rigor mortis	enumerate	patron
mortal	numerical	expatriate
mortgage	numerator	patriarch

For more information on word sorts and spelling stages, see pages 5–31 in the *Word Study Manual.*

Focus on . . .

Use one or more activities in this section to focus on a particular area of need in your students.

Comprehension STRATEGY SUPPORT

To help those students who need more practice using the strategies covered in this lesson, work one-on-one or in small groups to apply the strategy prompts below. Apply the prompts to a *Reading Advantage* paperback, a classroom library book, or a new or familiar selection in the magazine. Always model your own thinking first.

Making Connections

- What does this story (article, passage) remind me of?
- What do I already know about this topic?
- Where have I heard about this topic before?
- What do I have in common with the characters, people, or situations in the text?
- What other books, stories, articles, movies, or TV shows does this text make me think about?

Understanding Text Structure

- What kind of text is this? (book, story, article, guidebook, play, manual)
- How does the author organize the text? (cause-effect, problem-solution, chronological order, description, question-answer, comparison-contrast)
- What details support my thoughts about the text structure?
- What is the cause (effect, problem, solution, order, question, answer)?
- If fiction, who are the characters? What is the setting, plot, conflict, and resolution?

Writing Character Portrait

Ask students how they would describe Naomi to a friend. Have partners write a brief character portrait of Naomi. Have them first complete a character map to organize their thoughts. (See TE page 388 for a BLM.)

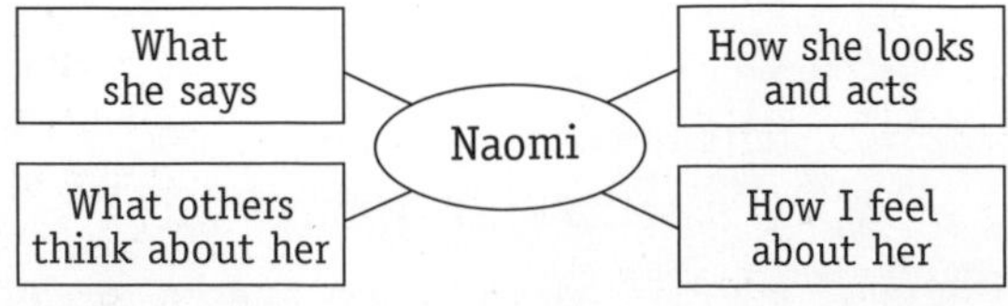

For more practice writing descriptive paragraphs, see lessons in *Writing Advantage* pages 114–151.

Fluency: Expression

After students have read "Senior Year" at least once, read aloud the introductory paragraph above the poem on page 35. Ask students to work in small groups to practice reading the poem chorally. Groups may choose to read the poem aloud as one voice or choose to have half the group read the narration and the other half read the dialogue. Remind students that words within quotation marks show dialogue. These words should be read with expression, as though someone were actually speaking them.

When students read aloud, do they—

✓ reflect an understanding of the text?
✓ demonstrate appropriate timing, stress, and intonation?
✓ incorporate appropriate speed and phrasing?

English Language Learners

To support students' comprehension of "An Unexpected Revolution," review the meaning of figures of speech.

1. Discuss how figurative speech cannot be taken literally, or word for word.
2. Have partners write one example of literal and figurative speech. (raining hard, raining cats and dogs)
3. Then, discuss the literal and figurative meanings of these expressions from the story.

A hush came over the gym.
Shaking off her dream . . .
Naomi couldn't escape the posters.
Naomi's voice trailed off.
I'll catch you sixth period, and you can tell me then.

Independent Activity Options

While you work with individuals or small groups, others can work independently on one or more of the following options:

- Level D paperback books, see TE pages 367–372
- Level D *eZines*
- Repeat word sorts from this lesson
- *Student Journal* pages for this lesson
- *Writing Advantage* independent lessons

Assessment

Strategy Assessment

To help you and your students assess their use of comprehension strategies, ask the following questions. Students can complete a written response or provide verbal answers in a one-on-one reading conference.

1. **Making Connections** What connections did you make to this story? (Answers will vary. Possible responses may include that students know of girls who excel in sports and participate on boys' teams.)
2. **Understanding Text Structure** What are the main problems in this story? How are they resolved? (Problems include that Naomi wants to be on an all-boys wrestling team. Her parents don't want her to wrestle because her brother died while wrestling. Solutions include that she proves that she is more fit than most of the boys, so she is allowed on the team. When her parents see that she has started a "revolution," in which girls want inclusion in all sports, her parents allow her to wrestle.)

For ongoing informal assessment, use the checklists on pages 61–64 of *Level D Assessment*.

Word Study Assessment

Use these steps to help you and your students assess their understanding of Latin roots.

1. Present the chart below. Read the roots and words aloud.
2. Have students explain how the meaning of each word is related to the root.

mort "death"	*numer* "number"	*pater/pat* "father"
mortal	numeral	paternal
mortified	numerical	patriarch
postmortem	enumerate	patron

LESSON **19**

On the Chase

Revolutions, pages 44–49

SUMMARY

This **first-person account** of a storm chaser describes two days spent following storms in Kansas and Missouri.

COMPREHENSION STRATEGIES

Determining Importance
Monitor Understanding

WRITING

Journal Entry

VOCABULARY

Word Relationships

PHONICS/WORD STUDY

Latin Roots *ped, pop/pub, prim/princ*

Lesson Vocabulary

pursues	downdraft
severe	exhilarated
dissipated	intensity
jet stream	

MATERIALS

Revolutions, pp. 44–49
Student Journal, pp. 66–69
Word Study Manual, p. 54
Writing Advantage, pp. 30–55

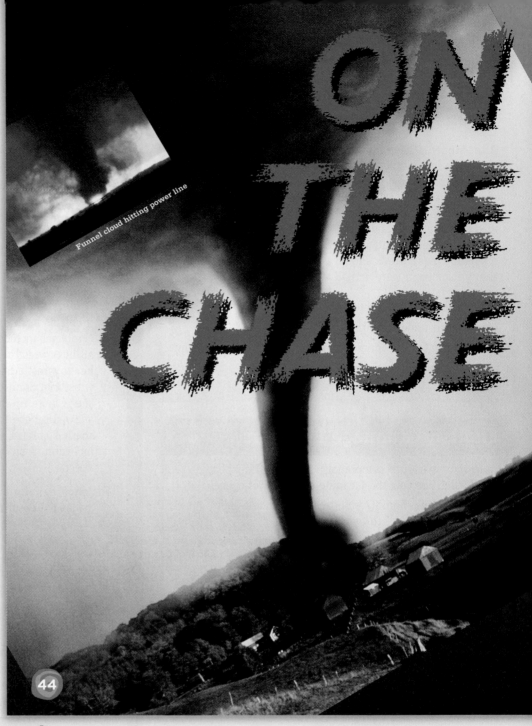

Funnel cloud hitting power line

ON THE CHASE

44

Before Reading  Use one or more activities.

Make an Association Web

Tell students they are going to read about a storm chaser. Then start for students an association web about storm chasers. See the example. Use the four question words to prompt students for answers. (See Differentiated Instruction.)

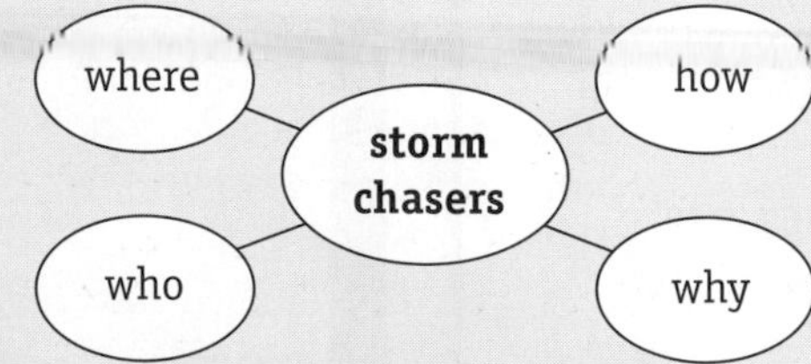

Vocabulary Preview

Display the selection vocabulary. Have students find each word in the text and use context clues to discover the meaning. Assess prior knowledge by asking students to complete the synonym/antonym chart on *Student Journal* page 66. Students work first with the vocabulary word *severe* and then with one other word they choose from the remaining vocabulary. Students may use a dictionary or a thesaurus to complete the chart.

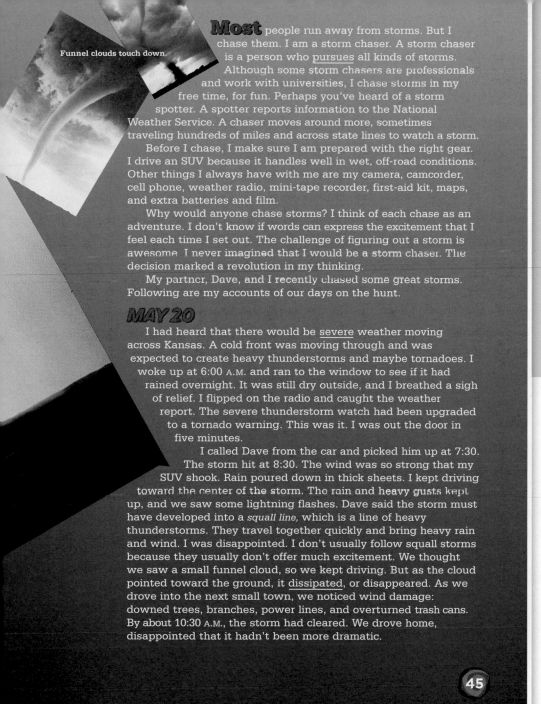

Funnel clouds touch down.

Most people run away from storms. But I chase them. I am a storm chaser. A storm chaser is a person who <u>pursues</u> all kinds of storms. Although some storm chasers are professionals and work with universities, I chase storms in my free time, for fun. Perhaps you've heard of a storm spotter. A spotter reports information to the National Weather Service. A chaser moves around more, sometimes traveling hundreds of miles and across state lines to watch a storm.

Before I chase, I make sure I am prepared with the right gear. I drive an SUV because it handles well in wet, off-road conditions. Other things I always have with me are my camera, camcorder, cell phone, weather radio, mini-tape recorder, first-aid kit, maps, and extra batteries and film.

Why would anyone chase storms? I think of each chase as an adventure. I don't know if words can express the excitement that I feel each time I set out. The challenge of figuring out a storm is awesome. I never imagined that I would be a storm chaser. The decision marked a revolution in my thinking.

My partner, Dave, and I recently chased some great storms. Following are my accounts of our days on the hunt.

MAY 20

I had heard that there would be <u>severe</u> weather moving across Kansas. A cold front was moving through and was expected to create heavy thunderstorms and maybe tornadoes. I woke up at 6:00 A.M. and ran to the window to see if it had rained overnight. It was still dry outside, and I breathed a sigh of relief. I flipped on the radio and caught the weather report. The severe thunderstorm watch had been upgraded to a tornado warning. This was it. I was out the door in five minutes.

I called Dave from the car and picked him up at 7:30. The storm hit at 8:30. The wind was so strong that my SUV shook. Rain poured down in thick sheets. I kept driving toward the center of the storm. The rain and heavy gusts kept up, and we saw some lightning flashes. Dave said the storm must have developed into a *squall line*, which is a line of heavy thunderstorms. They travel together quickly and bring heavy rain and wind. I was disappointed. I don't usually follow squall storms because they usually don't offer much excitement. We thought we saw a small funnel cloud, so we kept driving. But as the cloud pointed toward the ground, it <u>dissipated</u>, or disappeared. As we drove into the next small town, we noticed wind damage: downed trees, branches, power lines, and overturned trash cans. By about 10:30 A.M., the storm had cleared. We drove home, disappointed that it hadn't been more dramatic.

45

DIFFERENTIATED INSTRUCTION

SMALL GROUP

MAKE AN ASSOCIATION WEB

To help students with the association web, use the following strategies.

1. Explain that a storm chaser is a person who follows all different kinds of storms.
2. Tell students that people chase storms for different reasons. Most of the time, professionals follow storms to find out new information about them.
3. Explain that in this selection, the storm chasers are not professionals, but chase storms as a hobby. Ask students why someone might like to be a storm chaser "just for fun."

Student Journal page 66

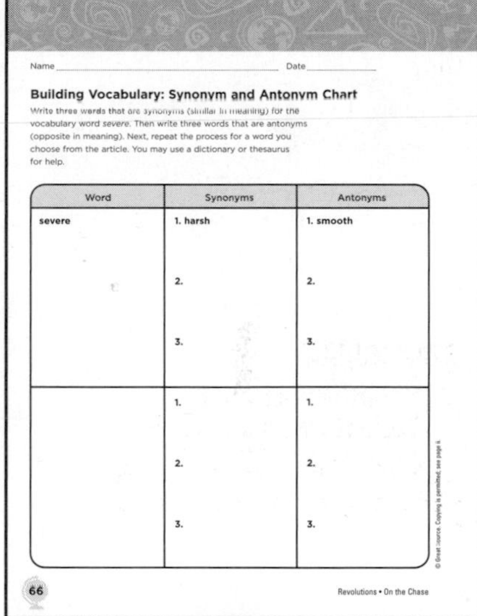

Name ______________________ Date __________

Building Vocabulary: Synonym and Antonym Chart

Write three words that are synonyms (similar in meaning) for the vocabulary word *severe*. Then write three words that are antonyms (opposite in meaning). Next, repeat the process for a word you choose from the article. You may use a dictionary or thesaurus for help.

Word	Synonyms	Antonyms
severe	1. harsh 2. 3.	1. smooth 2. 3.
	1. 2. 3.	1. 2. 3.

66 Revolutions • On the Chase

Preview the Selection

Have students look through the six pages of the article, pages 44–49 in the magazine. Use these or similar prompts to orient students to the article.

- What kind of selection is this? How do you know?
- What information do you get from the photographs?
- How is the information organized?

Teacher Think Aloud

When I preview this selection, I look at the dramatic photographs of storms, and I read the subheads. The subheads are dates. I guess that the writer is going to tell me what happened on those two days, in time order. I'll probably learn about storms that happened on those days.

Make Predictions/ Set Purpose

Students should use the information gathered in the selection preview to make predictions about what they will learn from the account. To help students set a purpose, suggest that they read to find out about the hobby of storm chasing.

DIFFERENTIATED INSTRUCTION

Comprehension

DETERMINING IMPORTANCE

To help students determine the importance of ideas in a text, follow these steps.

1. Have students reread the first paragraph on page 46.
2. Ask students to identify a sentence that contains an important detail.
3. Then ask: *Why is that sentence important? How can you prove its importance?*

MAY 23

After the thunderstorm, Dave and I decided to take a long weekend in Tornado Alley. Tornado Alley is the area in the United States where tornadoes most often occur. It includes the states from North Dakota south to Texas. From there, it includes the states east all the way to Ohio, then south to Kentucky and Tennessee. We packed the SUV and headed for Ellington, Missouri.

The weather will be perfect for making a tornado tomorrow. After supper, it was time for bed. Before going to sleep, I called Dave down the hall in the motel and told him to be ready to head out tomorrow morning at a moment's notice.

I woke up at dawn to a pinging noise. Big fat raindrops and balls of hail clunked against the metal roof of the motel. When I looked out the window, I saw hail hitting my car. I quickly got dressed and ran down the hallway. When I reached Dave's door, I banged loudly, but Dave was already up and dressed. We ran to the car, hopped in, and started driving south. The weather station reported a severe thunderstorm warning. I hoped for a *supercell*—a dangerous thunderstorm that occurs when the jet stream winds speed up.

Stormchasers display hail sto

A severe thunderstorm needs these three things:

- **Humidity—plenty of moisture in the air**
- **Unstable air—warm air close to the ground that is rising up and causing a lot of movement in the air**
- **Cool air moving into the area—cool air lifts the warm air and starts storms**

TORNADO ALLEY

North Dakota
Minnesota
South Dakota
Wyoming
Nebraska
Iowa
Illinois
Indiana
Ohio
Colorado
Kansas
Missouri
Kentucky
Tennessee
Oklahoma
Arkansas
Texas
Louisiana

46

During Reading

Comprehension

DETERMINING IMPORTANCE

Use these questions to model determining the importance of details in the first paragraph of the selection. Then have students determine the importance of details in the first paragraph of the entry for May 20.

- What are the most important ideas in the paragraph?
- How can I support my beliefs?

(See Differentiated Instruction.)

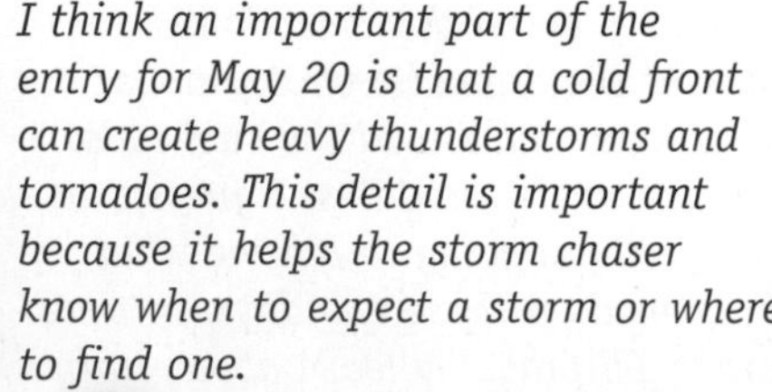

Teacher Think Aloud

I think an important part of the entry for May 20 is that a cold front can create heavy thunderstorms and tornadoes. This detail is important because it helps the storm chaser know when to expect a storm or where to find one.

Comprehension

MONITOR UNDERSTANDING

Use these questions to model visualizing. Then have students tell what they visualize as they read the account.

- What questions do I have as I read?
- Can I picture in my mind what it's like to be in the middle of a strong storm?
- Can I retell in my own words what is happening?

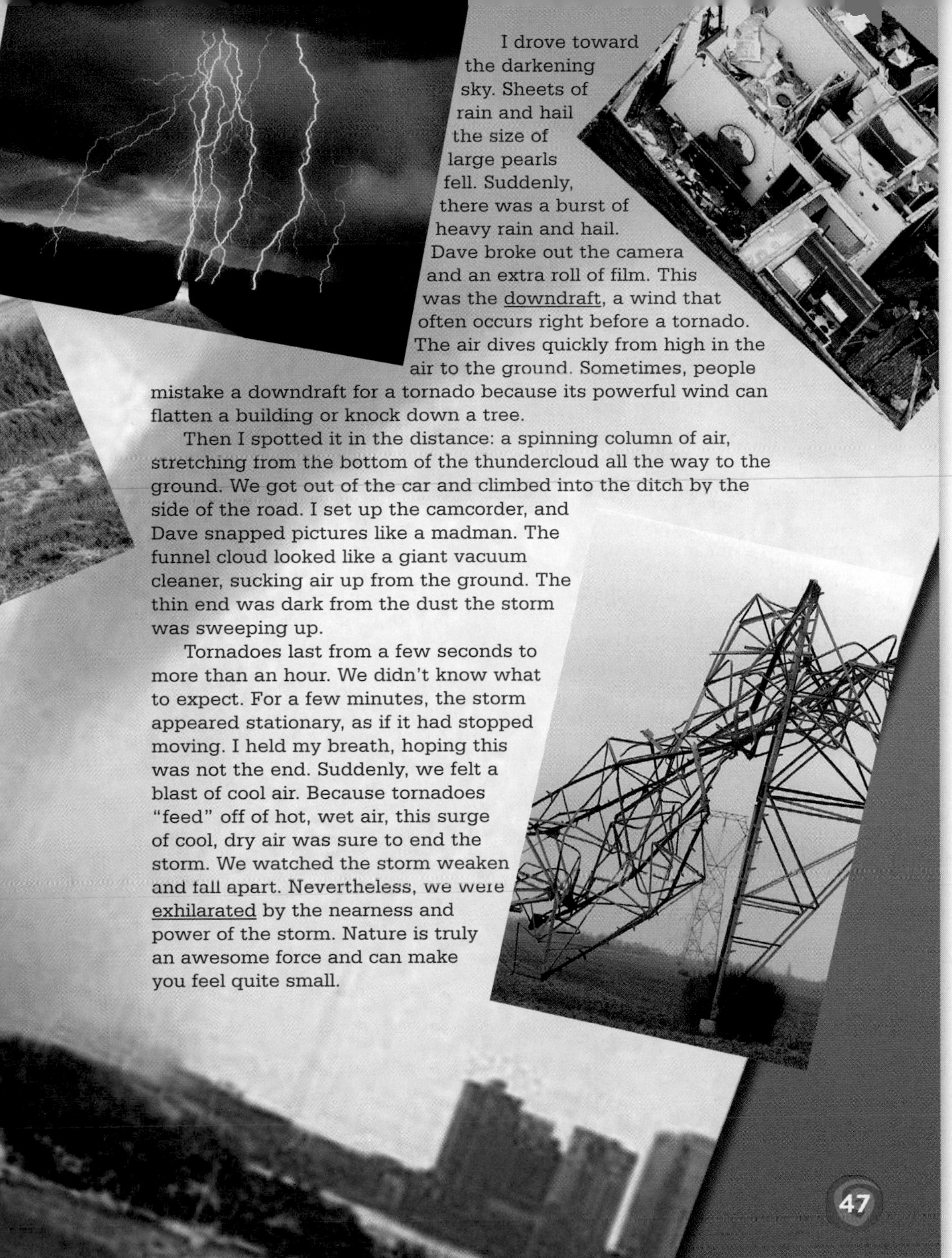

I drove toward the darkening sky. Sheets of rain and hail the size of large pearls fell. Suddenly, there was a burst of heavy rain and hail. Dave broke out the camera and an extra roll of film. This was the downdraft, a wind that often occurs right before a tornado. The air dives quickly from high in the air to the ground. Sometimes, people mistake a downdraft for a tornado because its powerful wind can flatten a building or knock down a tree.

Then I spotted it in the distance: a spinning column of air, stretching from the bottom of the thundercloud all the way to the ground. We got out of the car and climbed into the ditch by the side of the road. I set up the camcorder, and Dave snapped pictures like a madman. The funnel cloud looked like a giant vacuum cleaner, sucking air up from the ground. The thin end was dark from the dust the storm was sweeping up.

Tornadoes last from a few seconds to more than an hour. We didn't know what to expect. For a few minutes, the storm appeared stationary, as if it had stopped moving. I held my breath, hoping this was not the end. Suddenly, we felt a blast of cool air. Because tornadoes "feed" off of hot, wet air, this surge of cool, dry air was sure to end the storm. We watched the storm weaken and fall apart. Nevertheless, we were exhilarated by the nearness and power of the storm. Nature is truly an awesome force and can make you feel quite small.

47

Teacher Think Aloud

I have a lot of questions as I read this account. What kinds of storms does the author chase? How does he stay safe? Why does he chase storms? When I ask questions, it helps me focus on what I'm reading because I look for answers. It also helps me get more involved with the text.

Fix-Up Strategies

Offer these strategies to help students read independently.

If you don't understand what you're reading:

- Reread the difficult section to look for clues to help you comprehend.
- Read ahead to find clues to help you comprehend.
- Retell, or say in your own words, what you've read.
- Visualize, or form mental pictures of, what you've read.

If you don't understand a word:

- Reread the sentence. Look for ideas and words that provide meaning clues.
- Find clues by reading a few sentences before and after the confusing word.
- Look for the base or root word and think about its meaning.
- Think about the topic or plot at this point to see if either offers meaning clues.

DIFFERENTIATED INSTRUCTION

SMALL GROUP

Vocabulary

Word Relationships

To help students with this activity, use the steps below:

1. Remind students that words can mean the same thing but vary in the strength of that meaning.
2. Have students go to page 45 and find the word *chase*. Point out that *chase* is a word with many synonyms.
3. Ask students to come up with some synonyms of *chase*. Make a list on the board.
4. Using the list, have students arrange the words in order from weakest to strongest (example: *follow, chase, charge*).

Student Journal pages 67–68

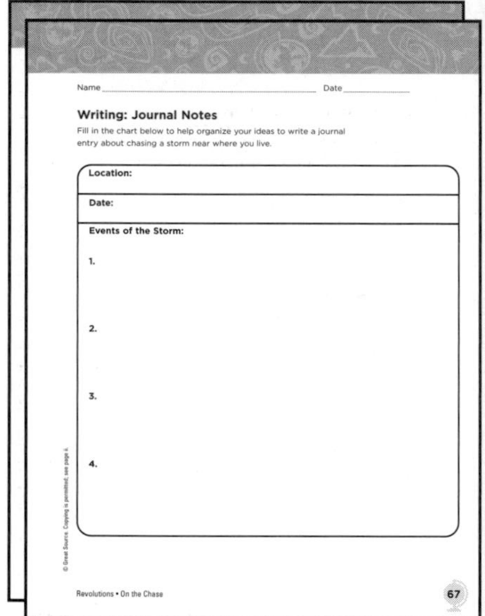

Name ______________ Date ________

Writing: Journal Notes

Fill in the chart below to help organize your ideas to write a journal entry about chasing a storm near where you live.

Location:

Date:

Events of the Storm:

1.

2.

3.

4.

© Great Source. Copying is permitted; see page ii.

Revolutions • On the Chase 67

We weren't done yet. We hopped back into the SUV and headed toward the storm sight to see the damage. While I drove, Dave turned on the radio to see if we could get the intensity rating of the tornado. The Fujita intensity scale measures tornado strength. This scale ranges from an F-0 tornado, one that causes light damage with winds up to seventy-two mph, to an F-5 tornado, one that causes great damage with winds above 261 mph. The weather report categorized this tornado as an F-2, with winds close to 140 mph.

Near where the tornado hit, we saw many blown-out windows in homes and buildings. Fallen trees blocked roads. A few cars were flipped over. We stopped at a gas station where the attendant said he watched the storm lift and toss a car down the block. The power was out, and schools were closed. Dave and I recorded everything and drank a soda with the attendant, while he told stories of other tornadoes he'd lived through.

As the sun dipped in the sky, we headed back to the motel and checked out. It's back to work tomorrow—but what an adventure! ◆

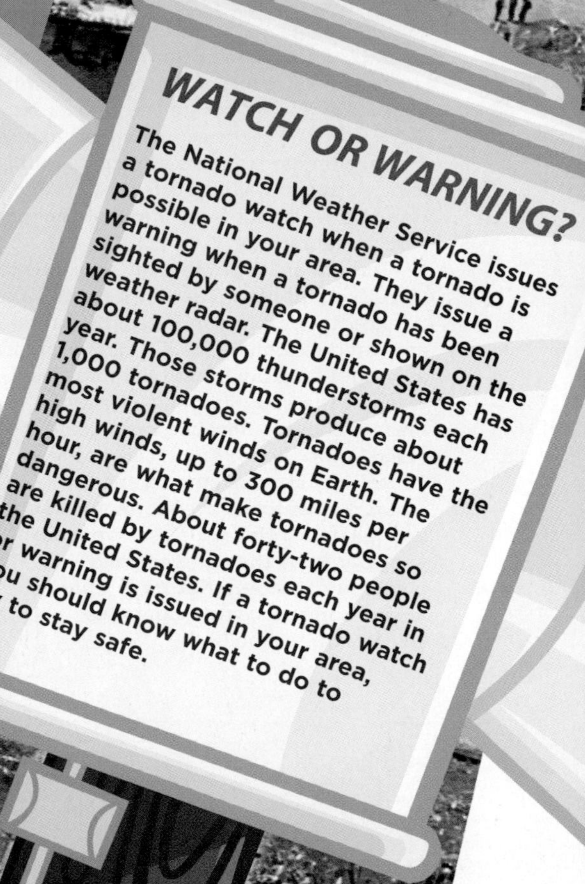

WATCH OR WARNING?
The National Weather Service issues a tornado watch when a tornado is possible in your area. They issue a warning when a tornado has been sighted by someone or shown on the weather radar. The United States has about 100,000 thunderstorms each year. Those storms produce about 1,000 tornadoes. Tornadoes have the most violent winds on Earth. The high winds, up to 300 miles per hour, are what make tornadoes so dangerous. About forty-two people are killed by tornadoes each year in the United States. If a tornado watch or warning is issued in your area, you should know what to do to try to stay safe.

48

After Reading

WHOLE CLASS

Use one or more activities.

Check Purpose

Have students decide if their purpose was met. What did they find out about the hobby of storm chasing?

Discussion Questions

Continue the group discussion with the following questions.

1. What are the primary natural causes of tornadoes and severe thunderstorms? (Cause-Effect)
2. Where in this country do most tornadoes occur? (Determining Importance)
3. After reading this selection, would you like to be a storm chaser? Why or why not? (Making Connections)

Revisit: Association Web

Revisit the association web about storm chasers. What new information can students add? What ideas might they like to change?

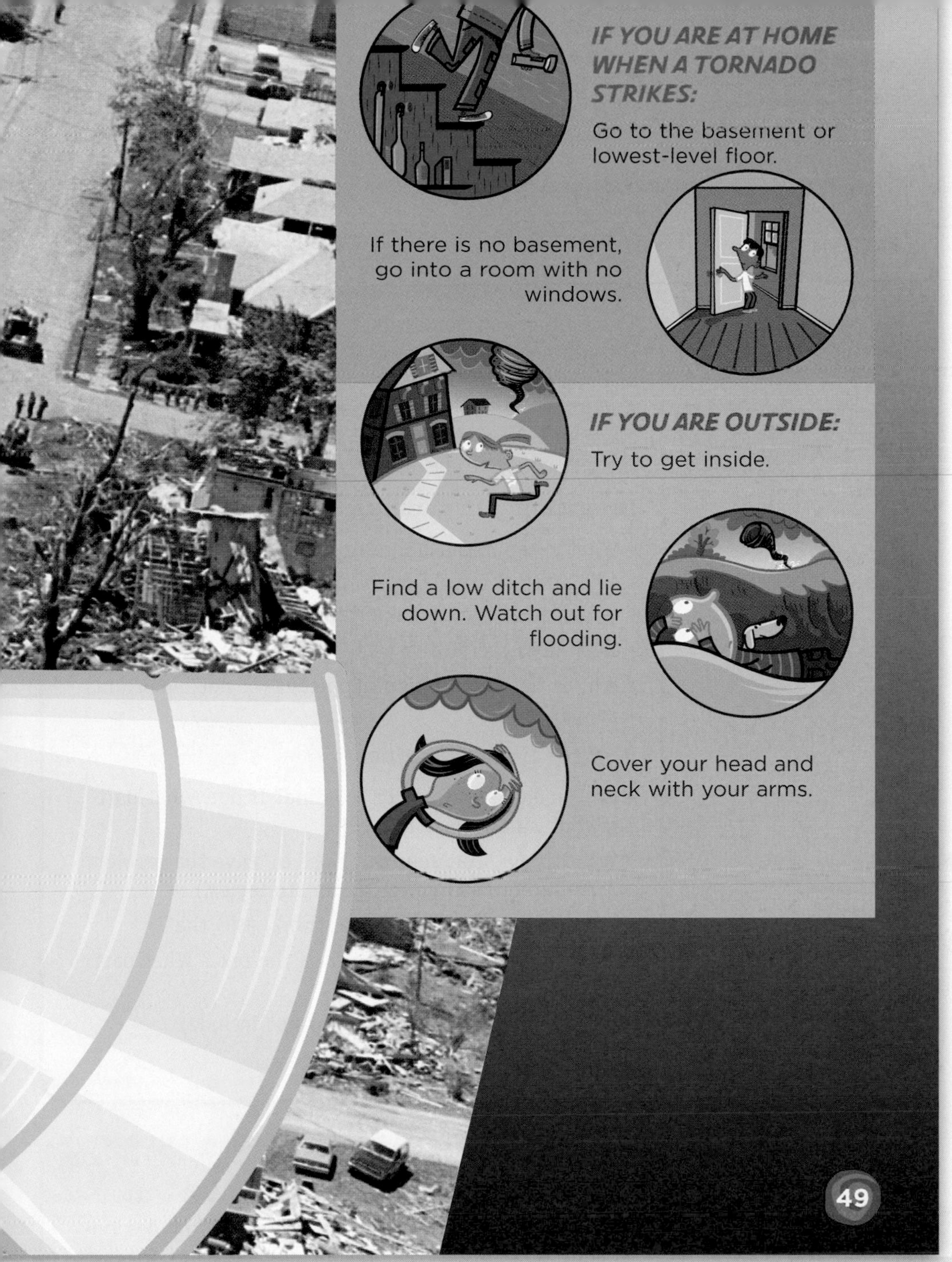

IF YOU ARE AT HOME WHEN A TORNADO STRIKES:
Go to the basement or lowest-level floor.
If there is no basement, go into a room with no windows.
IF YOU ARE OUTSIDE:
Try to get inside.
Find a low ditch and lie down. Watch out for flooding.
Cover your head and neck with your arms.
49

Student Journal page 69

Name ____________ Date ____________

Building Vocabulary: Word Relationships

When you list synonyms or antonyms, you will find that some words have stronger meanings than others. Using the two vocabulary words you chose for the chart on page 66, list either the three synonyms or antonyms you wrote. Rank all four words from weakest to strongest in meaning.

Vocabulary word: ____________

Selected synonyms or antonyms:

____

____

____

Rank the words by degree:

______ → ______ → ______ → ______

Vocabulary word: ____________

Selected synonyms or antonyms:

____

____

____

Rank the words by degree:

______ → ______ → ______ → ______

Revolutions • On the Chase 69

Writing Journal Entry

What might storm chasers who live in your area write in a journal? Have students write a journal entry about their hunt. Before writing the journal page, have students complete the planning activity on *Student Journal* page 67 to help organize their ideas. Students can then write the journal entry on *Student Journal* page 68.

Vocabulary

Word Relationships

Using the two words that were selected for the synonym/antonym chart, have students complete the activity on *Student Journal* page 69. Ask students to place the words on a continuum, from weakest to strongest in meaning, or from negative to more positive connotations. Discuss sample continuums as a group. Demonstrate with *coerced* from Lesson 13. (See Differentiated Instruction.)

Phonics/Word Study

Latin Roots

Ask: *When you pedal a bicycle, what part of your body do you use?* (foot) Explain that the root *ped* means "foot." Have students work in small groups to list as many words as they can that contain the root *ped*. Examples include *pedal*, *pedestrian*, and *moped*. Now, work with students to complete the in-depth Latin roots activity on TE page 158.

Phonics/Word Study

More Latin Roots

For instruction to introduce a root, see TE page 102. Work with students to discover the meaning of each root. See *Word Study Manual* page 54 for a related word sort.

ped **(foot)**

Write *pedal* and *petal*. If students know the meaning of the root *ped*, they will be able to choose the correct homophone for the context of their reading or writing.

biped	pedestal
centipede	pedestrian
moped	pedicure
orthopedic	pedigree
pedal	pedometer

pop/pub **(the people)**

popular	public
population	publicity
popularity	populace
publish	populate

prim/princ **(first)**

A *primer* is the first reader a child gets in school, and elementary school is also known as *primary* school. Words with the roots *prim, princ* are all around. Challenge students to use the meaning of *prim* to discover the meaning of the phrase *prima donna,* of Italian origin (first lady).

primeval	primer
primitive	prime
primary	prince/princess
prima donna	principle
primate	principal

Discovering the Roots

ped	*pop/pub*	*prim/princ*
pedestrian	popular	primeval
pedestal	populace	primary
pedicure	public	primate
centipede	publish	prince/princess
pedometer	population	prima donna

For more information on word sorts and spelling stages, see pages 5–31 in the *Word Study Manual.*

Focus on . . .

Use one or more activities in this section to focus on a particular area of need in your students.

Comprehension STRATEGY SUPPORT

To help those students who need more practice using the strategies covered in this lesson, work one-on-one or in small groups to apply the strategy prompts below. Apply the prompts to a *Reading Advantage* paperback, a classroom library book, or a new or familiar selection in the magazine. Always model your own thinking first.

Determining Importance

- What is the most important idea in the paragraph? How can I prove it?
- Which details are unimportant? Why?
- What does the author want me to understand?
- Why is this information important (or not important) to me?

Monitor Understanding

- Do I understand what I'm reading? If not, what part is confusing to me?
- What fix-up strategies can I use to solve the problem? (See During Reading for fix-up strategies.)
- Why did a character say (do, think, ask) that?
- What images do I visualize from the text? What parts can't I visualize?
- Why did the author include (or not include) those details?

Writing News Story

Have students write a news story about a storm, describing any resulting damage. Remind students to answer *who, what, where, when,* and *why*—the 5Ws. Have students use a 5Ws chart to organize their ideas. (See TE page 384 for a BLM.)

5Ws	Information for News Story
Who	damage to city's residents' homes
What	a tremendous thunderstorm
Where	my city
When	last night
Why	necessary weather conditions

To help students include sensory details in their writing, see lessons in *Writing Advantage*, pages 30–55.

Fluency: Expression

After students have read the selection at least once, ask them to put themselves in the place of the storm chaser who wrote these accounts. Have them practice reading the text silently, as if they were that person. Then in small groups or pairs, have them agree on one day to read about, taking turns reading aloud.

As you listen to students, use these prompts to guide them.

- Read expressively. Think how the writer might feel and sound. Punctuation such as exclamation points will help guide your expression as you read.
- When explaining terms and phrases, read with confidence. This will help the listener better understand what you are trying to convey.

When students read aloud, do they—

✓ reflect an understanding of the text?

✓ demonstrate appropriate timing, stress, and intonation?

✓ incorporate appropriate speed and phrasing?

English Language Learners

Guide students in forming questions about the text.

1. Choose a section and have partners read it together.
2. Have pairs come up with questions about their reading.
3. As students work, ask: *Is there a word or idea you don't understand? Is there something you want to learn more about?*

Allow partners to share their questions with the class.

Independent Activity Options

While you work with individuals or small groups, others can work independently on one or more of the following options.

- Level D paperback books, see TE pages 367–372
- Level D *eZines*
- Repeat word sorts from this lesson
- *Student Journal* pages for this lesson
- *Writing Advantage* independent lessons

Assessment

Strategy Assessment

To help you and your students assess their use of comprehension strategies, ask the following questions. Students can complete a written response or provide verbal answers in a one-on-one reading conference.

1. **Determining Importance** What were the most important parts of this selection to you? Why were those parts important? (Answers will vary. Possible responses may include that the descriptions of the different types of storms were the most important. The descriptions taught the reader about the power of storms, and why the writer finds them so exciting.)
2. **Monitor Understanding** What strategies did you use to fix-up your confusion while reading? (Answers will vary. Possible responses may include visualizing, such as trying to picture the balls of hail hitting the roof of the motel.)

For ongoing informal assessment, use the checklists on pages 61–64 of *Level D Assessment*.

Word Study Assessment

Use these steps to help you and your students assess their understanding of Latin roots.

1. Present the chart below. Read the roots and words aloud.
2. Have students explain how the meaning of each word is related to the root.

prim/princ "first"	*pop/pub* "the people"	*ped* "foot"
principal	public	pedal
primitive	population	pedicure
primary	popular	centipede

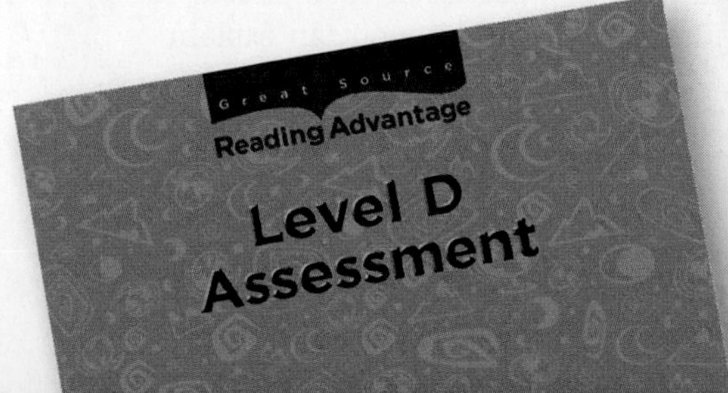

LESSON 20
Revolutions in Style: Fashion Through the Ages

Revolutions, pages 50–55

SUMMARY

This **nonfiction article** describes the changes in fashion over periods of time.

COMPREHENSION STRATEGIES

Monitor Understanding
Inferential Thinking

WRITING

Comparison Chart

VOCABULARY

Prefixes

PHONICS/WORD STUDY

Latin Roots *sign, son, spir*

Lesson Vocabulary

unseemly
accentuate
frivolous

MATERIALS

Revolutions, pp. 50–55
Student Journal, pp. 70–72
Word Study Manual, p. 55
Writing Advantage, pp. 152–169

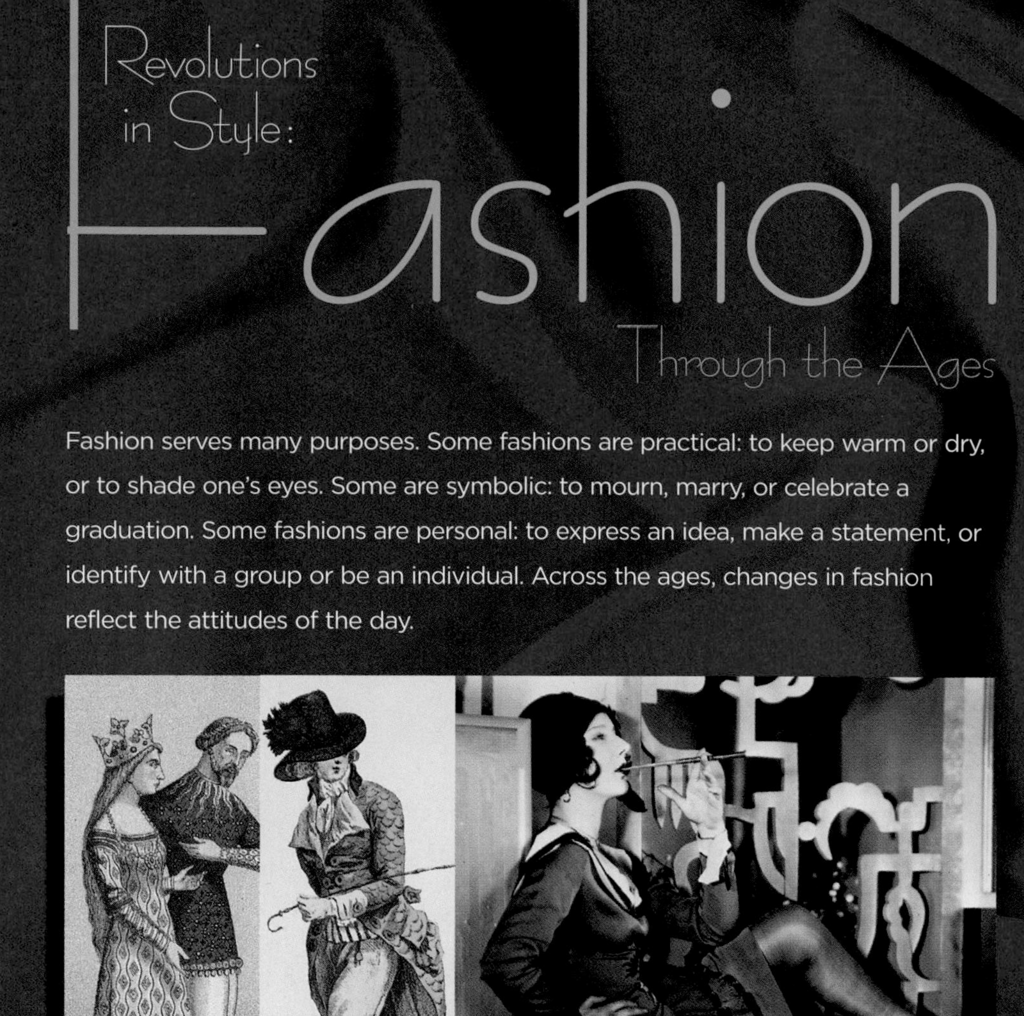

Revolutions in Style:
Fashion
Through the Ages
Fashion serves many purposes. Some fashions are practical: to keep warm or dry, or to shade one's eyes. Some are symbolic: to mourn, marry, or celebrate a graduation. Some fashions are personal: to express an idea, make a statement, or identify with a group or be an individual. Across the ages, changes in fashion reflect the attitudes of the day.
Civilian clothes of the Middle Ages
Mens fashion, 1780
1920s flapper
50

Before Reading

Use one or more activities.

Make a List

Introduce the subject of fashion. Tell students that fashion is what is popular to wear in a particular time period. To illustrate this point, you can explain that in the 1960s, the "hippie style" was the fashion trend. Almost everyone wore bell-bottom pants; long, straight hair; and many flowers. Ask students what today's beauty and fashion standards are. Record their responses in a list.

Today's Fashions

1. baggy pants
2. baseball caps
3.

Vocabulary Preview

Display the selection vocabulary. Assess prior knowledge by asking students to begin the word web activity on *Student Journal* page 70. Have students write in the definition box what they think their chosen word means. Students will revisit their definitions after they finish reading.

Europe in the Middle Ages (400–1200)

Holy wars, castles, and knights: the Middle Ages were anything but dark. But despite all this activity, fashion remained plain and practical. During the Middle Ages, the role of the tailor grew when scissors became common. Fashion was born.

During the Middle Ages, people used buttons for the first time. Buttons allowed for clothes to be more formfitting.

Beauty

To medieval people, beauty and looks were important. Pale skin was preferred. People bleached their skin to make it lighter. The ideal body was tall and thin with long hair, for both men and women.

Class Differences

Both the color and material of clothing told a person's class. Poor, country people made their own fabrics, using natural dyes that produced soft, earthy colors. In contrast, nobles bought or imported fine fabrics with brighter colors: reds, blues, greens, and white. It was during this time that black became associated with sorrow and mourning in European culture.

Women's Fashion

It was considered unseemly, or improper, for women to show their arms. So, women wore *cotes*, close fitting, long undergarments with sleeves. The basic over-dress was a *tunic*. Men and women wore tunics. A tunic had no set length. It varied from floor-length, to the ankle, or to the knee. Sleeves varied, too. They could be wide at the top, and narrow at the wrist or narrow at the top with a wide cuff. The outfit was finished with a belt around the waist called a *girdle*.

Young women wore their hair long and flowing, or in braids. Older and married women covered their hair with hats, scarves, or hairnets.

Men's Fashion

Men wore long shirts or tunics with different colored leggings, called *braies*. All classes of men wore linen or wool braies. Often, men draped a fur coat across their shoulders and wore a hat with a tail drooping down their back. Men had a wide variety of hats to choose from.

Hats during the Middle Ages ranged from pointy, elflike hats to hoods tied under the chin.

51

DIFFERENTIATED INSTRUCTION SMALL GROUP

Preview the Selection

To help students understand the text features, use these strategies.

1. List these text features: chronology, differentiation, and visual aids.
2. Explain each feature. *Chronology* refers to the order in which the article is written. For example, this author uses a verbal time-line to tell readers about the fashion trends of each time period. *Differentiation* is the distinction between women's and men's fashion. Each time period has visual aids (pictures) to help readers see how fashion standards have changed through time.

Student Journal page 70

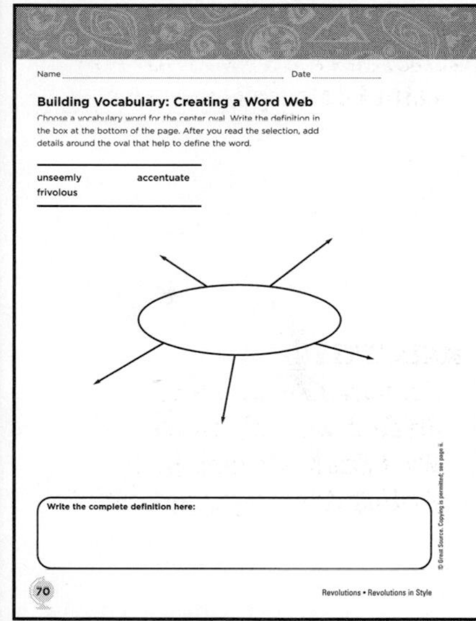

Name ______ Date ______

Building Vocabulary: Creating a Word Web

Choose a vocabulary word for the center oval. Write the definition in the box at the bottom of the page. After you read the selection, add details around the oval that help to define the word.

unseemly accentuate
frivolous

Write the complete definition here:

70 Revolutions • Revolutions in Style

Preview the Selection

Have students look through the six pages of the article, pages 50–55 in the magazine. Use these or similar prompts to guide students to notice important features of the text.

- What do you think you will like or dislike about the topic?
- How has the author organized the information in the article?

(See Differentiated Instruction.)

Teacher Think Aloud

When I preview this selection, I look at the outfits in the pictures. Some of them look ridiculous to me! I wonder if this is going to be an article about crazy fashions. Then I notice that each page begins with a heading, for example, "Europe in the Middle Ages (400–1200)." I think each heading is giving me a clue about the text I'll read.

Make Predictions/ Set Purpose

Students should use the information gathered in the selection preview to make predictions about what they will learn from the article. To help students set a purpose, suggest that they read to learn about fashions and standards of beauty throughout history.

DIFFERENTIATED INSTRUCTION

Comprehension

INFERENTIAL THINKING

To help students think inferentially, ask these questions.

- What does the text tell you about the topic?
- What do you already know about the topic?
- What new information can you infer, using prior knowledge and the information in the text, that the author does not state directly?

Europe in the 1700s

The eighteenth century was a stable and prosperous time in Europe. Middle- and upper-class people had money to spend. Luxury goods—expensive, frivolous, or non-essential items—became popular. People carried fans and muffs. They wore wigs and make-up. Men's hats were designed to be carried rather than worn. Beauty was now very important.

Technology Affects Fashion
As machines to make clothes improved, luxury items became more available. With better looms, tailors were able to make fancy, patterned fabrics for everyone. With the invention of cut stone, diamond and rhinestone jewelry became more common. Not everyone welcomed this showiness. Religious people opposed fashion on the grounds that it promoted vanity.

Women
Eighteenth-century women were generally appreciated for their knowledge and abilities in the arts, including the art of conversation. In fact, it has been said that women were more respected in the 1700s than at any other time in European history. The size of women's clothes reflected this new attitude. The basic dress of the early 1700s was the *mantua* [MAN choo uh], a flowing garment pinched at the waist and having wide sleeves. As the century progressed, the mantua stiffened, and women wore large hoops underneath. In these large clothes, women appeared to be about three times as large as men. Around 1760, women's hairstyles went up, making women seem tall as well as wide. This large, imposing look lasted until the French Revolution in 1789.

Men
New ideas changed men's fashion, too. Because eighteenth century people favored intelligence over power, military styles were no longer fashionable. Everyday dress and high fashion became separate styles. In the evening, when fancy clothing was called for, a man might wear lace and velvet, while during the day, simple, dark clothes would do. Men's dress, like women's, expanded in size. Men wore long coats, buttoned at the waist, over breeches or knee pants. Wigs were so large that a man had to carry his hat. Often, men carried walking sticks to finish off an outfit.

52

During Reading

Comprehension

MONITOR UNDERSTANDING

Use these questions to model visualizing. Then have students tell what they visualize as they read.

- Can I "see" the different fashions in my mind?
- Which kinds of fashions do I have trouble picturing?
- How do the pictures help me visualize the text?

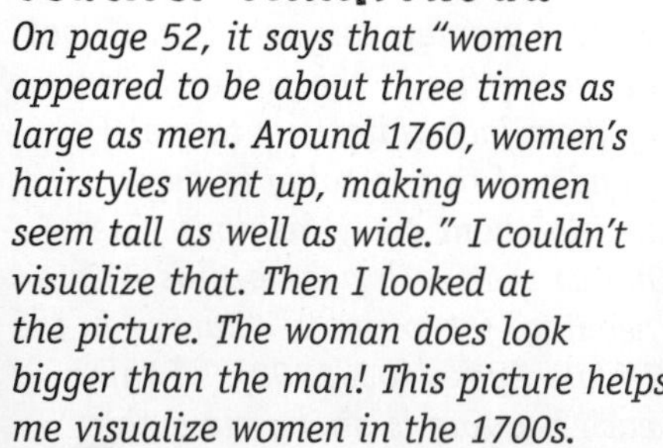

Teacher Think Aloud

On page 52, it says that "women appeared to be about three times as large as men. Around 1760, women's hairstyles went up, making women seem tall as well as wide." I couldn't visualize that. Then I looked at the picture. The woman does look bigger than the man! This picture helps me visualize women in the 1700s.

Comprehension

INFERENTIAL THINKING

Use these questions to model making inferences from the section "Women's Fashion." Then have students make inferences as they read another section.

- What does the text tell me about women's fashions in the Middle Ages?
- What do I already know about it?
- What ideas can I infer that the author has not stated directly?

(See Differentiated Instruction.)

Europe in the 1800s

Women

In the 1820s, women wore dresses with tight lacing to make their waists appear small. Overly large sleeves helped to <u>accentuate</u> the small-waist look. Skirts were long and full, with padding at the bottom to give them shape. Women wore large hats or bonnets and draped shawls over their shoulders.

By the mid-1850s, cheaper sewing machines made it easier for women to make their clothes at home. The crinoline, a stiff underskirt made of horsehair, became a must-have fashion item. One factory in Germany made more than 9 million crinolines between 1854 and 1866! Despite the crinoline's popularity, it was a dangerous item. It pinched a woman's waist so tightly that she couldn't work or walk for any length of time. Sometimes women fainted or suffered broken ribs from a corset tied too tightly. A corset was the undergarment that pulled in a woman's waistline.

By 1870 the crinoline fell out of style. It was replaced by the bustle, a pad that expanded the back of a woman's dress. Women wore several petticoats under their dresses. That style was fashionable until the end of the century. Many women carried fans and lace-trimmed parasols. Hats adorned with feathers were popular. By the 1880s, dresses became slimmer; sometimes, they were so tight around the knees that it was difficult to walk.

Men

Men did not have to endure the discomfort of crinolines and corsets. While women's clothing became fussier, men's clothing became simpler. During the mid-nineteenth century, men's jackets became a fashion staple, with ties offering the only hint of color. Most men wore a top hat when they went out. A well-groomed beard, sideburns, and mustache were all part of the look for men.

By the end of the nineteenth century, men's clothing became even more simplified. Jackets continued to be popular, especially the cutaway, with rounded corners in front, and the dinner jacket, black with satin lapels. Muted colors—gray, brown, black, and blue—dominated men's fashion.

53

Teacher Think Aloud

The text tells me that it was improper for women to show their bare arms in the Middle Ages. I know that some cultures still follow that guideline today. I infer that bare arms must symbolize something pretty important if some cultures still abide by that guideline.

Fix-Up Strategies

Offer these strategies to help students read independently.

If you don't understand what you're reading:

- Reread the difficult section to look for clues to help you comprehend.
- Read ahead to find clues to help you comprehend.
- Retell, or say in your own words, what you've read.
- Visualize, or form mental pictures of, what you've read.

If you don't understand a word:

- Reread the sentence. Look for ideas and words that provide meaning clues.
- Find clues by reading a few sentences before and after the confusing word.
- Look for the base or root word and think about its meaning.
- Think about the topic or plot at this point to see if either offers meaning clues.

America in the 1920s

World War I ended in 1918. Women won the right to vote in 1920. Henry Ford perfected the assembly line and started mass-producing cars. Mandatory education resulted in more people reading and spurred the growth of newspapers and magazines. Fashion advertising reached many people.

Beauty
Women of the 1920s plucked their eyebrows thin, outlined their eyes with thick, black eyeliner, and put drops of wax on their eyelashes to make them glisten. Short hair and slim lines were all the rage. The look was in stark contrast to the rounded, womanly look that had been fashionable earlier in the twentieth century.

Women
Flappers wanted to forget about World War I. They wore simple, shapeless dresses that showed their arms and legs. Some older people found bare arms and legs to be quite shocking. To further outrage the older generation, flappers smoked cigarettes, held in long, slim holders, and applied their make-up in public.

Men
Some men returning from World War I were not ready for a fashion change. Suits worn with light-colored shirts, popular before the war, remained fashionable. Silk ties and tie pins were still in vogue, as were black bowler hats. Other men wanted to look like the gangsters that ruled the city streets in the 1920s. For them, pinstripe suits were the rage.

Knickerbockers, or "knickers," were popular for casual wear. Knickers came in plus-fours, plus-sixes, plus-eights and plus-tens. The "plus" referred to the number of inches the pants hung below the knees. ◆

54

Student Journal page 71

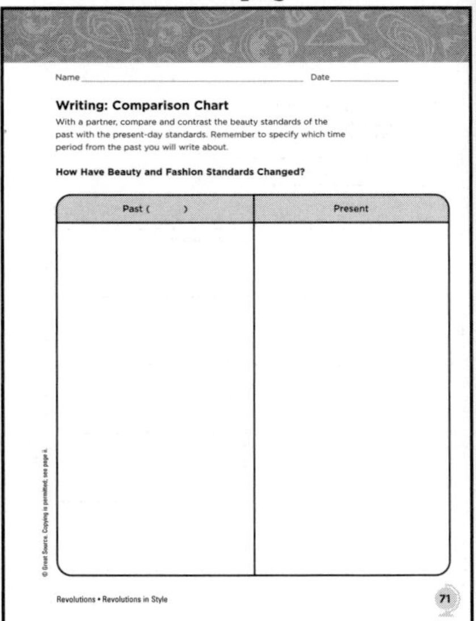

Name ______ Date ______

Writing: Comparison Chart

With a partner, compare and contrast the beauty standards of the past with the present-day standards. Remember to specify which time period from the past you will write about.

How Have Beauty and Fashion Standards Changed?

Past ( )	Present

Revolutions • Revolutions in Style 71

After Reading

Use one or more activities.

Check Purpose

Have students decide if their purpose was met. Were students' definitions correct? Did they learn about fashion and beauty from the past to the present?

Discussion Questions

Continue the group discussion with the following questions.

1. How was men's fashion affected when intelligence was favored over power? (Cause-Effect)
2. Which fashion trend do you think was the most practical? Why? (Evaluate)
3. From which time period would you choose a costume for a party? Why? (Making Connections)

Revisit: Word Web

Have students return to the word web on *Student Journal* page 70. Using a dictionary, the text, and previous knowledge, students should add various details to the web that help them define the vocabulary word. If their predicted definition was incorrect, have students revise it.

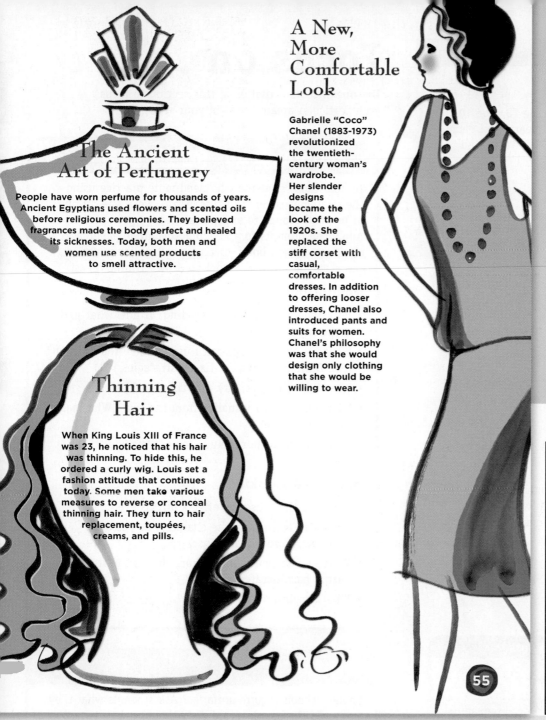

The Ancient Art of Perfumery

People have worn perfume for thousands of years. Ancient Egyptians used flowers and scented oils before religious ceremonies. They believed fragrances made the body perfect and healed its sicknesses. Today, both men and women use scented products to smell attractive.

Thinning Hair

When King Louis XIII of France was 23, he noticed that his hair was thinning. To hide this, he ordered a curly wig. Louis set a fashion attitude that continues today. Some men take various measures to reverse or conceal thinning hair. They turn to hair replacement, toupées, creams, and pills.

A New, More Comfortable Look

Gabrielle "Coco" Chanel (1883-1973) revolutionized the twentieth-century woman's wardrobe. Her slender designs became the look of the 1920s. She replaced the stiff corset with casual, comfortable dresses. In addition to offering looser dresses, Chanel also introduced pants and suits for women. Chanel's philosophy was that she would design only clothing that she would be willing to wear.

55

DIFFERENTIATED INSTRUCTION Vocabulary Prefixes

To help students with this activity, use the steps below:

1. Display the words *uncomfortable*, *unfriendly*, and *unprepared*. Read them aloud.
2. Ask students what they notice about the words. (All have the prefix *un-*.)
3. Read aloud the following sentences, having students fill each blank. *I was ___ for the exam; I think I might have failed it./This seat is so ___! I can't sit here for three hours!/ The salesperson was so ___, nobody wanted to speak to her.*
4. Ask students what they think *un-* means in each word.

Student Journal page 72

Name ________ Date ________

Building Vocabulary: Prefix *un-*

Write words you know that contain the prefix *un-*. Write a definition for each word. Use a dictionary to help you, if you wish.

***un-* means "not, to express negation"**

Words	Definitions
unseemly	inappropriate

72 Revolutions • Revolutions in Style

Writing Comparison Chart

Have students compare the beauty standards from the past with the beauty standards of today. Before students write, encourage them to pair up and choose a specific time period of the past to focus on. Encourage student pairs to brainstorm lists of beauty standards—past and present. Have students complete the comparison chart on *Student Journal* page 71.

Vocabulary Prefixes

Display the word *unseemly*. Have students find it on page 51. Ask them to use context clues and word parts to understand the word. Explain that *seemly* is an adjective that means "good-looking" or "appropriate." *Unseemly,* then, must mean "not attractive" or "inappropriate." Brainstorm a list of words that begin with *un-*. Then have students complete the prefixes chart on *Student Journal* page 72. (See Differentiated Instruction.)

Phonics/Word Study

Latin Roots

Display the following sentence: *I designed a significant insignia*. Ask which words in this sentence share a common root (*designed, significant, insignia*). Explain that the root *sign* means "sign." Have students discuss how the three words relate to each other. Now, work with students to complete the in-depth Latin roots activity on TE page 166.

Phonics/Word Study

More Latin Roots

For instruction to introduce a root, see TE page 102. Work with students to discover the meaning of each root. See *Word Study Manual* page 55 for a related word sort.

sign **(sign)**

This is a word to revisit later because it has a silent-sounded consonant connection. That is, the *g* in *sign* is not sounded, but it is sounded in the word *signature*.

assignment
significant
signature
resign
design
assign
signal
signify
insignia
resignation
designation
consign

son **(a sound)**

consonant
sonorous
resonate
sonar
sonic
unison
sonnet
ultrasonic

spir **(to breathe)**

Guide students to connect the meaning of the root to the words *inspire* and *spiritual*. Both words suggest "being filled with something," as humans' bodies are filled with air for breathing.

respiratory
inspire
spiritual
aspire
dispirited
perspire
transpire
conspire

Discovering the Roots

sign	*son*	*spir*
significant	sonorous	inspire
signature	sonic	conspire
resign	unison	perspire
consign	ultrasonic	spiritual
design	resonate	respiratory

For more information on word sorts and spelling stages, see pages 5–31 in the *Word Study Manual*.

Focus on . . .

Use one or more activities in this section to focus on a particular area of need in your students.

Comprehension Strategy Support

To help those students who need more practice using the strategies covered in this lesson, work one-on-one or in small groups to apply the strategy prompts below. Apply the prompts to a *Reading Advantage* paperback, a classroom library book, or a new or familiar selection in the magazine. Always model your own thinking first.

Monitor Understanding

- Do I understand what I'm reading? If not, what part is confusing to me?
- What fix-up strategies can I use to solve the problem? (See During Reading for fix-up strategies.)
- Why did a character say (do, think, ask) that?
- What images do I visualize from the text? What parts can't I visualize?
- Why did the author include (or not include) those details?

Inferential Thinking

- What are the causes or effects of this event?
- What do I learn from the character or person's thoughts, words, or actions?
- What do I know (or infer) from the text that the author hasn't stated directly?
- What conclusions can I draw?

Writing Persuasive Paragraph

Should schools require uniforms? Ask students what they think. On the board, record their thoughts in a two-column pro-con chart.

Then have students choose a side and write a persuasive paragraph defending their stand.

For more instruction on writing persuasively, see lessons in *Writing Advantage*, pages 152–169.

Fluency: Pacing

After students have read the selection at least once, have them work in pairs to read aloud parts of the article they liked best.

As you listen to pairs read, use these prompts to guide them.

- Keep your eyes on the text as you read so you don't miss any words.
- Let the punctuation be your guide.
- Reading too quickly, too slowly, or stumbling over words makes it difficult for listeners to understand the content.

When students read aloud, do they—

✓ demonstrate a smooth pace, not too fast or too slow?

✓ incorporate well-timed pauses between words and phrases?

✓ reflect an awareness and understanding of punctuation?

English Language Learners

To support students' understanding of prefixes, extend the vocabulary activity on TE page 165. Write *pre-* and *re-* at the top of a piece of chart paper. Explain that *pre-* means "before" and *re-* means "again" when added to the beginning of the word. Write the following words in list format on the chart paper: *preview*, *review*, *predict*, *remake*.

1. Have partners discuss the meanings of these words.
2. Have partners create sentences using these words.
3. Have partners brainstorm a list of other words they know that contain these prefixes.

Independent Activity Options

While you work with individuals or small groups, others can work independently on one or more of the following options.

- Level D paperback books, see TE pages 367–372
- Level D *eZines*
- Repeat word sorts from this lesson
- *Student Journal* pages for this lesson
- *Writing Advantage* independent lessons

Assessment

Strategy Assessment

To help you and your students assess their use of comprehension strategies, ask the following questions. Students can complete a written response or provide verbal answers in a one-on-one reading conference.

1. **Monitor Understanding** Which fashions could you visualize most easily? Which styles were harder to imagine? What did you do to help "see" them? (Answers will vary. Possible response: I could visualize the flapper's outfit the best, since I've seen this style before in movies. I had the hardest time imagining clothes from the Middle Ages. I reread the section and paused after each sentence to help me think about the describing words and imagine the clothes.)
2. **Inferential Thinking** What conclusions can you draw about fashions throughout history? (Answers will vary. Possible responses may include that fashions change depending on what goods are available and the different ideas of beauty. Fashions also change to reflect different attitudes and class structures.)

For ongoing informal assessment, use the checklists on pages 61–64 of *Level D Assessment*.

Word Study Assessment

Use these steps to help you and your students assess their understanding of Latin roots.

1. Present the chart below. Read the roots and words aloud.
2. Have students explain how the meaning of each word is related to the root.

son "a sound"	*sign* "sign"	*spir* "to breathe"
consonant	signature	respiratory
unison	signal	inspire
resonate	assignment	perspire

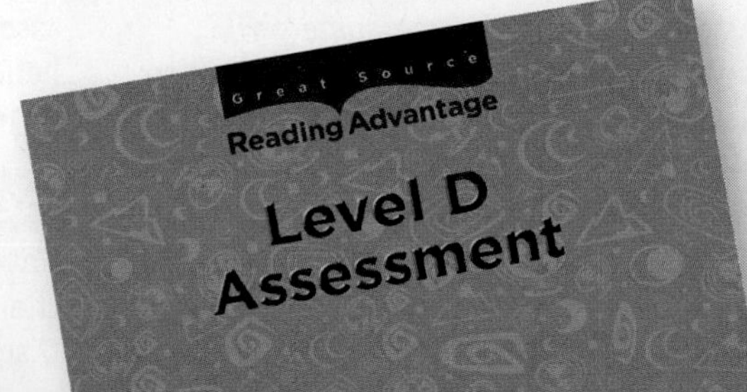

LESSON **21**

The Little Rock Nine, 1957

Revolutions, pages 56–59

SUMMARY

This **radio play** tells about nine black students who revolutionized the public school system by attending an all-white high school in Little Rock, Arkansas, in 1957.

COMPREHENSION STRATEGY

Understanding Text Structure

WRITING

Journal Entry

VOCABULARY

Context Clues

PHONICS/WORD STUDY

Latin Roots *terra, tort/torq, vac*

Lesson Vocabulary

unanimous	unruly
irate	deter
racist	taunted

MATERIALS

Revolutions, pp. 56–59
Student Journal, pp. 73–75
Word Study Manual, p. 56
Writing Advantage, pp. 56–93

CAST
Host
Mr. Edwards
Ms. Santana

The Little Rock Nine, 1957

HOST: Good Evening. Today we will spend our radio hour talking with two news reporters who covered the integration of Central High School in Little Rock, Arkansas, in 1957. Welcome, Mr. Edwards and Ms. Santana.

MR. EDWARDS & MS. SANTANA: Good evening.

HOST: Let's give our listeners some history. Could you explain *Brown vs. Board of Education?*

MS. SANTANA: Certainly. In the 1950s, American schools were segregated by race: white schools had all white teachers and students, and black schools had all black teachers and students. The schooling was supposed to be equal, but it wasn't. In Kansas, a girl named Linda Brown had to walk a mile to get to her black school even though there was a white elementary school just a few blocks from her house. Linda's father tried to sign her up in the white school but wasn't allowed. Mr. Brown complained in the courts. Eventually, the case went to the Supreme Court. The decision in *Brown vs. Board of Education* was unanimous. All the judges agreed that schools could not be segregated on the basis of race. They must be integrated—black and white students should be together.

Segregation

Often, we think of racial prejudice as a problem in the South. However, some schools in the North were still segregated in the 1970s. White children and black children attended different schools. Under a 1974 court order, the city of Boston bused black students to all-white schools. As in Arkansas, these students were met with anger and hatred. Persistent violence at some schools led to a major police presence. Some people said there was "a cop for every kid" during this period. Over the course of the next twenty-five years, many white families moved to the suburbs. White enrollment in Boston's public schools dropped dramatically—from more than 50 percent to just 15 percent. In 1999, the Boston School Committee voted to no longer consider race when making school assignments.

Before Reading

WHOLE CLASS Use one or more activities.

Make a Concept Web

Write the words *civil rights* in the center oval of a concept web. Discuss with students what *civil rights* means. Ask students: *What are some civil rights? Who has them? How do people get them?* Write students' responses to expand the web. (See Differentiated Instruction.)

Vocabulary Preview

Display the selection vocabulary. Ask students if they can make associations with any of the words. Model making associations with the word *unruly* to help students complete *Student Journal* page 73.

Preview the Selection

Have students read the title, look at the pictures, and read the headings. Discuss students' observations.

Make Predictions/ Set Purpose

Students should use the information gathered in the selection preview to make predictions about what they will learn from the radio play. To help students set a purpose, suggest that they read to learn how high-school students made a significant contribution to integrating schools in the American South.

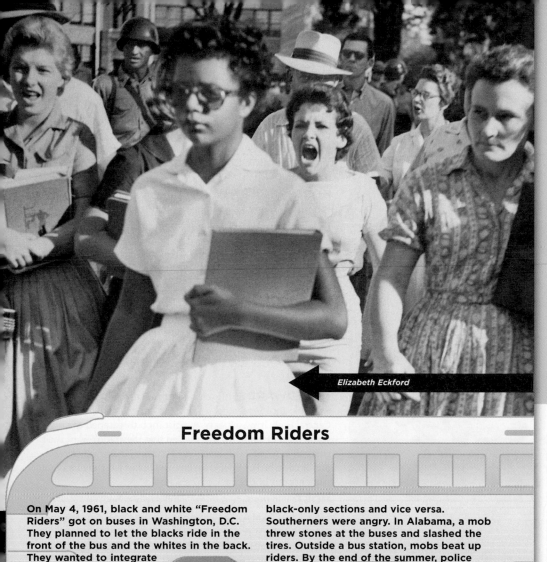

Elizabeth Eckford

Freedom Riders

On May 4, 1961, black and white "Freedom Riders" got on buses in Washington, D.C. They planned to let the blacks ride in the front of the bus and the whites in the back. They wanted to integrate Southern bus stations by sending the whites into black-only sections and vice versa. Southerners were angry. In Alabama, a mob threw stones at the buses and slashed the tires. Outside a bus station, mobs beat up riders. By the end of the summer, police had arrested more than 300 riders.

57

DIFFERENTIATED INSTRUCTION

SMALL GROUP

MAKE A CONCEPT WEB

To help students as they create the web, use these strategies.

1. Tell students that the civil rights movement was the effort, which began in the mid-1950s, to fight racial injustice.
2. At that time, in Southern states, many schools, buses, hotels, and restaurants were segregated, and blacks were denied their voting rights.
3. Martin Luther King Jr. and others fought a battle against racism and discrimination, using nonviolent protests, such as boycotts of buses, sit-ins at lunch counters, and mass demonstrations and marches.

Student Journal page 73

Name ____________ Date ________

Building Vocabulary: Making Associations

Pick two words from the vocabulary list below. Think about what you already know about each word. Then answer the following questions for each word.

unanimous	racist	deter
irate	unruly	taunted

Word ____________

What do you think about when you read this word? ____________

Who might use this word? ____________

What do you already know about this word? ____________

Word ____________

What do you think about when you read this word? ____________

Who might use this word? ____________

What do you already know about this word? ____________

Now watch for these words in the magazine selection. Were you on the right track?

Revolutions • The Little Rock Nine, 1957

73

During Reading

Comprehension

SMALL GROUP

UNDERSTANDING TEXT STRUCTURE

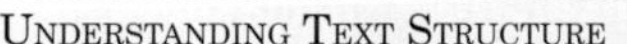

Use these questions to model how to understand the structure of a radio play. Then have students identify the parts of the radio play and explain how the parts help their understanding.

- How is this selection structured?
- How does this structure help me understand the information?

Teacher Think Aloud

I see a box that lists a cast. I know that a list of characters appears at the beginning of a play. Then I see the headings "Host," "Mr. Edwards," and "Ms. Santana." The text following each of these headings must be the character's words. This whole selection is a conversation among three people. I will need to pay attention so that I know who is speaking and can follow this conversation.

Fix-Up Strategies

Offer these strategies to help students read independently.

If you don't understand what you're reading:

- Reread the difficult section to look for clues to help you comprehend.
- Read ahead to find clues to help you comprehend.
- Retell, or say in your own words, what you've read.
- Visualize, or form mental pictures of, what you've read.

Hostile crowd outside Central High

HOST: That was a remarkable decision for 1954.

MR. EDWARDS: Yes, but remember that decision didn't address segregation in other public places, such as restaurants or buses. Also, the court gave no time frame for the changes. So, actually, nothing happened—even in schools—for a while.

HOST: How did Arkansas respond?

MR. EDWARDS: The school board wasn't happy and took their time—three years, in fact.

MS. SANTANA: The board didn't close or integrate the black high school. Instead, they let a few blacks come to Central High, the all-white school.

HOST: Those students became known as the Little Rock Nine. Why didn't they go to school on the first day?

MR. EDWARDS: Governor Faubus didn't allow them. He brought in the National Guard and threatened the lives of the black students who were supposed to enter Central High.

MS. SANTANA: That's right. But on the second day, the students were going to meet down the block from the school and walk in together. One girl, Elizabeth Eckford, didn't get the message. She tried to go in the front of the school on her own. A very irate, angry mob yelled threats at her. The National Guard looked on and did nothing.

HOST: Yes, the National Guard kept all nine students out. How did this end?

MR. EDWARDS: It took a court order against the Governor. It wasn't until September 23 that the Little Rock Nine entered Central High. It wasn't easy. A racist mob threatened the black students, and white mothers yelled that they didn't want their children in school with blacks. By 11:30 A.M., the unruly crowd was out of control. For safety reasons, the police led the black students out of the back of the school.

HOST: Did the nine ever get a full day of school?

MS. SANTANA: They did, but not until President Eisenhower sent the 101st Airborne to watch over them. A soldier was supposed to protect each black student. That soldier walked the student around school. But the presence of soldiers didn't deter the white students from yelling nasty remarks or beating up the black students.

58

Student Journal page 74

Name ____________ Date ________

Writing: Planning List and Journal Entry

Write a journal entry as if you were an eyewitness to the events told about in the radio play. First, list the events that took place.

List of Events

1.
2.
3.
4.

Now write your journal entry.

74 Revolutions • The Little Rock Nine, 1957

After Reading  Use one or more activities.

Check Purpose

Have students decide if their purpose was met. Did they learn more about how high-school students made a significant contribution to integrating schools in the South?

Discussion Questions

Continue the group discussion with the following questions.

1. What problems did the Little Rock Nine have to overcome? (Inferential Thinking)
2. How did the Little Rock Nine affect the lives of others? (Cause-Effect)
3. What do you admire about the Little Rock Nine? (Making Connections)

Revisit: Concept Web

Have students return to the concept web and invite them to add to it.

MR. EDWARDS: The hatred ran deep. When the 101st left, the black students had to take care of themselves. One girl was suspended after she dumped her lunch tray on two white boys who had insulted her. The principal let her come back, but she had to agree that she wouldn't respond to anything and would let the adults handle everything. Unfortunately, she was expelled after yelling back at some girls who taunted her with racist remarks. The other eight black students finished the school year.

HOST: After one of the nine graduated, didn't the people of Little Rock try to end integration?

MS. SANTANA: That's right. Governor Faubus tried to stop integration by shutting down all four high schools in Little Rock.

MR. EDWARDS: Yes, but a court found his actions to be illegal, and the schools reopened.

HOST: How did the events in Little Rock affect the rest of the United States?

MS. SANTANA: I'd say the integration of schools in Arkansas proved how deeply the prejudice of some Americans ran during those years.

MR. EDWARDS: Yes, but it also showed African Americans that the rights of Americans were their rights, too. If they protested loudly enough on the streets, in the courts, and in their towns, they'd be heard. I am sure that the Little Rock struggle helped other civil rights protests, such as the lunch counter sit-ins and the freedom rides that came later.

HOST: Thank you both so much for this information. ◆

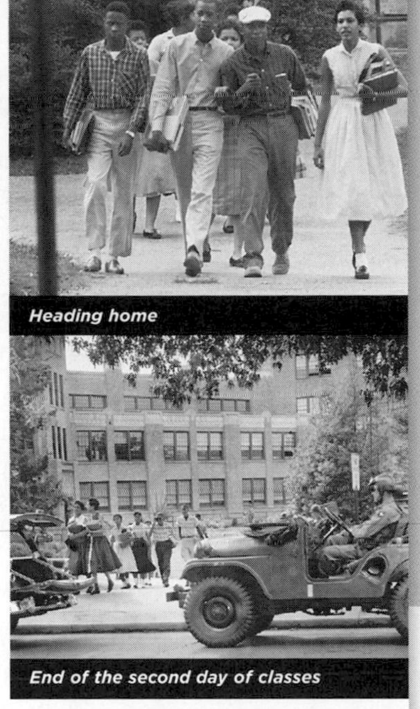

Heading home

End of the second day of classes

The Little Rock Nine

When asked to name the historical event that most affected him, former President Bill Clinton said that it was the events in Little Rock in 1957. In 1999, forty-two years after they entered Central High School, then-President Clinton presented the Little Rock Nine with Congressional Gold Medals. The awards were given in the name of "selfless heroism" in the face of horrible racial intolerance.

Little Rock 1997 Anniversary

59

DIFFERENTIATED INSTRUCTION

SMALL GROUP

Writing Journal Entry

To provide students with help in writing their journal entry, use these steps:

1. Remind students that a journal entry has these characteristics: a date, a first-person perspective, and an informal tone.
2. Also point out that a journal is a place to write thoughts and feelings as well as facts.

Student Journal page 75

Name ______ Date ______

Building Vocabulary: Using Context to Understand a Word

Look for the word *deter* in the radio play. Write in the box the sentences that help you know its meaning. Then complete the statements and answer the questions about the word.

My Word in Context:

I think this word means ______

because ______

My word is ______

My word is not ______

Where else might I find this word? ______

What makes this an important word to know? ______

Revolutions • The Little Rock Nine, 1957 75

Writing Journal Entry

Tell students they will write a journal entry as if they witnessed events in the radio play. Before they write, have them make a list of the events that took place. Encourage students to refer to the list as they complete the journal activity on *Student Journal* page 74. (See Differentiated Instruction.)

Vocabulary Context Clues

Draw students' attention to the following sentence on page 56: "*The decision in* Brown vs. Board of Education *was unanimous.*" Have students use context to figure out what *unanimous* means. Ask students which words help them figure out the meaning of *unanimous.* Then ask what *unanimous* means. Then have students complete the context activity for the word *deter* on *Student Journal* page 75.

Phonics/Word Study

Latin Roots

Write the following words on the board: *territory, terrestrial.* Ask students what these words have in common (a syllable and the word root, *terr*). Explain that *terra* means "earth." Ask what earth has to do with each of the words on the board. Now, work with students to complete the in-depth Latin roots activity on TE page 172.

Phonics/Word Study

More Latin Roots

For instruction to introduce a root, see TE page 102. Work with students to discover the meaning of each root. See *Word Study Manual* page 56 for a related word sort.

terra **(earth)**

terra cotta
terra firma
terrestrial
terrarium
terrain
terrace
Mediterranean
subterranean
terrier
territory

tort/torq **(to twist)**

Tortilla may be a surprise, but a dictionary definition describes the *twisting* of the dough to make the tortilla.

contort
extort
distort
retort
tortuous
contortion
extortion
distortion
torture
tortilla

vac **(empty)**

vacuous
vacuum
vacant
vacation
vacate
evacuate

Discovering the Roots

terra	*tort*	*vac*
terra cotta	contort	vacuum
subterranean	distort	vacate
terrestrial	retort	evacuate
terrain	torture	vacant
terrace	tortuous	vacuous

For more information on word sorts and spelling stages, see pages 5–31 in the *Word Study Manual.*

Focus on . . .

Use one or more activities in this section to focus on a particular area of need in your students.

Comprehension STRATEGY SUPPORT

To help those students who need more practice using the strategies covered in this lesson, work one-on-one or in small groups to apply the strategy prompts below. Apply the prompts to a *Reading Advantage* paperback, a classroom library book, or a new or familiar selection in the magazine. Always model your own thinking first.

Understanding Text Structure

- What kind of text is this? (book, story, article, guidebook, play, manual)
- How does the author organize the text? (cause-effect, problem-solution, chronological order, description, question-answer, comparison-contrast)
- What details support my thoughts about the text structure?
- What is the cause (effect, problem, solution, order, question, answer)?
- If fiction, who are the characters? What is the setting, plot, conflict, and resolution?

Writing Short Essay

Ask students to write a brief essay about a time when they, or someone they know, were treated unfairly. Before they begin writing, have them take notes about questions such as these.

- What happened?
- How did you (or the person) feel?
- How did you (or the person) react?
- What would you (or the person) do differently next time?

If you'd like students to edit their writing, see lessons in *Writing Advantage*, pages 56–93, for instruction on different kinds of editing.

Fluency: Expression

After students have read the radio play at least once, have groups of three read page 59 together. Then have students perform the dialogue. Have group members decide who will read which part. First, discuss with students the tone of the overall selection (informal and conversational, yet serious). Then, have students discuss the tone of each character. (Possible interpretations: Mr. Edwards, compassionate; the host, cordial; Ms. Santana, a bit angry.)

As you listen to students read, use these prompts to guide them in reading expressively.

- Read conversationally, or the way you talk.
- Ask yourself what your character is feeling.
- Match your tone of voice, facial expression, and gestures to the feelings of your character.

When students read aloud, do they—

✓ reflect an understanding of the text?
✓ demonstrate appropriate timing, stress, and intonation?
✓ incorporate appropriate speed and phrasing?

English Language Learners

To support students' understanding of prefixes, expand on the vocabulary context activity on TE page 171.

1. Display *unhappy* and *under*. Explain that *unhappy* contains the prefix *un-*, meaning "not." The *un* in *under* is not a prefix.
2. Display these words: *undo, unbuckle, uncle, until.* Discuss which words contain the prefix *un-*, meaning "not."

Independent Activity Options

While you work with individuals or small groups, others can work independently on one or more of the following options.

- Level D paperback books, see TE pages 367–372
- Level D *eZines*
- Repeat word sorts from this lesson
- *Student Journal* pages for this lesson
- *Writing Advantage* independent lessons

Assessment

Strategy Assessment

To help you and your students assess their use of comprehension strategies, ask the following questions. Students can complete a written response or provide verbal answers in a one-on-one reading conference.

- **Understanding Text Structure** What are the parts of a play? Would you rather read a play or a story? Why? (In this radio play, the parts include a cast and lines only. Other plays might have stage directions, scenes, and notes for sound effects. Students should be able to support their opinions with reasons.)

For ongoing informal assessment, use the checklists on pages 61–64 of *Level D Assessment*.

Word Study Assessment

Use these steps to help you and your students assess their understanding of Latin roots.

1. Present the chart below. Read the roots and words aloud.
2. Have students explain how the meaning of each word is related to its root.

terr "earth"	*vac* "empty"	*tort/torq* "to twist"
terrace	vacuum	distort
territory	vacant	contortion
terrain	vacation	torture

LESSON **22**

The Wheel . . . *and* Freedom of Speech

Revolutions, pages 60–end

SUMMARY

This **nonfiction article** explains the history of the wheel and its many uses. A **poem** follows.

COMPREHENSION STRATEGIES

Monitor Understanding
Inferential Thinking

WRITING

Notes for Visualizing

VOCABULARY

Concept Ladder

PHONICS/WORD STUDY

Latin Roots *val, ver, vid/vis*

Lesson Vocabulary

archaeological
maneuver
civilization

MATERIALS

Revolutions, pp. 60–end
Student Journal, pp. 76–78
Word Study Manual, p. 57
Writing Advantage, pp. 30–55

A Revolutionary Revolution

How do you define revolution?

A revolution is "an event that causes sudden, great change." The American Revolution caused great changes. However, another definition of the word is "the motion of a figure around a center or axis." The wheel works by revolving on an axle, a rod that goes through the center of the wheel. That makes the turning of a wheel a revolutionary revolution.

Many modern inventions have caused a revolution in the way we think and live, work, and play. The computer has opened up communication around the globe, and allowed us to do things faster. Many people have called the computer a revolutionary invention. But there are a few ancient inventions that have changed the entire course of human history. Consider the wheel. Can you imagine a world without it?

The wheel is believed to have been invented about 5,000 years ago. Wheels have been discovered in archaeological sites dating back that far. No one knows where the wheel was first used or who used it. Archaeologists believe that the wheel may have been invented as an improvement on the practice of using logs to roll things from one place to another. People would lay down several logs next to each other and roll heavy objects over the logs. The heavy stones used in the ancient pyramids of Egypt were transported this way. The rolling process took a long time, but it was better than having to carry heavy objects on your back.

People probably began using the spoked wheel about 4,000 years ago. Using spokes made the wheel lighter than one with a solid circle from edge to axis. Next came wheels with hubs and later, wheels with tires.

60

Before Reading

Use one or more activities.

Make a List

Tell students they are going to read a selection about the wheel. Have students brainstorm things that contain some type of wheel. List their responses on the board or on chart paper. Encourage students to think beyond the obvious. Offer some examples as shown.

What has wheels?

1. car
2. steering wheel
3. windmill

Vocabulary Preview

Display the selection vocabulary. Have students find each word in the text and use context clues to discover the meaning. Note that many words have more than one meaning, and words in English often come from other language sources.

Model for students how to investigate a word and its origin, using the word *course*. Now have students complete the word meanings and origins activity on *Student Journal* page 76.

In addition to its use as a device to transport things, the wheel is also a kind of tool. Here are some ways that the wheel is used as a tool:

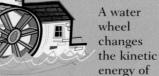

A water wheel changes the kinetic energy of falling water into mechanical energy. Kinetic energy is the energy of movement. Mechanical energy comes from a machine.

Cranks and doorknobs are kinds of wheels.

Gears are wheels with teeth around the edges. Clocks, watches, and bicycles are everyday items that rely on the use of gears.

Windmills use wind to power them, instead of water.

The steering wheel of a car makes it easy to turn a car.

A winch is a fixed wheel with a chain or rope used to lift heavy objects, such as buckets of water from a well.

61

DIFFERENTIATED INSTRUCTION SMALL GROUP

Make Predictions/ Set Purpose

To help students set a purpose for reading, use these strategies.

1. Note that personal interests often drive the reader's purpose for reading. Suggest that students browse through the article, looking for special features that grab their attention. Explain that any of these can help set a reading purpose.
2. Suggest that students talk with a partner. Discussion can spark new ideas and may raise new questions.

Student Journal page 76

Name ______ Date ______

Building Vocabulary: Word Meanings and Word Origins

Using a dictionary, write a short definition for each word. Also find the origin of the word. As you read the article, watch for each of the words. Did you select a definition that matches the way the word is used?

Word	Definitions	Language of Origin
archaeological		
civilization		
maneuver		

76 Revolutions • The Wheel

Preview the Selection

Have students look through the four pages of the article. Use these or similar prompts to orient students to the article.

- What do you think the article will be about?
- Do you think this is fiction or nonfiction? What clues help you know?
- What do the pictures tell you?

Teacher Think Aloud

The title and illustrations make me think this article will be about wheels and how they're everywhere. I don't understand the subtitle, though. How can a revolution be revolutionary? Wait, as I scan the first paragraph, I see that the word revolution *has two meanings!*

Make Predictions/ Set Purpose

Students should use the information gathered in the selection preview to make predictions about what they will learn from the article. To help students set a purpose, suggest that they read to learn about the importance of the wheel and to see if there are any surprising uses of wheels. (See Differentiated Instruction.)

DIFFERENTIATED INSTRUCTION

Comprehension

INFERENTIAL THINKING

To help students use their prior knowledge and the information from the text to make inferences, use the following steps:

1. Look at the three wheels on page 63.
2. Together, read the text next to each picture.
3. Ask: *What do you infer about how each invention changed people's lives?*
4. Then ask: *For each inference you made, what was your prior knowledge about it and what information did you use from the text?*

The invention of the wheel was a revolution in the development of human civilization. Lifting and carrying loads became easier. The wheel helped people use the strength of animals, by having them pull wheeled carts. Distant travel became possible, bringing together ideas and goods from faraway places. Water wheels helped create energy to power machines, such as sawmills and granaries. Using the wheel to work gave people time and energy to do things other than get and prepare food. In this way, the wheel may have given us the beginnings of recreation—spending time doing things other than surviving.

Wheels are essential to transportation. Trains, buses, cars, bicycles, and airplanes all need wheels in order to take people from one place to another. Our ability to explore the world is completely dependent on wheels, in one form or another.

The latest invention based on the wheel is the Segway Human Transporter (HT). This simply designed, two-wheeled machine was created as an alternative means of transportation. Because the Segway HT is about the same size as an average adult, it fits easily on city sidewalks. When riding a Segway HT, you can get places more quickly than if you were walking. At its slowest speed, the battery-powered Segway HT travels up to six miles per hour. At its fastest speed, it goes up to 12.5 miles per hour. Some city police forces are considering using the Segway HT to monitor city life. The company that created the Segway hopes that people will keep their cars at home and use a Segway to maneuver through crowded city streets. The company's goal is to encourage people to interact more with their community and to reduce traffic congestion and pollution.

The next time you use a wheel, think about where you'd be without it. ◆

During Reading

Comprehension

MONITOR UNDERSTANDING

Use these questions to model monitoring understanding. Then have students tell about how they monitor their understanding as they read the article.

- How do the pictures help me understand the text?
- What are the strongest images?
- Can I retell in my own words what I'm reading?

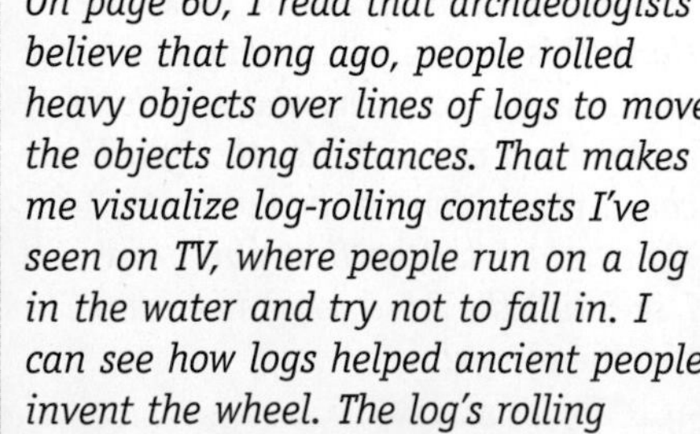

Teacher Think Aloud

On page 60, I read that archaeologists believe that long ago, people rolled heavy objects over lines of logs to move the objects long distances. That makes me visualize log-rolling contests I've seen on TV, where people run on a log in the water and try not to fall in. I can see how logs helped ancient people invent the wheel. The log's rolling motion is a lot like a wheel.

Comprehension

INFERENTIAL THINKING

Use these questions to model making inferences about the Segway (HT). Then have students reveal some inferences they make while reading about it.

- Why was the Segway (HT) invented?
- How might the Segway (HT) change our lives?

(See Differentiated Instruction.)

More Wheels at Work

Spinning Wheel

Spinning is the process of making threads from plant or animal fibers. Spinning wheels use a smooth stick, called a spindle, to make thread. The spindle spins like a top—driven by the turning of a large wheel using a foot pedal—and fibers are twisted around the spindle into fine thread. Very fine thread may require two spinnings.

The Turbine

In modern times, the traditional water wheel and windmill have given way to the turbine. A turbine is a wheel that is turned by moving fluid, such as water, steam, gas, or wind. Generators driven by turbines produce most of the electric power used in homes and factories. Turbines also turn propellers in ships, and are an essential part of jet engines.

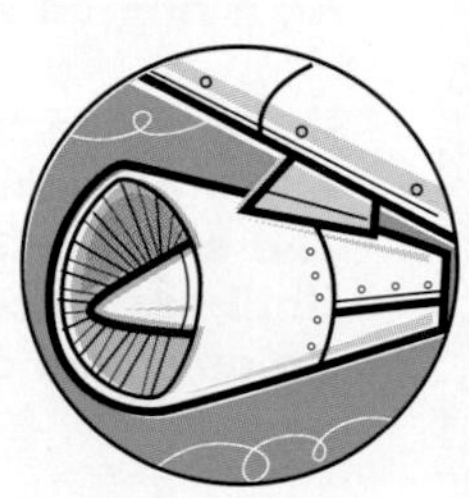

Potter's Wheel

The potter's wheel was possibly the first use of the wheel as a tool. This also is believed to date back about 5,000 years. A potter uses the wheel to shape clay into pottery. The potter puts a lump of clay onto the center of a horizontal, revolving wheel. As the wheel spins, the potter shapes the clay by using his or her hands or a variety of tools. Potters create bowls, dishes, cups, and utensils that people use to prepare and eat food.

Four Simple Machines

The wheel ❶ is one of the four simple machines. The other three are the lever ❷, the pulley ❸, and the inclined plane ❹. These four simple machines are the basis for all other machines.

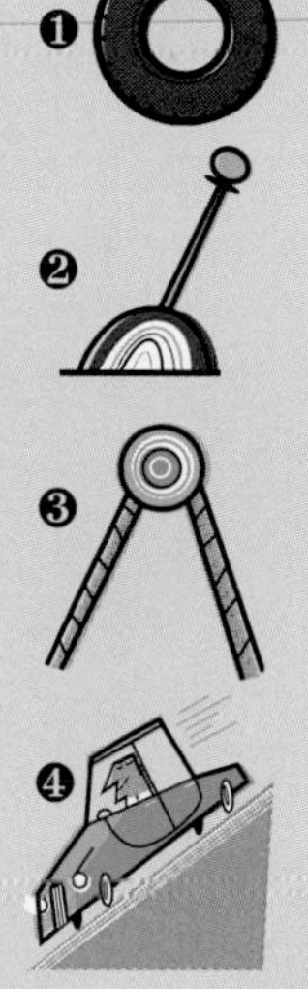

63

Teacher Think Aloud

When I read the section about the Segway and look at the picture of it, I "see" city streets filled with people using these machines, instead of walking, driving, or taking the bus. What effects would this have on city life? There would probably be less traffic and less pollution. But people would have to leave earlier because it might take longer to get to work.

Fix-Up Strategies

Offer these strategies to help students read independently.

If you don't understand what you're reading:

- Reread the difficult section to look for clues to help you comprehend.
- Read ahead to find clues to help you comprehend.
- Retell, or say in your own words, what you've read.
- Visualize, or form mental pictures of, what you've read.

If you don't understand a word:

- Reread the sentence. Look for ideas and words that provide meaning clues.
- Find clues by reading a few sentences before and after the confusing word.
- Look for the base or root word and think about its meaning.
- Think about the topic or plot at this point to see if either offers meaning clues.

Poem: Freedom of Speech

Have students read the poem silently. Use these or similar questions to discuss the poem as a group.

- What is the poem about?
- Why do you think the poem is paired with "The Wheel: A Revolutionary Revolution"?
- How would you describe the person's experience with the "turnstile" wheel?
- Do you like or dislike the poem? Why?

Student Journal page 77

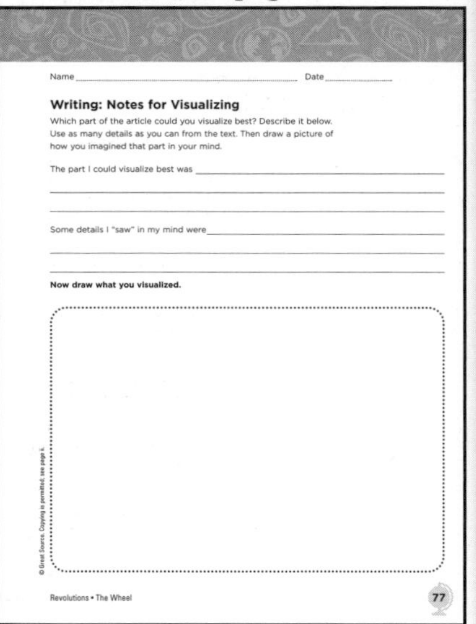

Name ________________ Date ________

Writing: Notes for Visualizing

Which part of the article could you visualize best? Describe it below. Use as many details as you can from the text. Then draw a picture of how you imagined that part in your mind.

The part I could visualize best was ________________

____

____

Some details I "saw" in my mind were ________________

____

____

Now draw what you visualized.

Revolutions • The Wheel 77

CREDITS

Program Authors
Laura Robb
James F. Baumann
Carol J. Fuhler
Joan Kindig

Editorial Board
Avon Cowell
Craig Roney
Jo Worthy

Magazine Writer
Anina Robb
Cara Lieb

Design and Production
Preface, Inc.

Photography
Inside front cover, cl © J. Pat Carter/AP Photo; c © Henry Diltz/Corbis; p. 1 cl © Jim Zuckerman/Corbis; c © John Springer Collection/Corbis; cr © Bettmann/Corbis; p. 7t © William Gottlieb/Corbis; bl © Bettmann/Corbis; br © L. Clarke/Corbis; p. 8 © AP Photo; p. 10 © Bettmann/Corbis; p. 11 © Corbis; p. 13 © Joan Miro/Art Resource NY; p. 14 © Bob Burch/Index Stock Imagery; p. 15 © R. Ian Lloyd/Masterfile; p. 16 © J. Pat Carter/AP Photo; p. 17 © Cary Wolinsky/IPN/Aurora; p. 18 © Pharos Tribune, Bruce Pyke/AP Photo; p. 19 © Bob Burch/Index Stock Imagery; pp. 21–22 © Henry Diltz/Corbis; p. 23 bkgd © Getty Images; l © Bettmann/Corbis; p. 23r, 25 © Corbis; p. 29 bkgd © Historical Picture Archive/Corbis; t © Swim Ink/Corbis; c © Hulton-Deutsch Collection/Corbis; b © Archivo Iconografico, S.A./Corbis; p. 34 © Stock Montage, Inc.; p. 35 © Brian A. Vikander/Corbis; p. 43 © Itsuo Inouye/AP Photo; p. 44 bkgd © Jim Zuckerman/Corbis; t © J. Pat Carter/AP Photo; p. 45l © Bettmann/Corbis; r © A & J Verkaik/Corbis; pp. 46–47 bkgd © Chris Golley/Corbis; p. 46c © Tom Bean/Corbis; p. 47tl © William James Warren/Corbis; tr © Wichita Eagle Beacon/Corbis SYGMA; b © Orban Thierry/Corbis SYGMA; p. 48 © Bettmann/Corbis; pp. 50–51 bkgd © PictureDisc, Inc.; p. 50l © The Art Archive/Musée des Arts Décoratifs Paris/Dagli Orti (A); c © Historical Picture Archive/Corbis; r © Getty Images; p. 51 © The Art Archive/Musée des Arts Décoratifs Paris/Dagli Orti (A); p. 52t © The Art Archive/Bibliothèque des Arts Décoratifs Paris/Dagli Orti; b © Christel Gerstenberg/Corbis; pp. 52–53 bkgd © PictureDisc, Inc.; p. 53 © Christel Gerstenberg/Corbis; p. 54 bkgd © PictureDisc, Inc.; t © John Springer Collection/Corbis; b © Getty Images; pp. 57–58, 59t, b © Bettmann/Corbis; p. 59c © AP Photo/Danny Johnston

Illustration
Inside front cover, l James Elston; cr Clint Hansen; r Chris Ellison; p. 1, l Ann Boyajian; r David Semple; pp. 2–6 James Elston; pp. 24–28 Clint Hansen; pp. 30–33 Chris Ellison; pp. 36–42 Ann Boyajian; pp. 48–49 Jim Paillot; p. 55 Ann Boyajian; pp. 60–63 David Semple; pp. 64–Inside back cover Bud Peen

Freedom of Speech

She can't complete the revolution
Inside the turnstile.
She's trapped, steel-armed,
While all around her, kids ease
Through the divide between token and travel.

She can't make it to the yellow line
Of halt, of shock-bright wait,
Where now, she watches other riders hinge
Their bodies into the darkness
Eyeing the dark tunnel.

She wants to yell to them, "Help!"
Yell that they are all cutting off the blood
To their heads, but her voice is wedged
Between her vocal chords, stuck tight
As a ring on a swollen finger.

If she could take one more step,
She'd be riding on the chords of the city,
The electric threads swallowing her up
Until her voice opened: a cough, a clang,
An unlocked channel of speech.

After Reading

WHOLE CLASS Use one or more activities.

Check Purpose

Have students decide if their purpose was met. What did they find out about the importance of the wheel?

Discussion Questions

Continue the group discussion with the following questions.

1. What effect has the invention of the wheel had on society? (Cause-Effect)
2. What are some different kinds of wheels? Pick one and explain how it works. (Details)
3. What kind of wheel do you use most often? (Making Connections)

Revisit: List

Revisit the list about wheels. What new information can students add?

A subway is a train that runs at least part of its route underground. Subways are used as a way for people to get around cities, such as New York, Boston, San Francisco, and Washington, D.C. To enter some subway stations, you pass through a turnstile. A turnstile has horizontal bars that revolve to let one person at a time enter a place. You may have gone through a turnstile at an amusement park or a sports stadium.

DIFFERENTIATED INSTRUCTION 

Vocabulary

Concept Ladder

To help students with the vocabulary activity, use these strategies.

1. Explain that one way to explore a word is to ask questions related to it. The questions and the answers build a "concept" view of the word.
2. Have students find the word *communication* on page 60. Ask them to suggest questions they have about it. Model one or two questions first. Suggest: *Who uses communication? When did communication start?*
3. Review students' questions and then work together to answer them.

Student Journal page 78

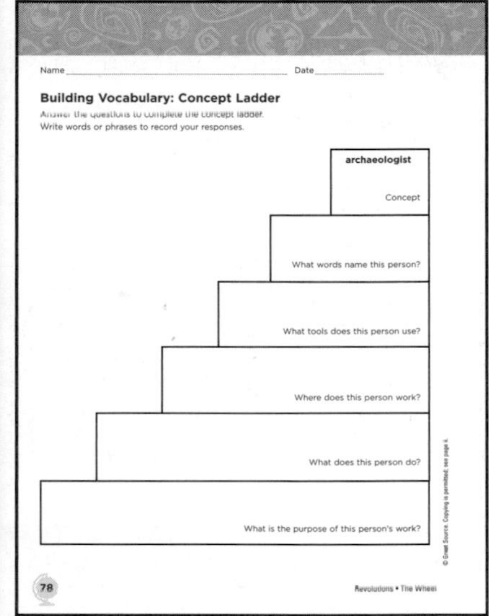
Name ____________ Date ________

Building Vocabulary: Concept Ladder

Answer the questions to complete the concept ladder.
Write words or phrases to record your responses.

archaeologist
Concept

What words name this person?

What tools does this person use?

Where does this person work?

What does this person do?

What is the purpose of this person's work?

© Great Source. Copying is permitted; see page ii.

78 Revolutions • The Wheel

Writing

Notes for Visualizing

Ask students which part of the article they could visualize best. Then have students write a description of that part and draw it to complete the visualizing activity on *Student Journal* page 77.

Vocabulary **Concept Ladder**

Display the word *civilization*. Ask students the following questions. Record the answers in the form of a concept ladder. (See TE page 379 for a BLM.) *Who belongs to a civilization? What are some characteristics of a civilization? When did civilizations begin? What is another word or words for* civilization*?* Then have students complete the concept ladder on *Student Journal* page 78 for the word *archaeologist*.

Phonics/Word Study

Latin Roots

Display the following sentence: *My dad supervised us when we made the home video for the television contest.* Ask students which words in this sentence share a common root (*supervised, video, television*). Explain that *vid* and *vis* mean "to see." Ask how the *vid/vis* words in the sentence relate to seeing. Now, work with students to complete the in-depth Latin roots activity on TE page 180.

Phonics/Word Study

More Latin Roots

For instruction to introduce a root, see TE page 102. Work with students to discover the meaning of each root. See *Word Study Manual* page 57 for a related word sort.

val (be strong, have worth)

The words *value* and *valor* are connected by their shared root

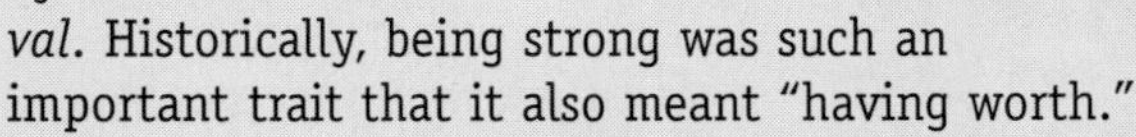

val. Historically, being strong was such an important trait that it also meant "having worth."

valor	devaluate
valiant	value
valid	invalid
validate	evaluate

ver **(true)**

verdict	verisimilitude
verify	veritable
very	veracity

vid/vis **(to see)**

video	advise
vision	visit
visibility	supervise
invisible	televise
revision	visionary

Discovering the Roots

val	*ver*	*vid/vis*
valor	veritable	video
value	veracity	supervise
evaluate	verdict	revision
valiant	verify	visit
validate	verisimilitude	invisible

For more information on word sorts and spelling stages, see pages 5–31 in the *Word Study Manual*.

Focus on . . .

Use one or more activities in this section to focus on a particular area of need in your students.

Comprehension STRATEGY SUPPORT

To help those students who need more practice using the strategies covered in this lesson, work one-on-one or in small groups to apply the strategy prompts below. Apply the prompts to a *Reading Advantage* paperback, a classroom library book, or a new or familiar selection in the magazine. Always model your own thinking first.

Monitor Understanding

- Do I understand what I'm reading? If not, what part is confusing to me?
- What fix-up strategies can I use to solve the problem? (See During Reading for fix-up strategies.)
- Why did a character say (do, think, ask) that?
- What images do I visualize from the text? What parts can't I visualize?
- Why did the author include (or not include) those details?

Inferential Thinking

- What are the causes or effects of this event?
- What do I learn from the character or person's thoughts, words, or actions?
- What do I know (or infer) from the text that the author hasn't stated directly?
- What conclusions can I draw?

Writing Short Essay

Tell students that there are many other inventions like the wheel that have had a huge impact on society. Ask students to pick one invention or simple machine that has changed their lives, and to then write a short essay about it. Ask students to think about how their lives would be different without that invention. Before writing, have students organize their ideas in a chart.

Invention or Simple Machine	How It Affects My Life	What I Think Life Would Be Like Without It

To provide instruction on writing techniques, see lessons in *Writing Advantage*, pages 30–55.

Fluency: Pacing

After students have read the poem "Freedom of Speech" at least once to themselves, have them use it in pairs to practice fluent reading.

As you listen to students read, use these prompts to guide them.

- Read at an even, natural pace.
- Notice how the punctuation does not always give you clues for when to pause. The meaning of the words and phrases are your main clue for when to pause.

When students read aloud, do they—

- ✓ demonstrate a smooth pace, not too fast or too slow?
- ✓ incorporate well-timed pauses between words and phrases?
- ✓ reflect an awareness and understanding of punctuation?

English Language Learners

To support students' comprehension as they read page 61 in "The Wheel: A Revolutionary Revolution," practice using several comprehension strategies. Use the prompts to practice the strategies of visualizing, making connections, and monitoring understanding.

- How do the pictures help you visualize the different types of wheels?
- Discuss a time when you have either seen or used any of these types of wheels.
- As you examine the information, what questions do you have?

Independent Activity Options

While you work with individuals or small groups, others can work independently on one or more of the following options.

- Level D paperback books, see TE pages 367–372
- Level D *eZines*
- Repeat word sorts from this lesson
- *Student Journal* pages for this lesson
- *Writing Advantage* independent lessons

Assessment

Strategy Assessment

To help you and your students assess their use of comprehension strategies, ask the following questions. Students can complete a written response or provide verbal answers in a one-on-one reading conference.

1. **Monitor Understanding** What strategies did you use when you had trouble understanding the text? (Answers will vary. Possible responses may include reading ahead, retelling a section in my own words, visualizing the text, and rereading a section.)
2. **Inferential Thinking** What conclusions can you draw about the invention of the wheel? (Answers will vary. Possible responses may include that this was one of the most important inventions in history. It helped people build, create, travel, and have more free time.)

See *Level D Assessment* page 26 for formal assessment to go with *Revolutions*.

Word Study Assessment

Use these steps to help you and your students assess their understanding of Latin roots.

1. Present the chart below. Read the roots and words aloud.
2. Have students explain how the meaning of each word is related to the root.

val "be strong, have worth"	*ver* "true"	*vid/vis* "to see"
value	verify	video
valid	verdict	invisible
evaluate	veritable	visit

Level D, Magazine 3

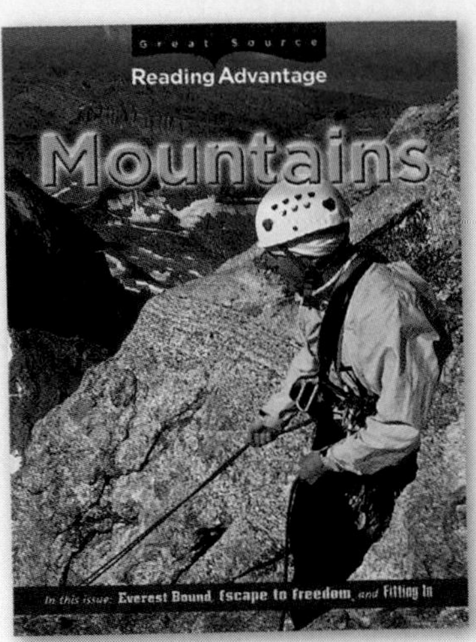

Mountains

Magazine Summary

Mountains magazine provides a variety of literature, including a travelogue, a photo-essay, a play, several articles, and poems. All of the selections focus on mountains, both physical and metaphorical. Through reading the magazine, students will come to grasp the concept of a mountain not only as a physical formation but also as a mental obstacle or challenge.

Content–Area Connection: social studies
Lexile measure: 890L

Mountains Lesson Planner

LESSON	BEFORE READING	DURING READING	AFTER READING
LESSON 23 **Nepal: Land of Mountains** (travelogue) page 186	Anticipation Guide Vocabulary Preview Preview the Selection Make Predictions/Set Purpose	Monitor Understanding Making Connections	Check Purpose Discussion Questions Writing: compare-contrast Vocabulary: synonyms Phonics/Word Study: Greek roots
LESSON 24 **Sherpas: Living and Leading in the Mountains** (profile) page 194	Concept Web Vocabulary Preview Preview the Selection Make Predictions/Set Purpose	Making Connections	Check Purpose Discussion Questions Writing: double-entry journal Vocabulary: homophones Phonics/Word Study: Greek roots
LESSON 25 **Higher than the Mountains** (photo-essay) page 198	Make a Web Vocabulary Preview Preview the Selection Make Predictions/Set Purpose	Understanding Text Structure Monitor Understanding	Check Purpose Discussion Questions Writing: notes for visualizing Vocabulary: multiple meanings Phonics/Word Study: Greek roots
LESSON 26 **Into the Darkness** *and* **The Blue Ridge Mountains** (historical fiction and poems) page 206	Anticipation Guide Vocabulary Preview Preview the Selection Make Predictions/Set Purpose	Understanding Text Structure Inferential Thinking	Check Purpose Discussion Questions Writing: character sketch Vocabulary: parts of speech Phonics/Word Study: Greek roots

Overview

Preview the Magazine

Give students time to look through the magazine. Have them read selection titles and look at the photographs and illustrations. Make sure that students look at the front and back covers. Tell students that the magazine contains a variety of literature, all related to the topic of mountains. Then have the class work together to fill in the chart using their knowledge of mountains

Physical Mountains	Other Kinds of Mountains
the Rockies	making new friends

PHONICS/ WORD STUDY	FOCUS ON	ASSESSMENT	HIGHER-ORDER THINKING QUESTIONS
Greek Roots	Writing: opinion paragraph Fluency: phrasing English Language Learners Independent Activity Options	Monitor Understanding Making Connections Greek Roots	Imagine you are planning a trip to Nepal. What would you need to take with you to have a happy adventure? Use information and specific details from the article to support your answer. How does the author support the idea that traveling to Nepal is unlike travel to any city or state in the United States? Use information and specific details from the article to support your answer.
Greek Roots	Writing: interview questions Fluency: pacing English Language Learners Independent Activity Options	Making Connections Greek Roots	What evidence does the author provide that Sherpas have physical qualities that suit their work as mountain climbers? Use information and specific details from the article to support your answer. What aspects of a Sherpa's village would make it difficult for most Americans to live there? Use information and specific details from the article to support your answer.
Greek Roots	Writing: friendly letter Fluency: pacing English Language Learners Independent Activity Options	Strategies: Understanding Text Structure Monitor Understanding Greek Roots	How does the author support the assertion that the International Space Station is a laboratory for many kinds of experiments? Use information and specific details from the article to support your answer. What image does the author convey about life on the space station? Use information and specific details from the article to support your answer.
Greek Roots	Writing: poem Fluency: punctuation English Language Learners Independent Activity Options	Understanding Text Structure Inferential Thinking Greek Roots	How does the author of "Into the Darkness" use specific language to make you feel what life as a slave was like? Use examples and specific details from the story to support your answer. Compare the ways the authors of "Into the Darkness" and "The Blue Ridge Mountains" write about nature. Use examples and specific details from the story and the poem to support your answer.

Mountains Lesson Planner

LESSON	BEFORE READING	DURING READING	AFTER READING
LESSON 27 **One Girl's Climb Out of Homelessness** (article) page 216	Concept Web Vocabulary Preview Preview the Selection Make Predictions/Set Purpose	Determining Importance	Check Purpose Discussion Questions Writing: letter Vocabulary: antonyms Phonics/Word Study: Greek roots
LESSON 28 **Dogs: More Than a Best Friend** (article) page 222	Make a List Vocabulary Preview Preview the Selection Make Predictions/Set Purpose	Determining Importance Making Connections	Check Purpose Discussion Questions Writing: opinion paragraph Vocabulary: synonyms Phonics/Word Study: Greek roots
LESSON 29 **Facing Personal Mountains: Maya Angelou & Frida Kahlo** (biographical sketches) page 230	Begin a List Vocabulary Preview Preview the Selection Make Predictions/Set Purpose	Making Connections Understanding Text Structure	Check Purpose Discussion Questions Writing: problem-solution Vocabulary: suffixes Phonics/Word Study: Greek roots
LESSON 30 **Raising the Monitor** (radio interview) page 238	K-W-L Chart Vocabulary Preview Preview the Selection Make Predictions/Set Purpose	Monitor Understanding Understanding Text Structure	Check Purpose Discussion Questions Writing: journal entry Vocabulary: synonyms and antonyms Phonics/Word Study: changes in vowels: long to schwa
LESSON 31 **The Ridge** *and* **Rock Climbing: Man and Mountain** (poem and first person account) page 247	Poem: The Ridge Begin a Web Vocabulary Preview Preview the Selection Make Predictions/Set Purpose	Inferential Thinking Monitor Understanding	Check Purpose Discussion Questions Writing: notes for visualizing Vocabulary: synonyms Phonics/Word Study: changes in vowels: long to short
LESSON 32 **Fitting In** (play) page 254	Rating Scale Vocabulary Preview Preview the Selection Make Predictions/Set Purpose	Making Connections Monitor Understanding	Check Purpose Discussion Questions Writing: play scene Vocabulary: idioms Phonics/Word Study: changes in vowels: short to schwa
LESSON 33 **Chained to a Mountain** (Greek myth) page 262	Concept Web Vocabulary Preview Preview the Selection Make Predictions/Set Purpose	Understanding Text Structure	Check Purpose Discussion Questions Writing: summarize Vocabulary: context clues Phonics/Word Study: silent-sounded consonants
LESSON 34 **Mountain Ranges** *and* **The Seven Summits** (poem and short feature) page 269	T-Chart Vocabulary Preview Preview the Selection Make Predictions/Set Purpose	Making Connections	Check Purpose Discussion Questions Writing: poem Vocabulary: homophones Phonics/Word Study: consonant alternations

PHONICS/ WORD STUDY	FOCUS ON	ASSESSMENT	HIGHER-ORDER THINKING QUESTIONS
Greek Roots	Writing: speech Fluency: pacing English Language Learners Independent Activity Options	Determining Importance Greek Roots	What are some causes of Elizabeth's success despite her homelessness? Use information and specific details from the article to support your answer. What were the effects of her parents' drug use on Elizabeth? Use information and specific details from the article to support your answer.
Greek Roots	Writing: news story Fluency: pacing English Language Learners Independent Activity Options	Making Connections Determining Importance Greek Roots	Compare the training described in the article for two of the jobs dogs do. Use information and specific details from the article to support your answer. What factors contribute to a dog's success as a therapy dog? Use information and specific details from the article to support your answer.
Greek Roots	Writing: autobiographical sketch Fluency: pacing English Language Learners Independent Activity Options	Making Connections Understanding Text Structure Greek Roots	How did having a difficult past contribute to the successes of Maya Angelou and Frida Kahlo? Use information and specific details from the article to support your answer. Select to write about Angelou or Kahlo. What conflict did she face in achieving her dream? Use information and specific details from the article to support your answer.
Changes in Vowels: long to schwa	Writing: interview Fluency: expression English Language Learners Independent Activity Options	Monitor Understanding Understanding Text Structure Changes in Vowels: long to schwa	What were the problems with diving the *Monitor* site at night? What were the benefits? Use information and specific details from the radio script to support your answer. After the Navy found the *Monitor*, what factors contributed to how long it took to bring parts of it to the surface? Use information and specific details from the radio script to support your answer.
Changes in Vowels: long to short	Writing: double-entry journal Fluency: punctuation English Language Learners Independent Activity Options	Inferential Thinking Monitor Understanding Changes in Vowels: long to short	How does the author of the poem "The Ridge" use specific language to convey how the feeling of climbing is like? Use information and specific details from the story to support your answer. What is the author's purpose in writing the article "Rock Climbing: Man and Mountain"? Is his/her purpose supported by the choice of a first-person narrative? Explain. Use information and specific details from the story to support your answer.
Changes in Vowels: short to schwa	Writing: jokes using idioms Fluency: expression English Language Learners Independent Activity Options	Making Connections Monitor Understanding Changes in Vowels: short to schwa	What conflicts does Maria face at her new school? Use information and specific details from the play to support your answer. How does the author use specific language to convey the difficulty of someone learning English? Use information and specific details from the play to support your answer.
Silent-Sounded Consonants	Writing: explanation Fluency: pacing English Language Learners Independent Activity Options	Understanding Text Structure Consonant Alternations: silent/sounded consonants	People remember Prometheus as a symbol of truth and justice. What did he do in his life to contribute to that reputation? Use information and specific details from the myth to support your answer. What were the effects of Prometheus disobeying Zeus? Use information and specific details from the myth to support your answer.
Consonant Alternations	Writing: explanation Fluency: pacing English Language Learners Independent Activity Options	Making Connections Consonant Alternations	In the poem "Mountain Ranges," the author describes the mountains as "barriers, guards, and doors." Why? Use information and specific details from the article and poem to support your answer. In what ways are the seven summits alike? In what ways are they different? Use information and specific details from the article to support your answer.

LESSON **23**

Nepal: Land of Mountains

Mountains, pages 2–7

SUMMARY

This **travelogue** describes the main attractions of Nepal, including the Himalaya Mountains.

COMPREHENSION STRATEGIES

Monitor Understanding
Making Connections

WRITING

Compare-Contrast

VOCABULARY

Synonyms

PHONICS/WORD STUDY

Greek Roots *aer, aster/astr, auto*

Lesson Vocabulary

summit	cutlery
treacherous	intricately
devastating	flourished
sacred	

MATERIALS

Mountains, pp. 2–7
Student Journal, pp. 80–82
Word Study Manual, p. 58
Writing Advantage, pp. 9–12

NEPAL

LAND OF MOUNTAINS

In Sanskrit, the word *Himalaya* means "house of snow." The Himalaya Mountains form the highest mountain range in the world. Mount Everest, the world's tallest peak, is part of the Himalayas. To climb Mount Everest, most people enter through the country of Nepal.

Before Reading

Use one or more activities.

Anticipation Guide

An anticipation guide is a series of statements that students respond to before reading a selection. It is not meant to quiz students, but rather to prompt discussion, build background, and create a purpose for reading. Create an anticipation guide for students. (See TE page 389 for a BLM.) Ask students to place a check in the AGREE or DISAGREE box before each statement. Students will revisit the guide after they finish the selection.

AGREE	DISAGREE	
		1. The Himalaya Mountains are in Nepal.
		2. Climbing the Himalaya Mountains is an easy task.
		3. Nepal is one of the safest places in the world.
		4. The customs in Nepal are similar to those in the United States.

Vocabulary Preview

List the selection vocabulary on an overhead transparency or on the board. Have students find each word in the text and use the surrounding words and sentences to discover the meaning. Ask students what associations they have with any of the words. Model the associations you might have with *cutlery*. Then have students complete the associations activity on *Student Journal* page 79.

When you think of traveling to a far-off land, what kind of adventures do you imagine? If you want to explore a new culture and take in beautiful scenery, you might consider a trip to Nepal. This mountainous country lies between India and Tibet. Nepal is home to the Himalaya Mountains, which contain eight of the world's ten highest peaks. At 29,035 feet, Mount Everest is the world's highest peak. People come from all over the world to climb Mount Everest. Every year, more than 20,000 hikers come for the challenge, the view, and the chance to say that they have conquered the world's tallest mountain. Since 1953, more than 1,200 men and women from 63 countries have reached the summit of Mount Everest. However, 175 people have died while attempting the treacherous climb. The lack of oxygen and severe cold can have devastating effects on hikers.

Mount Everest

Asia

The Himalayas

CHINA

GREAT HIMALAYA RANGE

TIBET

Mount Everest

INDIA

Bay of Bengal

Planning a Trip to Nepal

Safety Nepal is one of the safest places in the world, and so violent crime is rare. However, look out for pickpockets and the occasional luggage thief. Although it's generally safe to travel alone, women should be prepared for men to stare and whistle. If this happens, just ignore them, for the harassers are usually harmless.

Altitude Sickness

At the top of Mount Everest, climbers breathe in only 30 percent as much oxygen as when they are at sea level. When the brain doesn't get enough oxygen, people can suffer brain damage or go temporarily blind. In the thin, dry atmosphere, climbers risk becoming severely dehydrated. The extreme cold can cause frostbite. Any of these problems can cause climbers to fall. Most of the deaths on Mount Everest result from falls.

When traveling in Nepal, beware of the effects of the height of the land. If you travel more than 3,000 feet up at one time, or too quickly, you can become sick with headaches, loss of appetite, and sleeplessness. If you feel any of these symptoms, don't ignore them, because they could lead to more serious problems. The best thing to do is to get to lower ground.

3

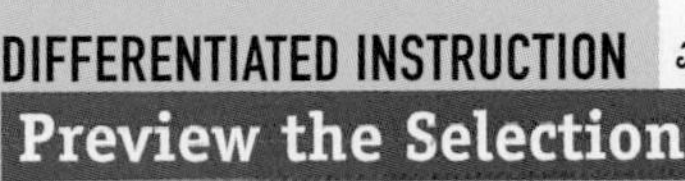

DIFFERENTIATED INSTRUCTION

SMALL GROUP

Preview the Selection

To help students understand the travelogue genre, use these steps:

1. Discuss travel materials students have seen—posters, brochures, TV ads. Ask: *What kinds of pictures do these materials usually include?*
2. Tell students that a travelogue uses pictures and words to create interest in a place and often provides helpful information for visitors.
3. List the types of information travelers might want—such as where to stay, what to eat, and the local customs and attractions. Have students scan the headings in the article to see what information is given.

Student Journal page 79

Name ______ Date ______

Building Vocabulary: Making Associations

Choose two vocabulary words. Think about what you already know about each word. Then answer the following questions for each word.

summit devastating sacred flourished
treacherous cutlery intricately

Word ______

What do you think about when you read this word? ______

Who might use this word? ______

What do you already know about this word? ______

Word ______

What do you think about when you read this word? ______

Who might use this word? ______

What do you already know about this word? ______

Now watch for these words in the magazine selection. Were you on the right track?

Mountains • Nepal: Land of Mountains 79

Preview the Selection

Have students look through the six pages of the travelogue. Use these or similar prompts to orient students to the selection.

- What do you think the selection is about?
- What form of writing will you read? How do you know?
- Do you think the selection is fiction or nonfiction? Why?

(See Differentiated Instruction.)

Teacher Think Aloud

By glancing at the title and pictures, I can see that this is a nonfiction article about Nepal, a country in Asia. As I preview further, however, I realize that the article is a travelogue, focusing on information for tourists to Nepal. Although I'm not planning a trip there myself, I'm sure the article will tell me what's special about this mountainous land.

Make Predictions/ Set Purpose

Students should use the information they gathered in previewing the selection to make predictions about what they will learn. If students have trouble generating a purpose for reading, suggest that they read to see if they were correct in their anticipation guide and to learn about the country of Nepal.

DIFFERENTIATED INSTRUCTION

Comprehension

MONITOR UNDERSTANDING

Help students monitor comprehension by visualizing sites in the travelogue. Ask:

- The roofs, windows, and doorways in Durbar Square are intricately carved. Can you think of other carvings you've seen that help you see this Square?
- The Hanuman Dhoka has many courtyards. What other buildings have courtyards? What are they like?
- What other mountainous regions help you visualize Pokhara?

WHEN TO MAKE THE TRIP

October is the start of the dry season in Nepal, and many travelers prefer this time of year. The weather is warm, and the clean air allows for great visibility. If you visit in October, you'll get to experience Dasain, Nepal's most important celebration. On Dasain, kites fill the sky, and goats, chickens, and buffalo roam the marketplaces. These animals will be sacrificed to the goddess Durga, to celebrate her victory of good over evil.

Customs Culture and customs are an important part of everyday life in Nepal. Here are some things you should know before you go.

1. **Greetings:** Don't be insulted if no one wants to shake your hand. The traditional way to greet someone in Nepal is called the *Namaste* (nah-mah-stay). Put your palms together as if you are praying and bow your head. Public displays of affection, like kissing or hugging, are frowned upon.
2. **Dress:** No matter how hot or tired a man is, he should not walk around without a shirt. Shorts are okay, but long pants are better. If possible, women shouldn't show their legs.
3. **Visiting Temples:** Foreigners are not usually allowed into major Hindu temples, so don't enter them or take pictures until you have permission. Leather isn't allowed inside of temples because cows are considered sacred "holy" animals.

A Hindu temple

JUST LIKE HOME?

Modern conveniences as we know them aren't part of everyday life in Nepal. Usually, the best place to go to the bathroom is an open field, as toilets tend to be dirty. Also, people in Nepal don't use toilet paper (only water) so bring your own and then bury or burn it. Don't bother bringing electronic gadgets to Nepal because there is electricity in only about ten percent of the country. Even where there is electricity, surges and blackouts often break off the service. Use your fingers to eat. Cutlery, such as spoons, knives, and forks, is rare.

4

During Reading

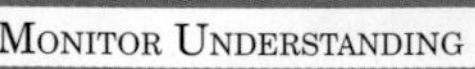

Comprehension

MONITOR UNDERSTANDING

Use these questions to model visualizing. Then have students tell what they visualize as they read.

- What's going on here?
- Is there an attraction I have a hard time picturing?
- What can I do to see things more clearly?

(See Differentiated Instruction.)

Teacher Think Aloud

When I first read the feature "Just Like Home?" on page 4, I didn't notice the question mark. So I thought the feature might show ways in which Nepal is like our country. What I read wasn't what I expected. So I asked myself, "What's going on here?" Then I understood that the author is actually pointing out ways in which Nepal is very, very different from the United States!

Comprehension

MAKING CONNECTIONS

Use these questions to model making connections. Then have students make their own connections with the text.

- Do I enjoy traveling or the idea of it?
- How does this selection compare with other travel writing I have read?
- Does this travelogue make me want to visit Nepal? Why or why not?

(See Differentiated Instruction.)

FOOD & DRINK

The main foods in the Nepalese diet are daal, tarkari, and bhaat—lentil soup, curried vegetables, and rice. The curry can be hot and spicy, so if you have a sensitive stomach, you might want to try just a little at first. In the larger cities of Kathmandu and Pokhara, you will also find restaurants serving Mexican, Chinese, and Italian food. Remember that since Nepal is a Hindu country, neither Hindus nor Buddhists eat beef. Therefore, you won't find it on a menu. But eating out in Nepal is cheap: for about $3, you can have a great dinner! Avoid drinking the local water; it might be unclean and make you sick. Stick to bottled water—it's available almost everywhere. You can also find soft drinks in most shops.

TWO CITIES TO SEE: KATHMANDU AND POKHARA

Mountains and snow-capped peaks surround the Kathmandu Valley. Almost 4,500 feet above sea level, this valley is a great way to get to know Nepal.

KATHMANDU—THE CULTURAL CENTER OF NEPAL

Attractions It takes a bit of creativity and a lot of patience to find your way through this ancient city's narrow and unmarked streets, but the sights are worth it. Here are some of the places you may want to check out when you visit Kathmandu.

The Namaste way of greeting

A street in Kathmandu

5

DIFFERENTIATED INSTRUCTION

Comprehension
MAKING CONNECTIONS

Help students make connections by having them answer these questions about the attractions mentioned in the travelogue.

- What customs are a special or important part of my life?
- What special rules about temples would I need to follow in Nepal?
- What might I order while eating in a restaurant in Nepal?
- What attraction might I like best in Kathmandu?
- Would I like Kathmandu more or less than Pokhara?

Teacher Think Aloud

I've read a lot about mountain climbers on Mount Everest and the Himalayas, but I never knew very much about the country just below these peaks. Now I do, and reading this travelogue reminds me of how many different cultures can be found around the world. I think it's important to learn about these cultures—even if we can't travel there—and to respect them.

Fix-Up Strategies

Offer these strategies to help students read independently.

If you don't understand what you're reading:

- Reread the difficult section to look for clues to help you comprehend.
- Read ahead to find clues to help you comprehend.
- Retell, or say in your own words, what you've read.
- Visualize, or form mental pictures of, what you've read.

If you don't understand a word:

- Reread the sentence. Look for ideas and words that provide meaning clues.
- Find clues by reading a few sentences before and after the confusing word.
- Look for the base or root word and think about its meaning.
- Think about the topic or plot at this point to see if either offers meaning clues.

DIFFERENTIATED INSTRUCTION SMALL GROUP

Vocabulary Synonyms

To help students with this activity, use these steps:

1. Remind students that the travelogue talks about Nepalese *customs* (established behaviors). Ask: *What other words have a similar meaning to* custom? Display responses. Students may suggest *practice, belief, habit, tradition.*
2. Have students use their synonyms in sentences related to the information they read. Example: The Nepalese have a *tradition* of putting their palms together and bowing when greeting someone.

Student Journal pages 80–81

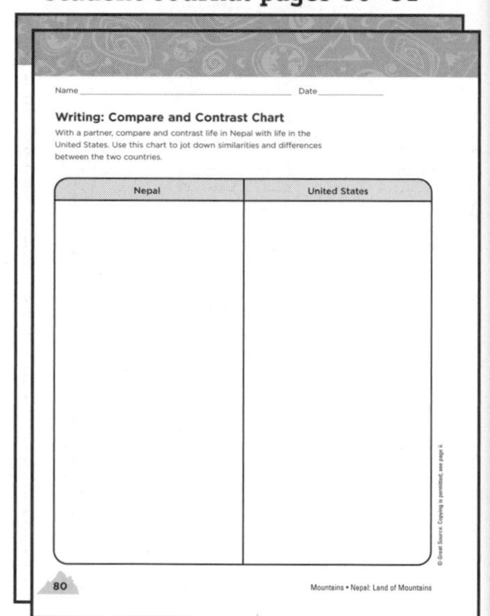

Name ____________ Date ____________

Writing: Compare and Contrast Chart

With a partner, compare and contrast life in Nepal with life in the United States. Use this chart to jot down similarities and differences between the two countries.

Nepal	United States

© Great Source. Copying is permitted; see page ii.

80 Mountains • Nepal: Land of Mountains

Durbar Square This is the center of old Kathmandu. Around it you will find many temples and shrines. Be sure to check out the intricately carved roofs, windows, and doorways. You will be amazed by the complex designs.

Hanuman Dhoka (Old Royal Palace) King Malla oversaw most of the building of this palace in the seventeenth century. At the entrance you will see a statue that honors the monkey god, Hanuman. Inside the palace, walk through one of the many *chowaks,* or courtyards. These courtyards were used for special events, such as coronations—ceremonies honoring a new king—and sacrifices to the gods.

Freak Street This is perhaps the most famous street in Kathmandu. Its real name is *Jochne,* but since hippies flocked to the city in the late 1960s, it has been known as Freak Street. Thirty years ago, you could stroll down the street and smell incense, gaze at praying children, and eat and sleep for next to nothing. All of these things attracted hippies, the longhaired "freaks" that gave the street its name.

POKHARA—THE ADVENTURE CENTER OF NEPAL

The remarkable city of Pokhara is rich with natural beauty. Nestled in a calm valley just 200 kilometers (about 124 miles) from Kathmandu, Pokhara is easy to get to. A thrilling airplane ride over the snowcapped Himalayas will take your breath away. With a population of 200,000, Pokhara is not particularly large. From here you will have amazing views of the snowy peaks. Many people who come to climb the mountains start in Pokhara because it is a wonderful place to rest and take in the scenery.

Lake Phewa and the Fishtail Mountains

After Reading

WHOLE CLASS Use one or more activities.

Check Purpose

Have students decide if their purpose was met. Were their responses correct in their anticipation guide? What did students learn about Nepal?

Discussion Questions

Continue the group discussion with the following questions.

1. What is Dasain? What happens on Dasain? (Monitor Understanding)
2. If you were to visit Nepal, what would you like to see most? (Making Connections)
3. Why do you think Nepal is a popular tourist destination? (Inferential Thinking)

Revisit: Anticipation Guide

Have students look back at their responses to the anticipation guide. Do they agree with their original choices? Discuss the choices with the class.

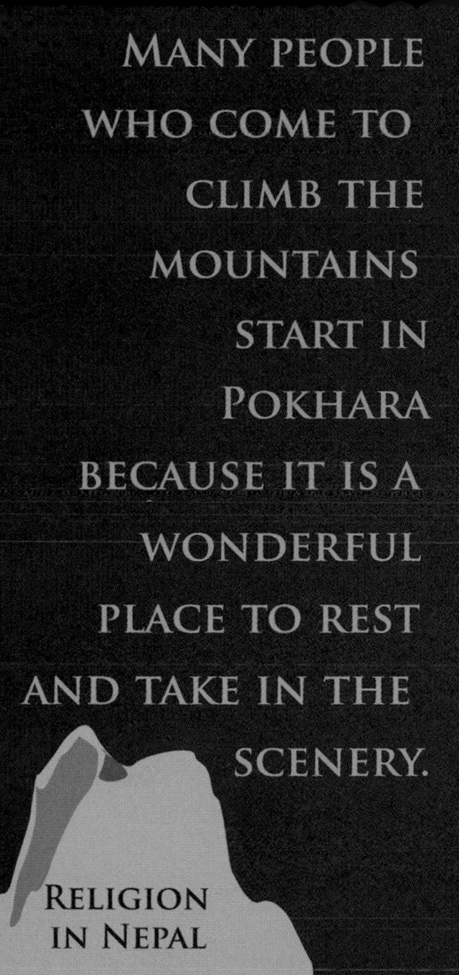

MANY PEOPLE WHO COME TO CLIMB THE MOUNTAINS START IN POKHARA BECAUSE IT IS A WONDERFUL PLACE TO REST AND TAKE IN THE SCENERY.

RELIGION IN NEPAL

Religion is very important to the Nepalese. Both Hinduism and Buddhism have flourished side by side there for a long time. About 90 percent of the population practices Hinduism. While Hindus believe in thousands of gods and goddesses, Buddhists believe in the teachings of one man who lived 2,500 years ago in India. His name was Siddhartha Gautama. In 1996, a team of archaeologists announced that they had found Siddhartha's birthplace, beneath a temple in southwestern Nepal.

When you visit Pokhara, be sure to see some of these sights:

Phewa Tal (Lake) This is the second largest lake in Nepal and the main attraction of Pokhara. Many tourists rent boats and float around the lake for the afternoon. Gazing up, you will see the splendid mountains, but don't forget to look down and see the mountains reflected in the water. Afterwards, walk along the row of shops, restaurants, and bookstores that line the lakeside.

Devil's Fall (Hell's Fall) Find this waterfall about a mile outside of Pokhara; it's worth the walk. According to modern legend, a foreigner named David went skinny-dipping in the river when the floodgates of the dam flew open. David was swept beneath the fall, never to be seen again.

The Old Bazaar In this old-fashioned market, you will find traders and sellers from many different ethnic backgrounds. Strolling the bazaar is a fun way to spend the afternoon and pick up a few souvenirs.

Chitwan National Park Take time to visit this national park, and you won't be disappointed. The oldest national park in Nepal, Chitwan is one of the best places to see wild animals. There are more than forty-three kinds of mammals in the park. Royal Bengal tigers, one-horned rhinoceroses, wild elephants, pythons, and more than 450 species of birds roam the park. ◆

7

Possible answers for **Student Journal page 82** include: *devastating*—overwhelming; *peak*—point, summit; *ancient*—old, old-fashioned; *sacred*—holy, respected; *bazaar*—market, fair; *culture*—society, behavior.

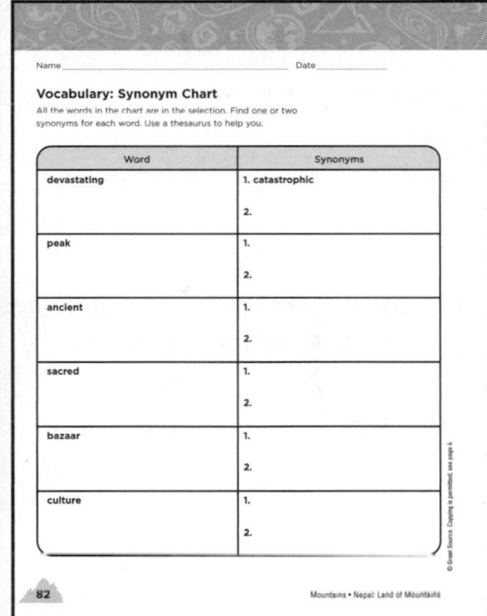

Name ____________ Date ________

Vocabulary: Synonym Chart

All the words in the chart are in the selection. Find one or two synonyms for each word. Use a thesaurus to help you.

Word	Synonyms
devastating	1. catastrophic 2.
peak	1. 2.
ancient	1. 2.
sacred	1. 2.
bazaar	1. 2.
culture	1. 2.

82 Mountains • Nepal: Land of Mountains

Writing Compare-Contrast

Have partners compare and contrast Nepal with the United States. Before they write, engage students in a brief discussion to have them think about the differences between the way people live in the United States and how they live in Nepal. Then have students begin the planning chart on *Student Journal* page 80. After pairs have finished their chart, have each student write about the differences on *Student Journal* page 81.

Vocabulary Synonyms

Display the word *devastating*. Ask: *What is the definition of* devastating*?* ("causing destruction" or "reducing to disorder or helplessness") *What other words have a similar meaning?* Display the words *destructive, catastrophic, disastrous, harmful,* and *dire,* explaining that these are all synonyms for the word *devastating*. Now have students complete the activity on *Student Journal* page 82. (See Differentiated Instruction.)

Phonics/Word Study

Greek Roots

Write this sentence on the board and read it aloud: *The astronomer saw an astronaut on an asteroid.* Ask students what they notice about the three nouns in the sentence. (They all begin with the word part *astr* or *ast*, meaning "star.") Have students tell what they know about these words. How does each word relate to the root? Now, work with students to complete the in-depth word root activity on TE page 192.

Phonics/Word Study

Introduce Greek Roots

Use the following steps to introduce Greek roots.

- Introduce the root that you are teaching by offering a few words containing that root. Discuss the words with students to see if they can come up with some kind of definition for each word. Discussion of each word should trigger some ideas as to what the root means.
- Ask what the words have in common. Through the processes of deduction and association, students should discover the meaning of the root.
- Ask students to identify other words with the same root. You can find word sorts in the *Word Study Manual* that will help students "see" the connections. (See *Word Study Manual* page 58 for a sort with *aer*, *aster/astr*, and *auto*.)
- Have students create a roots section in their Word Study notebooks. They should begin collecting words with each root they study.

aer **(air)**

Use the word *aerospace* to help students define the root and then discuss the other words.

aerial	aerate	aerobics
aerosol	aeronautics	aerospace
aerodrome	aerodynamic	

aster/astr **(star)**

Discuss *astronomy*. Ask what someone with an interest in astronomy studies.

astral	asteroid	astronomy
astrology	asterisk	astronomical
astronomer		

auto **(self)**

Begin by reviewing the meaning of *autobiography*.

autograph	autonomous	automatic
autoclave	autobiography	automobile
autocrat	auto-loading	auto-reverse

Discovering the Roots

aer	*aster/astr*	*auto*
aeronautics	astral	autograph
aerodynamic	astronomy	auto-reverse
aerospace	astrology	automobile
aerosol	asteroid	automatic
aerobics	asterisk	autobiography

For more information on word sorts and spelling stages, see pages 5–31 in the *Word Study Manual*.

Focus on . . .

Use one or more activities in this section to focus on a particular area of need in your students.

Comprehension STRATEGY SUPPORT

To help those students who need more practice using the strategies covered in this lesson, work one-on-one or in small groups to apply the strategy prompts below. Apply the prompts to a *Reading Advantage* paperback, a classroom library book, or a new or familiar selection in the magazine. Always model your own thinking first.

Monitor Understanding

- Do I understand what I'm reading? If not, what part is confusing to me?
- What fix-up strategies can I use to solve the problem? (See During Reading for fix-up strategies.)
- Why did a character say (do, think, ask) that?
- What images do I visualize from the text? What parts can't I visualize?
- Why did the author include (or not include) those details?

Making Connections

- What does this story (article, passage) remind me of?
- What do I already know about this topic?
- Where have I heard about this topic before?
- What do I have in common with the characters, people, or situations in the text?
- What other books, stories, articles, movies, or TV shows does this text make me think about?

Writing Opinion Paragraph

Ask students to think of a faraway place they would like to visit and to write a paragraph telling why they would like to go there. Draw the following chart on the board or on chart paper and have students copy it to help organize their thoughts.

Destination	Why It Interests Me	What I Know About It	What I Might Discover

For instruction and practice on brainstorming ideas before writing, see lessons in *Writing Advantage* pages 9–12.

Fluency: Phrasing

After students have read the selection at least once, have partners read parts of the travelogue to each other.

As you listen to students read, use these prompts to guide them.

- Read the headings with a strong voice so listeners will know you have started a new section.
- Pause after each heading. This will help listeners keep the information organized in their heads.
- Remember that sentences under a specific heading go together. Group these when you are reading. Pausing too long between sentences will make it harder for listeners to understand.

When students read aloud, do they—

✓ demonstrate quick recognition of words and phrases?

✓ exhibit an understanding of phrasal construction?

✓ incorporate appropriate timing, stress, and intonation?

English Language Learners

To support students' understanding of the travelogue genre, extend the Differentiated Instruction activity on TE page 187. With a partner, have students share information about their countries of origin. Allow students to use the library, Internet, or their parents as a resource to gain more information. Use these prompts as a guide for discussion.

- Where is the best place to eat?
- What are the local customs?
- When is the best time to travel?

Independent Activity Options

While you work with individuals or small groups, others can work independently on one or more of the following options.

- Level D paperback books, see TE pages 367–372
- Level D *eZines*
- Repeat word sorts from this lesson
- *Student Journal* pages for this lesson
- *Writing Advantage* independent lessons

Assessment

Strategy Assessment

To help you and your students assess their use of comprehension strategies, ask the following questions. Students can complete a written response or provide verbal answers in a one-on-one reading conference.

1. **Monitor Understanding** How did monitoring your understanding help you as you read this article? (Students may say that by asking themselves questions about the text, they identified passages that they did not fully understand and needed to reread.)
2. **Making Connections** As you read the article, what connections did you make? (Answers will vary. Students may mention that the descriptions of Nepal reminded them of how much they like to travel or made them realize how exciting travel to distant countries would be.)

For ongoing informal assessment, use the checklists on pages 61–64 of *Level D Assessment*.

Word Study Assessment

Use these steps to assess students' understanding of the Greek roots *aer, aster/astr,* and *auto*.

1. Write *aer, aster/astr,* and *auto* on the board.
2. Then write the following chart on the board.
3. Have students add the correct Greek root on the line to complete each word. (*astr*onomy, *auto*matic, *aster*isk, *auto*biography, *aer*ate, *aer*onautics)
4. Have students use the roots to generate other words and their meanings.

Word	Meaning
______onomy	"the study of the stars"
______matic	"by itself"
______isk	"a star-like symbol"
______biography	"the life story of yourself"
______ate	"to spray air into"
______onautics	"the study of air travel"

LESSON **24**

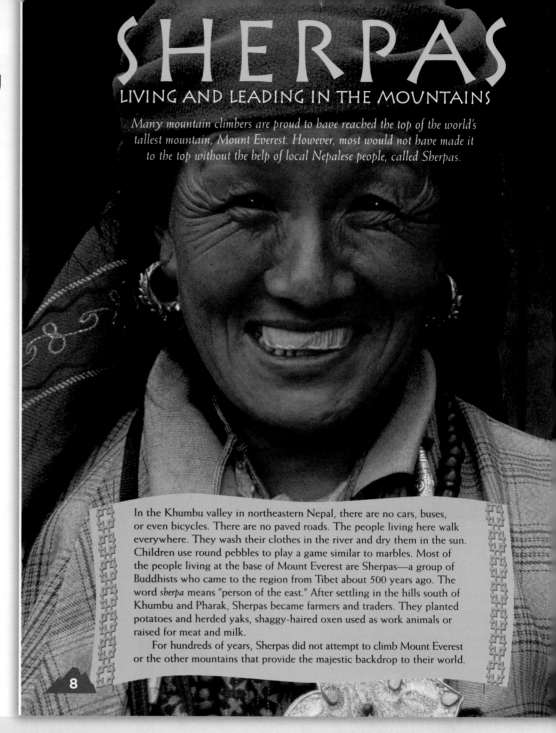

Sherpas: Living and Leading in the Mountains

Mountains, pages 8–9

SUMMARY

This **article** describes the lifestyle of the Sherpas, a people living in the mountains of Nepal.

COMPREHENSION STRATEGIES

Making Connections

WRITING

Double-Entry Journal

VOCABULARY

Homophones

PHONICS/WORD STUDY

Greek Roots *bio, chron, derm*

Lesson Vocabulary

compassion	benefited
adept	influx
obstacles	fatalities

MATERIALS

Mountains, pp. 8–9
Student Journal, pp. 83–85
Word Study Manual, p. 59
Writing Advantage, pp. 114–151

SHERPAS

LIVING AND LEADING IN THE MOUNTAINS

Many mountain climbers are proud to have reached the top of the world's tallest mountain, Mount Everest. However, most would not have made it to the top without the help of local Nepalese people, called Sherpas.

In the Khumbu valley in northeastern Nepal, there are no cars, buses, or even bicycles. There are no paved roads. The people living here walk everywhere. They wash their clothes in the river and dry them in the sun. Children use round pebbles to play a game similar to marbles. Most of the people living at the base of Mount Everest are Sherpas—a group of Buddhists who came to the region from Tibet about 500 years ago. The word *sherpa* means "person of the east." After settling in the hills south of Khumbu and Pharak, Sherpas became farmers and traders. They planted potatoes and herded yaks, shaggy-haired oxen used as work animals or raised for meat and milk.

For hundreds of years, Sherpas did not attempt to climb Mount Everest or the other mountains that provide the majestic backdrop to their world.

8

Before Reading

Vocabulary Preview

Display the selection vocabulary. Have students find each word in the text and use the surrounding words and sentences to discover the meaning. Have students begin *Student Journal* page 83.

Preview the Selection

Have students look through the two pages of the selection. Discuss what students notice.

Make Predictions/ Set Purpose

Students should use the information they gathered in previewing the selection to make predictions about what they will learn. If students have trouble generating a purpose for reading, suggest that they read to find out why Sherpas are important to the climbers of Mount Everest.

During Reading

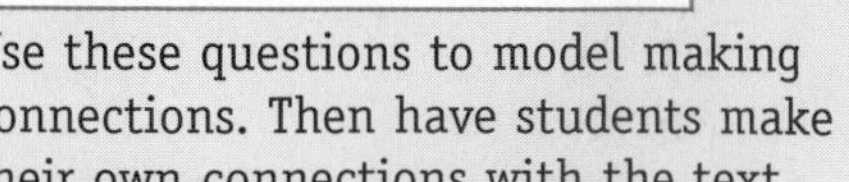

Comprehension

MAKING CONNECTIONS

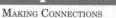

Use these questions to model making connections. Then have students make their own connections with the text.

- How is the topic of this article similar to that of the last article, "Nepal—Land of Mountains"?
- What ideas and vocabulary in the two articles can I connect?

Most Sherpas practice Mahayana Buddhism, a religion that stresses human compassion. For years, Sherpas believed that gods lived in the mountains, and they did not dare disturb the gods.

Beginning in the 1920s, however, Westerners began to come to the Khumbu valley to climb the Himalayas. In 1953 Sir Edmund Hillary and Sherpa Tenzing Norgay became the first climbers to reach the summit of Mount Everest. After their success, many foreigners flocked to the Khumbu valley in hopes of conquering the Big E (Mount Everest).

Because Sherpas were familiar with the terrain, they were hired to carry supplies. They brought supplies to base camps and prepared the camps in advance of climbers. Sherpas proved to be amazingly strong. It wasn't only young men who helped carry equipment up the mountains. Women, old men, boys, and girls all took part. Sometimes women carried their babies along with the supplies on their backs.

It soon became clear that Sherpas were valuable for much more than carrying supplies. They were adept climbers and had boundless energy and strength. Scientists who have studied the Sherpas have discovered that they possess some unusual traits. Because they have always lived at a high altitude, Sherpas breathe faster and take in more air per minute than people who live at lower altitudes. They seem to have a gene that enables their blood to carry more oxygen than other humans. Most Sherpas have a short, stocky build. Perhaps their body type makes it easier for them to hike up and down the rugged terrain.

Another feature that makes the Sherpas ideally suited to mountaineering is their positive attitude. Many observers have noted that Sherpas have an unusually bright outlook on life. Mountain climbing is filled with obstacles. Having a positive approach to a challenging situation makes it easier to find solutions to problems that arise.

Over the years, many Sherpas have benefited from the influx of foreign climbers. Sherpas own most of the lodges and hotels in the Khumbu valley. Some villages in the region now have electricity and modern conveniences, such as pizza parlors and video rental stores. The latest luxury is running hot water. However, when a family buys a solar heating tank to provide hot water, someone has to carry it up the mountains on his or her back. Despite the influence of modern life, there are no signs that the people of the Khumbu valley want to build roads.

While the Sherpas of Khumbu valley have had many successes, they have also suffered many losses. In 1922, an avalanche killed seven Sherpas participating in an expedition on Mount Everest. Forty-one of the first 100 fatalities on Everest were Sherpas. Despite their losses, Sherpas continue to be the backbone of the climbing industry that has turned Mount Everest into every mountaineer's dream-come-true. ◆

TENZING NORGAY

Sherpa Tenzing Norgay (1916–1986) planted the first flags on the summit of Mount Everest on May 29, 1953. Tenzing had devoted his life to reaching the top of Everest. For twenty years prior to reaching the world's tallest peak, Tenzing had climbed on every expedition up Mount Everest. He had started out as a porter, lugging supplies up the mountain. Over the years, he acquired a well-deserved reputation as one of the world's best climbers. Tenzing spoke seven languages but never learned how to write. He dictated several books, which offer a fascinating look at life in the Himalayas before Mount Everest became a major destination for climbers.

TIBET

Tibet is a country that also has access to Mount Everest. The Tibetan word for Mount Everest, Chomolungma, means "Goddess Mother of the Snows."

Student Journal page 83

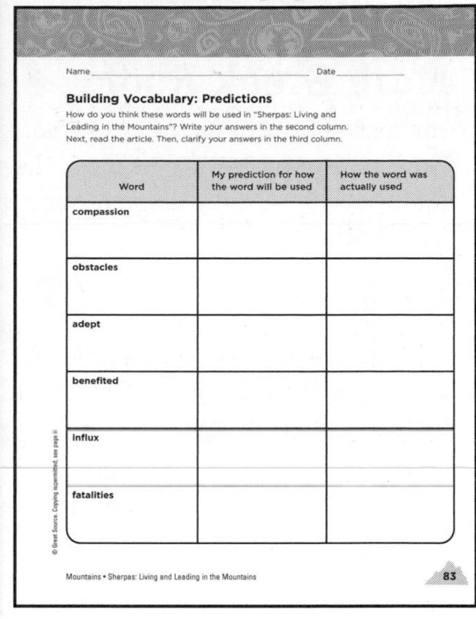
Name ______ Date ______

Building Vocabulary: Predictions

How do you think these words will be used in "Sherpas: Living and Leading in the Mountains"? Write your answers in the second column. Next, read the article. Then, clarify your answers in the third column.

Word	My prediction for how the word will be used	How the word was actually used
compassion		
obstacles		
adept		
benefited		
influx		
fatalities		

Mountains • Sherpas: Living and Leading in the Mountains 83

Student Journal pages 84–85

Name ______ Date ______

Double-entry Journal

In the first column, write phrases or sentences from "Sherpas: Living and Leading in the Mountains" that were meaningful to you. In the second column, explain the significance of each quotation.

Quotation	Why It Is Meaningful

84 Mountains • Sherpas: Living and Leading in the Mountains

After Reading

Use one or more activities.

Check Purpose

Ask students if their purpose was met. Did they find out why Sherpas are important to the climbers of Mount Everest?

Revisit: Predictions Chart

Have students return to *Student Journal* page 83 to complete the chart.

Writing Double-Entry Journal

Have students complete *Student Journal* page 84.

Vocabulary Homophones

Tell students that *gene* (page 9 of the article) and *jean* (cloth used for sportswear and work clothes) are *homophones*. Homophones are words that sound alike but are spelled differently and have different meanings. Give these additional examples of homophones: *eight, ate*; *horse, hoarse*. Have students complete *Student Journal* page 85.

Phonics/Word Study

Greek Roots

Display this sentence: *This biography is about a biologist with a bionic arm.* Ask students what they notice. (Three words begin with *bio*, meaning "life.") Ask what students know about these words. Repeat with the sentence: *The dermatologist healed the pachyderm's dermatitis.* Now work with students to complete the in-depth activity on TE page 196.

Phonics/Word Study

More Greek Roots

For instruction to introduce a root, see TE page 192. Work with students to discover the meaning of each root. See *Word Study Manual* page 59 for a related word sort.

bio **(life)**

Discuss the word *biodegradable*. To degrade something is to have it break down. If something biodegrades, it breaks down naturally.

biosphere
biochemical
biodegradable
bionic
macrobiotic
microbiology
biology
biography
biologist
symbiotic
biomedical

chron **(time)**

Chron is related to the notion of time and is, therefore, found in words such as *synchrony*, which means something that is done in unison, or in time, and *chronic*, which means ongoing.

chronology
chronicle
synchronize
chronograph
chronic
synchrony
chronometer

derm **(skin)**

Use familiar words, such as *hypodermic* and *dermatologist*, to help apply the meaning of the root to less familiar words.

pachyderm
subdermal
hypodermic
dermatitis
dermatology
taxidermist
dermatologist

Discovering the Roots

bio	*chron*	*derm*
biology	synchrony	subdermal
biohazard	chronometer	dermatitis
biotic	chronicle	taxidermy
biodegradable	chronology	hypodermic
biosphere	chronic	pachyderm

For more information on word sorts and spelling stages, see pages 5–31 in the *Word Study Manual*.

Focus on . . .

Use one or more activities in this section to focus on a particular area of need in your students.

Comprehension STRATEGY SUPPORT

To help those students who need more practice using the strategies covered in this lesson, work one-on-one or in small groups to apply the strategy prompts below. Apply the prompts to a *Reading Advantage* paperback, a classroom library book, or a new or familiar selection in the magazine. Always model your own thinking first.

Making Connections

- What does this story (article, passage) remind me of?
- What do I already know about this topic?
- Where have I heard about this topic before?
- What do I have in common with the characters, people, or situations in the text?
- What other books, stories, articles, movies, or TV shows does this text make me think about?

Writing Interview Questions

Have students think of three questions they would like to ask a Sherpa villager. Tell students to think about what they learned about the lifestyle of the Sherpas from the article to help them frame questions. The questions should be open ended and respectful of the Sherpa culture. Brainstorm some ideas with students to get them started, for example: *Why do you enjoy helping foreign mountain climbers? Do you think future generations will continue your lifestyle? Why or why not?* When finished, ask volunteers to role-play the interviews.

If you'd like students to write more about Sherpas and Nepal, see *Writing Advantage* pages 114–151 for lessons on expository writing structures.

Fluency: Pacing

After reading the article at least once, have student pairs alternate reading aloud the last two paragraphs of text on page 9. Use the special feature on Tenzing Norgay on the same page to model reading smoothly and at an even pace.

As you listen to students read, use these prompts to guide them.

- Try not to hesitate or repeat words.
- Preview the text to "troubleshoot" any difficult or unfamiliar words.
- Note how groups of words naturally go together.
- Notice the punctuation. It will help guide your reading.

When students read aloud, do they—

✓ demonstrate a smooth pace, not too fast or too slow?

✓ incorporate well-timed pauses between words and phrases?

✓ reflect an awareness and understanding of punctuation?

English Language Learners

To help students develop their understanding of homophones, extend the activity on TE page 195.

1. Review the concept of homophones with students, and write several examples of homophones on chart paper: *tail, tale; feet, feat; sail, sale.*
2. Discuss the meaning of each word.
3. Ask students to work in pairs and create a sentence for each pair that includes both words. For example, *I bought a new sail for my boat because it went on sale.*
4. Share the sentences with the entire class.

Independent Activity Options

While you work with individuals or small groups, others can work independently on one or more of the following options.

- Level D paperback books, see TE pages 367–372
- Level D *eZines*
- Repeat word sorts from this lesson
- *Student Journal* pages for this lesson
- *Writing Advantage* independent lessons

Assessment

Strategy Assessment

To help you and your students assess their use of comprehension strategies, ask the following questions. Students can complete a written response or provide verbal answers in a one-on-one reading conference.

- **Making Connections** As you read the article, what connections did you make? (Answers will vary. Students may mention that the previous article about Nepal provided them with facts and details about the country where the Sherpas live.)

For ongoing informal assessment, use the checklists on pages 61–64 of Level D Assessment.

Word Study Assessment

Use these steps to help you and your students assess their understanding of the Greek roots *bio*, *chron*, and *derm*.

1. Write *bio*, *chron*, and *derm* on the board.
2. Then write the following chart on the board.
3. Have students add the correct Greek root on the line to complete each word. (*derm*atology, *chron*ic, sub*derm*al, *bio*graphy, *chrono*meter, *bio*sphere)
4. Have students use the roots to generate other words and their meanings.

Word	Meaning
_____ atology	"the medical study of the skin"
_____ ic	"occurring over a long time"
sub _____ al	"under the skin"
_____ graphy	"the life story of someone"
_____ ometer	"an instrument to measure time"
_____ sphere	"the region on earth that supports life"

LESSON 25
Higher Than the Mountains
Mountains, pages 10–15

SUMMARY

This **photo-essay**, written in question-answer format, provides a brief overview of the International Space Station (ISS).

COMPREHENSION STRATEGIES

Understanding Text Structure
Monitor Understanding

WRITING

Notes for Visualizing

VOCABULARY

Multiple Meanings

PHONICS/WORD STUDY

Greek Roots *gram, graph, hydr*

Lesson Vocabulary

orbit	luminous
outweigh	assembling

MATERIALS

Mountains, pp. 10–15
Student Journal, pp. 86–88
Word Study Manual, p. 60
Writing Advantage, pp. 30–56

The International Space Station floats in space high above the highest mountain range. Building it and keeping it going is a mountain-sized challenge.

Before Reading

Use one or more activities.

Make a Space Station Web

Display the phrase *Space Station* in a centered oval on the board or on chart paper. Draw lines away from the oval, labeled with the words *Who? What? Where? Why?* Guide students in using these words to form concept questions about space stations, for example: *Who uses a space station?* List their ideas under the questions. (See Differentiated Instruction.)

Space Station
- Who?: astronauts, scientists, doctors
- What?:
- Where?:
- Why?:

Vocabulary Preview

List the vocabulary words and read each one aloud. Have volunteers define words they think they know. Tell students to choose a familiar word to begin the word web activity on *Student Journal* page 86. Have students draw or write to show the meaning of the word. Students will complete the web after reading. If students need help, have them read around the word in the article for context clues. Model the process using the word *assembling*.

WHAT IS THE ISS?

When completed, the International Space Station (ISS) will be about the size of two football fields, a small city in space. The ISS won't be built on Earth and launched into space. Instead, most of the ISS will be built in space. Shuttle missions will deliver different parts, and astronauts will put the station together on spacewalks.

The ISS circles at 250 miles above Earth. It travels at an amazing 17,500 miles per hour. At that speed, it takes the ISS only ninety minutes to orbit Earth! This giant laboratory is a temporary home to astronauts and scientists.

WHY ARE THEY FLOATING?

When astronauts say that they are floating in "zero gravity," this is not exactly true. Even though it might look and feel as if they have escaped the gravitational pull of Earth, they feel weightless because they are in a state of "free fall" around Earth. Imagine this: you are riding in an elevator. If the elevator drops freely, you will drop at the same speed as the elevator—in free fall—until someone hits the brakes. This is similar to what astronauts feel in space, except they have no brakes to stop their fall. So how do they stay up there without falling to Earth? The space station moves so quickly just out of Earth's atmosphere that it can keep orbiting around Earth without falling.

FACTS ABOUT THE ISS

Size	360 feet wide
Weight	1 million pounds
Cost	More than $60 billion
Date of Completion	April 2006
Time to Orbit the Earth	90 minutes
Speed	17,500 miles per hour

11

DIFFERENTIATED INSTRUCTION

SMALL GROUP

MAKE A SPACE STATION WEB

Use the following information to guide students in completing the Space Station web:

1. *What?* A space station is a place where people live and work in space. (Students may have heard about Skylab, MIR, or the International Space Station.)
2. *Where?* A space station orbits 200 to 300 miles above Earth.
3. *Why?* In a space station, scientists observe Earth, study stars and planets, and experiment to find the effects of space on different materials.
4. *Who?* Astronauts, scientists, doctors, and other workers.

Student Journal page 86

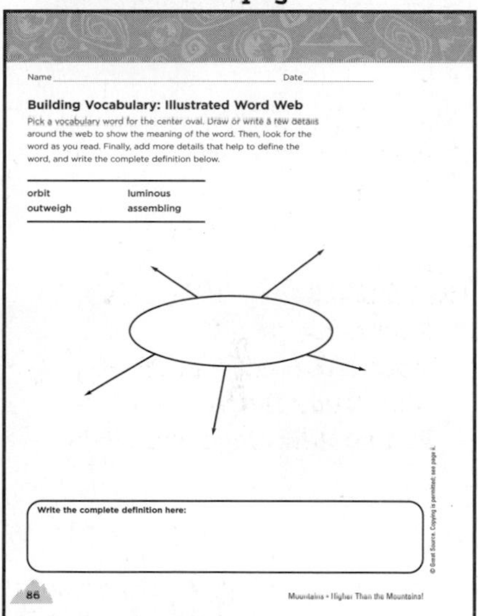

Name ______ Date ______

Building Vocabulary: Illustrated Word Web

Pick a vocabulary word for the center oval. Draw or write a few details around the web to show the meaning of the word. Then, look for the word as you read. Finally, add more details that help to define the word, and write the complete definition below.

orbit	luminous
outweigh	assembling

Write the complete definition here:

© Great Source. Copying is permitted; see page ii.

86 Mountains • Higher Than the Mountains!

Preview the Selection

Have students survey the six pages of the article. Use prompts such as these to guide students to notice features of the text.

- How is this article organized?
- How might the question-answer format affect your reading?
- What other features do you notice?
- Is this a fiction or nonfiction article? Why do you think that?

Teacher Think Aloud

It's easy to see that this selection is a nonfiction article about the International Space Station. In addition to great photographs of space, the article seems to contain lots of facts and details. I don't know much about the space station, but I bet this article will answer a lot of my questions.

Make Predictions/ Set Purpose

Students should use the information they gathered while previewing the selection to make predictions about what they will learn. If students have trouble setting a purpose for reading, suggest that they read to answer this question: *What is the International Space Station, and why is it such a challenge to keep the project going?*

DIFFERENTIATED INSTRUCTION

Comprehension

UNDERSTANDING TEXT STRUCTURE

Help students understand the text structure by asking:

- What is the purpose of the information in the white circle at the bottom of page 11? (to give basic facts about the ISS)
- What is the purpose of the white planets next to the text on page 12?
- What special feature do you notice in the text on page 14? (The labels Food, Sleep, Exercise, and Clothing give the topic of each paragraph.)

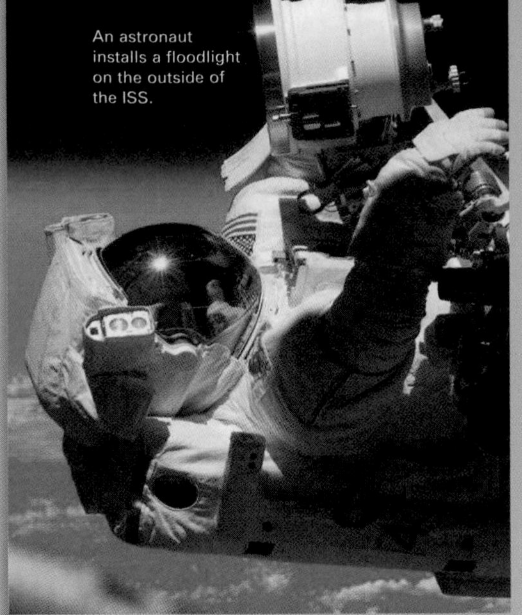

An astronaut installs a floodlight on the outside of the ISS.

An astronaut wraps up work on the outside of the *Unity* module.

12

WHY BUILD A SPACE STATION?

Will the benefits of this station outweigh its cost? Sixteen countries from around the world think so, and they are willing to spend the money and endure the risks of space travel to prove it. Scientists hope to achieve a number of important things with the ISS:

- Small groups of astronauts and scientists live and study for long periods of time in the weightless environment. Scientists are exploring the effect that zero gravity has on the human body and on plants and animals. Scientists hope to use the station as a base for future space travel.
- Without gravity, certain chemical reactions occur differently. In the ISS, scientists run experiments that may lead to treatments for cancer, AIDS, diabetes, and other diseases.
- Scientists are studying Earth from different angles and over long periods of time. They are also learning about space and its unique environment.

WHEN WILL IT BE FINISHED?

The first part of the space station launched into orbit on November 20, 1998. This was a Russian piece called Zarya. (In Russian, zarya describes the reddish color of the sky at sunrise or sunset.) An American piece called Unity was launched a few weeks later. Astronauts connected the two pieces while up in space. By the time the space station is completed, astronauts will have connected more than a hundred pieces. The work isn't simple. Astronauts have to go out in space, in teams of two, for as long as 6 1/2 hours at a time. Like construction workers, they connect beams, add lights, plug in wires, and bolt pieces together. A robotic arm helps them work.

During Reading

Comprehension

UNDERSTANDING TEXT STRUCTURE

Use these prompts to model how to identify and understand the question-answer text structure. Then have students retell one of the questions and the answer to it.

- What do you notice about the blue headings on each page?
- What does the text beneath each of these blue headings do?

(See Differentiated Instruction.)

Teacher Think Aloud

When I looked at the title of this article, the first question that popped into my head was "Why build a space station?" It's a question a lot of people must have. That's why the author used it as a heading on page 12. The other headings are commonly asked questions too. The text beneath each question does a good job of answering the question.

Comprehension

MONITOR UNDERSTANDING

Use these prompts to model for students how to monitor their understanding by visualizing the text.

- Can I visualize what the space station will look like?
- Can I visualize how the space station is being assembled?
- What details create this image in my mind?

(See Differentiated Instruction.)

Sixteen countries have joined together to build the ISS

 United States

 Russia

 Canada

 Japan

 Brazil

 Belgium

 Britain

 Denmark

 France

 Germany

 Italy

 Netherlands

 Norway

 Spain

 Sweden

Switzerland

What Astronauts See

From the ISS, astronauts are able to observe and photograph life in space, as well as life on Earth. In the winter of 2003, ISS astronaut Don Pettit photographed Canopus (kuh NOPE us), the second brightest star in the sky. Canopus is 65 times wider and 15,000 times more luminous than the sun. Pettit also photographed auroras—streamers of light that are sometimes visible in the night sky of northern regions. Auroras are also called "northern lights." Pettit saw blue auroras over Scandinavia. Usually, the lights are green or red.

Scientists hope to finish assembling the station by 2006. It will take about eight years to build the ISS for these reasons:

- There will need to be at least forty-six manned space missions to the station. Astronauts will have to complete 160 space walks and work for 1,900 hours to assemble the station. The station is made up of more than a hundred pieces that weigh more than a million pounds.
- When the space station is finished, an international crew of up to seven people will live and work in the station, and they will stay in space from three to six months. In case of an emergency, there will always be a return shuttle attached to the space station so everyone can get safely back to Earth.

DIFFERENTIATED INSTRUCTION

Comprehension

MONITOR UNDERSTANDING

If students have difficulty visualizing, they may be struggling with the vocabulary in the text. Offer these suggestions to help students monitor their understanding of what they read:

- Reread a confusing part. Then reread the sentences before and after this part.
- Is there a word you don't understand? If so, try to figure out its meaning. Continue reading to see if the word is defined.
- Look at the pictures or features in the selection. Do they clear up your questions?

Teacher Think Aloud

When I read the first question and answer in the article, I was amazed at how large the finished space station will be—about the size of two football fields. That's incredible! I know a football field is 100 yards long, so we're talking 200 yards, or 600 feet! That's about twenty times the size of a classroom. Imagine putting something that big—piece by piece—into space!

Fix-Up Strategies

Offer these strategies to help students read independently.

If you don't understand what you're reading:

- Reread the difficult section to look for clues to help you comprehend.
- Read ahead to find clues to help you comprehend.
- Retell, or say in your own words, what you've read.
- Visualize, or form mental pictures of, what you've read.

If you don't understand a word:

- Reread the sentence. Look for ideas and words that provide meaning clues.
- Find clues by reading a few sentences before and after the confusing word.
- Look for the base or root word and think about its meaning.
- Think about the topic or plot at this point to see if either offers meaning clues.

DIFFERENTIATED INSTRUCTION 

Vocabulary: Multiple Meanings

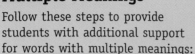

Follow these steps to provide students with additional support for words with multiple meanings:

1. As a group, define the word *space*. *Space* is "the area in which the solar system exists." It can also mean "the separation between objects," as in *the space* between words or "an area provided for a particular purpose" as in *parking space.*
2. Skim the article with students to help them find other words with multiple meanings. Possible words include *shuttle, station, base, study, angle,* and *exercise.*

Student Journal page 87

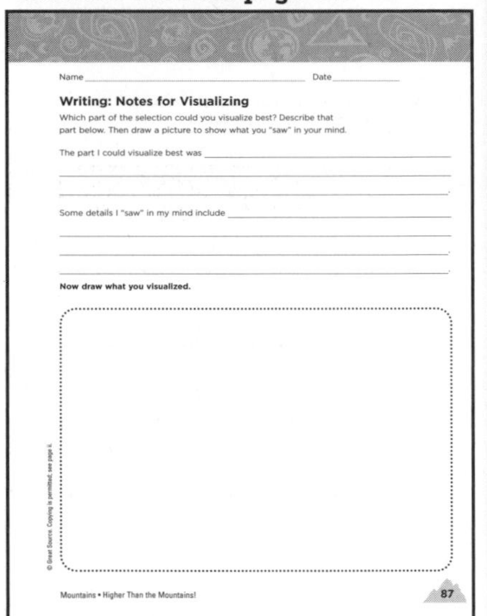

Name ______ Date ______

Writing: Notes for Visualizing

Which part of the selection could you visualize best? Describe that part below. Then draw a picture to show what you "saw" in your mind.

The part I could visualize best was ______

Some details I "saw" in my mind include ______

Now draw what you visualized.

Mountains • Higher Than the Mountains! 87

HOW WILL ASTRONAUTS LIVE IN THE SPACE STATION?

Life in the space station isn't easy. Scientists have tried to make the station as pleasant as possible, with bright rooms kept at seventy degrees Fahrenheit. The crew has to be comfortable, because they work hard all day. In a typical day, they work and exercise about 14 hours, make and eat meals for about 1 ½ hours, and sleep for the remaining 8 ½ hours. Life in space differs from life on Earth in many ways:

FOOD: Space explorers have more choices these days. Food is no longer just freeze-dried. The space station has water, a microwave oven, and refrigerators.

SLEEP: Each astronaut has a private room. At bedtime, the astronauts need to be tied down, so they don't float out of their beds.

EXERCISE: Weightlessness causes muscles to weaken and bones to wear away. Astronauts maintain a strict exercise program in space. They spend at least two hours every day on bikes, rowing machines, and other equipment.

CLOTHES: Inside the space station, astronauts wear regular clothes. When they make space walks, they wear special pressurized suits that keep out the flying debris and regulate the changing temperatures. In the cool shadow of the space station, the temperature can be −120 degrees Fahrenheit. In the sun, the temperature can soar to more than 250 degrees.

14

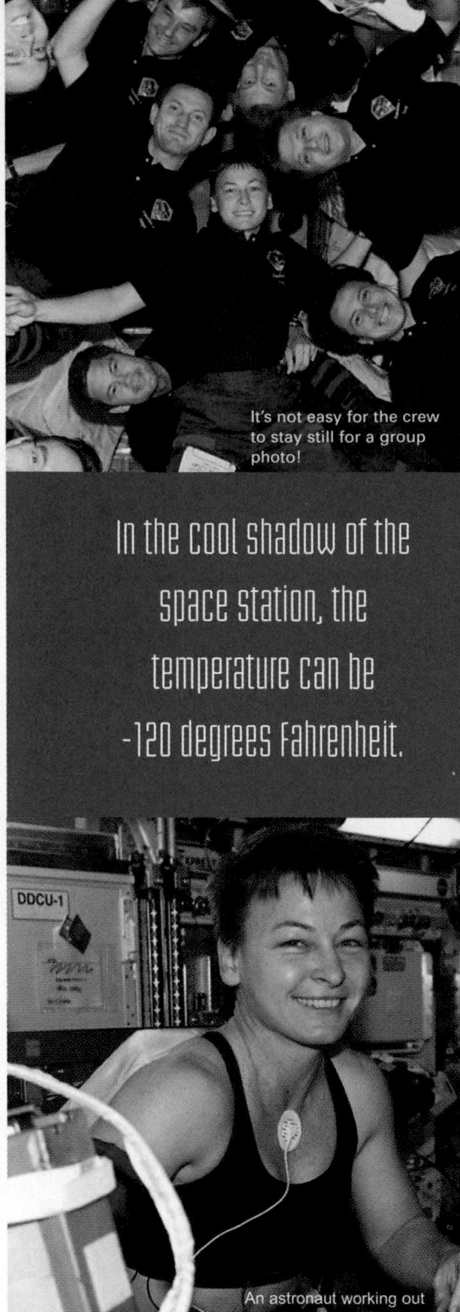

It's not easy for the crew to stay still for a group photo!

In the cool shadow of the space station, the temperature can be -120 degrees Fahrenheit.

An astronaut working out

After Reading  Use one or more activities.

Check Purpose

Have students decide if their purpose was met. Can students tell what the ISS is? Do they understand why it is such a challenge to keep the project going?

Discussion Questions

Continue the group discussion with the following questions.

1. What do you understand about astronauts or the space station that you didn't know before? (Making Connections)
2. What information did you learn from the features and captions? (Details)
3. Was the question-answer format an effective way to convey information about the ISS? Why or why not? (Evaluate)

Revisit: Space Station Web

Revisit the web that students began before reading. Discuss any additions students wish to make to the web.

Revisit: Illustrated Word Web

Have students complete the illustrated word web they began on *Student Journal* page 86. Students can use the information they learned in the article to complete the web.

VIEWING THE ISS

Satellites, including the ISS, are visible only when they are lit by the sun and the observer is in the darkness. This happens when the sun is just below the horizon, right before sunrise and after sunset. Satellites cannot be seen at night because the sun is too far below the horizon to light them. However, the sun never gets very far below the horizon during the summer in the far northern and southern latitudes. Therefore, satellites are visible all night from those locations.You can see the ISS fly overhead a few times each month. It looks like a bright, fast-moving star. If you are interested in finding out the best time to see it, check out the Web site at www.heavens-above.com. ◆

LIFE IMITATES ART

Movies have inspired scientists to build a talking, thinking, and flying robot to help astronauts in space. Scientists are building robots called "Personal Satellite Assistants" that look a lot like the one in the *Star Wars* movies. The robot will help astronauts with everyday chores, like checking the air temperature and monitoring changes in air pressure and quality.

15

Possible answers for **Student Journal page 88** include: *shuttle*—to cause to move back and forth/vehicle used for regular travel; *station*—to assign a position/place to stop; *base*—bottom part/headquarters; *study*—to pursue knowledge/a room for studying.

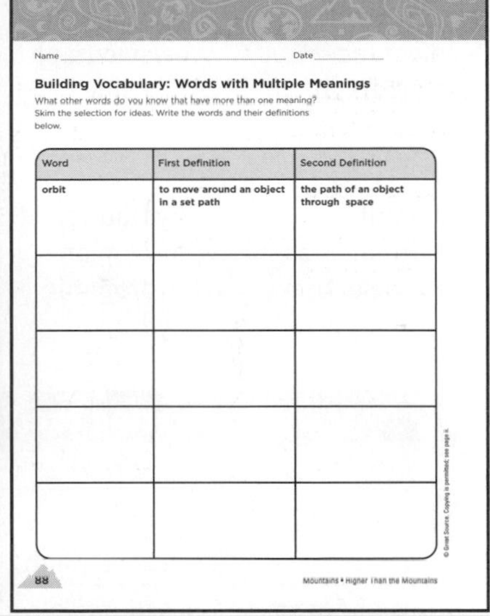

Name ______________________ Date ____________

Building Vocabulary: Words with Multiple Meanings

What other words do you know that have more than one meaning? Skim the selection for ideas. Write the words and their definitions below.

Word	First Definition	Second Definition
orbit	to move around an object in a set path	the path of an object through space

88 Mountains • Higher Than the Mountains

Writing Notes for Visualizing

Remind students that active readers visualize, or try to "see" in their minds what an author tells about. Ask students which part of the ISS they could visualize best. List their ideas on the board. Then have students complete the visualizing activity on *Student Journal* page 87. Students can refer to the list on the board for help in choosing a part of the article to draw and write about.

Vocabulary

Multiple Meanings

Point out *orbit* on page 11. Ask:

- What does the word *orbit* mean in this context? (to move around an object in a set path)
- What other meanings for *orbit* can you find in a dictionary?

Have students complete *Student Journal* page 88. Students can use *orbit* for their first entry. Brainstorm words as a group, if necessary. (See Differentiated Instruction.)

Phonics/Word Study

Greek Roots

Display this sentence and read it aloud: *Will you autograph the photograph in your biography for me?* Ask students what they notice about the underlined words. (They all contain the Greek root *graph*, meaning "writing.") Have students tell how the words relate to the root. Now, work with students to complete the in-depth activity on TE page 204.

Phonics/Word Study

More Greek Roots

For instruction to introduce a root, see TE page 192. Work with students to discover the meaning of each root. See *Word Study Manual* page 60 for a related word sort.

gram **(something written)**

telegram	grammar
phonogram	program
diagram	grammatical
monogram	gramophone

graph **(writing)**

phonograph	autograph
graphic	biography
calligraphy	photograph
telegraph	seismograph
monograph	digraph

hydr **(water)**

hydrant	hydraulic
hydrophobia	hydroplane
hydroelectric	hydroponic
hydrology	hydrous

Discovering the Roots

gram	*graph*	*hydr*
diagram	phonograph	hydrant
grammatical	seismograph	hydrophobia
monogram	digraph	hydraulic
telegram	graphic	hydroponic
program	calligraphy	hydroplane

For more information on word sorts and spelling stages, see pages 5–31 in the *Word Study Manual*.

Focus on . . .

Use one or more activities in this section to focus on a particular area of need in your students.

Comprehension STRATEGY SUPPORT

For students who need more practice using the strategies covered in this lesson, work one-on-one or in small groups to apply the strategy prompts below. Apply the prompts to a *Reading Advantage* paperback, a classroom library book, or a new or familiar selection in the magazine. Always model your own thinking first.

Understanding Text Structure

- What kind of text is this? (book, story, article, guidebook, play, manual)
- How does the author organize the text? (cause-effect, problem-solution, chronological order, description, question-answer, comparison-contrast)
- What details support my thoughts about the text structure?
- What is the cause (effect, problem, solution, order, question, answer)?
- If fiction, who are the characters? What is the setting, plot, conflict, and resolution?

Monitor Understanding

- Do I understand what I'm reading? If not, what part is confusing to me?
- What fix-up strategies can I use to solve the problem? (See During Reading for fix-up strategies.)
- Why did a person or character say (do, think, ask) that?
- What images do I visualize from the text? What parts can't I visualize?
- Why did the author include (or not include) those details?

Writing Friendly Letter

Have students imagine that they are going to live on the ISS. Ask students to write a letter in which they explain to family members or friends what their lives will be like. Before students begin, have them brainstorm a list of facts and details about the ISS that they might include in the letter. Then review the parts of a friendly letter with students (heading, greeting, body, closing, signature). Invite students to share their finished letters.

To provide instruction on writing techniques, see *Writing Advantage*, pages 30–56.

Fluency: Pacing

After students have read the article at least once, they can work with a partner to take turns reading alternate question-answer sections to practice fluent reading.

As students read, use these prompts to promote even pacing.

- Listen to me read. Then read it just like I did.
- Read a little faster (or slower) so readers can make sense of the words.
- Practice saying any words or names you are unfamiliar with so you don't hesitate or stumble over the words when you read.
- Use punctuation marks as clues to help you read evenly and smoothly. Remember to pause at commas and periods.

When students read aloud, do they—

✓ demonstrate a smooth pace, not too fast or too slow?

✓ incorporate well-timed pauses between words and phrases?

✓ reflect an awareness and understanding of punctuation?

English Language Learners

To prepare students for the writing activity, have them brainstorm and determine the most important ideas about living in the space station.

1. Model how to determine the main idea of the first paragraph on page 14. Remind students that headings tell the main idea of a section.
2. Have partners read the rest of page 14 and determine the main ideas of each section. Have them share their responses with the class.

Independent Activity Options

While you work with individuals or small groups, others can work independently on one or more of the following options.

- Level D paperback books, see TE pages 367–372
- Level D *eZines*
- Repeat word sorts from this lesson
- *Student Journal* pages for this lesson
- *Writing Advantage* independent lessons

Assessment

Strategy Assessment

To help you and your students assess their use of comprehension strategies, ask the following questions. Students can complete a written response or provide verbal answers in a one-on-one reading conference.

1. **Understanding Text Structure** The author used more than questions and answers to structure this text. What other features were used to present information in a simple and clear way? (Answers will vary and may include the white circles that present key facts, the small planet symbols beside each key point, and the sidebar on page 13 that lists nations that participated in building the ISS.)
2. **Monitor Understanding** As you read the article, what did you do to monitor your understanding? (Answers will vary. Students may say that they thought about whether the answers to each question made sense to them; or they may have tried to visualize information given in the article about the space station.)

For ongoing informal assessment, use the checklists on pages 61–64 of *Level D Assessment*.

Word Study Assessment

Use these steps to help you and your students assess their understanding of the Greek roots *gram*, *graph*, and *hydr*.

1. Write *gram*, *graph*, and *hydr* on the board.
2. Then write the following chart on the board.
3. Have students add the correct Greek root on the line to complete each word. (*hydro*ponics, *gram*mar, calli*graph*y, *hydr*ant, mono*gram*, di*graph*)
4. Have students use the roots to generate other words and their meanings.

Word	Meaning
_____ ponics	"growing plants in water"
_____ mar	"the study of rules for writing"
calli _____ y	"beautiful hand writing"
_____ ant	"a pipe for getting water"
mono _____	"a single written initial"
di _____	"two letters in writing with one sound"

LESSON 26
Into the Darkness *and* The Blue Ridge Mountains
Mountains, pages 16–23

SUMMARY

In this **historical fiction**, an enslaved African tells about her escape. A **poem** follows.

COMPREHENSION STRATEGIES

Understanding Text Structure
Inferential Thinking

WRITING

Character Sketch

VOCABULARY

Parts of Speech

PHONICS/WORD STUDY

Greek Roots *logo, meter/metr, micro*

Lesson Vocabulary

calluses	stifle
muffle	hitching post
ramshackle	nimbly

MATERIALS

Mountains, pp. 16–23
Student Journal, pp. 89–92
Word Study Manual, p. 61
Writing Advantage, pp. 30–55

Into the Darkness
The following story is historical fiction. Joanna Cook and the events that happen to her are fictional. However, the story is set during the Civil War in the United States and reflects the atmosphere of the time.

My name is Joanna Cook. It is 1862, and I am a slave. Nothing belongs to me, not my own body, not my time, not even my mother. I work as a field hand on a farm in Maryland, six long days a week. I watch as the farmer gets thick around the middle and rich in his big house and fancy carriage. For me, only the calluses on my hands grow thick. I have never tasted freedom. I wonder what it's like.

It's fall in Maryland, my favorite time of year. There is something about the leaves turning to fire and the days becoming shorter that I love. It reminds me of my mother. When I was a child, she used to bring me bouquets of leaves—maples, dogwoods, and oaks. I haven't seen her in four years.

16

Before Reading

Use one or more activities.

Anticipation Guide

Create an anticipation guide for students. (See TE page 389 for an anticipation guide BLM.) Ask students to read the statements and place a check in the AGREE or DISAGREE box before each statement. Students will have a chance to revisit their answers after they read the selection.

AGREE	DISAGREE	
		1. The Underground Railroad is an actual railroad.
		2. The Underground Railroad went from the South to the North.
		3. Going on the Underground Railroad was an easy task.
		4. A woman called "Moses" guided many slaves onto the Underground Railroad.

Vocabulary Preview

List the selection vocabulary on an overhead transparency or on the board. Assess prior knowledge by asking students to begin the knowledge rating chart on *Student Journal* page 89. Students should fill in as many boxes as they can. They can complete the chart after they finish reading.

We were separated at an auction in Richmond, Virginia. A farmer in Atlanta bought her, and I ended up here in Maryland. I'm sixteen and brave, and I'm not going to stay here forever, working for nothing but pain and disrespect.

At night, as I lay on my patch of hay, I hear Miss Winnie whispering to Miss Clarice about "Moses."

"We just have to get in touch with Moses," Miss Winnie sighs.

"Don't be talking crazy, now, Miss Winnie. We're too old to be walking miles and miles to the north. Besides, winter is coming."

DIFFERENTIATED INSTRUCTION SMALL GROUP

Preview the Selection

To introduce Harriet Tubman and the Underground Railroad, try the following:

1. As students look through the selection, point out the special features ("Moses" and "A Safe Place"). Ask volunteers to read these features aloud.
2. Tell students to look for mentions of Harriet Tubman and the concept of safe houses as they read "Into the Darkness."

Student Journal page 89

Name __________ Date __________

Building Vocabulary: Knowledge Rating Chart

Show your knowledge of each word by adding information to the other boxes in the row.

Word	Define or Use in a Sentence	Where Have I Seen or Heard It?	How Is it Used in the Selection?	Looks Like (Words or Sketch)
calluses				
muffle				
ramshackle				
stifle				
hitching post				
nimbly				

Preview the Selection

Have students look through the seven pages of the selection, pages 16–22 in the magazine. Use these or similar prompts to orient students to the selection.

- What do you think the selection is about?
- What form of writing will you read? How do you know?
- What feelings does the artwork convey?

(See Differentiated Instruction.)

Teacher Think Aloud

From the illustrations and dialogue in the text, I'm pretty sure this selection is a made-up story, or fiction. It seems to be set in the past, too. I notice, however, that page 18 has a picture of Harriet Tubman. She was a real person in history, but she could be a character in this story. I wonder whether the characters in this story will meet up with Harriet Tubman.

Make Predictions/ Set Purpose

Students should use the information they gathered in previewing the selection to make predictions about what they will learn. If students have trouble generating a purpose for reading, suggest that they read to see if they were correct in their responses in the anticipation guide and to learn how the Underground Railroad brought many slaves to freedom.

DIFFERENTIATED INSTRUCTION

Comprehension

UNDERSTANDING TEXT STRUCTURE

Help students understand this text as historical fiction by asking questions such as:

- What parts of the story do you think are real? Not real?
- Why do you think authors choose to write historical fiction?
- Do you think historical fiction is a good way to learn history? Why or why not?

"Clarice, don't be so stubborn. I can't take another season of this work. I ache all over—my bones, my skin, and my head all hurt. Moses isn't young either, but she escaped, and now she returns to help others get out. They say she has never lost a passenger, and she teaches you how to follow the North Star to freedom."

"Oh, Winnie, hush-up and go to sleep."

I want to jump out of my bed and shake Miss Winnie to learn more about this Moses lady. But I know better. I need to find Moses on my own. I am ready to follow the stars.

The next night, as the last embers of the fire are dying out, I hear a strange brushing sound at the door. At first, I think it's the wind and turn over to sleep. But then, I hear the sound again, and so do Miss Winnie and Miss Clarice.

"Joanna, go open that door," Winnie hisses.

"Who is it?" I ask her.

"How should I know? Go see."

I lift my weary legs over the side of my bed and put my blistered feet on the cool, dirt floor. Wrapping my arms around my body, I tiptoe to the door and crack it open. All at once, a strong hand pushes me back, and the door flings open, nearly hitting me in the nose.

"Ready?"

At first I don't know what's going on, but then I see Miss Winnie grab a tiny sack and give Clarice a look. Clarice silently shakes her head no and Winnie stands.

"It's just me, I guess," Winnie whispers. All I can do is stare, while inside, I am screaming *Take me! Take me!*

"I have arrangements for another," the mysterious woman says.

Moses

Harriet Tubman was known as Moses. Like Moses from the Bible, Tubman helped many slaves escape to freedom. Between 1850 and 1860, Tubman made nineteen trips to the South and led more than 300 slaves to freedom. Tubman traveled at night and was assisted by the "Underground Railroad." This secret network of people opened their homes to slaves on their way to Northern states and Canada. In 1856, Southern officials offered $40,000 for Tubman's capture. However, Harriet Tubman was never caught. During the Civil War, she worked as a cook, a nurse, and a spy for the Union army. Harriet Tubman settled in Auburn, New York, and died in 1913 in her early nineties.

18

During Reading

Comprehension

UNDERSTANDING TEXT STRUCTURE

Use these questions to model how to identify historical fiction. Then have students tell how story details help them recognize this genre.

- How do I know this is fiction and not nonfiction?
- What elements tell me this is a piece of historical fiction?

(See Differentiated Instruction.)

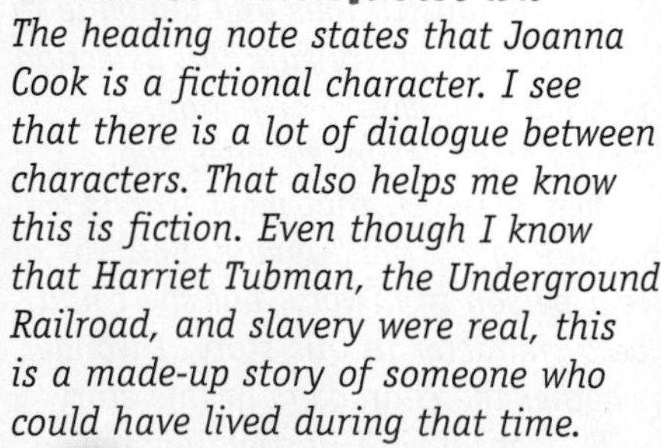

The heading note states that Joanna Cook is a fictional character. I see that there is a lot of dialogue between characters. That also helps me know this is fiction. Even though I know that Harriet Tubman, the Underground Railroad, and slavery were real, this is a made-up story of someone who could have lived during that time.

Comprehension

INFERENTIAL THINKING

Use these questions to model drawing conclusions about a story character. Then have students draw their own conclusions about Joanna Cook.

- What does Joanna do and say that shows me what she is like?
- What do I already know that helps me understand Joanna's words and actions?
- What words best describe Joanna?

Teacher Think Aloud

I know that runaway slaves were often recaptured and beaten. Yet Joanna is brave and determined enough to take this chance. I also know how hard it is to leave a familiar routine for the unknown. Clarice isn't willing to do it, but Joanna is positive enough to believe a new life is possible. So I can conclude that Joanna is brave, determined, and positive minded.

Fix-Up Strategies

Offer these strategies to help students read independently.

If you don't understand what you're reading:

- Reread the difficult section to look for clues to help you comprehend.
- Read ahead to find clues to help you comprehend.
- Retell, or say in your own words, what you've read.
- Visualize, or form mental pictures of, what you've read.

If you don't understand a word:

- Reread the sentence. Look for ideas and words that provide meaning clues.
- Find clues by reading a few sentences before and after the confusing word.
- Look for the base or root word and think about its meaning.
- Think about the topic or plot at this point to see if either offers meaning clues.

DIFFERENTIATED INSTRUCTION

Vocabulary

Parts of Speech

To help students with this activity, try the following steps:

1. Review these parts of speech: *noun* (naming word), *verb* (action word), *adjective* (describing word for nouns), *adverb* (describing word that tells where, when, or how).
2. Write the terms as column headings. Then write two examples of each: *noun*—friend, school; *verb*—sing, hear; *adjective*—good, funny; *adverb*—slowly, late.
3. Ask volunteers to suggest other words for each category.

Student Journal pages 90–91

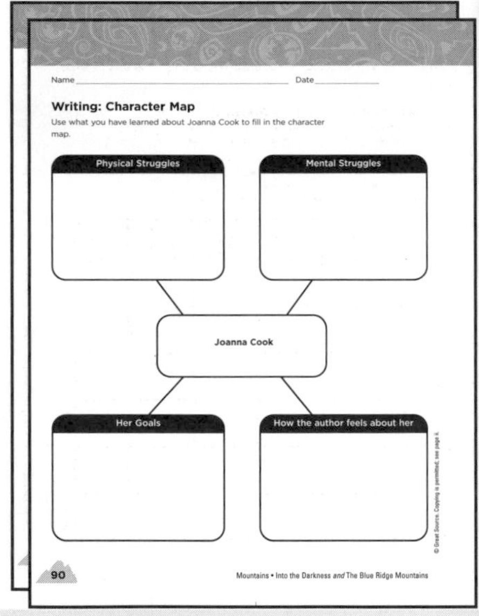

Name ________ Date ________

Writing: Character Map

Use what you have learned about Joanna Cook to fill in the character map.

Physical Struggles

Mental Struggles

Joanna Cook

Her Goals

How the author feels about her

90 Mountains • Into the Darkness *and* The Blue Ridge Mountains

After Reading

Use one or more activities.

Check Purpose

Ask students if their purposes were met. Were their responses correct in their anticipation guides? Did they learn how the Underground Railroad brought slaves to freedom?

Discussion Questions

Continue the group discussion with the following questions.

1. Why do you think Miss Clarice did not choose to escape with Miss Winnie? (Inferential Thinking)
2. Do you think it was right for people to help slaves to freedom, even though they were breaking the law? Explain. (Making Connections)
3. Do you think Joanna will reach freedom? Why or why not? (Predict)

Revisit: Knowledge Rating Chart

Have students revisit the knowledge rating chart on *Student Journal* page 89. Are there any adjustments or changes they would like to make? Students can add new notes if necessary.

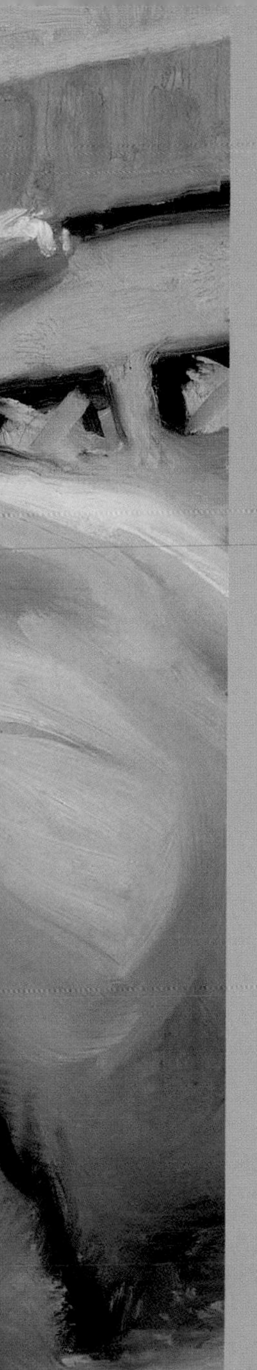

"I'll go." There, I say it. The words float in front of my face, echo in my ears.

There's only a beat of silence, and then the woman says, "Let's go then. You have miles to cover before first light."

As we step out onto the fields, my heart pounds so loudly I'm afraid it will wake the dogs. I hold my hand to my chest to muffle the noise, and Winnie and I follow the woman to the edge of the farm.

"Follow the maple trees until you get to the creek. Then follow the creek until you see a friendly face. He'll tell you what to do next."

Winnie and I turn to go, but the woman stops Winnie. She says, "Wait. You must go different ways. It's safer to split up."

She pulls Miss Winnie back with her and fixes her gaze on me. I want to protest. I can't find my way through strange woods by myself. Lord knows what or who might be lurking in the darkness. I want to cry. Maybe I don't know what I've gotten myself into. Maybe I should go back. I look into the dark trees and then back to the ramshackle huts. It takes me about a second to decide that the unknown darkness is better than what I know about the daylight here. I turn into the trees.

Every step I take seems loud, like my feet are beating drums. A twig snaps; leaves crackle. I walk along the line of maples, and bless my mother for teaching me about trees. After what seems like hours of walking, I notice a glimmer in the darkness. *It has to be water* I think as I pick up my pace. As I step nearer, I see the creek twist through the trees. On a big rock beside the creek, a man sits, twirling a twig. I don't know what I am supposed to do, so I step shyly up to him and ask, "Are you my friend?"

He turns his broad, open face to me and covers his mouth to stifle his laughter. "Well, I don't know about that, but I'm going to tell you how to cross that bridge into Delaware. Sit down."

Only when I bend my knees to sit do I realize how exhausted I am. The cool air tightens my muscles. But I sit next to this man and listen to him speak. He tells me that instead of going over the bridge, I'll be going under it. He explains how to hide in the shadow of the wooden planks. After he is silent for a few minutes, I stand to go.

"I better go before the light starts coming up," I say.

"One more thing. When you cross the bridge, walk along the road—hiding in the brush until you find a house with a lantern swinging on a hitching post. When you find that house, you can go in. The white folk there will hide you until nightfall. It will be a safe house."

I nod even though I have a million questions. How can I really trust any white folk? Why would they help me? I don't ask anything. Instead, I turn back to the creek.

Answers to **Student Journal page 92:** Noun (Person)—(none); Noun (Place)—(none); Noun (Thing)—calluses, hitching post; Verb—muffle, stifle; Adjective—ramshackle; Adverb—nimbly.

Name ______________ Date ______

Building Vocabulary: Parts of Speech Word Sort

Based upon what you already know about the words after reading "Into the Darkness," sort each word into the proper category below.

calluses ramshackle hitching post
muffle stifle nimbly

Noun			Verb	Adjective	Adverb
Person	Place	Thing			

Writing Character Sketch

Have students discuss what they know about Joanna Cook. Ask: *What were Joanna's physical struggles, her mental struggles, her goals? How does the author feel about her?* Record ideas as they are expressed. Then have students complete the character map on *Student Journal* page 90. When the character maps are completed, have students write character sketches of Joanna Cook on *Student Journal* page 91.

Vocabulary Parts of Speech

Display the words *hitching post,* and have students find them in the selection. Explain to students that a hitching post is "a post (or pole) to which people tied up their horses and carriages." Ask students whether *hitching post* is a noun or a verb. (noun) Review the terms *noun, verb, adjective,* and *adverb.* Then have students complete *Student Journal* page 92. (See Differentiated Instruction.)

Phonics/Word Study

Greek Roots

Write this sentence on the board and read it aloud: *In geometry we use the metric system to find the perimeter and diameter.* Ask students to identify the words formed with the Greek root *meter* or *metr,* meaning "measure." Ask students how each word relates to the root. Now, work with students to complete the in-depth word root activity on TE page 214.

I don't walk far before coming to the bridge. Luckily, it's still dark, although there's a hint of gray along the horizon. I crouch and climb down the bank to the water. Grabbing hold of a wooden support, I lower myself below the bridge and begin my dance. Nimbly, I dart from shadow to shadow, careful not to splash the water. I feel invisible, or maybe I'm not even really there. On the other bank, I scramble up and dash into the ditch beside the road. Here I feel exposed: the dusty road is wide enough for a carriage. I crouch down and run.

My stomach growls, and I look down at my bleeding arm. I must have cut myself on the brush in the woods. I don't feel any pain, though, until I see the blood. Holding my arm, tears welling in my eyes, I don't know what to do. Then I see it. There it is, just like the man in the woods had said: a lantern on a hitching post. I look up the walkway to the small house. Two brick chimneys smoke, and a light blazes in a room. I know I need to stop, to sleep, to eat, but I'm scared. In the distance I hear dogs snarling and men yelling. They're looking for me.

Before I can knock on the door, it opens. A white man, dressed all in black and with a big hat, leads me inside. I smell the warm bread and beans from the kitchen. He motions for me to follow him, and I do. At the table there is a place waiting for someone, and then I realize that it's for me. I sit and eat. The bread tastes like honey and warms my stomach and calms my head. When I can't eat another bite, the man takes me to a space hidden beneath the floorboards with a bed and blanket. "I'll wake you at next nightfall," he whispers, closing me into the darkness.

I sink into the bed. *Why would this man break the law to help me?* I wonder, as sleep hugs my eyes. In moments, I let myself go into the darkness. I can still hear the faint barking of the bloodhounds. Freedom is still a long way off. ◆

A Safe Place

Many slaves who traveled on the Underground Railroad tried to make it to Lake Erie in New York. They would cross the lake into the freedom of Canada, which was the only truly safe place. The Canadian government would not return runaway slaves to the United States, and in Canada, African Americans could vote and own land. It could take a strong runaway about two months to get from Maryland to Canada. For others, it could take as long as a year.

The Blue Ridge Mountains

I. The Skyline

Have you seen the Blue Ridge?
In the morning, the trees are violet gems;
In the twilight, they are hazy gray.
From afar I can't see
where one tree ends
and another begins.
Branches intertwine—
a stiff embrace as still as pond water,
the blueness, not really there.

II. Valley Fever

I cannot see forever,
the Blue Ridge blocks my view.
I cannot see behind me,
the mountains hide that, too.
I cannot see for miles,
up in the spring-blue sky.
But I can dream of a voyage
on the wings of a butterfly.

23

Poem: The Blue Ridge Mountains

Direct students' attention to the poem on page 23. Note that the poem is divided into two parts. Read each part aloud and discuss students' reactions to each one. Ask which part, "The Skyline" or "Valley Fever," students like better. Have students give reasons for their preference.

Phonics/Word Study

More Greek Roots

For instruction to introduce a root, see TE page 192. Work with students to discover the meaning of each root. See *Word Study Manual* page 61 for a related word sort.

***logo* (word, reason)**

Use the words *prologue* and *epilogue* to help students unlock other words in the list.

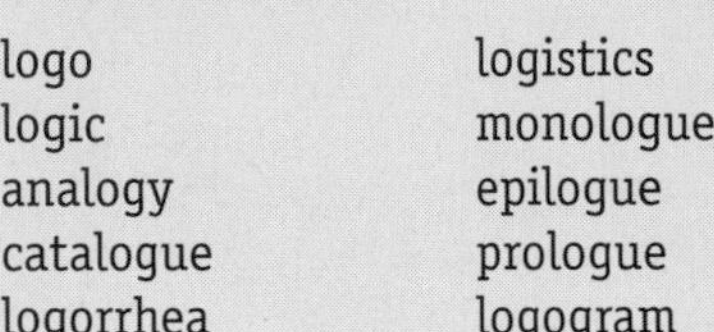

logo	logistics
logic	monologue
analogy	epilogue
catalogue	prologue
logorrhea	logogram

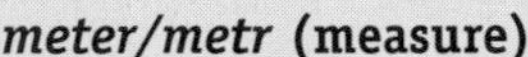

***meter/metr* (measure)**

Note that each word below defines a way of measuring something.

metronome	barometer
diameter	geometry
meter	perimeter
metric	symmetry

***micro* (small)**

micro-recorder	micromanage
microphone	microfiche
microscope	microbe
microwave	microcosm
microfilm	microorganism

Discovering the Roots

logo	*meter/metr*	*micro*
logo	metronome	microphone
logic	meter	microcosm
analogy	diameter	microwave
catalogue	symmetry	microscope
epilogue	barometer	microbe

For more information on word sorts and spelling stages, see pages 5–31 in the *Word Study Manual.*

Focus on . . .

Use one or more activities in this section to focus on a particular area of need in your students.

Comprehension STRATEGY SUPPORT

To help those students who need more practice using the strategies covered in this lesson, work one-on-one or in small groups to apply the strategy prompts below. Apply the prompts to a *Reading Advantage* paperback, a classroom library book, or a new or familiar selection in the magazine. Always model your own thinking first.

Understanding Text Structure

- What kind of text is this? (book, story, article, guidebook, play, manual)
- How does the author organize the text? (cause-effect, problem-solution, chronological order, description, question-answer, comparison-contrast)
- What details support my thoughts about the text structure?
- What is the cause (effect, problem, solution, order, question, answer)?
- If fiction, who are the characters? What is the setting, plot, conflict, and resolution?

Inferential Thinking

- What are the causes or effects of this event?
- What do I learn from the character or person's thoughts, words, or actions?
- What do I know (or infer) from the text that the author hasn't stated directly?
- What conclusions can I draw?

Writing Poem

Have students write a poem about a mountain. Before students begin to write, encourage them to reread "The Blue Ridge Mountains" and brainstorm a list of words that may be used to describe mountains. Remind students that a "mountain" does not only refer to a physical rock formation, but may be any huge, difficult problem people have to overcome.

For instruction on how to include strong verbs and sensory details, see lessons in *Writing Advantage* pages 30–55.

Fluency: Punctuation

After students have read "The Blue Ridge Mountains" at least once, have them read it aloud chorally. Half the class can read the first portion, "The Skyline," and the other half can read the second stanza, "Valley Fever."

As you listen to students read, use these prompts to guide them:

- Notice the different punctuation marks and what these signal to you. Pause at commas, periods, and semicolons. Let your voice rise at the end of sentences marked with a question mark.
- Reading too quickly or too slowly makes it difficult for listeners to understand the content.
- Try to read in unison.

When students read aloud, do they—

- ✓ demonstrate appropriate meaning and usage of punctuation marks?
- ✓ incorporate appropriate timing, stress, and intonation?
- ✓ exhibit well-timed pauses between words and phrases?

English Language Learners

To support students as they learn about parts of speech, examine words containing *-ing*.

1. Point out that words containing *-ing* are often verbs but can also be used as adjectives.
2. Write the following sentences on chart paper. Have partners discuss whether the *-ing* word in the sentence is used as an adjective or a verb.

   My mom is the most loving person I know.
   My dad is riding his bike to work today.
3. Have partners create their own sentences.

Independent Activity Options

While you work with individuals or small groups, others can work independently on one or more of the following options.

- Level D paperback books, see TE pages 367–372
- Level D *eZines*
- Repeat word sorts from this lesson
- *Student Journal* pages for this lesson
- *Writing Advantage* independent lessons

Assessment

Strategy Assessment

To help you and your students assess their use of comprehension strategies, ask the following questions. Students can complete a written response or provide verbal answers in a one-on-one reading conference.

1. **Understanding Text Structure** As you read the story, what details and information helped you know that this selection is an example of historical fiction? (Answers will vary. Students may say that the story blends historical facts, such as Moses, slavery, and the Underground Railroad, with made-up details and dialogue of imaginary characters.)
2. **Inferential Thinking** As you read this story, what conclusions did you draw about Joanna and her journey? (Answers will vary, but students might conclude that Joanna is brave and determined to undertake such a long, difficult, and dangerous journey.)

For ongoing informal assessment, use the checklists on pages 61–64 of Level D.

Word Study Assessment

Use these steps to help you and your students assess their understanding of the Greek roots *logo, meter/metr,* and *micro*.

1. Write the roots and sentences below on the board, or provide a copy for each student.
2. Have students use the correct root to complete the word in each sentence. *(barometer, monologue, microscope, analogy, perimeter)*
3. Then have students make a chart of the words and their meanings.

logo, meter/metr, micro
1. According to the baro _____, rain is likely.
2. We heard the comedian's opening mono ______ of jokes.
3. You can see blood cells with this _______ scope.
4. Your ana _____ compares football to a war.
5. We built a fence around the peri ______ of our yard.

LESSON 27

One Girl's Climb Out of Homelessness

Mountains, pages 24–27

SUMMARY

This **article** describes the obstacles Elizabeth Murray overcame to progress from homelessness to acceptance at Harvard College.

COMPREHENSION STRATEGY

Determining Importance

WRITING

Letter

VOCABULARY

Antonyms

PHONICS/WORD STUDY

Greek Roots *mono, phil, phon*

Lesson Vocabulary

paraphernalia	financially
retrieved	unique
succumb	inspirational
scoured	

MATERIALS

Mountains, pp. 24–27
Student Journal, pp. 93–95
Word Study Manual, p. 62
Writing Advantage, pp. 13–29

A homeless person sleeps in a doorway.

24

Before Reading

Use one or more activities.

Make a Concept Web

Ask students what associations they make with the word *homeless.* Make a web and add students' responses. Revisit the web when students finish the article.

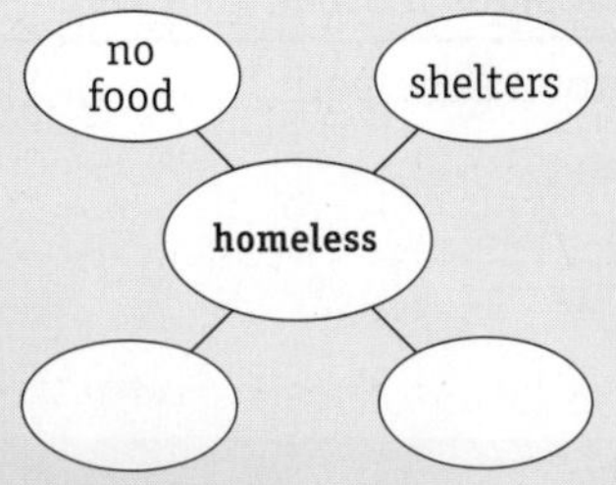

Vocabulary Preview

Review the vocabulary list with students. Ask students how they think the vocabulary words will be used in the selection. Then have students begin *Student Journal* page 93 by filling in only the prediction column. Students will complete the chart after they have finished the article.

Preview the Selection

Have students look through the four pages of the article.

Make Predictions/ Set Purpose

Students should use the information they gathered in previewing the selection to make predictions about what they will learn. If students have trouble generating a purpose for reading, suggest that they read to discover how a homeless girl turned her life around.

ONE GIRL'S CLIMB OUT OF HOMELESSNESS

AN EIGHTEEN-YEAR OLD WOMAN IS ACCEPTED AT HARVARD COLLEGE IN CAMBRIDGE, MASSACHUSETTS. THIS MIGHT NOT SOUND LIKE A BIG DEAL. HOWEVER, AFTER YOU LEARN ABOUT HER CIRCUMSTANCES, YOU'LL REALIZE THAT THIS IS AN AMAZING ACCOMPLISHMENT.

The young woman, Elizabeth Murray, grew up poor, often homeless, with drug-addicted parents. Yet, in an incredible show of will and desire, she made the steep climb out of poverty and homelessness.

Elizabeth Murray grew up in the Bronx, in New York City. She lived in a cramped, dirty apartment with her mother, father, and sister. There was rarely enough food to eat or warm clothes to wear in the winter. During her childhood, Elizabeth was surrounded by drugs. She witnessed her parents getting high in the kitchen. She grew accustomed to seeing their drug paraphernalia—needles, rubber tubes, and matches—scattered about. Welfare checks meant for food were spent on drugs before the money even arrived. Sometimes, her parents were so desperate for drug money that they sold Elizabeth's coats and shoes for extra cash.

25

DIFFERENTIATED INSTRUCTION

Comprehension

DETERMINING IMPORTANCE

Help students determine importance by finding the main idea of the second paragraph on page 26. Ask:

- What is the main topic of this paragraph? (Elizabeth's mother's AIDS)
- What are some details about this topic in the paragraph? (Accept all paragraph details.)
- What main idea do these details imply? (Possible response: When her parents got AIDS, Elizabeth's life became more difficult.)

Student Journal page 93

Name ______ Date ______

Building Vocabulary: Predictions

How do you think these words will be used in "One Girl's Climb Out of Homelessness?" Write your answers in the second column. Next, read the article. Then, clarify your answers in the third column.

Word	My prediction for how the word will be used	How the word was actually used
paraphernalia		
retrieved		
succumb		
scoured		
financially		
unique		
inspirational		

Mountains • One Girl's Climb Out of Homelessness 93

During Reading

Comprehension

SMALL GROUP

DETERMINING IMPORTANCE

Use these questions to model determining an implied main idea in the second paragraph. Then have students determine the main idea of other paragraphs.

- If the main idea is not stated, decide what the topic of the paragraph is by thinking about the details.
- In a sentence, state what the details tell you about the topic.

(See Differentiated Instruction.)

Teacher Think Aloud

In the second paragraph, the author doesn't state the main idea, but the topic is Elizabeth's childhood. Most of the details tell about Elizabeth's parents, their drug addiction, and its terrible impact on the family. These details imply a main idea that I might word this way: Due to drug addiction, Elizabeth's parents did not give her the care she needed in childhood.

Fix-Up Strategies

Offer these strategies to help students read independently.

If you don't understand what you're reading:

- Reread the difficult section to look for clues to help you comprehend.
- Read ahead to find clues to help you comprehend.
- Retell, or say in your own words, what you've read.
- Visualize, or form mental pictures of, what you've read.

Student Journal page 94

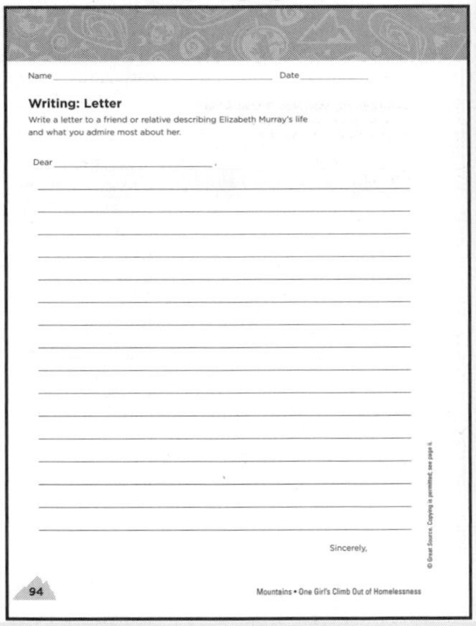

Name ______________________ Date __________

Writing: Letter

Write a letter to a friend or relative describing Elizabeth Murray's life and what you admire most about her.

Dear ______________________,

Sincerely,

94 Mountains • One Girl's Climb Out of Homelessness

Elizabeth realized at an early age that she would have to take care of herself. When she was nine, she took a job bagging groceries. She made about $22 a day and used this money to feed her family. Elizabeth attended school occasionally but faced constant teasing, because she was dirty and wore tattered clothes. A neighbor showed Elizabeth a set of encyclopedias that she had retrieved from the dumpster. Elizabeth read about a wide variety of topics. Although her parents were unable to educate her, Elizabeth found a way to learn. All through this time, though, Elizabeth says that she felt love from her parents and loved them back.

When she was ten, Elizabeth's world changed. Her mother became infected with HIV, and in a few years, her mother developed full-blown AIDS. After finishing the eighth grade, Elizabeth dropped out of school to care for her mother. Eventually, her mother was hospitalized. When Elizabeth was only fifteen years old, her mother died. Elizabeth wanted to give her mother a proper funeral, so she had to beg for money from her mother's drinking buddies. Soon after,

26

After Reading

Use one or more activities.

Check Purpose

Have students decide if their purpose was met. Did students discover how a homeless girl turned her life around?

Discussion Questions

Continue the group discussion with the following questions.

1. What do I understand now about homelessness that I didn't before? (Making Connections)
2. Do you think the author admires Elizabeth Murray? Why or why not? (Inferential Thinking)
3. What kind of a person do you think Elizabeth is? (Inferential Thinking)

Revisit: Concept Web

Revisit the web. Were students' associations with the term *homeless* correct? What new information might they add?

Revisit: Predictions Chart

Have students complete the third column in the predictions chart on *Student Journal* page 93. How were the words actually used?

Elizabeth's father also developed AIDS and was forced to live on the streets.

Although she was without a family, Elizabeth did not succumb to despair. She never gave up. Instead, she figured out how to avoid ending up like her mother and father. Elizabeth decided to return to school. However, she was seventeen and only had an eighth grade education. To make matters worse, she had another large hurdle to overcome; she was homeless. During this time, Elizabeth rode the subways at night and tried to sleep on the trains. Sometimes she slept on park benches. She scoured dumpsters and trash cans for food. Despite these obstacles, she applied to a public high school called the Humanities Preparatory Academy and was accepted.

SOMETIMES SHE SLEPT ON PARK BENCHES. SHE SCOURED DUMPSTERS AND TRASH CANS FOR FOOD.

Elizabeth did not tell the school that she was homeless.

Elizabeth dove into her schoowork. She doubled up on her classes to catch up and used the stairwells in the school as her study rooms. Even though the odds were stacked against her, Elizabeth succeeded in school, receiving straight A's. She earned her diploma in just two years.

Each year *The New York Times* offers scholarships to students in the New York area who are motivated, studious, and financially needy. The award is often given to students who have overcome great obstacles and have made learning a priority in their lives. This scholarship seemed like a perfect fit for Elizabeth, so she applied for one of these special awards to pay for college.

Her unique story inspired the editors at *The New York Times.* They awarded Elizabeth a $12,000 scholarship for each year she attended college. But Elizabeth's story did not stop with the scholarship. It was printed in *The New York Times* and inspired so many readers that they donated an additional $200,000, enough for fifteen more scholarships for other needy students.

Elizabeth Murray applied and was accepted to Harvard College as a member of the class of 2004. After completing her first year at Harvard, she decided to take time off to travel around the country, giving inspirational speeches to teachers and students. In the spring of 2003, the Lifetime Network aired *Homeless to Harvard,* a movie based on her life. Around the same time, Elizabeth left Harvard to care for her ailing father. She said that although she and Harvard were not a perfect fit, she plans to continue her studies at another college. ◆

SOUP KITCHENS

SOUP KITCHENS AND FOOD PANTRIES SUPPLY MORE THAN FIVE MILLION MEALS TO NEW YORK CITY RESIDENTS EVERY MONTH. IN THE LAST TEN YEARS, THE NUMBER OF SOUP KITCHENS AND SHELTERS IN MAJOR AMERICAN CITIES HAS INCREASED. ONE BIG REASON FOR THE NEED FOR SOUP KITCHENS: THE NUMBER OF AMERICANS LIVING BELOW THE POVERTY LINE JUMPED FROM 25 MILLION IN 1980 TO 36.9 MILLION IN 2000.

27

DIFFERENTIATED INSTRUCTION

SMALL GROUP

Vocabulary Antonyms

To help students with this activity, use these steps:

1. Write the following word pairs on the board or on chart paper and read them aloud: *poor/rich, dirty/clean, finish/start.*
2. Ask students what the relationship is between the word pairs. Students should notice that the word pairs are antonyms, or words with opposite meanings.
3. Have students suggest other antonym pairs.

Possible answers to **Student Journal page 95** include: *unique*—common, average, unoriginal; *retrieved*—lost, kept, forgot; *inspirational*—discouraging, dissuading, depressing.

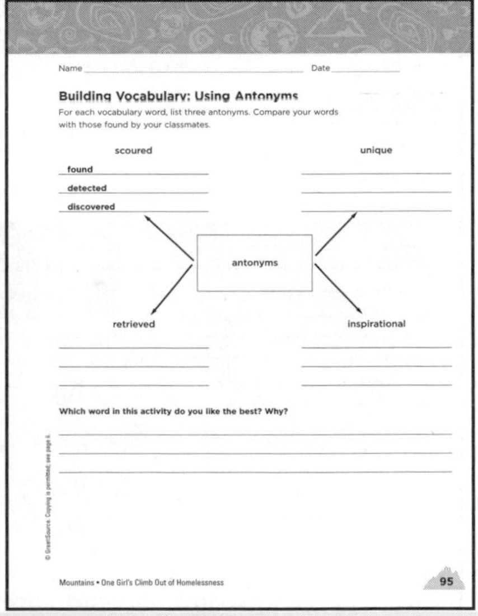

Name ______ Date ______

Building Vocabulary: Using Antonyms

For each vocabulary word, list three antonyms. Compare your words with those found by your classmates.

scoured
- found
- detected
- discovered

unique

antonyms

retrieved

inspirational

Which word in this activity do you like the best? Why?

© GreatSource. Copying is permitted; see page ii.

Mountains • One Girl's Climb Out of Homelessness 95

Writing Letter

Have students write a letter to a friend or relative in which they describe what they learned about Elizabeth Murray and what they admire most about her. Before they write, instruct students to look back through the article and jot down some problems Elizabeth had to overcome. Then have students write the letter on *Student Journal* page 94.

Vocabulary Antonyms

Display the word *scoured* and ask:

- What is the definition of *scoured* as it is used in the article? (searched through)
- What words can you think of that are opposite in meaning?

With students' help, make a list of words that mean the opposite of *scoured*. Explain that these are antonyms of *scoured*. Now have students complete *Student Journal* page 95. (See Differentiated Instruction.)

Phonics/Word Study

Greek Roots

Write *tone, rail, harmonic, syllable,* and *mega* on the board. Then write the Greek roots *mono, phil,* and *phon(e)*. Challenge students to create words by adding the roots to the words on the board. Discuss how the meanings of the words change when the roots are added. Now, work with students to complete the in-depth activity on TE page 220.

Phonics/Word Study

More Greek Roots

For instruction to introduce a root, see TE page 192. Work with students to discover the meaning of each root. See *Word Study Manual* page 62 for a related word sort.

mono **(one, single)**

monolingual	monologue
monotone	monastery
monotonous	monk
monosyllabic	monorail
monochrome	monolith

phil **(love)**

Philadelphia is referred to as the "City of Brotherly Love." Use that to help unlock the meanings of the other words.

philosophy	philharmonic
philanthropic	Philadelphia
philately	audiophile

phon **(sound)**

phonetic	phoneme
phonological	phonics
telephone	homophone
megaphone	symphony

Discovering the Roots

mono	*phil*	*phon*
monastery	philosophy	phoneme
monologue	philanthropic	symphony
monotony	Philadelphia	homophone
monk	audiophile	telephone
monolingual	anglophile	megaphone

For more information on word sorts and spelling stages, see pages 5–31 in the *Word Study Manual*.

Focus on . . .

Use one or more activities in this section to focus on a particular area of need in your students.

Comprehension STRATEGY SUPPORT

To help those students who need more practice using the strategies covered in this lesson, work one-on-one or in small groups to apply the strategy prompts below. Apply the prompts to a *Reading Advantage* paperback, a classroom library book, or a new or familiar selection in the magazine. Always model your own thinking first.

Determining Importance

- What is the most important idea in the paragraph? How can I prove it?
- Which details are unimportant? Why?
- What does the author want me to understand?
- Why is this information important (or not important) to me?

Writing Speech

Have students write a brief speech, introducing Elizabeth Murray to an audience. Before students begin to write, have them make a list of examples from Elizabeth's life that they would like to include in their introductory speech. Remind students that this speech should pique the audience's interest in Elizabeth. Encourage students to use some of the vocabulary words in their speeches.

For instruction and practice on writing different kinds of introductions, see lessons in *Writing Advantage* pages 13–29.

Fluency: Pacing

After students have read the selection at least once silently, have students pair up to read aloud parts of the article.

As you listen to students read, use these prompts to guide them.

- Read at a smooth and even pace.
- Notice the different punctuation marks and what these signal to you. Pause at commas and periods.
- Remember that sentences under a specific heading go together. Group these when you are reading.

When students read aloud, do they—

✓ demonstrate a smooth pace, not too fast or too slow?
✓ incorporate well-timed pauses between words and phrases?
✓ reflect an awareness and understanding of punctuation?

English Language Learners

To support students as they learn about antonyms (*Student Journal* page 95), review correct use of a thesaurus.

1. Have students examine several thesaurus entries. Remind students that a thesaurus is typically used as a resource for finding synonyms of a word.
2. Point out that a thesaurus can also be used to find antonyms, and show students how to find antonyms within a thesaurus entry.
3. Write the following words on the board: *unique, retrieved, inspirational, scoured.* Have partners look up the words and find synonyms and antonyms for each.

Independent Activity Options

While you work with individuals or small groups, others can work independently on one or more of the following options.

- Level D paperback books, see TE pages 367–372
- Level D *eZines*
- Repeat word sorts from this lesson
- *Student Journal* pages for this lesson
- *Writing Advantage* independent lessons

Assessment

Strategy Assessment

To help you and your students assess their use of the comprehension strategy, ask the following questions. Students can complete a written response or provide verbal answers in a one-on-one reading conference.

- **Determining Importance** As you read a paragraph in a nonfiction article, how would you go about determining the main idea if it is not stated directly? (Answers will vary. Students may say they would determine the topic of the paragraph, think about what the details say about this topic, and then state a sentence that tells what the paragraph is all about.)

For ongoing informal assessment, use the checklists on pages 61–64 of *Level D Assessment*.

Word Study Assessment

Use these steps to help you and your students assess their understanding of the Greek roots *mono*, *phil*, and *phon*.

1. Place the following chart on the board. Write the three roots, *mono*, *phil*, and *phon*, near the chart.
2. Ask students to add one of the three roots to create the word with the listed meaning. (audio*phile*, *mono*tone, homo*phone*, *mono*lingual, *phil*anthropic)

Word	Meaning
audio _____	"a lover of sound reproduction, or stereo"
_____ tone	"speaking in one tone"
homo _____	"two words that sound alike"
_____ lingual	"speaking one language"
_____ anthropic	"love of people, or humankind"

LESSON **28**

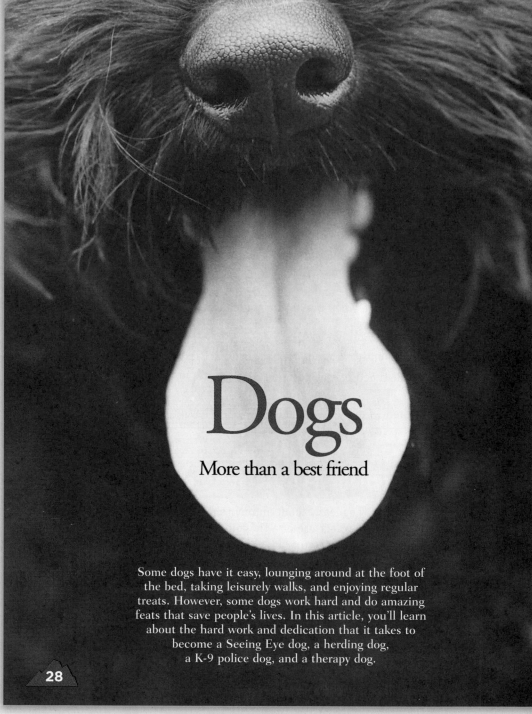

Dogs: More Than a Best Friend

Mountains, pages 28–33

SUMMARY

This **article** tells about four different dogs that help people in some way: a Seeing Eye dog, a herding dog, a K-9 police dog, and a therapy dog.

COMPREHENSION STRATEGIES

Determining Importance
Making Connections

WRITING

Opinion Paragraph

VOCABULARY

Synonyms

PHONICS/WORD STUDY

Greek Roots *pol/polis, photo/phos, scope*

Lesson Vocabulary

innate	grueling
unauthorized	interact
agile	isolated

MATERIALS

Mountains, pp. 28–33
Student Journal, pp. 96–98
Word Study Manual, p. 63
Writing Advantage, pp. 114–151

Dogs

More than a best friend

Some dogs have it easy, lounging around at the foot of the bed, taking leisurely walks, and enjoying regular treats. However, some dogs work hard and do amazing feats that save people's lives. In this article, you'll learn about the hard work and dedication that it takes to become a Seeing Eye dog, a herding dog, a K-9 police dog, and a therapy dog.

28

Before Reading

Use one or more activities.

Make a List

Write the following question on the board or on chart paper and read it aloud: *How do dogs help people?* Have students share their ideas. List their responses. Revisit the chart later.

How do dogs help people?

1. Seeing Eye dogs help blind people get around.
2. Herd dogs move livestock.
3.

Vocabulary Preview

Write the vocabulary words on the board and read them aloud to clarify pronunciations. Then have students choose one of the vocabulary words to create a word web on *Student Journal* page 96. Have students write a brief definition of the word before reading the selection. When they finish reading, students can add details to the web to help define the word.

Another Set of Eyes

Seeing Eye dogs act as a set of eyes for blind people or people with limited sight. Usually, Seeing Eye dogs are German shepherds, Labradors, or golden retrievers. Training one of these dogs is a long and important process.

The Puppy Raiser

The first step in training a Seeing Eye dog involves a specially trained person known as the puppy raiser. When a puppy is about eight weeks old, the puppy raiser begins to teach basic obedience skills, such as staying and heeling. Trainers also teach social skills, such as riding in a car, walking in traffic, and lying quietly in an office.

Training the Dog

When the dog is about a year and a half old, it starts a four to six month training process. Veterinarians check the dog's medical condition by conducting bone, eye, and stress tests. If a dog is healthy, it begins to practice skills in many environments: city sidewalks, beaches, malls, subways, trains, and construction sites. When the dog is ready, it is matched with a blind or vision-impaired partner.

A Seeing Eye dog can usually work for seven or eight years. People often think that the guide dog knows where to go, but it is the responsibility of the human to direct the dog. The human listens for the sound of traffic or other sounds and then determines if it's safe to go. If the person instructs the dog to go, but the dog senses it is unsafe, the dog will refuse the command. This is called "intelligent disobedience."

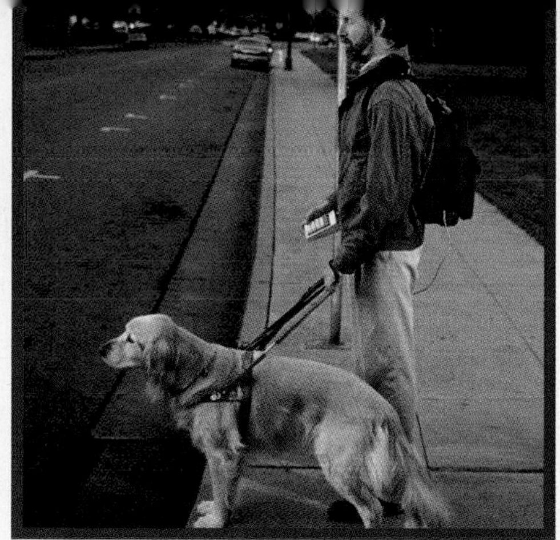

An Extra Farm Worker

Herd dogs help move livestock, such as sheep and cattle. In fact, dogs have been used to herd animals for thousands of years. Dogs help farmers or animal handlers with jobs like gathering animals, sorting them, moving them to another place, and keeping them in one place. Here are three of the basic skills that a herd dog must master:

Fetching: If a dog is told to fetch an animal, he must bring the animal back to the handler.

Driving: Driving is when the dog pushes the animals away from the handler.

Gathering: Dogs are trained to keep the animals together. They do this by circling around the edges of the herds to "gather" the animals into an area.

DIFFERENTIATED INSTRUCTION SMALL GROUP

Preview the Selection

To support the preview, use the steps below:

1. Have students look at the photographs in the article.
2. Have students compare the photographs. What details do students notice about them? Discuss as a group what the photographs have in common.
3. Ask students what they think they will learn about in this article.

Student Journal page 96

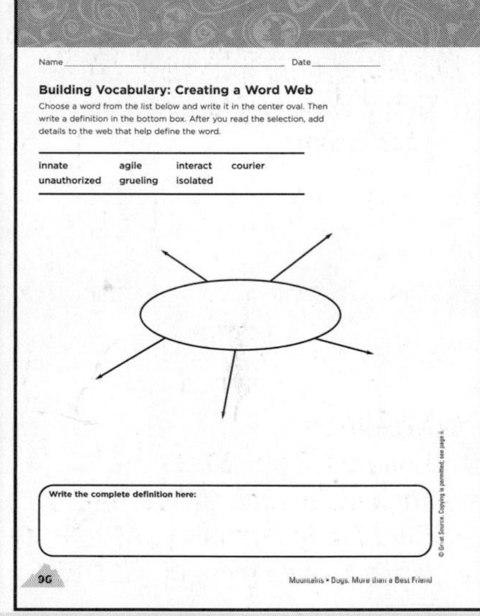

Name_______________ Date_______

Building Vocabulary: Creating a Word Web

Choose a word from the list below and write it in the center oval. Then write a definition in the bottom box. After you read the selection, add details to the web that help define the word.

innate agile interact courier
unauthorized grueling isolated

Write the complete definition here:

© Great Source. Copying is permitted; see page ii.

96 Mountains • Dogs: More than a Best Friend

Preview the Selection

Have students look through the six pages of the article. Use these prompts to orient students to the article.

- What do you think the article will be about?
- Is this fiction or nonfiction? What clues help you know?
- How is the information organized?
- What do the photographs tell you?

(See Differentiated Instruction.)

Teacher Think Aloud

I've seen Seeing Eye dogs and police dogs, and I've often wondered how they are trained to be so reliable. The first page also mentions herding dogs and therapy dogs, but I don't know much about them. I am interested in finding out what these dogs can do, and how dogs, in general, can be trained to have so many useful skills.

Make Predictions/ Set Purpose

Students should use the information they gathered in previewing the selection to make predictions about what they will learn. If students have trouble generating a purpose for reading, suggest that they read to learn different ways in which dogs help people.

DIFFERENTIATED INSTRUCTION

Comprehension

DETERMINING IMPORTANCE

Help students use subheadings to determine the importance of information. Ask:

- Who can turn this heading "Easing People's Pain" into a question about dogs? (Possible response: How do dogs ease people's pain?)
- After rereading this section of the article, how would you answer this question?
- Does your answer contain the important information? How do you know?

A Good Breed

The Border Collie is generally thought of as the ideal dog for herding sheep, cows, goats, pigs, and even geese. These dogs tend to be calm, easy to command, and passionate about their jobs.

Once a herd dog has repeated a task a number of times, it will know what to do without being guided by a human. For example, dogs that are trained to bring in cattle to be milked twice a day will do this task on their own.

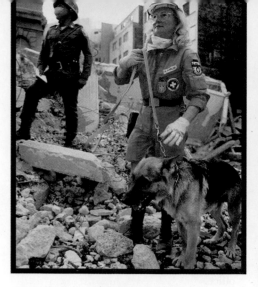

Keeping People Safe

K-9 (a play on the word canine) police dogs are true public servants. Properly trained police dogs help police officers prevent and solve crimes.

Why Dogs?

Dogs are sensitive to scents that people cannot smell. In the natural world, dogs use their strong sense of smell to find food or avoid enemies. It's this innate sensitivity to scents, along with positive reinforcements like praise and treats, that trainers use to train a police dog.Trainers teach police dogs to do the following jobs:

- Search buildings for unauthorized people
- Track criminals
- Search for missing children
- Find evidence dropped by criminals
- Search for explosives and drugs

30

During Reading

Comprehension

DETERMINING IMPORTANCE

Use these steps to model how to determine the importance of information in "An Extra Farm Worker." Then have students determine importance in another section.

1. Find a heading or subheading.
2. Reword the heading as a question.
3. Read to find the answer.

(See Differentiated Instruction.)

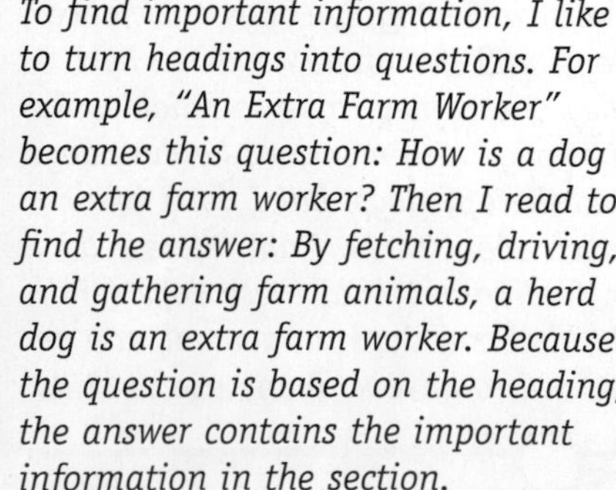

Teacher Think Aloud
To find important information, I like to turn headings into questions. For example, "An Extra Farm Worker" becomes this question: How is a dog an extra farm worker? Then I read to find the answer: By fetching, driving, and gathering farm animals, a herd dog is an extra farm worker. Because the question is based on the heading, the answer contains the important information in the section.

Comprehension

MAKING CONNECTIONS

Use these prompts to model for students how to make connections with the text. Then have students make their own connections with the text.

- What do I know about training dogs?
- Have I had any experience with the types of dogs mentioned in the text?
- What information from the article will I most likely remember?

Different dogs are trained for specific jobs. Below is a list of four "job titles" for police dogs:

Patrol K-9: Fully trained in obedience, this dog specializes in searching buildings, neighborhoods, and woods. Patrol dogs are agile, alert, and well trained to protect their handlers.

Detection K-9: Detection dogs specialize in finding drugs and recovering evidence. They can also be trained to search for a person who is alive or dead.

Search and Rescue K-9: These dogs search on both land and water in order to find people in trouble or already dead.

Dual Purpose K-9: A broadly trained animal, this dog can search buildings and outside areas, trail an escaped person, search for evidence, and detect drugs.

Easing People's Pain

A dog's job doesn't always involve grueling work. Some dogs help people by simply visiting them. These dogs, sometimes called *therapy dogs,* add to the quality of a sick person's life. Almost any breed of dog can be trained to become a therapy dog.

A Short History

Pet therapy is a relatively new job for dogs, and the term "pet therapy" was not used until 1964. A child psychiatrist named Boris Levinson observed that dogs helped children who didn't speak and weren't social. After Levinson's experiments, other scientists tested his ideas. Many studies showed that people who interact with animals smile and laugh more, are more alert, and are more hopeful about life than people who are isolated. Today, many health care centers use therapy dogs to help sick and depressed patients feel better.

Teacher Think Aloud

As I read "Dogs: More Than a Best Friend," I'm reminded of a time when I was at the airport and saw police officers walking around with dogs. I realized that the dogs were using their sense of smell to make sure there were no explosives or illegal substances in the airport. Despite all the people and noise, the dogs were completely calm. I think it's great that these dogs help keep people safe!

Fix-Up Strategies

Offer these strategies to help students read independently.

If you don't understand what you're reading:

- Reread the difficult section to look for clues to help you comprehend.
- Read ahead to find clues to help you comprehend.
- Retell, or say in your own words, what you've read.
- Visualize, or form mental pictures of, what you've read.

If you don't understand a word:

- Reread the sentence. Look for ideas and words that provide meaning clues.
- Find clues by reading a few sentences before and after the confusing word.
- Look for the base or root word and think about its meaning.
- Think about the topic or plot at this point to see if either offers meaning clues.

DIFFERENTIATED INSTRUCTION

SMALL GROUP

DISCUSSION QUESTIONS

To help students with the first discussion question, use the steps below:

1. Review with students the first question about comparing a Seeing Eye dog with a therapy dog.
2. On the board, make a Venn diagram with either side labeled "Seeing Eye Dog" and "Therapy Dog," and the middle section labeled "Both."
3. With students, brainstorm similarities and differences. Record their ideas on the Venn diagram.

Qualities of a Good Therapy Dog

Sociability: Dogs that are used for therapy enjoy being with people. A dog that turns away from a person can do more harm than good. If a dog is calm and friendly, it will make a good therapy dog.

Politeness: A polite dog will not touch someone unless it is invited to touch. Therapy dogs need to be trained not to invade someone's personal space. A polite dog that respects a person's space will make a good therapy dog.

Calmness and Friendliness: Finding the balance between these two traits can be difficult. An obedient, calm dog might not make a good therapy dog because it may not interact well with people. An overly friendly dog may become too excited and cause injuries or upset a patient. A dog that has a balance of both qualities makes an ideal therapy dog.

How Dogs Help

Dogs can help sick people in many ways:

- Dogs that visit hospitals or nursing homes help the patients feel less lonely and depressed.
- Interacting with dogs makes people become more interested in the world.
- Dogs distract people from their pain or illness.
- People talk to dogs and share their hopes, fears, and feelings with them without fear of being judged.
- Petting a dog can reduce a person's blood pressure and provide exercise for weak hands and arms.

Whether helping a sick person by giving love or keeping an older person company, therapy dogs have an important job.

Perhaps in addition to being a best friend, dogs should be known as a best helper. ◆

Portuguese Water Dogs

The Portuguese Water Dog is an ancient breed of working dog. There is archaeological evidence that these dogs were used to herd sheep and cattle thousands of years ago during the Stone Age. The dogs migrated from Asia to Spain and Portugal. In fishing villages along the coast of Portugal, the dogs were used to herd fish into a net, dive for lost equipment, guard a sailor's property, and carry messages from one boat to another. Portuguese water dogs were so helpful to sailors that they were paid for their work! Some historians think that in 1588, the Spanish Armada, the fleet of armed ships, took these dogs along and used them as couriers between ships.

Student Journal page 97

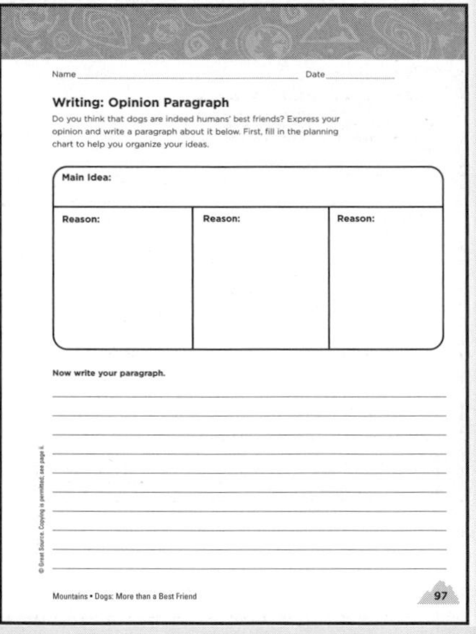

Name ________ Date ________

Writing: Opinion Paragraph

Do you think that dogs are indeed humans' best friends? Express your opinion and write a paragraph about it below. First, fill in the planning chart to help you organize your ideas.

Main Idea:		
Reason:	Reason:	Reason:

Now write your paragraph.

© Great Source. Copying is permitted; see page ii.

Mountains • Dogs: More than a Best Friend 97

After Reading

Use one or more activities.

Check Purpose

Have students decide if their purpose was met. What did they learn about how dogs help people?

Discussion Questions

Continue the group discussion with the following questions.

1. How do you think a Seeing Eye dog and a therapy dog are similar? How are they different? (Compare-Contrast)
2. What different kinds of things are police dogs trained to do? (Details)
3. Which helping dog did you find the most interesting? (Making Connections)

(See Differentiated Instruction.)

Revisit: List

Revisit the list about how dogs help people. What new information can students add?

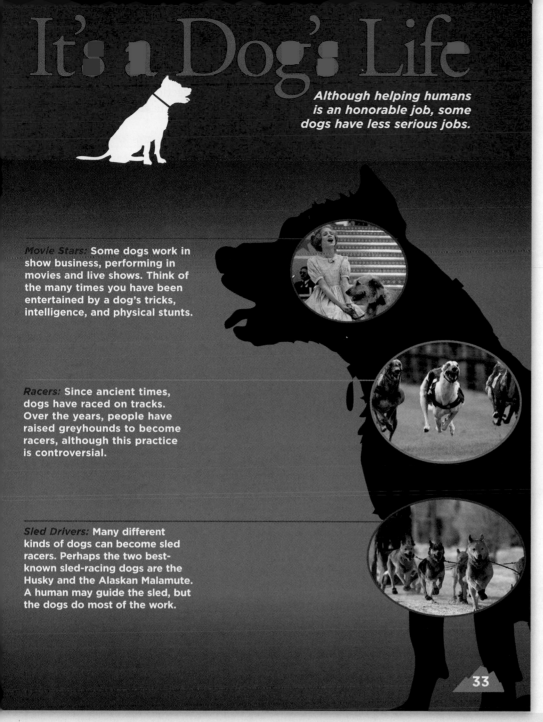

It's a Dog's Life

Although helping humans is an honorable job, some dogs have less serious jobs.

Movie Stars: **Some dogs work in show business, performing in movies and live shows. Think of the many times you have been entertained by a dog's tricks, intelligence, and physical stunts.**

Racers: **Since ancient times, dogs have raced on tracks. Over the years, people have raised greyhounds to become racers, although this practice is controversial.**

Sled Drivers: **Many different kinds of dogs can become sled racers. Perhaps the two best-known sled-racing dogs are the Husky and the Alaskan Malamute. A human may guide the sled, but the dogs do most of the work.**

33

Possible answers for **Student Journal page 98** include *agile—nimble, quick, spry; grueling—difficult, challenging, exhausting; interact—socialize, act together, consort.*

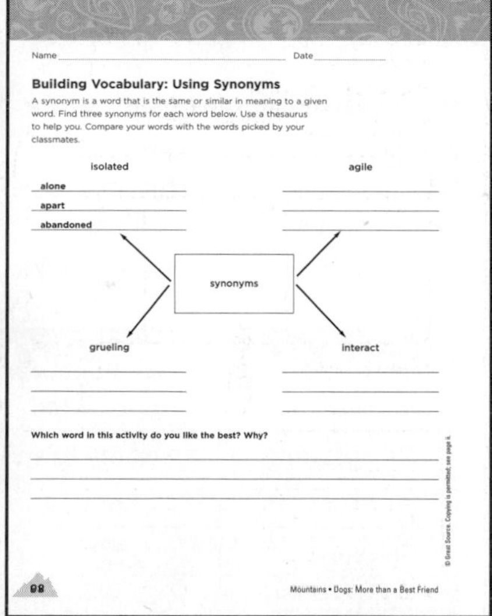

Name ______ Date ______

Building Vocabulary: Using Synonyms

A synonym is a word that is the same or similar in meaning to a given word. Find three synonyms for each word below. Use a thesaurus to help you. Compare your words with the words picked by your classmates.

isolated: alone, apart, abandoned

agile: ______

synonyms

grueling: ______

interact: ______

Which word in this activity do you like the best? Why?

______

Writing Opinion Paragraph

Do students think dogs are indeed our best friends? Have students express their opinions and write a paragraph about it on *Student Journal* page 97. Ask students to support their ideas with information they learned from the article. Tell students they can also use information and experiences from their own lives to help them form an opinion.

Vocabulary Synonyms

Write *isolated* on the board or on chart paper. Ask students to find it on page 31 and tell what it means. (cut off from other people) Recall that synonyms are words with the same or similar meaning. Ask volunteers to suggest synonyms for *isolated*. List their responses. (*alone, apart, abandoned, separate*) Using three of the vocabulary words, students should complete the synonyms activity on *Student Journal* page 98.

Phonics/Word Study

Greek Roots

Write this sentence on the board: *The cosmopolitan politician talked politics with the police.* Invite students to tell what they notice about the words in the sentence. (four words include the root *pol/polis*, which means "city, state") Discuss how each word is related to the root. Now, work with students to complete the in-depth Greek root activity on TE page 228.

Phonics/Word Study

More Greek Roots

For instruction to introduce a root, see TE page 192. Work with students to discover the meaning of each root. See *Word Study Manual* page 63 for a related word sort.

photo/phos **(light)**

Start by discussing the word *photosynthesis*.

phosphorous	
photojournalist	
photosynthesis	photogenic
telephoto	photograph

pol/polis **(city, state)**

police	cosmopolitan
metropolis	politician
politics	metropolitan

scope **(instrument or procedure for viewing)**

microscope	periscope
telescope	stethoscope
kaleidoscope	oscilloscope
laparoscopy	colonoscopy

Discovering the Roots

photo/phos	*pol/polis*	*scope*
phosphorous	metropolitan	stethoscope
photosynthesis	police	periscope
telephoto	politics	colonoscopy
photojournalist	cosmopolitan	kaleidoscope
photogenic	metropolis	microscope

For more information on word sorts and spelling stages, see pages 5–31 in the *Word Study Manual*.

Focus on . . .

Use one or more activities in this section to focus on a particular area of need in your students.

Comprehension STRATEGY SUPPORT

INDEPENDENT

To help those students who need more practice using the strategies covered in this lesson, work one-on-one or in small groups to apply the strategy prompts below. Apply the prompts to a *Reading Advantage* paperback, a classroom library book, or a new or familiar selection in the magazine. Always model your own thinking first.

Determining Importance

- What is the most important idea in the paragraph? How can I prove it?
- Which details are unimportant? Why?
- What does the author want me to understand?
- Why is this information important (or not important) to me?

Making Connections

- What does this story (article, passage) remind me of?
- What do I already know about this topic?
- Where have I heard about this topic before?
- What do I have in common with the characters, people, or situations in the text?
- What other books, stories, articles, movies, or TV shows does this text make me think about?

Writing News Story

INDEPENDENT

Have students write a fictional news story about a dog that rescues someone in a dangerous situation. As a group, brainstorm some rescue situations: a fire, a capsized boat, an accident, and so on. Remind students that news stories always contain answers to the 5Ws—*who*, *what*, *when*, *where*, and *why*. Have students use a 5Ws chart to help organize their ideas. You can find a 5Ws BLM on TE page 384. Encourage students to create attention-getting headlines for their stories.

For instruction and lessons on expository writing structures, see lessons in *Writing Advantage*, pages 114–151.

Fluency: Pacing

After students have read the selection at least once, they can use it to practice fluent reading. Students can work in pairs to read aloud a section of "Dogs: More Than a Best Friend."

As you listen to students read, use these prompts to guide them.

- Read at an even, natural pace. Preview the text as needed to avoid stops and starts.
- Let the punctuation guide your pauses and the expression in your voice.

When students read aloud, do they—

✓ demonstrate a smooth pace, not too fast or too slow?

✓ incorporate well-timed pauses between words and phrases?

✓ reflect an awareness and understanding of punctuation?

English Language Learners

To support students' understanding of multiple meaning words found in "Dogs: More than a Best Friend," review correct use of the dictionary.

1. Have students examine several dictionary entries. Point out how different meanings are differentiated within an entry in a dictionary.
2. Write the following sentence on the board: *Some dogs have it easy, lounging around at the foot of the bed.* Have partners look up the underlined word and find the definition that matches the context of the sentence.

Independent Activity Options

While you work with individuals or small groups, others can work independently on one or more of the following options.

- Level D paperback books, see TE pages 367–372
- Level D *eZines*
- Repeat word sorts from this lesson
- *Student Journal* pages for this lesson
- *Writing Advantage* independent lessons

Assessment

Strategy Assessment

To help you and your students assess their use of comprehension strategies, ask the following questions. Students can complete a written response or provide verbal answers in a one-on-one reading conference.

1. **Determining Importance** As you read this article, what did you do to find the important information in each section? (Answers will vary. Students may say that they tried to turn headings and subheadings into questions and then read for the information that answered these questions.)
2. **Making Connections** What connections did you make as you read this article? (Students may mention that the article may have reminded them of Seeing Eye dogs or K-9 dogs that they have seen working in their communities.)

See *Level D Assessment* page 34 for formal assessment to go with *Mountains*.

Word Study Assessment

To help you and your students assess their understanding of the Greek roots, review the meanings of *photo/phos, pol/polis,* and *scope*.

1. Write the Greek roots *photo/phos, pol/polis*, and *scope* on the board or on chart paper.
2. Under the roots, write the sentences below.
3. Have students add the correct Greek root to complete a word in each sentence. *(photosynthesis, Metropolis, stethoscope, photojournalist, politicians)*
4. Ask students to add similar sentences to the chart.

During ______synthesis, plants use light to make food.
*Metro*______ is a synonym for *a large city*.
A doctor uses a stetho______ to listen to your heart.
A ______journalist reports a story with pictures.
The first ______iticians were chosen in the Greek city-states.

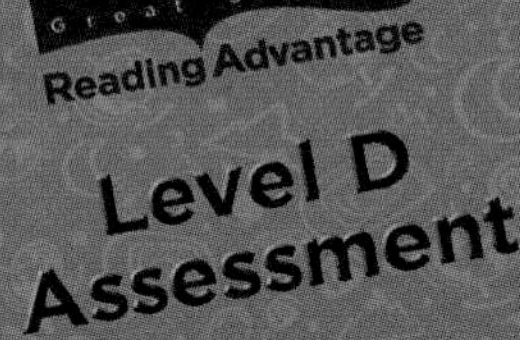

LESSON **29**

Facing Personal Mountains

Mountains, pages 34–39

SUMMARY

These **biographical sketches** tell how Maya Angelou and Frida Kahlo overcame obstacles to become accomplished artists.

COMPREHENSION STRATEGIES

Making Connections
Understanding Text Structure

WRITING

Problem-Solution

VOCABULARY

Suffixes

PHONICS/WORD STUDY

Greek Roots *techn, therm, zoo*

Lesson Vocabulary

transformed	controversial
voraciously	mischievousness
shuffling	tumultuous
optimistic	

MATERIALS

Mountains, pp. 34–39
Student Journal, pp. 99–101
Word Study Manual, p. 64
Writing Advantage, pp. 8–12

FACING PERSONAL MOUNTAINS

Maya Angelou and Frida Kahlo

Angelou and Kahlo both overcame personal obstacles to make contributions to society, one in literature and one in art.

MAYA ANGELOU

Today, critics and fans praise Maya Angelou as one of the strongest voices in literature. However, her talents go beyond writing poetry and novels. She is an actress, playwright, civil-rights activist, producer, and director. From a humble, poor beginning, she has become a powerful spokeswoman for women and minorities all over the world.

Maya Angelou was born Marguerite Johnson in St. Louis, Missouri, on April 4, 1928. When she was almost three years old, her parents divorced. Maya and her brother, Bailey, were sent to live with their grandmother in the small town of Stamps, Arkansas. This grandmother, on her father's side, raised the two children. Angelou was close to her grandmother and called her Momma. Her grandmother provided the love Maya needed as a child.

Angelou says that she learned many tough lessons while growing up in the segregated South. She learned what it was like to be a black girl in a world where whites made the rules. She learned the hard lesson of humility when she had to wear hand-me-down clothing from white women and when a white dentist would not treat her because she was black.

Angelou has said that as a child she often dreamed of waking up to find herself transformed: her hair bouncing on her shoulders in a blond bob. Angelou dreamed that

34

Before Reading

Use one or more activities.

Begin a List

Tell students that they are about to read about two women who overcame obstacles to make contributions to society. Write *overcoming obstacles* on the board or on chart paper and discuss with students what character traits are needed to overcome obstacles. As students respond, make a list. Tell students that they will come back to the list, after reading the biographical sketches, to add what they have learned.

Overcoming Obstacles

1. strong desire to succeed
2. willingness to work hard
3. help from others
4. luck
5. belief in yourself

Vocabulary Preview

Display the selection vocabulary. Assess prior knowledge by asking students to complete the making associations activity on *Student Journal* page 99. Ask students if they can make associations with any of the words. Have students think about times they may have seen, heard, or used the words.

I Know Why the Caged Bird Sings

"If growing up is painful for the Southern Black girl, being aware of her displacement is the rust on the razor that threatens the throat. It is an unnecessary insult."

—Maya Angelou

her life would be better if she were white. Despite these negative experiences and feelings, Angelou's grandmother was able to teach her pride and the importance of religion and prayer. These important values gave Angelou the inner strength that she needed to get through her childhood.

During this time with her grandmother, Angelou took comfort in the imaginary worlds of books and poems. She read voraciously and could not get enough books. When Angelou was twelve, in 1940, she and her brother were sent to San Francisco to live with their mother again. Life with her mother didn't run smoothly, and Angelou's teen years were difficult. In need of money for food and rent, she worked as a cocktail waitress.

When life became too much for her, she ran away to live with her father. He was living in a rundown trailer with his girlfriend, and life there was not much better. She ran away again, this time to a parking lot for wrecked cars where many homeless children lived. She lived on the streets for a month and then returned to her mother. The constant shuffling between her grandmother, mother, and father and the tough experiences of her youth left Angelou aching to prove that she was old enough to take care of herself.

In her rush to be a grown-up, Angelou became pregnant. At the young age of seventeen, she gave birth to a son, Guy Johnson.

In her early twenties, Angelou became a dancer in a cabaret act. It was then that she changed her name from Marguerite to Maya.

The first book that Angelou wrote is perhaps her most famous one. She didn't publish this book, *I Know Why the Caged Bird Sings,* until 1970, when she was forty-two years old. Her autobiography reflects the many challenges that Angelou overcame. In the end, though, hers is an optimistic story.

Angelou speaks many languages and always challenges herself by taking on new projects. She has traveled to Europe, the Middle East, and Africa to learn about different cultures. She has won numerous awards. In 1993 she became the second poet to write and read an original poem at the inauguration of a United States president.

Today, Maya Angelou is still quite active. She appears on television and writes for the theater. Angelou has developed her own line of greeting cards for Hallmark. A truly brave woman, Maya Angelou faced her personal mountains and shines in the glory of her successes.

35

DIFFERENTIATED INSTRUCTION SMALL GROUP

Preview the Selection

Review characteristics of a biographical sketch with students:

- A *biography* tells the true story of a person's life. A *biographical sketch* is a shorter, more succinct presentation of a person's life.
- Biographical texts present facts about a person, including specific dates, names, places, events, and accomplishments.
- Biographical texts are usually arranged chronologically to reflect the progression of a person's life.

Student Journal page 99

Name ____________ Date ________

Building Vocabulary: Making Associations

Pick two words from the vocabulary list below. Think about what you already know about each word. Then answer the following questions for each word.

transformed	shuffling	controversial	tumultuous
voraciously	optimistic	mischievousness	

Word ____________

What do you think about when you read this word? ____________

Who might use this word? ____________

What do you already know about this word? ____________

Word ____________

What do you think about when you read this word? ____________

Who might use this word? ____________

What do you already know about this word? ____________

Now watch for these words in the magazine selection. Were you on the right track?

Mountains • Facing Personal Mountains 99

Preview the Selection

Have students look through the six pages of the article, pages 34–39 in the magazine. Use these or similar prompts to orient students to the text.

- What does the title phrase "Facing Personal Mountains" mean?
- What information does the text under the title give you?
- Do you think the selection is fact or fiction? How do you know?

(See Differentiated Instruction.)

Teacher Think Aloud

I see this article is about the writer Maya Angelou and the artist Frida Kahlo. I've heard of them, but I don't know much about their lives and work. The note under the title says both women had to overcome personal obstacles to reach success. I'm glad that artists and writers are willing to struggle so hard to express themselves creatively. We all benefit from their work!

Make Predictions/ Set Purpose

Students should use the information they gathered in previewing the selection to make predictions about what they will learn. If students have trouble generating a purpose for reading, suggest that they read to see how two creative people overcame obstacles in their lives.

DIFFERENTIATED INSTRUCTION

Comprehension

MAKING CONNECTIONS

Help students make connections with the text by asking these questions:

- What books or movies have you read or seen lately in which real people or characters overcame obstacles?
- How did these people solve the problems in their lives?
- What generalizations can you make about the traits one needs in order to overcome obstacles?

She found a way to use the emotions that these obstacles produced to inspire her art.

FRIDA KAHLO

Frida Kahlo was born in Mexico City, Mexico; however, the year of her birth is unclear. She claimed that she was born in 1910. However, her birth certificate reads 1907. This is only one of many controversial details of Kahlo's life.

When she was six years old, Kahlo was infected with polio, a crippling disease. The disease weakened her right leg, causing it to become much thinner than her left leg. Despite her illness, Kahlo was full of energy, and her high spirits often led to mischievousness and trouble. At the National Preparatory School, Kahlo often played pranks on her teachers and friends.

When Kahlo was eighteen, she was struck by a streetcar. The accident resulted in a broken spine, collarbone, ribs, and pelvis. The accident also crushed

36

During Reading

Comprehension

MAKING CONNECTIONS

Use these prompts to model how to make text-to-text connections. Then have students make their own connections with the text.

- How is this selection similar to "One Girl's Climb Out of Homelessness"?
- What can I learn from reading both texts that I couldn't learn from one?

(See Differentiated Instruction.)

Teacher Think Aloud

This biographical sketch about Maya Angelou is very much like the earlier selection about Elizabeth Murray's climb out of homelessness. (See TE page 216.) Both women had heartbreakingly difficult childhoods. They basically had to take care of themselves. Yet, they both went on to do amazing things. It inspires me that people can overcome terrible hardship.

Comprehension

UNDERSTANDING TEXT STRUCTURE

Use these prompts to model how to determine the text structure of the two biographical sketches. Then have students compare the text structures.

- What does the first part of each biographical sketch focus on? What does the second part focus on?
- How are the two women's problems similar? How are the solutions to their problems similar?

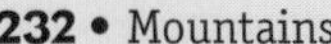

Self-portrait by Frida Kahlo

her right foot. She lay flat on her back, wrapped in a plaster cast, for a month. During her recovery, Kahlo began to paint to distract herself. She gave these paintings away to friends and relatives. At the time, Kahlo did not realize that she would eventually become a serious artist.

Kahlo's strong desire to live helped her recover from the accident. However, she was often in pain and had to be hospitalized many times. In the course of her lifetime, she underwent more than thirty operations.

Frida Kahlo and Diego Rivera

In 1929, Kahlo married a fellow artist, Diego Rivera. Although Rivera was twenty years older than Kahlo, they shared a passion for painting. A year after they married, they traveled together to San Francisco, where Rivera painted two murals. While he worked, Kahlo explored the city and painted portraits of friends and herself. In San Francisco, Kahlo began to see a doctor who would become a lifelong friend.

Kahlo and Diego's marriage was tumultuous, full of strong and sometimes negative emotions. Although they loved each other deeply, they hurt each other by saying hateful things. Yet Rivera encouraged Kahlo's now famous personal style: traditional Mexican clothes of long, colorful dresses and big, showy jewelry. More important, he supported her desire to paint.

Teacher Think Aloud

Most biographical sketches proceed in chronological, or time, order, beginning with childhood and moving on to adulthood. These sketches do that, too, but they also have a problem-solution structure. That is, the first half of each sketch presents the serious problems that each woman faced in childhood and adolescence. The second half shows how she overcame her problems largely by doing creative work.

Fix-Up Strategies

Offer these strategies to help students read independently.

If you don't understand what you're reading:

- Reread the difficult section to look for clues to help you comprehend.
- Read ahead to find clues to help you comprehend.
- Retell, or say in your own words, what you've read.
- Visualize, or form mental pictures of, what you've read.

If you don't understand a word:

- Reread the sentence. Look for ideas and words that provide meaning clues.
- Find clues by reading a few sentences before and after the confusing word.
- Look for the base or root word and think about its meaning.
- Think about the topic or plot at this point to see if either offers meaning clues.

DIFFERENTIATED INSTRUCTION

Vocabulary Suffixes

To help students understand suffixes, use the following steps:

1. Show this list of words: *coastal, dangerous, critical, poisonous, educational, humorous.* Ask what the words have in common. (They end with *-al* or *-ous.*)
2. Explain that all the words are adjectives, or describing words, and that *-al* or *-ous* at the end of a base word often signals an adjective.
3. Have students suggest other adjectives that end with *-al* and *-ous.*

Over the years, Kahlo painted many portraits—of herself, her friends, and relatives. In her many self-portraits, Kahlo often showed herself with pets or other meaningful objects. Although she was largely self-taught, she studied the work of famous European painters. Kahlo was also influenced by Mexican artists and owned hundreds of Mexican religious paintings.

In 1953, Kahlo's right leg was amputated because of an infection. In 1954, Kahlo died after suffering a bout of pneumonia. Kahlo had faced many mountains, including physical pain and marital difficulties. Yet, she found a way to use the emotions that these obstacles produced to inspire her art. ◆

Polio

Polio is an infectious viral disease that can lead to paralysis or death. In the 1950s, the polio vaccine was developed. The vaccine almost eliminated polio in developed countries. Although polio is seldom seen today in the United States, it is still a threat in other parts of the world. In the spring of 2003, there was a large polio epidemic in India. More than 80 million Indian children were vaccinated to protect them from the disease.

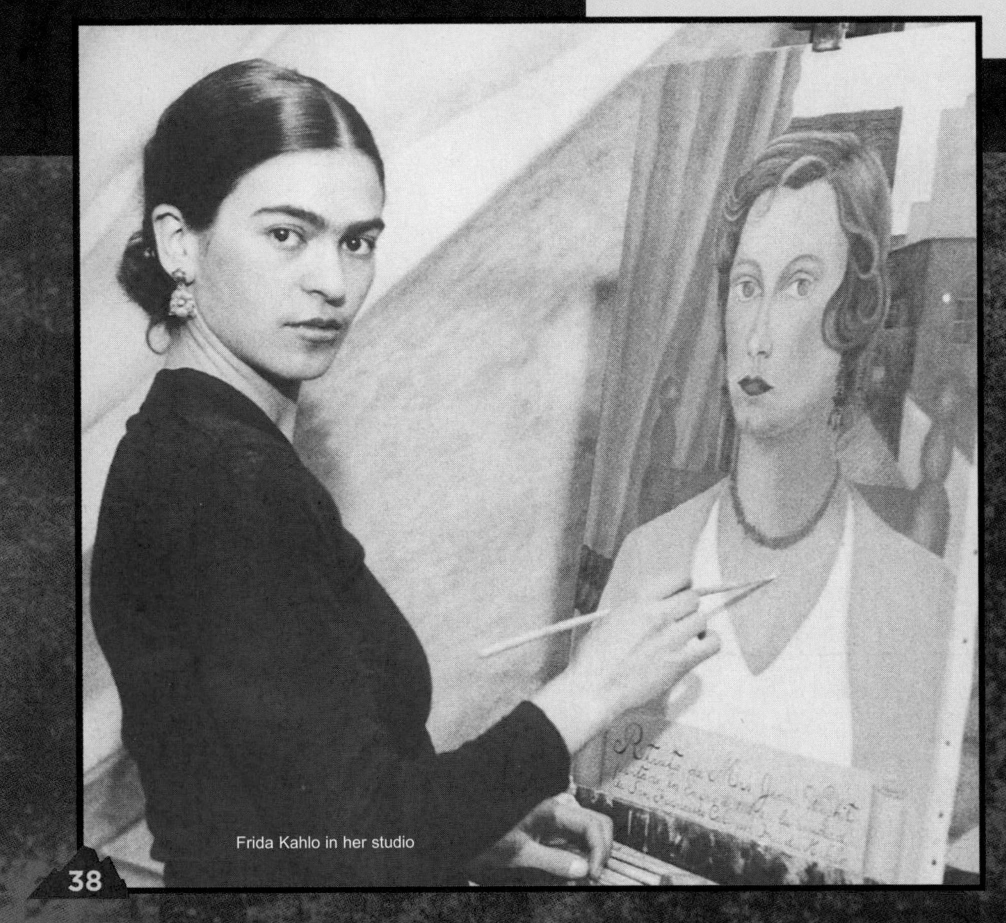

Frida Kahlo in her studio

38

Student Journal page 100

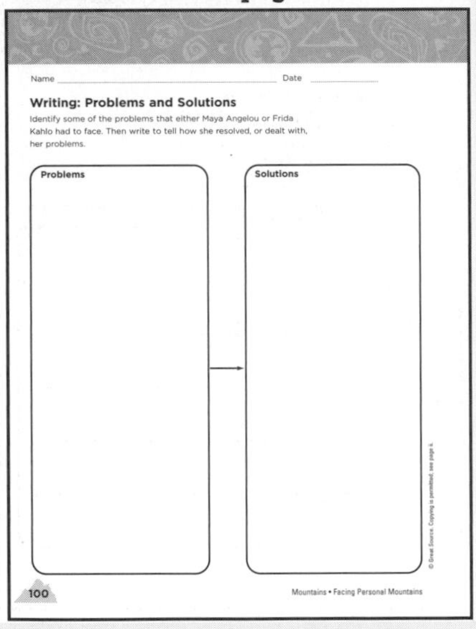

Name ______ Date ______

Writing: Problems and Solutions

Identify some of the problems that either Maya Angelou or Frida Kahlo had to face. Then write to tell how she resolved, or dealt with, her problems.

Problems	Solutions

100 Mountains • Facing Personal Mountains

After Reading

Use one or more activities.

Check Purpose

Have students decide if their purposes were met. Did they learn about how two creative women overcame obstacles in their lives?

Discussion Questions

Continue the group discussion with the following questions.

1. Who helped Maya Angelou and Frida Kahlo to succeed? How? (Monitor Understanding)
2. What do you admire about the two women? Explain. (Making Connections)
3. Which woman do you think had a more difficult life? Explain. (Compare-Contrast)

Revisit: List

Revisit the list about the traits needed to overcome obstacles. Can students add anything new to the list?

Art as Therapy

Mt. Sinai hospital in New York City believes in the healing power of art. This famous hospital has an Art Committee, which decided to hang art on the walls of its pain management center. After the artwork was put up, the whole atmosphere changed. Suddenly, patients were talking about the paintings. The art took their minds off their pain. In other hospitals, patients don't just look at art. They create it.

Diego Rivera

From the time he was a young child, it was clear that Diego Rivera had artistic talent. When he was twelve years old, Rivera began taking painting classes. By the time he was twenty, Rivera was an established painter. Rivera painted many public murals, often depicting common workers in a positive light. Sometimes his work expressed strong political feelings. In 1933 he created a mural for Rockefeller Center in New York City. He included a figure that looked like Lenin, who led the Russian revolution. Because of Lenin's inclusion, the mural was destroyed.

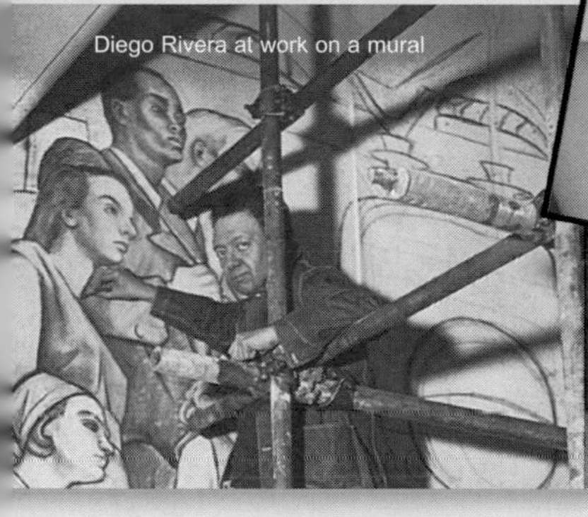

Diego Rivera at work on a mural

39

Answers for **Student Journal page 101** include *personal*—person, relating to one's private life; *famous*—fame, full of fame; *victorious*—victory, full of success; *traditional*—tradition, relating to customs; *outrageous*—outrage, full of scandalousness; and *original*—origin, relating to creation.

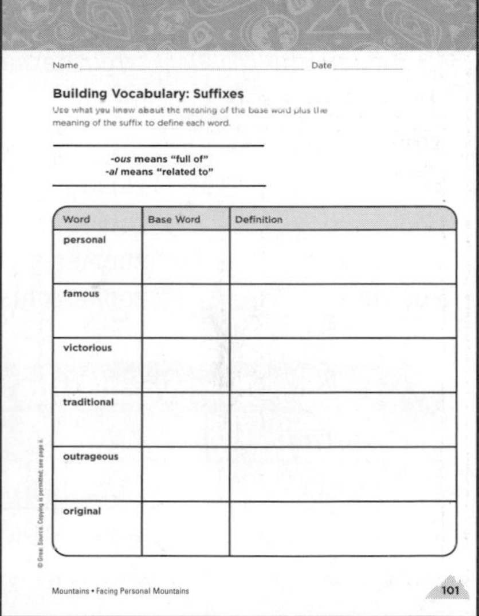

Name _______________ Date _______

Building Vocabulary: Suffixes

Use what you know about the meaning of the base word plus the meaning of the suffix to define each word.

***-ous* means "full of"**
***-al* means "related to"**

Word	Base Word	Definition
personal		
famous		
victorious		
traditional		
outrageous		
original		

Mountains • Facing Personal Mountains 101

Writing Problem-Solution

Explain to students that an author sometimes uses a problem-solution structure to organize information. Discuss with students the problems that the author describes in the lives of Maya Angelou and Frida Kahlo. Then discuss the solutions. Write ideas on the board or on a chart as students make responses. Then have students complete the problem-solution chart on *Student Journal* page 100.

Vocabulary Suffixes

Write *controversial* and *tumultuous* on the board. Underline the *-al* and *-ous* suffixes. For each word, ask volunteers to identify the base word and its meaning. (*controversy*—debate; *tumult*—uproar, confusion) Give the meanings the suffixes. (*-al*—relating to; *-ous*—full of) Ask volunteers to define each adjective. Then have students complete *Student Journal* page 101. (See Differentiated Instruction.)

Phonics/Word Study

Greek Roots

Display the following sentence and read it aloud: *To avoid hypothermia, put on some thermal underwear or turn up the thermostat.* Ask students which words contain the Greek root *therm*, meaning "heat." Ask students to define each word and how it relates to the root. Now, work with students to complete the in-depth Greek root activity on TE page 236.

Phonics/Word Study

More Greek Roots

For instruction to introduce a root, see TE page 192. Work with students to discover the meaning of each root. See *Word Study Manual* page 64 for a related word sort.

techn **(art, skill, craft)**

technical
technician
technically
technology
technological
high-tech
pyrotechnic
low-tech

therm **(heat)**

thermometer
thermal
thermoelectric
thermonuclear
thermostat
hypothermia

zoo **(animal)**

zoo
zoologist
zoolatry
zootomy
zoology
zoological
zoometry
zoomorphism

Discovering the Roots

techn	*therm*	*zoo*
technical	thermal	zoology
technician	thermometer	zoologist
pyrotechnic	thermonuclear	zoo
high-tech	hypothermia	zoological
technology	thermostat	zoomorphism

For more information on word sorts and spelling stages, see pages 5–31 in the *Word Study Manual.*

Focus on . . .

Use one or more activities in this section to focus on a particular area of need in your students.

Comprehension Strategy Support

To help those students who need more practice using the strategies covered in this lesson, work one-on-one or in small groups to apply the strategy prompts below. Apply the prompts to a *Reading Advantage* paperback, a classroom library book, or a new or familiar selection in the magazine. Always model your own thinking first.

Making Connections

- What does this story (article, passage) remind me of?
- What do I already know about this topic?
- Where have I heard about this topic before?
- What do I have in common with the characters, people, or situations in the text?
- What other books, stories, articles, movies, or TV shows does this text make me think about?

Understanding Text Structure

- What kind of text is this? (book, story, article, guidebook, play, manual)
- How does the author organize the text? (cause-effect, problem-solution, chronological order, description, question-answer, comparison-contrast)
- What details support my thoughts about the text structure?
- What is the cause (effect, problem, solution, order, question, answer)?
- If fiction, who are the characters? What is the setting, plot, conflict, and resolution?

Writing Autobiographical Sketch

Discuss with students the personal "mountains " they struggle to climb. Write down notes on the board or on chart paper. Then have students write a brief autobiographical sketch about obstacles they've overcome or are working to overcome. They can structure their sketch according to these three questions:

- What are the obstacles?
- What did you or are you doing to overcome them?
- What have you learned in the process?

Have students brainstorm ideas before beginning to write. To provide more practice with the brainstorming process, see lessons in *Writing Advantage,* pages 8–12.

Fluency: Pacing

After students have read the biographical sketch of Maya Angelou at least once, have partners read aloud the sketch to each other. Explain to students that in order for the information to be clearly understood, they must read at an even pace, not too quickly or too slowly.

As you listen to students read, use these prompts to guide them in reading at an even pace.

- Use punctuation clues, especially commas and periods, to tell you where to pause.
- Read conversationally, or the way you talk.
- To avoid stumbling over difficult words, practice reading them aloud to yourself first.

When students read aloud, do they—

- ✓ demonstrate a smooth pace, not too fast or too slow?
- ✓ incorporate well-timed pauses between words and phrases?
- ✓ reflect an awareness and understanding of punctuation?

English Language Learners

To support students' comprehension of "Facing Personal Mountains: Maya Angelou and Frida Kahlo," help students build background knowledge.

1. Tell students that they will be reading about women who overcame obstacles.
2. Write the word *obstacle* on chart paper. Discuss the meaning of the word as a group.
3. Have partners use the following prompts to share about overcoming obstacles in their own lives.

   What was the problem?

   How did you solve your problem?

Independent Activity Options

While you work with individuals or small groups, others can work independently on one or more of the following options.

- Level D paperback books, see TE pages 367–372
- Level D *eZines*
- Repeat word sorts from this lesson
- *Student Journal* pages for this lesson
- *Writing Advantage* independent lessons

Assessment

Strategy Assessment

To help you and your students assess their use of comprehension strategies, ask the following questions. Students can complete a written response or provide verbal answers in a one-on-one reading conference.

1. **Making Connections** As you read these two biographical sketches, what connections did you make? (Answers will vary. Students may name other writers, artists, or entertainers who overcame difficult childhoods to enjoy success.)
2. **Understanding Text Structure** Besides the chronological order of these biographies, what else did you notice about how they were organized? (Answers will vary. Students may note that the first half of each sketch outlined the problems of the individual, and the second half summarized how she overcame these problems.)

For ongoing informal assessment, use the checklists on pages 61–64 of *Level D Assessment*.

Word Study Assessment

Use these steps to help you and your students assess their understanding of the Greek roots.

1. Write *techn*, *therm*, and *zoo* on the board.
2. Then write the lists of words and meanings shown below.
3. Have students use the correct Greek root to complete each word. *(zoology, low-tech, thermometer, technician, thermal, zoolatry)*
4. Ask students to generate other words with these roots for the list.

Word	Meaning
_____ology	the study of animals
low-_____	not showing much skill or craft
_____ ometer	a device to measure heat
_____ ician	a person with a special skill
_____ al	having to do with heat
_____ latry	animal worship

LESSON **30**

Raising the *Monitor*

Mountains, pages 40–46

SUMMARY

This **radio interview** explores the problems encountered in locating and raising the Civil War–era ship the U.S.S. *Monitor*.

COMPREHENSION STRATEGIES

Monitor Understanding
Understanding Text Structure

WRITING

Journal Entry

VOCABULARY

Synonyms and Antonyms

PHONICS/WORD STUDY

Changes in Vowels:
Long to Schwa

Lesson Vocabulary

innovative relevant
imperative

MATERIALS

Mountains, pp. 40–46
Student Journal, pp. 102–105
Word Study Manual, p. 65
Writing Advantage, pp. 170–181

Raising the Monitor

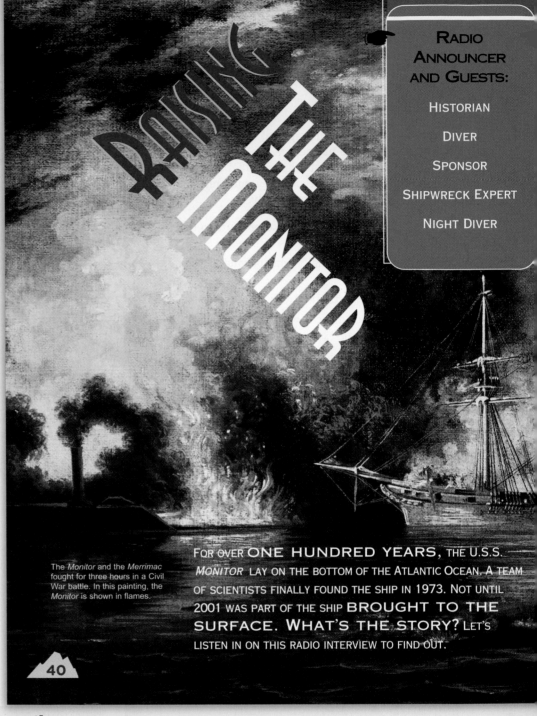

Radio Announcer and Guests:

Historian

Diver

Sponsor

Shipwreck Expert

Night Diver

The *Monitor* and the *Merrimac* fought for three hours in a Civil War battle. In this painting, the *Monitor* is shown in flames.

FOR OVER **ONE HUNDRED YEARS,** THE U.S.S. *MONITOR* LAY ON THE BOTTOM OF THE ATLANTIC OCEAN. A TEAM OF SCIENTISTS FINALLY FOUND THE SHIP IN 1973. NOT UNTIL 2001 WAS PART OF THE SHIP **BROUGHT TO THE SURFACE. WHAT'S THE STORY?** LET'S LISTEN IN ON THIS RADIO INTERVIEW TO FIND OUT.

40

Before Reading

Use one or more activities.

Make a K-W-L Chart

Create a K-W-L chart on the process of recovering shipwrecks. Then help students formulate questions about what they want to learn about recovering shipwrecks. Use the chart shown as a model.

Suggest that students read the interview to try to learn the answers to their questions. Have students return to the chart, after reading the selection, to record what they have learned. (See Differentiated Instruction.)

Locating and Recovering Shipwrecks

What We Know	What We Want to Learn	What We Learned
Divers use SCUBA gear and other special equipment. Some ships are too deep for divers, so small subs are used.	How are shipwrecks found? What dangers do divers face? Why do people look for shipwrecks?	

Vocabulary Preview

List the selection vocabulary on the board. Assess prior knowledge by asking students to begin the knowledge rating chart on *Student Journal* page 102. Students should fill in as many boxes as they can. They can complete the chart after they finish reading.

ANNOUNCER: On today's program, we will talk about the discovery and raising of the U.S.S. *Monitor.* Many people consider this Civil War ship to be the first modern warship. Let's ask a historian for a little background on the *Monitor.*

HISTORIAN: In its time, the *Monitor* was a new kind of ship. It had no masts or sails and was run entirely by steam. The ship was made of iron and heavy armor. An armor belt that was five feet high and six inches thick circled the ship at the waterline. One of the more innovative features of the ship was its spinning gun turret. This tower was near the middle of the ship and held two cannons.

ANNOUNCER: It sounds like a strong ship. If it was so well protected, why did it sink?

HISTORIAN: It didn't sink in battle. In fact, the *Monitor* fought in only one major battle. Less than a year after it set sail, it was lost at sea in a storm.

ANNOUNCER: But the *Monitor* impressed so many people that engineers modeled many more ships on its design. Let's turn now to a diver to get some information on how and when the ship was found.

DIVER: The *Monitor* remained underwater for more than a century. People searched for it but were uncertain of its exact location. Eventually, scientists from Duke University found it in 1973 by taking a "footprint" of the wreck. The footprint included information about the size and shape of the hull, the armor belt, the gun turret, and other features of the deck. Identifying the ship was difficult, because there were twenty-two other shipwrecks in the area. The scientists used the process of elimination—but there was one more complication: The *Monitor* was upside down. It took a year to be sure that the wreck off the North Carolina coast was the *Monitor.*

The *Monitor's* crew

The U.S.S. *Monitor*

41

DIFFERENTIATED INSTRUCTION

SMALL GROUP

MAKE A K-W-L CHART

To encourage a discussion about shipwrecks, ask students the following questions:

- Do you know of any shipwrecks or ships that have sunk? Have you heard of the *Titanic*? The *Andrea Doria*? The U.S.S. *Monitor*? The *Lusitania*?
- How do you think people explore shipwrecks?
- Why do you think people want to explore shipwrecks?

Student Journal page 102

Name ________________ Date ________

Building Vocabulary: Knowledge Rating Chart

Show what you know about each word by completing the other boxes in the row.

Word	Define or Use in a Sentence	Where Have I Seen or Heard It?	How Is it Used in the Selection?	Looks Like (Words or Sketch)
innovative				
imperative				
relevant				

102 Mountains • Raising the *Monitor*

Preview the Selection

Have students survey the seven pages of the radio interview. Use these prompts to help students notice the important features of this selection.

- What do you notice about the way this interview is organized?
- What does the format tell you about the way the information will be presented?
- Do you think the information is factual? Why do you think that?

Teacher Think Aloud

As I look over the "Raising the Monitor," I see that it's a little different from most interviews. The radio announcer here interviews at least four different people about their experiences raising the Civil War–era ship. Getting information from the perspectives of four different experts should give me a very full and interesting account of this unusual event.

Make Predictions/ Set Purpose

Students should use the information they gathered in previewing the selection to make predictions about what they will learn. If students have trouble generating a purpose for reading, suggest that they read to learn about the challenges of raising the Civil War–era ship called the *Monitor.*

DIFFERENTIATED INSTRUCTION

Comprehension

UNDERSTANDING TEXT STRUCTURE

Help students recognize the radio interview format by sharing these definitions and questions.

- An interview is a series of questions between two or more people. Who takes part in this interview? (interviewer, interviewees)
- A transcript is a written record of an interview. How does the transcript identify the speakers? (by their names)

HISTORIAN: Once the wreck was found, it was imperative to find a way to protect the wreckage sight from looters and troublemakers. The governor of North Carolina named the area a Marine Sanctuary, and then the U.S. Secretary of the Interior made the area a National Historic Place.

ANNOUNCER: What were the goals of the Navy's mission?

DIVER: The Navy made a plan for the dives: Phase 1—survey and prepare the site for dives; Phase 2—send divers to raise the ship's engine and the hull.

ANNOUNCER: I suppose removing the engine was difficult since the boat was upside down. We'll be back to talk more about the wreck after a word from our sponsor.

SPONSOR: Tired of spending your summer the same old way? Spend this summer at Marine Camp off the coast of Florida. Learn to snorkel and dive, identify fish, track currents, and steer a sailboat. Call 1-555-FUN-DIVE today!

ANNOUNCER: We're back to learn more about the wreck of the *Monitor.* Please welcome to our studio an expert on shipwrecks.

SHIPWRECK EXPERT: Thank you. The *Monitor* wasn't in great shape when it was found. Most of the hull had worn away, most of the frame was gone, and the engine room had been exposed to the ocean. Ocean currents passed right through the wreck, leaving a huge hole in the wooden deck, and much of the inside of the ship spilled out onto the seafloor.

ANNOUNCER: What could you do to slow down the deterioration while divers were working on raising the engine?

Diver investigating the *Monitor*

42

During Reading

Comprehension

MONITOR UNDERSTANDING

Use these prompts to model for students how to monitor their understanding. Then have students monitor their own understanding of the text.

- Does what I am reading make sense?
- Can I visualize what the *Monitor* looks like?
- Can I visualize what it would be like to explore a ship underwater?

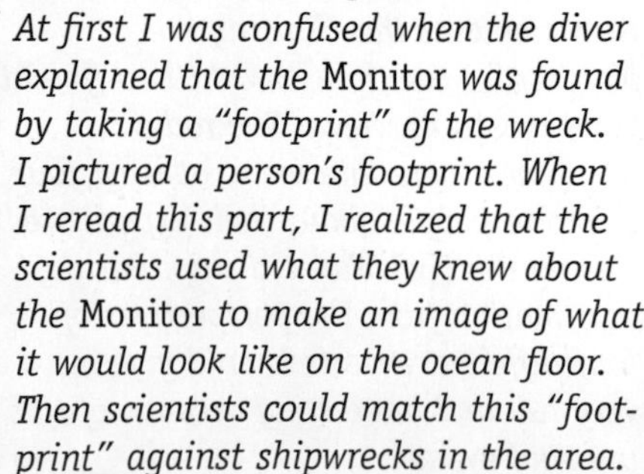

Teacher Think Aloud

At first I was confused when the diver explained that the Monitor *was found by taking a "footprint" of the wreck. I pictured a person's footprint. When I reread this part, I realized that the scientists used what they knew about the* Monitor *to make an image of what it would look like on the ocean floor. Then scientists could match this "foot-print" against shipwrecks in the area.*

Comprehension

UNDERSTANDING TEXT STRUCTURE

Use these prompts to model how to determine the question-answer or problem-solution text structure of the interview. Then have students tell how the text structure helps them understand the information.

- What features do I expect in an interview? What about a radio show?
- What patterns do I notice in the text?

(See Differentiated Instruction.)

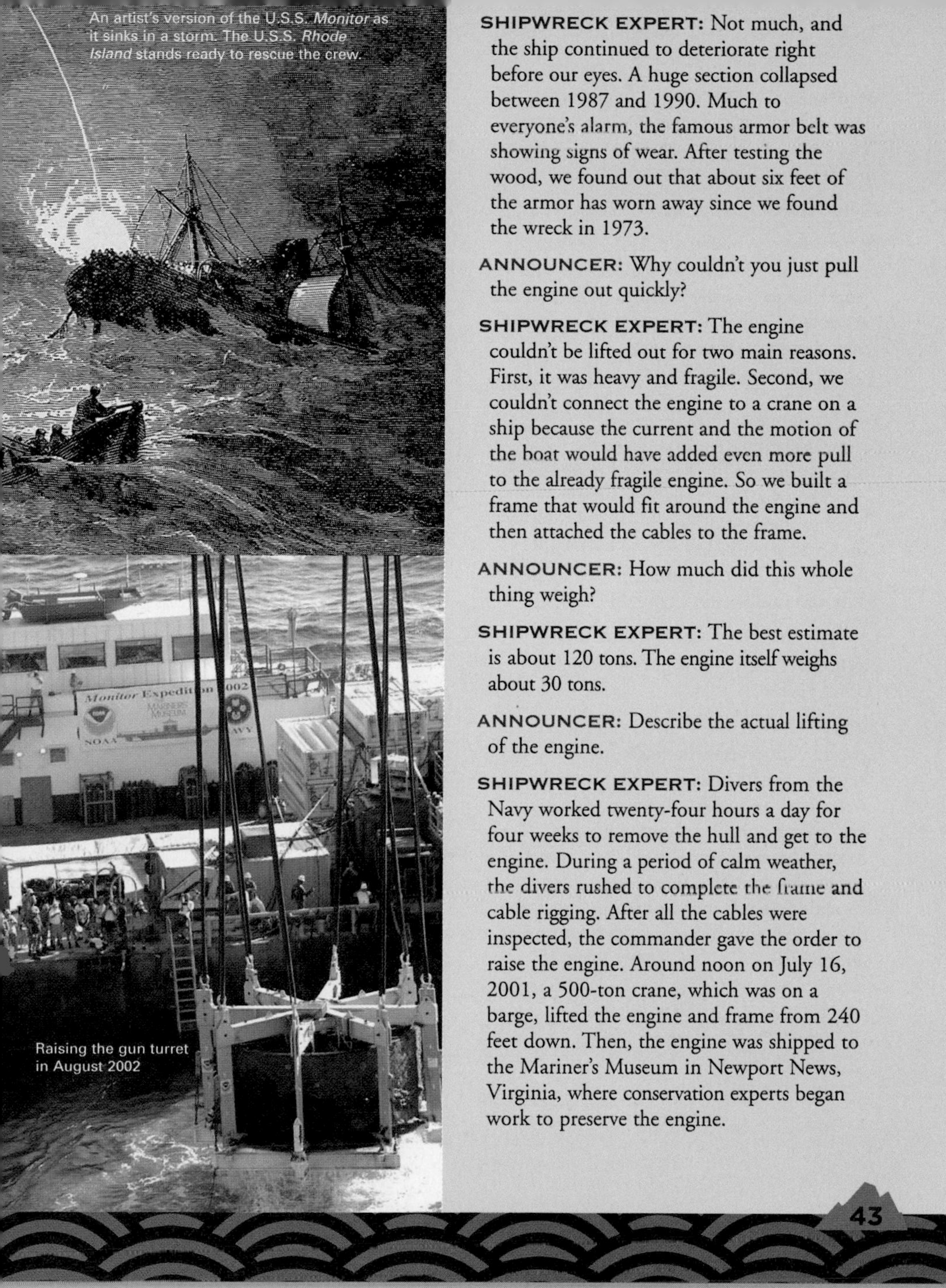
An artist's version of the U.S.S. *Monitor* as it sinks in a storm. The U.S.S. *Rhode Island* stands ready to rescue the crew.

Raising the gun turret in August 2002

SHIPWRECK EXPERT: Not much, and the ship continued to deteriorate right before our eyes. A huge section collapsed between 1987 and 1990. Much to everyone's alarm, the famous armor belt was showing signs of wear. After testing the wood, we found out that about six feet of the armor has worn away since we found the wreck in 1973.

ANNOUNCER: Why couldn't you just pull the engine out quickly?

SHIPWRECK EXPERT: The engine couldn't be lifted out for two main reasons. First, it was heavy and fragile. Second, we couldn't connect the engine to a crane on a ship because the current and the motion of the boat would have added even more pull to the already fragile engine. So we built a frame that would fit around the engine and then attached the cables to the frame.

ANNOUNCER: How much did this whole thing weigh?

SHIPWRECK EXPERT: The best estimate is about 120 tons. The engine itself weighs about 30 tons.

ANNOUNCER: Describe the actual lifting of the engine.

SHIPWRECK EXPERT: Divers from the Navy worked twenty-four hours a day for four weeks to remove the hull and get to the engine. During a period of calm weather, the divers rushed to complete the frame and cable rigging. After all the cables were inspected, the commander gave the order to raise the engine. Around noon on July 16, 2001, a 500-ton crane, which was on a barge, lifted the engine and frame from 240 feet down. Then, the engine was shipped to the Mariner's Museum in Newport News, Virginia, where conservation experts began work to preserve the engine.

43

Teacher Think Aloud

The introduction says that the Monitor *was found in 1973 but that its parts weren't recovered until 2001. Why did it take so long? As I read, I realized that this interview is organized in a problem-solution format. As soon as scientists and divers solved one problem, another arose. Recognizing this problem-solution format helped me better understand the information.*

Fix-Up Strategies

Offer these strategies to help students read independently.

If you don't understand what you're reading:

- Reread the difficult section to look for clues to help you comprehend.
- Read ahead to find clues to help you comprehend.
- Retell, or say in your own words, what you've read.
- Visualize, or form mental pictures of, what you've read.

If you don't understand a word:

- Reread the sentence. Look for ideas and words that provide meaning clues.
- Find clues by reading a few sentences before and after the confusing word.
- Look for the base or root word and think about its meaning.
- Think about the topic or plot at this point to see if either offers meaning clues.

DIFFERENTIATED INSTRUCTION SMALL GROUP

Writing Journal Entry

Try these steps:

1. Point out to students that journal entries include facts, as well as personal observances and opinions. As students take notes, encourage them to jot down ideas about how their character might have felt at that time.
2. Review the following characteristics of a journal entry before students begin to write: a date line, a first-person perspective, and an informal tone.
3. As students write, remind them to include both facts and personal observances in their journal entries.

Student Journal pages 103–104

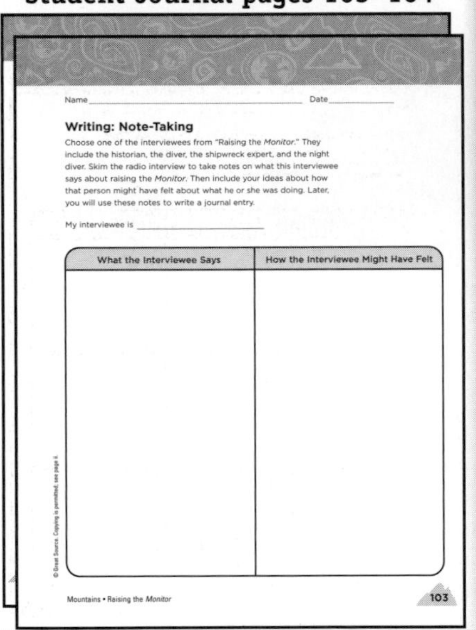
Name ________ Date ________

Writing: Note-Taking

Choose one of the interviewees from "Raising the *Monitor*." They include the historian, the diver, the shipwreck expert, and the night diver. Skim the radio interview to take notes on what this interviewee says about raising the *Monitor*. Then include your ideas about how that person might have felt about what he or she was doing. Later, you will use these notes to write a journal entry.

My interviewee is ________

What the Interviewee Says	How the Interviewee Might Have Felt

© Great Source. Copying is permitted; see page ii.

Mountains • Raising the Monitor 103

ANNOUNCER: Once the engine was raised, what was the next goal?

SHIPWRECK EXPERT: The most interesting feature of the *Monitor* was the gun turret, so we hoped to bring it up from the ocean floor.

ANNOUNCER: And were you successful?

SHIPWRECK EXPERT: Yes, a year after we raised the engine, we brought up the gun turret. As part of the mission, divers worked around the clock. That meant that some of the diving was done at night.

ANNOUNCER: What is it like to dive at night?

NIGHT DIVER: Diving at night is a completely different experience from day diving, even for highly trained divers. In the darkness, the *Monitor* looked different because the view of the wreck is limited to the small section that the light on your helmet illuminates. Sometimes the hardest part was finding the section of the wreck I was supposed to be working on.

ANNOUNCER: How did you stay safe down there?

NIGHT DIVER: New divers were always paired with divers who had a lot of experience with the wreck site. Before diving, we studied the models, drawings, videotapes, and photographs that other divers had recorded earlier. Sometimes, there was a person on deck directing a night diver by watching a small film from a camera in the diver's helmet and speaking to him through an earpiece.

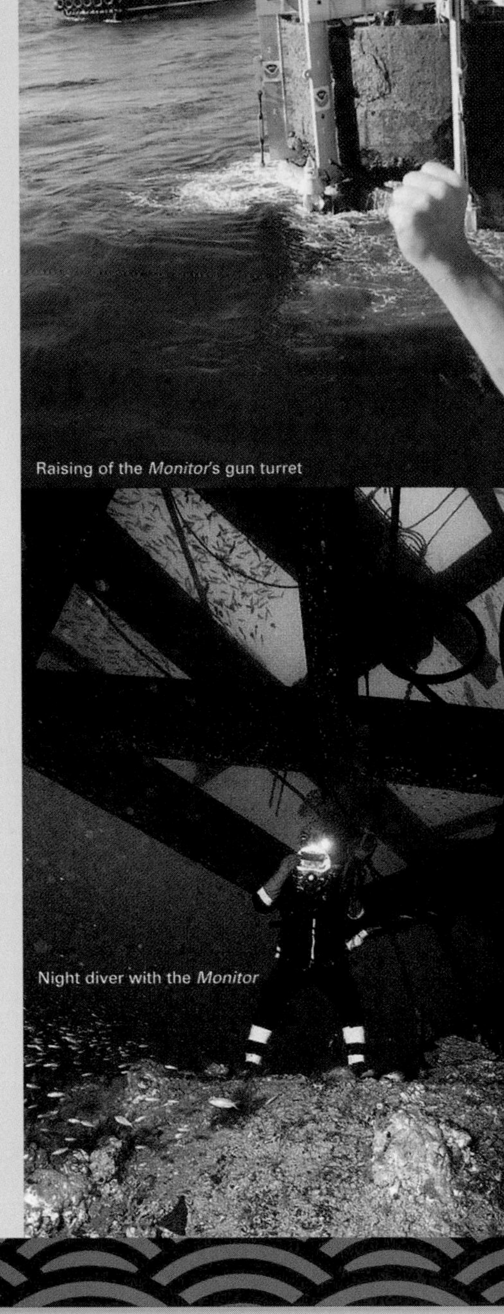
Raising of the *Monitor*'s gun turret

Night diver with the *Monitor*

44

After Reading

Use one or more activities.

Check Purpose

Have students decide if their purpose was met. Were students able to predict what the radio interview was about? Are they able to describe some of the challenges of raising the Monitor?

Discussion Questions

Continue the group discussion.

1. Recovery work on the *Monitor* is still taking place. What problems might scientists, engineers, and divers face in the future? (Inferential Thinking)
2. How important do you think it is to recover and preserve artifacts? (Making Connections)
3. How did the text format help you understand the challenges faced in recovering the *Monitor*? (Understanding Text Structure)

Revisit: K-W-L Chart

Revisit the K-W-L chart that students began in Before Reading. Were all students' questions answered? What new information can they add to the chart?

Revisit: Knowledge Rating Chart

Have students complete the knowledge rating chart on *Student Journal* page 102 and share what they wrote. Do students need to change any meanings?

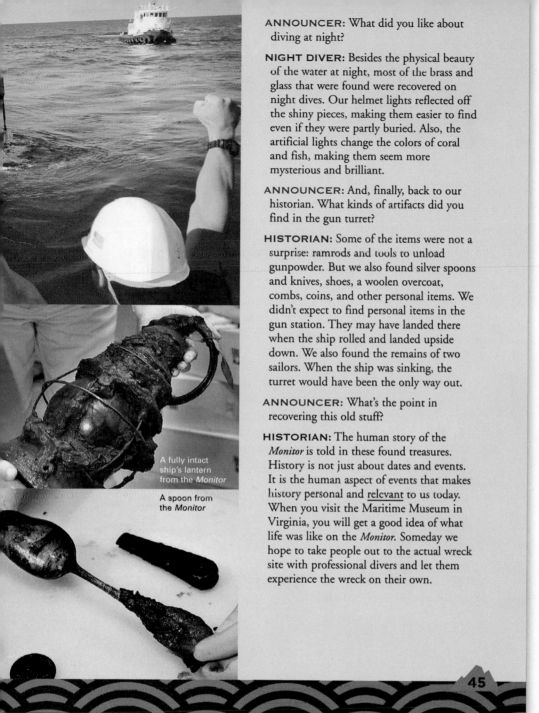

ANNOUNCER: What did you like about diving at night?

NIGHT DIVER: Besides the physical beauty of the water at night, most of the brass and glass that were found were recovered on night dives. Our helmet lights reflected off the shiny pieces, making them easier to find even if they were partly buried. Also, the artificial lights change the colors of coral and fish, making them seem more mysterious and brilliant.

ANNOUNCER: And, finally, back to our historian. What kinds of artifacts did you find in the gun turret?

HISTORIAN: Some of the items were not a surprise: ramrods and tools to unload gunpowder. But we also found silver spoons and knives, shoes, a woolen overcoat, combs, coins, and other personal items. We didn't expect to find personal items in the gun station. They may have landed there when the ship rolled and landed upside down. We also found the remains of two sailors. When the ship was sinking, the turret would have been the only way out.

ANNOUNCER: What's the point in recovering this old stuff?

HISTORIAN: The human story of the *Monitor* is told in these found treasures. History is not just about dates and events. It is the human aspect of events that makes history personal and relevant to us today. When you visit the Maritime Museum in Virginia, you will get a good idea of what life was like on the *Monitor*. Someday we hope to take people out to the actual wreck site with professional divers and let them experience the wreck on their own.

A fully intact ship's lantern from the *Monitor*

A spoon from the *Monitor*

45

Possible answers for **Student Journal page 105** include *imperative*—essential, urgent, necessary/unnecessary, not required, optional; *relevant*—connected, applicable, pertinent/unrelated, immaterial, irrelevant.

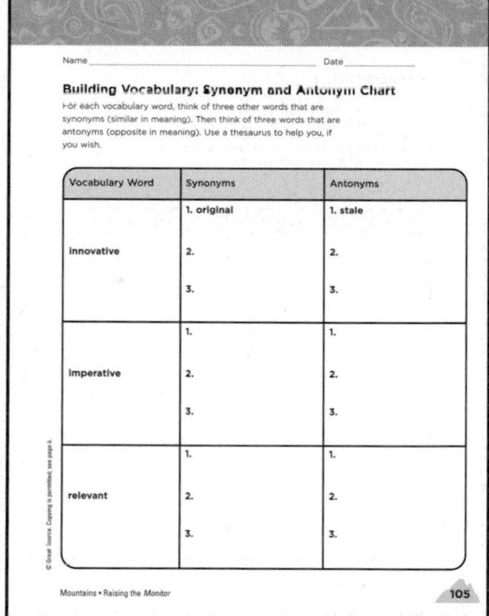

Name________ Date________

Building Vocabulary: Synonym and Antonym Chart

For each vocabulary word, think of three other words that are synonyms (similar in meaning). Then think of three words that are antonyms (opposite in meaning). Use a thesaurus to help you, if you wish.

Vocabulary Word	Synonyms	Antonyms
innovative	1. original 2. 3.	1. stale 2. 3.
imperative	1. 2. 3.	1. 2. 3.
relevant	1. 2. 3.	1. 2. 3.

Mountains • Raising the *Monitor* 105

Writing Journal Entry

Ask students to write a journal entry from the perspective of one of the interviewees, such as the diver or the shipwreck expert. Have students skim the radio interview and take notes on *Student Journal* page 103 about the work their character did to help raise the *Monitor*. Students should then use their notes to write their journal entries on *Student Journal* page 104. (See Differentiated Instruction.)

Vocabulary Synonyms and Antonyms

Display *innovative* and ask:

- What is the definition of *innovative*? (new and original)
- What other words come to mind when you hear or see *innovative*?

List the words students suggested and ask if any are synonyms for *innovative*. Then ask students to suggest antonyms. Now have students complete *Student Journal* page 105.

Phonics/Word Study Changes in Vowels

Display the following sentences. Ask students what they notice in the sound of the underlined vowels. *I can't explain his explanation. Did you compose this composition? You're invited without an invitation.* (The long vowel sound in *explain, compose,* and *invited* becomes a schwa sound when the suffix is added.) Now, work with students to complete the in-depth vowel change activity on TE page 245.

THE *MONITOR* AND THE *MERRIMACK*

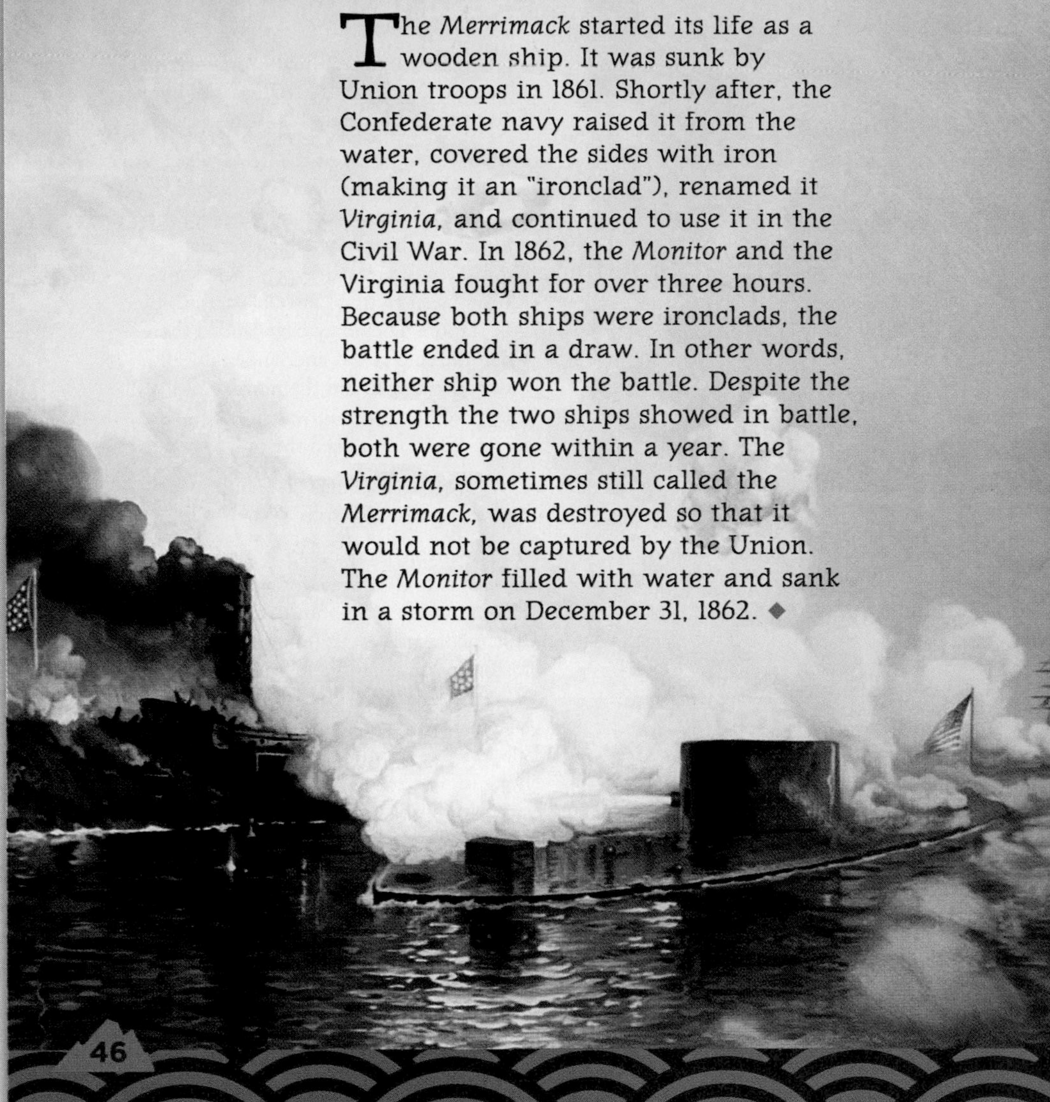

The *Merrimack* started its life as a wooden ship. It was sunk by Union troops in 1861. Shortly after, the Confederate navy raised it from the water, covered the sides with iron (making it an "ironclad"), renamed it *Virginia*, and continued to use it in the Civil War. In 1862, the *Monitor* and the Virginia fought for over three hours. Because both ships were ironclads, the battle ended in a draw. In other words, neither ship won the battle. Despite the strength the two ships showed in battle, both were gone within a year. The *Virginia*, sometimes still called the *Merrimack*, was destroyed so that it would not be captured by the Union. The *Monitor* filled with water and sank in a storm on December 31, 1862. ◆

Phonics/Word Study

Changes in Vowels: Long to Schwa

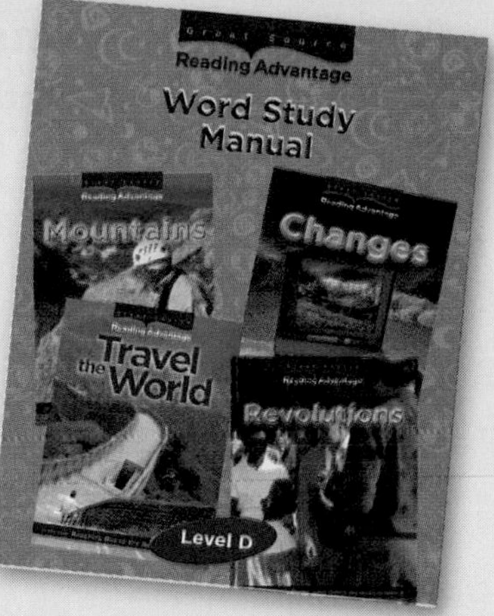

The words *compete* and *competition* are examples of how the vowel sound represented by *e* changes from the long *e* sound (*compete*) to the schwa sound (*competition*).

What is the schwa sound? The schwa sound can be represented by any short vowel letter. It generally is found in unstressed syllables. When the word is pronounced, the vowel sound in that unstressed syllable sounds as if it could be any short vowel sound. So how can students decide which vowel letter to write when they spell the word? The answer is in the base word. Think about *compete* and *competition*. The vowel letter in the second syllable of *compete*, the base word, is key. *Competition* is spelled with an *e* in the second syllable, too.

In preparation for a sort across all of the changes in vowels, follow these steps.

- Write *compete* and *competition* on the board and share the information above with students. Once they demonstrate understanding, write *suppose* and *supposition* on the board. Ask students to apply what they know about the vowel sound changes.
- Have students practice with the following similar word pairs.

explain	explanation	compose	composition
oppose	opposition	confide	confident
contrite	contrition	reside	resident
suppose	supposition	invite	invitation
repeat	repetition	erudite	erudition

See *Word Study Manual* page 65 for word list.

- A sort using all of the changes in vowels will follow at the end of Lesson 32.

For more information on word sorts and spelling stages, see pages 5–31 in the *Word Study Manual*.

Focus on . . .

Use one or more activities in this section to focus on a particular area of need in your students.

Comprehension STRATEGY SUPPORT

To help those students who need more practice using the strategies covered in this lesson, work one-on-one or in small groups to apply the strategy prompts below. Apply the prompts to a *Reading Advantage* paperback, a classroom library book, or a new or familiar selection in the magazine. Always model your own thinking first.

Monitor Understanding

- Do I understand what I'm reading? If not, what part is confusing to me?
- What fix-up strategies can I use to solve the problem? (See During Reading for fix-up strategies.)
- Why did a character say (do, think, ask) that?
- What images do I visualize from the text? What parts can't I visualize?
- Why did the author include (or not include) those details?

Understanding Text Structure

- What kind of text is this? (book, story, article, guidebook, play, manual)
- How does the author organize the text? (cause-effect, problem-solution, chronological order, description, question-answer, comparison-contrast)
- What details support my thoughts about the text structure?
- What is the cause (effect, problem, solution, order, question, answer)?
- If fiction, who are the characters? What is the setting, plot, conflict, and resolution?

Writing Interview

Ask students to rewrite the feature "The *Monitor* and the *Merrimack*" in interview format. Suggest that students have the announcer ask the "historian" about the history of the *Merrimack*, its battle with the *Monitor*, and its ultimate fate. Remind students that interview format should include speech tags and dialogue. When they are finished, have students read their interviews aloud to a partner.

To provide more practice and instruction on extracting information from text, see the lessons in *Writing Advantage*, pages 170–181.

Fluency: Expression

After students have read the selection at least once, they can focus on reading expressively by working in small groups to practice and then to present the interview. Before students begin, discuss how an interview is conversational in nature. The dialogue should be smooth, as if students were speaking instead of reading.

Use these prompts to help students read expressively:

- Read your lines several times so you are comfortable with them.
- Read with expression. Put yourself in the role of the announcer or specific expert.
- Use the punctuation marks for clues to expression. Raise your voice slightly at the end of a question. Pause when you see a comma or a period.
- Put energy into your voice as you read. It will make the interview more interesting and understandable.

When students read aloud, do they—

✓ reflect an understanding of the text?
✓ demonstrate appropriate timing, stress, and intonation?
✓ incorporate appropriate speed and phrasing?

English Language Learners

To support students as they develop fluency skills, read "Raising the Monitor" aloud together.

1. Model appropriate pacing, intonation, and expression as you read a section out loud.
2. Have students form groups of five. Have each group read the selection out loud together, each member of the group reading a different role in the radio interview.
3. Spend time listening to each group. Provide feedback and suggestions on how to improve intonation, pacing, etc.

Independent Activity Options

While you work with individuals or small groups, others can work independently on one or more of the following options.

- Level D paperback books, see TE pages 367–372
- Level D *eZines*
- Repeat word sorts from this lesson
- *Student Journal* pages for this lesson
- *Writing Advantage* independent lessons

Assessment

Strategy Assessment

To help you and your students assess their use of comprehension strategies, ask the following questions. Students can complete a written response or provide verbal answers in a one-on-one reading conference.

1. **Monitor Understanding** As you read the radio interview, what information did you visualize to better understand it? (Answers will vary. Students may say they visualized the *Monitor*'s footprint, the divers working underwater at night, or the cage that was built to contain the *Monitor*'s engine.)
2. **Understanding Text Structure** In addition to the typical question-answer format of an interview, what did you notice about how the text was organized? (Answers will vary, but students should point out that the text describes a series of problems associated with raising the *Monitor,* and their solutions.)

For ongoing informal assessment, use the checklists on pages 61–64 of *Level D Assessment*.

Word Study Assessment

Follow these steps to help you and your students assess their understanding of the change in long vowels to a schwa sound.

1. Have students say the five long vowel sounds as well as the schwa sound.
2. Write these word pairs on the board or on word cards: *depose/deposition; recite/recitation; declaim/declamation; deprive/deprivation.*
3. Have students say the words and identify the long vowel sound in the first word and the schwa sound in the second word of each pair.

depose	deposition
recite	recitation
declaim	declamation
deprive	deprivation

THE RIDGE

From the high ridge I look down
on the valley I grew up in.
It's as tiny as a train-set model,
perfect rows of houses,
parallel lines of streets.
I want it to be a puzzle—
the way I remember.

Around me: disorder
Flies buzz, ticks crawl, robins sing,
and a white-tailed deer darts over the hill.
Each animal flits off in its own direction,
not held in by roads, stoplights, or signs.
For a moment I think I will follow them
into the woods, but—
I want to know which way to go.

47

LESSON **31**

The Ridge *and* Rock Climbing

Mountains, pages 47–51

SUMMARY

The **poem** describes looking at a hometown from high on a ridge. The **first-person account** describes two friends' arduous rock climb.

COMPREHENSION STRATEGIES

Inferential Thinking
Monitor Understanding

WRITING

Notes for Visualizing

VOCABULARY

Synonyms

PHONICS/WORD STUDY

Changes in Vowels: Long to Short

Lesson Vocabulary

accomplishment crevice

MATERIALS

Mountains, pp. 47–51
Student Journal, pp. 106–108
Word Study Manual, p. 66
Writing Advantage, pp. 94–113

Before Reading

Use one or more activities.

Poem: The Ridge

Have students read the poem "The Ridge" on page 47. Discuss the meaning of the poem and student interpretations.

Begin a Web

Write "Why go rock climbing?" in the center of a word web. Write students' responses in the web. Suggest that students look for other reasons for going rock climbing as they read the selection. Add more ideas to the web after students read the selection.

Vocabulary Preview

Display the vocabulary. Have students complete *Student Journal* page 106.

Preview the Selection

Have students look through selection pages 48–51. Discuss what students notice.

Make Predictions/ Set Purpose

Students should use the information they gathered in previewing the selection to make predictions about what they will learn. If students have trouble generating a purpose for reading, suggest that they read to learn about the personal challenges of rock climbing.

DIFFERENTIATED INSTRUCTION

Comprehension

MONITOR UNDERSTANDING

Help students monitor their understanding by asking them to visualize these steps of the climb.

1. To begin their climb, Joe and Jim scramble up a crevice and the first pitch. How do you visualize these actions?
2. The climbers next face and climb a chimney. Can you picture this in your mind?
3. Joe and Jim belay up the next pitch. What do you see when you read about this?

Student Journal page 106

Name ______________________ Date __________

Building Vocabulary: Making Associations

Think about what you already know about each vocabulary word. Then answer the following questions for each word.

Word **accomplishment**

What do you think about when you read this word? ____________

Who might use this word? ____________

What do you already know about this word? ____________

Word **crevice**

What do you think about when you read this word? ____________

Who might use this word? ____________

What do you already know about this word? ____________

Now watch for these words in the selection. Were you on the right track?

Rock Climbing

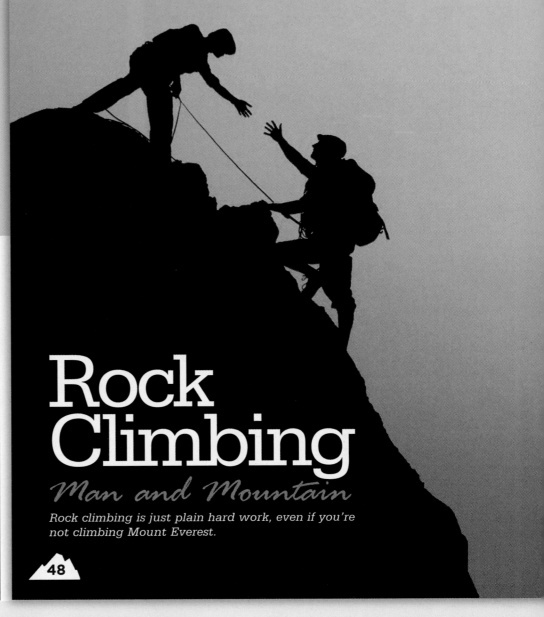

Man and Mountain

Rock climbing is just plain hard work, even if you're not climbing Mount Everest.

48

During Reading

Comprehension

INFERENTIAL THINKING

Use these prompts to model how to make inferences from the first paragraph. Then have students make inferences as they read another section.

- What does the text say about Joe's feelings about rock climbing?
- What do I already know about rock climbing?
- Using what I read and my experience, what inferences can I make?

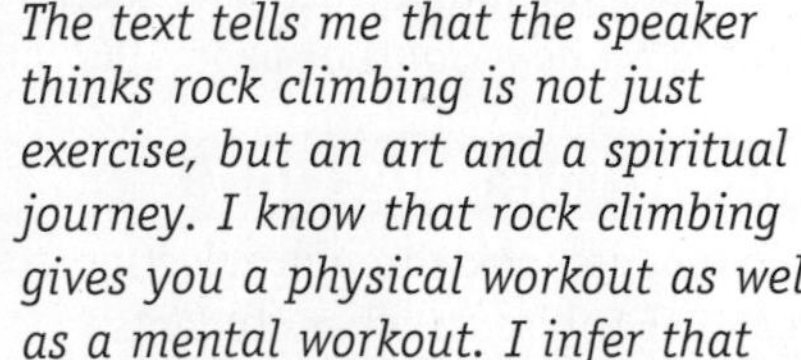

Teacher Think Aloud

The text tells me that the speaker thinks rock climbing is not just exercise, but an art and a spiritual journey. I know that rock climbing gives you a physical workout as well as a mental workout. I infer that the speaker must be a pretty healthy person doing activities that help both his body and his mind.

Comprehension

MONITOR UNDERSTANDING

Use these prompts to model how to monitor understanding of the text. Then have students monitor their own understanding.

- What can I visualize? Which parts are difficult to picture?
- Which parts are confusing? I'll mark them with a self-stick note and a question mark.

(See Differentiated Instruction.)

When I rock climb, I'm free. To me, rock climbing isn't just exercise; it's an art and a spiritual journey. I climb because I find satisfaction in the movement—it's almost like a dance. Also, I feel tremendous strength and a sense of accomplishment when I reach my goal.

Climbing has taught me that there is a difference between good fears and bad fears. Good fears keep you safe and make you double-check what you are doing, while bad fears stop you from doing something that really is safe.

My name is Joe, and I started rock climbing when I found out that I could do it. I'd walked by the "rock climbing wall" at my gym dozens of times before I even considered trying to climb. Then, one day I heard an instructor say that anyone who can walk up a few flights of stairs without having to rest could rock climb. I was worried that I didn't have enough upper body strength. After my first lesson, though, I learned that my legs would push me up the rocks, and my arms just balanced me.

Now, my friend Jim and I are fanatic climbers. Last Friday night we drove up to the Catskill Mountains for a Saturday morning hike starting at 5:30. As we started out, I thought we were making good time up the four-mile trail that followed a babbling creek. The gurgling sounds of the water calmed me. Before long, the sun was rising in the sky.

We were close to reaching the rock face, the "wall," we were going to climb. I was surprised by the steady incline we had to climb to get to the real climbing spot. We'd already broken a good sweat. Usually, we don't have to work so hard before "really" climbing. I was relieved that some other climbers had left their ropes, and Jim and I used them, even though they did not lead straight up to our route. We zigzagged up until we came to a level spot. Jim stumbled up behind me, and when I asked him how he was feeling, he answered by throwing up on my boots. I suggested that we remove our backpacks and sit down and rest for a while. Jim agreed.

When I asked him how he was feeling, he responded by throwing up on my boots.

We took a break and listened to the birds chattering and the wind whistling. After a while, I told Jim that I understood if he wanted to quit. But being a determined fellow, he shook his head *no* and slung his backpack over his shoulders.

From the level ground, we scrambled up a dirt crevice until we reached the base of our climb. The gap was dirty and slick. I checked my watch; we had about nine hours of daylight left. I was annoyed that we'd wasted all that time just getting to this spot, so I quickly climbed the first *pitch*. A pitch is about fifteen feet of climbing. This pitch wasn't too steep, so I didn't bother to put any gear in the rock to help me. I looked over my shoulder for Jim, and, although he looked ghostly, he shimmied up the pitch. Soon we were at the base of the *chimney*, a wide crack in the rock big enough to fit most of your body.

The chimney was a little scary to climb, and I was glad I was wearing kneepads. Getting out of the chimney and onto the next ledge was tough, so I fixed a rope to a tree and pulled myself up. I stopped to wipe the sweat out of my eyes and wait for Jim.

Teacher Think Aloud

When Joe said that he walked by a rock-climbing wall in his gym, I was confused. Aren't rocks and rock walls outside? Then I stopped for a moment to visualize what he was talking about: an artificial surface used to learn how to climb. Then I read on about the gym instructor who teaches indoor climbing, and this confirmed what I had visualized.

Fix-Up Strategies

Offer these strategies to help students read independently.

If you don't understand what you're reading:

- Reread the difficult section to look for clues to help you comprehend.
- Read ahead to find clues to help you comprehend.
- Retell, or say in your own words, what you've read.
- Visualize, or form mental pictures of, what you've read.

If you don't understand a word:

- Reread the sentence. Look for ideas and words that provide meaning clues.
- Find clues by reading a few sentences before and after the confusing word.
- Look for the base or root word and think about its meaning.
- Think about the topic or plot at this point to see if either offers meaning clues.

DIFFERENTIATED INSTRUCTION SMALL GROUP

DISCUSSION QUESTIONS

To support the discussion of Joe and Jim's friendship, provide the following steps:

1. Ask students what makes a good friendship. (Possible answers: consideration, support, sharing good times, understanding)
2. Then ask students if Joe and Jim are good friends. Have students support their answers. (Possible answer: They are good friends. They have a mutual goal, climbing rocks, and help each other attain it. They count on each other during steep ascents. They're considerate of each other. When Jim was sick, Joe told him to take it easy.

Student Journal page 107

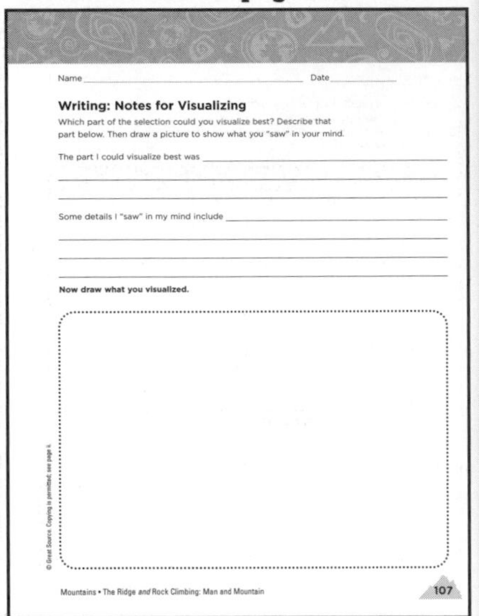

Name _____ Date _____

Writing: Notes for Visualizing

Which part of the selection could you visualize best? Describe that part below. Then draw a picture to show what you "saw" in your mind.

The part I could visualize best was _____

Some details I "saw" in my mind include _____

Now draw what you visualized.

© Great Source. Copying is permitted; see page ii.

Mountains • The Ridge *and* Rock Climbing: Man and Mountain 107

The next pitch was steep so I pulled out my climbing aids. We were going to have to *belay*, or assist each other. I secured my ropes through a harness and tied myself in it. I was the lead climber, so I went first and climbed to the ledge. Then I helped Jim up the slope.

We climbed the next section with protection—solid cams. *Camming devices*—also called cams or friends—are used mainly to protect the lead climber from falling. A cam has a trigger that allows it to widen to fit into different-sized cracks. I use cams so I can shift my weight onto them while I climb up a steep slope. I moved very slowly to make sure that the cams didn't pull out, and, finally, I reached the ledge.

When Jim caught up with me, we prepared our camp. First, we made sure that everything, including ourselves, was carefully clipped and secured so nothing would roll away at night. Since I'm bigger than Jim, I slept on a flat boulder while Jim squeezed in a slot between my boulder and the wall face. Then exhaustion hit.

I'd gone for so long without food or water that I felt dizzy, but I forced myself to eat, drink, and soak in the warm evening. I fell asleep watching the stars—even though the boulder was not a comfortable bed.

Waking at dawn, Jim and I both felt worn out, but we knew that we had to get climbing if we were going to have any chance of reaching the mountaintop. ◆

After Reading

WHOLE CLASS Use one or more activities.

Check Purpose

Have students decide if their purposes were met. Did they learn more about the personal challenges of rock climbing?

Discussion Questions

Continue the group discussion with the following questions. (See Differentiated Instruction.)

1. Would you like to go rock climbing? Why or why not? (Making Connections)
2. Do you think Joe and Jim are good friends to each other? What makes you say so? (Inferential Thinking)
3. Do you think the author has strong views about rock climbing? Explain. (Inferential Thinking)

Revisit: Web

Revisit the word web about reasons for rock climbing. Do students want to add any new ideas to the web?

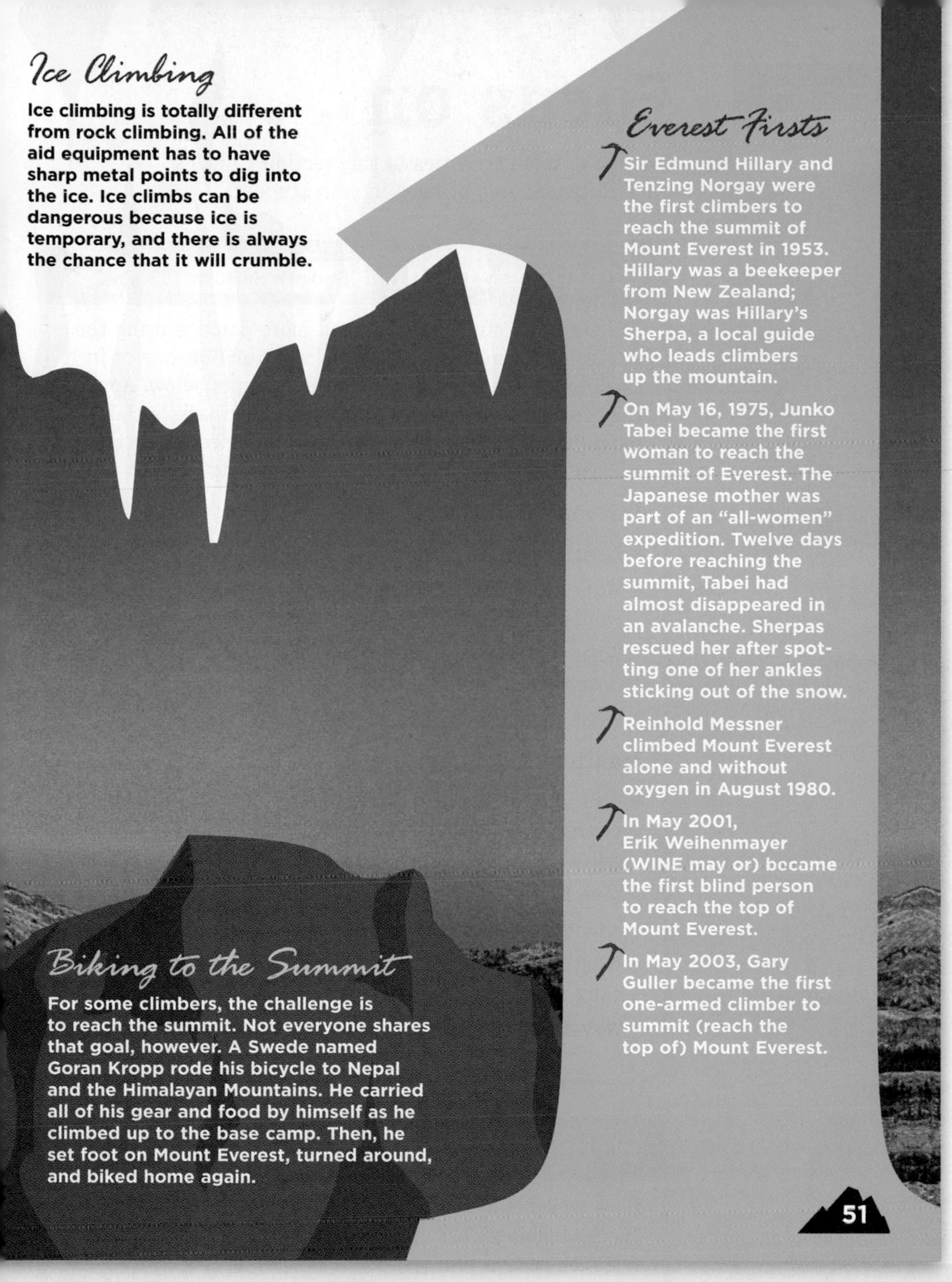

Ice Climbing

Ice climbing is totally different from rock climbing. All of the aid equipment has to have sharp metal points to dig into the ice. Ice climbs can be dangerous because ice is temporary, and there is always the chance that it will crumble.

Everest Firsts

- Sir Edmund Hillary and Tenzing Norgay were the first climbers to reach the summit of Mount Everest in 1953. Hillary was a beekeeper from New Zealand; Norgay was Hillary's Sherpa, a local guide who leads climbers up the mountain.
- On May 16, 1975, Junko Tabei became the first woman to reach the summit of Everest. The Japanese mother was part of an "all-women" expedition. Twelve days before reaching the summit, Tabei had almost disappeared in an avalanche. Sherpas rescued her after spotting one of her ankles sticking out of the snow.
- Reinhold Messner climbed Mount Everest alone and without oxygen in August 1980.
- In May 2001, Erik Weihenmayer (WINE may or) became the first blind person to reach the top of Mount Everest.
- In May 2003, Gary Guller became the first one-armed climber to summit (reach the top of) Mount Everest.

Biking to the Summit

For some climbers, the challenge is to reach the summit. Not everyone shares that goal, however. A Swede named Goran Kropp rode his bicycle to Nepal and the Himalayan Mountains. He carried all of his gear and food by himself as he climbed up to the base camp. Then, he set foot on Mount Everest, turned around, and biked home again.

51

Possible answers to **Student Journal page 108** include *steep*—inclined; *carefully*—cautiously, mindfully, attentively; *exhaustion*—fatigue, tiredness, weakening; *comfortable*—cozy, soothing, snug; *chance*—opportunity, possibility, occasion.

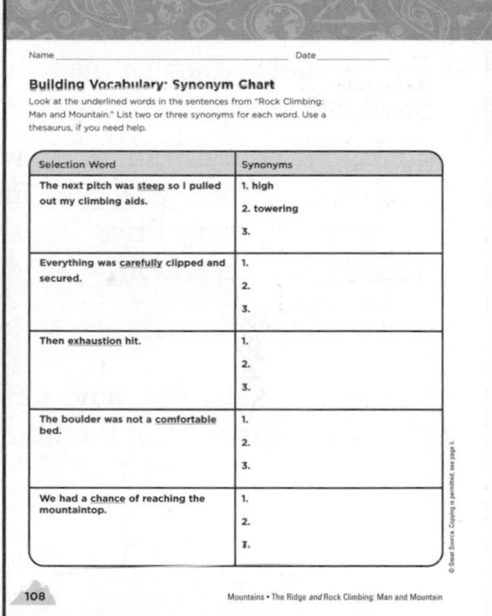

Name ______________________ Date __________

Building Vocabulary: Synonym Chart

Look at the underlined words in the sentences from "Rock Climbing: Man and Mountain." List two or three synonyms for each word. Use a thesaurus, if you need help.

Selection Word	Synonyms
The next pitch was steep so I pulled out my climbing aids.	1. high 2. towering 3.
Everything was carefully clipped and secured.	1. 2. 3.
Then exhaustion hit.	1. 2. 3.
The boulder was not a comfortable bed.	1. 2. 3.
We had a chance of reaching the mountaintop.	1. 2. 3.

© Great Source. Copying is permitted; see page ii.

108 Mountains • The Ridge *and* Rock Climbing: Man and Mountain

Writing

Notes for Visualizing

Remind students that active readers visualize, or try to "see" what an author tells about. Have students complete the notes for the visualizing activity on *Student Journal* page 107, to verbalize what they "saw" most clearly in the selection. Then have students draw what they "saw" to share with others.

Vocabulary Synonyms

Draw students' attention to the sentence with the word *crevice* and the sentence after it on page 49. Ask students to find the synonym, or word similar in meaning, for *crevice*. (*gap*) Ask students for another synonym for *crevice*. (*crack*) Then ask students to name synonyms for *level* (*flat, smooth, even*), *base* (*bottom*), and *dirty* (*unclean, filthy*). Finally, have students complete *Student Journal* page 108.

Phonics/Word Study

Changes in Vowels

Display the following sentence: *The wise monk shared his wisdom.* Ask students to identify the related words in the sentence and describe the vowel sounds they hear in these words. Ask: *How is the* i *in* wise *different from the* i *in* wisdom*?* Now, work with students to complete the in-depth vowel changes activity on TE page 252.

Phonics/Word Study

Changes in Vowels: Long to Short

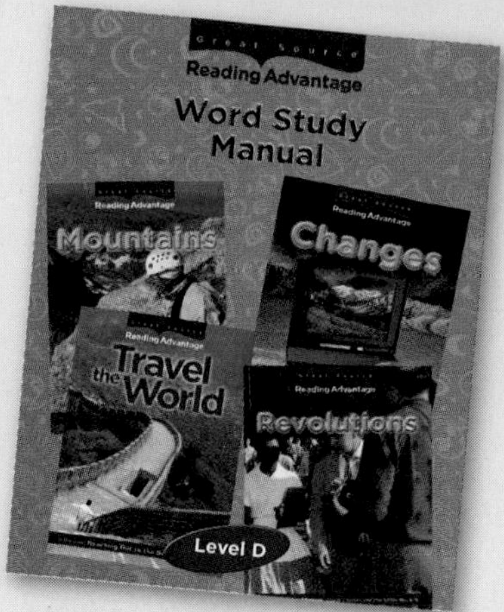

In some related words, the vowel sound changes from a long one to a short one. *Crime* and *criminal* are examples. The long *i* vowel sound in *crime* changes to the short *i* vowel sound in the first syllable of *criminal.*

In preparation for a sort across all of the changes in vowels, follow these steps.

- Write the words *crime* and *criminal* on the board. Share the information above with students. Once they demonstrate understanding of the vowel sound change, write *nation* and *national* on the board. Have students explain the vowel change in their own words.
- Have students examine the following similar word pairs.

contrite	contrition	wise	wisdom
sublime	subliminal	insane	insanity
compete	competitive	sign	signal
repeat	repetition	divine	divinity

(See *Word Study Manual* page 66 for a word list.)

For more information on word sorts and spelling stages, see pages 5–31 in the *Word Study Manual.*

Focus on . . .

Use one or more activities in this section to focus on a particular area of need in your students.

Comprehension STRATEGY SUPPORT

To help those students who need more practice using the strategies covered in this lesson, work one-on-one or in small groups to apply the strategy prompts below. Apply the prompts to a *Reading Advantage* paperback, a classroom library book, or a new or familiar selection in the magazine. Always model your own thinking first.

Inferential Thinking

- What are the causes or effects of this event?
- What do I learn from the character or person's thoughts, words, or actions?
- What do I know (or infer) from the text that the author hasn't stated directly?
- What conclusions can I draw?

Monitor Understanding

- Do I understand what I'm reading? If not, what part is confusing to me?
- What fix-up strategies can I use to solve the problem? (See During Reading for fix-up strategies.)
- Why did a character say (do, think, ask) that?
- What images do I visualize from the text? What parts can't I visualize?
- Why did the author include (or not include) those details?

Writing Double-entry Journal

Have students make double-entry journal notes about "Rock Climbing." Ask students to look back through the selection to find phrases, passages, and ideas that they felt were especially interesting. Explain to students that, in the first column, they should write down these interesting quotations. Then, in the second column, they should write their thoughts and feelings about the quotations. Students can interpret, disagree with, or make an association with each quotation.

Set a two-column chart with the following heads:

Quotations	My Thoughts and Feelings

To help students reveal their opinions or respond to literature through a book review, see lessons in *Writing Advantage,* pages 94–113.

Fluency: Punctuation

After students have read the poem "The Ridge" at least once, have partners read it silently and then aloud. Tell students to read the poem at an even pace—not too fast and not too slowly. Suggest that they adjust their pace, however, to punctuation cues. Ask students to identify the punctuation marks in the poem that indicate a pause (commas, periods, a colon, and dashes).

As students read aloud, use these prompts.

- Look for punctuation marks to help you adjust your pace. Remember that a colon and a dash are less of a pause than a period but more of a pause than a comma.
- Reread until you can read the text at the appropriate pace without effort. With practice, you won't stumble over words or have to slow down.

When students read aloud, do they—

- ✓ demonstrate appropriate meaning and usage of punctuation marks?
- ✓ incorporate appropriate timing, stress, and intonation?
- ✓ exhibit well-timed pauses between words and phrases?

English Language Learners

To support students as they improve their fluency, discuss words containing silent consonants in "Rock Climbing: Man and Mountain." Write *climb*, *whistle*, and *straight* on chart paper. Write words with similar spelling patterns (*bomb*, *hustle*, *light*) beneath each word.

1. Discuss the meanings and model proper pronunciations of these words.
2. Have partners create sentences using the words.
3. Have partners share their sentences with the group.

Independent Activity Options

While you work with individuals or small groups, others can work independently on one or more of the following options.

- Level D paperback books, see TE pages 367–372
- Level D *eZines*
- Repeat word sorts from this lesson
- *Student Journal* pages for this lesson
- *Writing Advantage* independent lessons

Assessment

Strategy Assessment

To help you and your students assess their use of comprehension strategies, ask the following questions. Students can complete a written response or provide verbal answers in a one-on-one reading conference.

1. **Inferential Thinking** After reading this article, what inferences can you make about rock climbing? (Answers will vary. Students may say that because the speaker talked about sweating, and that hard physical activity is known to make a person sweat, they may infer that rock climbing is tough work. Be sure students mention a specific text detail and related personal knowledge or experience to support their inference.)
2. **Monitor Understanding** As you read the article, what did you do to monitor your comprehension? (Answers will vary. Students may mention that they visualized the features of the mountain, such as the pitch, chimney, and crevice, or the special equipment the climbers used.)

For ongoing informal assessment, use the checklists on pages 61–64 of *Level D Assessment*.

Word Study Assessment

Use these steps to help you and your students assess their understanding of changes in long vowels to short vowels.

1. Create a chart like the one below.
2. Ask students to read each pair of words on a line and think about the change in vowel sound that occurs from Word 1 to Word 2.
3. Ask students to use the third column to describe the vowel sound change they hear.

Word 1	Word 2	
contrite	contrition	long *i* to short *i*
insane	insanity	long *a* to short *a*
repeat	repetition	long *e* to short *e*
divine	divinity	long *i* to short *i*

LESSON **32**
Fitting In
Mountains, pages 52–57

SUMMARY
This **play** is about a new student named Maria and how she tries to fit in with her peers at school.

COMPREHENSION STRATEGIES
Making Connections
Monitor Understanding

WRITING
Play Scene

VOCABULARY
Idioms

PHONICS/WORD STUDY
Changes in Vowels: Short to Schwa

Lesson Vocabulary
idiomatic heritage

MATERIALS
Mountains, pp. 52–57
Student Journal, pp. 109–111
Word Study Manual, pp. 67–68
Writing Advantage, pp. 114–151

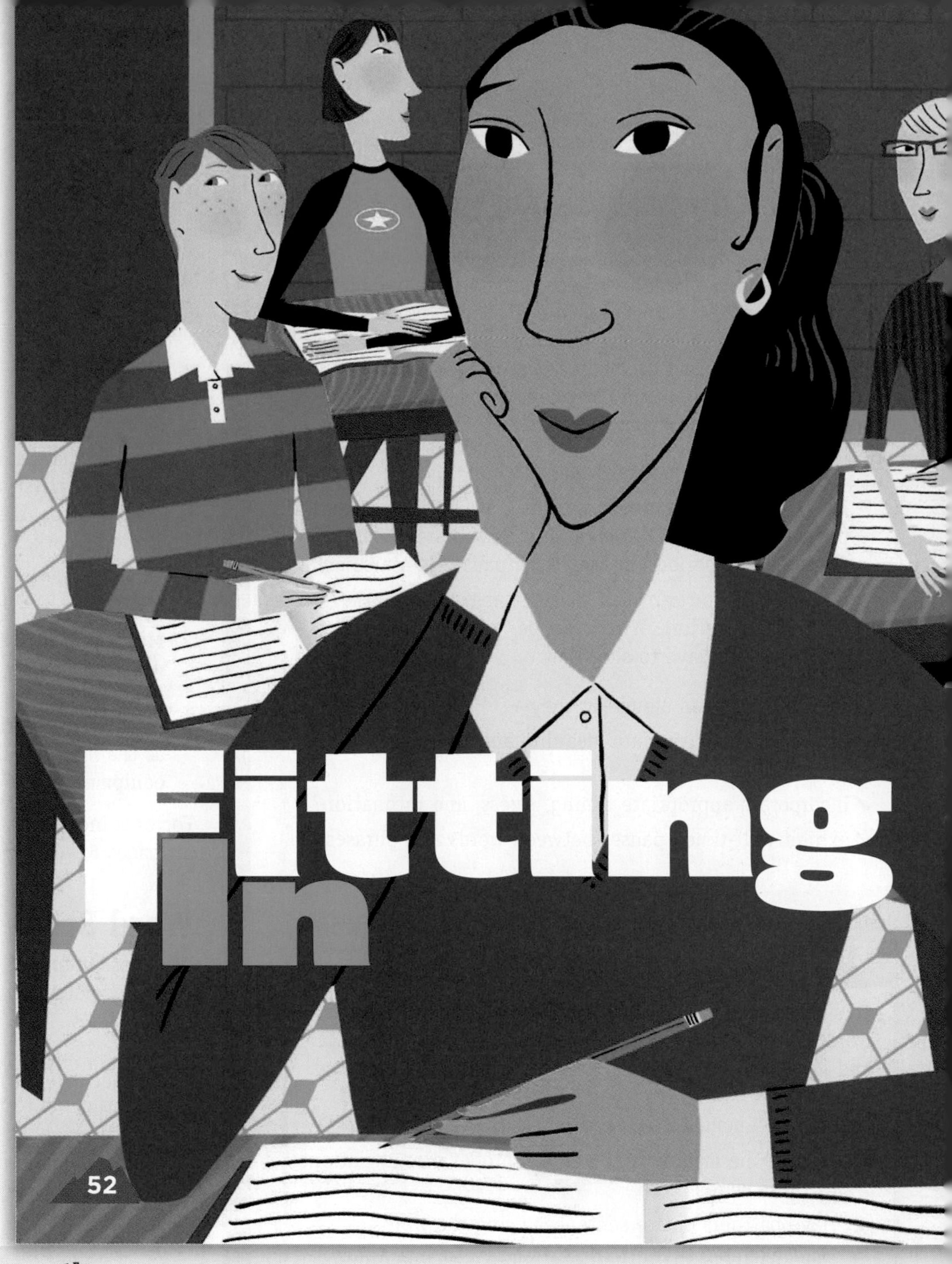

Before Reading

WHOLE CLASS Use one or more activities.

Make a Rating Scale

Display the phrase *fitting in*. Ask students what the phrase means to them. Then tell students they will rate the extent to which they think they "fit in" with their peers. Show the following scale.

1	2	3	4
seldom	sometimes	usually	always

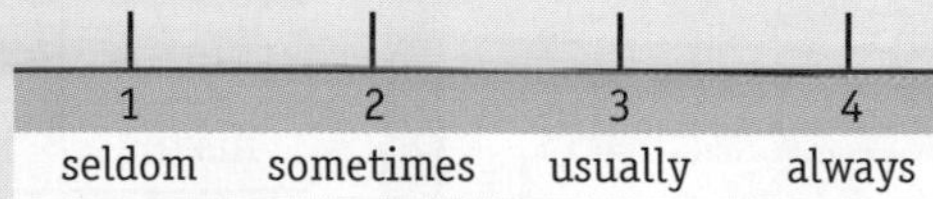

On a slip of paper, have students anonymously choose their rating number. After each slip is folded, collect them and tally the responses for each rating. Report and discuss the results.

Vocabulary Preview

List the selection vocabulary on an overhead transparency or on the board. Then have students complete the making associations chart on *Student Journal* page 109. Model the process of making associations with the word *heritage*.

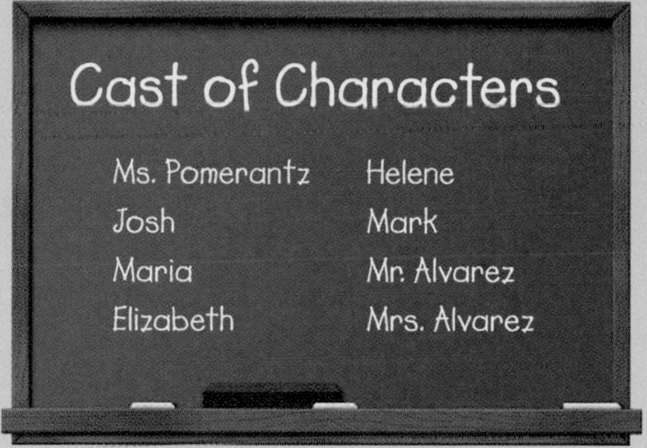

Cast of Characters
Ms. Pomerantz
Josh
Maria
Elizabeth
Helene
Mark
Mr. Alvarez
Mrs. Alvarez

SCENE I

Ms. Pomerantz's homeroom at the beginning of the school day. As the students enter the room, they notice Maria, a new girl sitting alone at the front of the room.

Ms. Pomerantz: Everyone, come in. Find your seats and sit down. I'd like to introduce you all to a new student. Please meet Maria Alvarez, who just moved here from Mexico. Maria is still learning English, so please speak slowly and clearly to her.

Josh: *Buenas días*, Maria!

Maria: *(laughing) Buenas días*!

Ms. Pomerantz: Thanks, Josh, for that nice icebreaker. *(Ms. Pomerantz turns to Maria.)* Maria, you can always count on Josh to begin a conversation. He's never at a loss for words.

Maria: *(looking puzzled)* Icebreaker? Loss for words? What do you mean?

Ms. Pomerantz: An icebreaker is something that you say to ease the tension in an uncomfortable situation.

53

DIFFERENTIATED INSTRUCTION (SMALL GROUP)

Preview the Selection

To help students understand the characteristics of a play, use the following steps:

1. List these play features: cast of characters, dialogue, and scenes.
2. Explain each feature. The cast of a play refers to the different characters. The dialogue is what each character says. The scenes are the different sections of the play, similar to chapters in books.
3. Have students talk about plays they have seen performed or read. Discuss how readers can learn about characters, setting, and plot through dialogue.

Student Journal page 109

Name ____________ Date ________

Building Vocabulary: Making Associations

Think about what you already know about each vocabulary word. Then answer the questions for each word.

Word idiomatic

What do you think about when you read this word? ____________

Who might use this word? ____________

What do you already know about this word? ____________

Word heritage

What do you think about when you read this word? ____________

Who might use this word? ____________

What do you already know about this word? ____________

Now watch for these words in the selection. Were you on the right track?

Mountains • Fitting In 109

Preview the Selection

Have students look through the six pages of the play, pages 52–57 in the magazine. Use these or similar prompts to orient students to the selection.

- In what form is the selection written?
- What information does the cast of characters give you?
- What are the two settings for the action?

(See Differentiated Instruction.)

Teacher Think Aloud

This play is called Fitting In, *and the pictures with it show that the setting is a classroom in a school. I'm interested to find out why it is in* Mountains *magazine. Sometimes "climbing a mountain" is a metaphor, or comparison, for doing something difficult. Maybe one of the characters in the play will have a hard time fitting in at school.*

Make Predictions/ Set Purpose

Students should use the information they gathered in previewing the selection to make predictions about what they will learn. If students have trouble generating a purpose for reading, suggest that they read to find out why Maria thinks she will have a hard time fitting in with her peers.

DIFFERENTIATED INSTRUCTION

Comprehension

MAKING CONNECTIONS

Help students make connections with the text by asking these questions:

- If you were new in school, how would you try to make friends?
- How might you make a newcomer to your class feel welcome and comfortable?
- Do you think a member of the class or the newcomer should make the first move toward starting a friendship? Why?

As students read, ask them to look for connections between their discussion and what happens in the play.

When I said that Josh is never at a loss for words, I meant that he always has something to say. For example, when I want to discuss a book that we are reading, I can always count on Josh to say something interesting.

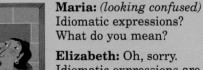

Elizabeth: Ms. Pomerantz, may I take Maria on a tour of the school?

Ms. Pomerantz: I think that's a great idea, Elizabeth, but not right now. Maybe you could do that during your lunch period. We need to take attendance and listen to morning announcements now.

SCENE II

In the cafeteria at lunchtime

Elizabeth: Hey, Maria. Do you want to sit with me?

Maria: Thank you, Elizabeth. That is so kind of you.

Elizabeth: Maria, this is my friend Helene. We always eat lunch together.

Maria: So kind to meet you.

Helene: *(laughing)* You mean "So *nice* to meet you."

Maria: *(feeling embarrassed)* So sorry. I'm not so good at my English.

Elizabeth: No, no. You're doing fine. English is really hard. There are so many exceptions to the rules and strange idiomatic expressions.

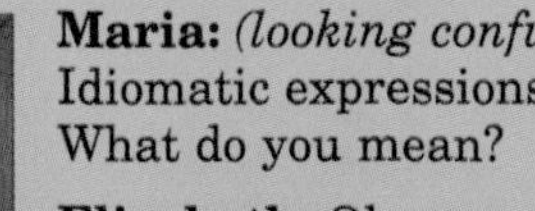

Maria: *(looking confused)* Idiomatic expressions? What do you mean?

Elizabeth: Oh, sorry. Idiomatic expressions are phrases that you can't really understand unless you know what they mean. For example, if you say that you "put your foot in your mouth," it doesn't mean that you really picked up your foot and stuck it in your mouth. Instead, it means that you said something embarrassing.

Maria: Okay, I think I understand.

Helene: I think it must be really hard to learn English. Hey, what are you eating, Maria? That looks really good.

Maria: I'm eating corn tamales.

Mark: *(peering over Maria's shoulder from the next table)* Ugh, gross!

Elizabeth: Go away, Mark! *(whispering to Maria)* He's such a dweeb.

Maria: A dweeb? What's that?

Elizabeth: Oh, a dweeb is someone who doesn't know how to act around other people. Take Mark. He's really smart, but when it comes to people skills, Mark doesn't seem to really have any.

Maria: *(laughing)* Okay, I get it. My cousin Pedro is a dweeb, too. He's very smart, but he doesn't know how to talk to people, except for teachers and other grown-ups.

During Reading

Comprehension

MAKING CONNECTIONS

Use these questions to model how to make connections with the text. Then have students make their own connections with the text.

- Do the characters and setting remind me of my classmates and classroom?
- Are the characters' words and actions believable?
- Have I ever had trouble fitting in?

(See Differentiated Instruction.)

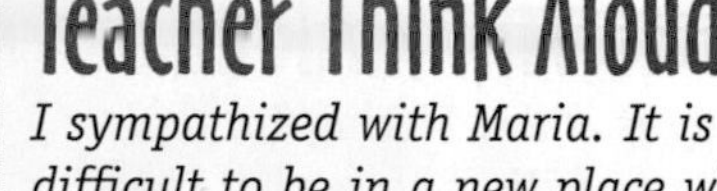

Teacher Think Aloud

I sympathized with Maria. It is difficult to be in a new place where you don't speak the language very well. When I was in France on vacation, I had a hard time. Even though I knew how to speak some French, I never fully understood what people were saying. And they all spoke so fast!

Comprehension

MONITOR UNDERSTANDING

Use these questions to model how to monitor understanding. Then have students monitor their understanding of the play.

- Can I keep track of which characters are speaking when?
- Can I distinguish the characters' lines from the stage directions that tell how the characters should speak and act?

SCENE III

Dinnertime at Maria's house

Mrs. Alvarez: So, Maria, how was your first day at your new school?

Maria: It was okay, but I don't think I will ever understand all their strange expressions. Most of the kids seem nice, but they all talk so fast. There's this one girl, Elizabeth, who was very nice to me. But I am so different from these American kids. I don't think I'll ever fit in.

Mr. Alvarez: Maria, you don't have to fit in. Remember your heritage. You are different, and that's okay. You have to learn that it's all right not to look and act the same as all the kids at school. They will respect you once they understand that you are Mexican and proud of it.

Maria: Daddy, you don't understand. I don't want to be different from the other kids. Today I was eating tamales for lunch, and this boy Mark made fun of me. I don't want to be teased because I eat different food.

Mr. Alvarez: Maria, you must not turn away from our culture. You must be proud to be Mexican.

Maria: *(getting angry)* I *am* proud to be Mexican, but I also want to fit in. You just don't get it! *(stomps away from dinner table)*

55

Teacher Think Aloud

I think the words in parentheses are the stage directions because they describe what the characters are doing, not what they're saying out loud. For example, in scene one, a stage direction for Maria says "looking puzzled." Her lines that follow are questions, so it would make sense for Maria to deliver the lines with a puzzled, or confused, look on her face.

Fix-Up Strategies

Offer these strategies to help students read independently.

If you don't understand what you're reading:

- Reread the difficult section to look for clues to help you comprehend.
- Read ahead to find clues to help you comprehend.
- Retell, or say in your own words, what you've read.
- Visualize, or form mental pictures of, what you've read.

If you don't understand a word:

- Reread the sentence. Look for ideas and words that provide meaning clues.
- Find clues by reading a few sentences before and after the confusing word.
- Look for the base or root word and think about its meaning.
- Think about the topic or plot at this point to see if either offers meaning clues.

DIFFERENTIATED INSTRUCTION 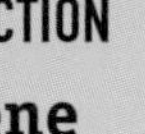

Writing Play Scene

To help students imagine what characters might say in the next scene, use these steps:

1. Have students think about how Maria's peers act. Ask students to identify two characteristics that describe Josh, Elizabeth, Helene, and Mark. As students discuss the characteristics, list their suggestions in a chart.
2. Have students suggest what the main characters might say in the scene. On the board or on chart paper, write the ideas for dialogue beside each corresponding cast member.

Student Journal page 110

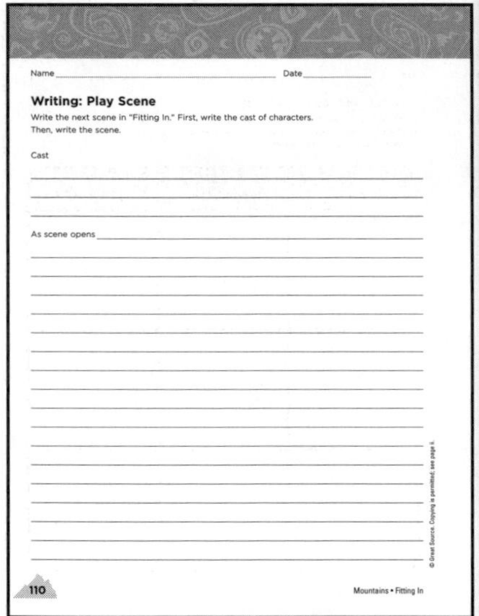

Name ________________ Date ________

Writing: Play Scene

Write the next scene in "Fitting In." First, write the cast of characters. Then, write the scene.

Cast ________________

As scene opens ________________

110 Mountains • Fitting In

Scene IV

In Maria's room, later that night

Mrs. Alvarez: May I come in?

Maria: Yes, Mama. Come in.

Mrs. Alvarez: Maria, I just want you to know that I understand how hard it is for you at school. I know it's important for you to fit in with the other kids. I want to help you feel comfortable here. I remember being thirteen years old and feeling like I was different from other kids because my parents always made me wear old-fashioned Mexican dresses until I was fifteen. Imagine how I must have felt!

Maria: I know, Mama. It must have been hard for you, too. I just want to blend in and understand what the kids are saying. I feel like it's going to take forever to know all of their strange expressions.

Mrs. Alvarez: You're a smart girl, Maria. You'll catch on quickly. Listen, I was thinking that this weekend, you and I could go shopping for some new clothes.

Maria: *(beaming)* Oh, thank you, Mama. My old clothes are so different from what all the girls here are wearing. I'd love to go shopping!

Scene V

At school the next morning, in homeroom

Elizabeth: Hi, Maria.

Maria: Hi, Elizabeth.

Josh: *Buenas días*, Elizabeth! So, I was wondering. Does your mom make tacos all the time? I really love tacos.

Maria: Well, not *all* the time, but sometimes. She is a really good cook.

Josh: Maybe one day you could bring in some Mexican food.

Maria: *(with hesitation in her voice)* Yes, maybe.

Elizabeth: Don't worry about it, Maria. If you want to bring in some Mexican food to share, that would be cool. But don't make Josh talk you into it.

Maria: Okay, I'll think about it. Maybe it would be fun.

Ms. Pomerantz: Excuse me. May I have everyone's attention, please? This morning we're going to change the schedule around. Instead of going by a B-day schedule, today will be an A-day. Check your schedules and make sure you know where you're going. Your first and third period classes will each be an hour long, and you'll only have one elective. Any questions?

After Reading  Use one or more activities.

Check Purpose

Have students decide if their purpose was met. Did students find out why Maria thinks she will have a hard time fitting in with her peers?

Discussion Questions

Continue the group discussion with the following questions.

1. Why do you think Elizabeth is so kind and helpful to Maria? (Inferential Thinking)
2. How does Mr. Alvarez's viewpoint differ from Maria's and her mother's? (Compare-Contrast)
3. If you were Maria, would you be as anxious to fit in? Why or why not? (Making Connections)

Revisit: Associations Chart

Have students revisit the making associations activity on *Student Journal* page 109. Are students' associations close to the actual meanings of the words? Would students like to revise their answers?

Mark: Cool, we have an extra long math class today. I am so psyched!

Maria: *(whispering to Elizabeth)* What does *psyched* mean?

Elizabeth: Mark is really happy, because he loves math. You say that you're psyched about something when you're really excited about it.

Maria: Thanks for being my interpreter, Elizabeth. I feel like every day here is like climbing a mountain. I never know what might happen to block my way or confuse me.

Elizabeth: Don't worry. I feel like that, too, sometimes, and I've lived here my whole life! ◆

57

DIFFERENTIATED INSTRUCTION

Vocabulary Idioms

Explain to students that idiomatic expressions are phrases that a person might not understand unless he or she knows its meaning.

1. With students, brainstorm a list of idiomatic expressions, such as the ones below.
2. Talk about what each one means.

List of Popular Idioms		
catch his eye	save face	lift her spirits
foot the bill	head over heels	raise some eyebrows
out in left field	skeleton in the closet	have cold feet
threw in the towel	hitting the books	pulled a fast one

Student Journal page 111

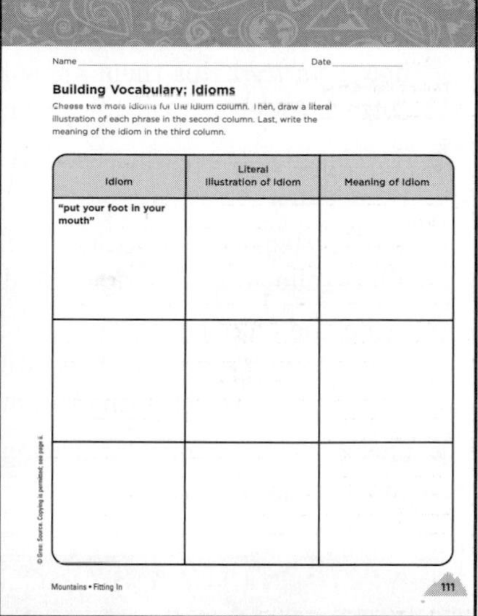

Name ______________________ Date __________

Building Vocabulary: Idioms

Choose two more idioms for the idiom column. Then, draw a literal illustration of each phrase in the second column. Last, write the meaning of the idiom in the third column.

Idiom	Literal Illustration of Idiom	Meaning of Idiom
"put your foot in your mouth"		

© Great Source. Copying is permitted; see page ii.

Mountains • Fitting In 111

Writing Play Scene

Have partners write the next scene of *Fitting In*. Before they write, engage students in a brief discussion about how Maria's classmates might react if she brings Mexican food to class the next day. Remind students to continue the same text format, paying close attention to the dialogue between characters. Have students write the next scene on *Student Journal* page 110. (See Differentiated Instruction.)

Vocabulary Idioms

Point out to students that *put your foot in your mouth* is an idiomatic expression that means "to say something that is embarrassing." Ask students what other idioms they know. Then have students complete the idiom chart on *Student Journal* page 111. (See Differentiated Instruction.)

Phonics/Word Study

Changes in Vowels

Display the words *legal* and *legality*. Ask students what they notice about the sound of the vowel *a* in each word. (It has a schwa sound in *legal,* but a short *a* sound in *legality*.) Next, display the words *addict* and *addiction* and elicit that *addict* begins with a short *a,* whereas *addiction* begins with a schwa sound. Now, work with students to complete the in-depth vowel changes activity on TE page 260.

Phonics/Word Study

Changes in Vowels: Short to Schwa

When students are trying to determine the vowel in any number of difficult polysyllabic words, encourage them to look at other forms of the words. For example, look at the word *personal*. The *-al* at the end of the word contains the schwa sound. This makes it difficult to decide which vowel is correct there. If students think of other forms of the word they are trying to spell, they may have some success in finding the right vowel. In the case of *personal*, the word *personality* helps. Listen to the difference between *personal* and *personality* as you say it aloud. In *personality*, the syllable containing the letters *-al* sounds like the short *a* that it is. It changes to schwa in *personal*. This is true for other words, as well. (See *Word Study Manual* page 67.)

In preparation for a sort across all of the changes in vowels, follow these steps.

- Share the example of *personal* and *personality*, providing the information given above.
- Then write the words *polar* and *polarity* on the board. Ask students to explain in their own words how *polarity* helps them know how to choose the correct vowel to spell the second syllable of *polar*.
- Have students examine the following similar word pairs.

  legality/legal adapt/adaptation
  allege/allegation rigid/rigidity

- Using the Changes in Vowels Sort sheet on *Word Study Manual* page 68, have students cut up their words and sort according to how the vowel changes.
- Check the final sorts by sharing the columns together as a class.

Changes in Vowels Sort

Long-to-Schwa impose/imposition	Long-to-Short divine/divinity	Short-to-Schwa locality/local
compete/competition	nation/national	fatality/ fatal
suppose/supposition	volcano/volcanic	hospitality/hospital
pose/position	cave/cavity	hypocrisy/hypocrite
	recite/recitation	metallic/metal
	parasite/parasitic	prohibit/prohibition
	apply/application	
	classify/ classification	

For more information on word sorts and spelling stages, see pages 5–31 in the *Word Study Manual*.

Focus on . . .

Use one or more activities in this section to focus on a particular area of need in your students.

Comprehension STRATEGY SUPPORT

To help those students who need more practice using the strategies covered in this lesson, work one-on-one or in small groups to apply the strategy prompts below. Apply the prompts to a *Reading Advantage* paperback, a classroom library book, or a new or familiar selection in the magazine. Always model your own thinking first.

Making Connections

- What does this story (article, passage) remind me of?
- What do I already know about this topic?
- Where have I heard about this topic before?
- What do I have in common with the characters, people, or situations in the text?
- What other books, stories, articles, movies, or TV shows does this text make me think about?

Monitor Understanding

- Do I understand what I'm reading? If not, what part is confusing to me?
- What fix-up strategies can I use to solve the problem? (See During Reading for fix-up strategies.)
- Why did a character say (do, think, ask) that?
- What images do I visualize from the text? What parts can't I visualize?
- Why did the author include (or not include) those details?

Writing Jokes Using Idioms

Have students use idioms to write jokes or riddles. Explain that "having cold feet" means "to be afraid to do something." The phrase can be made into a joke by making the punch line about someone who might really have cold feet. For example, *Why didn't the snowman ask the girl for a date? He had cold feet!* Brainstorm a list of common idioms and what each joke might be about.

Idiom	Joke Topic
getting into someone's hair	a clumsy barber
walking on air	a skydiver in love
monkeying around with something	a curious monkey on the loose

To help students add descriptive language to their writing, see lessons in *Writing Advantage*, pages 114–151.

Fluency: Expression

After students have read the selection at least once, have students form groups to expressively read scenes from the play.

As you listen to students read, use these prompts to guide them.

- Preview what you will read. Notice the different punctuation marks and what these signal to you. Let your voice rise at the end of sentences marked with a question mark. Put excitement in your voice when exclamation marks are present.
- Put yourself in the situation of the character. How would a frustrated teenager sound? How would a caring friend sound? Read with expression.
- Watch for cues in parentheses and stage directions that tell you how to say your lines.

When students read aloud, do they—

✓ reflect an understanding of the text?
✓ demonstrate appropriate timing, stress, and intonation?
✓ incorporate appropriate speed and phrasing?

English Language Learners

To support students' understanding of idioms, extend the activity on page 111 of the *Student Journal*.

1. Review the idioms presented in the lesson.
2. Provide students with examples of other common idioms. Discuss their meanings together.
3. Have partners use the idioms to complete a chart similar to the one on *Student Journal* page 111.

Encourage students to continually add to their charts as they encounter other idioms in their reading.

Independent Activity Options

While you work with individuals or small groups, others can work independently on one or more of the following options.

- Level D paperback books, see TE pages 367–372
- Level D *eZines*
- Repeat word sorts from this lesson
- *Student Journal* pages for this lesson
- *Writing Advantage* independent lessons

Assessment

Strategy Assessment

To help you and your students assess their use of comprehension strategies, ask the following questions. Students can complete a written response or provide verbal answers in a one-on-one reading conference.

1. **Making Connections** What connections can you make with any of the relationships, conflicts, feelings, or dialogue in this play? (Answers will vary. Students may make a connection with Maria's feelings of anger toward her father when she thinks he doesn't understand how she feels. Students may identify with being upset with parents because they think their parents just don't *get* it.)
2. **Monitor Understanding** How did you resolve any confusion as you read the play? What fix-up strategies did you use? (Answers will vary. Students may say that they were confused at first by the words in parentheses. But then they reread some parts and realized that the phrases were stage directions.)

For ongoing informal assessment, use the checklists on pages 61–64 of *Level D Assessment*.

Word Study Assessment

Use these steps to help you and your students assess their understanding of short to schwa vowel changes.

1. Write on the board the following pairs of words: *fatal, fatality; idol, idolatry; adapt, adaptation; insular, insularity*.
2. Have students pronounce the words in each pair and identify the vowel that goes from having a short vowel to a schwa, or vice versa.
3. Have students tell how these changes might be helpful when thinking about how to spell a word.

Word 1	Vowel Sound	Word 2	Vowel Sound
fatal	schwa	fatality	short
idol	schwa	idolatry	short
adapt	schwa	adaptation	short
insular	schwa	insularity	short

LESSON 33

Chained to a Mountain

Mountains, pages 58–62

SUMMARY

This is a retelling of the **myth** of Prometheus, who is said to have given fire to humankind.

COMPREHENSION STRATEGIES

Understanding Text Structure

WRITING

Summarize

VOCABULARY

Context Clues

PHONICS/WORD STUDY

Silent-Sounded Consonants

Lesson Vocabulary

cunning	putrid
confer	fumed
decreed	deceptive

MATERIALS

Mountains, pp. 58–62
Student Journal, pp. 112–114
Word Study Manual, p. 69
Writing Advantage, pp. 30–57

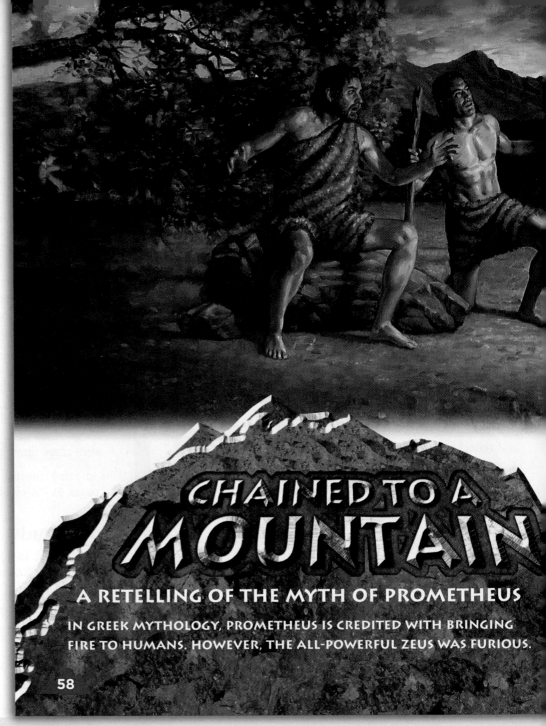

CHAINED TO A MOUNTAIN

A RETELLING OF THE MYTH OF PROMETHEUS

IN GREEK MYTHOLOGY, PROMETHEUS IS CREDITED WITH BRINGING FIRE TO HUMANS. HOWEVER, THE ALL-POWERFUL ZEUS WAS FURIOUS.

58

Before Reading

Use one or more activities.

Make a Concept Web

On the board or on chart paper, write the word *fire* in the center oval of a concept web. Ask students to talk about the importance of fire to humankind. (heat, cooking, light) Add their ideas to the web. End by asking students to suggest how prehistoric peoples might have learned about fire. (by observing natural phenomena: lightning, the sun, volcanoes, sparks from hitting two rocks together)

Vocabulary Preview

Display the selection vocabulary. Have students begin *Student Journal* page 112. They will return to the page after reading.

Preview the Selection

Have students look through "Chained to a Mountain" and tell what they notice. (See Differentiated Instruction.)

Make Predictions/Set Purpose

Students should use the information they gathered in previewing the selection to make predictions about what they will learn. If students have trouble generating a purpose for reading, suggest that they read to find out why Zeus punished Prometheus so harshly.

According to Greek mythology, Zeus sent two brothers, Prometheus and Epimetheus, to earth. He ordered them to create mankind and animals and to give each a gift, a unique quality. Prometheus formed men in the image of the gods of Olympus. He shaped man out of mud, and the goddess Athena breathed life into man's clay body.

Epimetheus created animals and gave them gifts such as cunning and slyness, swiftness, strength, fur, and wings. The two brothers finally finished their work, but Prometheus had not yet given man a gift. When he went to confer with his brother about the gift, his brother admitted that he had used up all of the gifts, and there was nothing left to give to man.

Prometheus knew that man must have a gift, for he loved mankind more than he loved the Olympians. After much thought, he decided to give man the gift of fire, even though he knew that fire was meant only for the gods. Prometheus waited for Apollo, the sun god, to ride across the morning sky. When the sun's chariot passed, Prometheus lit a torch of fire and brought it to earth. He taught man how to use fire, and then Prometheus left earth.

DIFFERENTIATED INSTRUCTION SMALL GROUP

Preview the Selection

To support students' preview of the selection, follow these steps:

1. Introduce the characters Prometheus and Epimetheus by reading aloud the feature "The Titans" on page 62. Have students read along silently.
2. Introduce the Greek gods who are characters in the myth. Tell students that Zeus was the ruler of the twelve gods of Mount Olympus (home to the gods), Athena was the goddess of wisdom, and Apollo was the sun god and one of the sons of Zeus.

Student Journal page 112

Name ____________ Date ________

Building Vocabulary: Knowledge Rating Chart

Show your knowledge of each word by adding information to the other boxes in the row.

Word	Define or Use in a Sentence	Where Have I Seen or Heard It?	How Is it Used in the Selection?	Looks Like (Words or Sketch)
cunning				
fumed				
confer				
decreed				
putrid				
deceptive				

112 Mountains • Chained to a Mountain

During Reading

Comprehension SMALL GROUP

UNDERSTANDING TEXT STRUCTURE

Use these questions to model for students how to identify and understand the text structure of a myth. Then have students tell how the text structure helps them understand this myth.

- What are this myth's story elements?
- Who are the main characters, and what are their conflicts?
- How are the conflicts resolved?
- What theme does the myth teach?

Teacher Think Aloud

One way to appreciate myths is to think about their story elements. Myths have plots, characters, settings, and themes, just like other stories. The characters and the conflicts, or problems, they face are always important in myths. I also need to be aware of the theme, or underlying message, that the myth expresses.

Fix-Up Strategies

Offer these strategies to help students read independently.

If you don't understand what you're reading:

- Reread the difficult section to look for clues to help you comprehend.
- Read ahead to find clues to help you comprehend.
- Retell, or say in your own words, what you've read.
- Visualize, or form mental pictures of, what you've read.

Student Journal page 113

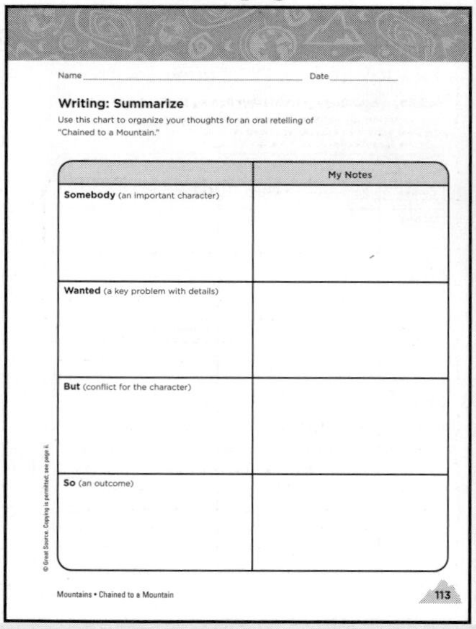

Name_______________ Date_______

Writing: Summarize

Use this chart to organize your thoughts for an oral retelling of "Chained to a Mountain."

	My Notes
Somebody (an important character)	
Wanted (a key problem with details)	
But (conflict for the character)	
So (an outcome)	

Mountains • Chained to a Mountain 113

Origins of Fire

Cultures around the world have different myths explaining the origin of fire:

- According to Hawaiian legend, Pele, the goddess of fire, lived in the volcano Kilauea on Hawaii. Her jealous rages were believed to cause the volcano's eruptions.
- According to Apache legend, fire was discovered when a fox outwitted a village of fireflies and scattered fire around the earth.
- African folklore states that the god Tore possessed fire, and his mother, Matu, guarded the fire. Doru, a magician, attached feathers to his shoulders and swooped down and stole the fire from Matu. Doru then distributed fire to the people.

Zeus was furious when he heard what Prometheus had done. Zeus decreed that when man killed an animal, he must sacrifice part of the animal to the gods. Prometheus didn't think this command was fair and decided to trick Zeus. He gathered together two different piles. In one pile, Prometheus put the edible, good parts of an ox but disguised the meat in putrid manure. In the other pile, he placed the ox bones and covered them in sweet-smelling fat. Prometheus showed the two piles to Zeus and asked him to choose one. Zeus chose the sweet-smelling pile but grew furious when he discovered that it was only a pile of bones. From that time on, only fat and bones were sacrificed to the gods, and man kept the meat for himself.

Zeus accepted that he had been tricked, but he would not give up. As punishment, he took fire away from mankind. However, Prometheus went to the sun, lit another torch, and brought it to man again. Zeus fumed and burned with anger, but he thought of another way to punish man and Prometheus.

60

After Reading

Use one or more activities.

Check Purpose

Have students decide if their purpose was met. Did they find out why Zeus chained Prometheus to a mountain?

Discussion Questions

Continue the group discussion with the following questions.

1. What things did Prometheus do to anger Zeus? (Details)
2. What was the result of Pandora's disobeying Zeus? (Cause-Effect)
3. Which part of the myth did you find the most exciting? Why? (Making Connections)

Revisit: Knowledge Rating Chart

Have students return to the knowledge rating chart on *Student Journal* page 112. Encourage them to review their initial notes and make any adjustments as needed.

To punish man, Zeus had one of the gods create a beautiful mortal. Each of the gods gave this mortal a gift: wealth; beauty; and the gifts of a deceptive, dishonest heart and a lying tongue. She was the first woman, and her name was Pandora. Zeus gave Pandora one last gift, a box, and ordered her never to open it. Zeus then presented Pandora to Epimetheus as a bride. Prometheus warned his brother not to accept any gifts from Zeus, but Pandora was so beautiful that Epimetheus couldn't resist.

Pandora and Epimetheus lived happily, except that she longed to open the box. She told herself that since the gods and goddesses had given her such wonderful gifts,this one must be wonderful, too. One day when her husband was gone, she opened the box.

All at once, out of the box flew the evils, horrors, and troubles that still curse the world today: pain, sickness, old age, and greed. Pandora screamed so loudly that Epimetheus heard her from town. He rushed home and shut the lid, but it was too late; all of the evils had already escaped.

Later that night, they heard a small voice coming from the box. It said, "Let me out. It is I, hope."

61

DIFFERENTIATED INSTRUCTION

Vocabulary

Context Clues

To help students find and use context clues, follow these steps:

1. Tell students that the first place to look for context clues is in the sentence in which the unfamiliar word appears. If the sentence itself does not yield clues, students should look at sentences just before and just after the sentence with the unfamiliar word.
2. Explain that clues may be a synonym (word with similar meaning), an antonym (opposite), a definition, or an example.

Student Journal page 114

Name ________ Date ________

Building Vocabulary: Using Context to Understand a Word

Look for the word *cunning* in the myth "Chained to a Mountain." Write in the box the sentences that help you know its meaning. Then complete the statements and answer the questions about the word *cunning*.

My Word in Context:

I think this word means ________

because ________

My word is ________

My word is not ________

Where else might I find this word? ________

What makes this an important word to know? ________

114 Mountains • Chained to a Mountain

Writing Summarize

Have students work cooperatively to complete the "somebody wanted but so" chart on *Student Journal* page 113. Then have partners retell the myth of Prometheus. Provide coaching, as needed, to be certain students include the important features of characters, setting, and plot events.

Vocabulary Context Clues

Display the word *deceptive*. Have students find the word on page 61. Ask them to tell what the word means. (dishonest) Have volunteers identify the context clues that helped them figure out the meaning. Ask students to complete the context activity, which focuses on *cunning*, on *Student Journal* page 114. (See Differentiated Instruction.)

Phonics/Word Study

Silent-Sounded Consonants

Display the following sentences, underlining the *n* as shown: *Zeus condemned Prometheus to a life of pain. Zeus's condemnation of Prometheus seems very harsh.* Ask students what they notice about the sound of this *n* in each word. (It is silent in *condemned* but sounded in *condemnation*.) Now, work with students to complete the in-depth activity on TE page 267.

Pandora and Epimetheus opened the lid, and a small spirit flew out of the box and into the world, bringing hope to humankind.

When Zeus was satisfied that he had punished man with the horrors from Pandora's box, he turned his thoughts to punishing Prometheus. Zeus was furious with Prometheus for tricking him with the sacrifices and for giving man fire. Zeus ordered two servants, Force and Violence, to capture Prometheus and chain him to a mountain. While Prometheus was chained to the mountain, a giant eagle came to him every day and pecked out his liver. At night, his liver grew back, but each morning, the eagle returned to torture him again.

Zeus hoped this punishment might make Prometheus say which one of his sons would take the throne from him, for only Prometheus knew. But Prometheus would not tell. He said to Zeus, "My body may be bound to this mountain, but my spirit and my mind are free."

Prometheus never broke in his spirit or his mind, and to this day, people remember him as a symbol of truth and justice. Even while chained to a mountain and tortured, Prometheus held on to his beliefs. ◆

THE TITANS

According to Greek mythology, the giant Titans ruled the earth before the Olympians, led by Zeus, defeated them. Prometheus was supposed to have been the wisest of the Titans. His name means "forethought," and he could tell the future. His brother, Epimetheus, was a stupid Titan. His name means "afterthought." Nowadays, someone of tremendous size or strength is referred to as a titan. The ship's name *Titanic* comes from the word *titan*.

Phonics/Word Study

Silent-Sounded Consonants

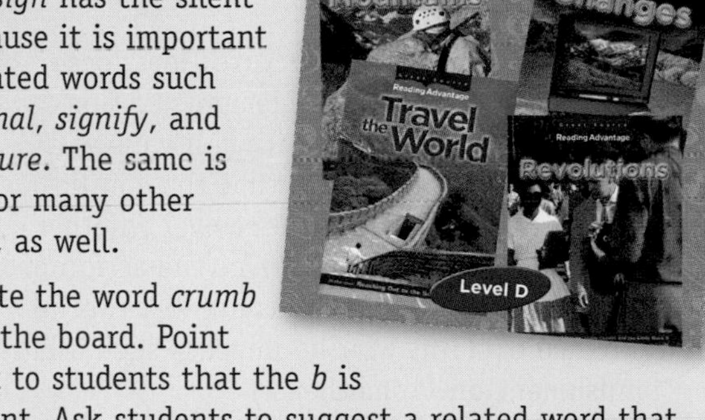

Many students wonder why there is a silent *g* in the word *sign*. The word *sign* has the silent *g* because it is important in related words such as *signal*, *signify*, and *signature*. The same is true for many other words, as well.

- Write the word *crumb* on the board. Point out to students that the *b* is silent. Ask students to suggest a related word that has a sounded *b* in it. Wait for a response and then, as needed, write *crumble* on the board.
- Display the words *soft* and *soften*. Have students identify the word that has a silent *t*.
- Ask students to generate more silent-sounded words if they can.
- Using the Silent-Sounded Consonant Sort, have students think of words related to the base words in the pairs listed below. (See *Word Study Manual* page 69.)

resign	resignation	condemn	condemnation
design	designate	debt	debit
sign	signal	hymn	hymnal

- Have students cut the words up and sort according to pairs.
- Have students create a section in their Word Study notebooks for silent-sounded changes and list the pairs they have worked with.

For more information on word sorts and spelling stages, see pages 5–31 in the *Word Study Manual*.

Focus on . . .

Use one or more activities in this section to focus on a particular area of need in your students.

Comprehension STRATEGY SUPPORT

To help those students who need more practice using the strategies covered in this lesson, work one-on-one or in small groups to apply the strategy prompts below. Apply the prompts to a *Reading Advantage* paperback, a classroom library book, or a new or familiar selection in the magazine. Always model your own thinking first.

Understanding Text Structure

- What kind of text is this? (book, story, article, guidebook, play, manual)
- How does the author organize the text? (cause-effect, problem-solution, chronological order, description, question-answer, comparison-contrast)
- What details support my thoughts about the text structure?
- What is the cause (effect, problem, solution, order, question, answer)?
- If fiction, who are the characters? What is the setting, plot, conflict, and resolution?

Writing Explanation

Have students think about some of the idioms they listed in the previous lesson. (See TE page 260.) Give these quick examples: *He's hot under the collar. She hit the roof.* (They both mean "got angry.") Then have students discuss the meaning of *Pandora's box* in this sentence: *To do what you're suggesting is like opening Pandora's box.* Have students reread the part of the myth that deals with the character Pandora. As a follow-up to the discussion, have students write an explanation of what it means "to open Pandora's box." Then have students identify one or two situations when the idiom would be appropriate to use.

To help strengthen students' writing, see lessons on writing techniques in *Writing Advantage*, pages 30–55.

Fluency: Pacing

After reading the myth at least once, have students listen as you model reading smoothly and at an even pace. Then have partners take turns reading self-selected sections of the myth.

As you listen to students read, use these prompts to guide them.

- Read smoothly; not too quickly and not too slowly.
- Use the punctuation, especially commas and periods, to regulate your pace.
- Preview the text to "troubleshoot" any difficult or unfamiliar words. It will also help you to notice, in advance, which groups of words naturally go together.

When students read aloud, do they—

✓ demonstrate a smooth pace, not too fast or too slow?
✓ incorporate well-timed pauses between words and phrases?
✓ reflect an awareness and understanding of punctuation?

English Language Learners

To support students' use of text features, guide them in analyzing the information in the list included on page 60 of "Chained to a Mountain." Have partners use the following questions as prompts as they analyze the information.

- How is the information organized (list, chart, table, and so on)?
- What features of the list help you understand the main idea?
- What examples does the author provide in the list?

Independent Activity Options

While you work with individuals or small groups, others can work independently on one or more of the following options.

- Level D paperback books, see TE pages 367–372
- Level D *eZines*
- Repeat word sorts from this lesson
- *Student Journal* pages for this lesson
- *Writing Advantage* independent lessons

Assessment

Strategy Assessment

To help you and your students assess their use of comprehension strategies, ask the following question. Students can complete a written response or provide verbal answers in a one-on-one reading conference.

- **Understanding Text Structure** How does thinking about the story elements of this myth help you appreciate it? (Answers will vary. Students might note that the conflict between Zeus and Prometheus over whether humans should have fire drives the action of the plot; Zeus's character, as an all-powerful god, also explains why he imposes such a harsh punishment on Prometheus.)

For ongoing informal assessment, use the checklists on pages 61–64 of *Level D Assessment*.

Word Study Assessment

Use these steps to help you and your students assess their understanding of silent/sounded consonants.

1. Write each of the following words on a word card: *resign*, *resignation*, *design*, *designation*, *sign*, *signal*, *condemn*, *condemnation*, *debt*, *debit*, *hymn*, and *hymnal*.
2. Have students sort the words into two groups; those with silent consonants and those without silent consonants.
3. Have students explain why the sound changes in the longer word of each related pair. (Adding a suffix affects the pronunciation of each word.)

MOUNTAIN RANGES

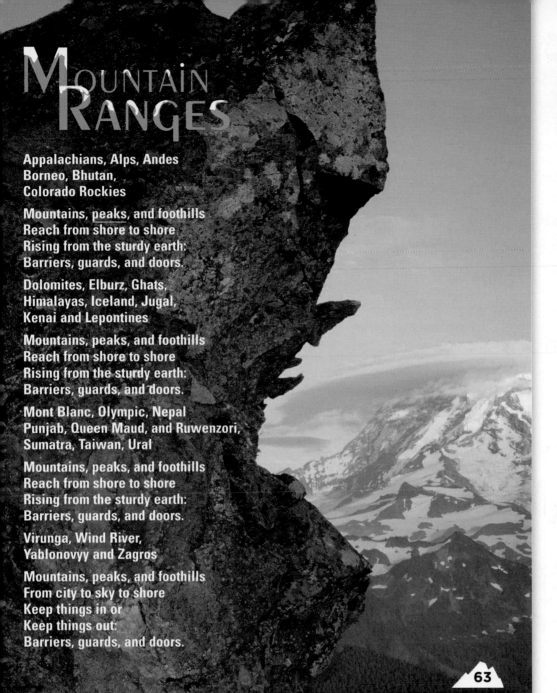

Appalachians, Alps, Andes
Borneo, Bhutan,
Colorado Rockies

Mountains, peaks, and foothills
Reach from shore to shore
Rising from the sturdy earth:
Barriers, guards, and doors.

Dolomites, Elburz, Ghats,
Himalayas, Iceland, Jugal,
Kenai and Lepontines

Mountains, peaks, and foothills
Reach from shore to shore
Rising from the sturdy earth:
Barriers, guards, and doors.

Mont Blanc, Olympic, Nepal
Punjab, Queen Maud, and Ruwenzori,
Sumatra, Taiwan, Ural

Mountains, peaks, and foothills
Reach from shore to shore
Rising from the sturdy earth:
Barriers, guards, and doors.

Virunga, Wind River,
Yablonovyy and Zagros

Mountains, peaks, and foothills
From city to sky to shore
Keep things in or
Keep things out:
Barriers, guards, and doors.

63

LESSON 34

Mountain Ranges *and* The Seven Summits

Mountains, pages 63–end

SUMMARY

The **poem** names some of the world's peaks. The **short feature** identifies and gives a brief description of the highest mountain peak in each of the seven continents.

COMPREHENSION STRATEGY

Making Connections

WRITING

Poem

VOCABULARY

Homophones

PHONICS/WORD STUDY

Consonant Alternations

Lesson Vocabulary

peaks

MATERIALS

Mountains, pp. 63–end
Student Journal, pp. 115–117
Word Study Manual, p. 70
Writing Advantage, pp. 114–151

Before Reading

Use one or more activities.

Poem: Mountain Ranges

Read aloud the poem "Mountain Ranges," while students follow along silently. Then ask: *What does the author have to say about mountains?*

Make a T-Chart

Begin a two-column chart labeled "Continents." With students' help, fill in the first column with the names of the seven continents. After students read the selection, have them record in the second column the name of the highest mountain on each continent.

Vocabulary Preview

Write *peaks* on the board. Encourage students to find the word in the selection and look for context clues to figure out its definition. Have students complete *Student Journal* page 115.

Preview the Selection

Have students look through pages 63–the end of the magazine. Ask them what text features they notice and what they think they will learn about and why.

Make Predictions/Set Purpose

Students should use the information they gathered in previewing the selection to make predictions about what they will learn. If students have trouble generating a purpose for reading, suggest that they read to find out more about the mountains on each of the seven continents.

DIFFERENTIATED INSTRUCTION

Comprehension

MAKING CONNECTIONS

Help students connect with the text by asking these questions:

- Which of these seven mountains were you familiar with? What did you know?
- Which peak would you most like to climb?
- Which climb might be the most difficult and dangerous?

Call on volunteers to explain their answers, using what they have read in the article and what they already know.

Student Journal page 115

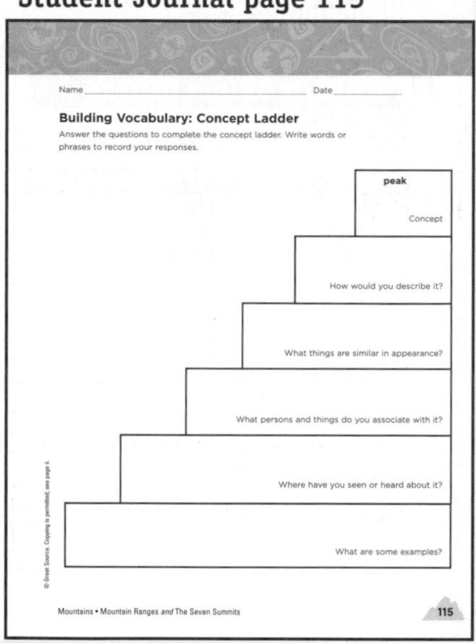

Name_______________ Date_______

Building Vocabulary: Concept Ladder

Answer the questions to complete the concept ladder. Write words or phrases to record your responses.

peak

Concept

How would you describe it?

What things are similar in appearance?

What persons and things do you associate with it?

Where have you seen or heard about it?

What are some examples?

© Great Source. Copying is permitted; see page ii.

Mountains • Mountain Ranges *and* The Seven Summits

115

CREDITS

Program Authors
Laura Robb
James F. Baumann
Carol J. Fuhler
Joan Kindig

Editorial Board
Avon Cowell
Craig Roney
Jo Worthy

Magazine Writers
Anina Robb
Lauren Kaufmann

Design and Production
Preface, Inc.

Photography
Inside front cover, l © Galen Rowell/Corbis; cl Earl & Nazima Kowall/Corbis; cr © AFP/Corbis; r © D. Falconer/PhotoLink/Photodisc; p. 1l © Bettmann/Corbis; r © Warren Morgan/Corbis; cl © AP Photo/U.S. Navy, Martin Maddock; pp. 2–3b © Galen Rowell/Corbis; p. 3t © Sheldan Collins/Corbis; c © S. P. Gillette/Corbis; p. 4 © David Samuel Robbins/Corbis; p. 5l © Craig Lovell/Corbis; r © Tibor Bognar/Corbis; p. 6t © Macduff Everton/Corbis; b © Cath Mullen, Frank Lane Picture Agency/Corbis; p. 7 © Kurt Stier/Corbis; p. 8 © Earl & Nazima Kowall/Corbis; p. 9 © Hulton-Deutsch Collection/Corbis; p. 10 © NASA; p. 12 © AFP/Corbis; pp. 13–15 © NASA; p. 15b © Trapper Frank/Corbis SYGMA; p. 18 © Corbis; p. 22 © Bettmann/Corbis; p. 23 © Owaki - Kulla/Corbis; p. 24 © Andrew Holbrooke/Corbis; pp. 25–26 © AP Photo/Bebeto Matthews; p. 27 © Lightenstein Andrew/Corbis SYGMA; p. 28 © Henry Horenstein/Corbis; p. 29t © Mark Richards/PhotoEdit, Inc.; b © D. Falconer/PhotoLink/Getty Images; p. 30l © AFP/Corbis; r © Owen Franken/Corbis; p. 31 Ronnie Kaufman/Corbis; p. 32t © Reuters NewMediaInc./Corbis; b © Yann Arthus-Bertrand/Corbis; p. 33t © Lynn Goldsmith/Corbis; c © Reuters NewMedia Inc./Corbis; b © Patrick Chauvel/Corbis SYGMA; pp. 34–36 © Bettmann/Corbis; p. 37t © Albright-Knox Art Gallery/Corbis; b © Hulton Archive/Getty Images; p. 38 © Bettmann/ Corbis; p. 39 © Jeff Greenberg/PhotoEdit, Inc.; p. 40 © Christie's Images/Corbis; pp. 41–42 © Corbis; p. 42b © AP Photo/US Navy, PHC Eric J. Tilford; pp. 42–43 © Corbis; p. 43b © AP Photo/ U.S. Navy, Martin Maddock; pp. 44–45 © AP Photo/Steve Early, Pool; p. 44b © AP Photo/US Navy, PHC Eric J. Tilford; p. 45c © AP Photo/Newport News Daily Press, Joe Fudge; b © AP Photo/Daily Press, Kenneth D. Lyons; p. 46 © Christie's Images/Corbis; pp. 48–49 © Warren Morgan/Corbis; pp. 50–51 © Galen Rowell/Corbis; p. 63 © Pat O'Hara/Corbis; p. 64t © Jeff Vanuga/Corbis; c © Corbis; b © David Keaton/Corbis; Inside back cover, tl © Marc Garanger/Corbis; tr © Sheldan Collins/Corbis; bl © Corbis; br © Wayne Lawler, Ecoscene/Corbis

Illustration
Inside front cover–1 bkgd, Preface, Inc.; Inside front cover, r Peter Sylvada; p. 1cr Violet Lemay; r Philip Howe; pp. 16–20 Peter Sylvada; p. 39 Preface, Inc.; p. 47 John Pirman; pp. 52–57 Violet Lemay; pp. 58–62 Philip Howe; p. 58b, pp.64–Inside back cover, Preface, Inc.

THE SEVEN SUMMITS

Each of the seven continents has a mountain that boasts of being the highest on the continent. These seven mountains are known as the Seven Summits.

North America

MOUNT McKINLEY

The highest peak in North America is in Alaska. Also known as Denali, meaning "the great one," Mount McKinley reaches 20,320 feet high. Climbing it, you will find a snow-covered mountain surrounded by five giant glaciers. Bad weather makes Mount McKinley difficult to climb, and many people have died trying to climb to its peak.

ATLANTIC OCEAN

South America

ACONCAGUA

At 22,841 feet, Aconcagua is the highest peak in the Western Hemisphere. The mountain's top is swept clean of snow by the brisk wind, which makes many of the hikes to the top look easy. But, beware—this is also the reason Aconcagua has one of the highest death rates of the Seven Summits. Hikers who climb too quickly, without respect for the elevation or the weather, find themselves breathing in too-thin air and freezing to death.

Antarctica

VINSON MASSIF

Thirteen miles long, eight miles wide, and 16,066 feet high, the Vinson Massif is Antarctica's highest mountain. Although the climb itself is not difficult, the weather conditions in Antarctica make the climb more challenging. At the top, climbers gaze out over miles of ice caps and glaciers. In the distance they can see the curved horizon of the earth. In 1966 Vinson Massif became the last of the Seven Summits to be climbed. As of 1999, only 400 people had climbed this peak, located 600 miles from the South Pole.

During Reading

Comprehension

MAKING CONNECTIONS

Use these prompts to model how to make connections with the text. Then have students make connections.

- What mountains have I seen?
- What do I know about how mountains are formed?
- What do the poem and short article remind me of?

(See Differentiated Instruction.)

Teacher Think Aloud

This article makes me recall facts from a geography class. Australia's Mount Kosciuszko, for example, is a plateau. I recall that that's a mountain so old that its top has eroded away. Africa's Mount Kilimanjaro was formed by a volcano, but I seem to recall that most tall mountains were formed by the folding or breaking of the earth's crust. It's hard to imagine such powerful forces at work under the earth!

Fix-Up Strategies

Offer these strategies to help students read independently.

If you don't understand what you're reading:

- Reread the difficult section to look for clues to help you comprehend.
- Read ahead to find clues to help you comprehend.
- Retell, or say in your own words, what you've read.
- Visualize, or form mental pictures of, what you've read.

Europe

MONT BLANC

Europe's highest mountain is in France and rises about 15,800 feet high. Sometimes called La Dame Blanche, or the white lady, Mont Blanc is a snow-covered beauty. Hikers like to start their climb at 2 A.M. before the sun softens the snowy surface and makes the climb slippery and dangerous. The hike to the summit takes about two days and leads through treacherous areas such as the Grand Coulier, where avalanches often occur.

Asia

MOUNT EVEREST

Also known by the Tibetan name Chomolungma (Goddess Mother of the Snows) and by the Nepali name Sagarmatha (Mother of the Universe), Mount Everest is the highest mountain in the world, rising 29,035 feet. People began trying to climb Mount Everest in 1921, but its peak was not reached until 1953. Climbers of all nationalities and ages attempt to climb Mount Everest. More than 600 people have made it to the top and at least 100 people have died trying. The dangers of Mount Everest are many: avalanches, falls, extreme cold, and the harsh effects of thin air.

PACIFIC OCEAN

Africa

KILIMANJARO

At 19,340 feet, almost 3 1/2 miles, Kilimanjaro is the highest mountain peak in Africa and the tallest freestanding mountain on Earth. In fact, Kilimanjaro is an inactive volcano with a crater 1 1/2 miles wide. Located near the equator, snowcapped Kilimanjaro gazes out over the desert of East Africa and takes climbers through temperatures that range from Arctic freeze to equatorial heat. People climb Kilimanjaro during every season, usually spending about six days to reach the top.

Australia

MOUNT KOSCIUSZKO

Rising only 7,310 feet, the climb up the highest peak in Australia is more like a pleasant hike than a dangerous trek. In fact, this mount is not a mountain at all but a plateau with steep sides. Located conveniently between the cities of Melbourne and Sydney, Mount Kosciuszko's rocky and forest-covered terrain attracts many hikers, skiers, and climbers. How did an Australian mountain get a Polish name? Some say that the first man to climb the mountain in 1840 named the peak after the Polish patriot, Tadeusz Kosciuszko because the mountain's round shape reminded him of Kosciuszko's tomb.

Student Journal page 116

Name __________ Date __________

Writing: Poem

Think about words and phrases you would use to describe a mountain. Write those in the box at the top of the page. Then use the remaining space to write a short descriptive poem about a mountain.

Descriptive Words and Phrases:

Now write your poem.

116 Mountains • Mountain Ranges *and* The Seven Summits

Student Journal page 117

Name __________ Date __________

Building Vocabulary: Homophones

Write a short definition for each word in the homophone pair. Then use each word in a sentence to show its meaning.

Words	Definitions
1. weather	1.
2. whether	2.
Sentence 1:	
Sentence 2:	
1. feat	1.
2. feet	2.
Sentence 1:	
Sentence 2:	
1. scene	1.
2. seen	2.
Sentence 1:	
Sentence 2:	

Mountains • Mountain Ranges *and* The Seven Summits 117

After Reading

Use one or more activities.

Check Purpose

Have students decide if their purpose was met.

Discussion Questions

Ask students to compare the highest mountains in Australia and Asia. Then ask: *Which of the seven mountains would you like to climb? Why?* (Making Connections)

Revisit: T-Chart

Have students add the names of the highest mountains to the chart.

Writing Poem

Have students complete *Student Journal* page 116, to write a descriptive poem about a mountain.

Vocabulary Homophones

Display the word *peak,* and have students define it. (mountaintop or point) Then ask students to name a word that sounds the same as *peak*. (*peek*) Explain that words such as *peak* and *peek* are called *homophones*. Have students complete *Student Journal* page 117.

Phonics/Word Study

Consonant Alternations

Write the words *music* and *musician* on the board. Ask students what they notice about the sound of the letter *c* in each word. (It has a /k/ sound in *music* and a /sh/ sound in *musician*.) Now, to explore more examples of these types of sound changes, work with students to complete the in-depth activity on page 272.

Phonics/Word Study

Other Consonant Alternations

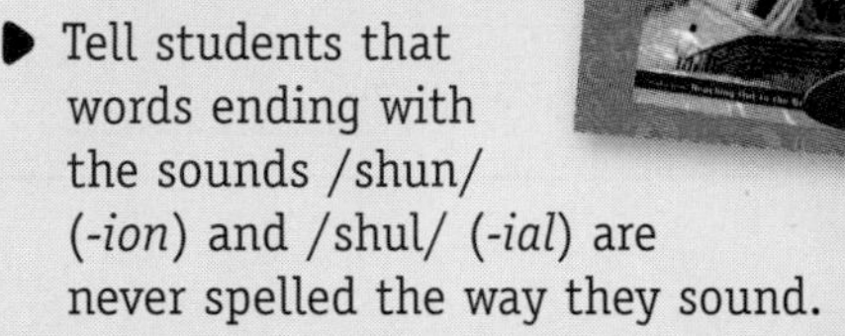

When endings such as *-ion* and *-ial* are added to words, the final consonant sound in the word changes. The chart that follows shows the four changes that can occur. Once students learn how the changes work, their spelling of the endings should improve.

- Tell students that words ending with the sounds /shun/ (*-ion*) and /shul/ (*-ial*) are never spelled the way they sound.
- Write these four words on the board: *refract*, *magic*, *critic*, and *office*.
- Ask students to change the words, one by one, as follows. Change *refract* to *refraction*, *magic* to *magician*, *critic* to *criticize*, and *office* to *official*.
- Ask students to explain the changes to the words when the endings were added. In the case of *refract*, the hard /t/ sound changes to the /sh/ sound, but the final letter *t* remains as a vestige of its meaning. In *magic*, the hard sound /k/ changes to the soft sound /sh/. But the letter *c* remains as a meaning marker. In *office*, the final sound changes from /s/ to /sh/ and the silent *e* is dropped when *-ial* is added.
- Using the Consonant Alternations Sort, have students sort the words shown in the chart above according to their respective endings. (See *Word Study Manual* page 70.)
- Check the final sorts.

Other Consonant Alternations Sort

/t/ to /sh/	/k/ to /sh/	/k/ to /s/	/s/ to /sh/
refract refraction	magic magician	critic criticize	prejudice prejudicial
intent intention	logic logician	politic politicize	office official
reflect reflection	clinic clinician		
perfect perfection	statistic statistician		

For more information on word sorts and spelling stages, see pages 5–31 in the *Word Study Manual*.

Focus on . . .

Use one or more activities in this section to focus on a particular area of need in your students.

Comprehension STRATEGY SUPPORT

To help those students who need more practice using the strategies covered in this lesson, work one-on-one or in small groups to apply the strategy prompts below. Apply the prompts to a *Reading Advantage* paperback, a classroom library book, or a new or familiar selection in the magazine. Always model your own thinking first.

Making Connections

- What does this story (article, passage) remind me of?
- What do I already know about this topic?
- Where have I heard about this topic before?
- What do I have in common with the characters, people, or situations in the text?
- What other books, stories, articles, movies, or TV shows does this text make me think about?

Writing Explanation

Have each student draw a mountain that has yet to be discovered. Tell them that the mountain can be anywhere in the world and can look any way they wish. Then tell them that they will create a name for their mountains. Note that mountains are named in different ways. Some, such as Mount Everest, are named for people—in this case, Sir George Everest, a British surveyor. Other names for mountains are descriptive. Mount Blanc in France is an example. Once students' names and drawings are completed, they should write a paragraph explaining their choices.

For more instruction on writing descriptive paragraphs, see lessons in *Writing Advantage*, pages 114–151.

Fluency: Pacing

After students have read the feature at least once, have student pairs alternate reading aloud the information about two different summits. Use the text about Mount McKinley to model reading smoothly and at an even pace.

When students read aloud, do they—

✓ demonstrate a smooth pace, not too fast or too slow?

✓ incorporate well-timed pauses between words and phrases?

✓ reflect an awareness and understanding of punctuation?

English Language Learners

To support students as they expand their vocabulary, extend the homophones lesson on TE page 271. Brainstorm a list of homophones on chart paper (*beat, beet; flee, flea*).

1. Have partners divide their paper into four columns, titled *word, picture, definition,* and *sentence*.
2. Have partners work together to complete the chart using several homophones on the list.
3. Have partners share their work with the group.

Independent Activity Options

While you work with individuals or small groups, others can work independently on one or more of the following options.

- Level D paperback books, see TE pages 367–372
- Level D *eZines*
- Repeat word sorts from this lesson
- *Student Journal* pages for this lesson
- *Writing Advantage* independent lessons

Assessment

Strategy Assessment

To help you and your students assess their use of comprehension strategies, ask the following question. Students can complete a written response or provide verbal answers in a one-on-one reading conference.

- **Making Connections** What connections did you make with the poem and the short article? (Answers may vary. Students may mention that they've already visited or they would like to visit a particular mountain or area.)

See *Level D Assessment* page 38 for formal assessment to go with *Mountains*.

Word Study Assessment

Use these steps to help you and your students assess their understanding of consonant alternations.

1. Write the following pairs of words on the board: *detect, detection; pediatric, pediatrician; public, publicize; circumstance, circumstantial.*
2. Ask these questions:
   - What change do you hear in the final sound of *detect* when it changes to *detection*? (the /t/ changes to /sh/)
   - In which pair does the final /k/ sound change to /sh/? (*pediatric, pediatrician*)
   - In which pair does the final /k/ sound change to /s/? (*public, publicize*)
   - What change do you hear in the final sounds of *circumstance* when it changes to *circumstantial*? (the /s/ changes to /sh/)

Level D, Magazine 4

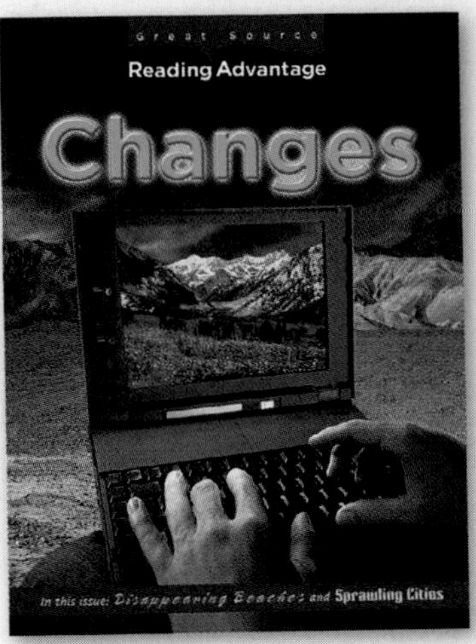

Changes

Magazine Summary

Changes magazine contains articles, poetry, a play, a short story, and a myth—all related to the theme of change. Students will read about personal change, climate change, political change, and the changes that come with a move to a new place.

Content–Area Connection: social studies
Lexile measure: 920L

Changes Lesson Planner

LESSON	BEFORE READING	DURING READING	AFTER READING
LESSON 35 **Crossing to the New World** (personal essay) page 278	Concept Web Vocabulary Preview Preview the Selection Make Predictions/Set Purpose	Making Connections	Check Purpose Discussion Questions Writing: journal entry Vocabulary: context Phonics/Word Study: suffixes
LESSON 36 **Change *and* Counterfeit Money** (article and poem) page 284	Poem: Change Features List Vocabulary Preview Preview the Selection Make Predictions/Set Purpose	Monitor Understanding Making Connections	Check Purpose Discussion Questions Writing: public service notice Vocabulary: synonyms and antonyms Phonics/Word Study: absorbed prefixes
LESSON 37 **Beach Erosion in the United States** (article) page 292	Anticipation Guide Vocabulary Preview Preview the Selection Make Predictions/Set Purpose	Monitor Understanding	Check Purpose Discussion Questions Writing: letter to the editor Vocabulary: prefix *re-* Phonics/Word Study: additional absorbed prefixes
LESSON 38 **Something's Changed** (play) page 299	Make a Graph Vocabulary Preview Preview the Selection Make Predictions/Set Purpose	Making Connections Understanding Text Structure	Check Purpose Discussion Questions Writing: play scene Vocabulary: synonyms and antonyms Phonics/Word Study: additional absorbed prefixes

Overview

Preview the Magazine

Give students time to look through the magazine. Have them read selection titles and look at the photographs and illustrations. Suggest that students also take time to become familiar with the front and back covers. Tell students that the magazine features literature about many different kinds of changes. Begin a discussion about two kinds of change—world change and personal change. Create a chart like the one shown.

World Changes	Personal Changes
a new president	new haircut
war	new school
the Internet	new friends

PHONICS/ WORD STUDY	FOCUS ON	ASSESSMENT	HIGHER-ORDER THINKING QUESTIONS
Suffixes	Writing: informational letter Fluency: expression English Language Learners Independent Activity Options	Making Connections Suffixes	What factors did immigration officials on Ellis Island use to determine whether or not a new immigrant could stay in the United States? Use information and specific details from the article to support your answer. What details support how confusing Ellis Island must have been for people arriving there? Use information and specific details from the article to support your answer.
Absorbed Prefixes	Writing: What if? Fluency: punctuation English Language Learners Independent Activity Options	Monitor Understanding Making Connections Absorbed Prefixes	In early America, why was paper money so easily counterfeited? Did it pass for genuine currency? Use information and specific details from the article to support your answer. What evidence did Detective Murray use to catch the Johnson family counterfeiters? Use information and specific details from the article to support your answer.
Additional Absorbed Prefixes	Writing: summary Fluency: phrasing English Language Learners Independent Activity Options	Monitor Understanding Understanding Text Structure Absorbed Prefixes	What factors contribute to beach erosion along the United States coastline? Use information and specific details from the article to support your answer. Imagine that you are a coastal engineer. What methods would you use to stop beach erosion along a section of coastline? Use information and specific details from the article to support your answer.
Additional Absorbed Prefixes	Writing: opinion paragraph Fluency: expression English Language Learners Independent Activity Options	Making Connections Understanding Text Structure Absorbed Prefixes	What conflict does Sylvia face in the play? Use information and specific details from the play to support your answer. What are some causes of Sylvia's dissatisfaction with her appearance? Use information and specific details from the play to support your answer.

Changes Lesson Planner

LESSON	BEFORE READING	DURING READING	AFTER READING
LESSON 39 **Changing the Definition of Pop Star: Stevie Wonder** (biographical sketch) page 307	Make a List Vocabulary Preview Preview the Selection Make Predictions/Set Purpose	Determining Importance Making Connections	Check Purpose Discussion Questions Writing: acceptance speech Vocabulary: context clues Phonics/Word Study: suffixes *-ible* and *-able*
LESSON 40 **The Next Move** (short story) page 315	Begin a List Vocabulary Preview Preview the Selection Make Predictions/Set Purpose	Inferential Thinking Monitor Understanding	Check Purpose Discussion Questions Writing: character map Vocabulary: context clues Phonics/Word Study: suffixes *-ible* and *-able*
LESSON 41 **From Carbon to Jewel: The Many Faces of Diamonds** (play) page 323	K-W-L Chart Vocabulary Preview Preview the Selection Make Predictions/Set Purpose	Making Connections Understanding Text Structure	Check Purpose Discussion Questions Writing: advertisement Vocabulary: suffix *-ist* Phonics/Word Study: suffixes *-ible* and *-able*
LESSON 42 **Changing Governments: Hong Kong No Longer Under British Rule** (play) page 330	Association Web Vocabulary Preview Preview the Selection Make Predictions/Set Purpose	Monitor Understanding	Check Purpose Discussion Questions Writing: compare-contrast Vocabulary: synonyms-antonyms Phonics/Word Study: doubling with polysyllabic words
LESSON 43 **Changing Landscapes: Urban Sprawl** (first person account) page 336	Anticipation Guide Vocabulary Preview Preview the Selection Make Predictions/Set Purpose	Monitor Understanding Determining Importance	Check Purpose Discussion Questions Writing: pro-con chart Vocabulary: antonyms Phonics/Word Study: suffixes *-ant* and *-ent*
LESSON 44 **Tiger Woods: Changing the Face of Golf** (biographical sketch) page 344	K-W-L Chart Vocabulary Preview Preview the Selection Make Predictions/Set Purpose	Making Connections	Check Purpose Discussion Questions Writing: timeline Vocabulary: multiple meanings Phonics/Word Study: eponymous words
LESSON 45 **Roots** *and* **Echo and Narcissus** *and* **Thirteen** (Greek myth and poems) page 350	Features of Mythology Chart Vocabulary Preview Preview the Selection Make Predictions/Set Purpose	Inferential Thinking Making Connections	Check Purpose Discussion Questions Writing: character map Vocabulary: denotation and connotation Phonics/Word Study: more eponyms
LESSON 46 **The Name of the Game: What's in a Name** *and* **Watch Your Words!** (articles) page 358	Names Chart Vocabulary Preview Preview the Selection Make Predictions/Set Purpose	Making Connections Understanding Text Structure	Check Purpose Discussion Questions Writing: journal Vocabulary: multiple meanings Phonics/Word Study: word trees

PHONICS/ WORD STUDY	FOCUS ON	ASSESSMENT	HIGHER-ORDER THINKING QUESTIONS
Suffixes *-ible* and *-able*	Writing: illustrated timeline Fluency: pacing English Language Learners Independent Activity Options	Determining Importance Making Connections Suffixes	What evidence does the author give to support the idea that Stevie Wonder never stopped growing as a musical artist? Use information and specific details from the article to support your answer. How did Stevie Wonder contribute to social issues of his time? Use information and specific details from the article to support your answer.
Suffixes *-ible* and *-able*	Writing: interior monologue Fluency: expression English Language Learners Independent Activity Options	Inferential Thinking Monitor Understanding Suffixes	How does Sela's opinion of moving change from the beginning of the story to the end? Use information and specific details from the story to support your answer. What did Sela realize about her life when she attended the Alterations meeting? Use information and specific details from the story to support your answer.
Suffixes *-ible* and *-able*	Writing: opinion essay Fluency: expression English Language Learners Independent Activity Options	Making Connections Understanding Text Structure Suffix *-able* with Exceptions	What leads to the formation of diamonds from carbon? Use information and specific details from the radio play to support your answer. What are some uses of diamonds throughout history? Use information and specific details from the radio play to support your answer.
Doubling with Polysyllabic Words	Writing: news story Fluency: pacing English Language Learners Independent Activity Options	Monitor Understanding Doubling with Polysyllabic Words	How has the drug opium affected the history of Hong Kong? Use information and specific details from the article to support your answer. What conflict arises from the change of government in Hong Kong from British rule to Communist Chinese? Use information and specific details from the article to support your answer.
Endings *-ant* and *-ent*	Writing: visualizing Fluency: phrasing English Language Learners Independent Activity Options	Monitor Understanding Determining Importance Suffixes *-ant* and *-ent*	What kinds of changes are brought on by urban sprawl? Use information and specific details from the article to support your answer. What causes the expansion of urban areas? Use information and specific details from the article to support your answer.
Eponymous Words	Writing: character map Fluency: pacing English Language Learners Independent Activity Options	Making Connections Eponymous Words	What obstacles did Tiger Woods face in his career as a professional golfer? Use information and specific details from the article to support your answer. How does the author support the conclusion that Tiger Woods has benefited the sport of golf? Use information and specific details from the article to support your answer.
More Eponyms	Writing: double-entry journal Fluency: pacing English Language Learners Independent Activity Options	Inferential Thinking Making Connections Eponyms	How do the lives of Echo and Narcissus show the principle that personality flaws can determine what happens to people? Use information and specific details from the myths to support your answer. What specific language does the author use to make Echo and Narcissus interesting to the reader? Use information and specific details from the myths to support your answer.
Word Trees	Writing: opinion paragraph Fluency: punctuation English Language Learners Independent Activity Options	Making Connections Understanding Text Structure Word Trees	What factors were behind the name changes talked about in the article? Use information and specific details from the article to support your answer. Language changes come from invention and usage. How does the author support that idea in the poem "Watch Your Words"? Use information and specific details from the article to support your answer.

LESSON **35**

Crossing to the New World

Changes, pages 2–5

SUMMARY

The unnamed author of this **personal essay** describes his experiences crossing the Atlantic Ocean and entering the United States at Ellis Island as an Arab immigrant in 1907.

COMPREHENSION STRATEGIES

Making Connections

WRITING

Journal Entry

VOCABULARY

Context

PHONICS/WORD STUDY

Suffixes *-crat, -ician, -logy, -phobia*

Lesson Vocabulary

crammed	transporting
disembark	lured
quarantine	impatient
contagious	vouch

MATERIALS

Changes, pp. 2–5
Student Journal, pp. 118–120
Word Study Manual, p. 71
Writing Advantage, pp. 30–55

CROSSING to the NEW WORLD

More immigrants arrived in the United States in 1907 than in any year before. Here's the story of one immigrant's arrival at Ellis Island, the first stop in the new country.

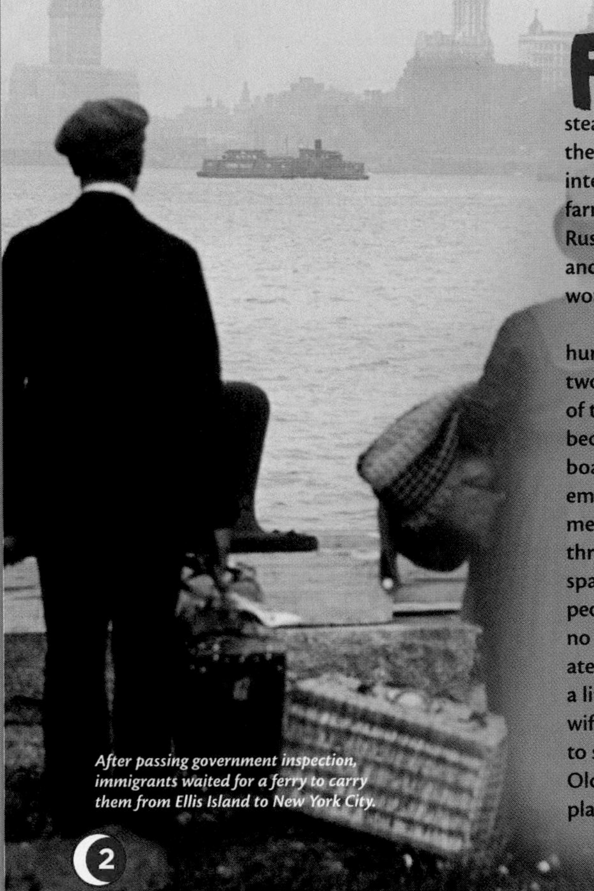

For days I traveled from the Middle East to the city of Liverpool, England. There, many like me stood and waited in line to board a steamship and sail across the Atlantic Ocean to the New World. My fellow travelers were an interesting and varied group. There were Irish farmers whose hands were stained with soil, Russian Jews with long beards, Greeks in slippers, and Englishmen in knee pants. I, being an Arab, wore a long robe.

After days of waiting to leave, the boat crew hurried passengers on board and jammed over two thousand people into the steerage section of the ship. This section is called the steerage because the parts and instruments that steer the boat used to be stored there. Now, it is a large, empty space divided into two sections, one for men and one for women. Bunk beds, stacked three and four high, took up most of the floor space, and the crammed room smelled of people, spoiled food, and seasickness. There was no privacy, no toilets, and nowhere to bathe. I ate my meals of soup, potatoes, and eggs off of a little tin tray as I sat on my bunk. Luckily, my wife had packed me some dried fish and prunes to snack on. I left my wife and family back in the Old World. Once I found a job and a decent place to live, I'd send for them.

After passing government inspection, immigrants waited for a ferry to carry them from Ellis Island to New York City.

2

Before Reading

Use one or more activities.

Make a Concept Web

Tell students that they are going to read about someone who left his own country to move to the United States, a country he had never seen. With students' help, create a word web around the word *immigrate*. Ask students what *immigrate* means to them, and write their responses in the web.

Vocabulary Preview

Display the selection vocabulary. Ask students to predict how each word might be used in the essay. Have students complete the second column of the predictions chart on *Student Journal* page 118. They will complete the activity later.

Preview the Selection

Have students preview the essay and tell what they notice.

Make Predictions/ Set Purpose

Students should use the information they gathered in previewing the selection to make predictions about what they will learn. If students have trouble generating a purpose for reading, suggest that they read to learn about the immigration experience in the early 1900s.

BUT INSTEAD OF HEADING TO THE MAINLAND, THE BOAT TURNED TOWARD FOUR BRICK TOWERS. THIS WAS THE PLACE I'D HEARD ABOUT: **ELLIS ISLAND.**

After almost two weeks of sailing, the ship arrived in New York Harbor. I scurried up to the boat deck like a mouse to cheese. There, Lady Liberty, the beautiful sea green statue, welcomed me. But instead of heading to the mainland, the boat turned toward four brick towers. This was the place I'd heard about: Ellis Island. I knew that there I'd be questioned and checked for diseases.

To get to Ellis Island, I boarded a smaller riverboat. The loud chatter of different languages confused me, and I strained my ears to hear a familiar word. This boat was worse than the steamship. It was an open-air barge, and, because it was winter, I shivered. I'd heard that many people, especially children, died because they were not used to the cold air that slammed them in the face as they crossed the Hudson River.

This riverboat ride should have taken less than an hour. However, there were so many steamships in the harbor that we had to wait several hours on this open barge. Before I was allowed off the boat, an official-looking man asked me questions about my country, age, health, job, and plans in the New World. He wrote my answers down, and I had to swear that I was telling the truth before I could disembark at Ellis Island.

On Ellis Island, a man pinned a numbered tag onto my clothes. Then the yelling began. I couldn't understand any of the directions, so I tried my best just to follow what everyone else did. My group lined up, and slowly the line moved to the second floor of the immigration building. As we walked, doctors looked us over and pulled out anyone who was sneezing, coughing, or limping. At the top of the stairs, a group of inspectors sent us, three at a time, to a private room. This was quarantine, the place where doctors checked your health. A doctor yelled at me to see if I could hear and looked me over for a few seconds. Friends who had been rejected and sent back to the old country had warned me that the doctors checked carefully to see if you were crazy or had contagious diseases, like tuberculosis, that would spread.

I passed the medical inspection. Months later, I learned that if I'd been sick, the doctor would have marked me with blue chalk and put me in a holding cell to be rechecked. Doctors sent dangerously sick people to the Ellis Island Hospital to be cured. But if the doctors couldn't make the people well, they sent them back to the steamship. Americans tried to discourage the ships from transporting,

Immigrants endured crowded conditions on the ships.

3

DIFFERENTIATED INSTRUCTION

Comprehension

MAKING CONNECTIONS

To help students make connections with the text, use one or both of these activities.

1. Ask students to tell about other stories, articles, or movies that describe immigrants' experiences.
2. Have students tell about a time that they were surrounded by people speaking another language. What did that feel like?

Student Journal page 118

Name_____________ Date_______

Building Vocabulary: Predictions

How do you predict these words will be used in "Crossing to the New World"? Write your answers in the second column. Next, read the essay. Then, clarify your answers in the third column.

Word	My prediction for how the word will be used	How the word was actually used
crammed		
disembark		
quarantine		
contagious		
transporting		
lured		
impatient		
vouch		

118 Changes • Crossing to the New World

During Reading

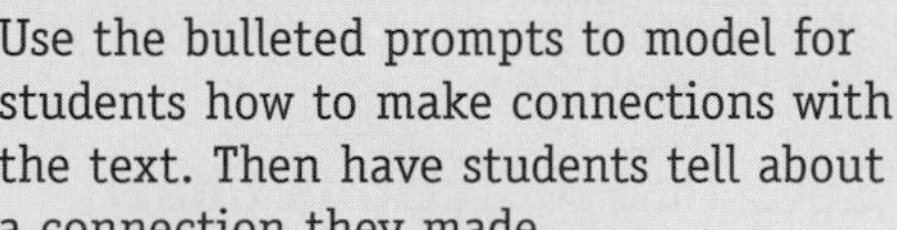

Comprehension

MAKING CONNECTIONS

Use the bulleted prompts to model for students how to make connections with the text. Then have students tell about a connection they made.

- What issues does this raise that I've already read about or heard about?
- How does my prior knowledge help me understand this selection?

(See Differentiated Instruction.)

Teacher Think Aloud

I've heard a lot about immigration recently. People seem to be worried about too many people coming to the United States, and people coming illegally. Yet, everyone who isn't Native American in this country is descended from immigrants. I know that from history class, and this selection supports the idea by mentioning all the different nationalities who came in 1907.

Fix-Up Strategies

Offer these strategies to help students read independently.

If you don't understand what you're reading:

- Reread the difficult section to look for clues to help you comprehend.
- Read ahead to find clues to help you comprehend.
- Retell, or say in your own words, what you've read.
- Visualize, or form mental pictures of, what you've read.

or carrying, sick passengers by fining the ship $100 for every passenger that had to be sent back.

After quarantine, the guards shuffled me into a great, airy hall filled with more guards and giant iron cages. These cages weren't jail cells but places to change money or buy a railroad ticket. I was so hungry that I decided to change some money and get something to eat, but I was nervous because I didn't know how to count the new money. The guards rushed me along to a restaurant, but I couldn't ask the price of the food. I saw some posters that looked like price lists, but I couldn't read them and couldn't ask what was on the menu. So, I gave the man behind the counter some money, and he gave me some change and a paper bag filled with bread. Many others were lured by the tempting smell of pies, bologna, and bread, and they lined up to buy food, too.

Guards pushed me into another line. Someone's suitcase kept hitting my knee, and I grew angry and impatient. Finally, I reached a desk at the end of the hall where a man who spoke my language asked me many of the same questions that I was asked on the riverboat. He checked to see if the answers I gave him matched the ones that were written down.

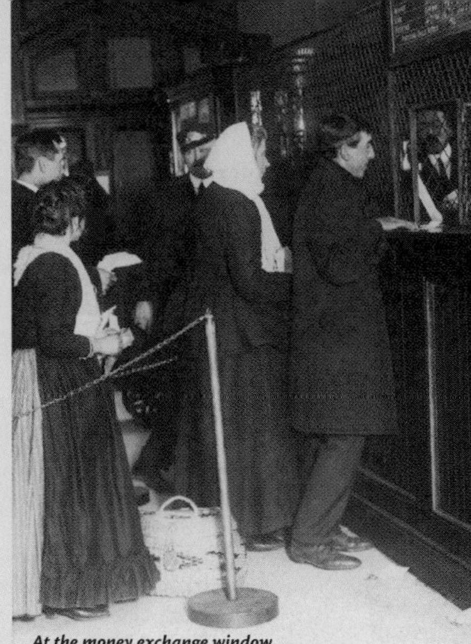

At the money exchange window, immigrants received U. S. dollars in exchange for money from other countries.

I KNEW THAT I MUST HAVE MONEY OR A RELATIVE...

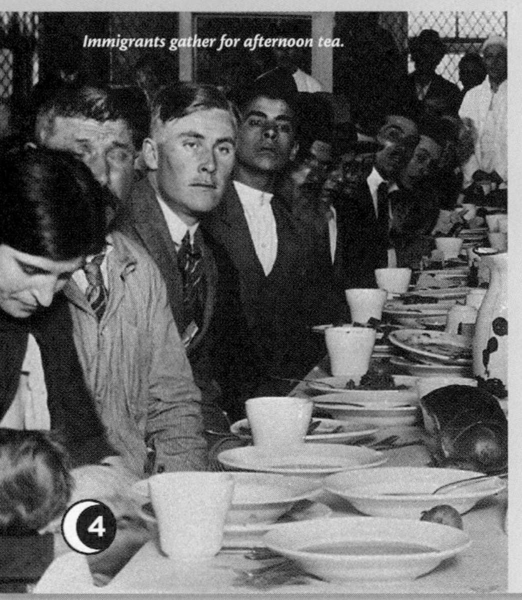

Immigrants gather for afternoon tea.

After that questioning, a guard led me downstairs. I felt like a prisoner with all of the guards yelling, as if loud English would be easier to understand. Someone said that now people were deciding if we could come to this country or not. To be allowed in I knew that I must either have money or a relative who already lived here. Luckily, my great-uncle came here a few years ago, and he promised that he would vouch for me and give his word that he would help support me.

Finally, the guards led me outside. The sun in the New World seemed brighter than on the ship or on Ellis Island. A whole crowd of people cried, screamed, and waved pictures. I gazed over the crowd for my uncle, and I saw him standing by a building that looked like a castle. He smiled and held up his hand to wave.

I was on my way to New York City. ◆

Student Journal page 119

Name ______ Date ______

Writing: Journal Entry

Imagine you are a teenage immigrant crossing into the New World. Write a journal entry about the immigration process from your perspective.

Today I have crossed into the New World: ______

Changes • Crossing to the New World 119

After Reading

Use one or more activities.

Check Purpose

Have students decide if their purpose was met. What did they learn about the immigration experience in the early 1900s?

Discussion Questions

Continue the group discussion with the following questions.

1. What was the immigrant experience like in 1907? (Evaluate)
2. What personal qualities did it take to immigrate to the United States in the early 1900s? (Inferential Thinking)
3. How did this essay make you feel about the process of immigration in the early 1900s? (Making Connections)

Revisit: Concept Web

Have students go back to the web they created in Before Reading and add what they learned.

Revisit: Predictions Chart

Give students time to reread each word in context and write each word's definition in the third column of *Student Journal* page 118.

MANY NAMES, ONE PLACE

Through history, there have been many names for one place.

- **Native Americans originally called Ellis Island *KIOSHK,* which means Gull Island. Then, only sea gulls lived on the three-acre, muddy island. The island sat so low that at high tide the land barely stayed above water.**
- **When the Dutch bought New York from the Native Americans, they called it Little Oyster Island because they found many delicious oysters in its mud and sand.**
- **During most of the 1700s, the British called it Bucking Island. No one knows where the name Bucking came from.**
- **After 1765, people called the island Anderson's Island (after a pirate named Anderson who was hanged there) or Gibbet Island because of all the hangings that took place there. *Gibbet* is a slang word for the gallows.**

- **Sam Ellis, a farmer, bought the island during the American Revolution. When he died, his family sold the land to New York City, and soon the American government took control of the island. The island still carries his name.**

Ellis Island in New York Harbor

ELLIS ISLAND TIME LINE

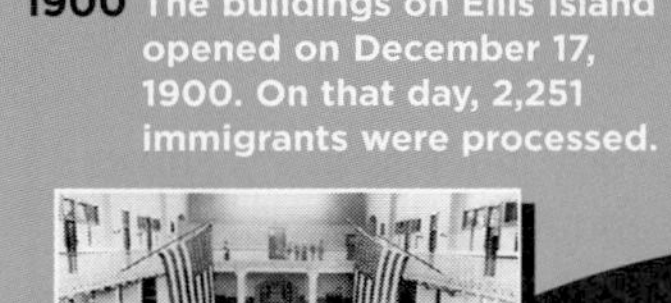

1900 The buildings on Ellis Island opened on December 17, 1900. On that day, 2,251 immigrants were processed.

1907 The year 1907 was a peak year of immigration. That year, 1,285,349 people entered the United States. Of that number, 1,004,756 came through Ellis Island.

1954 The island was vacated.

1970 Native Americans tried to occupy the island to bring attention to how European immigrants destroyed the native peoples.

1976 Ellis Island opened as a museum for visitors. It is run by the National Park Service.

5

DIFFERENTIATED INSTRUCTION

Vocabulary Context

To be sure students understand how context clues can define words, follow these steps:

1. Remind students that context clues are often in the form of a synonym, an antonym, or a definition.
2. Think aloud how you can figure out the meaning of the vocabulary word *transporting* by finding a synonym, and the word *lured* by looking at context clues—the information that surrounds the word in the selection.
3. Then have volunteers think aloud about how they can figure out the meaning of the word *disembark* by using context clues.

Student Journal page 120

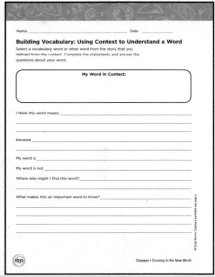

Name ____________________ Date __________

Building Vocabulary: Using Context to Understand a Word

Select a vocabulary word or other word from the story that you defined from the context. Complete the statements and answer the questions about your word.

My Word in Context:

I think this word means ____________________

because ____________________

My word is ____________________

My word is not ____________________

Where else might I find this word? ____________________

What makes this an important word to know? ____________________

Writing Journal Entry

Have students use the information in "Crossing to the New World" to write on *Student Journal* page 119 a journal entry from the perspective of a teenage immigrant.

Vocabulary Context

Display the word *contagious*. Then read the sentence on page 3 in which the word appears. Explain that students can use information in the text to figure out challenging words. For example, the text on page 3 tells them that "contagious" diseases are diseases "that would spread." Have students work together to complete *Student Journal* page 120. (See Differentiated Instruction.)

Phonics/Word Study

Suffixes

Display the words *arachnophobia* and *claustrophobia*. Ask: *What do you know about these words? What is similar about these words?* Point out that the suffix *-phobia* means "fear." Now explain that the word root *triskaideka* means "thirteen." So *triskaidekaphobia* means "fear of the number thirteen." Now, work with students to complete the in-depth suffixes activity on TE page 282.

Phonics/Word Study

Suffixes

When students recognize common suffixes, they have one more way to understand the meanings of unfamiliar words. Students will encounter these four common suffixes repeatedly in their reading.

-crat **(advocate of a specific theory of government)**

plutocrat democrat
autocrat bureaucrat

-ician **(practitioner)**

physician beautician
magician technician
statistician musician

-logy **(doctrine, science, theory)**

etymology geology
biology psychology
physiology

-phobia **(fear)**

graphophobia hydrophobia
claustrophobia arachnophobia

Quite a few words with the suffix *-phobia* include Greek or Latin roots, and the analysis of the words can afford a good review of previously learned roots. For example, the word *graphophobia* is one students can figure out. They have already studied the root *graph* (writing), so students should recognize that *graphophobia* means "fear of writing." Have students complete the word sort. See *Word Study Manual* page 71. Discuss together the meanings of the words and roots.

Discovering the Suffixes

-crat	*-ician*	*-logy*	*-phobia*
autocrat	physician	etymology	claustrophobia
bureaucrat	statistician	entomology	agoraphobia
plutocrat	musician	geology	arachnophobia
democrat	magician	biology	acrophobia
	beautician	psychology	graphophobia

For more information on word sorts and spelling stages, see pages 5–31 in the *Word Study Manual*.

Focus on . . .

Use one or more activities in this section to focus on a particular area of need in your students.

Comprehension STRATEGY SUPPORT

To help those students who need more practice using the strategies covered in this lesson, work one-on-one or in small groups to apply the strategy prompts below. Apply the prompts to a *Reading Advantage* paperback, a classroom library book, or a new or familiar selection in the magazine. Always model your own thinking first.

Making Connections

- What does this story (article, passage) remind me of?
- What do I already know about this topic?
- Where have I heard about this topic before?
- What do I have in common with the characters, people, or situations in the text?
- What other books, stories, articles, movies, or TV shows does this text make me think about?

Writing Informational Letter

The author of "Crossing to the New World" planned to bring his family to the United States after he got settled. What would his relatives need to know about the trip across the Atlantic? About the inspection at Ellis Island? Have each student write a letter to the author's family, telling them what to expect. Suggest that students use a T-chart like the one shown, to help them organize the information they want to include in their letters.

What to Expect	What to Write
Paragraph 1: For the Trip	Clothes to pack, food to take
Paragraph 2: For Ellis Island	Questions to answer, inspections to pass

To help students use strong verbs and specific nouns in their writing, see lessons in *Writing Advantage*, pages 30–55.

Fluency: Expression

Talk with students about how the narrator's feelings changed at different points during his immigration process. At the beginning of the trip, he was in awe of the number and variety of people making the journey across the Atlantic Ocean. Aboard the ship, he was disappointed with or upset about the crowded and unsanitary conditions. Have students work with partners and take turns reading aloud different paragraphs of the essay. Partners should listen to each other and coach the correct use of expression.

As students read, use these prompts to guide them.

- Think about how the author might have felt. Show his feelings in your voice.
- Ask your partner if he or she hears the expression in your voice.

When students read aloud, do they—

✓ reflect an understanding of the text?

✓ demonstrate appropriate timing, stress, and intonation?

✓ incorporate appropriate speed and phrasing?

English Language Learners

To support students' comprehension of "Crossing to the New World," guide them in determining the author's perspective. Have partners reread page 4 of "Crossing to the New World" and answer the following questions.

- How did the author feel as he was trying to buy food?
- When did the author feel angry?
- How did the author's feelings change as he was led outside?

Independent Activity Options

While you work with individuals or small groups, others can work independently on one or more of the following options.

- Level D paperback books, see TE pages 367–372
- Level D *eZines*
- Repeat word sorts from this lesson
- *Student Journal* pages for this lesson
- *Writing Advantage* independent lessons

Assessment

Strategy Assessment

To help you and your students assess their use of comprehension strategies, ask the following questions. Students can complete a written response or provide verbal answers in a one-on-one reading conference.

- **Making Connections** How do you think you would feel if you learned your family was moving to a country where you didn't know the language? (Answers will vary. Students may mention fears of getting lost, of being embarrassed, of having trouble making friends, and so on. Students who have experienced such a move can describe their own feelings.)

For ongoing informal assessment, use the checklists on pages 61–64 of *Level D Assessment*.

Word Study Assessment

Use these steps to help you and your students assess their understanding of the four suffixes studied in this lesson.

1. Write the following words on the board or on word cards: *zoology*, *electrophobia*, *democrat*, *politician*.
2. Ask students to find the suffixes and tell what each one means. Then have them use the suffixes to help them define the words. Compare their definitions with the ones provided.

Word and Suffix	Suffix Definition	Word Definition
zoology (*-logy*)	doctrine, science, theory	scientific study of animals
electrophobia (*-phobia*)	fear	fear of electricity
democrat (*-crat*)	advocate of a special theory of government	advocate of democracy
politician (*-ician*)	practitioner	one actively involved in politics

LESSON **36**

Change *and* Counterfeit Money . . .

Changes, pages 6–11

SUMMARY

The **poem** is about coins in pockets and piggybanks. It is followed by an **informational article** about paper money and how counterfeiters try to copy it.

COMPREHENSION STRATEGIES

Monitor Understanding
Making Connections

WRITING

Public Service Notice

VOCABULARY

Synonyms and Antonyms

PHONICS/WORD STUDY

Absorbed Prefixes

Lesson Vocabulary

counterfeit	bogus
circulation	genuine
rampant	surveillance

MATERIALS

Changes, pp. 6–11
Student Journal, pp. 121–124
Word Study Manual, p. 72
Writing Advantage, pp. 56–93

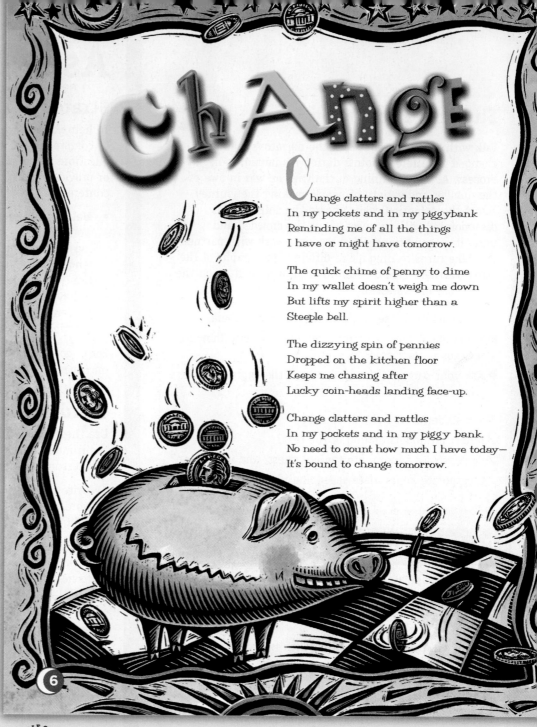

Change

Change clatters and rattles
In my pockets and in my piggybank
Reminding me of all the things
I have or might have tomorrow.

The quick chime of penny to dime
In my wallet doesn't weigh me down
But lifts my spirit higher than a
Steeple bell.

The dizzying spin of pennies
Dropped on the kitchen floor
Keeps me chasing after
Lucky coin-heads landing face-up.

Change clatters and rattles
In my pockets and in my piggy bank.
No need to count how much I have today—
It's bound to change tomorrow.

6

Before Reading

Use one or more activities.

Read a Poem

Read "Change" on page 6 to students, and then have them read it aloud with you. Ask students if their change "clatters and rattles." What sounds does it make? What do students do with their change? Some people save it in containers for a long time and then cash it in. Others simply carry it around.

Begin a Features List

Write "Features of U.S. Bills" on the board. Explain to students that the U.S. government tries to make its paper money hard to counterfeit by printing many features on its bills. Show students one or two bills and ask them to identify their distinctive features. Use students' responses to make a list. Tell students that they can add to the list after reading the article.
(See Differentiated Instruction.)

Vocabulary Preview

Display the selection vocabulary and help students pronounce each word. Direct attention to the word associations activity on *Student Journal* page 121. Then use a word selected from the article to model how you make associations or connections. Ask students to complete the journal page with two of the lesson's vocabulary words.

Changing the Real Thing

The government changes the design of paper money every so often so that counterfeiters cannot learn to perfect their fake money. Each year in America, an average of $250 million in <u>counterfeit</u> money is pulled from <u>circulation</u> so that it cannot be passed off as real. But, counterfeiting continues: people are always looking for an easy way to make a buck.

7

DIFFERENTIATED INSTRUCTION
FEATURES OF U.S. BILLS

- amount of bill worth
- portrait of early leaders
- picture of public buildings
- U.S. motto
- "Federal Reserve Note"
- serial number
- signatures of Treasurer of the United States and Secretary of the Treasury

Student Journal page 121

Name ______ Date ______

Building Vocabulary: Making Associations

Pick two words from the vocabulary list below. Think about what you already know about each word. Then answer the following questions.

counterfeit	rampant	genuine
circulation	bogus	surveillance

Word ______

What do you think about when you read this word? ______

Who might use this word? ______

What do you already know about this word? ______

Word ______

What do you think about when you read this word? ______

Who might use this word? ______

What do you already know about this word? ______

Now watch for these words in the magazine selection. Were you on the right track?

Changes • Change and Counterfeit Money 121

Preview the Selection

Have students preview the five pages of the article, pages 7–12 in the magazine. Use these or similar prompts to guide students to notice the important features of the text.

- What is the first thing you notice about the article?
- Do you think this selection is fiction or nonfiction? Why?
- How is the information organized?
- What do you think you will learn?

Teacher Think Aloud

By looking at the photographs, I know right away that this article is about money. The title tells me that it is actually about counterfeit *money. I am sure it is nonfiction because it begins with a history of counterfeiting that is presented by time period.*

Make Predictions/ Set Purpose

Students should use the information they gathered in previewing the selection to make predictions about what they will learn. If students have trouble generating a purpose for reading, suggest that they read to learn how paper money has changed over the years and what counterfeiters do to make fake money.

DIFFERENTIATED INSTRUCTION SMALL GROUP

Comprehension

MONITOR UNDERSTANDING

Help students monitor their understanding by following these steps:

1. Ask: *Did you understand what the phrase "track down" on page 10 means?* (See section called "A False Lead," first paragraph.) Have students who understood it explain whether they already knew the meaning or figured it out from context clues.
2. Explain that the phrase is an *idiom*—a phrase that can't be understood just by reading the words. The meaning must be learned.

Counterfeiting— A Short History

Counterfeiting is not a new crime. In America, counterfeiting was rampant, way out of control, before the American Revolution. Each colony printed its own money, called notes. These notes were usually small in size and printed on only one side. It was easy for counter-feiters to copy the simple designs. Another thing that made counterfeiting easy before the Revolution was that the general public was not very well educated. Passing off fake notes to people wasn't hard to do. Some historians guess that over half of the notes that circulated in the colonies were fakes.

The 1770s

In 1775, right before the Revolutionary War, Paul Revere minted the first American money. It was called a Continental. However, during the war, the British counterfeited so much of the new American money that the Continental became worthless. After the war, private banks printed and circulated their own paper money. At one point, there were over 7,000 different kinds of these bank notes, and each one had a different design! These bank bills were easy to counterfeit because it was impossible to keep track of 7,000 varieties and designs of money. To combat the uncontrolled crime of counterfeiting, the government created the Secret Service.

▲ A chemical bath at the Secret Service detects bad bills.

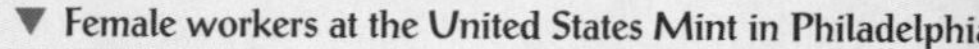

▼ Female workers at the United States Mint in Philadelphia

▲ A bank note for five hundred dollars from the Boylston Bank (c.1862)

During Reading

Comprehension

SMALL GROUP

MONITOR UNDERSTANDING

Use these questions to model how to monitor understanding by asking questions. Then have students ask their own questions to resolve any confusion.

- What is the author talking about?
- Why did the author include this detail?
- What fix-up strategy can I use?

(See Differentiated Instruction.)

Teacher Think Aloud

As I read the section titled "The 1770s," I got confused when I read the last sentence about the Secret Service. How did creating it help? I've never understood what the Secret Service does. I decided to read ahead, and in the section titled "The 1930s," I learned more about the purpose of the agency. I know that authors don't always explain things right away.

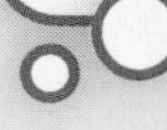

Comprehension

SMALL GROUP

MAKING CONNECTIONS

Use the bulleted prompts to model for students how to make connections with the text. Then have students share connections they have made.

- What do I know after reading this selection that I didn't know before?
- How can I apply this information to my own life?

The 1860s

The government did not make money, as we know it, until the 1860s. Right before the Civil War, the government needed money, so a law was passed allowing the Treasury Department to print and circulate one kind of standard money. When a national currency (bills), was printed in 1862, some people thought the counterfeiting problem would be solved. However, lawbreakers saw forging the standard bills as a challenge, and counterfeiting continued. In fact, the number of fake bills in circulation increased.

The 1930s

During the Great Depression of the 1930s, when Americans were desperate for money, counterfeiting increased. So did the effort to stop it. The Secret Service provided information about the fake bills to banks. Some people thought this was a bad idea because they believed it would encourage and teach people how to counterfeit. However, the Secret Service decided that only an educated public could help stop fake money from passing hands.

Today, counterfeiting is still a problem. Today's counterfeiters have a lot of technology, such as computers, special printers, and ink, at their fingertips. The mistakes that detectives used to find on counterfeit bills aren't present anymore, which makes the bogus bills harder to detect.

How to Spot Counterfeit Bills

You have a role in protecting the worth of our money. The more familiar you become with the money in your pocket, the more likely you will be able to detect fake money. Here are a few things to look for to make sure your money is the real thing:

- The Portrait: On your paper money, each picture of a president has certain qualities that let you know the bill is genuine, or real. Make sure the portrait looks lifelike and stands out from the background. A counterfeit portrait will appear flat and lifeless on a dark background.
- The Seals: Each bill has a seal from the Federal Reserve and the Treasury. On a real bill, the seals' saw-toothed edges should look sharp and clear. The shape of a seal on a bogus bill may look uneven, and some of the saw-teeth may be dull or broken.
- The Border: The border on a genuine bill should be clear and unbroken. An unclear, blurry, or broken line signals a counterfeit.
- The Serial Numbers: On real money, each numeral in the serial number should be evenly spaced, and the ink should be the same color as the Treasury Seal. On a counterfeit bill, the numbers are often not spaced correctly or the ink is a different shade from the seal.
- The Paper: The paper that genuine money is printed on has tiny red and blue fibers running through it. Counterfeiters try to reproduce this paper by printing tiny red and blue lines on the paper. However, if you look closely at a bogus bill, you can tell that the lines are not set in the paper but rather printed on it.

9

Teacher Think Aloud

I never had any idea that counterfeit money was such a big problem in this country. After reading the part about spotting fake bills, I wanted to examine some money and try to find all those items. But then I thought: What if I actually find a bill that's fake? What will I do with it? Then I read the instructions on page 11 and learned that it should be turned in to the police. That's good to know.

Fix-Up Strategies

Offer these strategies to help students read independently.

If you don't understand what you're reading:

- Reread the difficult section to look for clues to help you comprehend.
- Read ahead to find clues to help you comprehend.
- Retell, or say in your own words, what you've read.
- Visualize, or form mental pictures of, what you've read.

If you don't understand a word:

- Reread the sentence. Look for ideas and words that provide meaning clues.
- Find clues by reading a few sentences before and after the confusing word.
- Look for the base or root word and think about its meaning.
- Think about the topic or plot at this point to see if either offers meaning clues.

Student Journal pages 122–123

Name ______________________ Date ________

Writing: Organizing Information

Organize what you want newcomers to this country to know about counterfeit money. Write your ideas in the chart.

Topic: Counterfeit Money

Main Idea 1: What to Look For

Details:

Main Idea 2: What to Do

Details:

Student Journal page 124 (See possible answers on TE page 289.)

Name ______________________ Date ________

Building Vocabulary: Synonym and Antonym Chart

Read each word. Think of two or three other words that are synonyms (similar in meaning) for it. Then think of two or three words that are antonyms (opposites) for the word. Use a thesaurus to help you.

Vocabulary Word	Synonyms	Antonyms
counterfeit	1. fake 2. bogus 3.	1. real 2. genuine 3.
genuine	1. 2. 3.	1. 2. 3.
bold	1. 2. 3.	1. 2. 3.
easy	1. 2. 3.	1. 2. 3.

The Case of the Million Dollar Counterfeiting: How one detective solved a counterfeiting crime

A Canadian detective, John Wilson Murray, spent his career tracking down counterfeiters. He is best known for solving a case that had stumped the U.S. Secret Service for years, a case known as The Million Dollar Counterfeiting.

In 1880, Canada was flooded with counterfeit American bills. These bills were so perfect looking that even bankers could not spot them. All of this bogus money, over one million dollars worth, was a problem because it was causing the Canadian dollar to lose its value.

One of the counterfeit bills was a five-dollar bill. A Treasury worker discovered it by accident. He came across the bogus bill and commented that it was better looking than any five-dollar bill he had ever seen. That was its fault: it was too perfect. The worker checked the bill's serial number and found out it was a fake. Immediately, the Secret Service went to work to find the counterfeiters. They did not have any luck. Soon after, however, fake Canadian bills were found. The counterfeiting scam became an international crime.

These counterfeiters were daring and bold, and they were not afraid to spend their fake money. They bought over $200,000 worth of furs with counterfeit money. They went to banks and passed off the counterfeit money as real.

A False Lead

Detective John Murray set out on the case. First he traveled to New York City and Philadelphia to look for a trail of bogus bills. He went to bars and clubs that were known hangouts for criminals and counterfeiters, but he found nothing. The Secret Service wasn't having any luck either. Murray went back to New York to track down counterfeiters he had known when he was a young detective. One of these men gave Murray his first lead. After praising the beauty of the forgeries, the man said it looked like the work of John Hill.

Murray knew Hill. He was an old engraver who had done time in jail twice for counterfeiting. He found Hill but quickly decided that he had nothing to do with this counterfeiting scheme. Murray was looking for a master, not a small-time engraver like Hill. Hill wouldn't have the time or skill to carve the detailed designs of the fake printing plates.

Following the Trail

Murray's mind turned to the educated Englishman Ed Johnson, who had counterfeited bills during the Civil War. Murray found out that a family named Johnson had been living in a grand style in Indianapolis. They spent money freely and lived in luxury with a big house, servants, and horse-drawn carriages. Accused of being counterfeiters, the family left Indianapolis. Murray tracked the Johnson family from Ohio to Kentucky to Connecticut and then to New York.

The trail Murray was following grew cold, and he was afraid that the Johnson family had returned to England. Then, he had a brainstorm: perhaps the family was back in Canada, where the counterfeiting began. Murray hurried back to Canada. Resting at a bar in Toronto, Murray got a break when in walked Johnnie Johnson, Ed's son. Murray followed Johnson until he found out where the family lived. He arranged with the neighbors to set up a surveillance spot so he could watch the Johnson's house.

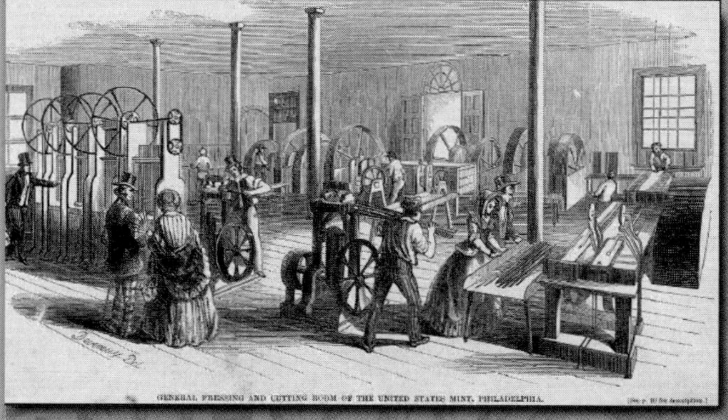

GENERAL PRESSING AND CUTTING ROOM OF THE UNITED STATES MINT, PHILADELPHIA.

▲ Workers press and cut currency at the mint in Philadelphia (1852).

10

After Reading

Use one or more activities.

Check Purpose

Have students decide if their purpose was met. How has paper money changed over the years? What do counterfeiters do to make fake money?

Discussion Questions

Continue the group discussion with the following questions.

1. Why was money so easy to counterfeit in the early years of the United States? (Cause-Effect)
2. What has the government done to stop counterfeiting? (Details)
3. How did this article make you feel about counterfeiting money? (Making Connections)

Revisit: Features List

Revisit the list of the features on U.S. bills. Can students add anything new to the list?

Revisit: Making Associations Activity

After reading the article, have students check the word associations activity on *Student Journal* page 121. Are there any changes they would like to make?

One evening when Ed Johnson headed out, Murray shadowed him, following just far enough behind not to be noticed. Johnson stopped at a bar for a drink and gave the bartender a dollar bill. Murray waited for Johnson to leave. Then he went into the bar and asked for the dollar bill. He examined it closely and knew he had his man. Murray followed Johnson into many stores and asked the clerks for the bills. Each time he collected a forgery.

Closing In

One night, Murray tapped Johnson on the shoulder, told him he was under arrest, searched him, and found more bogus bills. Johnson tried to make a deal with Murray, offering him a lot of money. But Murray insisted that Johnson give up the plates that he was using to make the counterfeit money. Johnson finally agreed. However, he had buried the plates, and they had to be dug up from the ground. It is said that Johnson lifted the plates from the ground as tenderly as a mother lifts a baby from a cradle.

Johnson told Murray the story of the plates. He had made them many years earlier when he lived in the United States. His daughters had forged the signatures because he had trained them since childhood in copying signatures. They printed large numbers of bills once a year. After each printing, they sealed the plates in wax and buried them. Everything else—pens, paper, and ink—was destroyed.

Johnson went on trial in the fall of 1880 and pleaded guilty to all seven charges brought against him. Lawyers asked for Johnson's sentence to be suspended, and it was. He was released and brought to the United States. However, if the Johnsons ever set foot in Canada again, they would be put in prison.

The Johnsons' counterfeiting scam lives on, for to this day, up in Northern Canada, Johnsons' bills still pass for real ones. ◆

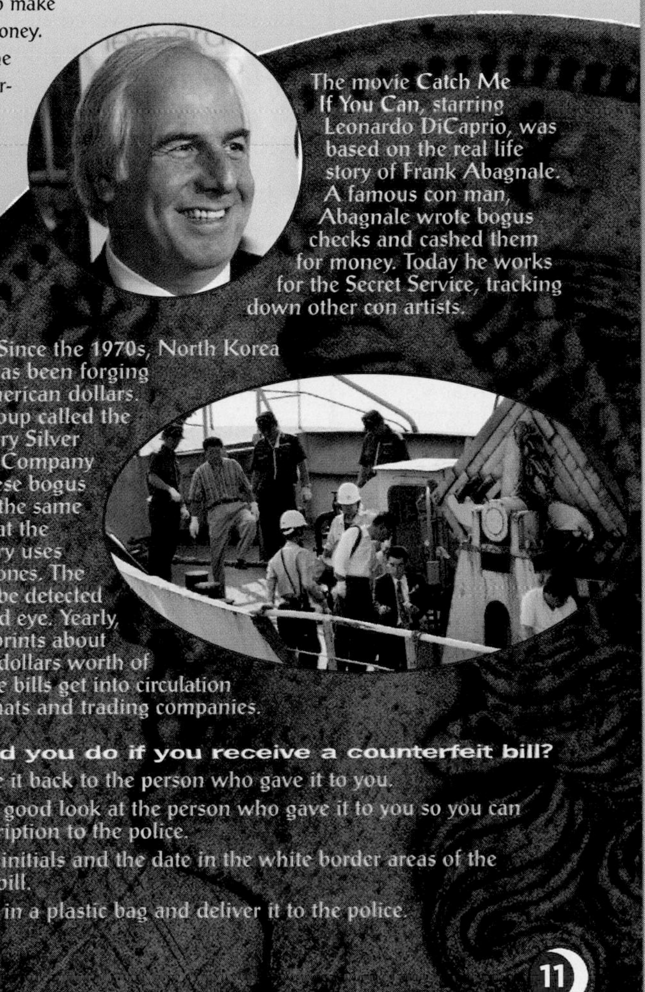

The movie Catch Me If You Can, starring Leonardo DiCaprio, was based on the real life story of Frank Abagnale. A famous con man, Abagnale wrote bogus checks and cashed them for money. Today he works for the Secret Service, tracking down other con artists.

Since the 1970s, North Korea has been forging American dollars. A group called the February Silver Trading Company prints these bogus bills with the same method that the U.S. Treasury uses to print real ones. The fakes cannot be detected with the naked eye. Yearly, North Korea prints about fifteen million dollars worth of forged bills. The bills get into circulation through diplomats and trading companies.

What should you do if you receive a counterfeit bill?

1. Do not give it back to the person who gave it to you.
2. Try to get a good look at the person who gave it to you so you can give a description to the police.
3. Write your initials and the date in the white border areas of the suspicious bill.
4. Put the bill in a plastic bag and deliver it to the police.

11

DIFFERENTIATED INSTRUCTION

Writing

Public Service Notice

Use these steps to help students with writing and designing their public service notices.

1. Brainstorm attention-getting words students can use as eye-catching titles for their notices, such as *warning*, *alert*, *caution*, and *beware*.
2. Provide magazines for students to browse through, noting colors and designs that attract attention.
3. Discuss keeping a reader's attention by using short sentences, questions, and answers. (Example: *Are you carrying counterfeit money?*)

Possible answers for **Student Journal page 124** include *counterfeit*—forged/original; *genuine*—real, true, authentic/phony, imitative, copy; *bold*—daring, risky, brave/timid, cautious, fearful; *easy*—effortless, uncomplicated, undemanding/hard, difficult, demanding.

Writing Public Service Notice

Ask students to write a public service notice warning newcomers to the United States about counterfeit money. Students can use the chart on *Student Journal* page 122 to help organize the information into two major categories. On *Student Journal* page 123, students can write final versions of their notices. Encourage students to include eye-catching titles. (See Differentiated Instruction.)

Vocabulary Synonyms and Antonyms

Display the word *counterfeit.* Ask students to scan the selection to find other words that mean the same. (*fake, bogus*) List the words and explain that words with similar meanings are synonyms. Then have students find selection words that mean the opposite of *counterfeit.* (*real, genuine*) List those words, explaining that they are antonyms. Students can practice identifying synonyms and antonyms on *Student Journal* page 124.

Phonics/Word Study

Absorbed Prefixes

Explain that a *prefix* is a letter or group of letters added to the beginning of a word to make a new word. For example, when *in-* is added to *active*, the new word is *inactive*, or "not active." Sometimes the prefix changes to make the new word easier to pronounce (*irregular* instead of *inregular).* In this case the prefix is said to be "absorbed." Work with students to complete the in-depth prefixes activity on TE page 290.

Phonics/Word Study

Absorbed Prefixes

Write the words *incapable* and *inactive* on the board. Ask students what the words have in common. Discuss the meaning of the words' shared prefix *in-* (not).

- Write *illegal* on the board. Ask students to define the word. (not legal) Because *inlegal* is difficult to say, the sound /n/ in the prefix *in-* is absorbed. (*illegal* rather than *inlegal*)
- Write the word *irregular*. Ask students to tell its meaning. (not regular) Have students explain why they think it is *irregular* rather than *inregular*. Point out that in some words, the prefix *in-* changes for the sake of fluent pronunciation.
- Using the Absorbed Prefix Sort One sheet, model the sorting process. (See *Word Study Manual* page 72.) Place a few words in the appropriate columns. Complete the sort with students.
- Discuss the sort and what students learned. Ask what they noticed about words in the Oddball column. Explain that *p* in a base word such as *perfect* is a "stop" consonant and is not easily absorbed.
- Have students sort on their own or in groups. Check the final sorts.

Prefix	Meaning	Base word or root	Before absorption	After absorption
ad-	to, toward	breviate	adbreviate	abbreviate
com-	with, together	ruption	comruption	corruption
dis-	opposite of	fidere	disfidence	diffidence
ex-	out, from	centric	excentric	eccentric
in-	not	legal	inlegal	illegal
in-	not	responsible	inresponsible	irresponsible
in-	not	measurable	inmeasurable	immeasurable
ob-	to, toward	fend	obfend	offend
sub-	under	plant	subplant	supplant

Absorbed Prefix Sort One

in- + base word	absorbed prefix + base word	Oddball
infinite	illegal	imperfect
inordinate	irrational	impossible
inactive	immeasurable	impatient
inconsolable	illicit	
inadvertent	irregular	
inconsequential	irrelevant	

For more information on word sorts and spelling stages, see pages 5–31 in the *Word Study Manual.*

Focus on . . .

Use one or more activities in this section to focus on a particular area of need in your students.

Comprehension STRATEGY SUPPORT

To help those students who need more practice using the strategies covered in this lesson, work one-on-one or in small groups to apply the strategy prompts below. Apply the prompts to a *Reading Advantage* paperback, a classroom library book, or a new or familiar selection in the magazine. Always model your own thinking first.

Monitor Understanding

- Do I understand what I'm reading? If not, what part is confusing to me?
- What fix-up strategies can I use to solve the problem? (See During Reading for fix-up strategies.)
- Why did a character say (do, think, ask) that?
- What images do I visualize from the text? What parts can't I visualize?
- Why did the author include (or not include) those details?

Making Connections

- What does this story (article, passage) remind me of?
- What do I already know about this topic?
- Where have I heard about this topic before?
- What do I have in common with the characters, people, or situations in the text?
- What other books, stories, articles, movies, or TV shows does this text make me think about?

Writing What If?

Discuss with students why bills and coins are a more convenient form of money than gold and silver. (They don't have to be weighed or measured each time they're used; they're easy to carry; they can be divided so people can make exact purchases and get exact change.) Have students write an extended answer to the questions: *What if you had to buy things using gold? What would that be like?*

To help students edit their writing, see the editing lessons in *Writing Advantage,* pages 56–93.

Fluency: Punctuation

Read "Change" aloud in a lighthearted manner as students follow along. Tell them to pay attention to the groups of words you read together and to note that you don't pause at the end of a line unless there is a period. Have students practice reading the poem silently so that they can "hear" which groups of words go together. Then have students work with partners and take turns reading the poem aloud to each other. Listeners can prompt readers to read with the correct phrasing and expression.

Use these prompts to guide students as they read.

- Read at an even, natural pace.
- Notice how the punctuation does not always give you clues for when to pause. The meaning of the words and phrases are your main clue for when to pause.

When students read aloud, do they—

✓ demonstrate appropriate meaning and usage of punctuation marks?

✓ incorporate appropriate timing, stress, and intonation?

✓ exhibit well-timed pauses between words and phrases?

English Language Learners

To support students' understanding of different text features included in "Counterfeit Money: Changing the Real Thing," guide them in analyzing visual aids and captions.

1. Have partners find the pictures and captions in the text.
2. Have them discuss each picture and read the captions together.
3. Have partners share their responses with the group.

Independent Activity Options

While you work with individuals or small groups, others can work independently on one or more of the following options.

- Level D paperback books, see TE pages 367–372
- Level D *eZines*
- Repeat word sorts from this lesson
- *Student Journal* pages for this lesson
- *Writing Advantage* independent lessons

Assessment

Strategy Assessment

To help you and your students assess their use of comprehension strategies, ask the following questions. Students can complete a written response or provide verbal answers in a one-on-one reading conference.

1. **Monitor Understanding** What questions do you still have about this article? How could you find out the answers? (Answers will vary. Possible questions: *Do the police give you a real bill when you turn in a fake one? Why was Ed Johnson's sentence suspended?* Students could do research online or in a library.)
2. **Making Connections** What in your own experience helped you understand the information in this article? (Answers will vary. Students may mention a movie or TV show they have seen about counterfeiting.)

For ongoing informal assessment, use the checklists on pages 61–64 of *Level D Assessment*.

Word Study Assessment

Use these steps to help you and your students assess their understanding of absorbed prefixes.

1. Write the following words on the board or on word cards: *immeasurable, inconsequential, irrational, infinite*.
2. Ask students to tell which words have absorbed prefixes, and to explain how the word would be spelled if the prefix hadn't been absorbed.

Word	Is the prefix absorbed?	If yes, what was the old word?
immeasurable	yes	*in*measurable
inconsequential	no	
irrational	yes	*in*rational
infinite	no	

LESSON 37
Beach Erosion in the United States
Changes, pages 12–16

SUMMARY

This **informational article** discusses the causes and effects of beach erosion, linking it to global warming, and describes attempts to slow the process.

COMPREHENSION STRATEGY

Monitor Understanding

WRITING

Letter to the Editor

VOCABULARY

Prefix *re-*

PHONICS/WORD STUDY

Additional Absorbed Prefixes

Lesson Vocabulary

erosion
in flux
continuous
obliterated
replenish

MATERIALS

Changes, pp. 12–16
Student Journal, pp. 125–127
Word Study Manual, p. 73
Writing Advantage, pp. 94–113

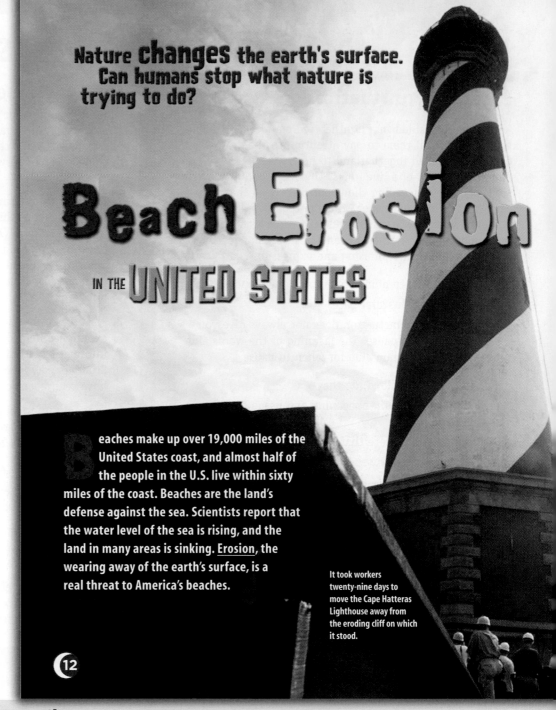

Nature changes the earth's surface. Can humans stop what nature is trying to do?

Beach Erosion IN THE UNITED STATES

Beaches make up over 19,000 miles of the United States coast, and almost half of the people in the U.S. live within sixty miles of the coast. Beaches are the land's defense against the sea. Scientists report that the water level of the sea is rising, and the land in many areas is sinking. Erosion, the wearing away of the earth's surface, is a real threat to America's beaches.

It took workers twenty-nine days to move the Cape Hatteras Lighthouse away from the eroding cliff on which it stood.

12

Before Reading

Use one or more activities.

Anticipation Guide

Create an anticipation guide for students. (See TE page 389 for an anticipation guide BLM.) Ask students to read the statements and check whether they agree or disagree with each statement. Then discuss the responses. (See Differentiated Instruction.)

Vocabulary Preview

Display the selection vocabulary. Assess students' prior knowledge of the words by having them begin the knowledge rating chart on *Student Journal* page 125. Students should fill in as many boxes as they can. They can fill in any empty boxes after reading. Model part of the process for one of the words.

Preview the Selection

Have students survey the article and tell what they think they will learn about.

Make Predictions/ Set Purpose

Students should use the information they gathered in previewing the selection to make predictions about what they will learn. If students have trouble generating a purpose for reading, suggest that they read to find out the causes and effects of beach erosion, and what measures are being taken to prevent it.

A SIGN OF TROUBLE

A lighthouse built in 1870 on the coast of North Carolina used to be 1,500 feet from the sea. In 1999, workers had to move the Cape Hatteras Lighthouse inland a quarter of a mile from where it first stood. Beach erosion had worn away nearly 1,300 feet of the shore. In 1996, Nauset Light in Eastham, Massachusetts, was moved 350 feet for the same reason. Beach erosion is not limited to a single beach.

DISAPPEARING BEACHES

Healthy beaches have a lot of sand. This sand comes from the ocean and the land. However, the beach-line is constantly in flux. Nothing stays the same. Beaches build up and then erode as waves wash up on the shore, as wind and storms blow sand around, and as the sea level changes. Danger develops when storms and rising sea levels cause beaches to wear away faster than they can repair themselves. As a result, some beaches have become smaller, and seaside homes are in danger of disappearing.

Many people like to drive their cars on the beach. However, beach traffic adds to the problem of erosion. Cars crush and press the sand into a hard mat. The beach flattens out, and this makes it easier for storm waves to cut away at the dunes. Some beaches ban the use of any kind of vehicle on the beach. Other beaches restrict the type of vehicle to a dune buggy or similar vehicle.

Erosion damages the plants and animals that live at the beach. The roots of the plants help hold the sand down so it isn't blown away by wind. Less space for beach grasses can actually add to the erosion process. Plants also provide food and shelter for animals that live in the sand. As shorelines disappear, there are fewer places where birds and sea turtles can lay their eggs.

THREE CAUSES OF EROSION

Storms

Most beach erosion happens when waves break on the beach and a thin layer of sand slips back into the sea. However, when there is a strong storm, the waves become larger and more powerful, and these big waves take more sand off the beaches, dropping it on the ocean floor. Also, strong storm winds carry sand that has piled up in the dunes back out to sea.

People

People also cause beach erosion. Hotels, beach homes, and roads that are built too close to the shore interfere with the natural movement of sand and water. These human-made "improvements" block sand from moving back up onto the shore. The sand has nowhere to go but back out to sea. Plans to halt erosion have backfired and made erosion worse.

13

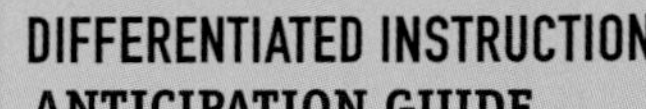

DIFFERENTIATED INSTRUCTION

ANTICIPATION GUIDE

Here's an example of an anticipation guide.

AGREE	DISAGREE	
		1. You can never step on the same beach twice.
		2. The coastline is a linked system; if you change one area, you will cause a change elsewhere.
		3. Breakwaters destroy the beach and benefit only the people who live along it.
		4. Global warming increases the earth's temperature and causes beach erosion.

Student Journal page 125

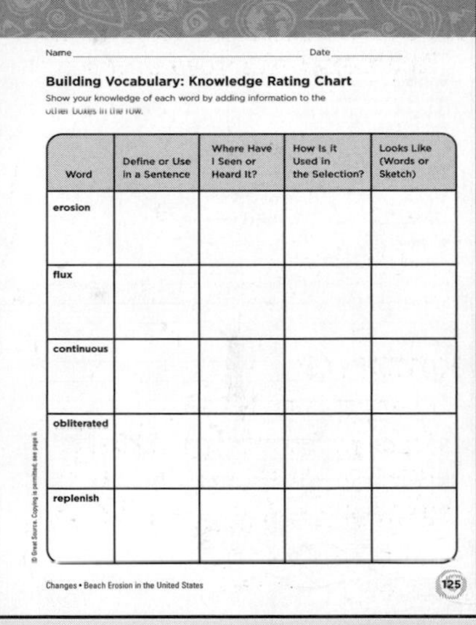

Name ______ Date ______

Building Vocabulary: Knowledge Rating Chart

Show your knowledge of each word by adding information to the other boxes in the row.

Word	Define or Use in a Sentence	Where Have I Seen or Heard It?	How Is It Used in the Selection?	Looks Like (Words or Sketch)
erosion				
flux				
continuous				
obliterated				
replenish				

Changes • Beach Erosion in the United States 125

During Reading

Comprehension

SMALL GROUP

MONITOR UNDERSTANDING

Use the bulleted prompts to model for students how to visualize what they are reading about. Then have students tell about a part they visualized and what details helped them visualize it.

- What do I picture in my mind as I read, and what details create this image?
- How does visualizing help me understand what I am reading?

Teacher Think Aloud

When I read the section subtitled "Storms," on page 13, I could clearly visualize big coastal storms. I pictured wind and rain and huge waves pounding the shore. The details about how the waves and wind cause the sand to go back into the sea helped me visualize the way sand can disappear.

Fix-Up Strategies

Offer these strategies to help students read independently.

If you don't understand what you're reading:

- Reread the difficult section to look for clues to help you comprehend.
- Read ahead to find clues to help you comprehend.
- Retell, or say in your own words, what you've read.
- Visualize, or form mental pictures of, what you've read.

Global Warming

Over the last 100 years, the sea level has risen about one foot. Why? Some people say global warming is the cause. Global warming is an increase of the earth's temperature that also increases the air temperature. Global warming can change the sea level because, as the air warms, the huge glaciers of ice at the North and South Poles melt. That water runs off into the oceans, and the sea level rises.

Perhaps a foot doesn't seem like that much, but consider the price of continuous, steady global warming and a higher sea level:

- Islands and cities by the coast could be obliterated, or wiped out.
- Groundwater that people drink could become polluted with salt water.
- Tunnels, bridges, and beaches could be destroyed.

THREE ATTEMPTS to Slow Beach Erosion

Sea Walls

Many cities by the sea try to stop beach erosion by building sea walls. Sea walls are made of concrete, rock, or wood. They are usually built at the edge of the beach to keep water and sand on the beach. People hope these walls will slow the erosion process. Sea walls do protect expensive homes built near the coast. However, some of them are not only ugly to look at, but they may actually speed up beach erosion. The walls reflect the energy of the waves back into the sea, causing the water to pull more sand from the beach back into the ocean.

Sand Replacement

Some people have dumped new sand on the shore to replenish, or refill, the beaches. Others try digging up sand from deep on the ocean floor, cleaning it, and dumping it on the beaches. This process is expensive and only works for a while. Eventually, the same erosion that first wore away the beach will eat away at the new sand.

Breakwaters

Breakwaters are huge walls of rocks built in the ocean. As the waves roll toward shore, they crash onto the break-waters instead of the beach. This takes away some of their power by the time they hit the beach. Many people don't like the way breakwaters look, so scientists are studying underwater breakwaters. Underwater, the rocks would take power from the crashing waves the way a coral reef does; however, there is evidence that breakwaters change the pattern of the waves, which causes beach erosion. Again, the breakwaters mainly benefit people who live along the beach.

Student Journal page 126

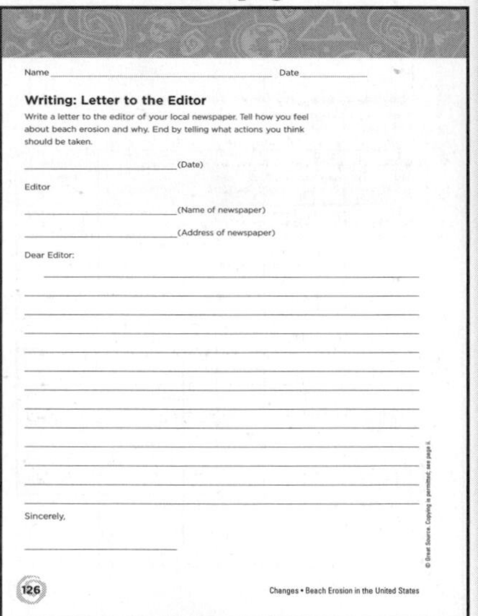

Name ______________________ Date __________

Writing: Letter to the Editor

Write a letter to the editor of your local newspaper. Tell how you feel about beach erosion and why. End by telling what actions you think should be taken.

______________________(Date)

Editor

______________________(Name of newspaper)

______________________(Address of newspaper)

Dear Editor:

Sincerely,

____

126 Changes • Beach Erosion in the United States

After Reading

Use one or more activities.

Check Purpose

Have students decide if their purpose was met. What are the causes and effects of beach erosion? How have people tried to prevent beach erosion?

Discussion Questions

Continue the group discussion with the following questions.

1. What are the main causes of beach erosion? (Cause-Effect)
2. What did you like about this article? Why? (Making Connections)
3. How did the organization of the article help you answer the questions on page 15? (Understanding Text Structure)

Revisit: Anticipation Guide

Have students return to their anticipation guides after reading the article. Do students want to change any of their opinions because of what they learned? Encourage discussion.

Revisit: Knowledge Rating Chart

Have students look over their knowledge rating charts on *Student Journal* page 125 and fill in the empty boxes that they left before reading the selection.

A dune buggy crosses a sand dune.

Erosion

THE FUTURE

What *can* be done about beach erosion? The ocean is a powerful force. There is little humans can do to hold it back. Scientists are still working on ways to do just that. However, as you just read, some of the solutions actually make erosion worse. Clearly, more work is needed.

What *should* be done about beach erosion? You may have noticed that most of the problems resulting from beach erosion have to do with development—houses, hotels, roads—along the ocean. People fear that they will lose their property—and rightly so. Many people have already lost property. Either the ocean has covered their land, or land and buildings have fallen into the ocean. Should millions of dollars be spent to repair or rebuild buildings that have been damaged or claimed by the ocean? Should building near and on beaches be restricted? What do *you* think? ◆

DIFFERENTIATED INSTRUCTION

Writing

Letter to the Editor

To help students write their letters, use these steps:

1. Provide copies of several editorial pages for students to browse through to see how letters to the editor are written.
2. Suggest that students use an organizer similar to the following to help them with the prewriting process.

Main Idea (state your feelings)
↓
Most important supporting fact
↓
Other supporting facts
↓
Conclusion (give a possible course of action)

Student Journal page 127

Name ______ Date ______

Vocabulary: Prefix *re-*

There are many common words that use the prefix *re-*, such as *reread* and *recall*. See how many you can think of. Write the word in the first column and the definition in the second column.

***-re* means "to do again"**

Words	Definitions
reread	read something again

Changes • Beach Erosion in the United States 127

Writing Letter to the Editor

Review the questions at the end of the article: *Should millions of dollars be spent to repair or rebuild buildings that have been damaged or claimed by the ocean? Should building near and on beaches be restricted?* Ask students to take a position in response to the questions and write a letter to the editor of a newspaper, explaining his or her stance. Have them write their letter on *Student Journal* page 126. (See Differentiated Instruction.)

Vocabulary Prefix *re-*

Explain that a prefix is a group of letters added to the beginning of a word to make a new word. The vocabulary word *replenish* is made up of the prefix *re-*, which means "do again," and the word *plenish*, which means "to stock or fill." So if a grocer buys more vegetables, he *replenishes* his supply. Have students write on *Student Journal* page 127 as many words using this prefix as they can. Possible answers include *rebuild*, *reactivate*, *reheat*, *recheck*, *reconnect*.

Phonics/Word Study

Additional Absorbed Prefixes

Review what students learned in the last lesson about absorbed prefixes. Display the following words: *irrelevant*, *illegal*, and *immeasurable*. Ask students to identify the absorbed prefix *in-* in each word. (*ir-*; *il-*; *im-*) Discuss the meaning of each word. (not relevant; not legal; not measurable) Now, work with students to complete the in-depth additional absorbed prefixes activity on TE page 297.

Global Warming Is Here!

Temperatures have risen since the 1970s.

Some scientists fear that polar ice sheets will melt as global temperatures rise.

Scientists who keep track of temperatures around the world have seen a warming trend. Ten of the warmest years on record have occurred since 1987. Nine of those years have occurred since 1990. Some scientists see this as the fastest temperature rise since the Ice Age. They are worried about how the earth might change as a result of warmer temperatures.

What does global warming mean for the earth? One effect is that the sea level is rising. If the polar ice continues to melt, the water will drain into the oceans. This could cause coastal flooding around the world. Global warming also affects animals. For example, insects searching for cooler weather have moved to Alaskan forests. The forests are now dying because the insects are damaging the trees.

On the Record

Warmest Century: **1900s**
Warmest Decade: **1990s**
Warmest Year: **1998**

16

Phonics/Word Study

Additional Absorbed Prefixes

- Write the words *eccentric*, *correspond*, and *supplant* on the board. Ask students what the words have in common. As needed, discuss with students what they have already learned about the absorbed prefix feature.
- Have students use a dictionary to identify the prefix in each word and to see how it changes the base word. (prefixes: *ex-*, *com-*, and *sub-*)
- Point out that the prefix *in-* is not the only prefix associated with the absorbed prefix feature.
- Using the Absorbed Prefix Sort Two sheet, model the sorting process for students. (See *Word Study Manual* page 73.) Place the first few words under the appropriate columns (*ad-* + base word, *con-* + base word, *dis-* + base word, non-absorbed prefixes). Have students complete the sort with you.
- Discuss the sort and what students learned.
- Hand out the Absorbed Prefix Sort Two sheet. Have students cut up the sheets and do the sort on their own or in groups.
- Check the final sorts and have students copy the sort into their Word Study notebook.

Absorbed Prefix Sort Two

ad- + base word	*con-* + base word	*dis-* + base word	non-absorbed prefixes
accommodate	combine	difference	advantage
appendix	collide	difficulty	advent
alleviate	connect	differ	confluence
appeal	correct		content
assimilate	collusion		distant
afflict			disappear
			disseminate
			dissolve
			dissonance

For more information on word sorts and spelling stages, see pages 5–31 in the *Word Study Manual.*

Focus on . . .

Use one or more activities in this section to focus on a particular area of need in your students.

Comprehension STRATEGY SUPPORT

To help those students who need more practice using the strategies covered in this lesson, work one-on-one or in small groups to apply the strategy prompts below. Apply the prompts to a *Reading Advantage* paperback, a classroom library book, or a new or familiar selection in the magazine. Always model your own thinking first.

Monitor Understanding

- Do I understand what I'm reading? If not, what part is confusing to me?
- What fix-up strategies can I use to solve the problem? (See During Reading for fix-up strategies.)
- Why did a character say (do, think, ask) that?
- What images do I visualize from the text? What parts can't I visualize?
- Why did the author include (or not include) those details?

Writing Summary

Remind students that a good way to check how well they have understood a text is to write a summary of it. A summary contains the most important ideas from the reading and leaves out extraneous details and examples. Have students write a summary of "Beach Erosion in the United States." Suggest that students use a main idea organizer before they begin writing. (See TE page 385 for a main idea organizer BLM.)

Main Idea:		
Detail:	**Detail:**	**Detail:**
Conclusion:		

For more instruction on planning and writing summaries, see lessons in *Writing Advantage,* pages 94–113.

Fluency: Phrasing

After students have had a chance to reread sections of the article silently, have them work with partners and take turns reading different paragraphs aloud. Remind students to use punctuation clues to help them know when to pause and when to stop. Also model for students how to keep words that belong together in phrases: *Beaches make up over 19,000 miles/of the United States coast,/and almost half of the people/in the U.S./live within 60 miles/ of the coast.*

Monitor partners as they read, and provide prompts to encourage fluent reading.

- Keep your eyes on the text so that you can anticipate words that go together.
- Don't come to a complete stop when you see a comma; just pause slightly and continue reading.

When students read aloud, do they—

✓ demonstrate quick recognition of words and phrases?

✓ exhibit an understanding of phrasal construction?

✓ incorporate appropriate timing, stress, and intonation?

English Language Learners

To support students' comprehension of "Beach Erosion in the United States," help them build background knowledge. Gather resources from the library or Internet that provide pictures of different forms of erosion.

1. Have partners discuss what they see in each picture.
2. Have them work together to draw and label a picture that shows the effects of erosion.
3. Have partners share their illustrations with the group.

Independent Activity Options

While you work with individuals or small groups, others can work independently on one or more of the following options.

- Level D paperback books, see TE pages 367–372
- Level D *eZines*
- Repeat word sorts from this lesson
- *Student Journal* pages for this lesson
- *Writing Advantage* independent lessons

Assessment

Strategy Assessment

To help you and your students assess their use of comprehension strategies, ask the following questions. Students can complete a written response or provide verbal answers in a one-on-one reading conference.

- **Monitor Understanding** What were some strong images for you in the article? Why? What images did you have difficulty visualizing? Explain why you think you had trouble. (Answers will vary. For example, students may mention the lighthouses that were moved, or what a breakwater looks like. For the second question, they may say that there were not enough details to help them form a mental image.)

For ongoing informal assessment, use the checklists on pages 61–64 of *Level D Assessment*.

Word Study Assessment

Use these steps to help you and your students assess their understanding of the additional absorbed prefixes.

1. Write the following words on the board or on word cards: *appendix, difference, correct, afflict, compare*.
2. Ask students to identify the absorbed prefix in each word.

Word	Absorbed Prefix
appendix	*ad-*
difference	*dis-*
correct	*con-*
afflict	*ad-*
compare	*con-*

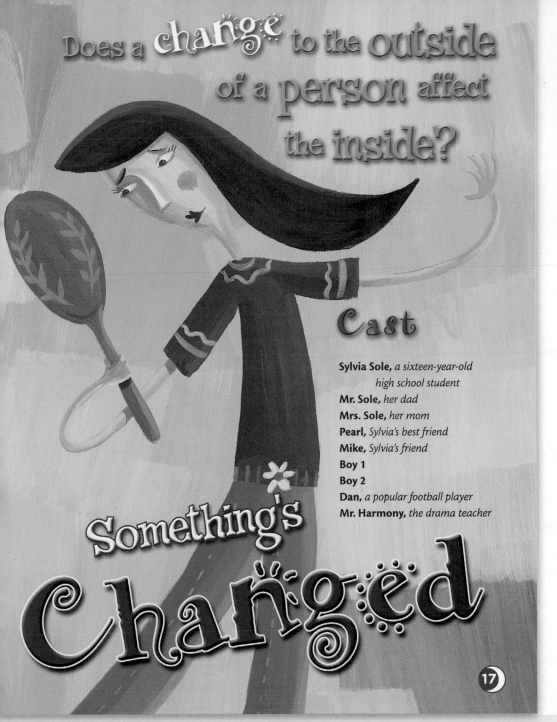

Does a change to the outside of a person affect the inside?

Cast

Sylvia Sole, *a sixteen-year-old high school student*
Mr. Sole, *her dad*
Mrs. Sole, *her mom*
Pearl, *Sylvia's best friend*
Mike, *Sylvia's friend*
Boy 1
Boy 2
Dan, *a popular football player*
Mr. Harmony, *the drama teacher*

Something's Changed

17

LESSON **38**

Something's Changed

Changes, pages 17–22

SUMMARY

In this **play**, a high-school girl changes her hair color in hopes of changing her life. Instead, she finds that real changes can only happen from within.

COMPREHENSION STRATEGIES

Making Connections
Understanding Text Structure

WRITING

Play Scene

VOCABULARY

Synonyms and Antonyms

PHONICS/WORD STUDY

Additional Absorbed Prefixes

Lesson Vocabulary

bravado	devastated
correlation	classic

MATERIALS

Changes, pp. 17–22
Student Journal, pp. 128–131
Word Study Manual, p. 74
Writing Advantage, pp. 152–169

Before Reading

Use one or more activities.

Make a List

Begin a discussion with students about changes that may affect the way a person looks, thinks, or acts. Create a list of students' responses. Keep the list so you can revisit it later.

Changes That May Affect How You Look, Think, or Act

1. new hairstyle
2. new family member
3. changing schools

Vocabulary Preview

List the vocabulary words and read each one aloud. Tell students to choose a familiar word to begin the illustrated word web activity on *Student Journal* page 128. Students will complete the web after reading. Model the process for students, using the word *classic*.

Preview the Selection

Have students preview the play. Ask students what they notice.

Make Predictions/ Set Purpose

Students should use the information they gathered in previewing the selection to make predictions about what they will learn. If students have trouble generating a purpose for reading, suggest that they read to find out what truly changes Sylvia.

DIFFERENTIATED INSTRUCTION

Comprehension

UNDERSTANDING TEXT STRUCTURE

To help students better understand the structure of a play, follow these steps.

1. Ask: *Did you notice that there is a new scene whenever the location of the action changes? Why do you think that is?*
2. Discuss students' responses. Guide them to the realization that each scene location requires different props, and that the time between scenes is often when stage sets are changed.

Student Journal page 128

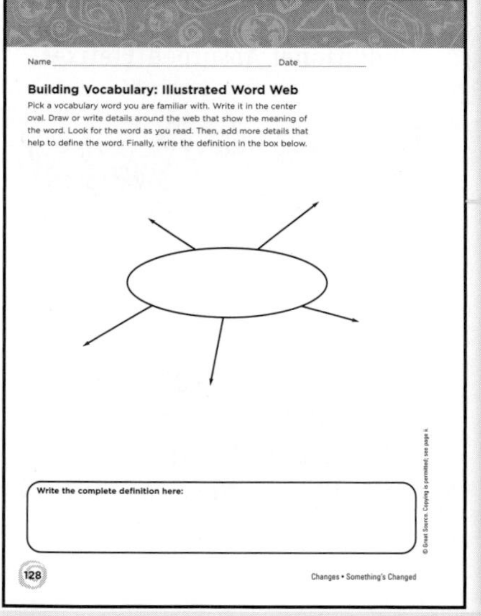

Name ______________________ Date __________

Building Vocabulary: Illustrated Word Web

Pick a vocabulary word you are familiar with. Write it in the center oval. Draw or write details around the web that show the meaning of the word. Look for the word as you read. Then, add more details that help to define the word. Finally, write the definition in the box below.

Write the complete definition here:

128 Changes • Something's Changed

Scene i

The Soles's kitchen at breakfast before school

SYLVIA: I can't go to school today.

MR. SOLE: *(not looking up from his paper)* Why not, Sweetheart?

SYLVIA: I'm joining the Marines.

MR. SOLE: That's nice, dear, so what time do you need to be picked up?

SYLVIA: No one listens to me in this house! *(She storms out to the bathroom beside the kitchen, looks in the mirror, and speaks to the mirror.)* Look at that. I mean just look at yourself, Sylvia. No one in school has hair as dark as yours. Come to think of it, does anyone else have dark brown hair? Hmm…not Kelly, Christine, or Janice. And look at your eyebrows, Sylvia. Could they be bushier? Oh my gosh, are they connecting over my nose? It's hopeless; I'll never be like those other girls. Who's going to look at me? I'll never, ever have a life, and THEY don't even care.

MRS. SOLE: Is everything all right in there, Sylvia?

SYLVIA: *(storming out of the bathroom)* Fine, and what kind of name is Sylvia anyway? We're in the twenty-first century, have you noticed?

18

Scene ii

A hallway in school. Sylvia walks with her friends Pearl and Mike.

PEARL: I can't believe you got the lead in the musical, Sylvia!

SYLVIA: What are you talking about, Pearl?

PEARL: It's posted on the door. I mean, Mr. Harmony posted the cast list this morning, but I thought you knew! Oh, I've ruined another great moment for you.

SYLVIA: Quit it, Pearl. Nothing is ruined. I am just in shock. Wow—I thought he'd definitely give the lead to a senior.

MIKE: You have the best voice in school, Sylvia. No one else could be Maria in *West Side Story* but you.

SYLVIA: *(suddenly shy)* Do you really think so? Oh, I am going to be so busy learning lines and music! Maybe this is too much for me.

(Lights fade on the three friends.)

During Reading

Comprehension

MAKING CONNECTIONS

Use the bulleted prompts to model for students how to make connections with the text. Then have students share connections they've made.

- What does this selection remind me of?
- How does my past experience help me to understand the selection?

Teacher Think Aloud

Sylvia's conversation with her mirror reminds me a lot of when I was in high school. I worried about how my hair looked all the time. My friend Maggie used a cream to try to make her freckles disappear. Joey always wore bulky clothes because he thought he was too skinny. There probably wasn't a single person in school who didn't think there was something wrong with the way he or she looked.

Comprehension

UNDERSTANDING TEXT STRUCTURE

Use the bulleted prompts to model for students how to identify and understand the elements of the play. Then have students describe the conflict and resolution of the play.

- What is the text structure of this selection?
- What is the conflict and resolution of the play?

(See Differentiated Instruction.)

Scene iii

Pearl and Sylvia in Sylvia's bedroom after school. Pearl brushes her blonde hair at Sylvia's vanity.

SYLVIA: I wish I had your hair color because maybe then Dan would notice me.

PEARL: I can't believe you're into Dan. He is *so* not your type—I mean, football—come on, Sylvia, you've never sat through one whole game.

SYLVIA: He is just so cute. I'd ask him out if I were bold and had the <u>bravado</u>, but I know he'd laugh in my face.

PEARL: Bravado—what a theater word! Just call it guts. But, I can't believe I'm hearing this. I think Mike likes you.

SYLVIA: No, no way. We're all just friends. Hey, Pearl, will you help dye my hair? *(Sylvia pulls out a bottle of peroxide bleach.)*

PEARL: Wow, are you serious about this? You know, Sylvia, blonde hair isn't going to change your life.

SYLVIA: Oh, yes, it is. I just know it. Come with me.

(The two girls disappear into the bathroom as the lights fade.)

Scene iV

The Soles's kitchen, dinner that same night

MRS. SOLE: Honey, did you know Sylvia got the lead in the school musical?

MR. SOLE: Was there ever a doubt? She's so talented.

MRS. SOLE: *(shouting)* Sylvia, supper is ready!

SYLVIA: Here I am. *(Sylvia walks into the kitchen. Her hair is Marilyn Monroe blonde. Her parents stare.)*

MRS. SOLE: Oh, your beautiful coffee-colored hair!

SYLVIA: Brown is so dull, so normal. I am sick of being normal! This hair is going to change my whole life.

MR. SOLE: Don't hold your breath.

SYLVIA: What is that supposed to mean? *You* notice me now.

MR. SOLE: I always notice you. I was just saying that I don't think you can make a <u>correlation</u>—uh, I mean a connection—between hair color and the quality of your life.

SYLVIA: You've never grown up in THIS town or gone to THIS high school.

MRS. SOLE: Let's just eat before dinner gets cold.

(Lights fade.)

Teacher Think Aloud

As I look through this selection, I recognize all the elements of a play: a cast list, different scenes, and the speaker's name before each piece of dialogue. I'm sure this is fiction because plays always seem to tell a story. I find them easier to read than many stories, though, because I can easily tell who is saying the words and where the action is taking place.

Fix-Up Strategies

Offer these strategies to help students read independently.

If you don't understand what you're reading:

- Reread the difficult section to look for clues to help you comprehend.
- Read ahead to find clues to help you comprehend.
- Retell, or say in your own words, what you've read.
- Visualize, or form mental pictures of, what you've read.

If you don't understand a word:

- Reread the sentence. Look for ideas and words that provide meaning clues.
- Find clues by reading a few sentences before and after the confusing word.
- Look for the base or root word and think about its meaning.
- Think about the topic or plot at this point to see if either offers meaning clues.

Student Journal pages 129–130

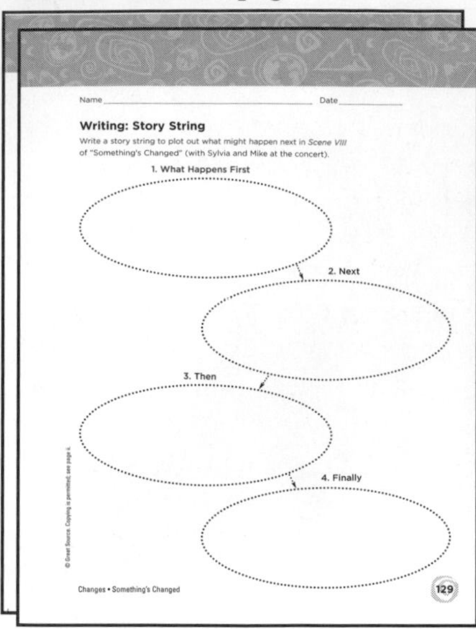
Name ______ Date ______

Writing: Story String

Write a story string to plot out what might happen next in *Scene VIII* of "Something's Changed" (with Sylvia and Mike at the concert).

1. What Happens First
2. Next
3. Then
4. Finally

© Great Source. Copying is permitted; see page ii.

Changes • Something's Changed 129

Student Journal page 131

Name ______ Date ______

Building Vocabulary: Synonym and Antonym Chart

For each vocabulary word, think of two or three other words that are synonyms (similar in meaning). Then think of two or three words that are antonyms (opposite in meaning). Use a thesaurus to help you, if you wish.

Vocabulary Word	Synonyms	Antonyms
bravado	1. daring 2. 3.	1. cowardice 2. 3.
correlation	1. 2. 3.	1. 2. 3.
classic	1. 2. 3.	1. 2. 3.
devastated	1. 2. 3.	1. 2. 3.

© Great Source. Copying is permitted; see page ii.

Changes • Something's Changed 131

Scene V

School the next day

MIKE: Man, Sylvia, what happened to you?

PEARL: Doesn't she look absolutely great?

MIKE: I guess that's a word for it. Why did you dye your hair, Sylvia?

SYLVIA: *(ignoring him)* Look, there's Dan. He's alone at his locker. I'm going to do it, now. I am going to walk over there and … *(She starts toward a group of "popular" boys.)*

BOY 1: Whoa, turn down the lights!

BOY 2: I thought the sun rose at 6 A.M.

DAN: Who is that anyway? Is that the girl who does all of those geeky shows?

(Hearing this, Sylvia turns back to her friends, devastated.)

SYLVIA: *(to herself)* How can they make fun of me? Now I look like all of their girlfriends!

MIKE: Are you okay, Sylvia?

SYLVIA: No, I'm not okay. Nothing is ever going to change for me. Instead, I'm always going to be boring, brown-haired Sylvia.

(Inside Mr. Harmony's classroom)

MR. HARMONY: I assume everyone has seen the cast list. We're going to have a read-through on … *(He stops when he looks up and sees Sylvia.)* Wow, Sylvia, what happened to you? *(The class laughs.)*

SYLVIA: Just trying out a new look, Sir.

MR. HARMONY: Well, I need that brown hair back right now. I've never heard of a bleached blonde Maria before.

SYLVIA: Sure thing, Mr. Harmony.

MR. HARMONY: Good, now, where was I? Oh, yes, Wednesday night at 5 P.M. …

(Lights fade.)

After Reading

WHOLE CLASS

Use one or more activities.

Check Purpose

Have students decide if their purpose was met. Did they learn more about the kinds of changes that can affect a person on the inside? Were they able to understand what truly changes Sylvia?

Discussion Questions

Continue the group discussion with the following questions.

1. What did Mr. Sole mean when he told Sylvia that she couldn't make a correlation between hair color and the quality of her life? (Inferential Thinking)
2. Think of a time you felt like Sylvia and wanted to make a change. What did you do, and how did it affect you? (Making Connections)

Revisit: List

Revisit the list that students began in Before Reading. Did students list changes similar to the ones Sylvia experienced? Do students want to add to the list?

Revisit: Illustrated Word Web

Have students complete the illustrated word web they began on *Student Journal* page 128. Students can use the information they learned in the article to complete it.

Scene VI

Sylvia's bedroom that evening

SYLVIA: *(talking to a stuffed animal)* I can't believe Dan didn't know who I was. And there is nothing "geeky" about the shows I'm in. They are classic, timeless theater. What a dork he must be. But the whole drama class laughed at me, too, so I must be a bigger idiot than I thought.

MRS. SOLE: *(knocking on door)* May I come in?

SYLVIA: Yes, Mom, come on in.

MRS. SOLE: Ah, I do think brown hair suits you best, Sylvia, but I want you to know how proud your father and I are of you for getting the lead in the school play. You have such a talent, and we are proud that you go after your dreams. Oh, yes, and this letter came for you in the mail today. It looks like a response to your audition for the Millville Summer Music Theater.

SYLVIA: Oh, forget it. There is no way I will get in, Mom. Did you see all of the girls trying out? And there were two other audition days.

MRS. SOLE: Well, I'll just leave it right here then. *(She places the letter next to Sylvia on her bed and leaves. Sylvia fingers the envelope and then tears it open and reads aloud.)*

SYLVIA: Dear Ms. Sole, I am pleased to inform you that the directors of the Millville Summer Music Theater are proud to offer you a role in the cast of this year's summer musical. Our first meeting will be May 21. At that time we will present you with...

(Lights fade on a giddy Sylvia.)

West Side Story

The musical *West Side Story* is a modern retelling of the classic romance *Romeo and Juliet* written by Shakespeare. The Broadway musical version opened in 1957. The movie came out in 1962. Both stories follow the relationship of a young couple who fall in love but are kept apart by their families and friends. Both stories end tragically.

21

DIFFERENTIATED INSTRUCTION

SMALL GROUP

Vocabulary Synonyms and Antonyms

Review the terms *synonym* (word with similar meaning) and *antonym* (word with opposite meaning).

1. Write the word *change* on the board or on chart paper. Ask volunteers to suggest synonyms for *change*. (*alter, vary, modify, adjust, improve, transform*)
2. Ask volunteers to suggest antonyms for the word *change*. (*stay, remain, leave, endure, last*)
3. Model for students how to use a thesaurus to help them find synonyms and antonyms.

***bravado:** courageousness, fearlessness; cowardice, timidity*

***correlation:** relationship, connection, relevance; irrelevance, contrast, disparity*

***classic:** timeless, legendary, tasteful; modern, contemporary, craze*

***devastated:** humiliated, deflated, crushed; inflated, elevated, bolstered*

Writing Play Scene

Have partners write a scene in which Sylvia and Mike go to the concert. First, have students discuss what Sylvia and Mike might talk about or what might happen at the concert, given the changes Sylvia has gone through. Then, have partners work together to record their scene ideas in the story string on *Student Journal* page 129. Once partners have completed the story string, have them write their scene on *Student Journal* page 130.

Vocabulary Synonyms and Antonyms

Display the word *bravado*. Ask students:

- What is the definition of the word *bravado*? (a false show of bravery)
- What other words come to mind when you hear or see *bravado*?

Ask if any of these words are synonyms for *bravado*. Then ask students for antonyms. Invite students to complete *Student Journal* page 131. (See Differentiated Instruction.)

Phonics/Word Study

Additional Absorbed Prefixes

Tell students that they are going to learn three more absorbed prefixes in this lesson. Review the prefixes they studied in the last lesson: *ad-*, *con-*, and *dis-*. Remind them of how these prefixes are absorbed when they form new words: *ad-/appeal, con-/combine, dis-/differ*. Now, work with students to complete the in-depth additional absorbed prefixes activity on TE page 305.

Scene VII

School the next day

PEARL: What happened to you? You look different.

SYLVIA: Of course I do. I dyed my hair back.

PEARL: No, it's something else. I can't quite put my finger on it.

(Sylvia smiles knowingly. Mike walks up to them.)

SYLVIA: Hey, do you two want to go to the concert with me tonight?

MIKE: *(shocked)* Uh, I mean, yeah, sure.

PEARL: Of course. *(Sylvia elbows her friend.)* What am I saying? I have to watch my little sister tonight, so you two go. Have fun! ◆

22

Phonics/Word Study

Additional Absorbed Prefixes

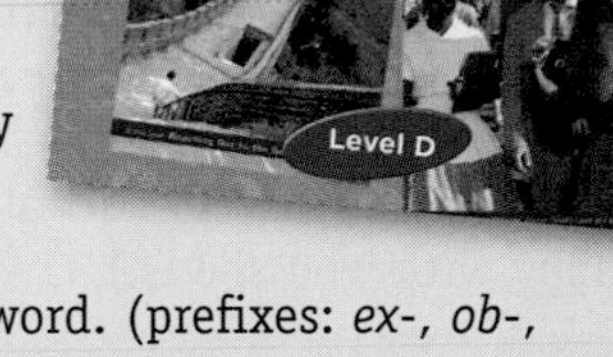

- Write *eccentric*, *offend*, and *difference* on the board. Ask students what the words have in common. As needed, discuss with students what they have already learned about the absorbed prefix feature.
- Have students use a dictionary to identify the prefix in each word and to see how it changes the base word. (prefixes: *ex-*, *ob-*, and *dis-*)
- Using the Absorbed Prefix Sort Three sheet, model the sorting process for the students. (See *Word Study Manual* page 74.) Place the first few words under the appropriate columns (*ex-* + base word, *ob-* + base word, *sub-* + base word, non-absorbed prefixes). Have students complete the sort with you.
- Discuss the sort and what students learned.
- Hand out the Absorbed Prefix Sort Three sheet. Have students cut up the sheets and do the sort on their own or in groups.
- Check the final sorts and have students copy the sort into their Word Study notebook.

Absorbed Prefix Sort Three

ex- + base word	*ob-* + base word	*sub-* + base word	non-absorbed prefixes
eccentric	occasion	suggest	exchange
effect	occupy	supplant	exhibit
effigy	occur	surreptitious	oblige
effective	offer	surrogate	obstruct
efficiency	opponent	succinct	suburban
ecclesiastic	opposite	succumb	subparticle

For more information on word sorts and spelling stages, see pages 5–31 in the *Word Study Manual.*

Focus on . . .

Use one or more activities in this section to focus on a particular area of need in your students.

Comprehension STRATEGY SUPPORT

To help those students who need more practice using the strategies covered in this lesson, work one-on-one or in small groups to apply the strategy prompts below. Apply the prompts to a *Reading Advantage* paperback, a classroom library book, or a new or familiar selection in the magazine. Always model your own thinking first.

Making Connections

- What does this story (article, passage) remind me of?
- What do I already know about this topic?
- Where have I heard about this topic before?
- What do I have in common with the characters, people, or situations in the text?
- What other books, stories, articles, movies, or TV shows does this text make me think about?

Understanding Text Structure

- What kind of text is this? (book, story, article, guidebook, play, manual)
- How does the author organize the text? (cause-effect, problem-solution, chronological order, description, question-answer, comparison-contrast)
- What details support my thoughts about the text structure?
- What is the cause (effect, problem, solution, order, question, answer)?
- If fiction, who are the characters? What is the setting, plot, conflict, and resolution?

Writing Opinion Paragraph

Write the following expressions on the board: *You can't judge a book by its cover. You only have one chance to make a first impression.*

Discuss both expressions relating to making judgments about people from their appearance. Then ask each student to choose one of the expressions to write about. Students should include a main idea statement telling whether they agree or disagree with the expression, and then include at least three details to support their opinions. Students can use a main idea organizer to help them plan their writing. (See TE page 385 for a main idea BLM.)

For further instruction on writing persuasive essays, see lessons in *Writing Advantage,* pages 152–169.

Fluency: Expression

After students have read the selection at least once, have them form groups to read scenes from the play.

As you listen to students read, use these prompts to guide them:

- Put yourself in the character's place. How would a frustrated teenager sound? How would a caring friend sound? Read with expression.
- Watch for the stage directions, or the cues in parentheses, that tell you a character's feelings so that you know how to say your lines.

When students read aloud, do they—

✓ reflect an understanding of the text?
✓ demonstrate appropriate timing, stress, and intonation?
✓ incorporate appropriate speed and phrasing?

English Language Learners

To support students' use of the making connections strategy, extend the comprehension activity on TE page 300. Remind students that making personal connections will help improve their understanding of the text.

1. Have students think about what the selection reminds them of.
2. Have them take about 5–10 minutes to write down their personal connection.
3. Have students share their responses with a partner.

Independent Activity Options

While you work with individuals or small groups, others can work independently on one or more of the following options:

- Level D paperback books, see TE pages 367–372
- Level D *eZines*
- Repeat word sorts from this lesson
- *Student Journal* pages for this lesson
- *Writing Advantage* independent lessons

Assessment

Strategy Assessment

To help you and your students assess their use of comprehension strategies, ask the following questions. Students can complete a written response or provide verbal answers in a one-on-one reading conference.

1. **Making Connections** What connections were you able to make to the characters or situations in the play? (Answers will vary.)
2. **Understanding Text Structure** What was the problem in the play, and how was it resolved? (Sylvia wants to be different—more like everyone else. Gaining pride in her talent helps her become happy with who she is.)

For ongoing informal assessment, use the checklists on pages 61–64 of *Level D Assessment*.

Word Study Assessment

Use these steps to help you and your students assess their understanding of the additional absorbed prefixes.

1. Write the following words on the board or on word cards: *suggest*, *effective*, *occasion*, *eccentric*, *supplant*, *opposite*.
2. Ask students to identify the absorbed prefix in each word.

Word	Absorbed Prefix
suggest	*sub-*
effective	*ex-*
occasion	*ob-*
eccentric	*ex-*
supplant	*sub-*
opposite	*ob-*

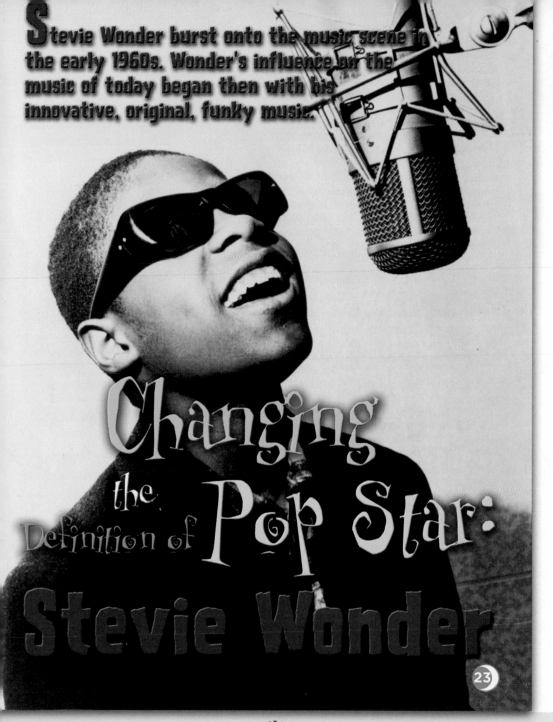

Stevie Wonder burst onto the music scene in the early 1960s. Wonder's influence on the music of today began then with his innovative, original, funky music.

Changing the Definition of Pop Star: Stevie Wonder

23

LESSON 39

Changing . . . Pop Star: Stevie Wonder

Changes, pages 23–28

SUMMARY

This **biographical sketch** details the exceptional career of musician Stevie Wonder.

COMPREHENSION STRATEGIES

Determining Importance
Making Connections

WRITING

Acceptance Speech

VOCABULARY

Context Clues

PHONICS/WORD STUDY

Suffixes *-ible* and *-able* Words with Exceptions

Lesson Vocabulary

genius	coveted
incubator	inductees
genre	innovation
arbitrary	

MATERIALS

Changes, pp. 23–28
Student Journal, pp. 132–134
Word Study Manual, p. 75
Writing Advantage pp. 170–181

Before Reading

Use one or more activities.

Make a List

Brainstorm with students a list of ways a popular musician can effect change in society. Students will revisit the list after they read the selection.

How can musicians effect change?
1. Play benefit concerts
2. Start foundations
3. Raise awareness about an issue

Vocabulary Preview

Review the vocabulary list. Write the words on the board or on chart paper and read them aloud. Then have students complete *Student Journal* page 132. Students will answer questions for two of the vocabulary words.

Preview the Selection

Have students look through the six pages of the biographical sketch, pages 23–28 in the magazine. Discuss students' impressions.

Make Predictions/Set Purpose

Students should use the information they gathered in previewing the selection to make predictions about what they will learn. If students have trouble generating a purpose for reading, suggest that they read to find out how Stevie Wonder changed the definition of pop star.

DIFFERENTIATED INSTRUCTION

Comprehension

DETERMINING IMPORTANCE

Use this activity to help students determine importance.

1. Have students read the paragraph on page 26 that is under the "Stevie Wonder" heading.
2. Ask: *Which do you think is the most important idea in this paragraph: (1) Stevie contributes to society; (2) He helps other visually impaired people;* or *(3) The Kurzweil reader converts text into speech? Why?* (Number 2, because 1 is too vague, and 3 is not directly about Wonder.)

Student Journal page 132

Name ______________ Date ______

Building Vocabulary: Making Associations

Pick two words from the vocabulary list below. Think about what you know about each word. Then answer the following questions for each word.

genius genre coveted innovation
incubator arbitrary inductees

Word ______________

What do you think about when you read this word? ______________

Who might use this word? ______________

What do you already know about this word? ______________

Word ______________

What do you think about when you read this word? ______________

Who might use this word? ______________

What do you already know about this word? ______________

Now watch for these words in the magazine selection. Were you on the right track?

If you were asked to name a musical genius, perhaps you would include musicians like Mozart, Louis Armstrong, and Yo Yo Ma.

Not far down on the list might also be music maker Stevie Wonder. Critics praise Wonder's music, and his fans are loyal and great in number. Throughout his life, he has found ways to overcome his physical handicaps and use both his music and his fame to promote causes that concern him.

Stevie Wonder hasn't always been known by that name. Steveland Judkins was born May 13, 1950, in Saginaw, Michigan. At birth, the doctors placed him in an incubator, a medical machine that keeps small babies warm and helps them develop. This machine that was supposed to help save Stevie's life blew too much oxygen into the air around the small baby. As a result, Stevie became permanently blind.

In interviews Stevie has often said that his blindness was a blessing because it made him focus on the sense of sound instead of sight.

While many people might consider blindness a handicap, Stevie never looked at it that way. In fact, in interviews he's often said that his blindness was a blessing because it made him focus on the sense of sound instead of sight. Being blind didn't stop Stevie from following any of his dreams. At the age of seven, he began to learn piano. By the age of nine, he was playing the harmonica and drums. Not much later, Stevie joined a church choir and began to sing.

The musical genre, or style, that interested Wonder was R&B, Rhythm and Blues. Rhythm and Blues is the name used to describe the African American music that grew out of American cities in the 1930s. R&B mixed the traditional Blues style with the jazz of the modern city. In the 1950s, R&B became connected to black popular music, but it wasn't aimed only at teenagers like rock 'n' roll was. However, these musical categories often seem arbitrary, or random, and many artists, including Stevie Wonder, fit into more than one category.

During Reading

Comprehension

DETERMINING IMPORTANCE

Use the bulleted prompts to model for students how to determine the importance of ideas in the third paragraph of the selection. Then have students determine the importance of ideas in the fourth paragraph.

- What are the most important ideas in the paragraph?
- How can I support my beliefs?

(See Differentiated Instruction.)

Teacher Think Aloud

I think the most important idea in the third paragraph on page 24 is that blindness didn't stop Wonder from being a music maker or following any of his dreams. The other details in the paragraph support my beliefs by describing how Wonder's blindness has helped him focus on his sense of sound. Also, they describe his early involvement in a variety of musical experiences.

Comprehension

MAKING CONNECTIONS

Use the bulleted prompts to model for students how to make connections with the text. Then have students share a connection they made.

- What do I already know about this topic?
- How does my knowledge help me understand it?

• **Wolfgang Amadeus Mozart**
(1756–1791) was a composer who lived in Austria. He wrote many symphonies, operas, piano concertos, and choral works. Famous works of his include the opera The Magic Flute and Symphony Number 40.

• **Louis "Satchmo" Armstrong**
(1900–1971) was an American jazz musician. He was known for his smooth style of playing the trumpet and his trademark gravelly voice. Well-known vocal performances of Armstrong's include "Hello, Dolly" and "What a Wonderful World."

• **Yo Yo Ma**
(born 1955) is a well-known and well-respected cellist. He lives in Massachusetts and has performed live all over the world and on TV. He was even on an episode of "Mr. Rogers' Neighborhood"!

"I love touching people with songs but I also want to reach people's consciences and trigger some emotion on matters other than the heart."

25

Teacher Think Aloud

I saw Stevie Wonder perform on TV. I remember that he seemed to really enjoy performing and to be a happy person. Although I can't remember the songs he sang, I liked listening to them. I don't think I would have gotten as much out of this article if I didn't know who Stevie was. I was able to think about him performing as I read, and that made the article more interesting.

Fix-Up Strategies

Offer these strategies to help students read independently.

If you don't understand what you're reading:

- Reread the difficult section to look for clues to help you comprehend.
- Read ahead to find clues to help you comprehend.
- Retell, or say in your own words, what you've read.
- Visualize, or form mental pictures of, what you've read.

If you don't understand a word:

- Reread the sentence. Look for ideas and words that provide meaning clues.
- Find clues by reading a few sentences before and after the confusing word.
- Look for the base or root word and think about its meaning.
- Think about the topic or plot at this point to see if either offers meaning clues.

In 1961, the music producer Ronnie White discovered Stevie Wonder. White had arranged a coveted, much desired audition for Stevie with Berry Gordy, Jr., at Motown Records. Motown was a successful, independent record company made up of producers, musicians, and song-writers. Berry immediately liked the eleven-year-old singer and signed a contract with him. After being renamed "Little Stevie Wonder," at the age of twelve, Stevie recorded his first album and became one of the first mainstream African American musicians. Because of his overflowing energy and exciting live shows, Stevie Wonder was a big star by the time he was just fifteen.

After being renamed "Little Stevie Wonder," at the age of twelve, Stevie recorded his first album.

When he turned twenty-one and his Motown contract ended, Wonder decided to try some new things. He built his own recording studio, and he enrolled in college at the University of Southern California. Never happy being "good enough," Wonder wanted to improve his music writing skills; so in college, he studied music theory.

At this time, Wonder also decided that he wanted more control over his own career. On his own, he recorded two albums at the studio he built. When they were finished, he showed the records to the producers at Motown. Motown, and especially its founder, Berry Gordy, Jr., had a reputation for controlling musicians. Wonder was about to change this. Motown badly wanted to claim Wonder as one of its artists, so the company agreed to pay Wonder more and, most importantly, give him artistic freedom.

By 1972 Wonder was back at the top of the charts with an album that contained the now-classic hits "Superstition" and "You Are the Sunshine of My Life." Wonder also added political and social messages to his music, a big change for R&B songs. Many of Wonder's songs took on issues such as the harsh life in the ghetto and unfair politics.

In 1973 Wonder was sidetracked by an auto accident. A tree crashed onto his car, and he fell into a coma. After the accident, Wonder made a full recovery; however, the head injury left him without his sense of smell. With the same hope-fulness Wonder had as a child, he faced his recovery and music head on. Wonder released another smash album in 1974. And in the years 1972 through 1974, Wonder won more Grammy awards than any other artist. He collected awards in almost every category: Best R&B Artist, Best Song, Best Male Vocalist, and Best Album.

Stevie Wonder

Stevie Wonder contributes to society in many ways. Wonder founded an award program called SAP/Stevie Wonder Vision Awards. The program's mission is to spotlight computer technology that helps people who are blind and visually impaired in the workplace. One of the inventions, the Kurzweil reader system, allows blind people to put written documents into a machine that converts the writing into speech.

26

Student Journal page 133

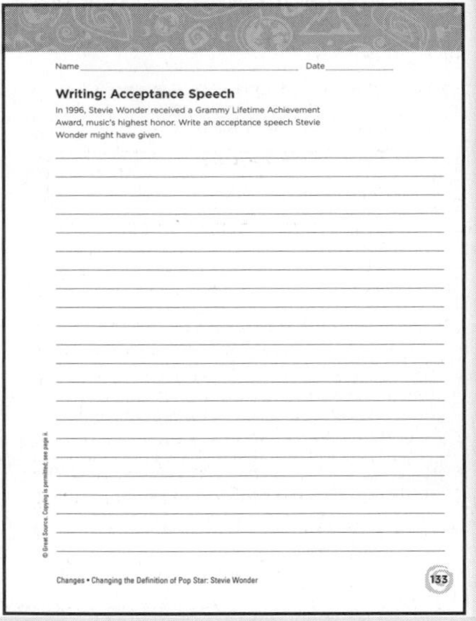

Name ____________ Date ________

Writing: Acceptance Speech

In 1996, Stevie Wonder received a Grammy Lifetime Achievement Award, music's highest honor. Write an acceptance speech Stevie Wonder might have given.

© Great Source. Copying is permitted; see page ii.

Changes • Changing the Definition of Pop Star: Stevie Wonder 133

After Reading

Use one or more activities.

Check Purpose

Have students decide if their purpose was met. Did they find out how Stevie Wonder changed the definition of pop star?

Discussion Questions

Continue the group discussion with the following questions.

1. What effect did Stevie Wonder's blindness have on his career? (Cause-Effect)
2. How are the events of Stevie Wonder's life arranged in the article? (Sequence)
3. Which of Stevie Wonder's qualities do you admire? (Making Connections)

Revisit: List

Revisit the list about pop musicians effecting change in society. What new information can students add?

Gold and Platinum Albums

In the recording industry, it is extremely important to sell a lot of recordings. The more you sell, the more opportunities you have to further your career and the more money you will make. That's why the recording industry has gold and platinum albums. When a record "goes gold," it means that over 500,000 units have been sold. A platinum album has sold at least 1,000,000 copies. The sales are certified by the Record Industry Association of America (RIAA).

During the late 1970s and early 1980s, Wonder tried out many different styles of music. Critics and fans didn't always praise or welcome these new styles. However, the failure of a few albums didn't slow down Stevie Wonder; he kept on making music. In the mid-1980s, he returned to his hit R&B style and put out a platinum album, Hotter Than July.

At this time in his career, Wonder also began working with other top artists. In 1982 he sang a duet with former Beatle, Paul McCartney. Their hit single, "Ebony and Ivory," was a song about peace between different races of people. It pointed out that the beautiful harmonies of the black and white piano keys should be a lesson for the way that black and white people can get along.

Wonder also worked with Michael Jackson in 1987. After taking a short break, Wonder returned to songwriting by composing the soundtrack for the Spike Lee movie Jungle Fever.

27

DIFFERENTIATED INSTRUCTION

Vocabulary

Context Clues

To help students with context clues, use the steps below:

1. Tell students that the first place to look for context clues is in the sentence in which the unfamiliar word appears.
2. Explain that clues may be a synonym (word with similar meaning), an antonym (word with opposite meaning), a definition, or an example.
3. If the sentence itself does not provide clues, students should look at sentences just before and just after the sentence with the unfamiliar word.

Student Journal page 134

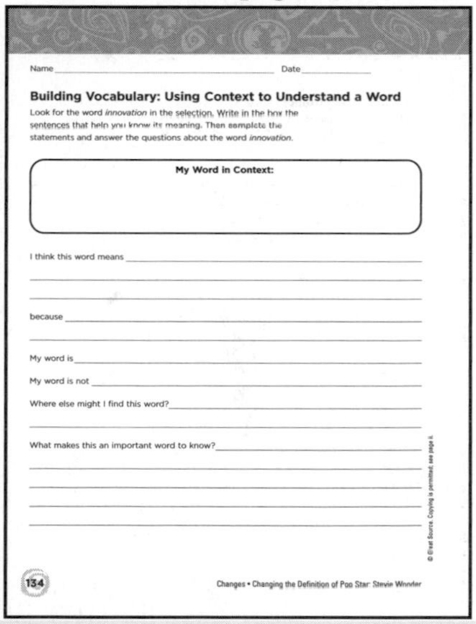

Name ______ Date ______

Building Vocabulary: Using Context to Understand a Word

Look for the word *innovation* in the selection. Write in the box the sentences that help you know its meaning. Then complete the statements and answer the questions about the word *innovation*.

My Word in Context:

I think this word means ______

because ______

My word is ______

My word is not ______

Where else might I find this word? ______

What makes this an important word to know? ______

© Great Source. Copying is permitted; see page ii.

134 Changes • Changing the Definition of Pop Star: Stevie Wonder

Writing Acceptance Speech

Remind students that they read about Stevie Wonder receiving a Grammy Lifetime Achievement Award, music's highest honor. Ask students what Wonder might have said in his acceptance speech. Encourage students to use information they learned from this article, along with personal experience, to come up with ideas. Write students' ideas on the board. Then have students complete *Student Journal* page 133.

Vocabulary Context Clues

Have students look on page 26 for the following sentence: *White had arranged a* <u>*coveted,*</u> *much desired audition for Stevie . . . at Motown Records.* Explain that reading context clues, or the words surrounding *coveted,* helps to figure out its meaning. Point out that the phrase *much desired* immediately follows the word *coveted,* giving its meaning. Then have students complete *Student Journal* page 134. (See Differentiated Instruction.)

Phonics/Word Study

Suffixes *-ible* and *-able*

Display these words and root words: *question, profit, terr, vis*. Ask students to add the suffixes *-ible* or *-able* correctly to each word. (*questionable, profitable, terrible,* and *visible*) Explain that words that take *-able* are base words that can stand on their own, and words that take *-ible* are roots. Now, work with students to complete the in-depth suffixes activity on TE page 313.

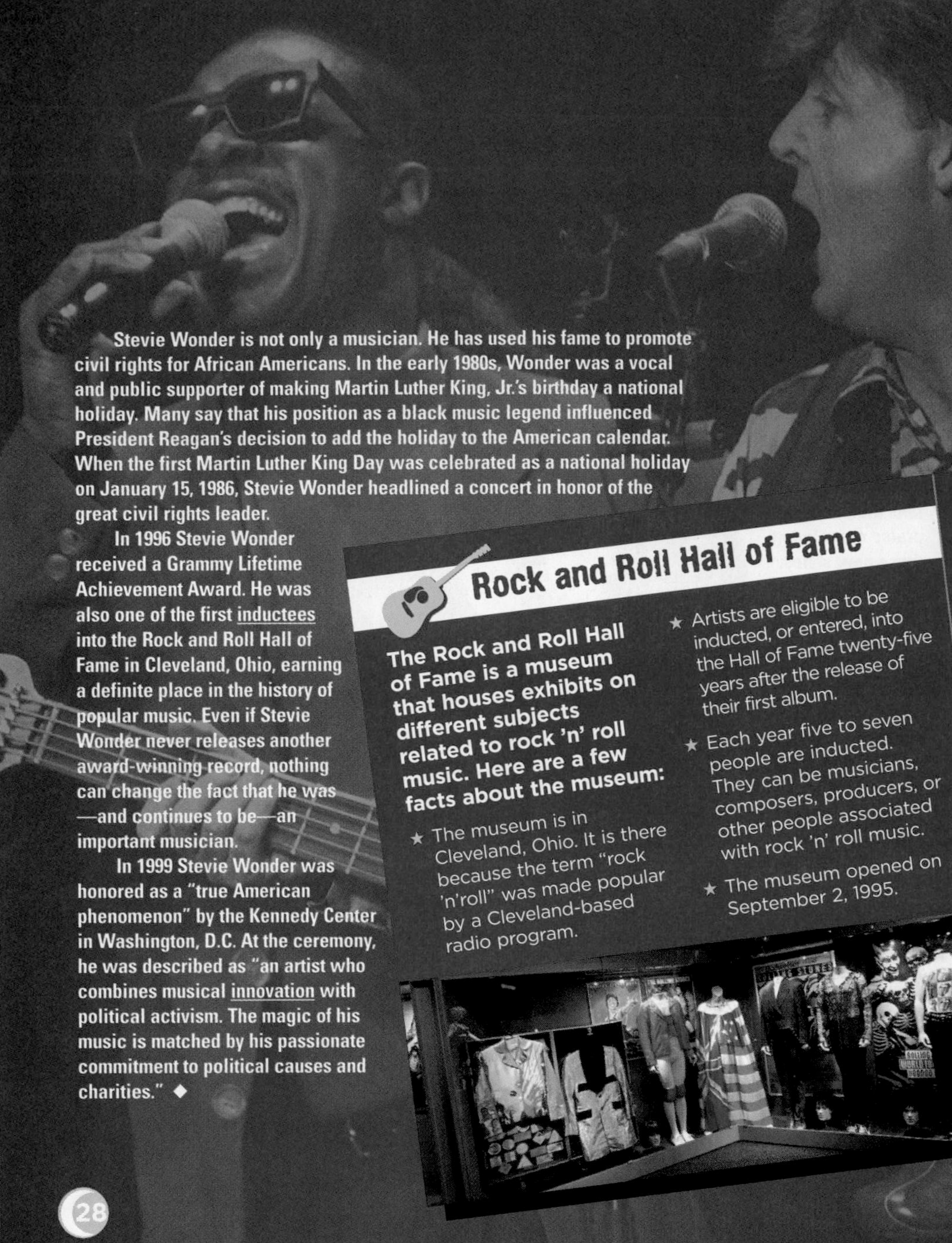

Stevie Wonder is not only a musician. He has used his fame to promote civil rights for African Americans. In the early 1980s, Wonder was a vocal and public supporter of making Martin Luther King, Jr.'s birthday a national holiday. Many say that his position as a black music legend influenced President Reagan's decision to add the holiday to the American calendar. When the first Martin Luther King Day was celebrated as a national holiday on January 15, 1986, Stevie Wonder headlined a concert in honor of the great civil rights leader.

In 1996 Stevie Wonder received a Grammy Lifetime Achievement Award. He was also one of the first inductees into the Rock and Roll Hall of Fame in Cleveland, Ohio, earning a definite place in the history of popular music. Even if Stevie Wonder never releases another award-winning record, nothing can change the fact that he was—and continues to be—an important musician.

In 1999 Stevie Wonder was honored as a "true American phenomenon" by the Kennedy Center in Washington, D.C. At the ceremony, he was described as "an artist who combines musical innovation with political activism. The magic of his music is matched by his passionate commitment to political causes and charities." ◆

Rock and Roll Hall of Fame

The Rock and Roll Hall of Fame is a museum that houses exhibits on different subjects related to rock 'n' roll music. Here are a few facts about the museum:

- ★ The museum is in Cleveland, Ohio. It is there because the term "rock 'n'roll" was made popular by a Cleveland-based radio program.
- ★ Artists are eligible to be inducted, or entered, into the Hall of Fame twenty-five years after the release of their first album.
- ★ Each year five to seven people are inducted. They can be musicians, composers, producers, or other people associated with rock 'n' roll music.
- ★ The museum opened on September 2, 1995.

28

Phonics/Word Study

Suffixes *-ible* and *-able* Words with Exceptions

Great Source
Reading Advantage
Word Study Manual
Mountains
Changes
Travel the World
Revolutions
Level D

One of the most difficult features of derivational constancy stage that students have to deal with is the issue of when to use *-ible* versus *-able*.

- Display the words shown in the first two columns below. Ask students to figure out what the words in each column have in common. Students should note that the words have been presorted by suffix.
- Once students recognize that the suffix is the sort criterion, help them notice that the words with the *-able* suffix are base words that can stand on their own. Words with the *-ible* suffix are generally roots.
- Using the Suffix Sort One sheet, model the sorting process for students. (See *Word Study Manual* page 75.) Place the first few words under the appropriate columns (*-able*, *-ible*, Oddball). Have students complete the sort with you.
- Discuss the sort and what students learned.
- Hand out the Suffix Sort One sheet. Have students cut up the sheets and do the sort on their own or in groups.
- Check the final sorts and have students copy the sort into their Word Study notebook.

Suffix Sort One: *-ible* and *-able* Words with Exceptions

-able	*-ible*	Oddball
movable	negligible	tolerable
durable	possible	combustible
profitable	terrible	flammable
presentable	edible	distractible
agreeable	visible	
unconscionable	legible	
desirable	plausible	
forgettable	invincible	
questionable	audible	

For more information on word sorts and spelling stages, see pages 5–31 in the *Word Study Manual.*

Focus on . . .

Use one or more activities in this section to focus on a particular area of need in your students.

Comprehension STRATEGY SUPPORT

INDEPENDENT

To help those students who need more practice using the strategies covered in this lesson, work one-on-one or in small groups to apply the strategy prompts below. Apply the prompts to a *Reading Advantage* paperback, a classroom library book, or a new or familiar selection in the magazine. Always model your own thinking first.

Determining Importance

- What is the most important idea in the paragraph? How can I prove it?
- Which details are unimportant? Why?
- What does the author want me to understand?
- Why is this information important (or not important) to me?

Making Connections

- What does this story (article, passage) remind me of?
- What do I already know about this topic?
- Where have I heard about this topic before?
- What do I have in common with the characters, people, or situations in the text?
- What other books, stories, articles, movies, or TV shows does this text make me think about?

Writing Illustrated Timeline

INDEPENDENT

Have students use the information from the biographical sketch to make an illustrated timeline of Stevie Wonder's accomplishments. Students can work with a partner and then take notes about Wonder's achievements and when they took place. Then students can transfer the information to a timeline. See example below.

Timeline

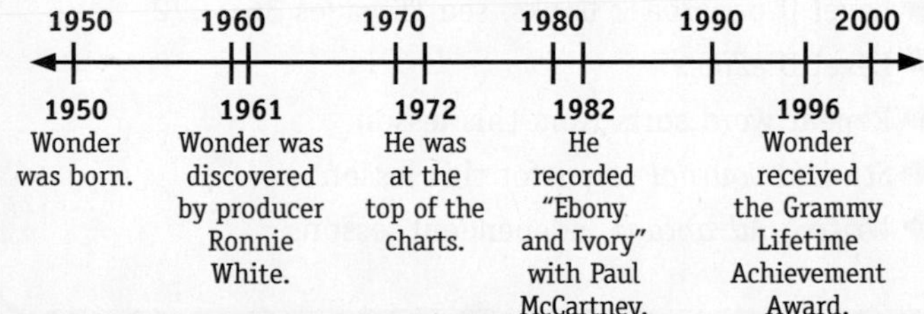
1950
1960
1970
1980
1990
2000
1950 Wonder was born.
1961 Wonder was discovered by producer Ronnie White.
1972 He was at the top of the charts.
1982 He recorded "Ebony and Ivory" with Paul McCartney.
1996 Wonder received the Grammy Lifetime Achievement Award.

For further instruction on taking notes, see lessons in *Writing Advantage,* pages 170–181.

Fluency: Pacing

After students have read the selection at least once, they can use a portion of it to practice fluent reading. Students can work in pairs.

As you listen to students read, use these prompts to guide them.

- Read at an even pace, as this will help keep your partner's attention. Preview the text, as needed, to avoid stops and starts.
- Let the punctuation guide your pauses and the expression in your voice.

When students read aloud, do they—

✓ demonstrate a smooth pace, not too fast or too slow?
✓ incorporate well-timed pauses between words and phrases?
✓ reflect an awareness and understanding of punctuation?

English Language Learners

Work with students to extend the Determining Importance activity on page 308. Use the paragraph under the "Stevie Wonder" heading, on page 26 of the article, to model the skill. Then have students practice the skill.

1. Assign a paragraph from the page to each pair.
2. Have partners read the paragraph together and discuss the main idea.
3. Have students share how they determined the main idea of each paragraph.

Independent Activity Options

While you work with individuals or small groups, others can work independently on one or more of the following options.

- Level D paperback books, see TE pages 367–372
- Level D *eZines*
- Repeat word sorts from this lesson
- *Student Journal* pages for this lesson
- *Writing Advantage* independent lessons

Assessment

Strategy Assessment

To help you and your students assess their use of comprehension strategies, ask the following questions. Students can complete a written response or provide verbal answers in a one-on-one reading conference.

1. **Determining Importance** What do you think is one important idea about Stevie Wonder to take away after reading this biographical sketch? (Answers will vary, but students should be able to support their responses by referring to the text. The key idea is probably that he overcame many odds to pursue his dream.)
2. **Making Connections** From reading this article, what did you learn about Stevie Wonder that you didn't already know? (Answers will vary. Some students may not have known about him at all. Others can explain the most interesting new fact they learned.)

For ongoing informal assessment, use the checklists on pages 61–64 of *Level D Assessment*.

Word Study Assessment

Use these steps to help you and your students assess their understanding of the suffixes *-ible* and *-able*.

1. Write the following words or word parts on the board or on word cards: *account*, *invis*, *elig*, *honor*, *collect*, *poss*. Note that these words were not part of the sort.
2. Ask students to add the suffix *-ible* or *-able* correctly to each word, using what they've learned.

Word/Word Part	Word with Suffix *-ible, -able*
account	account*able*
invis	invis*ible*
elig	elig*ible*
honor	honor*able*
collect	collect*able*

The Next Move

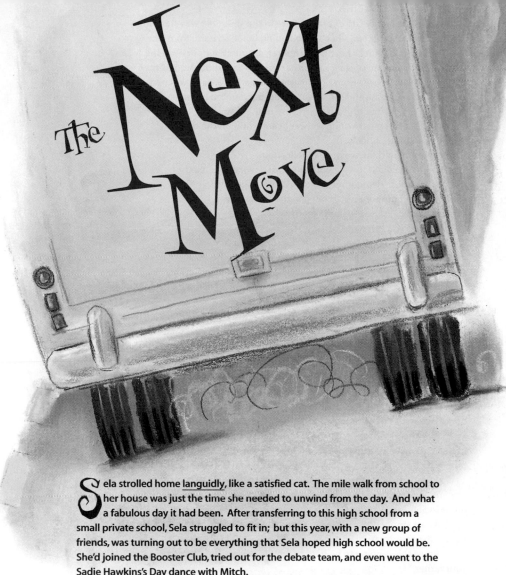

Sela strolled home languidly, like a satisfied cat. The mile walk from school to her house was just the time she needed to unwind from the day. And what a fabulous day it had been. After transferring to this high school from a small private school, Sela struggled to fit in; but this year, with a new group of friends, was turning out to be everything that Sela hoped high school would be. She'd joined the Booster Club, tried out for the debate team, and even went to the Sadie Hawkins's Day dance with Mitch.

All around her, golden October leaves danced from the tree limbs, spiraling to the earth. Unself-consciously, Sela stepped up her pace and ran right through a pile of swept-up leaves. The brushing sound reminded her of when she was little and spent hours with her father raking their backyard, swinging her miniature rake beside him. She smiled, looked up at the blue sky, and sighed happily.

LESSON 40
The Next Move

Changes, pages 29–34

SUMMARY

This **short story** tells about the difficult adjustments a teenage girl makes when her family moves to California and she goes to a new school.

COMPREHENSION STRATEGIES

Inferential Thinking
Monitor Understanding

WRITING

Character Map

VOCABULARY

Context Clues

PHONICS/WORD STUDY

Suffixes *-ible* and *-able* Words with Exceptions

Lesson Vocabulary

languidly	anxious
feigning	stucco
prefaced	

MATERIALS

Changes, pp. 29–34
Student Journal, pp. 135–137
Word Study Manual, p. 76
Writing Advantage, pp. 30–55

Before Reading

Use one or more activities.

Begin a List

Display the heading *Difficulties of Moving*. Discuss why it's difficult to move to a new location, listing students' responses. Tell students that they will come back to the list later.

Difficulties of Moving
1. lose contact with old friends
2. other students know skills you weren't taught
3.

Vocabulary Preview

Display the selection vocabulary. Discuss each word and its meaning. Assess prior knowledge by asking students to complete the second column of the predictions chart on *Student Journal* page 135. They will complete the chart later.

Preview the Selection

Have students read the title and look at the pictures on the six pages of the short story, pages 29–34.

Make Predictions/ Set Purpose

Students should use the information they gathered in previewing the selection to make predictions about what they will learn. If students have trouble generating a purpose for reading, suggest that they read to discover why Sela was angry and upset about moving, and what changed her feelings.

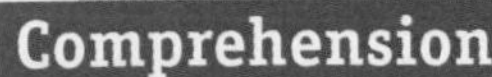

DIFFERENTIATED INSTRUCTION

Comprehension

INFERENTIAL THINKING

Use this activity to help students make a prediction based on what they've learned about a character.

1. Have students read the fourth paragraph on page 33. Ask: *Do you predict that Sela will join the staff of the literary magazine? Why or why not?*
2. Possible answers are yes, because the beginning of the story shows that Sela enjoys getting involved in school activities, or no, because Sela is too unhappy to take part.

Student Journal page 135

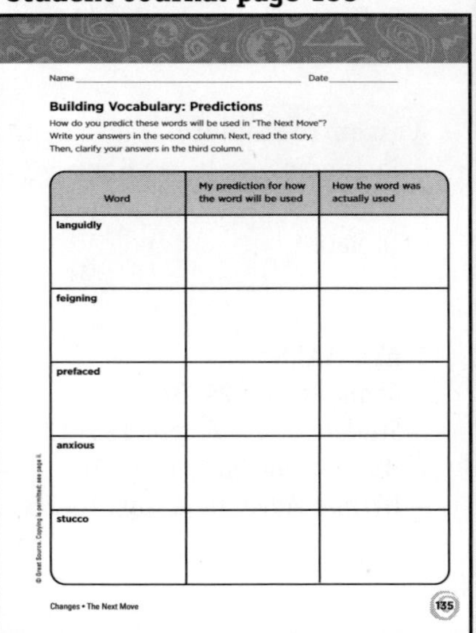

Name ______________________ Date __________

Building Vocabulary: Predictions

How do you predict these words will be used in "The Next Move"? Write your answers in the second column. Next, read the story. Then, clarify your answers in the third column.

Word	My prediction for how the word will be used	How the word was actually used
languidly		
feigning		
prefaced		
anxious		
stucco		

© Great Source. Copying is permitted; see page ii.

Changes • The Next Move 135

Placing the empty cup of orange juice in the sink, Sela was startled by the door opening. "Mom, what are you doing home so early from work?" Mrs. Trop, feigning not to hear her daughter, dropped her purse on the kitchen table, and ran upstairs. Adults are weird, Sela thought, and then thought nothing more about it. She grabbed her book bag, switched on the overhead light, and sat down to start her algebra homework.

"Sela," her mother called from the top of the stairs.

"Yeah," Sela replied instinctively, concentrating on the math problems in front of her.

"There's something we need to talk about."

That made Sela stop. She put her pencil down and looked toward the stairs. Her mother's voice was like a shadow, with no body, but those words hung in the air like the smell of mothballs. Sela waited silently.

"Sela, are you listening?"

"Yes, I'm listening." Sela thought she could hear her mother shifting her weight impatiently at the top of the stairs. She knew no conversation was going to be shouted across the house, especially one prefaced with *we need to talk*.

"Come upstairs, now, please."

As if she were carrying a weight around her neck, Sela shuffled upstairs. The light in her parent's room flickered as her mother walked in front of it, away from it, and then in front again. Sela's mind flashed to the dance, the strobe light, and Mitch.

"Sit here." Mrs. Trop patted the end of the bed. Looking her mother in the eyes, Sela became anxious and nervous for a moment. Had someone died? Was it Grandpa? Thoughts of disasters swirled in her mind and a light sweat broke out on her forehead.

"Okay, there's no easy way to tell you this, so I am just going to say it." Bracing herself, Sela looked straight into her mother's teary eyes. "Your father just called me from his cell phone. The company he interviewed with last week offered him a job."

"Mom, that's great! Dad has been so down since he was laid off last summer."

"Yes, it is great, but it's also not great. The office they want your father to run is in San Jose, California."

Sela sat stunned. She didn't know what to say. California was on the other side of the country from Rhode Island. It was 3,000 miles away.

"I know this is going to be hard for you to accept, but we are going with your father."

"What?" was all Sela could manage to ask even though she had heard her mother clearly.

"Sela, we can't afford to pay two rents, and I don't want our family to be separated until June." Mrs. Trop put her hand on her daughter's back, but Sela pulled away.

30

During Reading

Comprehension

INFERENTIAL THINKING

Use the bulleted prompts to model for students how to draw conclusions from the text on page 29. Then have students draw conclusions from another section of text.

- What do I learn from the character's thoughts, words, or actions?
- What conclusions do I draw?

(See Differentiated Instruction.)

Teacher Think Aloud

From Sela's thoughts, I learn that she worked hard to fit into a new school, and that things are finally coming together for her. All her thoughts and actions show how happy she is. The text doesn't say where she lives, but I can conclude from the description of the falling leaves that it is someplace with lots of trees and that it gets cool in the fall and probably cold in the winter.

Comprehension

MONITOR UNDERSTANDING

Use these questions to model monitoring understanding. Then have students apply a fix-up strategy to another part of the text that is unclear or confusing.

- Do I understand what I'm reading? If not, what part is confusing me?
- Why did the author include those details?
- What fix-up strategy can I try?

"You are going to ruin my life!" Sela gasped between sobs and ran out of the room. The next thing her mother heard was the sound of Sela's bedroom door slamming.

Sela woke in an unfamiliar room and lay motionless under the sheets, not wanting to move. Her eyes gazed from the blank, white walls to the stacked cardboard boxes. All of the contents of my life, she thought, packed away. Throwing her legs over the side of the bed, Sela sighed. It was hot, hotter than Rhode Island in October. It was nothing like fall was supposed to be.

Sela ran over the blur of the last three days in her head: her father's whistling, the movers going through her room, turning in her textbooks, the airport. Sela whispered to herself, "I can't believe I'm here." She was testing out her voice because she had made a vow of silence when she stepped onto the airplane. If her parents were going to uproot her life, then they would have to suffer, too. The childishness of her vow did not embarrass her.

Sela did not like this change.

"Sela!" Mrs. Trop called from another room. "You need to be ready in twenty minutes. I called the guidance counselor, and the school wants you to start today."

What? Sela thought to herself. *I don't even get a few days to mope, to sightsee? This whole thing is a nightmare.*

31

Teacher Think Aloud

I was confused when I read the second paragraph on page 31. In the first paragraph, Sela was upset and slammed the door to her bedroom. I thought she was still in her bedroom, but why were there packing boxes there already? I decided to reread the paragraph. When I did, I noticed the part about it being hotter than Rhode Island. I realized that Sela had moved to California already.

Fix-Up Strategies

Offer these strategies to help students read independently.

If you don't understand what you're reading:

- Reread the difficult section to look for clues to help you comprehend.
- Read ahead to find clues to help you comprehend.
- Retell, or say in your own words, what you've read.
- Visualize, or form mental pictures of, what you've read.

If you don't understand a word:

- Reread the sentence. Look for ideas and words that provide meaning clues.
- Find clues by reading a few sentences before and after the confusing word.
- Look for the base or root word and think about its meaning.
- Think about the topic or plot at this point to see if either offers meaning clues.

"We know she is just going to love our school," the guidance counselor, Mr. Weeble, said as he shook Mrs. Trop's hand.

Adults are so fake, Sela wanted to scream. *He doesn't care if I love it here or not, and Mom knows I hate it already.*

"Taylor will show Sela around today." Mr. Weeble waved his hand and a tan, thin girl bounded up beside him, her teeth gleaming like icicles.

"Hi! I'm Taylor." Sela nodded and hugged her arms to her chest. She felt pale and unfashionable next to Taylor. "We're off!" Taylor started out of the office, and Sela followed her like a lost puppy. At the door she turned to look at her mother, who stood, nervously biting her fingernails.

32

Student Journal page 136

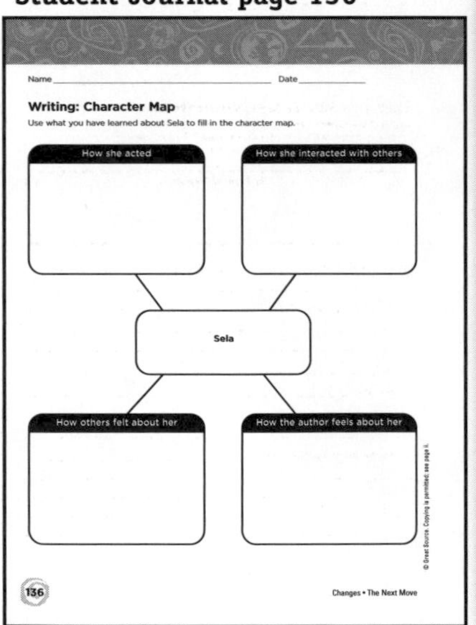
Name ______ Date ______

Writing: Character Map

Use what you have learned about Sela to fill in the character map.

How she acted

How she interacted with others

Sela

How others felt about her

How the author feels about her

136

Changes • The Next Move

After Reading

Use one or more activities.

Check Purpose

Have students decide if their purpose was met. Did they learn why Sela was angry and upset about moving, and what changed her feelings?

Discussion Questions

Continue the group discussion with the following questions.

1. What was the effect of Sela's "silent treatment" on her mom? (Cause-Effect)
2. Did you predict that things would turn around for Sela in California? Explain. (Predict)
3. How would you have reacted if you were in Sela's place? (Making Connections)

Revisit: List

Revisit the list about why it's difficult to move. Do students want to add anything new to the list?

Revisit: Predictions Chart

Have students revisit the predictions chart on *Student Journal* page 135. How were the words actually used? Have students fill in the third column.

Sela turned up the walkway to her new house, 1156 Pathway Lane. The white stucco ranch looked exactly like all of the other houses on the block, and the only way that Sela was certain this was the right one was the pyramid of empty cardboard boxes on the curb.

"How was it?" Mrs. Trop sang out as the screen door clicked shut. Sela was not about to end her vow of silence. She slipped down the hall to her room and shut the door. From the living room she heard her mother cry out, "Where is my daughter?" Collapsing on her bed, Sela cried. She cried for her old room, the violet walls and the dusty shelves. She cried for her friends, for the first snow, for the Atlantic Ocean. She cried for everything she had lost. She even cried for Madame—the strictest French teacher in the state of Rhode Island. Sitting up, she looked into the mirror propped up against her desk. Her brown eyes were puffed, swollen, and red. Her hair hovered above her head in a static haze. She stuck her tongue out at herself.

The next morning, dressed in black from head to toe, Sela slipped out of the house before breakfast. The sun shone, sparkling off the shiny chrome of cars. Sela hated California. This was the third straight day of perfect weather, and Sela longed for rain. She had settled into a comfortable routine of silence. In every class she attended yesterday, she tried to sink into the desk chair, unnoticed. A new student, the new girl, Sela had worked for months trying to fit in at her old high school, and she was too tired to reinvent herself again. After all, who was to say that she'd be at this school very long. Sela decided the best way to make it through was just to be no one and pass the time. The schoolwork wouldn't be a problem, and she told herself she didn't need friends. As she turned the corner to the high school, Sela noticed a flyer stapled to a telephone pole.

Sela passed the same flyer for the literary magazine on Wednesday and Thursday. By Friday morning she was almost curious to see if the flyer would still be posted. And it was. *Who am I kidding?* she thought to herself. *This is trouble.* I am not getting involved in anything here. But all day, the thought of the meeting stuck inside her head. When the final bell rang, Sela headed for her locker. Walking down the hallway, she slowed as she passed Ms. Ali's room. Inside, the young English teacher paced in circles, her flowing skirt kicking out behind her, her long braids bouncing off her back. What a hippie, Sela thought.

"Come on in." Ms. Ali's voice was like a high-pitched whistle. "My first editor!"

Join the staff of Alterations,
the Senior High's new literary magazine.
First meeting is Friday at 3:30
in Ms. Ali's room.

33

DIFFERENTIATED INSTRUCTION

Writing

Character Map

To provide students with help writing their character map, use these steps:

1. Ask students what words or phrases they would use to describe their friends.
2. If needed, give these examples of categories used to describe friends: what personal qualities they have, what they like to do, what ambitions they have for the future, how they deal with disappointments, how they get along with others.

Student Journal page 137

Name ______________________ Date __________

Building Vocabulary: Using Context to Understand a Word

Look for the word *anxious* in "The Next Move." Write in the box the sentence or sentences that help you know its meaning. Then complete the statements and answer the questions about the word *anxious*.

My Word in Context:

I think this word means ______________________

because ______________________

My word is ______________________

My word is not ______________________

Where else might I find this word? ______________________

What makes this an important word to know? ______________________

Changes • The Next Move 137

Writing Character Map

Have students discuss what they know about Sela. Jot down ideas on the board or on a chart as they are expressed. Then have students use their discussion to help them complete the character map on *Student Journal* page 136. (See Differentiated Instruction.)

Vocabulary Context Clues

Draw students' attention to the very first sentence on page 29 of the story. Discuss using context to figure out what *languidly* and *strolled* mean. Ask how a satisfied cat moves (sluggishly, slowly, drooping). Then ask students to retell in their own words the way Sela is moving. Remind students that "reading around" a word is one way to figure out what a word means. Have students complete *Student Journal* page 137.

Phonics/Word Study

Suffixes *-ible* and *-able*

Remind students that standalone words like *present* and *agree* take the suffix *-able* rather than *-ible*. (*presentable*, *agreeable*) But there are some exceptions. Write these words on the board: *impress*, *access*. They take the suffix *-ible*. (*impressible*, *accessible*) Ask what is similar about *impress* and *access*. (Both end in *-ess*.) Now, work with students to complete the in-depth suffixes activity on TE page 321.

Caught off guard, Sela allowed herself to be guided into the classroom. Two other girls and a guy walked in behind her and sat toward the back.

"Oh—four will be fine! One for poetry, one for short stories, one for essays, and one to oversee you all!" Ms. Ali talked as if the students were already a team of editors. Sela got up to leave. "Oh, do you have something you'd like to share Miss, Miss?"

"Trop, I mean Sela. Uh, no, I was just going to..." Sela looked toward the door. And as she did, she saw Ms. Ali's smile drop into a frown. At once, she felt sorry for being rude and sat back down. Ms. Ali smiled again.

"Fabulous. To get started, I'd like us to decide if we are going to keep the name *Alterations* or vote on a new name. Any thoughts?" No one said anything. "Well let's try this, then. Everyone say why the name should stay the same." She looked around the room, finally pointing to Sela, who sank into her desk. The last thing she wanted to do was offer an opinion, but she was on the spot.

"*Alterations* is a good name, I guess, because things change. People get older and graduate, teachers retire, friends move; in a way, I guess, the only thing that any of us can be certain about is that things will *not* stay the same, no matter how badly we want them to."

"Very nicely put," Ms. Ali beamed.

Sela felt her face flush red, as if she'd just uncovered something secret about herself.

"We'll meet again in two days—same time, same place."

At the door, a girl touched Sela on the shoulder, "Hi, I'm Jenna. We're going to stop by Nick's Place before heading home. Do you want to come?"

"Sure." The word slipped out of Sela's mouth before she had time to think. "I just need to call my parents and let them know I'll be late."

Jenna handed Sela her cell phone, "We'll meet you on the steps!"

Sela phoned home, wondering how she would start this conversation. She hadn't spoken to her parents in nearly a week. The phone rang and rang. Finally, Mrs. Trop picked up.

"Hello," she sang into the receiver.

Sela waited a beat. "Hi, Mom, it's me." ◆

34

Phonics/Word Study

Suffixes *-ible* and *-able* Words with Exceptions

- Display these words:

admit	apprehend	comprehend
suppress	access	remit
permit	repress	impress

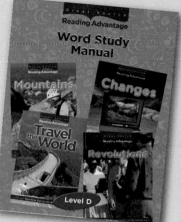

- Point out to students that all the words are either standalone words or complete base words. So if students were to simply follow the rule that complete words take the *-able* suffix, then the spelling of these particular words would be incorrect.
- Have students consult a dictionary to find out what suffix all these words take. They will discover that all the words take the *-ible* suffix. Make the point that these words are exceptions to the rule that students learned previously about choosing either *-able* or *-ible*.
- Hand out the Suffix Sort Two sheet. (See *Word Study Manual* page 76.) Ask students to cut up the sheets and do the sort on their own or in groups.
- Check the final sorts. Have students copy the sort into their Word Study notebook.

Suffix Sort Two: *-ible* and *-able* Words with Exceptions

-ess	*-it*	Oddball
accessible	admissible	confessable
repressible	permissible	forgettable
impressible	remissible	presentable
suppressible		comprehensible
compressible		apprehensible

For more information on word sorts and spelling stages, see pages 5–31 in the *Word Study Manual*.

Focus on . . .

Use one or more activities in this section to focus on a particular area of need in your students.

Comprehension Strategy Support

To help those students who need more practice using the strategies covered in this lesson, work one-on-one or in small groups to apply the strategy prompts below. Apply the prompts to a *Reading Advantage* paperback, a classroom library book, or a new or familiar selection in the magazine. Always model your own thinking first.

Inferential Thinking

- What are the causes or effects of this event?
- What do I learn from the character or person's thoughts, words, or actions?
- What do I know (or infer) from the text that the author hasn't stated directly?
- What conclusions can I draw?

Monitor Understanding

- Do I understand what I'm reading? If not, what part is confusing to me?
- What fix-up strategies can I use to solve the problem? (See During Reading for fix-up strategies.)
- Why did a character say (do, think, ask) that?
- What images do I visualize from the text? What parts can't I visualize?
- Why did the author include (or not include) those details?

Writing Interior Monologue

Draw students' attention to this paragraph on page 31:

> *What?* Sela thought to herself. *I don't even get a few days to mope, to sightsee? This whole thing is a nightmare.*

Point out the words in italics. Ask students who Sela is talking to. (herself) Explain that the words that a single character speaks are called a monologue. Words that a character is thinking silently to him- or herself are called an interior monologue. Have students write a short interior monologue about feelings they've experienced around an event. Remind them to use phrases such as "I thought to myself" or "thoughts swirled in my mind," before or after the words they are thinking.

For instruction on writing techniques, such as adding details with prepositional phrases or using strong verbs and specific nouns, see *Writing Advantage*, pages 30–55.

Fluency: Expression

After students have read "The Next Move" at least once, have small groups read aloud scenes from the story. Ask students how Sela's feelings change. (Possible responses may cover the gamut from satisfied to worried to resentful to despair to hopeful.) Ask students to recall times when they felt the same emotions. Ask: *How did you sound when you were worried? How did you sound when you were hopeful?* Tell students that they can use what they know about feelings and voice intonation to help them speak the way all the characters might speak.

When students read aloud, do they—

✓ reflect an understanding of the text?

✓ demonstrate appropriate timing, stress, and intonation?

✓ incorporate appropriate speed and phrasing?

English Language Learners

To support students as they analyze characters, extend the character map activity on TE page 319.

1. Discuss the ideas presented by the class about Sela.
2. Have partners work together to complete the character map on page 136 of the *Student Journal*.
3. Have partners work together to write a simple paragraph, including a topic sentence and supporting details, about Sela.

Independent Activity Options

While you work with individuals or small groups, others can work independently on one or more of the following options.

- Level D paperback books, see TE pages 367–372
- Level D *eZine*
- Repeat word sorts from this lesson
- *Student Journal* pages for this lesson
- *Writing Advantage* independent lessons

Assessment

Strategy Assessment

To help you and your students assess their use of comprehension strategies, ask the following questions. Students can complete a written response or provide verbal answers in a one-on-one reading conference.

1. **Inferential Thinking** After reading the story, what conclusions can you draw about Sela's character? (Answers will vary. Students may mention that she is not really a loner, but would prefer to be involved in activities with others; that she tries to make the best of bad situations.)
2. **Monitor Understanding** What parts of the story, if any, were confusing to you? What did you do to clear up the confusion? (Answers will vary. Students may mention using fix-up strategies such as rereading a part or reading on.)

See *Level D Assessment* page 46 for formal assessment to go with *Changes*.

Word Study Assessment

Use these steps to help you and your students assess their understanding of exceptions to the use of the suffixes *-ible* and *-able*.

1. Write the following words on the board or on word cards: *accessible*, *transmissible*, *remissible*, *compressible*, *permissible*, *repressible*.
2. Ask students to identify and correctly spell the base word that is used to form each longer word. Remind them that the endings of some of the base words will be different when the suffix is removed.

Word	Base Word
accessible	access
transmissible	transmit
remissible	remit
compressible	compress
permissible	permit
repressible	repress

From Carbon to Jewel:

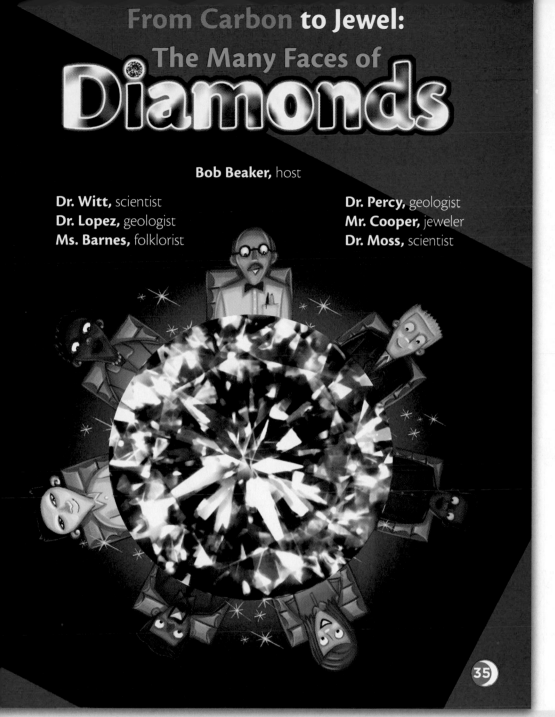

The Many Faces of Diamonds

Bob Beaker, host

Dr. Witt, scientist
Dr. Lopez, geologist
Ms. Barnes, folklorist

Dr. Percy, geologist
Mr. Cooper, jeweler
Dr. Moss, scientist

35

LESSON **41**

From Carbon to Jewel

Changes, pages 35–39

SUMMARY

Diamond facts and folklore are discussed in a **television talk show format.**

COMPREHENSION STRATEGIES

Making Connections
Understanding Text Structure

WRITING

Advertisement

VOCABULARY

Suffix *-ist*

PHONICS/WORD STUDY

Suffixes *-ible* and *-able* Words with Exceptions

Lesson Vocabulary

core	synthesize
encased	manipulate
originated	elite
transformation	trigger
fabricate	

MATERIALS

Changes, pp. 35–39
Student Journal, pp. 138–140
Word Study Manual, p. 77
Writing Advantage, pp. 152–169

Before Reading

Use one or more activities.

Make a K-W-L Chart

Create a K-W-L chart about diamonds. In this chart, students will record what they know about diamonds, what they want to know about diamonds, and, after they have read the selection, what they have learned about diamonds. Tell students that as they read the article, they should pay close attention to see if their questions are answered in the text. Students will finish the chart later.

Vocabulary Preview

Display the selection vocabulary. Have students start *Student Journal* page 138. They can complete the chart after they have finished reading. For definition help, students can use context clues. Use the vocabulary word *transformation* to model a response for the page.

Preview the Selection

Have students look through the play. What do students think they will learn? (See Differentiated Instruction.)

Make Predictions/ Set Purpose

Students should use the information they gathered in previewing the selection to make predictions about what they will learn. If students have trouble generating a purpose for reading, suggest that they read to find out why diamonds are so valuable.

DIFFERENTIATED INSTRUCTION SMALL GROUP

Preview the Selection

Help students understand the different purposes for reading:

1. Have students look through the cast of characters. Lead a discussion about the differences between their occupations.
2. Encourage students to think about the purpose each character has. Discuss the different types of information each character might contribute to a discussion about diamonds. Ask: *What would a geologist talk about compared with a jeweler? What kind of information would a scientist talk about? What would a folklorist say about diamonds?*

Student Journal page 138

Name_______________ Date__________

Building Vocabulary: Knowledge Rating Chart

Show your knowledge of each word by adding information to the other boxes in the row.

Word	Define or Use in a Sentence	Where Have I Seen or Heard It?	How Is It Used in the Selection?	Looks Like (Words or Sketch)
core				
encased				
originated				
transformation				
fabricate				
synthesize				
manipulate				
elite				
trigger				

138 Changes • From Carbon to Jewel

Join TV's favorite talk show, Science Corner, for the latest on diamonds, fact, and folklore.

BOB BEAKER: On *Science Corner* today, a few top scientists, folklorists, and geologists will talk about the many faces of diamonds. We start off today's show talking about diamonds in the earth. Then, we'll talk to some folklorists about legends that have grown up around diamonds. Finally, we'll explore how people have discovered how to change carbon into diamonds. For centuries, diamonds have dazzled men and women with their clear sparkle. Let's get some more information on the diamond. Dr. Percy?

DR. PERCY: Good afternoon. Did you know that diamonds are the hardest surface known to humans? And, if you own a diamond, it's probably the oldest thing you will ever own—maybe three billion years of age.

BOB BEAKER: When did people start mining and digging diamonds out of the earth?

DR. LOPEZ: We know that diamonds were mined in India about 4,000 years ago. The modern diamond mining business started when the great mines of South Africa were discovered in the late 1800s.

BOB BEAKER: Tell us about natural diamonds.

DR. PERCY: A diamond is a clear gem that is made up of carbon, one of the most common elements on earth. Geologists think that when the earth formed, billions of years ago, the materials at its core, or center, grew extremely hot and were put under very high pressure. These two factors (heat and pressure) caused the carbon to crystallize in the earth's core. When volcanoes erupted, they pushed up magma, or liquid rock, to the earth's surface. The magma carried the diamond crystals from the core of the earth to the surface, where they became encased in the hard, volcanic rock.

Who Are They?

A geologist is a person who studies geology. Geology is the study of the origin, history, and structure of the earth. Geology comes from two Greek words. Geo- is a prefix from a Greek word part that means "earth." The suffix -logy is from the Greek word logos, which means "word." Usually, -logy is defined as "the study of" something.

A folklorist is someone who collects and studies folklore. Folklore is the traditional beliefs, myths, and tales that develop in a particular place or about a certain subject.

36

During Reading

Comprehension

MAKING CONNECTIONS

Use the bulleted prompts to model for students how to make connections with the text. Then have students share a connection they have made.

- What does this play remind me of?
- What do I already know about diamonds?

Teacher Think Aloud

My father couldn't afford to buy my mother an engagement ring when they were young. Then, on their tenth anniversary, he surprised her with a beautiful diamond ring. I remember telling her to be careful not to scrape her new diamond. She laughed and said she didn't think she could damage it. She explained that diamonds are so hard, they are used in industry to cut metal.

Comprehension

UNDERSTANDING TEXT STRUCTURE

Use these questions to model how to identify the interview text structure of this play. Then have students discuss how this text structure helps them understand the information in the text.

- What kind of text structure does this selection have?
- Which details support my thoughts about the text structure?

(See Differentiated Instruction.)

DR. LOPEZ: However, not all diamonds are found where they first came to the surface. These volcanic eruptions happened billions of years ago. Since those times the earth's surface has worn away a lot, and rainstorms have washed the earth into rivers, streams, and the sea. So diamonds end up miles away from where they originated.

BOB BEAKER: That is an amazing natural transformation, from carbon to diamond. How can a person tell a high-quality diamond from one that isn't worth as much? Mr. Cooper?

MR. COOPER: In my line of work as a jeweler, we measure a diamond's worth by looking at the four C's: carat, clarity, color, and cut. Carat refers to the weight of the diamond. Clarity refers to the inclusion in a diamond. Inclusions are natural identifying marks like tiny cracks in the stone. The clearer a diamond is, the more it's worth. For the color rating, a jeweler looks for colorless diamonds. Diamonds range in color from icy white to almost yellow. Cut refers to the angles and size of the diamond's shape.

DIFFERENTIATED INSTRUCTION

Comprehension

UNDERSTANDING TEXT STRUCTURE

Use this activity to help students understand the text structure of a play.

1. Have students compare the structure of "Something's Changed" (page 17) with "From Carbon to Jewel."
2. Discuss students' responses. They should notice that "Something's Changed" has different scenes and less formal language. Both plays have a cast list and the speaker's name before each piece of dialogue.

Teacher Think Aloud

This selection has some of the elements of a play, like a list of characters and a person's name before each speech. But rather than action taking place in different scenes, it is set in one place. The picture on the first page shows people sitting around a table. One character asks questions about diamonds that the other characters answer. It reminds me of a television interview show.

Fix-Up Strategies

Offer these strategies to help students read independently.

If you don't understand what you're reading:

- Reread the difficult section to look for clues to help you comprehend.
- Read ahead to find clues to help you comprehend.
- Retell, or say in your own words, what you've read.
- Visualize, or form mental pictures of, what you've read.

If you don't understand a word:

- Reread the sentence. Look for ideas and words that provide meaning clues.
- Find clues by reading a few sentences before and after the confusing word.
- Look for the base or root word and think about its meaning.
- Think about the topic or plot at this point to see if either offers meaning clues.

BOB BEAKER: Now let's talk to our folklorist, Ms. Barnes, about diamond myth and legend.

MS. BARNES: Diamonds are fascinating stones. People once believed that they held magical powers or that the stone would cure the mentally ill and keep demons away. Some people believed that if you touched each corner in your home with a diamond, the diamond would protect your home from lightning and storms.

BOB BEAKER: Can you tell us about a famous diamond in history?

MS. BARNES: I enjoy the story of the Hope Diamond. Anything but hopeful, this diamond is famous because of the bad luck it seems to have caused its owners. This diamond was once part of a larger diamond called the Blue Tavernier. Louis XIV of France bought the 112 carat Blue Tavernier in 1668 and ordered his jewelers to cut it in half. During the French Revolution in 1789, the diamond was stolen and disappeared. It didn't turn up again until it was sold to an English banker, Henry Hope, in 1830. Then the bad luck began.

BOB BEAKER: Bad luck? What kind of bad luck?

MS. BARNES: When Hope's son got the diamond, he lost his fortune. When an American widow had the diamond, her only child was killed by accident, her family fell apart, she lost her money, and she killed herself. Harry Winston, the famous New York diamond buyer and seller, bought the Hope Diamond. His customers refused to touch it. Today, the diamond is on display at the Smithsonian Institution in Washington, D.C.

BOB BEAKER: Fascinating! Now let's turn to our other guests and see how humans fabricate, or make, diamonds.

DR. MOSS: People have been trying to synthesize, or create, diamonds for several hundred years. In 1770, a French scientist proved that diamonds were a crystal form of carbon. His discovery made scientists wonder if they could manipulate carbon in a laboratory to make it into a diamond. They tried using high temperatures and high pressure but had no luck.

38

Student Journal page 139

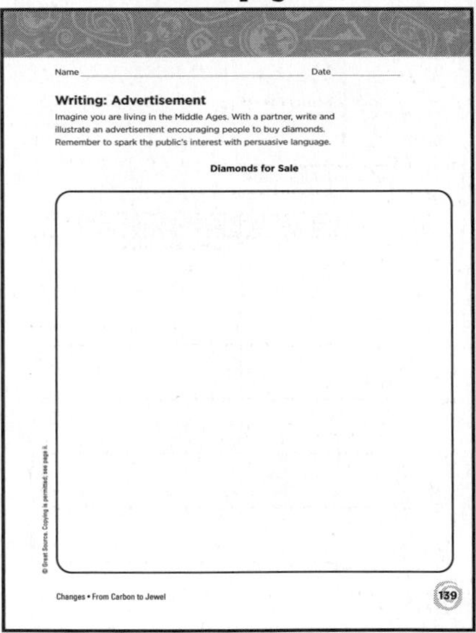

Name ____________ Date ________

Writing: Advertisement

Imagine you are living in the Middle Ages. With a partner, write and illustrate an advertisement encouraging people to buy diamonds. Remember to spark the public's interest with persuasive language.

Diamonds for Sale

Changes • From Carbon to Jewel 139

After Reading

Use one or more activities.

Check Purpose

Have students decide if their purpose was met. Did students find out why diamonds are valuable?

Discussion Questions

Continue the group discussion with the following questions.

1. Why are diamonds valuable? (Draw Conclusions)
2. How do the views of the geologist and the folklorist differ? (Compare-Contrast)
3. If someone gave you a diamond, would you sell it, keep it, or give it as a gift? Why? (Making Connections)

Revisit: K-W-L Chart

Revisit the K-W-L chart. Have students complete the third column in the chart.

Revisit: Knowledge Rating Chart

Encourage students to take another look at their responses to the knowledge rating chart on *Student Journal* page 138. Are there any adjustments or changes they would like to make? Students can add new notes, if necessary.

DR. WITT: In the 1940s, a Harvard scientist ran experiments that recreated the high pressure and high temperatures that might be found deep in the earth's core. He heated the carbon to 3,000 degrees and put it under 600,000 pounds of pressure. But he wasn't able to make a diamond.

BOB BEAKER: During the 1950s and the Cold War between the United States and the former Soviet Union, scientists started diamond experiments again because diamonds were needed for weapons and tools. The only diamonds available came from foreign countries.

DR. WITT: The General Electric Company (GE) took up the challenge. An <u>elite</u> team of the best physicists, chemists, and mechanical engineers experimented for over three years with temperatures and pressures. A breakthrough came when they tried adding certain minerals to <u>trigger</u> the carbon to change to diamond. When they found the right mineral to set off the change, they were able to make diamonds.

DR. MOSS: In 1955, this was a huge announcement to the world. GE made a diamond that scratched glass and didn't dissolve in acid. It had all of the characteristics of a natural diamond. The diamonds that were manufactured are used in industry, never for jewelry.

BOB BEAKER: It must have been an exciting and thrilling discovery. I'd like to thank all of my guests for a fascinating show. Until next time, this is the *Science Corner.* ◆

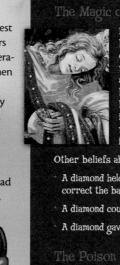

The Meaning of Diamond

The word diamond comes from the Greek word adamas meaning unrelenting or not giving up. The Greeks thought everyone should try to be adamas, like a diamond. The ancient Greeks placed diamonds on their shields before they went to battle because they believed the stones would protect them.

The Magic of Diamonds

During the Middle Ages, people believed that a diamond could cure sickness. The sick person would take a diamond to bed and warm the stone with his body heat. Then he would breathe on the stone and keep it close to his skin. All of this was done while the ill person fasted or went without food.

Other beliefs about diamonds:

- A diamond held in the mouth would correct the bad habit of lying.
- A diamond could protect a person from poison.
- A diamond gave one strength in battle.

The Poison of Diamonds

In the Middle Ages, people discovered that diamond powder was poisonous:

- A royal son murdered his father, a Turkish sultan, by mixing ground diamond into his father's food.
- In 1532 doctors thought they were helping Pope Clement VII by treating him with powdered diamond by the spoonful, but the pope died.

39

DIFFERENTIATED INSTRUCTION SMALL GROUP

Writing Advertisement

To help students prepare for the writing activity, use these steps:

1. Ask: *What kind of language do advertisements use?* Students should respond that ads use emotional, persuasive language.
2. Explain the following advertising techniques. *Bandwagon* is the suggestion that everyone is using the product and that you should, too. *Propaganda* is words and ideas with positive connotations used to suggest that such positive qualities should be associated with the product and its users. *Testimonial* is when a famous celebrity endorses the product.

Student Journal page 140

Name ______ Date ______

Building Vocabulary: Suffix *-ist*

Complete the chart by thinking of five additional words that end in *-ist*. Write each word in the first column and its definition in the second column.

-ist means "one who does something"

Word	Definitions
novelist	one who writes novels

140 Changes • From Carbon to Jewel

Writing Advertisement

Discuss what people in the Middle Ages believed about diamonds. (Diamonds could cure sickness, provide protection from poison, cure lying, provide strength in battle.) Have students suppose that they are diamond merchants during the Middle Ages. Remind them to point out one or more ways in which diamonds supposedly help people as they complete *Student Journal* page 139. (See Differentiated Instruction.)

Vocabulary Suffix *-ist*

Display the word *geologist*. Underline the suffix *-ist*. Explain that this suffix means "one who does something." A *geologist* is one who studies geology. Ask students if they remember another word in the text with the suffix *-ist*. (*folklorist*) Ask: *What does a folklorist do?* (studies folklore) Have students suggest other words that end in *-ist*. (*tourist*, *biologist*) Have partners complete *Student Journal* page 140. For help, they can use a dictionary.

Phonics/Word Study

Suffixes *-ible* and *-able* Words with Exceptions

Display these word pairs: *love/lovable* and *present/presentable*. What do students notice about the spelling changes? Explain that most standalone words, like *present*, will not have a spelling change when a suffix is added. But standalone words that end in silent *e*, *-ate*, or *y* will. Now help students complete the in-depth suffixes activity on TE page 328.

Phonics/Word Study

Suffixes *-ible* and *-able* Words with Exceptions

One of the most difficult features of the derivational constancy stage that students have to deal with is the issue of when to use *-ible* versus *-able*.

- Write the words *admire*, *navigate*, and *rely* on the board. Ask students to change each to an adjective by adding either *-ible* or *-able*. Have students share their responses.
- Now write the words *admirable*, *navigable*, and *reliable* on the board. Have students explain how the base words changed when the suffix *-able* was added. Ask students to explain why *-able* was added instead of *-ible*. (All the words are base words that can stand on their own.) Discuss the base word changes: drop final silent *e*, drop *-ate*, change *y* to *i*.
- Model adding *-able* or *-ible* to the words below to form adjectives. (*achieve/achievable*) Using the Suffix Sort Three sheet, model the sorting process for students by writing the headings (*ends in silent* e, *ends in* -ate, *ends in* y, *Oddball*) and placing the first few words under the appropriate columns. (See *Word Study Manual* page 77.) Have students complete the sort with you.

achieve	observe	dispose	classify
comply	notice	size	trace
calculate	separate	pity	
manage	vary	love	
operate	educate	excite	

- Hand out the Suffix Sort Three sheet. Ask students to cut up the sheets and do the sort on their own or in groups.
- Check the final sorts and have students copy the sort into their Word Study notebook.

Suffix Sort Three: *-ible* and *-able* Words with Exceptions

ends in silent *e*	ends in *-ate*	ends in *y*	Oddball
achievable	calculable	variable	traceable
observable	separable	compliable	manageable
disposable	operable	pitiable	noticeable
lovable	educable	classifiable	
sizable			
excitable			

For more information on word sorts and spelling stages, see pages 5–31 in the *Word Study Manual.*

Focus on . . .

Use one or more activities in this section to focus on a particular area of need in your students.

Comprehension STRATEGY SUPPORT

To help those students who need more practice using the strategies covered in this lesson, work one-on-one or in small groups to apply the strategy prompts below. Apply the prompts to a *Reading Advantage* paperback, a classroom library book, or a new or familiar selection in the magazine. Always model your own thinking first.

Making Connections

- What does this story (article, passage) remind me of?
- What do I already know about this topic?
- Where have I heard about this topic before?
- What do I have in common with the characters, people, or situations in the text?
- What other books, stories, articles, movies, or TV shows does this text make me think about?

Understanding Text Structure

- What kind of text is this? (book, story, article, guidebook, play, manual)
- How does the author organize the text? (cause-effect, problem-solution, chronological order, description, question-answer, comparison-contrast)
- What details support my thoughts about the text structure?
- What is the cause (effect, problem, solution, order, question, answer)?
- If fiction, who are the characters? What is the setting, plot, conflict, and resolution?

Writing Opinion Essay

Have students search online or use reference books to find out why diamonds became traditional for engagement rings. Then have them write an opinion essay about whether people should feel that they have to get engaged with a diamond. Before students write, have them organize their thoughts in a chart like this:

My Opinion:
Details that support my opinion: 1. 2.

To provide more instruction and practice on writing personal essays, see *Writing Advantage*, pages 152–169.

Fluency: Expression

After students have read the selection at least once, have students form groups to read paragraphs from the talk show script expressively.

As you listen to students read, use these prompts to guide them.

- Put yourself in the situation of the character. How would experts sound? How would an interested host sound?
- Preview what you will read. Notice the different punctuation marks and what these signal to you. Pause when you see periods or commas. Let your voice rise slightly at the end of sentences marked with a question mark.

When students read aloud, do they—

✓ reflect an understanding of the text?
✓ demonstrate appropriate timing, stress, and intonation?
✓ incorporate appropriate speed and phrasing?

English Language Learners

To support students' understanding of suffixes, build on the vocabulary activity on TE page 327. Remind students that *-ist* means "one who does something." Tell students that *-er* and *-or* also mean "one who does something."

1. Write the following words on chart paper: *sailor, examiner, instructor, organizer*.
2. Then, have partners predict the meaning of each word.

Encourage students to look for other words in their reading that contain these suffixes.

Independent Activity Options

While you work with individuals or small groups, others can work independently on one or more of the following options.

- Level D paperback books, see TE pages 367–372
- Level D *eZines*
- Repeat word sorts from this lesson
- *Student Journal* pages for this lesson
- *Writing Advantage* independent lessons

Assessment

Strategy Assessment

To help you and your students assess their use of comprehension strategies, ask the following questions. Students can complete a written response or provide verbal answers in a one-on-one reading conference.

1. **Making Connections** What do you think is the most fascinating thing about diamonds? Explain. (Answers will vary.)
2. **Understanding Text Structure** Do you think a play with a question-answer format is a good way to present information about diamonds? Why or why not? (Answers will vary. Students may have found the information more accessible in this format than in a straight nonfiction article, or they may have found it more confusing. They should give examples from the text as they respond.)

For ongoing informal assessment, use the checklists on pages 61–64 of *Level D Assessment*.

Word Study Assessment

Use these steps to help you and your students assess their understanding of spelling changes that occur when adding the suffix *-able*.

1. Write the following words on the board or on word cards: *love, educate, size, comply, pity, operate*.
2. Ask students to add the suffix *-able* to each word. Have students identify the spelling changes that occur.

Word	Word with *-able* Added
love	lovable
educate	educable
size	sizable
comply	compliable
pity	pitiable
operate	operable

LESSON **42**

Changing Governments

Changes, pages 40–43

SUMMARY

This **article** explains the history of Hong Kong and how China regained control of the city from the British in 1997.

COMPREHENSION STRATEGIES

Monitor Understanding

WRITING

Compare-Contrast

VOCABULARY

Synonyms and Antonyms

PHONICS/WORD STUDY

Doubling with Polysyllabic Words

Lesson Vocabulary

perpetuity	regain
tyrannous	preserve
resumed	

MATERIALS

Changes, pp. 40–43
Student Journal, pp. 141–143
Word Study Manual, p. 78
Writing Advantage, pp. 114–151

Hong Kong
No Longe
Unde

40

Before Reading

Use one or more activities.

Make an Association Web

Tell students that they are going to read about Hong Kong. Then start an association web about the city. Ask:

- Where is Hong Kong?
- What do you know about the city?

Hong Kong: China, city, crowded, shopping

Vocabulary Preview

Review the vocabulary list with students. Clarify pronunciations. Then have students complete the second column of the chart on *Student Journal* page 141. Have students fill in the third column after they finish reading.

Preview the Selection

Have students look through the article. Discuss with students what they notice and what they think they will learn.

Make Predictions/ Set Purpose

Students should use the information they gathered in previewing the selection to make predictions about what they will learn. If students have trouble generating a purpose for reading, suggest that they read to find out why Hong Kong is now ruled by China.

Changing Governments

I t was midnight in the island city of Hong Kong, and the Union Jack (the British flag) was lowered for the last time. As the rain fell, a Chinese leader stepped into Hong Kong and legally took control of the city from the British.

British Rule July 1, 1997

DIFFERENTIATED INSTRUCTION

Comprehension

MONITOR UNDERSTANDING

Follow these steps to help students understand the importance of rereading.

1. Give students two minutes to read the feature "Opium" on page 43. Ask which details they can recall. List their responses.
2. Then have students carefully reread the feature, using as much time as they need. Which new details can they add to the list?
3. How did rereading slowly help them find more details?

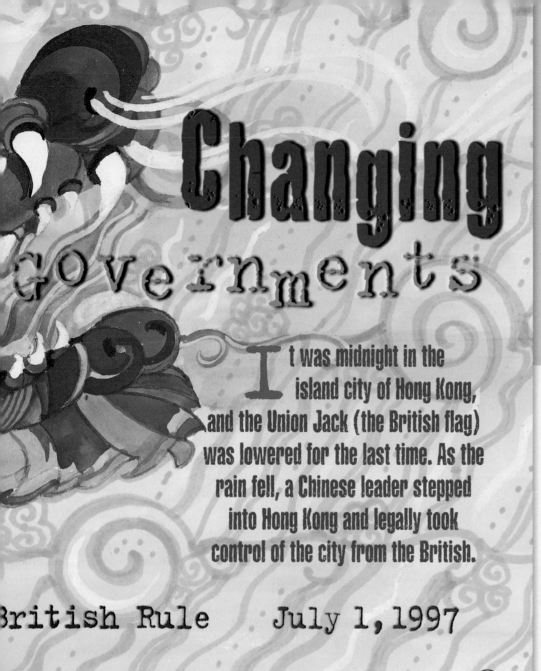

Student Journal page 141

Name ______________ Date ______

Building Vocabulary: Predictions

How do you predict these words will be used in "Changing Governments"? Write your answers in the second column. Next, read the article. Then clarify your answers in the third column

Word	My prediction for how the word will be used	How the word was actually used
perpetuity		
tyrannous		
resumed		
regain		
preserve		

During Reading

Comprehension

SMALL GROUP

MONITOR UNDERSTANDING

Use these questions to model how to monitor understanding of the first paragraph on page 42. Then have students read the second paragraph and retell it in their own words.

- Do I understand what I am reading? If not, what part is confusing me?
- What fix-up strategies can I use to solve the problem?

(See Differentiated Instruction.)

Teacher Think Aloud

I always thought that Hong Kong was a good city to live in when the British governed it. I was confused when I read that the British traded opium to the people of Hong Kong, and many of them became addicts. I decided to reread the paragraph more slowly. When I did, I discovered it was talking about the 1800s. Maybe things improved later under British rule. I'll read on to find out.

Fix-Up Strategies

Offer these strategies to help students read independently.

If you don't understand what you're reading:

- Reread the difficult section to look for clues to help you comprehend.
- Read ahead to find clues to help you comprehend.
- Retell, or say in your own words, what you've read.
- Visualize, or form mental pictures of, what you've read.

When did the British take control of Hong Kong?

In the early nineteenth century, Hong Kong was only a small fishing village. But, in 1841 during the first Opium War between China and England, an English sailor raised the Union Jack on Hong Kong Island and claimed Hong Kong for England. England won the war and signed the Treaty of Nan-chiang with Hong Kong. Under this treaty, England took control of Hong Kong "in perpetuity," or forever. The British traded opium to the Chinese for precious Chinese tea, silk, and spices. This hurt the people of Hong Kong because many of them became addicted to opium.

In 1937 the Japanese invaded China and took control of many parts of China. They also took control of Hong Kong from the British. Many Chinese went hungry and some tried to escape to other countries. Chinese people who were left behind were taken as prisoners of war. Japan didn't end its tyrannous, cruel, and controlling rule until after World War II. Then, England resumed its control of Hong Kong once again.

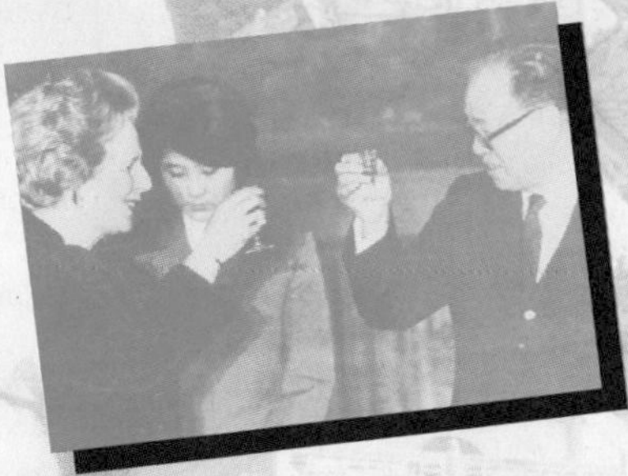

British Prime Minister Margaret Thatcher toasts the Sino-British Joint Declaration with Chinese Premier Zhao Ziyang in 1984.

Communism

A communist government is one in which the state owns all property. A single party rules the country, unlike the United States where the Congress contains representatives of both major political parties. In a communist country, most aspects of a person's life are controlled by the government. The goal of a communist government is for everyone to share goods and wealth equally in order to achieve higher social order. Some people view communism as a threat to world peace. Other people consider it the only hope for their country.

- Hong Kong **means "fragrant harbor."**
- **The population of Hong Kong is about six million. Hong Kong is one of the world's most crowded places.**
- **Hong Kong consists of a peninsula, which is part of mainland China, and over 235 islands.**

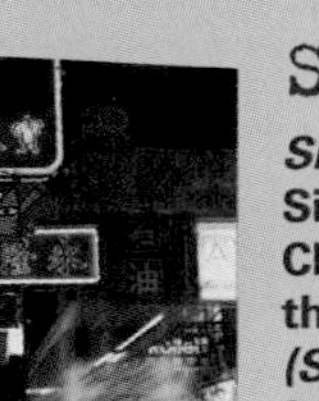

Sino

***Sino* means "Chinese." The term Sino-British refers to a combination of Chinese and British. *Sino* comes from the French and Greek words for *Chinese (Sinae and Sinai)* and the Arabic word for *China, Sin*.**

Student Journal page 142

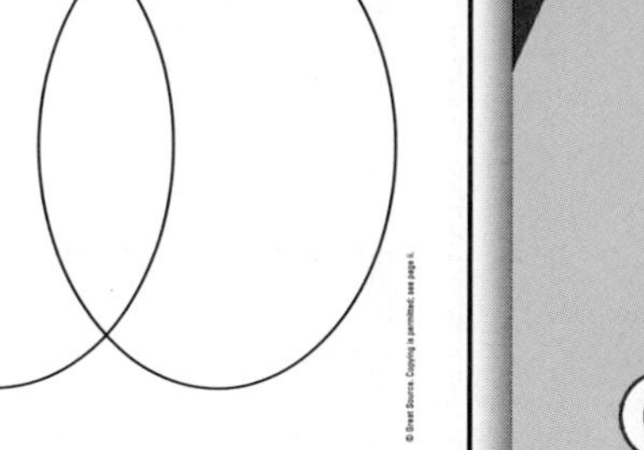

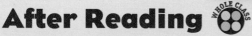

Name ____________ Date ______

Writing: Compare and Contrast

Compare and contrast the city or town in which you live with the city of Hong Kong. Fill in the Venn diagram below. Use what you know from the article, your group discussion, and your own life to help you make comparisons.

______ Both Hong Kong

142 Changes • Changing Governments

After Reading

Use one or more activities.

Check Purpose

Have students decide if their purpose was met. Did they find out why Hong Kong is now ruled by China?

Discussion Questions

Continue the group discussion with the following questions.

1. What was the effect of opium on the Chinese people? (Cause-Effect)
2. What are some things that make Hong Kong a unique city? (Details)
3. Do you think it was difficult for China to take back Hong Kong? Why or why not? (Making Connections)

Revisit: Association Web

Revisit the association web about Hong Kong. What new information can students add?

What events led to this night of independence for Hong Kong?

By the 1950s Hong Kong had grown rich as a trading and business center. It was the connecting city between China and the western world.

In 1972 China was a world power and became a member of the United Nations. The leaders of China wanted to take back Hong Kong peacefully, so they began talks with Britain about the future of Hong Kong. But it wasn't until 1984 that the British Prime Minister, Margaret Thatcher, signed the Sino-British Joint Declaration with the Chinese Premier Zhao Ziyang (shou she ANG). This agreement stated that China would regain, or take back, control of Hong Kong in 1997. In another part of the treaty, China also promised that it wouldn't change Hong Kong's social structure and the way it ran for fifty years.

On July 1, 1997, as millions of people watched from all around the world, history was made: Hong Kong was returned to China.

Hong Kong is indeed a special place. It mixes the cultures and traditions of the Far East with the conveniences and services of the West. Many think of Hong Kong as a shopper's paradise, but there are also world-class restaurants, museums, theaters, and sporting events. Residents and tourists enjoy the beaches, camping, boating, and hundreds of miles of hiking trails in and around Hong Kong. This city of over six million people is safe, the crime rate is low, and the people who live here are respectful and helpful.

China, a communist country, has pledged that for fifty years it will preserve, or keep, the democratic, capitalist lifestyle that thrived in Hong Kong under the British rule. However, it has been only a few years since the change in government. Time will tell. ◆

Opium comes from certain kinds of poppies.

Opium

Opium is a drug from which other medicines are made, most commonly codeine and morphine. Codeine is used to stop coughing. Morphine stops pain. Opium drugs are highly addictive; that is, once people start taking them, they have a very hard time stopping. People who become addicted to drugs tend to neglect their own health and the care of other people. The United States, as well as other countries, has many laws that control the making, selling, and use of opium and opiates (drugs made from opium).

Opium use began at least 6,000 years ago in the Middle East. Arabian traders took opium to China probably about 1,400 years ago. At first, the Chinese used the drug mainly as a medicine. Over time, though, many Chinese used it as a drug and became addicted. So many people were addicted that the Chinese government outlawed opium in 1729. European traders continued to trade opium for Chinese silk and tea. Since opium was illegal in China, the trading became smuggling. Widespread opium addiction caused many Chinese people to ignore their jobs and other responsibilities. The great amounts of money needed to pay for the opium caused economic problems in China. To try to stop opium smuggling, China fought the first Opium War in 1839. Britain easily won the war. At the end of the war, in 1842, Britain and China signed the Treaty of Nan-chiang. Among other things, the treaty gave the island of Hong Kong to Britain until July 1, 1997.

43

Possible answers for **Student Journal page 143** include *regain—find, retrieve/recede, regress; perpetuity—ceaselessness, endlessness, duration/briefly, shortly, for a while; resume—continue, carry on, proceed/cease, stop, discontinue.*

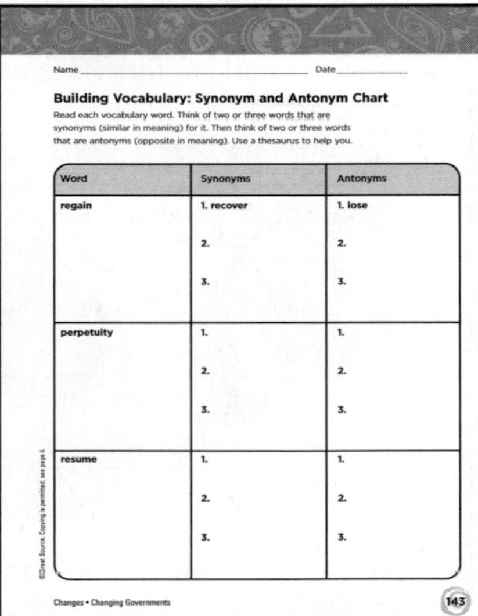

Name________ Date________

Building Vocabulary: Synonym and Antonym Chart

Read each vocabulary word. Think of two or three words that are synonyms (similar in meaning) for it. Then think of two or three words that are antonyms (opposite in meaning). Use a thesaurus to help you.

Word	Synonyms	Antonyms
regain	1. recover 2. 3.	1. lose 2. 3.
perpetuity	1. 2. 3.	1. 2. 3.
resume	1. 2. 3.	1. 2. 3.

Changes • Changing Governments 143

Writing Compare-Contrast

Have students compare-contrast the city of Hong Kong with the city in which they live. Ask for ideas and write them on the board or on chart paper. Then have students fill in the Venn diagram on *Student Journal* page 142.

Vocabulary Synonyms and Antonyms

Ask students if they can think of a word that is a synonym for *preserve*. (*keep*) If they have difficulty, refer them to the last paragraph on page 43 of the selection. Ask if they know any words that are antonyms of *preserve*. (*waste, use, exhaust*) To continue practice with synonyms and antonyms, have students complete the chart on *Student Journal* page 143. Students can use a thesaurus if they need help.

Phonics/Word Study

Doubling with Polysyllabic Words

Display these words: *exit, equip, enter,* and *embed*. Ask which syllable is stressed in each word. (EXit, eQUIP, ENter, emBED) Then write each word in the past tense: *exited, equipped, entered, embedded*. What do students notice? The words that have the second syllable stressed have doubled letters when *-ed* is added. Help students complete the in-depth words activity on TE page 334.

Phonics/Word Study

Doubling with Polysyllabic Words

- Write *equip*, *infer*, and *credit* on the board. Ask students to form the past tense of each by adding *-ed*. Have students share their responses. Write *equipped*, *inferred*, and *credited*. Note that the first two words have doubled letters because doubling preserves the vowel sound. The third word, however, does not need doubling. The second syllable in *credit* is unstressed, and that syllable contains the schwa sound. It is not necessary to double to preserve a schwa sound.
- Have students use Polysyllabic Doubling Sort One sheet to sort words by whether the final consonant before the *-ed* ending is doubled. (See *Word Study Manual* page 78.) Once that is done, have students check to see if the stressed syllable is the same throughout each column.
- Turn students' attention to the Oddball column. Ask them if they see any similarities among the words. As needed, guide students to see that all the words have a second syllable that ends in two consonants. The two consonants preserve the vowel sound, so nothing further is needed.

Polysyllabic Doubling Sort One

doubled	not doubled	Oddball
compelled	entered	pretended
repelled	exited	repented
embedded	suffered	existed
submitted	developed	attended
preferred		prevented
formatted		

For more information on word sorts and spelling stages, see pages 5–31 in the *Word Study Manual.*

Focus on . . .

Use one or more activities in this section to focus on a particular area of need in your students.

Comprehension STRATEGY SUPPORT

To help those students who need more practice using the strategies covered in this lesson, work one-on-one or in small groups to apply the strategy prompts below. Apply the prompts to a *Reading Advantage* paperback, a classroom library book, or a new or familiar selection in the magazine. Always model your own thinking first.

Monitor Understanding

- Do I understand what I'm reading? If not, what part is confusing to me?
- What fix-up strategies can I use to solve the problem? (See During Reading for fix-up strategies.)
- Why did a character say (do, think, ask) that?
- What images do I visualize from the text? What parts can't I visualize?
- Why did the author include (or not include) those details?

Writing News Story

Have students write a news story about the day Hong Kong was returned to China in 1997. Suggest that students include some of the effects this must have had on the Chinese people. Brainstorm some ideas as a group. Remind students that news stories always contain the answers to the 5Ws—*who*, *what*, *where*, *when*, and *why*. Have students use a 5Ws chart such as the one below to help organize their ideas. You can find a 5Ws BLM on TE page 384.

5Ws	Information for News Story
Who	
What	
Where	
When	
Why	

For more instruction on expository writing structures, see lessons in *Writing Advantage,* pages 114–151.

Fluency: Pacing

After students have read the selection at least once, they can use it to practice fluent reading. Students can work in pairs to read a section of "Changing Governments." Monitor partners as they read, and provide prompts to encourage fluent reading.

As you listen to students read, use these prompts to guide them.

- Read at an even, natural pace—neither too quickly nor too slowly. Preview the text, as needed, to avoid stops and starts.
- Let punctuation such as commas and periods guide your pauses. Let question marks and exclamation points guide the expression in your voice.

When students read aloud, do they—

✓ demonstrate a smooth pace, not too fast or too slow?

✓ incorporate well-timed pauses between words and phrases?

✓ reflect an awareness and understanding of punctuation?

English Language Learners

To support students as they develop their vocabulary, provide additional support for the synonyms and antonyms activity on TE page 333.

1. Allow students to use a thesaurus as you complete the chart together.
2. Discuss the slight differences in the meanings of each of the words. Also discuss appropriate contexts in which each of the words is typically used.
3. Have partners create sentences using several of the words.

Independent Activity Options

While you work with individuals or small groups, others can work independently on one or more of the following options.

- Level D paperback books, see TE pages 367–372
- Level D *eZines*
- Repeat word sorts from this lesson
- *Student Journal* pages for this lesson
- *Writing Advantage* independent lessons

Assessment

Strategy Assessment

To help you and your students assess their use of comprehension strategies, ask the following questions. Students can complete a written response or provide verbal answers in a one-on-one reading conference.

- **Monitor Understanding** Which aspects were confusing to you regarding the events that led to Hong Kong's return to Chinese rule in 1997? What did you do to try to resolve the confusion? (Answers will vary. Maybe students reread, read ahead, or asked another student for help.)

For ongoing informal assessment, use the checklists on pages 61–64 of *Level D Assessment*.

Word Study Assessment

Use these steps to help you and your students assess their understanding of doubling with polysyllabic words.

1. Write the following words on the board or on word cards: *infer, enter, suffer, repel, submit, develop*.
2. Ask students to form the past tense of each word by adding *-ed*, doubling letters when necessary.

Word	Word with *-ed* Added
infer	inferred
enter	entered
suffer	suffered
repel	repelled
submit	submitted
develop	developed

LESSON **43**

Changing Landscapes: Urban Sprawl

Changes, pages 44–49

SUMMARY

In this **first-person account,** a student discusses the causes and effects of urban sprawl.

COMPREHENSION STRATEGIES

Monitor Understanding
Determining Importance

WRITING

Pro-Con Chart

VOCABULARY

Antonyms

PHONICS/WORD STUDY

Suffixes *-ant* and *-ent*

Lesson Vocabulary

altered	scrape by
inconsequential	interact
phenomenon	loitering

MATERIALS

Changes, pp. 44–49
Student Journal, pp. 144–146
Word Study Manual, p. 79
Writing Advantage, pp. 30–55

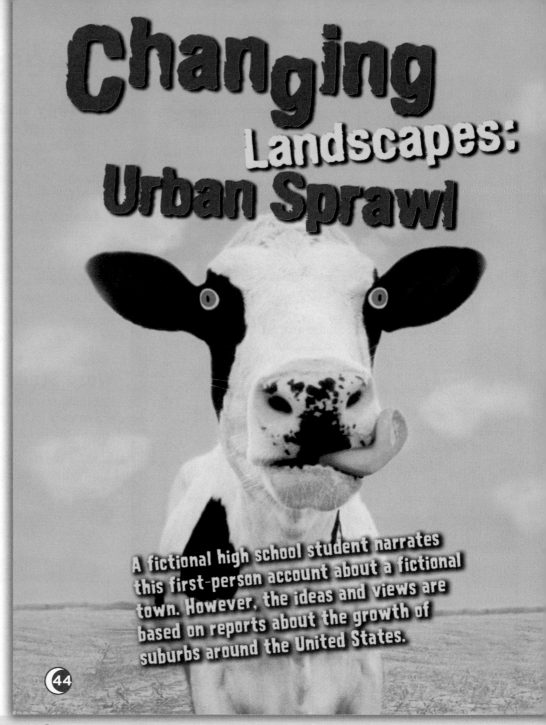

Changing Landscapes: Urban Sprawl

A fictional high school student narrates this first-person account about a fictional town. However, the ideas and views are based on reports about the growth of suburbs around the United States.

44

Before Reading

Use one or more activities.

Anticipation Guide

Create an anticipation guide for students. (See TE page 389 for an anticipation guide BLM.) Ask students to read the statements and place a check in the AGREE or DISAGREE box before each statement. Then discuss their responses. Revisit the guide later.

AGREE	DISAGREE	
		1. More Americans live in the city than in the suburbs.
		2. Overpopulated suburbs are a result of urban sprawl.
		3. New highways are indicators of urban sprawl.
		4. Because of urban sprawl, most suburban people go downtown to shop.

Vocabulary Preview

List the selection vocabulary on an overhead transparency or on the board. Then have students choose a word for the word web activity on *Student Journal* page 144. Have students write in the definition box what they think their chosen word means. Students can revise their definitions, if necessary, and write details about the word after they finish reading the selection. Model the process with the word *altered*.

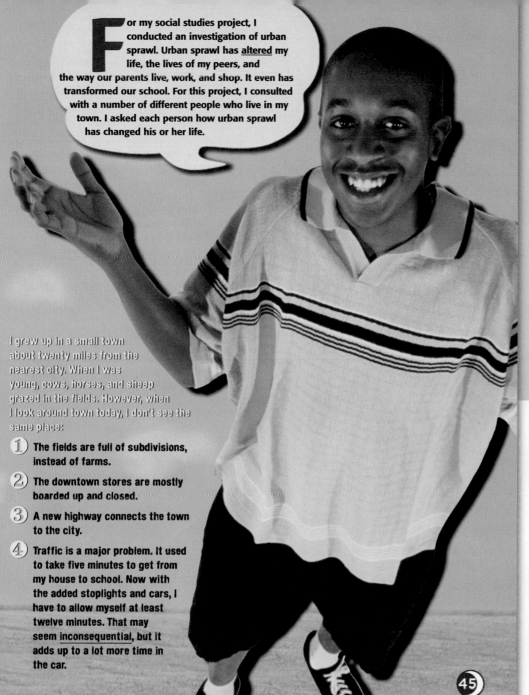

For my social studies project, I conducted an investigation of urban sprawl. Urban sprawl has altered my life, the lives of my peers, and the way our parents live, work, and shop. It even has transformed our school. For this project, I consulted with a number of different people who live in my town. I asked each person how urban sprawl has changed his or her life.

I grew up in a small town about twenty miles from the nearest city. When I was young, cows, horses, and sheep grazed in the fields. However, when I look around town today, I don't see the same place:

1. **The fields are full of subdivisions, instead of farms.**
2. **The downtown stores are mostly boarded up and closed.**
3. **A new highway connects the town to the city.**
4. **Traffic is a major problem. It used to take five minutes to get from my house to school. Now with the added stoplights and cars, I have to allow myself at least twelve minutes. That may seem inconsequential, but it adds up to a lot more time in the car.**

45

DIFFERENTIATED INSTRUCTION

Preview the Selection

Help students understand the first-person narrative.

1. Explain that the first-person pronouns *I*, *me*, *my*, *we*, *us*, and *our* signal that this is a first-person narrative, or told from the speaker's point of view.
2. Ask students: *Who presents the information in "Changing Landscapes: Urban Sprawl"?* Students should note that a high-school student narrates this selection. Suggest that students look back through previously read magazine selections to find another first-person narrative. ("Changing Culture: Crossing to the New World")

Student Journal page 144

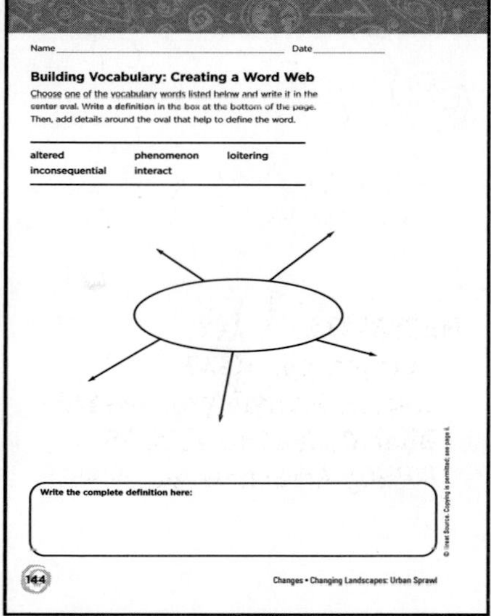
Name ______ Date ______

Building Vocabulary: Creating a Word Web

Choose one of the vocabulary words listed below and write it in the center oval. Write a definition in the box at the bottom of the page. Then, add details around the oval that help to define the word.

altered	phenomenon	loitering
inconsequential	interact	

Write the complete definition here:

144 Changes • Changing Landscapes: Urban Sprawl

Preview the Selection

Have students look through the selection. Use these or similar prompts to orient students to it.

- What information does the title page provide?
- In what format is the selection written?
- Do you think the selection is fiction or nonfiction? Why?

(See Differentiated Instruction.)

Teacher Think Aloud

From the title page, I learn that this selection is about urban sprawl. I'm not sure exactly what urban sprawl is, but I guess I will find out. This is a nonfiction selection. The author presents facts, and he interviews people for information. I also like the use of pictures in the diagrams. It makes the diagrams easier to understand.

Make Predictions/ Set Purpose

Students should use the information they gathered in previewing the selection to make predictions about what they will learn. If students have trouble generating a purpose for reading, suggest that they read to see if they were correct in their anticipation guide responses and to find out what urban sprawl is.

DIFFERENTIATED INSTRUCTION

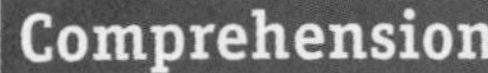

Comprehension

MONITOR UNDERSTANDING

Use this activity to help students develop their visualizing skills.

1. Tell students that many families in their town or city may own at least one car. Ask them to close their eyes and visualize the busiest local road at rush hour.
2. Then refer students to page 46 and ask: *How many people owned a car in 1920?* (one out of thirteen) Have students visualize how that same road might look with that few cars.

Urban sprawl has changed their lives.

I asked the town manager what he thinks happened to our town. He said that people from the nearby city began moving here because they wanted a quieter, calmer, and greener life. However, the more people who moved out here, the less quiet, clean, and green life in town became. New neighborhoods, highways, shopping malls, and gas stations have replaced parks and farms.

This phenomenon fascinates me: Why do people leave the city? News reports explain how the quality of life in American cities has been getting worse. Cities are dirty, crowded, expensive, and dangerous. Inner-city public schools are overcrowded and under-funded. City governments have a hard time providing simple services like trash collection. The list goes on, but for many people, these reasons are good enough to lead them to a simpler life in the "country."

The problem is that, eventually, these new communities become as bad as the cities that people wished to escape. So people keep moving even farther outside of the city, taking the problems with them.

The "progress" of urban sprawl in America

1920: Only one out of every thirteen people owned a car.

1921: The first drive-in restaurant opens in Texas.

1947: The first suburb with similar, low-cost homes is built in Levittown, NY.

46

During Reading

Comprehension

MONITOR UNDERSTANDING

Use these questions to model how to visualize what you are reading about. Then have students tell about a part they visualized.

- What do I picture in my mind?
- Which details help me create this image in my mind?
- How does seeing this picture in my mind help me? (See Differentiated Instruction.)

Teacher Think Aloud

As I read the first paragraph on page 46, I pictured highways gradually spreading out and malls eventually springing up across open land. The details "more people" making "less . . . green" helped me picture land decreasing as people on it increase and highways and malls slowly take over. Here, visualizing helps me understand how populated and busy our land is getting.

Comprehension

DETERMINING IMPORTANCE

Use these questions to model for students how to determine the importance of ideas in the paragraph about Mr. Washington, on page 47. Then have students determine the importance of ideas in the next paragraph, about Ms. Holly.

- What are the most important ideas in the paragraph?
- How can I support my beliefs?

The following is a summary of the conversations that I had with different people in town about how urban sprawl has changed their lives.

Mr. Washington, small business owner: Mr. Washington didn't have many good things to say about urban sprawl. For over twenty years his family ran the local hardware store downtown. People went to Washington's if they needed anything from a light bulb to a garden hose. But with more people in town, the demand has increased for more stores with a bigger selection of items at lower prices. Now, with a Hardware Heaven on the edge of town, people hop in their cars, drive out to the super store, and stock up. With business near a standstill, Washington's will close after the holiday season.

Ms. Holly, middle school principal: Ms. Holly sees two sides to urban sprawl. At first, the increase in the number of students overwhelmed her. Class sizes grew. The school needed to buy extra desks and books and hire new teachers. But Ms. Holly is happy to see the diversity of the student body. With different people moving into town, students are exposed to a wide range of cultures and new ways of thinking.

Mr. Lentz, construction worker: Mr. Lentz is very happy about the growth of the town. For a while he scraped by and took odd jobs during the winter to make ends meet. But as soon as people began fleeing from the city, his business boomed. There are new houses to build, and people who move into the older homes want to fix them up but don't have time to do the work themselves. He is busy all the time.

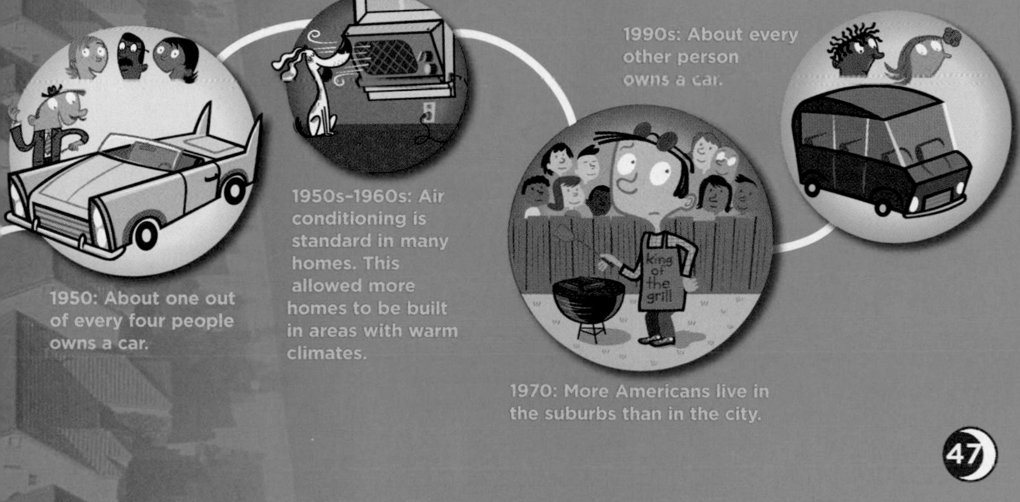

1950: About one out of every four people owns a car.

1950s–1960s: Air conditioning is standard in many homes. This allowed more homes to be built in areas with warm climates.

1970: More Americans live in the suburbs than in the city.

1990s: About every other person owns a car.

Teacher Think Aloud

I think the important ideas in this paragraph are that bigger stores have lower prices and more stock. More people shopping at superstores hurts the small stores. I can support my beliefs because Mr. Washington, a small-business owner, is going to have to close his store, as he is losing business to Hardware Heaven. Also, I know that this has happened to a lot of good stores in my area, too.

Fix-Up Strategies

Offer these strategies to help students read independently.

If you don't understand what you're reading:

- Reread the difficult section to look for clues to help you comprehend.
- Read ahead to find clues to help you comprehend.
- Retell, or say in your own words, what you've read.
- Visualize, or form mental pictures of, what you've read.

If you don't understand a word:

- Reread the sentence. Look for ideas and words that provide meaning clues.
- Find clues by reading a few sentences before and after the confusing word.
- Look for the base or root word and think about its meaning.
- Think about the topic or plot at this point to see if either offers meaning clues.

DIFFERENTIATED INSTRUCTION

SMALL GROUP

Vocabulary Antonyms

To help students with this vocabulary activity, follow these steps:

1. Explain to students that antonyms are words with opposite meanings.
2. Write the following word pairs on the board or on chart paper: *urban/suburbs*, *narrates/tells*, *downtown/uptown*, *car/vehicle*, and *public/private*. Tell students to identify the antonym pairs in the list.
3. Ask students what antonym pairs they know. Write their suggested pairs on the board or on chart paper.

Student Journal page 145

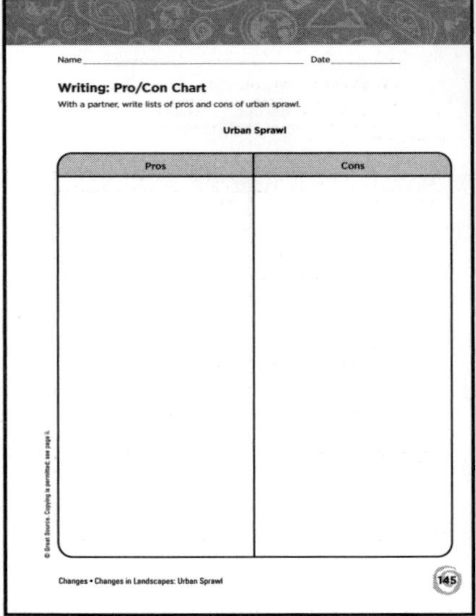

Name ____________________ Date __________

Writing: Pro/Con Chart

With a partner, write lists of pros and cons of urban sprawl.

Urban Sprawl

Pros	Cons

© Great Source. Copying is permitted; see page ii.

Changes • Changes in Landscapes: Urban Sprawl 145

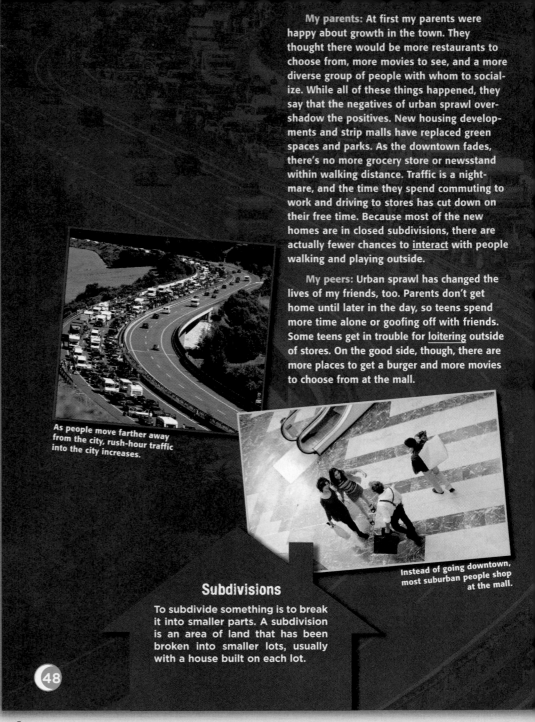

My parents: At first my parents were happy about growth in the town. They thought there would be more restaurants to choose from, more movies to see, and a more diverse group of people with whom to socialize. While all of these things happened, they say that the negatives of urban sprawl overshadow the positives. New housing developments and strip malls have replaced green spaces and parks. As the downtown fades, there's no more grocery store or newsstand within walking distance. Traffic is a nightmare, and the time they spend commuting to work and driving to stores has cut down on their free time. Because most of the new homes are in closed subdivisions, there are actually fewer chances to interact with people walking and playing outside.

My peers: Urban sprawl has changed the lives of my friends, too. Parents don't get home until later in the day, so teens spend more time alone or goofing off with friends. Some teens get in trouble for loitering outside of stores. On the good side, though, there are more places to get a burger and more movies to choose from at the mall.

As people move farther away from the city, rush-hour traffic into the city increases.

Instead of going downtown, most suburban people shop at the mall.

Subdivisions

To subdivide something is to break it into smaller parts. A subdivision is an area of land that has been broken into smaller lots, usually with a house built on each lot.

48

After Reading

WHOLE CLASS

Use one or more activities.

Check Purpose

Have students decide if their purpose was met. Were their responses correct in their anticipation guide? Did students find out what urban sprawl is?

Discussion Questions

Continue the group discussion with the following questions.

1. What are the causes and effects of urban sprawl? (Cause-Effect)
2. What is a solution to the traffic problem between cities and suburbs? (Problem-Solution)
3. What do you understand now that you didn't understand before reading the selection? (Making Connections)

Revisit: Anticipation Guide

Look back with students at the anticipation guide. How accurate were their responses? Which would they like to adjust?

Revisit: Word Web

Have students return to the word web on *Student Journal* page 144. Using a dictionary, the text, and prior knowledge, students can add details that help them define their word.

The leaders in our town and other towns had some ideas about how to slow down the damage created by urban sprawl:

- **Planning:** Communities need to control growth and plan it. They need to make sure they have the roads, water pipes, and money to support growth. Good planning will help make growing towns more pleasant places to live.
- **Public Transportation:** Americans will always want to drive, and highways will always be built and repaired. However, if there are good trains and buses, people will use them. This will help cut down on traffic and pollution.

In conclusion, urban sprawl is here to stay. Our focus should be on finding a way to control it and not letting it control us.

Urban sprawl has caused problems in my town and in other towns around the country.

Too much traffic. As people move out into the suburbs, they have to drive longer distances to work. Each year, average Americans spend about fifty-five eight-hour days in their cars. That's over two weeks behind the wheel every year!

Too much pollution. Because of all of the cars on the roads, pollution has become a real problem for big cities and for smaller towns, too.

Not as many places to farm. In the 1990s, more than three million acres of farmland in America were lost to new houses and malls. What will happen to our country if there isn't room to grow enough food?

Wildlife in danger. As highways and new neighborhoods cover open spaces, many animals' homes are destroyed. As a result, wildlife such as deer, bears, and coyotes now live in or near the suburbs.

Possible answers for **Student Journal page 146** may include *altered: unchanged, the same; interact: avoid, disconnect, keep quiet; loiter: work, be diligent; allow: deny, refuse, oppose.*

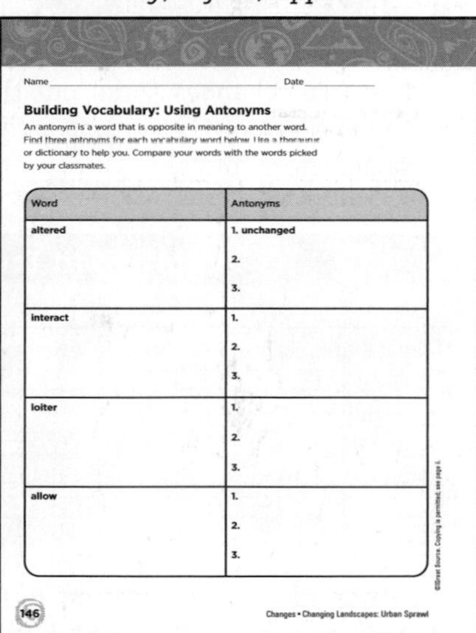

Name__________ Date__________

Building Vocabulary: Using Antonyms

An antonym is a word that is opposite in meaning to another word. Find three antonyms for each vocabulary word below. Use a thesaurus or dictionary to help you. Compare your words with the words picked by your classmates.

Word	Antonyms
altered	1. unchanged 2. 3.
interact	1. 2. 3.
loiter	1. 2. 3.
allow	1. 2. 3.

©Great Source. Copying is permitted; see page ii.

146 Changes • Changing Landscapes: Urban Sprawl

Writing Pro-Con Chart

Have students do *Student Journal* page 145. Before they write, encourage them to pair up and reread the selection to look for appropriate information. After students have completed their lists, divide the class into two groups—the "Pros" and the "Cons." Conduct an informal debate weighing the positive and negative aspects of urban sprawl. Have students in each group work cooperatively, sharing ideas from their lists.

Vocabulary Antonyms

Display the word *inconsequential*. Ask:

- What is the definition of *inconsequential*? (lacking importance)
- What words mean the opposite of *inconsequential*? (*important, major, significant, valuable*)

Display the words. Explain that words that are opposite in meaning are called antonyms. Have students complete *Student Journal* page 146. (See Differentiated Instruction.)

Phonics/Word Study

Suffixes *-ant* and *-ent*

Display *relev*, say *relevant*, and ask students to spell the word. Many will be unsure whether *-ant* or *-ent* is the ending. Display the correct spelling. Then display *relevance* and *relevancy*, pointing out the *a* in each. Explain how one form of a word will help them spell the other forms. Now, work with students to complete the in-depth endings *-ant* and *-ent* activity on TE page 342.

Phonics/Word Study

Suffixes *-ant* and *-ent*

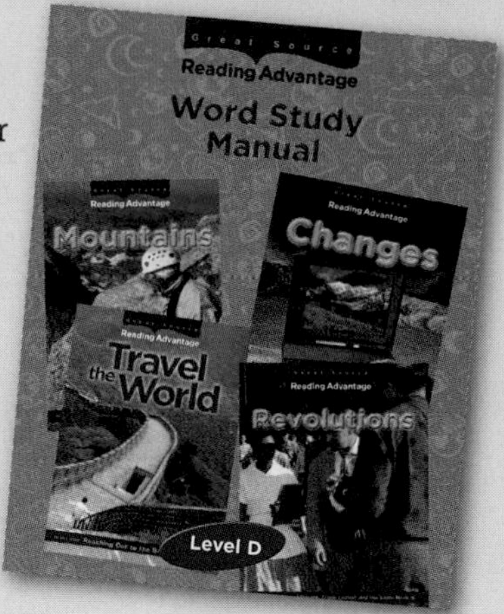

Words ending with *-ant* or *-ent* can be problematic for students. One way to help students decide which spelling is the correct way to end a given word is to look at all the various forms of the word in question. For example, to spell correctly the end of *brilliant*, students should think about *brilliance* and *brilliancy*. To spell *emergent*, students should think about *emergence* and *emergency*.

- Using the Suffix Sort Four sheet, students should begin by sorting by the *-ant* and *-ent* endings. (See *Word Study Manual* page 79.)
- Next, have students sort by noun and adjective. Discuss how the form of the word changes when the usage changes. Point out that, no matter what, the spelling of the *-ant* or *-ent* ending remains the same across forms.

Suffix Sort Four

-ant	*-ance*	*-ancy*	*-ent*	*-ence*	*-ency*
brilliant	brilliance	brilliancy	emergent	emergence	emergency
compliant	compliance	compliancy	permanent	permanence	permanency
reliant	reliance		competent	competence	competency
defiant	defiance		excellent	excellence	excellency
relevant	relevance	relevancy	coherent	coherence	coherency

For more information on word sorts and spelling stages, see pages 5–31 in the *Word Study Manual.*

Focus on . . .

Use one or more activities in this section to focus on a particular area of need in your students.

Comprehension STRATEGY SUPPORT

To help those students who need more practice using the strategies covered in this lesson, work one-on-one or in small groups to apply the strategy prompts below. Apply the prompts to a *Reading Advantage* paperback, a classroom library book, or a new or familiar selection in the magazine. Always model your own thinking first.

Monitor Understanding

- Do I understand what I'm reading? If not, what part is confusing to me?
- What fix-up strategies can I use to solve the problem? (See During Reading for fix-up strategies.)
- Why did a character say (do, think, ask) that?
- What images do I visualize from the text? What parts can't I visualize?
- Why did the author include (or not include) those details?

Determining Importance

- What is the most important idea in the paragraph? How can I prove it?
- Which details are unimportant? Why?
- What does the author want me to understand?
- Why is this information important (or not important) to me?

Writing Visualizing

Ask students which aspects of urban sprawl they could visualize best. Have students review the selection to pick an aspect of urban sprawl that made a clear impression on them. Have students draw what they "see" in their minds and then write a matching description.

To give students more practice in using sensory details in their writing, see lessons in *Writing Advantage,* pages 30–55.

Fluency: Phrasing

After students have read the selection at least once, have pairs choose two paragraphs to alternate reading aloud to each other.

As you listen to students read, use these prompts to guide them.

- Preview what you will read. Look for groups of words that naturally go together. Many times, words are held together or "chunked" with commas. Reading these words in "chunks" will help you sound natural.
- Be aware of end punctuation marks that signal pauses.
- Pause briefly before and after reading headings to indicate to listeners that you've started a new section.

When students read aloud, do they—

✓ demonstrate quick recognition of words and phrases?

✓ exhibit an understanding of phrasal construction?

✓ incorporate appropriate timing, stress, and intonation?

English Language Learners

To support students as they develop the skill of visualizing, extend the comprehension activity on TE page 338.

1. Have students discuss what they "saw" as they visualized the busiest local road at rush hour.
2. Have them write a brief paragraph describing the scene at this busy local road at rush hour, encouraging them to use strong verbs and adjectives.
3. Have students share their work with a partner.

Independent Activity Options

While you work with individuals or small groups, others can work independently on one or more of the following options.

- Level D paperback books, see TE pages 367–372
- Level D *eZines*
- Repeat word sorts from this lesson
- *Student Journal* pages for this lesson
- *Writing Advantage* independent lessons

Assessment

Strategy Assessment

To help you and your students assess their use of comprehension strategies, ask the following questions. Students can complete a written response or provide verbal answers in a one-on-one reading conference.

1. **Monitor Understanding** What is urban sprawl? Which details helped you visualize and understand this term? (Answers will vary. Students may describe urban sprawl as an overcrowding of rural areas, with people, highways, and buildings. The descriptions of heavy traffic may have helped students visualize.)
2. **Determining Importance** Why do you think knowing about urban sprawl is important? (Answers will vary. Possible responses include that knowing the reasons behind something, such as more wild animals showing up in towns, can help you better understand it. You can work to help control the effects of urban sprawl by encouraging people to use public transportation and by pushing to develop more bicycle lanes.)

For ongoing informal assessment, use the checklists on pages 61–64 of *Level D Assessment*.

Word Study Assessment

Use these steps to help you and your students assess their understanding of the use of the suffixes *-ant* and *-ent*.

1. Write the following words on the board or on word cards: *reliance*, *compliancy*, *competency*, *excellence*, *coherency*, *emergency*.
2. Ask students to write the correct *-ant*/*-ent* form of each word by paying attention to the spelling of the form given.

Word	*-ant* or *-ent*
reliance	reliant
compliancy	compliant
competency	competent
excellence	excellent
coherency	coherent
emergency	emergent

LESSON **44**

Tiger Woods: Changing the Face of Golf

Changes, pages 50–53

SUMMARY

This **biographical sketch** tells about the life and career of Tiger Woods, whose success has sparked great interest in golf.

COMPREHENSION STRATEGIES

Making Connections

WRITING

Timeline

VOCABULARY

Multiple Meanings

PHONICS/WORD STUDY

Eponymous Words

Lesson Vocabulary

identifies	accomplishing
discrimination	sensation
previous	legacy

MATERIALS

Changes, pp. 50–53
Student Journal, pp. 147–149
Word Study Manual, p. 80
Writing Advantage, pp. 114–151

Before Reading

Use one or more activities.

Begin a K-W-L Chart

Write *Golf and Tiger Woods* on the board. Then begin a brief discussion about what students know about Woods and the game of golf. Draw a K-W-L chart on the board or on chart paper. Ask students to suggest entries for the first two columns. Tell students that they will come back to the chart to list what they have learned after reading the biographical sketch.

Vocabulary Preview

Display the selection vocabulary. Have students do *Student Journal* page 147. Students may adjust definitions after reading. Use the word *legacy* to model.

Preview the Selection

Have students look through the biographical sketch. Discuss the features that students notice.

Make Predictions/ Set Purpose

Students should use the information they gathered in previewing the selection to make predictions about what they will learn. If students have trouble generating a purpose for reading, suggest that they read to learn how Tiger Woods changed the sport of golf.

Changing the Face of Golf

Golf usually brings to mind stuffy, middle-aged white men wearing pink and green checked pants and button-front sweaters. Boring, we think, as we click past the TV station airing a tournament. However, in the last few years, all of that seems to have changed. Now, golf seems dramatic, exciting, and fun. People read about golf in magazines and check for scores on TV. Why the sudden change? His name is Tiger Woods.

Born Eldrick "Tiger" Woods on December 30, 1975, Tiger grew up in a middle-class town south of Los Angeles with his mother and father, Kultida and Earl. Looking at Tiger, many people assume that he is African American; however, Tiger's background is a real mix. His father is half African American, one-quarter Chinese, and one-quarter Native American, and his mother is half Thai, one-quarter Chinese, and one-quarter Caucasian. Tiger identifies and connects with all of his different heritages, and it bothers him when people do not recognize the different cultures that make up his background.

Tiger's father, Earl, picked up the game of golf for fun when he was forty-two. With a new son with whom he wanted to spend time, Earl took Tiger out to the garage with him every day when he practiced hitting balls. Even though Tiger was only a baby, he watched his father closely. This pleased Earl, and he made Tiger a special baby-sized putter, which Tiger took with him everywhere. Then one day something amazing happened. While Earl practiced hitting balls into the net, Tiger climbed out of his chair, picked up his mini-putter, and began hitting balls into the net with his father. He wasn't even a year old!

By the time Tiger was two, word of his talent spread, and he was invited onto a TV talk show for a putting competition. Tiger was a hit with the audience. When he was four, he entered a local golf contest, and even though he was in the group with ten- and eleven-year-olds, Tiger won, surprising everyone.

Tiger's game was progressing and improving smoothly, but the world around him wasn't always kind. More than once, Tiger was kicked off a golf course because of the color of his skin. In fact, it wasn't until the year that Tiger was born, in 1975, that the Professional Golf Association (PGA) allowed Lee Elder, an African American golfer, to play in The Masters tournament. But Tiger loved golf and would not be stopped by racial discrimination.

DIFFERENTIATED INSTRUCTION

Comprehension

MAKING CONNECTIONS

Follow these steps to help students make connections with the text.

1. Say: *On page 52, we learn that Tiger liked other things besides golf, such as video games, music, and friends.*
2. Ask: *Do you think it is important for people to be involved in different activities, even though they may have a special talent? Why? Do you know someone who is obsessed with one activity? What do you think about that?*

Student Journal page 147

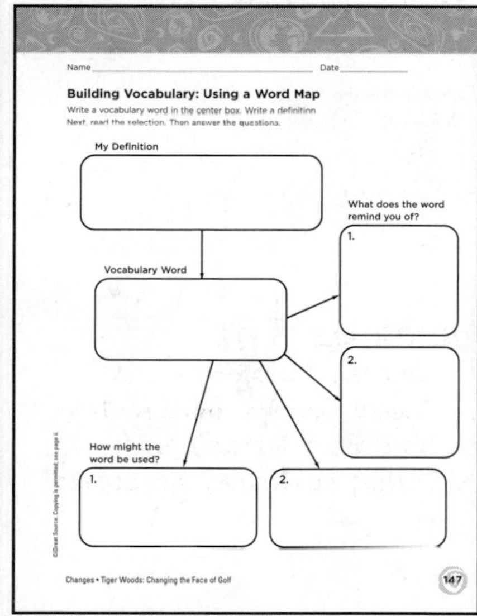

Name ______ Date ______

Building Vocabulary: Using a Word Map

Write a vocabulary word in the center box. Write a definition. Next, read the selection. Then answer the questions.

My Definition

Vocabulary Word

What does the word remind you of?

1.

2.

How might the word be used?

1.

2.

©Great Source. Copying is permitted; see page ii.

Changes • Tiger Woods: Changing the Face of Golf 147

During Reading

Comprehension

MAKING CONNECTIONS

Use these questions to model for students how to make connections with the text, using the first paragraph as an example. Then have students make their own connections to the selection.

- What does this selection remind me of?
- How does my past experience help me understand the selection?

(See Differentiated Instruction.)

Teacher Think Aloud

I really related to the discussion of Tiger Woods's cultural heritage. I had a friend in high school named Elena whose mother was Native American and whose father was Cuban. People always assumed Elena was African American. It bothered her not only because she was proud of her heritage, but also because people made assumptions about her from the way she looked.

Fix-Up Strategies

Offer these strategies to help students read independently.

If you don't understand what you're reading:

- Reread the difficult section to look for clues to help you comprehend.
- Read ahead to find clues to help you comprehend.
- Retell, or say in your own words, what you've read.
- Visualize, or form mental pictures of, what you've read.

YOUNG PRO

Tiger won six PGA tournaments in a row, matching the record Ben Hogan set in 1948.

While Tiger's father encouraged him to practice and practice, his mother balanced his life by encouraging him to relax and have some fun. During junior high school, Tiger's own desire to practice and play grew. He entered tournament after tournament and won. People began to notice him. He won six Junior World Amateur Tournaments, breaking the previous record of four.

In high school, Tiger joined the golf team, but he also liked the other activities that teenagers enjoy: video games, music, and hanging out with friends. He continued to play in many tournaments, but spending most of the summers on the road often left him homesick. Toward the end of his high-school golf career, Tiger was contacted by many colleges that wanted to enroll him in their programs. In the end, Tiger chose Stanford University because he liked their golf coach and knew that he would get a great education there.

In college, Tiger struggled to balance tournaments with school. After accomplishing all that he could as an amateur golfer, he decided to turn professional during his junior year of college. In only a few days, without even hitting one shot as a professional, Tiger won a forty-million dollar contract with Nike and a twenty-million dollar contract with Titleist, a major golf ball company.

As a young pro, Tiger's career had its ups and downs. After a year of disappointing games, Tiger won The Masters in 1997. Overnight he became a sensation, a star, and found himself in a whirlwind of media and interviews. At the beginning of the 1998 golf season, the press and the public were all eager to see Tiger play. TV ratings for golf were soaring. Unfortunately, all of the attention and fame wore Tiger out, so he spent the end of the year reworking his golf game. By the end of the 1999 season, Tiger had won so many tournaments that the Associated Press named him Male Athlete of the Year.

Still a young man, Tiger continues to win and break records, and he is on track to become the first athlete in any sport to win a billion dollars. But perhaps a more important legacy, or gift, that Tiger has left to the world is a renewed interest in the game of golf. People love to watch him grow, develop, and change as a golfer and a person. Tiger reminds us that maybe there is another young player out there who can also rise to greatness. In fact, it could be you. ◆

52

Student Journal page 148

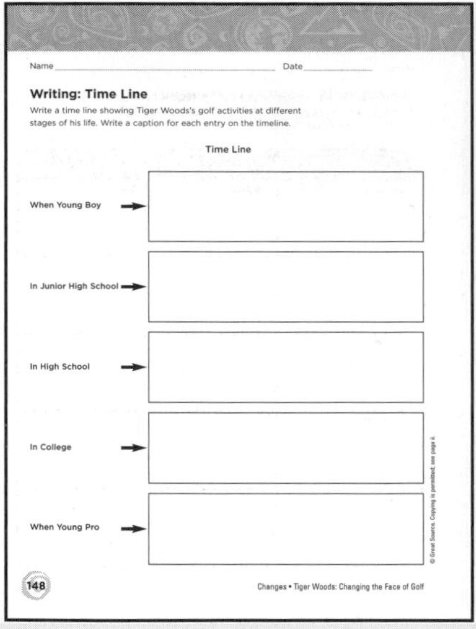

Name ______ Date ______

Writing: Time Line

Write a time line showing Tiger Woods's golf activities at different stages of his life. Write a caption for each entry on the timeline.

Time Line

When Young Boy →

In Junior High School →

In High School →

In College →

When Young Pro →

148 Changes • Tiger Woods: Changing the Face of Golf

After Reading  Use one or more activities.

Check Purpose

Have students decide if their purpose was met. Did they learn how Tiger Woods changed the sport of golf?

Discussion Questions

Continue the group discussion with the following questions.

1. What character traits does Tiger Woods have that helped him succeed? (Inferential Thinking)
2. Which ideas in this biographical sketch are important to remember? Why? (Determining Importance)
3. Would you like to be a professional athlete? If so, in what sport? (Making Connections)

Revisit: K-W-L Chart

Revisit the K-W-L chart. Ask students to suggest entries for the third column in the chart.

Revisit: Word Map

Have students return to the word map activity on *Student Journal* page 147. Tell them to review their original definition and adjust it, as needed. Then have them complete the page.

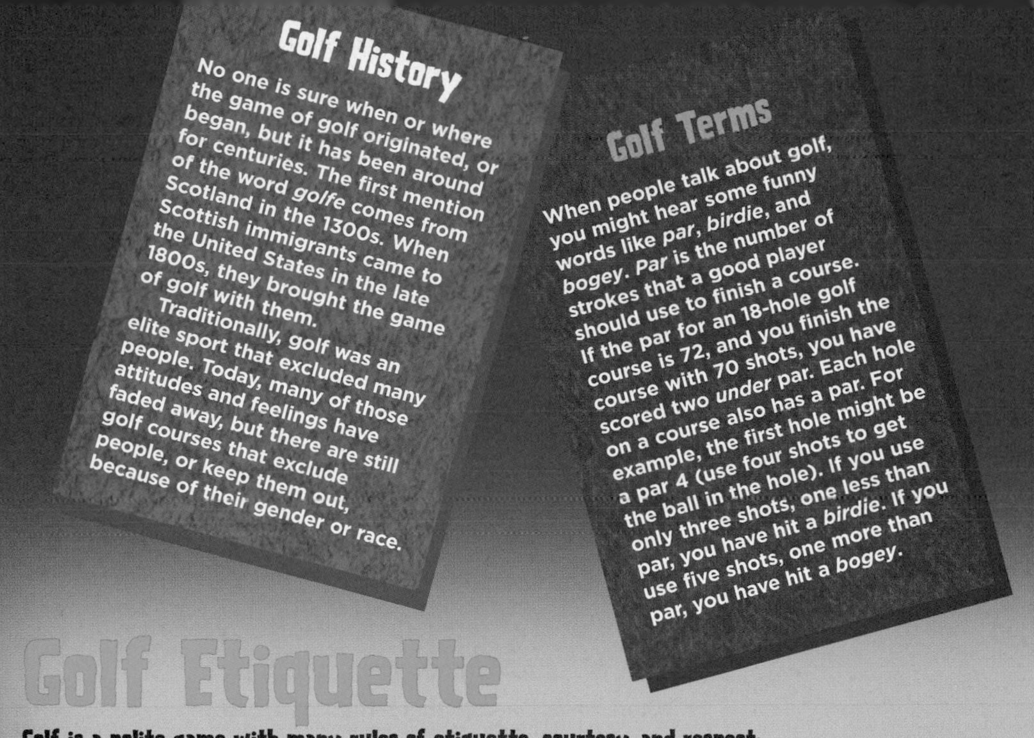

Golf History

No one is sure when or where the game of golf originated, or began, but it has been around for centuries. The first mention of the word *golfe* comes from Scotland in the 1300s. When Scottish immigrants came to the United States in the late 1800s, they brought the game of golf with them.

Traditionally, golf was an elite sport that excluded many people. Today, many of those attitudes and feelings have faded away, but there are still golf courses that exclude people, or keep them out, because of their gender or race.

Golf Terms

When people talk about golf, you might hear some funny words like *par*, *birdie*, and *bogey*. *Par* is the number of strokes that a good player should use to finish a course. If the par for an 18-hole golf course is 72, and you finish the course with 70 shots, you have scored two *under* par. Each hole on a course also has a par. For example, the first hole might be a par 4 (use four shots to get the ball in the hole). If you use only three shots, one less than par, you have hit a *birdie*. If you use five shots, one more than par, you have hit a *bogey*.

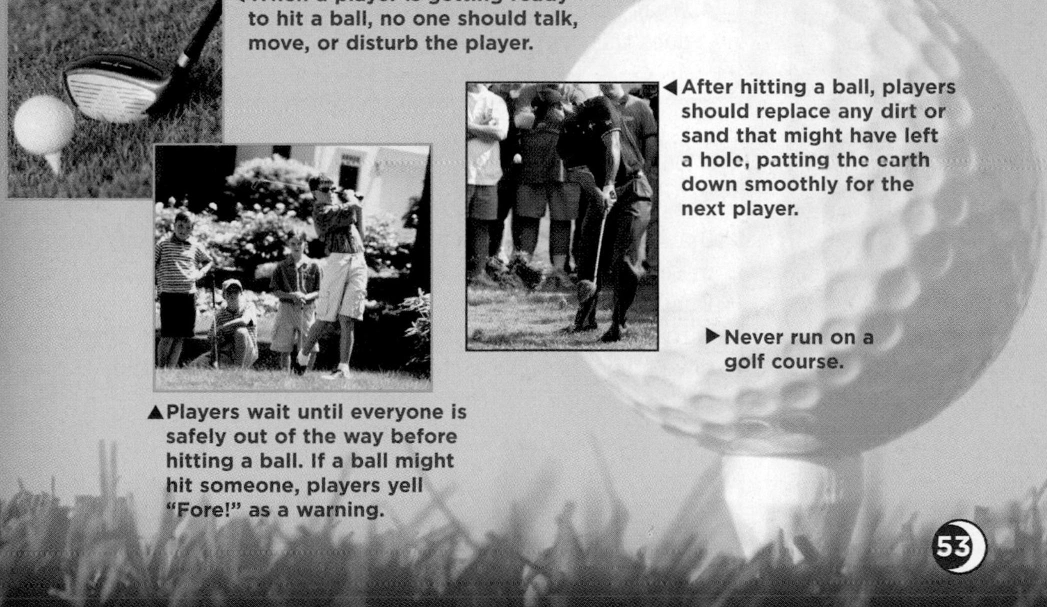

Golf Etiquette

Golf is a polite game with many rules of etiquette, courtesy, and respect:

◀ When a player is getting ready to hit a ball, no one should talk, move, or disturb the player.

◀ After hitting a ball, players should replace any dirt or sand that might have left a hole, patting the earth down smoothly for the next player.

▶ Never run on a golf course.

▲ Players wait until everyone is safely out of the way before hitting a ball. If a ball might hit someone, players yell "Fore!" as a warning.

DIFFERENTIATED INSTRUCTION

Vocabulary

Multiple Meanings

Help students with this activity.

1. Explain that many words have multiple meanings, and that the meanings change depending on how a word is used.
2. Draw attention to this sentence on page 51: *Tiger identifies and connects with . . .* Ask what *identifies* means here. (makes a connection with) Provide a sentence with another meaning of *identifies*. (*He identifies the book bag in the office.*) Ask what *identifies* means here. (recognizes something) Then ask a volunteer to use *identifies* defined this way in a sentence.

Student Journal page 149

Name ______________________ Date __________

Building Vocabulary: Words with Multiple Meanings

The words in the left column have more than one meaning. Write two definitions for each word.

Word	First Definition	Second Definition
checked	verified	inspected
change		
course		
sensation		
break		

Changes • Tiger Woods: Changing the Face of Golf 149

Writing Timeline

Tell students that a timeline shows the order in which events happen. A reader can see at a glance what the key events are and when they happened. Have students use *Student Journal* page 148 to create a timeline for the golfing career of Tiger Woods. To help prepare, students can work with partners to identify the five key events for the timeline.

Vocabulary Multiple Meanings

Have students complete *Student Journal* page 149. They can use a dictionary, the text, or prior knowledge to write two definitions for each word. Then have students share their responses. Possible answers include *change*—coins, to alter; *course*—path, to run through; *sensation*—big hit, feeling; *break*—opportunity, to surpass. (See Differentiated Instruction.)

Phonics/Word Study

Eponymous Words

Explain that many English words come from the names of real or fictional people. These are called "eponymous words," or "eponyms." Examples are *August*, named for Roman emperor Augustus Caesar; and *teddy bear*, named for president Theodore Roosevelt. Now, work with students to complete the in-depth eponymous words activity on TE page 348.

Phonics/Word Study

Eponymous Words

By definition, eponymous words are those that have come into English through someone's name. Here are some examples. (A more comprehensive chart can be found in the *Word Study Manual* on page 80.) Have students use encyclopedias or the Internet to find the origin of each term.

Term	Definition	Source
Doberman pinscher	a breed of dog	Ludwig Dobermann, 19th-Century German dog breeder
Fahrenheit	temperature scale used in U.S. and other countries	Gabriel Daniel Fahrenheit (1686–1736), German scientist
forsythia	ornamental shrub with yellow bell-shaped flowers	William Forsyth (1737–1804), British botanist
Gothic	relating to a style of architecture or a style of macabre fiction	the Goths, a Germanic people who originated in Scandinavia
graham crackers	slightly sweet whole-wheat crackers	Sylvester Graham (1794–1851), American dietary reformer
jumbo	very large	Jumbo, 62-ton African elephant exhibited at London Zoo from 1865 to 1882
Morse code	an early means of communicating across phone lines using a series of tapping sounds	Samuel Finley Breese Morse (1791–1872), American artist and inventor
pasteurize	a process that kills bacteria in milk	Louis Pasteur (1822–1895), French chemist and bacteriologist
teddy bear	stuffed animal	a bear named after Theodore Roosevelt (1858–1919), American president

There are several books filled with the origins of certain words and expressions. Charles Earle Funk has a number of titles, including *A Hog on Ice and Other Curious Expressions; Horsefeathers and Other Curious Words;* and *Thereby Hangs a Tale: Stories of Curious Word Origins.*

For more information on word sorts and spelling stages, see pages 5–31 in the *Word Study Manual.*

Focus on . . .

Use one or more activities in this section to focus on a particular area of need in your students.

Comprehension Strategy Support

To help those students who need more practice using the strategies covered in this lesson, work one-on-one or in small groups to apply the strategy prompts below. Apply the prompts to a *Reading Advantage* paperback, a classroom library book, or a new or familiar selection in the magazine. Always model your own thinking first.

Making Connections

- What does this story (article, passage) remind me of?
- What do I already know about this topic?
- Where have I heard about this topic before?
- What do I have in common with the characters, people, or situations in the text?
- What other books, stories, articles, movies, or TV shows does this text make me think about?

Writing Character Map

Draw a character map on the board with "Tiger Woods" in the center. Label six ovals: Birthplace and Early Life, Family, Education, Goals, Obstacles, Achievements. Discuss with students each of these aspects of Woods's life. Then have students make a character map and write in the ovals about each of the subtopics.

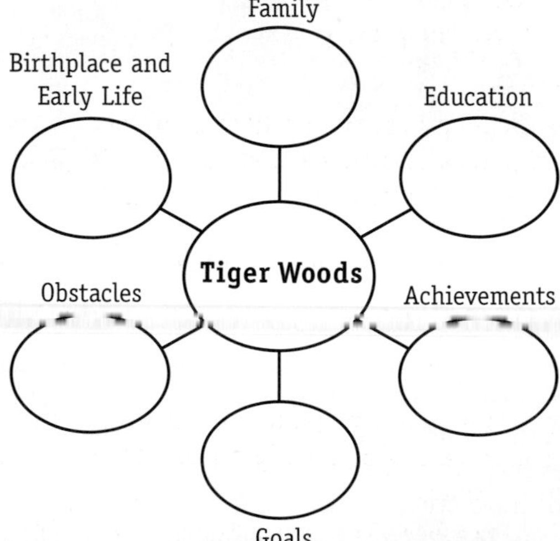

To give students more practice in writing descriptive paragraphs, see lessons in *Writing Advantage,* pages 114–151.

Fluency: Pacing

After students have read "Golf History" and "Golf Terms" at least once, have partners alternate reading the features aloud. Tell students that when they convey information, it's important to read at an even pace, not too fast and not too slow. Note the terms in italics. Tell students that italics indicate that a word is important and needs to be emphasized.

As students read aloud, use these prompts.

- Remember that the words in italics should be slightly emphasized.
- Reread until you can read the text at an even pace without effort. With practice, you can emphasize words without having to slow down.

When students read aloud, do they—

- ✓ demonstrate a smooth pace, not too fast or too slow?
- ✓ incorporate well-timed pauses between words and phrases?
- ✓ reflect an awareness and understanding of punctuation?

English Language Learners

To support students as they respond to the discussion questions on TE page 346, provide background knowledge relating to character traits.

1. Have students discuss what they already know about character traits.
2. Brainstorm a list of character traits and discuss their meanings.
3. Have partners sort the traits into categories: positive and negative. Encourage students to share their rationale for placing their words into each category.

Independent Activity Options

While you work with individuals or small groups, others can work independently on one or more of the following options.

- Level D paperback books, see TE pages 367–372
- Level D *eZines*
- Repeat word sorts from this lesson
- *Student Journal* pages for this lesson
- *Writing Advantage* independent lessons

Assessment

Strategy Assessment

To help you and your students assess their use of comprehension strategies, ask the following questions. Students can complete a written response or provide verbal answers in a one-on-one reading conference.

- **Making Connections** In what ways are you like and unlike Tiger Woods? (Answers will vary. Students should use examples from the text to support their answers.)

For ongoing informal assessment, use the checklists on pages 61–64 of *Level D Assessment*.

Word Study Assessment

Use these steps to help you and your students assess their understanding of eponymous words.

1. Write these eponymous words on the board or on word cards: *ammonia, maverick, leotard, boycott, dahlia, sideburns*.
2. Ask students to use a library or the Internet to find the origin of each word. The URL of one website with many eponyms listed alphabetically is http://users.tinyonline.co.uk/gswithenbank/eponyms.htm.

Word	Source
ammonia	the Egyptian god Ammon
maverick	Samuel Maverick, American pioneer
leotard	Jules Léotard, French acrobat
boycott	Charles Boycott, Irish land agent
dahlia	Anders Dahl, Swedish botanist
sideburns	Ambrose Burnside, American general

LESSON **45**

Roots; Echo and Narcissus; Thirteen

Changes, pages 54–59

SUMMARY

The **myth** explains each character's personality flaw. The **poems** are about growing up.

COMPREHENSION STRATEGIES

Inferential Thinking
Making Connections

WRITING

Character Map

VOCABULARY

Denotation and Connotation

PHONICS/WORD STUDY

More Eponyms

Lesson Vocabulary

frolic	shunned
seethed	despondent
vain	mourned
notorious	

MATERIALS

Changes, pp. 54–59
Student Journal, pp. 150–152
Word Study Manual, p. 80
Writing Advantage, pp. 170–181

Roots

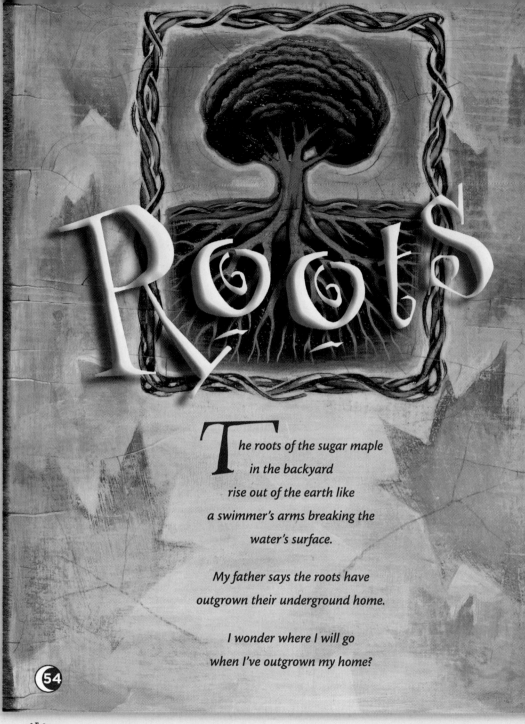

The roots of the sugar maple
in the backyard
rise out of the earth like
a swimmer's arms breaking the
water's surface.

My father says the roots have
outgrown their underground home.

I wonder where I will go
when I've outgrown my home?

54

Before Reading

Use one or more activities.

Features of Mythology Chart

Write the word *myth* on the board or on chart paper. Remind students that myths are one kind of folk literature. Ask them to identify any myths they have read or heard. Students who have read the *Mountains* magazine may recall the myth about Prometheus and how he gifted the human world with fire. Work with students to identify some of the features of myths. Start a chart as shown. (See Differentiated Instruction.)

Features of Mythology

Characters	Settings	Kinds of Events
gods, goddesses, Titans, humans	Earth, Olympus, underworld	heroic human deeds; gods punish or reward humans

Vocabulary Preview

Review the vocabulary list. Write the words on the board and read them aloud to clarify pronunciations. Ask students to think about how the words might be used in the selection, and then have them begin the predictions chart on *Student Journal* page 150. Students will complete the chart after reading the selection.

Echo and Narcissus

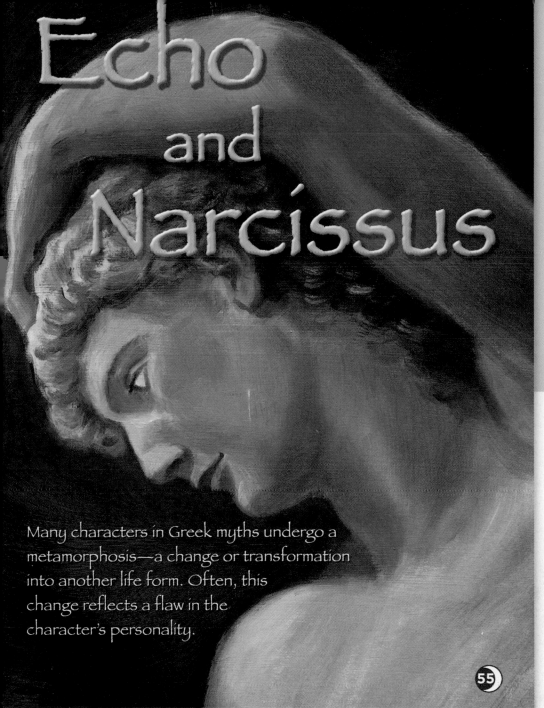

Many characters in Greek myths undergo a metamorphosis—a change or transformation into another life form. Often, this change reflects a flaw in the character's personality.

55

DIFFERENTIATED INSTRUCTION

FEATURES OF MYTHOLOGY CHART

Help students understand the features of myths.

- Myths are one kind of oral folk literature that was passed down over generations.
- Myths are stories about immortal gods and goddesses and their interactions with humans. The stories dramatize and explain natural events in the world.
- Myths are narratives with all the basic story elements—characters, setting, plot with conflict, and theme. The themes often offer advice on how to live morally or wisely.

Student Journal page 150

Name ______________________ Date ____________

Building Vocabulary: Prediction Chart

How do you think these words will be used in the selection "Echo and Narcissus"? Write your answers in the second column. Next, read the article. Then, clarify your answers in the third column.

Word	My prediction for how the word will be used	How the word was actually used
frolic		
seethed		
vain		
notorious		
shunned		
despondent		
mourned		

150 Changes • Echo and Narcissus

Preview the Selection

Have students look through the four pages of the myth. Use these or similar prompts to guide students to notice the important features of the text.

- What do you learn from the title and the heading note on page 55?
- What elements of a myth do you recognize? What clues do you have?
- What do you think the relationship is between Echo and Narcissus?

Teacher Think Aloud

The introduction tells me that this is a Greek myth, which means it is fiction. I have heard of Echo and Narcissus, but I don't know much about them or their relationship. I see on page 56 that the goddess Hera also plays a role. I know that gods and goddesses are a big part of Greek myths. I am glad to see an explanation of nymphs on the last page. I never really understood what they were.

Make Predictions/ Set Purpose

Students should use the information they gathered in previewing the selection to make predictions about what they will learn. If students have trouble generating a purpose for reading, suggest that they read to discover why the Greek youth Narcissus turned into a flower.

DIFFERENTIATED INSTRUCTION

Comprehension

INFERENTIAL THINKING

To help students make inferences from the text, follow these steps:

1. What does the text tell you about the topic? (Narcissus, who was stuck on himself, shunned others and was reduced to a flower.)
2. What do you already know about the topic? (I know that myths have an underlying message.)
3. Using your prior knowledge, along with information in the text, what new information can you infer that the author does not state directly? (Students may infer that one should not be haughty or snub admirers.)

Long, long ago there was a beautiful nymph named Echo who loved to frolic and play in the woods. Echo had one downfall: she talked too much. Whether she was arguing or chatting, she always had to have the last word.

Zeus, the father of the gods, liked to spend time with the nymphs in the woods, and this made his wife, Hera, very jealous.

Once when Hera was looking for Zeus, Echo hid him and lied to Hera about where he was. When Hera found out that Echo had lied to her, she seethed and boiled with anger and cursed Echo saying, "You shall not use that tongue that cheated me, except to repeat someone's last words. You shall have no power to speak first."

Unable to speak, Echo became very sad and hid alone in the forest. One day she saw a handsome young man named Narcissus running through the woods. Narcissus was known throughout his town for being both attractive and vain: he thought he was the greatest. He had rejected the maidens of the village many times, saying they were not beautiful enough to stand beside him.

When Echo laid eyes on Narcissus, she fell in love with him and followed him through the forest. Echo longed to speak to him but could not speak first because of the curse that Hera had put on her. So she waited and waited for Narcissus to speak.

One day, Narcissus shouted out into the woods, "Who is here?"

Echo answered, "Here!"

Narcissus waited, but no one came out of the woods. He called again, "Why do you reject me?"

"Reject me," Echo replied.

"No, let us join together," he cried.

Echo answered with all her heart, using his same words, "Join together!"

She ran to where Narcissus stood. But when she stood before him, he rejected her and ran back to the village. Saddened, Echo went to live in the deep woods and caves.

Narcissus became notorious, or known, throughout his village for his vanity. He shunned the lovely nymphs and maidens who fell in love with him. One day, a girl whom he rejected prayed to a goddess that Narcissus should feel what it is like to love someone and not be loved in return. The goddess granted her wish.

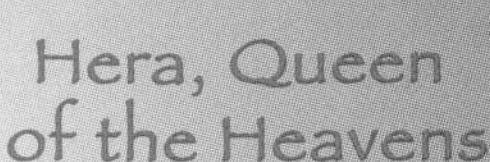

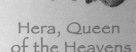

Hera, Queen of the Heavens

Hera was the queen of the heavens and the wife of Zeus. She was the goddess of marriage and of the sacred wedding vows between men and women. Hera was also a master of magic and could "will" anything to happen. Curses and hexes were her specialty, and she was cruel when she felt that she had to be.

56

During Reading

Comprehension

INFERENTIAL THINKING

Use these questions to model how to make inferences about the first three paragraphs of the myth. Have students make inferences about another section.

- What does the text tell me?
- What do I already know about myths?
- Using what I know, what ideas can I infer that are not stated directly?

(See Differentiated Instruction.)

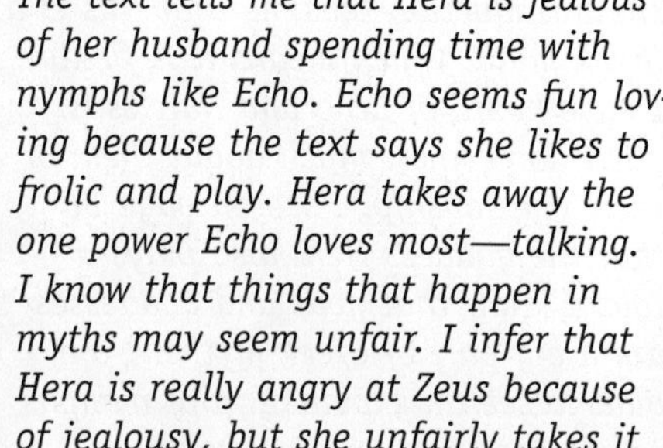

Teacher Think Aloud

The text tells me that Hera is jealous of her husband spending time with nymphs like Echo. Echo seems fun loving because the text says she likes to frolic and play. Hera takes away the one power Echo loves most—talking. I know that things that happen in myths may seem unfair. I infer that Hera is really angry at Zeus because of jealousy, but she unfairly takes it out on Echo.

Comprehension

MAKING CONNECTIONS

Use these questions to model how to make a connection with Echo and Narcissus. Then have students share a connection they make with those two characters or with Hera.

- Who do these characters remind me of?
- How are they similar to and different from the people I know?

Early that spring, Narcissus walked through the woods, and Echo watched him from high in a tree. He came to a clear pond and stopped for a drink. Leaning over the water, Narcissus saw his own reflection and thought his image was a beautiful water-spirit. He gazed at the blue eyes, the golden curls, the rosy cheeks, and the ivory skin. Narcissus fell in love with himself. He put his hand out to touch the lovely cheek, yet when he did, the water-spirit ran away. He tried again, yet each time he got too near, the image disappeared. Narcissus couldn't tear himself away from the beautiful reflection. He stayed beside the pond and didn't think of eating or sleeping. He became so despondent, so miserable, he began to talk to the image, saying, "Why do you run from me? All of the other nymphs loved me." Narcissus wept and his tears fell into the pond, making the image unclear. "Stay!" he cried. "If I cannot touch you, at least let me look at you."

"If I cannot touch you, at least let me look at you."

Day after day, Narcissus sat beside the pond. Soon he lost his color, his health, and his beauty. Echo watched over Narcissus until he died beside the pond. Echo mourned and cried for him, but when she went to gather his body for the funeral, it was gone. All that was left beside the pond was a small, white flower with an orange center that glowed like the sun. And to this day, that flower is called **Narcissus** and is one of the most delicate flowers of the spring.

Echo hid in a cave until her bones changed into the rocks and nothing was left of her except her voice. To this day she still answers people who call to her, and she always has the last word. ◆

57

Teacher Think Aloud

Echo reminds me of my friend who loves to talk. I can never get her off the phone. What she says is usually interesting, though. Unlike Echo, she doesn't argue a lot or feel that she has to have the last word. I know one or two people who remind me of Narcissus, too. They are also so fond of their looks that they seem to be in love with their reflections.

Fix-Up Strategies

Offer these strategies to help students read independently.

If you don't understand what you're reading:

- Reread the difficult section to look for clues to help you comprehend.
- Read ahead to find clues to help you comprehend.
- Retell, or say in your own words, what you've read.
- Visualize, or form mental pictures of, what you've read.

If you don't understand a word:

- Reread the sentence. Look for ideas and words that provide meaning clues.
- Find clues by reading a few sentences before and after the confusing word.
- Look for the base or root word and think about its meaning.
- Think about the topic or plot at this point to see if either offers meaning clues.

DIFFERENTIATED INSTRUCTION SMALL GROUP

Vocabulary Denotation and Connotation

To help students with the vocabulary activity, try these steps:

1. Write these words on the board: *snack, feast, banquet*. Tell students that the words all have the same simple definition, or denotation—"a meal."
2. Note that the words have different connotations, or associations. Have students decide which word is usually associated with each situation: a formal meal for a special occasion (*banquet*), a meal "on the run" while shopping (*snack*), a big meal with lots of good food. (*feast*)

Student Journal page 151

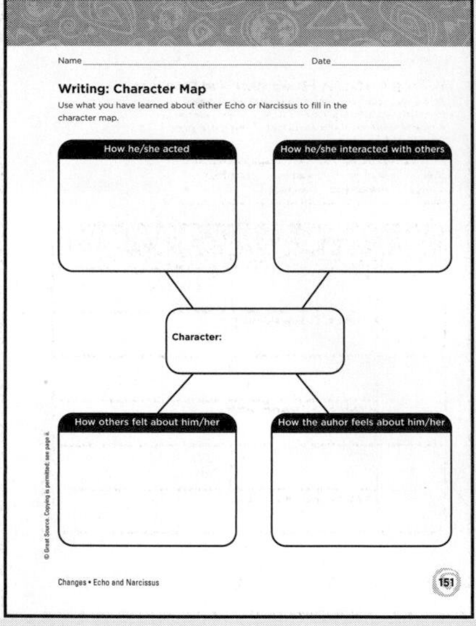
Name ______ Date ______

Writing: Character Map

Use what you have learned about either Echo or Narcissus to fill in the character map.

How he/she acted

How he/she interacted with others

Character:

How others felt about him/her

How the auhor feels about him/her

Changes • Echo and Narcissus

151

Nymphs

Nymphs were beautiful spirits of Greek mythology who were forever young. They were the spirits of natural things: mountains, rivers, trees, and meadows. The word *nymph* comes from a Greek word meaning "young woman," so nymphs are usually thought of as female.

Narcissus

The word *narcissist* comes from the myth of the vain youth, Narcissus. Today when you call a person a narcissist, you are saying that he or she is conceited, thinking only of him- or herself.

Echo

An echo is sound that is reflected back to you. The word *echo* comes from the Greek character Echo, who talked too much. Echo's punishment was to be doomed to only repeat someone else's words. She could no longer speak her own words.

Echo and Narcissus **by English artist John Waterhouse (1849–1917)**

58

After Reading

Use one or more activities.

Check Purpose

Have students decide if their purpose was met. Did they find out why the Greek youth Narcissus turned into a flower?

Discussion Questions

Continue the group discussion with the following questions.

1. Why did Narcissus reject the girls who fell in love with him? (Cause-Effect)
2. Who do you think was responsible for turning Narcissus into a flower? Explain. (Inferential Thinking)
3. Do you feel sympathy for Echo? For Narcissus? (Making Connections)

Revisit: Predictions Chart

Have students use context clues from the myth to complete the predictions chart on *Student Journal* page 150. How were the words actually used?

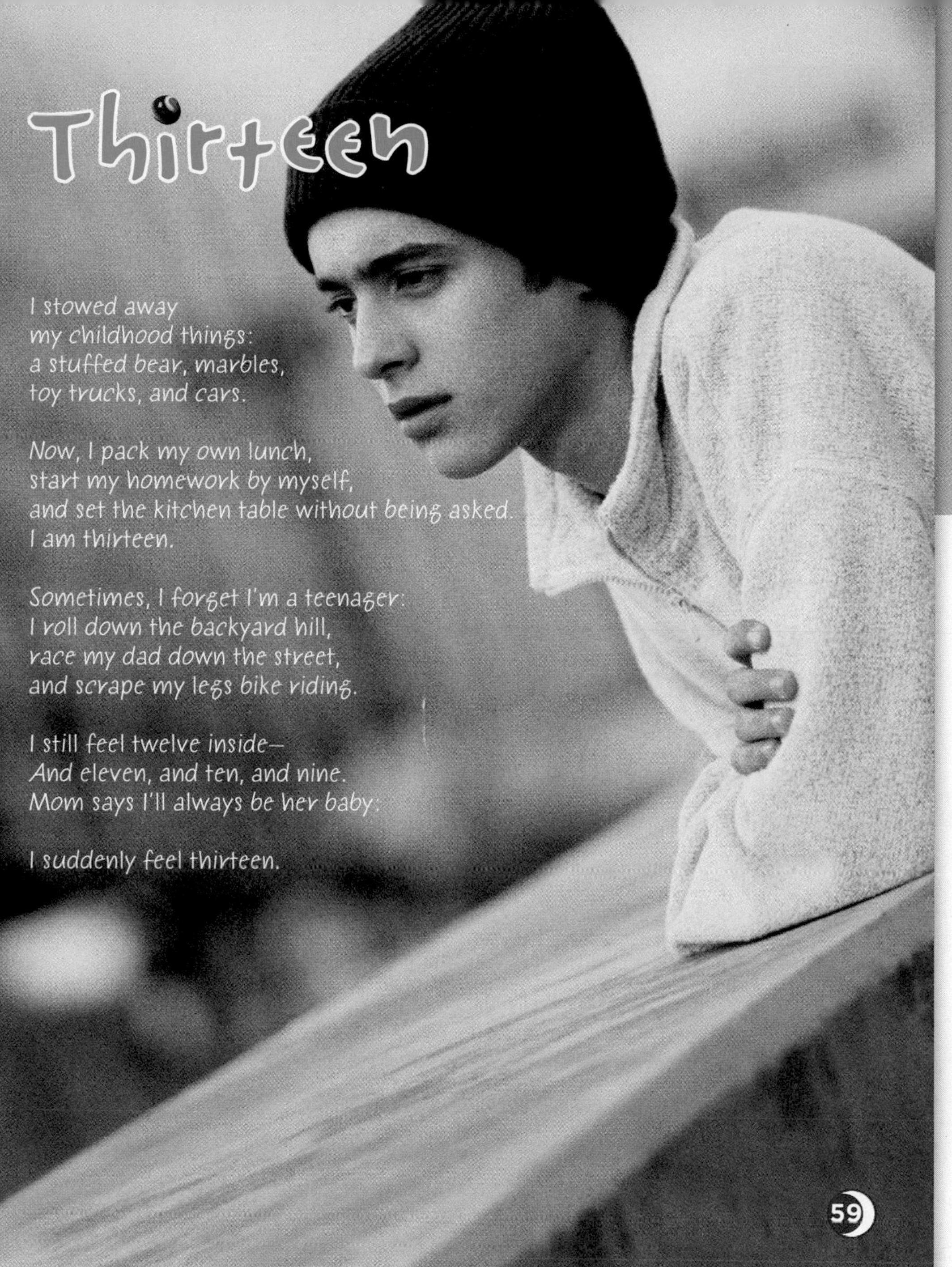

Thirteen

I stowed away
my childhood things:
a stuffed bear, marbles,
toy trucks, and cars.

Now, I pack my own lunch,
start my homework by myself,
and set the kitchen table without being asked.
I am thirteen.

Sometimes, I forget I'm a teenager:
I roll down the backyard hill,
race my dad down the street,
and scrape my legs bike riding.

I still feel twelve inside—
And eleven, and ten, and nine.
Mom says I'll always be her baby:

I suddenly feel thirteen.

59

Poems: Roots and Thirteen

Read the poems aloud as students follow along. Then discuss both poems.

- What main message do the two poems share?
- How does each poet express the idea that changes in life cause uncertainty?
- With which poem do you feel a more personal connection? Why?

Student Journal page 152

Name ______________________ Date __________

Building Vocabulary: Denotations and Connotations

Choose three vocabulary words. For each word, write a definition in the denotation box. Then, in the connotation box, write what personal associations you have with the word. Last, tell where you might see the word used.

frolic seethed vain notorious
shunned despondent mourned

Word	Denotation (general meaning)	Connotation (personal association)
	1.	
	Where might I see this word?	
	2.	
	Where might I see this word?	
	3.	
	Where might I see this word?	

152 Changes • Echo and Narcissus

Writing Character Map

Have students discuss what they know about Echo and Narcissus. Write ideas on the board or on a chart as they are expressed. Then have students use their discussion to help them complete the character map on *Student Journal* page 151 for one of the characters.

Vocabulary Denotation and Connotation

Words have denotations (general meanings) and connotations (personal associations). Explain that *vain* denotes "being exceptionally proud of oneself." Say: *Because he was so vain, the king believed he was the smartest person in the world. What does a vain person look like or act like?* These ideas are connotations of *vain*. Now have students complete *Student Journal* page 152. (See Differentiated Instruction.)

Phonics/Word Study

More Eponyms

Remind students that eponyms are words that come from people's names. Have students give clues for eponyms, such as *teddy bear*, *ritzy*, and *Gothic*, for others to guess the eponym and its source. As a warm-up, say: "a hot month of the year named after a famous Roman emperor" (*August*, Augustus Caesar). Now, work with students to complete the in-depth eponyms activity on TE page 356.

Phonics/Word Study

More Eponyms

Students can create a game using eponymous words.

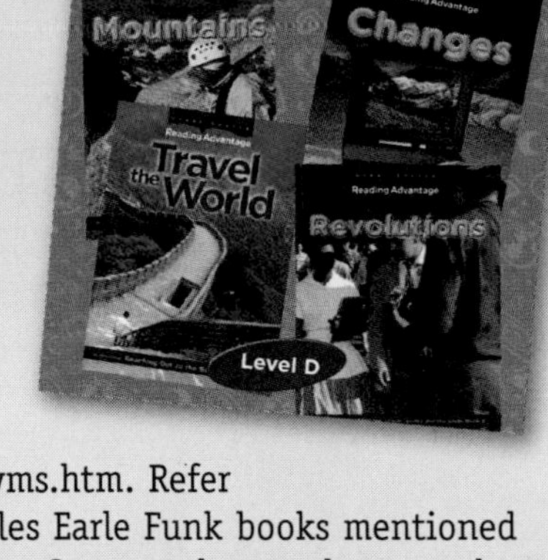

- Hand out the sheet with the list of eponymous words. (See *Word Study Manual* page 80.) Have students do research to add some new eponyms. An Internet source is http://users.tinyonline.co.uk/gswithenbank/eponyms.htm. Refer students to the Charles Earle Funk books mentioned in the previous lesson. Suggest that students work in small groups.
- Have each group choose an eponym and create a clue for it. Be sure there are no duplications among the groups. When all the clues have been compiled, collect them and create two decks. Have students form two teams. Give each team a deck of clues. Teams will alternate giving clues and making responses. A correct response must include the proper spelling of the eponymous word as well as the correct source of the word.

For more information on word sorts and spelling stages, see pages 5–31 in the *Word Study Manual.*

Focus on . . .

Use one or more activities in this section to focus on a particular area of need in your students.

Comprehension STRATEGY SUPPORT

To help those students who need more practice using the strategies covered in this lesson, work one-on-one or in small groups to apply the strategy prompts below. Apply the prompts to a *Reading Advantage* paperback, a classroom library book, or a new or familiar selection in the magazine. Always model your own thinking first.

Inferential Thinking

- What are the causes or effects of this event?
- What do I learn from the character or person's thoughts, words, or actions?
- What do I know (or infer) from the text that the author hasn't stated directly?
- What conclusions can I draw?

Making Connections

- What does this story (article, passage) remind me of?
- What do I already know about this topic?
- Where have I heard about this topic before?
- What do I have in common with the characters, people, or situations in the text?
- What other books, stories, articles, movies, or TV shows does this text make me think about?

Writing Double-entry Journal

Have students make double-entry journal notes about the poem "Thirteen." Display the headings for a double-entry journal chart. (See TE page 380 for a double-entry journal BLM.) Have students look back through the poem to find two or three quotations they think are important, or with which they had a personal connection, and write them in the first column of the chart. Then they should write their thoughts and feelings in the second column.

Quotations	My Thoughts and Feelings

To give students more practice in taking notes, see lessons in *Writing Advantage,* pages 170–181.

Fluency: Pacing

After students have read the poem "Thirteen" at least once, have them listen as you model how to read the poem at a smooth and even pace. Point out that reading too quickly or too slowly makes it difficult for listeners to understand the content. Then have partners take turns reading aloud to each other, following your model.

As you listen to students read, use these prompts to guide them.

- Notice how the line breaks and the punctuation in the poem help you read at an even pace. They signal where to pause slightly.
- Keep your eyes on the text as you read so you don't lose your place and either miss words or repeat them.
- Think about the message of the poem and its tone. Use your voice to create interest and hold attention.

When students read aloud, do they—

✓ demonstrate a smooth pace, not too fast or too slow?

✓ incorporate well-timed pauses between words and phrases?

✓ reflect an awareness and understanding of punctuation?

English Language Learners

To support students' comprehension of "Echo and Narcissus," guide students in making personal connections with the characters. Discuss what students know about each of the characters in "Echo and Narcissus." Have partners use the following questions as a guide as they make personal connections.

1. Which of the characters reminds me of myself?
2. Which of the characters is most different from me?

Independent Activity Options

While you work with individuals or small groups, others can work independently on one or more of the following options.

- Level D paperback books, see TE pages 367–372
- Level D *eZines*
- Repeat word sorts from this lesson
- *Student Journal* pages for this lesson
- *Writing Advantage* independent lessons

Assessment

Strategy Assessment

To help you and your students assess their use of comprehension strategies, ask the following questions. Students can complete a written response or provide verbal answers in a one-on-one reading conference.

1. **Inferential Thinking** Do you think the relationship between Echo and Narcissus would have been different if she could speak her love for him? (Answers will vary. Students should think about what they have learned and inferred about Echo and Narcissus. The logical answer is no. Echo would have talked too much, annoying Narcissus; Narcissus would have rejected her anyway for not being beautiful enough.)
2. **Making Connections** What connections did you make with the characters or events in this myth? (Answers will vary, but should show how students can relate to the text.)

For ongoing informal assessment, use the checklists on pages 61–64 of *Level D Assessment*.

Word Study Assessment

Use these steps to help you and your students assess their understanding of more eponyms.

1. On the board or on word cards, write the sources listed in the chart below.
2. Have students guess what eponym is derived from each source. They should be able to figure them out by logical thinking. For more sources and their eponyms, refer to the website http://users.tinyonline.co.uk/gswithenbank/eponyms.htm.

Source	Eponym
the naturalist R. J. Lechmere Guppy	guppy
Hygeia, the Greek goddess of health	hygiene
the Mexican state of Chihuahua	chihuahua dog
the town of Bologna, Italy	baloney
the naturalist Alexander Garden	gardenia
Moses Cleveland, American pioneer	Cleveland, Ohio

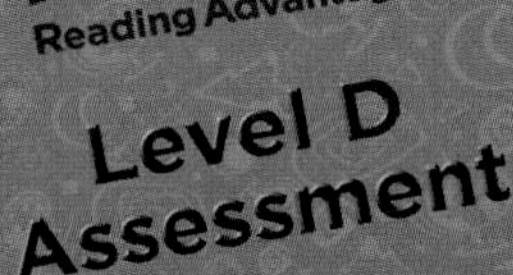

LESSON **46**

The Name Game *and* Watch Your Words!

Changes, pages 60–end

SUMMARY

These two **features** explore name changes and language changes.

COMPREHENSION STRATEGIES

Making Connections
Understanding Text Structure

WRITING

Journal

VOCABULARY

Multiple Meanings

PHONICS/WORD STUDY

Word Trees

Lesson Vocabulary

perceive	feminist
assume	abolitionist
majority	malodorous
retain	coincidentally

MATERIALS

Changes, pp. 60–end
Student Journal, pp. 153–156
Word Study Manual, p. 81
Writing Advantage, pp. 152–169

Before Reading

Use one or more activities.

Names Chart

List students' first names in a two-column chart with the labels *Names* and *Meanings Plus*. Go down the list of names, asking each student to tell what he or she knows about his or her name. (For additional information, many dictionaries have an appendix on biographical names.) Ask students to tell the meaning of the name, its origin, who named them, and what nicknames or family names they may have. Record the information.

Names	Meanings Plus
Margaret	pearl, Latin, Maggie
Dwight	fair, Germanic, D.W.

Vocabulary Preview

Review the vocabulary list. Write the words on the board and read them aloud to clarify pronunciations. Have students begin the knowledge rating chart on *Student Journal* page 153. They can complete the chart after reading. Model for students what you know about the word *malodorous*.

DIFFERENTIATED INSTRUCTION

SMALL GROUP

Preview the Selection

Help students get ready to read.

1. Have students look at each photograph in the article and identify each celebrity. List their names.
2. Ask: *Do you think the names on the list are the celebrities' birth names? Why? Why not?*
3. Have students talk about why they think these particular people changed their names. Ask students to suggest other celebrities they know about who have changed their names.
4. Point out that it is a relatively easy process for an adult to change a name. It takes a court order and costs $50–$100.

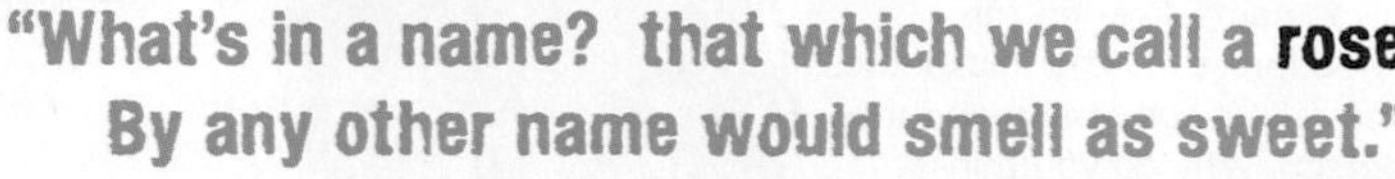

"What's in a name? that which we call a **rose**
By any other name would smell as sweet."

— Juliet, in William Shakespeare's *The Tragedy of Romeo and Juliet*

What do you like to be called? Do you have a nickname? Do your friends and family use different names for you? Often, the names we are given, or those we choose for ourselves, have special meaning for us. What if our names were changed? Would we feel any differently about ourselves? Would others perceive us differently?

Student Journal page 153

Name ______ Date ______

Building Vocabulary: Knowledge Rating Chart

Show your knowledge of each word by adding information to the other boxes in the row.

Word	Define or Use in a Sentence	Where Have I Seen or Heard It?	How Is it Used in the Selection?	Looks Like (Words or Sketch)
perceive				
assume				
majority				
coincidentally				
retain				
feminist				
abolitionist				
malodorous				

Changes • The Name Game: What's in a Name? 153

Preview the Selection

Have students look through the four pages of the main article, pages 60–63 in the magazine. Use these or similar prompts to prepare students for reading.

- What topic will you read about?
- What information do the section headings give you?
- What do you know by looking at the photographs?

(See Differentiated Instruction.)

Teacher Think Aloud

This article is all about names. I see some photographs of celebrities that I recognize in the title letters. That makes sense. It seems as though lots of celebrities have changed their names. The headings are kind of funny and don't really tell what each section is about, but the article seems very informative. I am sure it is nonfiction. I think people have strong feelings about names.

Make Predictions/ Set Purpose

Students should use the information they gathered in previewing the selection to make predictions about what they will learn. If students have trouble generating a purpose for reading, suggest that they read to find out why people change their birth names.

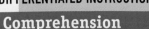

DIFFERENTIATED INSTRUCTION 

Comprehension

UNDERSTANDING TEXT STRUCTURE

Help students understand some of the different ways authors organize ideas in an informational article.

1. Write on the board the following ways of organizing nonfiction information: cause-effect, problem-solution, chronological order, description, question-answer, classification.
2. Ask students if they can describe any of the methods. Then define and discuss each one.

The Obscure and the Famous

There are many reasons people change their names. Sometimes when people immigrate, or come to live in the United States from a different country, they change their names. Their reasons may include wanting a name that's easier for others to pronounce. Some may want to assume, or adopt, a new name to reflect their fresh start in a new country.

Many celebrities change their names. They may feel their given names are too difficult to pronounce. This may have been in Demi Moore's mind when she changed her name from Demetria Guynes. If someone wants to become famous, he or she may want a name that sticks in people's minds. Perhaps that is why Caryn Johnson changed her name to Whoopi Goldberg or Gordon Sumner changed his to Sting.

Some people change their names to reflect their religious beliefs. When Cassius Clay adopted the Black Muslim religion in 1964, he became known as Muhammad Ali. He was the American heavyweight boxing champion in 1964, 1967, 1974, and 1978.

Many people like to be called by a nickname. Nicknames are usually shortened versions of a given name, like Ted for Theodore. But other nicknames can reflect something about a person. Why do you think Eldrick Woods prefers to be called "Tiger"? Or Earvin Johnson, "Magic"?

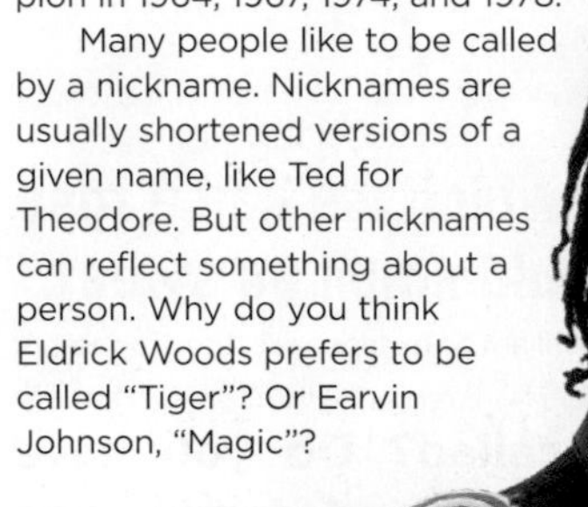

Caryn Johnson, a.k.a. Whoopi Goldberg

This Land Is Your Land

Many countries have come and gone throughout history, but some have merely changed their names. Sometimes when a country becomes independent from another's rule or has a change in government, its leaders decide on a new name. For example, in 1980, when the white-controlled government of the southern African country of Rhodesia handed over political power to the majority blacks, the new leaders renamed the country Zimbabwe.

Rhodesia had been named after a British financier named Cecil Rhodes. Zimbabwe means "house of stone" in the Shona language, spoken by the black African people who lived in and ruled the area beginning in about 1000.

Other countries that have changed names include Thailand (called Siam until 1939), Indonesia (known as the Dutch East Indies or the Netherlands Indies until 1945), and Burkina Faso (changed from Upper Volta in 1984).

Cities change their names, too. The city of St. Petersburg, Russia has had three names, one of them twice! The city was founded as St. Petersburg by Czar Peter the Great in 1703. One can easily see how it got its name. As Russia battled Germany in World War I, the city's name was changed to Petrograd ("Peter's City").

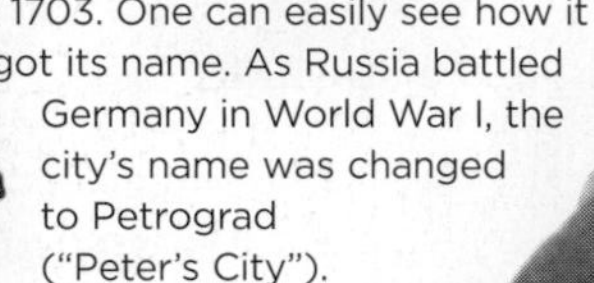

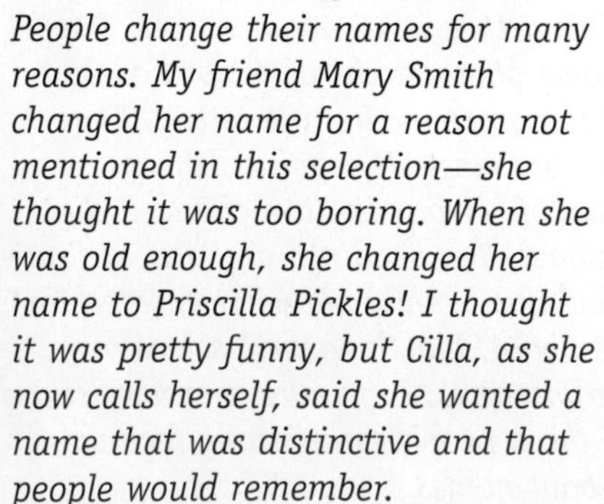

62

During Reading

Comprehension 

MAKING CONNECTIONS

Use these questions to model how to make connections with the section titled "The Obscure and the Famous," on page 62. Then have students make their own connections with the same section.

- What does this section remind me of?
- Was my experience the same as or different from those of people mentioned in the section?

Teacher Think Aloud

People change their names for many reasons. My friend Mary Smith changed her name for a reason not mentioned in this selection—she thought it was too boring. When she was old enough, she changed her name to Priscilla Pickles! I thought it was pretty funny, but Cilla, as she now calls herself, said she wanted a name that was distinctive and that people would remember.

Comprehension 

UNDERSTANDING TEXT STRUCTURE

Use these questions to model how to identify the classification text structure of the selection. Then have students identify the text structure of "Watch Your Words," beginning on page 64, and explain how they know.

- What is the structure of this text?
- What details support my thoughts about the text structure?

(See Differentiated Instruction.)

It was felt that the *-burg* in St. Petersburg sounded too German. The Soviet Communist Party took control of Russia in 1917, and in 1924 the city was renamed Leningrad, after the founder of the Soviet Communist Party, Vladimir Ilyich Lenin. With the decline of the influence of the Communist Party in Russia, the city went back to its original name of St. Petersburg in 1991.

To Change or Not to Change? That Is the Question.

There are situations in which *not* changing one's name makes a statement. It has been traditional in Western society for women to give up their "maiden" name and take their husband's last name when they marry. Today, more and more women are choosing to retain, or keep, their birth-family name. It all started with Lucy Stone, a nineteenth-century feminist and abolitionist. In 1855, Lucy Stone married Henry Blackwell, but she continued to use her maiden name, even refusing to open mail addressed to "Mrs. Henry Blackwell." Ever since then, women who keep their maiden names have been referred to as "Lucy Stoners."

A Rose Is a Rose Is a Rose, or Is It?

It seems that what we call ourselves—whether as individuals or whole countries—affects not only other people's ideas about us, but also the way we think and feel about ourselves. It may be true, as Juliet said: "That which we call a rose by any other name would smell as sweet." But if the rose were called "malodorous," would we even take the time to sniff? ◆

Coincidentally, Lenin changed his name. He was born Vladimir Ilyich Ulyanov on April 22, 1870, in Simbirsk, which is now called Ulyanovsk.

63

Teacher Think Aloud

The structure of this text isn't obvious at first because of the playful wording of the headings. But as I read, I realized that the information is organized by topic, or classification. That is, each section tells how one group changes names. "This Land Is Your Land" is about places changing names, whereas "To Change or Not to Change?" discusses married women keeping their "maiden" names.

Fix-Up Strategies

Offer these strategies to help students read independently.

If you don't understand what you're reading:

- Reread the difficult section to look for clues to help you comprehend.
- Read ahead to find clues to help you comprehend.
- Retell, or say in your own words, what you've read.
- Visualize, or form mental pictures of, what you've read.

If you don't understand a word:

- Reread the sentence. Look for ideas and words that provide meaning clues.
- Find clues by reading a few sentences before and after the confusing word.
- Look for the base or root word and think about its meaning.
- Think about the topic or plot at this point to see if either offers meaning clues.

Student Journal pages 154–155

Name ______________________ Date __________

Writing: Journal Notes

What's in your name? Answer the questions and make notes about how you feel about your name and what, if any other, name you might like to have. Then write a brief journal entry on the next page explaining your thoughts.

1. What does my name mean? ______________________

2. Have I ever wished I had a different name? Why or why not? ______________________

3. Whose names do I particularly like? Why? ______________________

4. If I could choose a new name, what would it be? Why ______________________

5. Do I know anyone who has ever changed their name? Why do I think they did it? ______________________

154 Changes • The Name Game: What's in a Name?

Possible answers to **Student Journal page 156** include: *ruler*—measuring device, king or queen; *box*—container, to fistfight; *sticks*—broken branches, pokes; *last*—at the end, to continue.

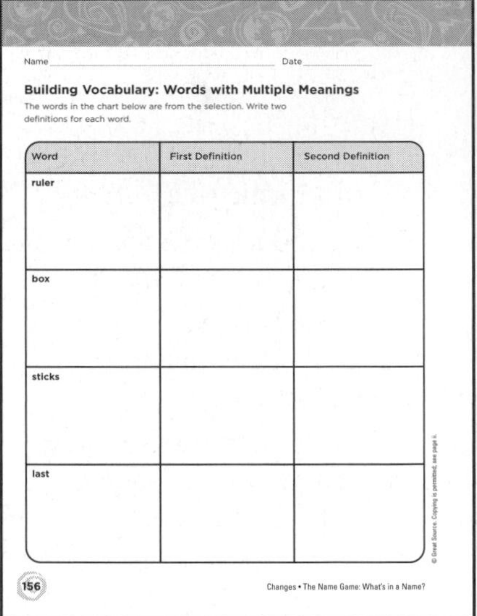

Name ______________________ Date __________

Building Vocabulary: Words with Multiple Meanings

The words in the chart below are from the selection. Write two definitions for each word.

Word	First Definition	Second Definition
ruler		
box		
sticks		
last		

156 Changes • The Name Game: What's in a Name?

CREDITS

Program Authors
Laura Robb
James F. Baumann
Carol J. Fuhler
Joan Kindig

Editorial Board
Avon Cowell
Craig Roney
Jo Worthy

Magazine Writers
Anina Robb
Cara Lieb

Design and Production
Preface, Inc.

Photography
Inside Front Cover, l © Bettmann/Corbis; c © AFP/Corbis; r © Matthew Mendelsohn/Corbis; tr © Ken Reid/Getty Images; tl © Fremont/Getty Images; p. 1l © D. Boone/Corbis; c © Cynthia Diane Pringle/Corbis; cr © Reuters NewMedia Inc./Corbis; tr © Corbis; tl © Larry Williams/Corbis; p. 2 © Bettmann/Corbis; p. 3t © Corbis; p. 3b © Bettmann/Corbis; p. 4 © Bettmann/Corbis; p. 5t © Michael S. Yamashita/Corbis; tr © Corbis; cl © Underwood & Underwood/Corbis; cr © Bettmann/Corbis; b © Bill Ross/Corbis; pp. 7, 8t © Charles O'Rear/Corbis; p. 8c, b © Corbis; p. 9 © Imagehunters/Corbis; p. 10b, pp. 10–11 bkgd © Corbis; p. 11c © Reuters NewMedia Inc./Corbis; p. 11b, p. 12 © AFP/Corbis; p. 11 bkgd © Photodisc; p. 13 © Annie Griffiths Belt/Corbis; p. 14t © Joseph Sohm; ChromoSohm Inc./Corbis; p. 14b © Corbis; pp. 14–15 bkgd © Bill Ross/Corbis; p. 16 © John Noble/Corbis; p. 21 © John Springer Collection/Corbis; p. 23 © Hulton Archive/Getty Images; pp. 24–25 © Bettmann/Corbis; p. 26 © Matthew Mendelsohn/Corbis; p. 27t © Hellestad Rune/Corbis SYGMA; c © Corbis; b © Neal Preston/Corbis; p. 28b © Kraft Brooks/Corbis SYGMA; bkgd © AP Photo; p. 35 © William Whitehurst/Corbis; pp. 36–37 bkgd © Steve Kaufman/Corbis; p. 38 © AP Photo/Ed Bailey; p. 39t © D. Boone/Corbis; c © Sandro Vannini/Corbis; b © Archivo Iconografico, S.A./Corbis; p. 42tl © Walter Hodge/Corbis; tc © Bettmann/Corbis; tr © Morton Beeb/Corbis; c © Setboun/Corbis; b © So Hing-Keung/Corbis; p. 43t © Bettmann/Corbis; b © Galen Rowell/Corbis; p. 44 © Cynthia Diane Pringle/Corbis; p. 45 © Photodisc; p. 46t © Kelly-Mooney Photography/Corbis; pp. 46–47 bkgd © Lester Lefkowitz/Corbis; p. 47 © J A Giordano/Corbis SABA; p. 48l, pp. 48–49 bkgd © W. Geiersperger/Corbis; p. 48r © Valerio De Berardinis/Corbis; p. 50 © Reuters NewMedia Inc./Corbis; p. 52t © Salvador Christina/Corbis SYGMA; pp. 52–53b © LWA-JDC/Corbis; p. 53cl © Corbis; c © Tom Stewart/Corbis; cr © Reuters NewMedia Inc./Corbis; p. 58t © Mimmo Jodice/Corbis; b © Walker Art Gallery, Liverpool, Merseyside, UK/Trustees of the National Museums & Galleries on Merseyside/Bridgeman Art Library; p. 59t © Corbis; bkgd © Gabriela Medina/SuperStock; p. 60l © Corbis; r © Mitchell Gerber/Corbis; p. 61l © Henry Diltz/Corbis; r © Bettmann/Corbis; p. 62 © Roger Ressmeyer/Corbis; p. 63 © Hulton-Deutsch Collection/Corbis; p. 64t © Tim Flach/Getty Images; b © Edward Holub/Corbis; p. 65tl, b © Georgina Bowater/Corbis; tr © Andrew McClosky/Time Life Pictures

Illustration
Inside Front Cover l, Jennifer Hewitson; r, Laura Huliska Beith; p. 1cr, Tim Zeltner; r, Rosanne Kaloustian; p. 6, Jennifer Hewitson; pp. 17–22, Laura Huliska Beith; pp. 29–34, Ann Boyajian; pp. 35–39, Brian White; 40-41, Gwen Connelly; pp. 46–49, Jim Paillot; p. 54, Tim Zeltner; pp. 55–57, Rosanne Kaloustian

Watch Your Words!

About 750,000 words make up the English language, but that number increases steadily. Why does a language change? A language changes because the people who speak it need to express new ideas.

How New Words Are Made

New words are made in many different ways. Following are types of new words in the English language.

Slang

Slang is language used by a group of people: young people, people in the theater, musicians, or politicians. Slang expressions are casual and are constantly being updated. Slang words used by teens in past decades, like groovy, swell, and neat-o, have been replaced by new slang words like cool, awesome, rad, phat, and bad.

bling-bling—expensive or showy clothing and jewelry or the wearing of them. This slang word is descriptive, expressing the sparkle of light reflecting off gold and gems. ▶

word—an affirmation like okay or yeah

Prefixes

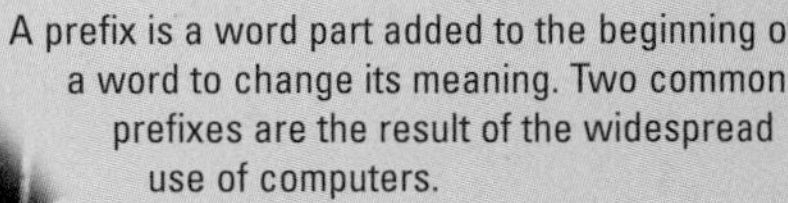

A prefix is a word part added to the beginning of a word to change its meaning. Two common prefixes are the result of the widespread use of computers.

cyber—relating to electronic or computer communications (cyberspace)

e-—relating to electronic communication (e-business, e-solutions, e-commerce)

◀ **cybercafe**— A cafe where the main attraction isn't coffee, but Internet access. Many people go to cybercafes with their laptops to work, hang out, surf the net, and drink coffee, making the Internet experience more social.

e-mail—mail sent from computer to computer across the Internet. E-mail is sent and received almost instantly, removing any lagtime. It makes the transfer of information almost immediate.

64

After Reading

WHOLE CLASS

Use one or more activities.

Check Purpose

Have students decide if their purpose was met. Did they find out why some people change their birth names?

Discussion Questions

Continue the group discussion with the following questions.

1. What are three possible reasons why a person may change his or her birth name? (Details)
2. What is unusual about Lenin's connection with city names? (Inferential Thinking)
3. Do you agree or disagree that a name affects how one is viewed by others? Why? (Making Connections)

Revisit: Knowledge Rating Chart

Have students return to the knowledge rating chart on *Student Journal* page 153. Encourage them to review their initial notes and make any adjustments as needed.

Compound Words

Compound words are the most common type of new word. They are formed when two existing words are combined to create a new meaning.

voice mail—a storage space of voice messages for a certain phone number. The messages are not only saved, they can also be rewound, played back, and deleted.

snail mail—the regular mail delivered by the post office. Compared to e-mail, letters travel at a snail's pace.

road rage—the anger people feel at being stuck in traffic. Road rage can sometimes become violent. People also refer to air rage, anger at waiting for or being stuck on an airplane; phone rage, fury over being put on hold or dealing with computerized menus; and store rage, irritation at having to wait in line for service. ▶

World Wide Web—the network of computers and servers that, like a filing cabinet, holds different documents and pages.

Words on Loan

A loan word is one that has been borrowed from another language and has made its way into everyday usage in English.

latte—an Italian word meaning hot, milky coffee. Today you can ask for a latte at almost any coffee shop, and everyone will understand what you are ordering. ▼

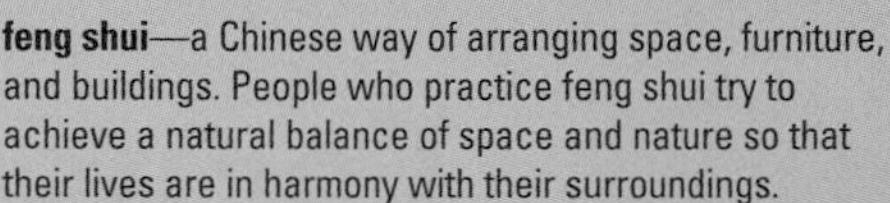

feng shui—a Chinese way of arranging space, furniture, and buildings. People who practice feng shui try to achieve a natural balance of space and nature so that their lives are in harmony with their surroundings.

oy vey—a Yiddish expression of weariness often expressed along with a sigh or a tinge of shock.

Portmanteau Words

Portmanteau words are similar to compound words. The difference is that sometimes only part of one or both original words is used in the new word.

infomercial—(information + commercial) An infomercial is an advertisement that provides information about a certain topic, product, or invention. It is usually much longer than thirty seconds. Often, infomercials blur the difference between commercials and news by using a talk-show or news-reporting format.

britpop—(British + pop music) popular music that comes from bands in England

New Meanings

Sometimes, new words can be made when people begin to expand the definition of words that already exist.

surf—Surfing used to refer only to riding the waves on a surfboard. Now, you can surf through the TV channels, as well as the Internet. ▶

vanilla—Because people think of vanilla as plain, vanilla also means computer software without any extra features.

Abbreviations

Abbreviations are shortened forms of words. Since e-mail messages are often short and quickly written, people have come up with many abbreviations to speed-up their writing. Here are a few handy ones that you might use in your future e-mails:

^5—high five

J4F—just for fun

ROTFL—rolling on the floor laughing

T+—think positive

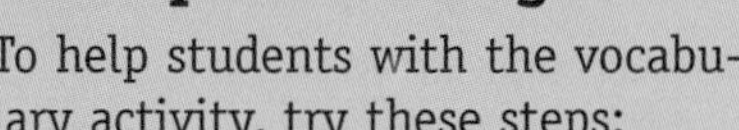

DIFFERENTIATED INSTRUCTION

Vocabulary

Multiple Meanings

To help students with the vocabulary activity, try these steps:

1. Write the following words in a vertical list (omitting the stars): *arm**, *trip**, *borrow*, *forget*, *table**.
2. Ask students to survey the list to find words that they think have more than one meaning. As words are identified, star them.
3. Discuss the multiple meanings of the starred words. Consult a dictionary if necessary.

Short Feature: Watch Your Words!

Read aloud the title of the article and the first two paragraphs. Then have students read the article silently. After students have read, have partners discuss the article. Follow up with these questions:

- What is the main idea or message of the article?
- Which words discussed in the article have you used? In what settings?
- Do you think every new word that comes into use should automatically be entered in dictionaries? Why? Why not?

Writing Journal

Ask students to think about what it might be like to have a new name. Write notes on the board as students discuss positive and negative aspects. Students should use the group discussion and their personal thoughts to write planning notes on *Student Journal* page 154. Then have them do *Student Journal* page 155. If students think that they already have the ideal name, they can write to explain why on the journal page.

Vocabulary Multiple Meanings

Display *assume*. Have students find the word on page 62. Ask a volunteer to read aloud the sentence in which *assume* appears. Ask: *What does* assume *mean as it is used in the text?* (to adopt) Ask students if they know any other meaning for *assume*. (to think you know something) Have pairs of students complete *Student Journal* page 156. (See Differentiated Instruction.)

Phonics/Word Study

Word Trees

Explain that a word tree is a good way of looking at all the forms of a word, at all the ways a root is used, or at all the words that are formed from certain prefixes. Display *re-*. Have students come up with words that have the prefix *re-*. Then have them define the words and say what they have in common. Now, work with students to complete the in-depth word trees activity on TE page 364.

Phonics/Word Study

Word Trees

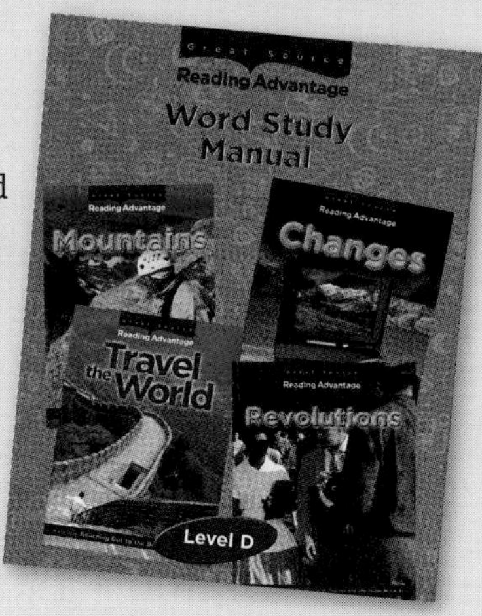

In doing this activity, students become more aware of how words are connected by spelling and meaning. A word tree BLM can be found in the *Word Study Manual* on page 81.

- Hand out copies of the BLM that show at the bottom a tree with a prefix, a root, or a base word that you have selected. You may prefer to have students self-select the word or word part. Have students create a word tree by adding words related to the designated one. Students can work independently, in pairs, or in small groups.
- Have students share their responses. They can make a transparency of their tree, duplicate it on a copier, or draw it on the board. As they present, students should be able to define the words and identify what all the words have in common.

For more information on word sorts and spelling stages, see pages 5–31 in the *Word Study Manual.*

Focus on . . .

Use one or more activities in this section to focus on a particular area of need in your students.

Comprehension STRATEGY SUPPORT

To help those students who need more practice using the strategies covered in this lesson, work one-on-one or in small groups to apply the strategy prompts below. Apply the prompts to a *Reading Advantage* paperback, a classroom library book, or a new or familiar selection in the magazine. Always model your own thinking first.

Making Connections

- What does this story (article, passage) remind me of?
- What do I already know about this topic?
- Where have I heard about this topic before?
- What do I have in common with the characters, people, or situations in the text?
- What other books, stories, articles, movies, or TV shows does this text make me think about?

Understanding Text Structure

- What kind of text is this? (book, story, article, guidebook, play, manual)
- How does the author organize the text? (cause-effect, problem-solution, chronological order, description, question-answer, comparison-contrast)
- What details support my thoughts about the text structure?
- What is the cause (effect, problem, solution, order, question, answer)?
- If fiction, who are the characters? What is the setting, plot, conflict, and resolution?

Writing Opinion Paragraph

Have students discuss the question: *Should people be allowed to change their birth names? Why? Why not?* As students respond, write their ideas on the board. Then have students use their discussion and the notes on the board to write a paragraph expressing their personal opinions.

To give students more practice in writing persuasive essays, see lessons in *Writing Advantage,* pages 152–169.

Fluency: Punctuation

After reading the article at least once, have students listen as you read the section with the heading "A Rose Is a Rose Is a Rose, or Is It?" to model reading smoothly and at an even pace, while using the punctuation as a guide for pausing. Then have partners take turns reading self-selected sections of the article, paying attention to the punctuation and injecting appropriate pauses.

As they read, guide students with the following prompts.

- Notice the punctuation. It will help guide your reading.
- Pause slightly at a comma, and a little longer at a period.
- Let your voice rise slightly as you come to the end of a question.

When students read aloud, do they—

- ✓ demonstrate appropriate meaning and usage of punctuation marks?
- ✓ incorporate appropriate timing, stress, and intonation?
- ✓ exhibit well-timed pauses between words and phrases?

English Language Learners

To support students as they learn about cause and effect, guide students in an extension of the understanding text structure activity on TE page 360. First, have students reread pages 62–63. Then, have partners respond to the following questions relating to cause and effect:

1. What are some reasons why a person might or might not change his or her name?
2. How might people be treated differently after they have changed their name?

Independent Activity Options

While you work with individuals or small groups, others can work independently on one or more of the following options.

- Level D paperback books, see TE pages 367–372
- Level D *eZines*
- Repeat word sorts from this lesson
- *Student Journal* pages for this lesson
- *Writing Advantage* independent lessons

Assessment

Strategy Assessment

To help you and your students assess their use of comprehension strategies, ask the following questions. Students can complete a written response or provide verbal answers in a one-on-one reading conference.

1. **Making Connections** What connections did you make to the information in this article? (Answers will vary. Students may mention that they get the names of countries confused with earlier names; that they would like to change their own names; that a woman should or should not hyphenate her name with her husband's name; and so on.)
2. **Understanding Text Structure** Did the text structure of the article make it easy and enjoyable to read, or not? Explain. (Answers will vary. In their responses, students should give examples from the text.)

See *Level D Assessment* page 50 for formal assessment to go with *Changes*.

Word Study Assessment

Use these steps to help you and your students assess their understanding of word trees.

1. Have student pairs self-select a word or word part to use for a word tree. Make sure they use a word or word part that differs from the one they used in the earlier activity.
2. Students can draw a tree of their own, or you can make more copies of the word tree BLM for them to use.
3. When partners complete the trees, have them share their work with the class. One partner can explain the relationship between the words, while the other defines each word.

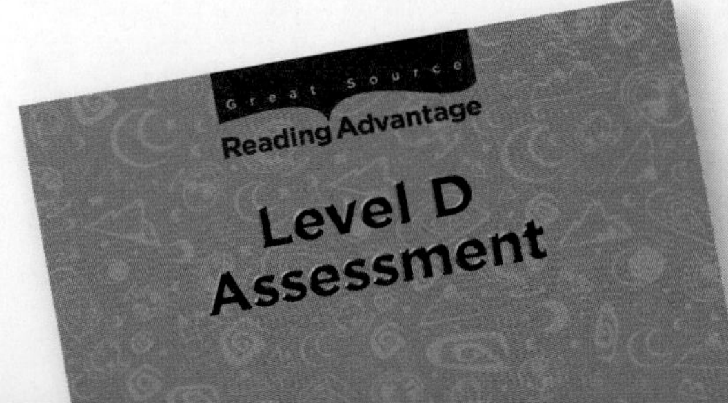

Great Source Reading Advantage
Appendix

Lessons for READING ADVANTAGE Paperbacks

The purpose of the paperbacks is to encourage independent reading. Minimal guidance is offered here and is optional. Additional sets of books can be ordered from Great Source.

Graphic Organizers (Blackline Masters)

Make photocopies or transparencies of the graphic organizers to use in your classroom instruction.

Going to Extremes

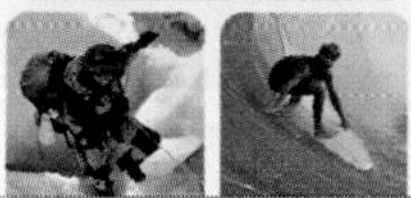

Synopsis In the world of sports, "extreme" athletes live on the edge of danger and keep inventing new sports, new tricks, and new ways of taking "old" sports, such as mountain-climbing, surfing, skiing, snowboarding, and roller-skating to new levels. *Going to Extremes* takes a look at cutting-edge sports, such as freestyle skiing, motorbike jumping, and air surfing, and examines the strengths and abilities stars in these sports need to have. The book examines how some of the most popular X sports came to be, the growing interest in X sports competitions, and why athletes around the world are becoming more and more interested in pushing their limits. 32 pages, *Lexile measure 780L*

Strategy Monitor Understanding (visualize)

Procedure Have students use three self-stick notes or fold a sheet of paper in thirds to provide places for them to respond to their reading.

- If students use self-stick notes, ask them to write their name, date, and book title on each of the self-stick notes. Tell students to place one self-stick note at the end of the first chapter, one halfway through the book (after Chapter 4), and a third at the end of the next-to-last chapter (Chapter 6).
- If students use a sheet of paper, have them write their name, date, and book title at the top of the paper. Students can then put the following headings on each third of the paper: After Chapter 1, After Chapter 4, After Chapter 6.
- For this strategy, ask students to draw a picture at each stopping point based on a description of a particular sport that interests them during their reading. Or students might choose to list some words and phrases from the book that help them to see, hear, and feel the excitement of an extreme sport or competition. After students have read the book, encourage them to share and compare their pictures or word descriptions.

Activity (Optional) Invite students to prepare a book talk to interest others in reading the book. Encourage students to highlight particular sections of the book they think would grab the attention of classmates.

Christopher Reeve: A Real-Life Superhero

Synopsis Christopher Reeve became famous for playing Superman in the 1978 movie of the same name. As Superman, he played a character with a double life, being both Clark Kent, the city newspaper reporter, as well as Superman, Man of Steel. Then, after a horse-jumping accident, Christopher Reeve became a hero in real life. This biography tells of his early years and reveals the double life he lived until his death in 2004. At home, he was a man paralyzed from the neck down who struggled every day to train his body to work again. In public, he was a leader in the heroic fight to help people with disabilities. *32 pages, Lexile measure 690L*

Strategy Making Connections

Procedure Have students use three self-stick notes or fold a sheet of paper in thirds to provide places for them to respond to their reading.

- If students use self-stick notes, ask them to write their name, date, and book title on each of the self-stick notes. Tell students to place one self-stick note at the end of the first chapter, one halfway through the book (after Chapter 3), and a third at the end of the next-to-last chapter (Chapter 4).
- If students use a sheet of paper, have them write their name, date, and book title at the top of the paper. Students can then put the following headings on each third of the paper: After Chapter 1, After Chapter 3, After Chapter 4.
- For this strategy, ask students to make notes at each stopping point to connect the information they are learning about Christopher Reeve with interests and experiences in their own lives. After students have read the book, encourage them to share their thoughts with classmates.

Activity (Optional) Invite students to write a book review that would interest others in reading this biography.

Whoppers!

Synopsis Eighth graders Rosa, Yolanda, and Darryl attend a weekend camp to build teamwork and cooperation skills. After a day of outdoor activities, they listen to a "whopper" of a tale and are inspired to create their own. Rosa writes about a colorful dragon that guards a museum in which paintings come to life and two knights joust for the hand of a princess. Yolanda dreams up a tale of an alien who takes a boy on a rocket ship trip into space, and Darryl writes about a robot that falls in love with a store mannequin. Their stories earn the kids recognition and lead to life-long friendships. Twenty years later, it appears that their adult lives have been shaped by their eighth-grade experience—or is that a "whopper" of an ending? *32 pages, Lexile measure 590L*

Strategy Making Connections

Procedure Have students use three self-stick notes or fold a sheet of paper in thirds to provide places for them to respond to their reading.

- If students use self-stick notes, ask them to write their name, date, and book title on each of the self-stick notes. Under this information, students should write the heading Predict. After leaving some space under Predict, students should write the heading Support. Tell students to place one self-stick note at the end of the first chapter, one halfway through the book (after Chapter 3), and a third at the end of the next-to-last chapter (Chapter 5).
- If students use a sheet of paper, have them write their name, date, and book title at the top of the paper. Students can then put the following headings on each third of the paper: After Chapter 1, After Chapter 3, After Chapter 5. Under each of these headings, students should write the heading Predict, leave some space, and then write the heading Support.
- For this strategy, students write a prediction at each stopping point. They also write the information (the support) that led them to make this prediction. The second and third predictions may or may not be a confirmation or an adjustment of the first one. When students finish the book, they can reread and discuss their predictions to review their thinking.

Activity (Optional) Invite students to make a portrait, collage, or other visual representation of a scene from one of the tales presented in the book.

Trapped!

Synopsis Seven incredible true stories of survival and rescue against all odds are presented in this book. These spellbinding accounts demonstrate daring and courage on the part of both victims and rescuers. The stories are as varied as the victims' traps, which include the landing gear of an airplane, a sinking car, and a flooded coal mine. Readers will be awed by the survival of a sailor trapped inside a whale, a teenager trapped in a factory fire with all exits locked, and the survival of and heroic rescues made by a New York City policewoman at the World Trade Center on September 11, 2001. *48 pages, Lexile measure 600L*

Strategy Monitor Understanding (visualize)

Procedure Have students use three self-stick notes or fold a sheet of paper in thirds to provide places for them to respond to their reading.

- If students use self-stick notes, ask them to write their name, date, and book title on each of the self-stick notes. Tell students to place one self-stick note at the end of the first chapter, one halfway through the book (after Chapter 3), and a third at the end of the next-to-last chapter (Chapter 6).
- If students use a sheet of paper, have them write their name, date, and book title at the top of the paper. Students can then put the following headings on each third of the paper: After Chapter 1, After Chapter 3, After Chapter 6.
- For this strategy, ask students to draw a picture at each stopping point based on a description of a setting or situation that "grabbed" them during their reading. Or students might choose to list some words and phrases from the book that help them to see, hear, and feel something being described in the book. After students have read the book, encourage them to share and compare their pictures or word descriptions.

Activity (Optional) Invite students to give a book talk that would convince other students to read this book.

A Guide to Mythical Creatures

Synopsis Along with myths, ancient peoples of the world created legends and stories of weird creatures such as dragons, goblins, and gnomes. Today's fantasies, such as the Harry Potter books and Tolkien's *The Lord of the Rings* series, draw on some of these ancient creatures as well as create their own. *A Guide to Mythical Creatures* is a compendium of fantastical creatures from long ago right up to the present, arranged in alphabetical order and guaranteed to inform and intrigue readers. *32 pages, Lexile measure 810L*

Strategy Making Connections

Procedure Have students use three self-stick notes or fold a sheet of paper in thirds to provide places for them to respond to their reading.

- If students use self-stick notes, ask them to write their name, date, and book title on each of the self-stick notes. Tell students to place one self-stick note at the end of page 9, one halfway through the book (after page 16), and a third self-stick note toward the end of the book (after page 26).
- If students use a sheet of paper, have them write their name, date, and book title at the top of the paper. Students can then put the following headings on each third of the paper: After Page 12, After Page 16, After Page 26.
- For this strategy, ask students to make notes at each stopping point to connect the information they are learning about with creatures they have met as a result of their own reading or TV/movie-viewing experiences. After students have read the book, encourage them to share what they know and have learned with classmates.

Activity (Optional) Invite students to prepare a poster, radio, or TV advertisement to generate interest in this book. Encourage students to capture interest and attention by describing some of the creatures introduced in the book.

Prisoner of War

Synopsis *Prisoner of War* is the true story of Harley Ross, who enlisted in the army during World War II to be a flying bomber and who became a prisoner of war after being shot down over enemy territory. The introduction serves to build background knowledge about World War II and to explain that Ross's experiences were related to his granddaughter (the author) in 1996 on the fiftieth anniversary of the Normandy Invasion. *48 pages, Lexile measure 740L*

Strategy Monitor Understanding

Procedure Have students use three self-stick notes or fold a sheet of paper in thirds to provide places for them to respond to their reading. (For the Question Strategy, students should have some extra self-stick notes. See the notations below for that strategy.)

- If students use self-stick notes, ask them to write their name, date, and book title on each of the self-stick notes. Tell students to place one self-stick note at the end of the first chapter, one halfway through the book (after Chapter 4), and a third at the end of the next-to-last chapter (Chapter 8).
- If students use a sheet of paper, have them write their name, date, and book title at the top of the paper. Students can then put the following headings on each third of the paper: After Chapter 1, After Chapter 4, After Chapter 8.
- At the first stopping point, ask students to write two or three questions about what they have read so far. If, in reading on, students discover answers to these questions, they can place extra self-stick notes on appropriate pages and jot down the answers. Have students repeat this process at the next two stopping points. For questions that the book doesn't answer, suggest to students that they do research to find the answers. Students might locate answers in books or on the Internet and discuss them with classmates.

Activity (Optional) Invite students to choose a scene from the book and write a script suitable for a TV or movie version of Harley Ross's war experience.

Major Disasters in U.S. History

Synopsis This book presents the stories behind some of the most memorable catastrophes of all time, including both natural disasters as well as those caused largely by human error. Events described are arranged in chronological order. The book includes the famous Chicago fire of 1871, the plague of locusts that descended on the Great Plains in the summer of 1874, New York's blizzard of 1888, the demise of the *Hindenburg* (biggest flying machine ever built) in 1937, the eruption of Mount Saint Helens in 1980, and 1989's furious Hurricane Hugo. *48 pages, Lexile measure 800L*

Strategy Monitor Understanding

Procedure Have students use three self-stick notes or fold a sheet of paper in thirds to provide places for them to respond to their reading. (For the Question Strategy, students should have some extra self-stick notes. See the notations below for that strategy.)

- If students use self-stick notes, ask them to write their name, date, and book title on each of the self-stick notes. Tell students to place one self-stick note at the end of the first chapter, one halfway through the book (after Chapter 3), and a third at the end of the next-to-last chapter (Chapter 5).
- If students use a sheet of paper, have them write their name, date, and book title at the top of the paper. Students can then put the following headings on each third of the paper: After Chapter 1, After Chapter 3, After Chapter 5.
- At the first stopping point, ask students to write two or three questions about what they have read so far. If, in reading on, students discover answers to these questions, they can place extra self-stick notes on appropriate pages and jot down the answers. Have students repeat this process at the next two stopping points. For questions that the book doesn't answer, suggest to students that they do research to find the answers. Students might locate answers in books or on the Internet and discuss them with classmates.

Activity (Optional) Invite students to choose a scene from the book and write a TV or movie script for an action-packed thriller.

Mummies

Synopsis The word *mummy* summons up a vision of a body tightly wrapped in cloth. However, the book *Mummies* reveals that not all mummies are alike. What they have in common is that they are not skeletons, but rather corpses with skin intact. The book features mummies from around the world, preserved in environments as varied as peat bogs, ice, and desert sand. What these places have in common is that they provide environments in which bacteria and fungi do not grow. *64 pages, Lexile measure 770L*

Strategy Monitor Understanding (visualize)

Procedure Have students use three self-stick notes or fold a sheet of paper in thirds to provide places for them to respond to their reading.

- If students use self-stick notes, ask them to write their name, date, and book title on each of the self-stick notes. Tell students to place one self-stick note at the end of the first chapter, one halfway through the book (after Chapter 3), and a third at the end of the next-to-last chapter (Chapter 6).
- If students use a sheet of paper, have them write their name, date, and book title at the top of the paper. Students can then put the following headings on each third of the paper: After Chapter 1, After Chapter 3, After Chapter 6.
- For this strategy, ask students to draw a picture at each stopping point based on a description of the places where mummies have been found. Or students might choose to list some words and phrases from the book that help them to see and understand what the people were like before they died. After students have read the book, encourage them to share and compare their pictures or word descriptions.

Activity (Optional) Invite students to prepare an advertisement (poster, radio, or TV) for the book.

Traces of a Crime: The Art and Science of Solving Crimes

Synopsis *Traces of a Crime: The Art and Science of Solving Crimes* offers an in-depth look at forensics—the science of solving a crime. The book presents actual criminal cases and describes the techniques that investigators use in gathering evidence and solving the crimes. These techniques include the latest advances in fingerprinting; bug, body, and bone trace evidence; DNA testing; and computer technology. Readers who follow TV shows such as *CSI: Crime Scene Investigation, CSI: Miami, Bones, and Law and Order* will especially be drawn to this book. *64 pages, Lexile measure 790L*

Strategy Monitor Understanding

Procedure Have students use three self-stick notes or fold a sheet of paper in thirds to provide places for them to respond to their reading. (For the Question Strategy, students should have some extra self-stick notes. See the notations below for that strategy.)

- If students use self-stick notes, ask them to write their name, date, and book title on each of the self-stick notes. Tell students to place one self-stick note at the end of the first chapter, one halfway through the book (after Chapter 4), and a third at the end of the next-to-last chapter (Chapter 6).
- If students use a sheet of paper, have them write their name, date, and book title at the top of the paper. Students can then put the following headings on each third of the paper: After Chapter 1, After Chapter 4, After Chapter 6.
- For this strategy, at the first stopping point, ask students to write two or three questions about what they have read so far. If, in reading on, students discover answers to these questions, they can place extra self-stick notes on appropriate pages and jot down the answers. Have students repeat this process at the next two stopping points. For questions that the book doesn't answer, suggest to students that they do research to find the answers. Students might locate answers in books or on the Internet and discuss them with classmates.

Activity (Optional) Invite students to give a book talk designed to interest others in reading the book. You might suggest that students relate recent events in the news or programs on TV that relate to the topic.

Baseball 101

Synopsis *Baseball 101* is a fun, all-inclusive primer to understanding the game of baseball and its history as well as improving one's playing skills. Fittingly, chapters are called "lessons" to support the game's basic strategies: pitching; hitting; getting on base; and catching and throwing. Lessons also provide interesting facts and anecdotes about the game's best and otherwise notable players from the United States and around the world. *64 pages, Lexile measure 790L*

Strategy Making Connections

Procedure Have students use three self-stick notes or fold a sheet of paper in thirds to provide places for them to respond to their reading.

- If students use self-stick notes, ask them to write their name, date, and book title on each of the self-stick notes. Tell students to place one self-stick note at the end of the first chapter, one halfway through the book (after Lesson 3), and a third at the end of the next-to-last chapter (Lesson 5).
- If students use a sheet of paper, have them write their name, date, and book title at the top of the paper. Students can then put the following headings on each third of the paper: After Lesson 1, After Lesson 3, After Lesson 5.
- For this strategy, ask students to make notes at each stopping point to connect the information they are learning about baseball with baseball facts and experiences from their own lives. After students have read the book, encourage them to share their thoughts with classmates.

Activity (Optional) Invite students to write a book review that is suitable for the sports section of a school or local newspaper.

The Boston Massacre Mystery

Synopsis As historical fiction, *The Boston Massacre Mystery* retells the events that led to and resulted from "The Boston Massacre" of March 5, 1770. This is the event in which five colonists were shot and killed in the street by British soldiers sent to the colonies to "maintain order." In truth, no one was ever able to determine what actually transpired on that fateful evening. But John Adams, a patriot lawyer and cousin to Sam Adams, a leader of the Sons of Liberty, defended the nine British soldiers. John Adams believed that everyone, even the hated Redcoats, is entitled to a fair trial. Within this true account is woven a compelling mystery: Who is behind the threats John Adams receives for taking the case? Although the fictional narrator Simon "Big Dog" Doggett first suspects Sam Adams and Paul Revere, Doggett later proves someone else is responsible. The issue of who is a real traitor at the time (a "Tory"—a British loyalist—or an American patriot) is central to the plot. *96 pages, Lexile measure 630L*

Strategy Making Connections

Procedure Have students use three self-stick notes or fold a sheet of paper in thirds to provide places for them to respond to their reading.

- If students use self-stick notes, ask them to write their name, date, and book title on each of the self-stick notes. Under this information, students should write the heading Predict. After leaving some space under Predict, students should write the heading Support. Tell students to place one self-stick note at the end of the first chapter, one halfway through the book (after Chapter 6), and a third at the end of the next-to-last chapter (Chapter 10).
- If students use a sheet of paper, have them write their name, date, and book title at the top of the paper. Students can then put the following headings on each third of the paper: After Chapter 1, After Chapter 6, After Chapter 10. Under each of these headings, students should write the heading Predict, leave some space, and then write the heading Support.
- For this strategy, students write a prediction at eachstopping point. They also write the information (the support) that led them to make this prediction. The second and third predictions may or may not be a confirmation or adjustment of the first one. When students finish the book, they can reread and discuss their predictions to review their thinking.

Activity (Optional) Invite students to make a portrait, collage, or other visual representation of either a character or a scene from the book.

Mystery at Canyon River Creek

Synopsis Jared, a seventh grader from Philadelphia, visits relatives in New Mexico and discovers a totally different way of life on his cousins Luke and Courtney's sheep ranch. In wanting to adapt, Jared tries to ride a horse, which proceeds to run wild and eventually dumps him against the stable wall. Part of the wall collapses, and much to Jared and his cousins' surprise, they discover an old map hidden within. Markings on the map turn out to be *petroglyphs* (symbols that ancestral Pueblo made on rocks and cliffs). The kids decipher the map and disarm a greedy ranch hand who wanted to locate the treasure, too. The kids find a true treasure—a cave of rare gems and rock formations that had been guarded and protected by the ancient Pueblo. Jared returns to Philadelphia with an appreciation of the southwest and its history as well as a newfound sense of confidence. *96 pages, Lexile measure 650L*

Strategy Making Connections

Procedure Have students use three self-stick notes or fold a sheet of paper in thirds to provide places for them to respond to their reading.

- If students use self-stick notes, ask them to write their name, date, and book title on each of the self-stick notes. Tell students to place one self-stick note at the end of the first chapter, one halfway through the book (after Chapter 4), and a third at the end of the next-to-last chapter (Chapter 6).
- If students use a sheet of paper, have them write their name, date, and book title at the top of the paper. Students can then put the following headings on each third of the paper: After Chapter 1, After Chapter 4, After Chapter 6.
- For this strategy, ask students to make notes at each stopping point to connect the information they are learning about the characters or setting with feelings or experiences in their own life. After students have read the book, encourage them to share their thoughts with classmates.

Activity (Optional) Create a storyboard of the book, highlighting its main events, for a movie version of the book. Suggest that students include ideas about how and where they would shoot the movie. Students might find the Story String graphic organizer useful in planning out their ideas. (See page 386.)

Knowledge Rating Chart

Show your knowledge of each word by adding information to the boxes.

Word	Define or Use in a Sentence	Where Have I Seen or Heard It?	How Is It Used in the Selection?	Looks Like (Words or Sketch)

Predictions

How do you predict these words will be used in the selection? Write your answers in the second column. Next, read the selection. Then, clarify your answers in the third column.

Word	My prediction for how the word will be used	How the word was actually used

Making Associations

Answer the questions for each word you write.

Word ______________________

What do you think about when you read this word? ______________________

____

Who might use this word? ______________________

____

What do you already know about this word? ______________________

____

____

Word ______________________

What do you think about when you read this word? ______________________

____

Who might use this word? ______________________

____

What do you already know about this word? ______________________

____

____

Word ______________________

What do you think about when you read this word? ______________________

____

Who might use this word? ______________________

____

What do you already know about this word? ______________________

____

____

Word Map

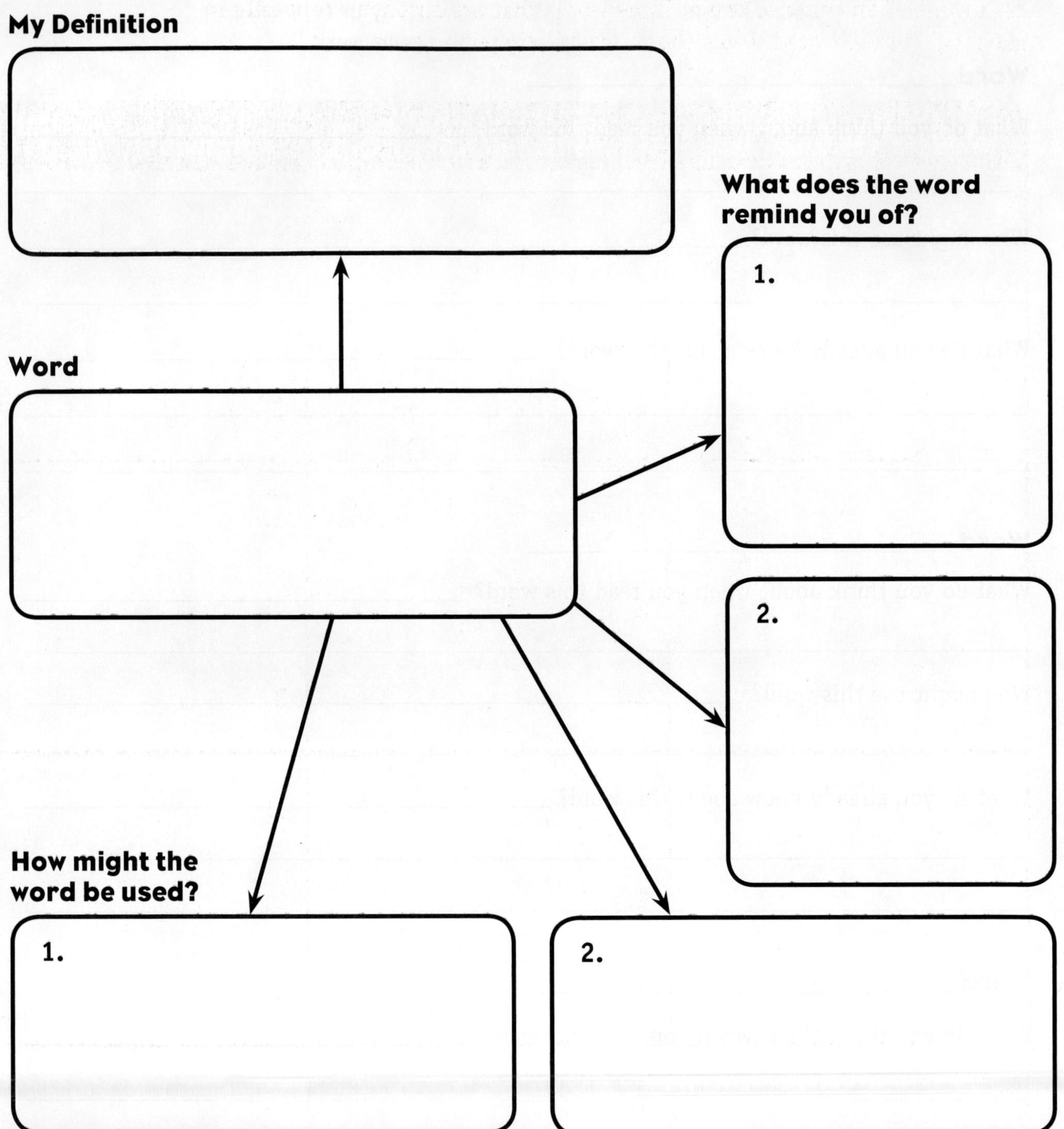
My Definition
What does the word remind you of?
1.
Word
2.
How might the word be used?
1.
2.

Synonym and Antonym Chart

Think of two or three other words that are synonyms (similar in meaning) for each word. Then think of two or three words that are antonyms (opposite in meaning) for each word. Use a thesaurus to help you in your work.

Word	Synonyms	Antonyms
	1. 2. 3.	1. 2. 3.
	1. 2. 3.	1. 2. 3.
	1. 2. 3.	1. 2. 3.
	1. 2. 3.	1. 2. 3.

Word Web

Write a word in the center oval. Add details around the oval that help to define the word. Then write the complete definition in the box at the bottom of the page.

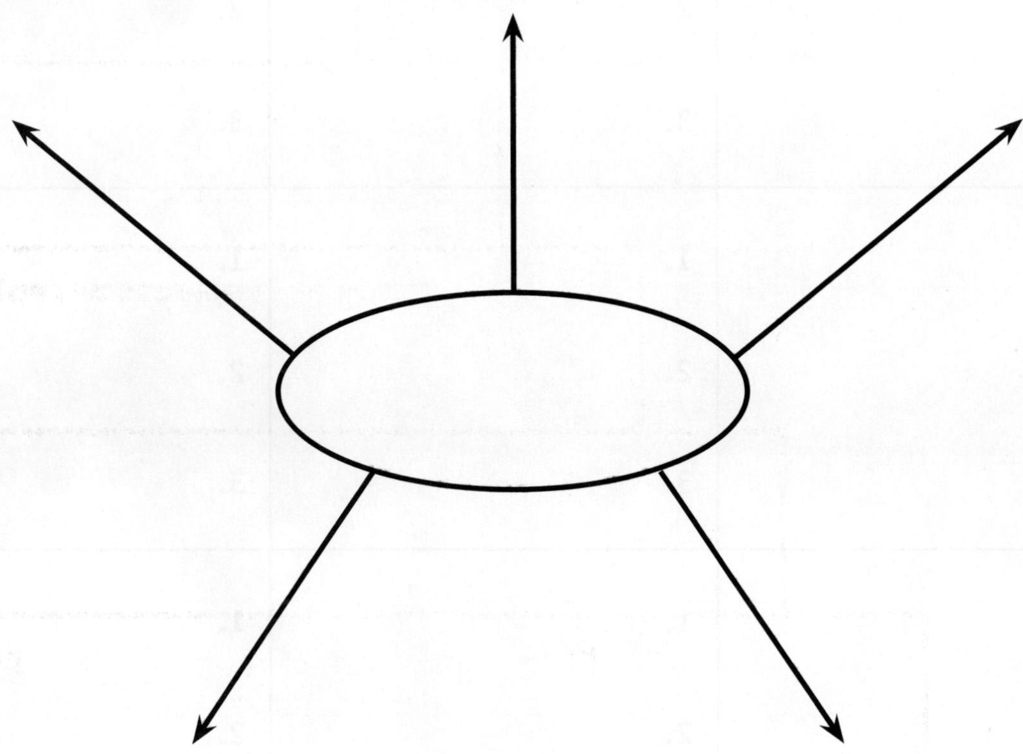

Write the complete definition here:

Concept Ladder

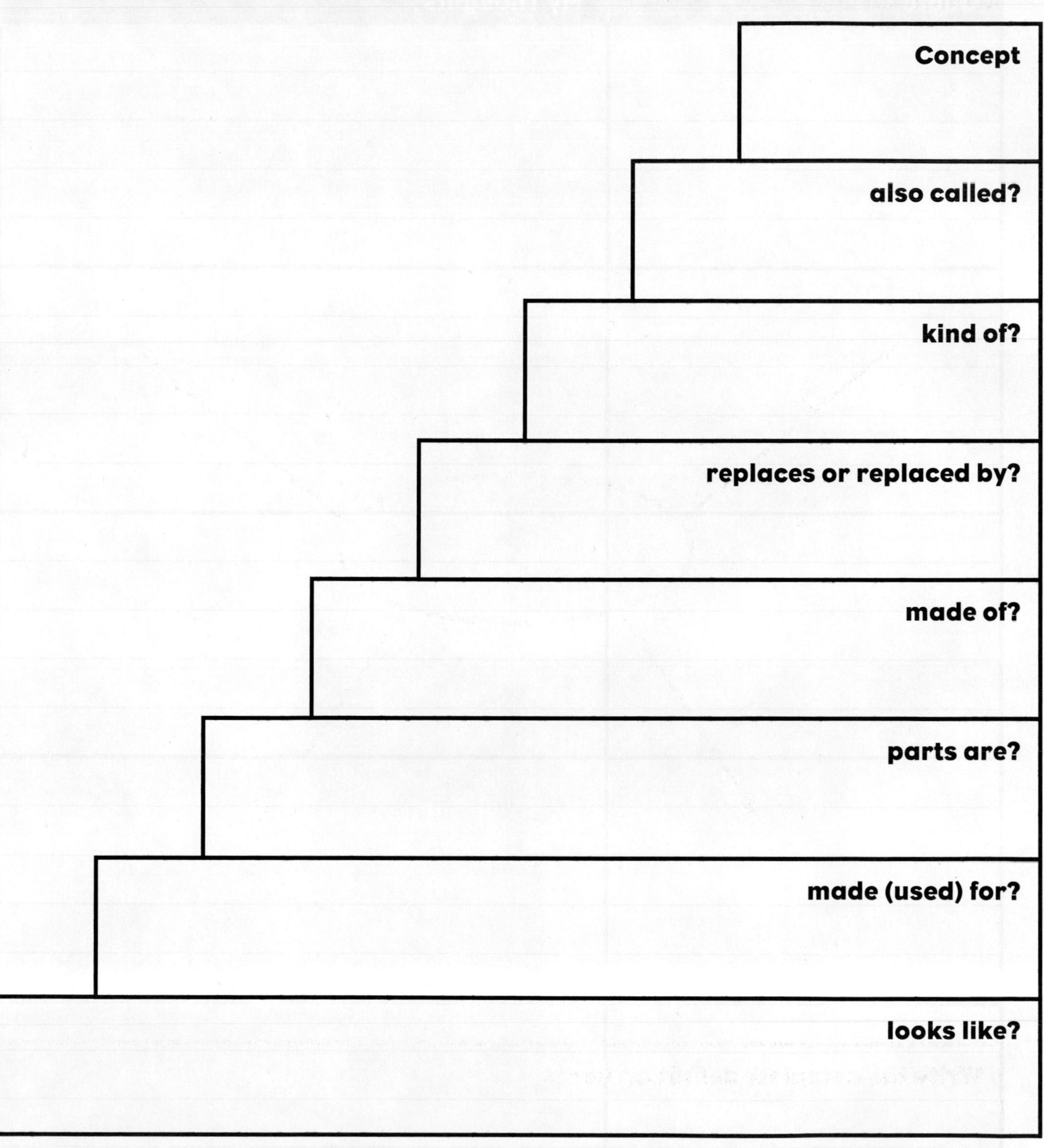

Double-entry Journal

Quote	My Thoughts

Word Relationships

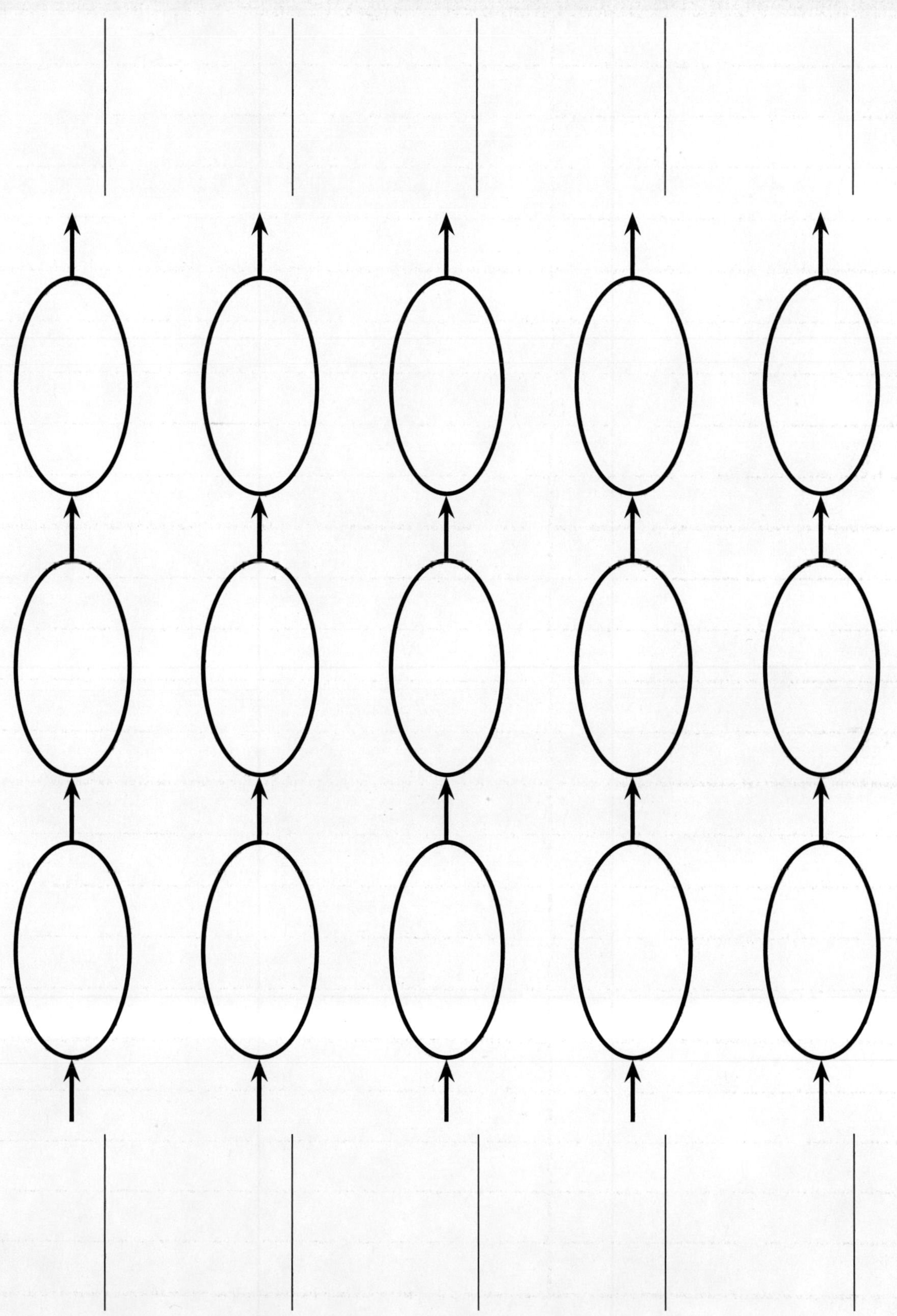

Words with Multiple Meanings

Word	First Definition	Second Definition

Somebody Wanted But So

Use this chart to help you organize your thoughts for a summary.

	My Notes
Somebody (an important character)	
Wanted (a key problem with details)	
But (conflict for the character)	
So (an outcome)	

Now write your summary.

5Ws Chart

The 5Ws—*who*, *what*, *where*, *when*, and *why*—give readers the basic information about what happens in a news story or informational article.

5Ws	Details from the Selection
Who is the article about?	
What happens in the article?	
Where does the major event of the article take place?	
When does the major event of the article take place?	
Why is this event important?	

Main Idea Organizer for ____________

First, write the details. They will help you figure out the main idea and conclusion.

Main idea:		
Detail:	**Detail:**	**Detail:**
Conclusion:		

Story String

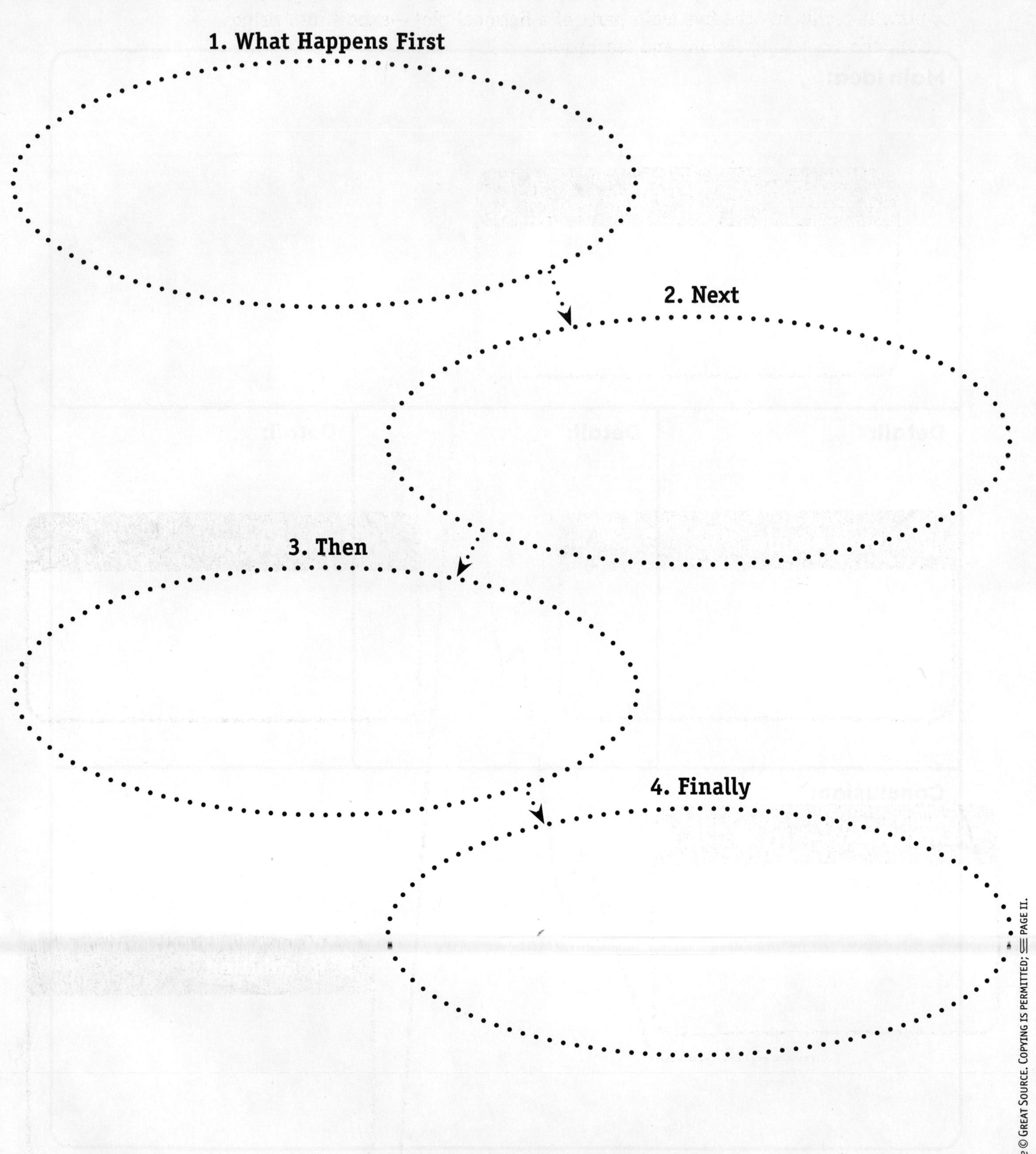

Plot Organizer

A plot diagram helps you to see the main plot stages of a folktale, story, novel, or play. It highlights the five main parts of a fictional plot—exposition, rising action, climax, falling action, and resolution.

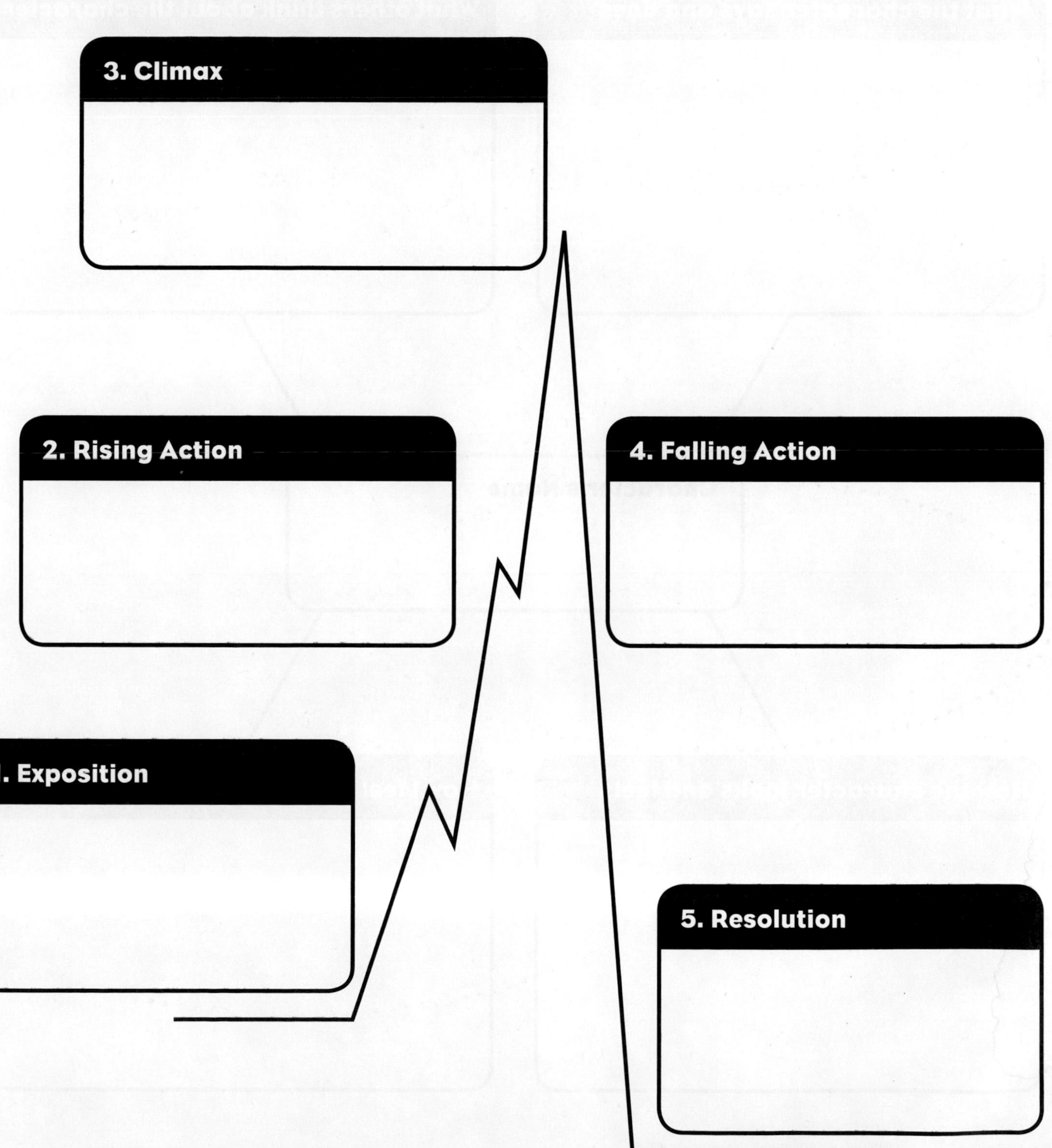

Character Map

A character map helps you understand and analyze a character in a story, play, or novel. This tool helps you see how you—and other characters—feel about the character.

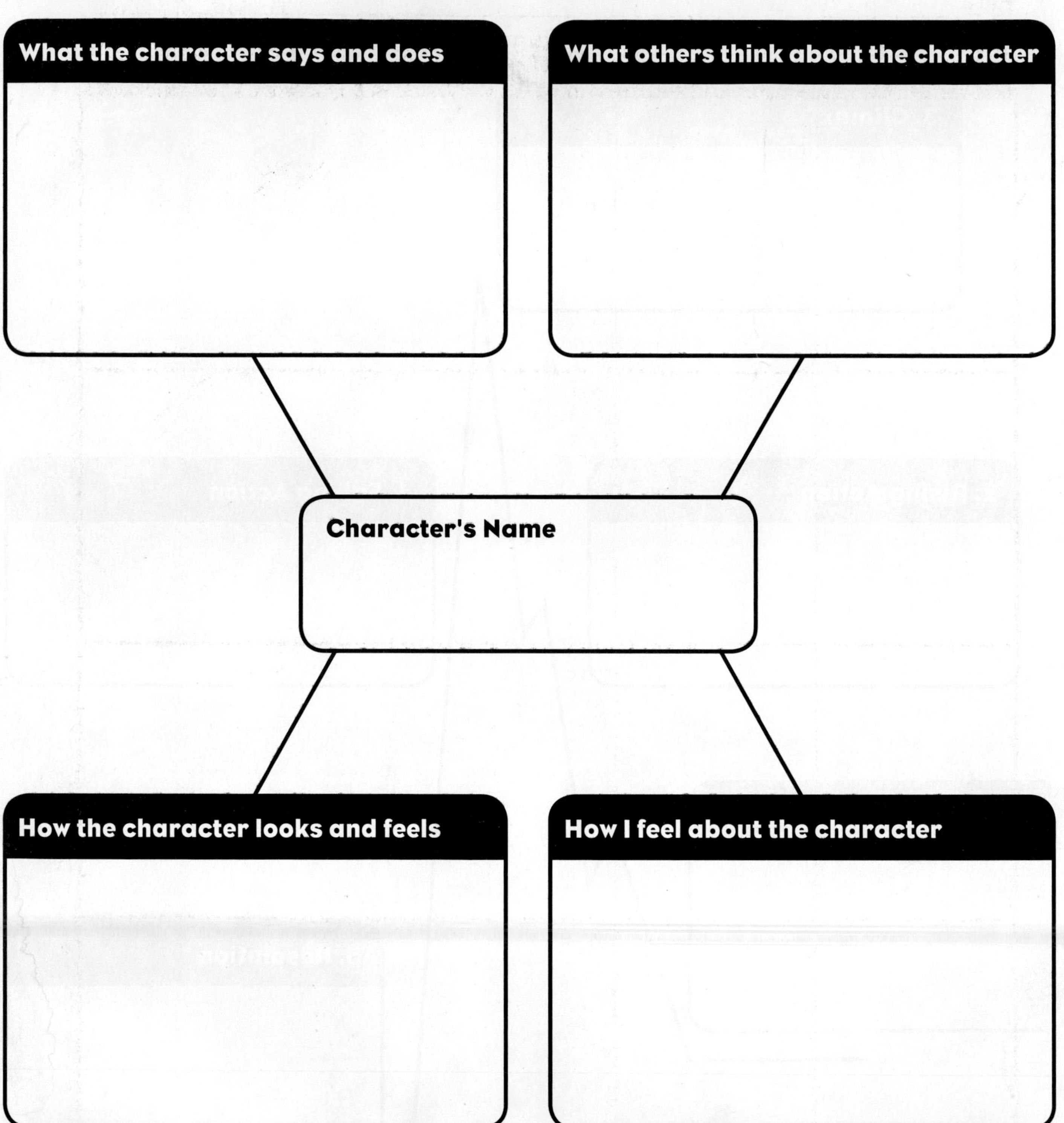